Exploring
Sport
and
Exercise
Psychology

3   796.019 VAN

American Psychological Association • Washington, DC

Published by
American Psychological Association
750 First Street, NE
Washington, DC 20002
www.apa.org

To order
APA Order Department
P.O. Box 92984
Washington, DC 20090-2984
Tel: (800) 374-2721; Direct: (202) 336-5510
Fax: (202) 336-5502; TDD/TTY: (202) 336-6123
Online: www.apa.org/pubs/books
E-mail: order@apa.org

In the U.K., Europe, Africa, and the Middle East, copies may be ordered from
American Psychological Association
3 Henrietta Street
Covent Garden, London
WC2E 8LU England

Typeset in Meridien by Circle Graphics, Inc., Columbia, MD

Printer: Edwards Brothers, Inc., Lillington, NC
Cover Designer: Mercury Publishing Services, Inc., Rockville, MD

The opinions and statements published are the responsibility of the authors, and such opinions and statements do not necessarily represent the policies of the American Psychological Association.

Library of Congress Cataloging-in-Publication Data

Exploring sport and exercise psychology / edited by Judy L. Van Raalte and Britton W. Brewer. — Third edition.
    pages cm
 Includes bibliographical references and index.
 ISBN 978-1-4338-1357-3 — ISBN 1-4338-1357-2 1. Sports—Psychological aspects. 2. Exercise—Psychological aspects. I. Van Raalte, Judy L. editor of compilation. II. Brewer, Britton W. editor of compilation.

 GV706.4.E96 2013
 796.01'9—dc23
                                            2013007796

British Library Cataloguing-in-Publication Data
A CIP record is available from the British Library.

Printed in the United States of America
Third Edition

http://dx.doi.org/10.1037/14251-000

In memory of Peter Van Raalte (1937–2000).

Contents

III

IV

V

Contributors

Mark B. Andersen, PhD, Victoria University, Footscray Park Campus, Melbourne, Australia

Patrick H. F. Baillie, PhD, LLB, Alberta Health Services, Calgary, Alberta, Canada

Beth C. Bock, PhD, Brown University, Providence, RI

Britton W. Brewer, PhD, Springfield College, Springfield, MA

Matthew M. Clark, PhD, Mayo Clinic, Rochester, MN

Karen D. Cogan, PhD, CC-AASP, U.S. Olympic Committee, Colorado Springs, CO

Kathryn A. Conley, PhD, Postdoctoral Fellow at Pace University Counseling Center, New York, NY

Nicole Damarjian, PhD, Eastern Connecticut State University, Willimantic

Steven J. Danish, PhD, ABPP, Virginia Commonwealth University, Richmond

Henry (Hap) Davis IV, PhD, RPsych, private practice, Calgary, Alberta, Canada

David A. Dzewaltowski, PhD, Kansas State University, Manhattan

Tanya Forneris, PhD, University of Ottawa, Ottawa, Ontario, Canada

Ronnesia B. Gaskins, PhD, University of Massachusetts Medical School, Worcester

Meredith Ginley, MS, The University of Memphis, Memphis, TN

Stephen P. Gonzalez, PhD, University of Utah, Salt Lake City

Daniel Gould, PhD, Michigan State University, East Lansing

Christy Greenleaf, PhD, University of Wisconsin–Milwaukee

Kate F. Hays, PhD, The Performing Edge, Toronto, Ontario, Canada

Maggie Hill, The University of Memphis, Memphis, TN

Barbi Law, PhD, Nipissing University, North Bay, Ontario, Canada

Jack J. Lesyk, PhD, CC-AASP, Ohio Center for Sport Psychology, Beachwood

Sarah E. Linke, PhD, University of California, San Diego, La Jolla

Bess H. Marcus, PhD, University of California, San Diego, La Jolla

Scott B. Martin, PhD, CC-AASP, FAASP, University of North Texas, Denton

Penny McCullagh, PhD, California State University, East Bay, Hayward

Andrew W. Meyers, PhD, The University of Memphis, Memphis, TN

Aidan Moran, PhD, University College Dublin, Belfield, Dublin 4, Ireland

Melissa A. Napolitano, PhD, George Washington University, Washington, DC

John M. Noble, PhD, University of Nebraska–Omaha

Bruce C. Ogilvie, PhD

Frank M. Perna EdD, PhD, private practice, Bethesda, MD

Albert J. Petitpas, EdD, Springfield College, Springfield, MA

Trent A. Petrie, PhD, CC-AASP, Fellow, AASP, University of North Texas, Denton

Steve Portenga, PhD, iPerformance Psychology, Denver, CO

Selen Razon, PhD, Ball State University, Muncie, IN

Wesley E. Sime, PhD, private practice, Lincoln, NE

Ronald E. Smith, PhD, University of Washington, Seattle

Ariane L. Smith Machin, PhD, CC-AASP, private practice, Ashburn, VA

Frank L. Smoll, PhD, University of Washington, Seattle

Harriet D. Speed, PhD, Victoria University, Melbourne, Victoria, Australia

Diane Ste-Marie, PhD, University of Ottawa, Ottawa, Ontario, Canada

Lauren M. Stoller, Boston University, Boston, MA

Jim Taylor, PhD, private practice, San Francisco, CA

Gershon Tenenbaum, PhD, CC-AASP, Florida State University, Tallahassee

Taunya Marie Tinsley, PhD, NCC, LPC, California University of Pennsylvania, California, PA

Judy L. Van Raalte, PhD, Springfield College, Springfield, MA

Dana K. Voelker, Ph.D, NCC, CC-AASP, State University of New York–Brockport

Robert S. Weinberg, PhD, Miami University, Oxford, OH

James P. Whelan, PhD, The University of Memphis, Memphis, TN

Gregory S. Wilson, PED, FACSM, University of Evansville, Evansville, IN

Leonard Zaichkowsky, PhD, private practice, Boston University, Boston, MA

Samuel Zizzi, EdD, West Virginia University, Morgantown

Preface

n preparing the first edition of this book, we attempted to survey the broad and ever-expanding field of sport and exercise psychology. We wanted to develop a highly readable text that would serve as a resource for professionals and students who were interested in learning more about the theoretical, empirical, and applied aspects of the field. To accomplish our goal, we enlisted experts across the diverse array of essential topics in sport and exercise psychology to write chapters.

Six years after the first edition was published, we updated *Exploring Sport and Exercise Psychology* in a new edition that highlighted the latest developments in the field, covered emerging areas of sport and exercise psychology, and addressed important topics that were not included in the first edition. The second edition featured an abundance of new references and case examples and several new chapters.

It has now been more than 15 years since the first edition was published. This third edition retains the focus of its predecessors, providing an overview of the field of sport and exercise psychology, connecting theory and practice, and discussing important practical issues related to credentialing and training. However, coverage of key areas such as assessment, diversity (with a focus on work with diverse groups, including master competitors), and international concerns has been expanded. New authors add fresh points of view to the topics covered, and current references and examples have been added to enrich this edition. We hope that this new edition will provide readers with a strong foundation in sport and exercise psychology and serve as a springboard for further exploration of the field.

Acknowledgments

Editing this edition of *Exploring Sport and Exercise Psychology* was an exciting but challenging task. It involved a limited time frame and a lot of work. We express our thanks to our chapter authors, who worked diligently to ensure that they included the most current information available, met deadlines, made revisions, made further revisions, and produced outstanding chapters.

We would again like to thank our mentors, Darwyn Linder and Paul Karoly, who taught us the basics and continue to inspire us. Our appreciation extends to our colleagues and students at Springfield College, especially Al Petitpas, who has been unflagging in his advocacy for our scholarly endeavors over the past two decades, and Eric Wall, who demonstrated immense patience and skill in deciphering editorial comments and typing manuscript corrections and edits.

We also thank the dedicated professionals at APA Books who made this book possible. In particular, we are grateful to Susan Reynolds and Beth Hatch, who guided this edition to completion. We also appreciate the thoughtful feedback we received from the anonymous reviewers.

Finally, we thank our families, who remained supportive throughout the preparation of this volume.

Exploring
Sport
and
Exercise
Psychology

for parents and youth sport coaches, and consult on the implementation of a community-based physical activity intervention. Although there may be no "typical" sport and exercise psychologist, all those who practice in this area should be familiar with a number of issues and content areas. Hence, this book is designed to acquaint psychologists, students, and other sport and mental health practitioners interested in sport and exercise psychology with basic interventions, clinical issues, special populations, and professional issues in the field.

The primary purpose of this chapter is to provide an introduction to sport and exercise psychology—its historical foundations, research trends, current controversies, client populations, and applied settings. After a summary of the history and current status of the field, an overview of this volume is presented.

A Brief History of Sport and Exercise Psychology

Despite the popular misconception that it is a novel area of inquiry, sport and exercise psychology has a rich history. Investigation of psychological factors associated with exercise is a relatively recent phenomenon (Gill, 1986, 1987); however, scientists have been studying psychological aspects of sport for more than 100 years (A. Kornspan, 2012). Examination of the evolution of sport and exercise psychology contributes to an enhanced understanding of the field as it stands today.

At the end of the 19th and the beginning of the 20th century, a number of theoretical and empirical works addressing sport-related topics appeared in the psychological literature (A. Kornspan, 2012). Notable among these works were the seminal reaction time investigations of athletes by E. W. Scripture and G. W. Fitz at Yale University and Harvard University, respectively (A. S. Kornspan, 2007a), the study by Norman Triplett (1898) of audience effects on cycling performance, which is considered the first experiment in social psychology (West & Wicklund, 1980), and the report of American Psychological Association (APA) founding president G. Stanley Hall (1908) extolling the psychological benefits of physical education. Sport psychology topics also began to be addressed in classrooms. It was in a psychology seminar for prospective YMCA physical training directors in 1891 that James Naismith was inspired to develop the game of basketball (Naismith, 1941). The International Congress of the Psychology and Physiology of Sport was convened by Pierre de Coubertin, founder of the modern Olympic Games, in 1913 (A. S. Kornspan, 2007b).

Britton W. Brewer and Judy L. Van Raalte

Introduction to Sport and Exercise Psychology

1

From the dusty reaches of human history and across each individual life span, physical activity is and has been a salient aspect of human experience, an important component of healthy lifestyles. Current evidence of the centrality of exercise and sport is reflected in the recreational and competitive sport and exercise organizations and leagues for children, adolescents, adults, and seniors. Given the centrality of physical activity to contemporary living, it is not surprising that psychologists are interested in sport and exercise behavior. This interest is reflected in sport and exercise psychology, a field that offers an abundance of exciting opportunities for research and practice in an inherently interesting domain of human behavior (Williams & Straub, 2010).

As is the case with many subfields of psychology, sport and exercise psychology encompasses a wide variety of clinical, educational, and research activities. A sport and exercise psychologist might work with elite or professional athletes, use exercise therapeutically with clients, conduct workshops

http://dx.doi.org/10.1037/14251-001
Exploring Sport and Exercise Psychology, Third Edition, J. Van Raalte and B. Brewer (Editors)
Copyright © 2014 by the American Psychological Association.
All rights reserved.

for parents and youth sport coaches, and consult on the implementation of a community-based physical activity intervention. Although there may be no "typical" sport and exercise psychologist, all those who practice in this area should be familiar with a number of issues and content areas. Hence, this book is designed to acquaint psychologists, students, and other sport and mental health practitioners interested in sport and exercise psychology with basic interventions, clinical issues, special populations, and professional issues in the field.

The primary purpose of this chapter is to provide an introduction to sport and exercise psychology—its historical foundations, research trends, current controversies, client populations, and applied settings. After a summary of the history and current status of the field, an overview of this volume is presented.

A Brief History of Sport and Exercise Psychology

Despite the popular misconception that it is a novel area of inquiry, sport and exercise psychology has a rich history. Investigation of psychological factors associated with exercise is a relatively recent phenomenon (Gill, 1986, 1987); however, scientists have been studying psychological aspects of sport for more than 100 years (A. Kornspan, 2012). Examination of the evolution of sport and exercise psychology contributes to an enhanced understanding of the field as it stands today.

At the end of the 19th and the beginning of the 20th century, a number of theoretical and empirical works addressing sport-related topics appeared in the psychological literature (A. Kornspan, 2012). Notable among these works were the seminal reaction time investigations of athletes by E. W. Scripture and G. W. Fitz at Yale University and Harvard University, respectively (A. S. Kornspan, 2007a), the study by Norman Triplett (1898) of audience effects on cycling performance, which is considered the first experiment in social psychology (West & Wicklund, 1980), and the report of American Psychological Association (APA) founding president G. Stanley Hall (1908) extolling the psychological benefits of physical education. Sport psychology topics also began to be addressed in classrooms. It was in a psychology seminar for prospective YMCA physical training directors in 1891 that James Naismith was inspired to develop the game of basketball (Naismith, 1941). The International Congress of the Psychology and Physiology of Sport was convened by Pierre de Coubertin, founder of the modern Olympic Games, in 1913 (A. S. Kornspan, 2007b).

Building on these early developments, laboratories dedicated to the psychological study of sport were established in Germany, Japan, Russia, and the United States in the 1920s (A. Kornspan, 2012). Coleman Griffith established what is regarded as the first sport psychology laboratory in North America in 1925 at the University of Illinois. Griffith conducted research on psychological aspects of sport performance, such as psychomotor learning, personality, and motivation. He also developed course work in sport psychology and later served as the sport psychologist for the Chicago Cubs (Kroll & Lewis, 1970).

Building on the advances of the 1920s, a steady stream of psychological research appeared in the physical education literature and graduate theses and dissertations in the 1930s, 1940s, and 1950s. Among the topics covered were the roles of intelligence, emotion, personality, anxiety, and relaxation in sport participation and performance. Paralleling this academic and scientific activity was continued effort directed at applying psychology to enhance performance in sport and other domains, such as business and the military. For example, Dorothy Yates, a clinical psychology professor in California, worked with boxers and naval aviators on progressive relaxation and positive affirmations. Hypnosis and other psychological techniques were applied with athletes in Australia, Brazil, England, Germany, Italy, Japan, and the Soviet Union (A. Kornspan, 2012).

It was not until the 1960s and 1970s that sport psychology began to flourish as a discrete discipline, separate from its parent disciplines, as evidenced by the emergence of textbooks, academic courses, professional organizations, and scholarly journals devoted to sport psychology (A. Kornspan, 2012; Williams & Straub, 2010). This occurred first in Europe, with the founding of the International Society of Sport Psychology (ISSP) in 1965 and the initial publication of the *International Journal of Sport Psychology* in 1970. Following the formation of ISSP, organizations focused on sport psychology mushroomed quickly around the world, with professional societies in the United States, Great Britain, France, Canada, and Germany emerging prior to 1970 (A. Kornspan, 2012) and in China, India, and Japan in the 1970s. Popular sport-specific research topics during this period included personality, arousal/anxiety, performance enhancement interventions (e.g., relaxation, imagery), achievement motivation, causal attributions, aggression, and team cohesion (Cox, Qiu, & Liu, 1993). Pioneering work on psychological testing and training with athletes by Ema Gerron in Bulgaria, Bruce Ogilvie and Thomas Tutko in the United States, Miroslav Vanek in Czechoslovakia, and others in the 1960s set the stage for more widespread application of psychology in elite sport in the 1970s (A. Kornspan, 2012).

On the heels of the developments of the 1960s and 1970s, sport and exercise psychology expanded into Asia and the South Pacific with the founding of the Asian South Pacific Association of Sport Psychology, the Korean Society of Sport Psychology, and the Chinese Psychological Society's Committee of Sport Psychology in the 1980s. The Sport Psychology Council, an informal collaboration among sport and exercise psychology organizations designed to share information and promote the field, was founded in the 1990s, and the Society for Sport and Exercise Psychology of Taiwan and the Hong Kong Society of Sport and Exercise Psychology were founded in the 2000s. Throughout the 1980s, 1990s, and 2000s, there were major trends toward investigation of psychological aspects of exercise; application of the growing knowledge base to assist sport participants in achieving maximal performance (Browne & Mahoney, 1984; Rejeski & Thompson, 1993); improvement of the quality of sport and exercise participants' involvement in physical activity (Hays, 1995; Williams & Straub, 2010); and the application of techniques common in sport psychology to other performance domains such as business, the performing arts, and the military (Hays, 2012). Reflecting these trends, the *Journal of Sport Psychology* became the *Journal of Sport & Exercise Psychology* (Gill, 1986, 1987) in 1988, the Association for the Advancement of Applied Sport Psychology (AAASP) was founded in 1985, and the Exercise and Sport Psychology division was formed in APA in 1987, constituting the first formal recognition of the field by mainstream psychology (Williams & Straub, 2010). Two journals focusing on applied issues in sport psychology, *The Sport Psychologist* and the *Journal of Applied Sport Psychology* debuted in 1987 and 1989, respectively. The proliferation of new scholarly journals continued through the 1990s and 2000s, with the addition of titles such as *Athletic Insight: The Online Journal of Sport Psychology;* the *International Journal of Sport & Exercise Psychology,* which added a Chinese language section in 2007; the *International Review of Sport and Exercise Psychology;* the *Journal of Clinical Sport Psychology;* the *Psychology of Sport & Exercise;* and, reflecting the foray of the field into the realm of performance in areas outside sport and exercise, *Sport, Exercise, and Performance Psychology,* a journal published by APA. Although sport and exercise psychology graduate programs in the United States have waxed (in the 1980s and early 1990s) and subsequently waned (in the late 1990s and early 2000s) as a function of economic and intradepartmental pressures in the university environment, academic programs fared better in Europe, especially the United Kingdom. In 1997, the European master's program in sport and exercise psychology enrolled its first students as a collaboration of 12 universities from 11 countries. Since 2010, the program has been funded by Erasmus Mundus and includes universities in Finland, Germany, Greece, and Sweden. On the whole, the sheer volume of scholarly productivity and educational opportunities clearly indicates that academic sport and exercise psychology has flourished over the past three decades and shows no signs of slowing down.

Substantial inroads were also made in the application of psychology in sport and exercise settings during the 1980s, 1990s, and 2000s. Consulting relationships with professional and collegiate sport teams and health service delivery organizations became commonplace. The employment of sport psychology consultants by the United States Olympic Committee (USOC) offers a vivid illustration of the gains made in terms of institutional recognition of the value of sport psychology services. After Richard Suinn and Jerry May served the USOC sports medicine staff in an official capacity in the 1970s, Dorothy Harris became the first sport psychologist in residence at the U.S. Olympic Training Center in 1980. Shane Murphy was hired as the USOC's first full-time sport psychologist in 1987. By 2008, the USOC sport psychology staff expanded to five full-time members (A. Kornspan, 2012), with a registry of approved sport psychology consultants offering satellite services nationwide.

The rise of sport and exercise psychology has not been without controversy. As a result of continued expansion over the latter half of the 20th century, the field experienced growing pains. In particular, because sport and exercise psychology encompasses professionals of varying educational background, issues of training, credentialing, and ethics came to the fore in the 1980s and 1990s. Debate was centered on the training needed to become a sport and exercise psychologist, competencies required to be labeled a sport and exercise psychologist, and standards of ethical professional conduct in sport and exercise psychology (Hays, 1995; Murphy, 1995; Silva, 2001; Taylor, 1991). Professional organizations sought to address these challenging issues by developing clearly specified credentialing procedures. In the early 1990s, a process for certifying sport and exercise psychology consultants was implemented by AAASP (renamed the Association of Applied Sport Psychology in 2006). Similar processes were established in Australia and Great Britain at about the same time. Since 2000, accreditation processes have been developed in China, France, Japan, the Netherlands, and Taiwan, and APA designated sport psychology as a proficiency area in 2003 (A. Kornspan, 2012). Although the fervor of the debate seemed to diminish gradually as credentialing procedures took hold, issues of title, training, competencies, and ethics are being raised once again in the realm of performance psychology (Hays, 2012).

Although its early history was dominated by the efforts of physical educators, sport and exercise psychology has evolved into an interdisciplinary field, involving both sport scientists and psychologists. From an initial focus on sport performance as the primary outcome of interest, sport and exercise psychology has broadened considerably. Although collegiate, professional, and elite amateur athletes have traditionally been the main recipients of sport and exercise psychology interventions, professionals in the field have expanded the horizon to include youth sport competitors, adult recreational sport participants, masters athletes, and other underserved populations (Hanrahan & Andersen, 2010). In keeping with the widening range of populations targeted for intervention, sport and exercise psychology research and practice have extended beyond the playing field and the laboratory to a host of other venues and include schools, health clubs, sports medicine clinics, counseling centers, and private practice offices. The current volume was created with these developments in mind.

Overview of the Volume

This volume provides an overview of the issues of potential interest to prospective and current sport and exercise psychology practitioners. It is designed to serve as a resource with theoretical and practical suggestions related to the practice of sport and exercise psychology. The sections of this volume are organized around three questions frequently asked about the field: What specifically do sport and exercise psychologists do? With whom do sport and exercise psychologists work? What does one need to do to become a sport and exercise psychologist? Chapter authors have adopted a scholarly yet practical approach in answering these critical questions. Where empirical data are limited or nonexistent, gaps in the knowledge base are acknowledged and sound recommendations for practice based on professional experience are provided.

The first three sections of the volume pertain primarily to what practitioners in sport and exercise psychology do. Part I, Performance Enhancement, addresses various cognitive–behavioral interventions designed to facilitate optimal sport performance. Interventions such as goal setting (Chapter 3, "Goal Setting in Sport and Exercise: Research to Practice"), imagery (Chapter 4, "Imagery Training for Peak Performance"), cognitive strategies (Chapter 5, "Cognitive Strategies in Sport Psychology"), intensity regulation (Chapter 6, "Intensity Regulation and Sport Performance"), and modeling (Chapter 7, "Modeling: Is What You See, What You Get?") are commonly considered the "meat and potatoes" of sport and exercise psychology. For each intervention, a theoretical rationale for using the intervention is provided, empirical support for the intervention is reviewed, and practical suggestions for implementing the intervention are given. Although the interventions featured in Part I are presented in individual chapters, professionals would most likely use them in combination in an integrated psychological skills training program, as described in Chapter 2, "Comprehensive Sport Psychology Services," which leads the section. Part I is most appropriate for practitioners interested primarily in assisting athletes to achieve favorable outcomes in sport tasks.

Reflecting the breadth of sport and exercise psychology, Part II, Promoting Well-Being, deals with psychological applications intended to enhance the physical and mental health of sport and general populations alike. Chapter 8, "Exercise Initiation, Adoption, and Maintenance in Adults: Theoretical Models and Empirical Support," describes interventions designed to increase exercise behavior in the general population, an issue with enormous public health ramifications. Complementing this chapter is Chapter 9, "Promotion of Physical Activity in Communities: Public Health Psychology of Physical Activity," which describes why community interventions are effective in promoting exercise and how community exercise interventions can best be implemented. Demonstrating the versatility of physical activity as a medium for promoting well-being, Chapter 10, "Clinical Applications of Exercise Therapy for Mental Health," considers the use of exercise to treat psychological problems. Chapter 11, "Counseling Interventions in Applied Sport Psychology," and Chapter 12, "Teaching Life Skills Through Sport: Community-Based Programs to Enhance Adolescent Development," employ developmental perspectives to examine ways in which sport participation can produce favorable psychosocial consequences. Both chapters provide further evidence of how sport and exercise psychology is concerned with outcomes beyond sport performance.

Part III, Clinical Issues, addresses aspects of practice that have been largely ignored in the sport and exercise psychology literature. That there has been little coverage of clinical issues such as assessment, psychopathology, and referral may seem surprising to practitioners with clinical training but is probably attributable to the fact that the field has traditionally been a subdiscipline of sport science rather than psychology. Chapter 13, "Measurement in Sport and Exercise Psychology," serves as a logical point of departure for this section, as consultation with sport and exercise participants often begins with assessment. In addition to identifying assessment instruments that are particularly useful in work with athlete clients, the chapter examines issues in applying traditional methods of psychological assessment to the sport and exercise milieu. Chapter 14, "Psychopathology in Sport and Exercise," and Chapter 15, "Referral Processes in Sport Psychology," highlight two possible outcomes of assessment: identification of pathological behavior in sport and exercise participants and recognition of the need to refer some clients to other professionals. The chapters in Part III are especially relevant to practitioners who lack clinical training or professional experience with sport and exercise populations.

Part IV, Working With Specific Populations, focuses on the individuals with whom sport and exercise psychology practitioners work. The chapters in this section present detailed information on several typical client populations in the field (Hanrahan & Andersen, 2010). Special considerations for working with children (Chapter 16, "Psychological Interventions in Youth Sports"), intercollegiate sport participants (Chapter 17, "Helping Intercollegiate Athletes In and Out of Sport"), and professional/elite amateur athletes (Chapter 18, "Working With Elite Athletes") are outlined. Chapter 19, "Diversity in Sport," addresses possible influences of selected individual difference factors (i.e., gender, race/ethnicity, sexual orientation, and physical disability status) on sport and exercise psychology consultation.

The final section of this volume, Part V, Professional Issues, addresses what individuals aspiring to become a sport and exercise psychologist need to know and do. In particular, issues central to the professionalization of sport and exercise psychology are explored. Chapters in this section tackle issues of training (Chapter 20, "Education for Sport and Exercise Psychology"), credentialing (Chapter 21, "Certification in Sport and Exercise Psychology"), and ethics (Chapter 23, "Ethics in Sport and Exercise Psychology") that have confronted the field (Hays, 1995; Murphy, 1995; Silva, 2001). Readers may be surprised to learn that the majority of training programs in sport and exercise psychology are in departments of physical education, that certification procedures in sport and exercise psychology are currently in place, and that there are a number of unique ethical challenges that can occur in sport and exercise psychology practice. Helpful "nuts and bolts" suggestions for diversifying a practice to include work with sport and exercise participants are given in Chapter 22, "Incorporating Sport and Exercise Psychology Into Clinical Practice."

Conclusion

Sport and exercise psychology is a growing field with a rich history. As a domain of research and practice, sport and exercise psychology is becoming increasingly diversified. The third edition of *Exploring Sport and Exercise Psychology* is designed to reflect this diversity and serve as a resource for professionals and students interested in the field.

References

Browne, M. A., & Mahoney, M. J. (1984). Sport psychology. *Annual Review of Psychology, 35*, 605–625. doi:10.1146/annurev.ps.35.020184.003133

Cox, R. H., Qiu, Y., & Liu, Z. (1993). Overview of sport psychology. In R. N. Singer, M. Murphey, & L. K. Tennant (Eds.), *Handbook of research on sport psychology* (pp. 3–31). New York, NY: Macmillan.

Gill, D. L. (1986). A prospective view of the *Journal of Sport (and Exercise) Psychology. Journal of Sport Psychology, 8,* 164–173.

Gill, D. L. (1987). Journal of Sport and Exercise Psychology. *Journal of Sport Psychology, 9,* 1–2.

Hall, G. S. (1908). *Physical education in colleges: Report of the National Education Association.* Chicago, IL: University of Chicago Press.

Hanrahan, S. J., & Andersen, M. B. (Eds.). (2010). *Routledge handbook of applied sport psychology: A comprehensive guide for students and practitioners.* New York, NY: Routledge.

Hays, K. F. (1995). Putting sport psychology into (your) practice. *Professional Psychology: Research and Practice, 26,* 33–40. doi:10.1037/0735-7028.26.1.33

Hays, K. F. (2012). The psychology of performance in sport and other domains. In S. M. Murphy (Ed.), *The Oxford handbook of sport and performance psychology* (pp. 24–45). New York, NY: Oxford University Press.

Kornspan, A. (2012). History of sport and performance psychology. In S. M. Murphy (Ed.), *The Oxford handbook of sport and performance psychology* (pp. 3–23). New York, NY: Oxford University Press.

Kornspan, A. S. (2007a). E. W. Scripture and the Yale Psychology Laboratory: Studies related to athletes and physical activity. *The Sport Psychologist, 21,* 152–169.

Kornspan, A. S. (2007b). The early years of sport psychology: The work of Pierre de Coubertin. *Journal of Sport Behavior, 30,* 77–93.

Kroll, W., & Lewis, G. (1970). America's first sport psychologist. *Quest, 13,* 1–4. doi:10.1080/00336297.1970.10519669

Murphy, S. M. (1995). Introduction to sport psychology interventions. In S. M. Murphy (Ed.), *Sport psychology interventions* (pp. 1–15). Champaign, IL: Human Kinetics.

Naismith, J. (1941). *Basketball: Its origins and development.* New York, NY: Association Press.

Rejeski, W. J., & Thompson, A. (1993). Historical and conceptual roots of exercise psychology. In P. Seraganian (Ed.), *Exercise psychology: The influence of physical exercise on psychological processes* (pp. 3–35). New York, NY: Wiley.

Silva, J. M. (2001). Current trends and future directions in sport psychology. In R. N. Singer, H. A. Hausenblas, & C. M. Janelle (Eds.), *Handbook of sport psychology* (2nd ed., pp. 823–832). New York, NY: Wiley.

Taylor, J. (1991). Career direction, development, and opportunities in applied sport psychology. *The Sport Psychologist, 5,* 266–280.

Triplett, N. (1898). The dynamogenic factors in pacemaking and competition. *The American Journal of Psychology, 9,* 507–533. doi:10.2307/1412188

West, S. G., & Wicklund, R. A. (1980). *A primer of social psychology theories.* Monterey, CA: Brooks/Cole.

Williams, J. M., & Straub, W. F. (2010). Sport psychology: Past, present, and future. In J. M. Williams (Ed.), *Applied sport psychology: Personal growth to peak performance* (6th ed., pp. 1–17). New York, NY: McGraw-Hill.

PERFORMANCE ENHANCEMENT

Harriet D. Speed and Mark B. Andersen

Comprehensive Sport Psychology Services 2

The title of this chapter is somewhat misleading. We cannot, within the space of this chapter, present a truly "comprehensive" description of services that sport psychology consultants might provide. Also, sport psychology practitioners come from a variety of backgrounds (e.g., exercise science, psychology, education) and use different service delivery models. There are, however, some important common components of consultation that sport psychology consultants should be familiar and comfortable with as they embark upon work with athletes (see also Poczwardowski & Sherman, 2011). These components include factors that affect the start of service delivery, the working alliance, assessment, intervention, record keeping, and the termination process.

http://dx.doi.org/10.1037/14251-002
Exploring Sport and Exercise Psychology, Third Edition, J. Van Raalte and B. Brewer (Editors)

Where to Begin

WHO IS THE CLIENT (WHO IS SERVED? WHO PAYS? WHO GETS TO KNOW WHAT?)

The question of "who" the client is has received considerable discussion in the sport psychology literature (e.g., Andersen, 2000, 2009; Perna, Neyer, Murphy, Ogilvie, & Murphy, 1995). At first glance, the answer seems obvious: the athletes. Upon closer examination, however, sport psychology services may have several other stakeholders, including coaches, parents, sporting clubs, and even institutions (e.g., universities, sporting institutes). Issues such as who employs (and pays) the sport psychology consultant to provide services; who directs the sport psychology consultant as to what services to provide; when, where, and to whom services are provided; and who we deliver those services to can all cloud and complicate the question of who the client is. In some cases, all that is involved in service delivery is consultation with a single person, the athlete (or coach). More often, however, several parties are involved, each potentially with its own agenda that the sport psychology consultant needs to identify and manage.

Determining who is the client is further complicated when sport psychology consultants slip into different service roles with the various stakeholders. Sport psychology consultants operate in environments that have looser physical and service boundaries than their colleagues in typical counseling and clinical psychology services (Andersen, 2000; Andersen, Van Raalte, & Brewer, 2001). As a consequence, they can be drawn into providing psychological services to individuals other than the primary, or original, client (e.g., the parent or coach of an athlete client). Such slipping into service delivery roles is not uncommon in sport psychology and is almost always fraught with boundary issues and dual role challenges (Andersen et al., 2001; Oliver, 2010). When sport psychology consultants find themselves veering into different service roles, it is important that they discuss and, if necessary, renegotiate their new roles with those involved so as to make the boundaries and scope of service clear to all.

GAINING ENTRY INTO SPORT SYSTEMS

Sport psychology services for athletes and coaches may begin in many ways. For example, a sport psychology consultant working for a university intercollegiate athletics department or sports club may begin services through coaches wanting some group sessions on mental preparation for competition; through athletes approaching the sport psychology consultant who is observing practice; through self, coach, or sports medicine referral; or through chance encounters in athletic facilities. Sport psychology consultants may also be contacted or "found" on the Internet. They need to be prepared for navigating the various avenues of entry into service.

Gaining entry into sport systems is also about the sport psychology consultant, as a person and as a practitioner. Coaches and athletes want support personnel who understand their sports and the demands that their sports place on them. Coaches and athletes want people they can trust and relate to and who can trust and relate to them. They want people who know what they are doing and can get on and do it. Being genuine, respectful, knowledgeable, and hardworking are all essential qualities for establishing a credible reputation as a sport psychology consultant, for building professional relationships with coaches and athletes, and ultimately for gaining work (Fifer, Henschen, Gould, & Ravizza, 2008; Ravizza, 1988).

Experienced athletes and coaches generally have expertise in the skills, techniques, and training methods of their sports and a good working knowledge of the psychological demands of their sports and of the mental skills necessary for performance (e.g., goal setting, imagery, positive self-talk). Therefore, it is appropriate for sport psychology consultants to take a collegial approach to their work with coaches. A willingness to share in and build on common ground with coaches or athletes is likely to engender trust, build positive relationships, and create work opportunities.

TALKING WITH COACHES

Often the starting point for sports psychology consultants is the "selling or telling" of sport psychology to coaches when the consultants talk with them about the doing of sport psychology, with the hope that their efforts will lead coaches to become interested in the services they provide, invite them to work with the athletes, and pay for services. How sport psychology consultants go about doing this selling or telling of sport psychology can be a major determinant of the outcome of these efforts (Speed, Andersen, & Simons, 2005).

Coaches come from diverse backgrounds and experiences and have many different views of sport psychology and of sport psychology consultants. Some coaches will be enthusiastic about including sport psychology services in their programs, some will be indifferent, and some will be outwardly hostile. Engaging with indifferent or hostile coaches can present numerous challenges to the sport psychology consultant both in their selling of sport psychology and their service delivery. What are some effective ways in which sport psychology consultants can talk to coaches, even those who may be skeptical or unreceptive?

It is not uncommon for neophyte sport psychology consultants (and some seasoned practitioners) to take a "shopping list" approach when talking to coaches about sport psychology and what they can do: the "here is a list of services I have to offer—goal setting, relaxation, imagery, self-talk, etc.—and here is how these interventions can be beneficial to you and your athletes" approach. The problem with this approach, aside from it rarely engaging coaches, is that often coaches do not know what to do with the list they have been given. Furthermore, the shopping list approach affords coaches little opportunity to get to know the sport psychology consultant as a person—his or her personal qualities and idiosyncrasies and, equally important, his or her method or style of working with athletes.

Coaches have a wealth of knowledge. When sport psychology consultants talk to coaches, they can use that knowledge both to engage the coach and to help get their messages about sport psychology, and themselves, across in meaningful ways. For example, practitioners may begin talking to coaches about sport psychology by focusing on something that coaches know and relate to well (i.e., coaching) and having the coaches talk about such things as important mental aspects of coaching or coach–athlete relationships or what they have observed as coaches to be important mental aspects of sport performance or team dynamics. The discussion that follows will typically evolve into sport psychology consultants and coaches sharing their stories and experiences of sport psychology. In this way, the coaches get to know the practitioners and what they do, and the sport psychology consultants get a feel for who the coaches are, what their expectations and needs are, and what their worlds are like.

Sharing stories can be one of the most powerful and meaningful forms of communication between the sport psychology consultant and the coach or athlete (e.g., Andersen & Speed, 2011; Leahy & Harrigan, 2006; Speed et al., 2005). Stories provide a mechanism for providing rich contexts to the shopping list of services that practitioners provide and for demonstrating not only what they do but also how they go about it. In stories, sport psychology consultants and sport psychology services come alive. Sharing stories with coaches can also help dispel some commonly held stereotypes and misunderstandings of sport psychology and convey the message that the parties share some common ground.

Effective relationships with coaches, like the working alliances sport psychology consultants have with athletes, are built on a foundation of trust and rapport. These early interactions between practitioners and coaches provide opportunities for making connections with coaches and for developing trust and rapport by communicating understanding and commitment.

TALKING WITH ATHLETES

The negative perceptions that some athletes have about psychology and psychological services (Van Raalte, Brewer, Brewer, & Linder, 1992) can affect the development of effective working relationships. In the early stages of service delivery, sport psychology consultants may need to spend time directly addressing some potential anxieties (e.g., I'll have to talk about my mother; the sport psychology consultant is going to see right through me; I'm going to have to dredge up my entire childhood) about the work. Consultants can put athletes at ease by letting them know that the territories that may be explored are the athletes' agenda and concerns and not those of the sport psychology consultant. In the following example, a sport psychology consultant sets the stage for a working relationship with a diver and discusses some anxieties the athlete may have about their working together:

> My job here is to talk to athletes about how things are going for them and see if there are ways we can work together to make their athletic involvement more enjoyable and to help with some of the mental aspects of training and competition. What I usually like to do is first hear about you, how you got into diving, what in diving really makes you happy, what's a pain in the butt, how things are going with teammates and coaches, and so forth. And everything we talk about is just between you and me. Nothing we say to each other has to go outside this room unless you want it to. (Andersen, 2000, p. 6)

The sport psychology consultant, in this example, has communicated a simple plan, telling the athlete that working together for the happiness and well-being of the athlete is the core of what the service is about. Thus, the message is, "Expect that we will be in a collaborative effort to help make your sporting experience even better than it already is."

The Working Alliance

Relationships in sport, between athletes and coaches, parents, health care providers, and officials, are the foundations upon which performance, satisfaction (or dissatisfaction) with participation, and happiness are built. Likewise, the working alliance between a sport psychology consultant and an athlete is the foundation upon which successful treatment or intervention outcomes are achieved (Andersen & Speed, 2010; Petitpas, Danish, & Giges, 1999).

The importance of the working alliance between psychology consultant and client has long been recognized in counseling and clinical psychology, first in clinical practice and theory and, more recently, in a wealth of psychotherapy outcome research (e.g., Horvath, 2000; Lambert & Barley, 2001; Norcross, 2011). The working alliance has also been explored in applied sport psychology (Andersen & Speed, 2010; Orlick & Partington, 1987; Petitpas et al., 1999; Strean & Strean, 1998), with findings generally in line with those of clinical practice and psychotherapy outcome research. That is, regardless of one's theoretical orientation, the relationship between therapist and client is consistently correlated with therapeutic outcomes, with positive relationships associated with positive outcomes (Horvath, 2000; Siegel, 2010). As long as the therapeutic relationship between therapist and client is warm, nurturing, nonthreatening, and mutually respectful, the likelihood of positive outcome is increased.

Intakes and Assessment

Intakes in sport psychology are much like those in other areas of psychological practice, such as counseling and clinical psychology. The practitioner wants to create a comfortable, supportive, warm, and safe welcoming space for the client and one in which the client can sense optimism for positive outcomes. The impression created by the intake session can significantly influence subsequent work with the client and is often the catalyst for therapeutic change (e.g., Simons, 2010).

Some practitioners (e.g., Taylor & Schneider, 1992) advocate a highly structured intake process in which the primary task is assessment of the client. From the start, practitioners take on a directive role and usually follow some form of interview and assessment schedule. At first glance, a standardized protocol may appear comforting and appealing to sport psychology consultants (particularly student or neophyte practitioners), as it sets up a relatively straightforward data gathering process and has well-defined directions and expectations. Sport psychology consultants ask questions (e.g., history, relationships with coaches, presenting problem), and athletes respond as best they can. More often, however, a rigid structure and focus create an environment that may be irrelevant and even alienating to clients. A highly structured, assessment-based intake is practitioner driven and practitioner relevant. The intake progresses according to the sport psychology consultant's agenda and may afford little opportunity for the athlete's agenda, or story, to surface. Jumping into assessment during an intake inherently focuses the context of the initial interview on mental problems, deficiencies, or pathologies, which may be perceived as threatening to athletes or serve to confirm their preconceptions of sport psychology as being primarily for "crazy people." In other cases, early assessment may be detrimental to athletes, pushing them in directions they are not ready or able to go at that time.

The intake approach many practitioners (e.g., Andersen, 2000; Simons, 2010) adopt and recommend is much more loosely structured and involves little direct assessment. The approach is primarily athlete driven and focuses on storytelling and relationship building. Throughout intake sessions, practitioners want to hear the athletes' stories, that is, their understandings of and perspectives on their situations and what is happening to them. At the same time, sport psychology consultants may want to convey to athletes that the consultants empathize with the athletes, do not judge them, are trustworthy and genuine, and care for them and can hear their stories. As Andersen (2000) stated, "Intakes are a process of building rapport, telling stories, and establishing working alliances . . . [and which] form the foundation for later work" (p. 13).

OBSERVATIONS

The world of the sport psychology consultant includes playing fields, strengthening and conditioning gyms, pool decks, buses to games, and sports medicine clinics. Observing athletes and coaches in these social and sporting situations supplies a wealth of information to sport psychology consultants and provides unique opportunities to gain understanding regarding individuals and teams in environments in which they may be less guarded and act more naturally than in a consulting room.

Field observations provide particularly rich data for assessment and can help practitioners to identify potential discrepancies or changes in athlete or team behavior (e.g., how players perform at home vs. away games, how coach behavior changes from practice to competition, how group dynamics work for or against team performance). They can also yield information that can be difficult, if not impossible, to obtain otherwise (e.g., issues that athletes are unwilling to discuss or are outside of their awareness).

Recently, Watson and Shannon (2010) stressed the importance of observational assessment in understanding how social environments influence athletes:

> Beyond practices and competitions, athletes often interact with each other in settings such as the locker room, weight room, training room, cafeteria, and during travel. Observing inter-actions in these settings can help practitioners garner a great deal of information. These observations can provide evidence about the athletic subculture of the team, athletes' personal identities, social networks of influence, motivation, communication patterns, cohesion, and social support. (p. 93)

According to Watson and Shannon (2010), these observations can provide the sport psychology consultant with understanding of how athletes and coaches affect one another and how "they fit, or don't fit, together" (p. 94). In addition, they can provide evidence of social support opportunities for athletes who struggle to cope in the performance or social environments of their sport.

Observing in the field also provides sport psychology consultants with valuable opportunities to hang out with athletes and coaches. In beginning relationships with athletes and coaches, "hanging out" is part of the process of entering into service delivery (Andersen, 2000; Andersen et al., 2001). Sport psychology consultants become part of the scene, which can help the athletes (and coaches) become comfortable with their presence. These early and indirect interactions provide the foundation upon which later therapeutic relationships develop, as they enable sport psychology consultants to make connections with athletes and begin the process of building rapport and trust.

NEEDS ASSESSMENT

In developing a sport psychology intervention with an athlete or team, it is particularly important to identify needs rather than to assume that the athlete or team should be provided with a particular preselected service or intervention such as precompetition mental preparation, goal setting, or anxiety management training. A needs assessment discussion with a coach might begin by asking about the strengths and weaknesses of the team collectively and players individually. Invariably, the stories will have psychological components that give entry points to let coaches know how the sport psychology consultant may be helpful for their specific needs. It is probably wise to keep in mind that "the customer is always right." The coaches and the athletes are the experts. They know what they need, and it is the job of sport psychology consultants to help them express their needs and then to provide services directed at fulfilling those needs and helping them get better at what they do.

ASSESSMENT INSTRUMENTS

The sport psychology literature is filled with a panoply of assessment tools, most of them in the "paper and pencil" category. One can assess competitive state and trait anxiety, physical self-description, mood, life events, sport motivation, and so forth. Most of these instruments have been used primarily in research settings. When one talks with applied sport psychology consultants about using standardized assessment tools, one often hears, "I find they are useful to help athletes talk about themselves." With a taciturn or laconic athlete, it is helpful to have an assessment tool that the athlete has completed, so one can say, "You know, this questionnaire is saying that when you are in pressure situations you seem to. . . . Does that sound like you?" Having a third party data source (the assessment tool) can help quiet athletes fill in the details of their stories.

Many applied sport psychology consultants use psychometric instruments; many do not. It is often a matter of taste and training. For reviews of the use of self-report measures and projective tests in sport, see Marchant (2010) and Gibbs (2010), respectively, as well as Chapter 13 in this volume.

Interventions

Effective interventions are developed from a foundation of understanding of athletes' or coaches' stories and the theoretical orientation of the sport psychology consultant. Theoretical orientations provide a framework for athletes' stories that leads sport psychologists to assessments and ultimately to goals and plans of action that play themselves out in the context of the working alliance.

Once the athletes' or coaches' stories have been constructed to the point where the sport psychologist can begin to see adaptive and maladaptive patterns of behavior and thinking, the questions become what sorts of interventions (e.g., relaxation, goal setting) will help and at what levels (e.g., individual, team, organization) to apply them. Regardless of the psychologist's theoretical orientation, the development of a cooperative two-way relationship between the sport psychologist and the athlete serves as the foundation for any intervention. Central to the success of interventions is the evolving of a "we," a kind of collaborative empiricism where sport psychologist and athlete (or coach, or team) are involved in a joint "investigation" of some phenomena (e.g., the athlete's behavior) in an effort to understand and change those phenomena in a manner that leaves the client with solid resources for the future (and probably makes them happier).

CHOOSING AND TIMING INTERVENTIONS

A variety of interventions are available for sport psychologists to use in congruence with their theoretical orientations (see Hanrahan & Andersen, 2010) and their comprehension of athletes' stories (e.g., cognitive skill development, somatic techniques, educational group [team] interventions, personal counseling, psychotherapy, family interventions). The number and kinds of interventions are legion, and several are described in the chapters in this volume. Before using any intervention, it would be best to have a clear picture of the situation from the athlete's point of view and to understand, as much as possible, the context of the situation. Without a complete picture, one may end up choosing an intervention doomed to failure.

Another reason to be cautious about intervening too quickly is that if the intervention fails, the athlete may not return for further consultation. Many athletes have time constraints, and when work with the sport psychologist seems unproductive, they will find something else to do. Due in part to the stigma attached to seeing a sport psychologist (Linder, Brewer, Van Raalte, & DeLange, 1991), athletes often begin by attempting to solve their problems themselves. They may have tried suggestions from teammates, parents, and coaches, and may have checked out assorted books, articles, and websites. Thus, the "obvious" intervention (e.g., relaxation) may have already been tried. It is useful for sport psychologists to discuss in detail with the athlete what solutions for the problem have already been attempted. If an intervention does fail, all is not lost. A failed intervention can be fertile ground for further collaborative efforts to try and figure out a solution.

SETTING INTERVENTION GOALS

Goal setting has repeatedly shown itself to be a strong and effective technique for initiating and maintaining behavior change. This section of the chapter, however, is not on goal setting for athletes; it is about the goals sport psychology consultants set for themselves and their athletes when they deliver service. When a sport psychology consultant and an athlete get together, goal setting has probably already begun on several conscious and unconscious levels. The athlete may have a conscious goal of getting over prerace anxiety and an unconscious one of finding someone to love and care for him. The sport psychologist may have a goal of securing another paying client or of connecting with someone who will admire her. Of course, some of these goals are never stated, or even fully understood, but they are goals nonetheless. Like the goals in a formal goal-setting exercise, they motivate behavior (see Marchant, 2000; Roberts & Kristiansen, 2010; see also Chapter 3, this volume).

The goals of interest in comprehensive sport psychology service delivery are the overall goals of service itself. Why are we in the sport psychology game? What are we trying to accomplish? What are the outcomes we hope to end up with when the athlete leaves our company for the last time?

There is also a dark side to sport psychologist goals. Some students and practitioners drop names of clients, are really looking for fame, want to rub shoulders with the international elite, and work hard at making athletes dependent on them. In these instances, the goal-setting program is focused on promoting the sport psychologists' needs at the expense of the athletes and coaches with whom they work. Careful examination of the sport psychologist's goals (both manifest and latent) in service is necessary. If one wants comprehensive care of athletes and coaches, then one needs comprehensive scrutiny of the main tool of service, the personality and character of the caregiver. The venue for such scrutiny to take place is supervision (Andersen, Van Raalte, & Brewer, 2000; Andersen, Van Raalte, & Harris, 2000; Van Raalte & Andersen, 2000; Watson, Zizzi, Etzel, & Lubker, 2004).

Keeping Records

Keeping adequate client records is a necessary part of being a sport psychologist. In many countries it is an ethical (or legal) requirement of regulatory boards and professional codes of conduct (e.g., American Psychological Association, 2007; Australian Psychological Society, 2007; British Psychological Society, 2008). Record keeping may also be necessary to meet workplace or contractual obligations with third parties (e.g., sporting clubs, academic institutions, insurance agencies). Equally important to the sport psychology consultant in the current climate of professional accountability, record keeping is an essential form of protection and risk management for both practitioners and clients.

There is another reason for keeping client records, one that is more intimately related to the practice of sport psychology: Records contribute, directly and indirectly, to the therapeutic process. Client records can enhance the continuity of care. Records convey key bits of information gleaned from previous sessions, reveal patterns and changes in clients' thoughts and behaviors, and present opportunities for the psychologist to analyze interactions with clients and what clients reveal in far more detail than is usually the case during consultation. Records can, and should, also form the bases for client assessments and appropriate intervention plans. And, as Luepker (2003, 2010) has pointed out, when records are shared with the client, they can become a dynamic therapeutic tool in themselves, contributing to both the therapeutic relationship and the treatment program.

How sport psychology consultants decide to maintain client records and in what form are mostly matters of personal preference or need. Regulatory boards and professional associations, such as those listed above, provide broad guidelines for record keeping, and several authors have supplemented these guidelines with specific format recommendations (e.g., the subjective, objective, assessment, and plan system of Kettenbach, 1995; see also Cameron and Turtle-Song, 2002).

Regardless of the system of record keeping that one uses, the following three questions are worth considering in deciding what information to include in a client record:

- Would I feel comfortable about my client or a third party reading what I have written?
- Would I be able to justify to my client or a third party what I have written in the record if my client or the third party views the record or challenges what I have written?
- If my records were subpoenaed, would I be comfortable having them entered into court evidence?

Endings: Termination of Services

Comprehensive care has three main phases, each with its own structure and function: a beginning phase (understanding the presenting issues, building relationships, formulating a treatment plan and determining interventions), a middle phase (working through the treatment plan and interventions), and a termination phase (preparing the client for conclusion of treatment and return to autonomous functioning). There are often built-in termination times in sport psychology service, especially for those who work with university teams (e.g., the athlete graduates and moves on). In some cases, termination occurs after two or three sessions because the athlete got what he or she needed, learned a new skill, and returned to his or her sport a bit more sure of himself or herself. In such cases, termination is relatively easy, although sport psychology consultants should still be sensitive to the emergence of termination issues. In other cases, where there has often been a long-term close relationship between sport psychology consultant and athlete, termination brings up several issues for both parties.

How do we know when termination of services with clients is nearing or has arrived? The answer is not straightforward. As Murdin (2000) stated, there is rarely a perfect recipe for ending. Such a determination depends on a number of factors, including the nature of client issues, the treatment or intervention objectives, the type of therapeutic tasks that are embarked upon, and how the client progresses through the therapeutic process. What is certain is that regardless of the criteria or process that sport psychology consultants use to determine the end point of service delivery, how they go about termination requires care. For some athletes, preparing for termination may create anticipation for new beginnings or resumed performance. For others, the prospect of ending treatment may evoke insecurity, feelings of abandonment, and a range of other negative emotions and reactions. In addition, sport psychology consultants and clients, because they have been in close, collaborative relationships, form connections and attachments to each other in the dance of transference and countertransference (e.g., Andersen, 2010; Strean & Strean, 1998). Letting go of that relationship, for either party, may be difficult, may be tinged with anger and sadness, or may be a time of client regression (Mainwaring, 2010; Quintana, 1993). Such feelings are normal, and acknowledging them is an important part of the termination process, for both client and consultant.

Preparing the athlete for termination should begin early in service delivery with conversations about the goals of the work together, the repeated assessment of those goals, and once goals are reached, the establishment of new goals or the initiation of termination. Recounting for the athlete all the gains made and letting him or her know how the sport psychology consultant feels and thinks about their time together can help the termination process along.

With early preparation, adverse reactions to ending relationships may be substantially reduced. Many sport psychology consultants offer a gradual "weaning" type of termination. First, instead of meeting once a week, the meetings become fortnightly, then monthly, and then on an as-needed basis, so there really is no defined termination point. Determining an end point in the therapeutic process (and relationship) with the client and discussing the lead-up to this end point help to identify the conclusion of treatment as a "real" event (Firestein, 2001) and can provide both client and sport psychology consultant with a comfortable transition to the end of the therapeutic alliance.

Summary

There are many possible models for comprehensive care of athletes. The topics presented and discussed in this chapter (e.g., how to get started, working alliances, assessment, interventions, record keeping, termination) provide an overview of some of the more important elements necessary for delivering holistic sport psychology services. The other chapters in this section of the book provide in-depth coverage of goal setting, imagery, cognitive strategies, arousal regulation, and observational learning. Continued thought, research, and discussion are warranted to inform comprehensive sport psychology practices that best serve the needs of athletes and coaches.

References

American Psychological Association. (2007). Record keeping guidelines. *American Psychologist, 62,* 993–1004. doi:10.1037/0003-066X.62.9.993

Andersen, M. B. (2000). Beginnings: Intakes and the initiation of relationships. In M. B. Andersen (Ed.), *Doing sport psychology* (pp. 3–16). Champaign, IL: Human Kinetics.

Andersen, M. B. (2009). Sport psychology in practice. In B. W. Brewer (Ed.), *Handbook of sports medicine and science: Sport psychology* (pp. 121–132). Oxford, England: Wiley-Blackwell.

Andersen, M. B. (2010). Psychodynamic models of therapy. In S. J. Hanrahan & M. B. Andersen (Eds.), *Routledge handbook of applied sport psychology: A comprehensive guide for students and practitioners* (pp. 160–167). London, England: Routledge.

Andersen, M. B., & Speed, H. D. (2010). Therapeutic relationships in applied sport psychology. In S. J. Hanrahan & M. B. Andersen (Eds.), *Routledge handbook of applied sport psychology: A comprehensive guide for students and practitioners* (pp. 3–11). London, England: Routledge.

Andersen, M. B., & Speed, H. D. (2011). The practitioner and client as storytellers: Metaphors and folktales in applied sport psychology practice. In D. Gilbourne & M. B. Andersen (Eds.), *Critical essays in applied sport psychology* (pp. 87–104). Champaign, IL: Human Kinetics.

Andersen, M. B., Van Raalte, J. L., & Brewer, B. W. (2000). When sport psychology consultants and graduate students are impaired: Ethical and legal issues in training and supervision. *Journal of Applied Sport Psychology, 12,* 134–150. doi:10.1080/10413200008404219

Andersen, M. B., Van Raalte, J. L., & Brewer, B. W. (2001). Sport psychology service delivery: Staying ethical while keeping loose. *Professional Psychology: Research and Practice, 32,* 12–18. doi:10.1037/0735-7028.32.1.12

Andersen, M. B., Van Raalte, J. L., & Harris, G. (2000). Supervision II: A case study. In M. B. Andersen (Ed.), *Doing sport psychology* (pp. 167–179). Champaign, IL: Human Kinetics.

Australian Psychological Society. (2007). *Code of ethics.* Melbourne, Australia: Author.

British Psychological Society. (2008). Access to records and record keeping. In *Generic professional practice guidelines* (2nd ed., pp. 12–15). London, England: Author.

Cameron, S. & Turtle-Song, I. (2002). Learning to write case notes using the SOAP format. *Journal of Counseling and Development, 80,* 286–292. doi:10.1002/j.1556-6678.2002.tb00193.x

Fifer, A., Henschen, K., Gould, D., & Ravizza, K. (2008). What works when working with athletes. *The Sport Psychologist, 22,* 356–377.

Firestein, S. K. (2001). *Termination in psychoanalysis and psychotherapy.* New York, NY: International Universities Press.

Gibbs, P. M. (2010). Psychological assessment: Projective techniques. In S. J. Hanrahan & M. B. Andersen (Eds.), *Routledge handbook of applied sport psychology: A comprehensive guide for students and practitioners* (pp. 101–110). London, England: Routledge.

Hanrahan, S. J., & Andersen, M. B. (Eds.). (2010). *Routledge handbook of applied sport psychology: A comprehensive guide for students and practitioners.* London, England: Routledge.

Horvath, A. O. (2000). The therapeutic relationship: From transference to alliance. *Journal of Clinical Psychology, 56,* 163–173.

Kettenbach, G. (1995). *Writing SOAP notes.* Philadelphia, PA: Davis.

Lambert, M. J., & Barley, D. E. (2001). Research summary on the therapeutic relationship and psychotherapy outcome. *Psychotherapy: Theory, Research, Practice, Training, 38,* 357–361. doi:10.1037/0033-3204. 38.4.357

Leahy, T., & Harrigan, R. (2006). Using narrative therapy in sport psychology practice: Application to a psychoeducational body image program. *The Sport Psychologist, 20,* 480–494.

Linder, D. E., Brewer, B. W., Van Raalte, J. L., & DeLange, N. (1991). A negative halo for athletes who consult sport psychologists: Replication and extension. *Journal of Sport & Exercise Psychology, 13,* 133–148.

Luepker, E. T. (2003). *Record keeping in psychotherapy and counseling: Protecting confidentiality and the professional relationship.* New York, NY: Routledge.

Luepker, E. T. (2010). Records: Purposes, characteristics, and contents for protecting our clients and ourselves. In S. J. Hanrahan & M. B. Andersen (Eds.), *Routledge handbook of applied sport psychology: A comprehensive guide for students and practitioners* (pp. 49–59). London, England: Routledge.

Mainwaring, L. (2010). Endings: More than saying goodbye. In S. J. Hanrahan & M. B. Andersen (Eds.), *Routledge handbook of applied sport psychology: A comprehensive guide for students and practitioners* (pp. 69–78). London, England: Routledge.

Marchant, D. (2000). Goal setting for professional sport. In M. B. Andersen (Ed.), *Doing sport psychology* (pp. 93–103). Champaign, IL: Human Kinetics.

Marchant, D. B. (2010). Psychological assessment: Objective/self-report measures. In S. J. Hanrahan & M. B. Andersen (Eds.), *Routledge handbook of applied sport psychology: A comprehensive guide for students and practitioners* (pp. 111–120). London, England: Routledge.

Murdin, L. (2000). *How much is enough? Endings in psychotherapy and counseling.* London, England: Routledge.

Norcross, J. C. (Ed.). (2011). *Psychotherapy relationships that work: Evidence-based responsiveness* (2nd ed.). London, England: Oxford University Press. doi:10.1093/acprof:oso/9780199737208.001.0001

Oliver, J. (2010). Ethical practice in sport psychology. In S. J. Hanrahan & M. B. Andersen (Eds.), *Routledge handbook of applied sport psychology: A comprehensive guide for students and practitioners* (pp. 60–68). London, England: Routledge.

Orlick, T., & Partington, J. (1987). The sport psychology consultant: Analysis of critical components as viewed by Canadian Olympic athletes. *The Sport Psychologist, 1,* 4–17.

Perna, F., Neyer, M., Murphy, S. M., Ogilvie, B. C., & Murphy, A. (1995). Consulting with sport organizations: A cognitive–behavioral approach. In S. M. Murphy (Ed.), *Sport psychology interventions* (pp. 235–252). Champaign, IL: Human Kinetics.

Petitpas, A. J., Danish, S. J., & Giges, B. (1999). The sport psychologist–athlete relationship: Implications for training. *The Sport Psychologist, 13,* 344–357.

Poczwardowski, A., & Sherman, C. P. (2011). Revisions to the Sport Psychology Service Delivery (SPSD) heuristic: Explorations with experienced consultants. *The Sport Psychologist, 25,* 511–531.

Quintana, S. M. (1993). Toward an expanded and updated conceptualization of termination: Implications for short-term, individual psychotherapy. *Professional Psychology: Research and Practice, 24,* 426–432. doi:10.1037/0735-7028.24.4.426

Ravizza, K. (1988). Gaining entry with athletic personnel for season-long consulting. *The Sport Psychologist, 2,* 243–254.

Roberts, G. C., & Kristiansen, E. (2010). Motivation and goal setting. In S. J. Hanrahan & M. B. Andersen (Eds.), *Routledge handbook of applied sport psychology: A comprehensive guide for students and practitioners* (pp. 490–499). London, England: Routledge.

Siegel, D. J. (2010). *The mindful therapist: A clinician's guide to mindsight and neural integration.* New York, NY: Norton.

Simons, J. (2010). The applied sport psychology intake. In S. J. Hanrahan & M. B. Andersen (Eds.), *Routledge handbook of applied sport psychology: A comprehensive guide for students and practitioners* (pp. 81–89). London, England: Routledge.

Speed, H. D., Andersen, M. B., & Simons, J. (2005). The selling or the telling of sport psychology: Presenting services to coaches. In M. B. Andersen (Ed.), *Sport psychology in practice* (pp. 3–16). Champaign, IL: Human Kinetics.

Strean, W. B., & Strean, H. S. (1998). Applying psychodynamic concepts to sport psychology practice. *The Sport Psychologist, 12,* 208–222.

Taylor, J., & Schneider, B. A. (1992). The Sport-Clinical Intake Protocol: A comprehensive interviewing instrument for sport. *Professional*

Psychology: Research and Practice, 23, 318–325. doi:10.1037/0735-7028. 23.4.318

Van Raalte, J. L., & Andersen, M. B. (2000). Supervision I: From models to doing. In M. B. Andersen (Ed.), *Doing sport psychology* (pp. 153–166). Champaign, IL: Human Kinetics.

Van Raalte, J. L., Brewer, B. W., Brewer, D. D., & Linder, D. E. (1992). NCAA Division II college football players' perceptions of an athlete who consults a sport psychologist. *Journal of Sport & Exercise Psychology, 14*, 273–282.

Watson, J. C., II, & Shannon, V. (2010). Individual and group observations: Purposes and processes. In S. J. Hanrahan & M. B. Andersen (Eds.), *Routledge handbook of applied sport psychology: A comprehensive guide for students and practitioners* (pp. 90–100). London, England: Routledge.

Watson, J. C., II, Zizzi, S. J., Etzel, E. F., & Lubker, J. R. (2004). Applied sport psychology supervision: A survey of students and professionals. *The Sport Psychologist, 18*, 415–429.

Robert S. Weinberg

Goal Setting in Sport and Exercise

Research to Practice

3

"My goal is to improve my free throw percentage from 70% to 80%."

"My objective is to reduce my unforced errors in tennis matches from 30 to 20."

"Our goal is to go to the conference championship."

"I want to be able to bench press 250 pounds."

"My goal in skateboarding is to do a 360° flip."

The above are just a few examples of different types of goals that athletes set in an attempt to improve their performance. Sport psychologists do not typically have a problem getting athletes to set goals. Rather, they have difficulty getting athletes to set the right kind of goals, goals that enhance motivation and direct attention toward goal completion. Athletes typically do not need to be convinced that goals are important; however, they may need to be instructed about the most effective types of goals to set and trained to develop a goal-setting program that works.

http://dx.doi.org/10.1037/14251-003
Exploring Sport and Exercise Psychology, Third Edition, J. Van Raalte and B. Brewer (Editors)

This chapter is designed specifically to help individuals involved in sport and exercise learn more about effective goal setting. A research-to-practice orientation is taken. The chapter begins with the definitions of goals, a brief discussion of goal-setting theory, and the presentation of goal-setting research. From this research, principles of effective goal setting are identified, and special cases related to goal setting for young athletes and people with injuries are described.

The Concept of Goal Setting

By definition, a *goal* is that which an individual is trying to accomplish; it is the object or aim of an action. For example, in most goal-setting studies, the term *goal* refers to attaining a specific level of proficiency on a task, usually within a specified time limit (Locke, Shaw, Saari, & Latham, 1981). From a practical point of view, goals focus on standards of excellence, such as improving free throw percentage by 5 points, losing 10 pounds, lowering one's time in the mile run by 4 seconds, or improving one's batting average by 20 points. In addition, goals have to be reached within a given time frame, such as by the end of the season or within a certain number of days, weeks, or months. In a more descriptive definition, Lessin argued:

> Goals are like magnets that attract us to higher ground and new horizons. They give our eyes a focus, our mind an aim, and our strength a purpose. Without their pull, we would remain forever stationary, incapable of moving forward. . . . A goal is a possibility that fulfills a dream. (As cited in Kennedy, 1998, p. 25)

Finally, from a definitional perspective, goals can be either *objective* or *subjective*. Although objective goals such as running a mile in 7 minutes are easily measurable, subjective goals, such as having more fun in competition, can also be assessed (e.g., How much fun did you have today? can be anchored from 1, *a lot less,* to 7, *a lot more*). This type of goal setting can be augmented by behavior changes such as the addition of training components that make practice more fun (e.g., more positive self-talk use, establishing more friendships on the team, working hard during drills).

Goal-Setting Theory

Locke and his colleagues (Locke, 1966, 1968, 1978; Locke & Latham, 1990, 2002, 2006; Locke, Shaw, Saari, & Latham, 1981) developed and continued to update a theory of goal setting that has served as the stimulus for literally hundreds of studies in industrial and organizational settings, and more recently in sport and exercise. The basic assumption of goal-setting theory is that task performance is regulated directly by the conscious goals that individuals set with regard to a particular task. Goals operate largely through internal comparison processes and require internal standards against which to evaluate ongoing performance. According to the theory, hard goals result in a higher level of performance and effort than easy goals, and specific hard goals result in higher levels of performance than no goals or generalized goals such as "do your best." Furthermore, goals mediate how performance is affected by monetary incentives, time limits, knowledge of results, degree of commitment, and competition. Locke argued that although goals can influence behavior, no simple correlation between goals and behavior can be assumed because people make errors and/or lack the ability to attain their objectives. Although most research investigating the goal-setting–performance relationship has set out to test the propositions put forth by Locke, other theories have been developed. These include cognitive mediation theory (Garland, 1985), goal orientation theory (Harwood, Spray, & Keegan, 2008; Nicholls, 1984a, 1984b), and the updated competitive goal-setting model (Burton & Weiss, 2008), which is discussed later in the chapter.

Goal Setting and Task Performance in Industrial Settings

Research on goal setting as a motivational strategy has proliferated so rapidly in the past 50 years that reviews have often used the statistical technique of meta-analysis to aggregate findings across studies (e.g., Klein, Wesson, Hollenbeck, & Alge, 1999; Locke & Latham, 1990, 2006; Mento, Steel, & Karren, 1987; Tubbs, 1986). There are now over 550 studies in the industrial/organizational psychology literature testing the effects of goal setting on performance. The most tested aspect of Locke's theory revolves around the relationship of goal difficulty/specificity and performance. As previously mentioned, Locke (1966, 1968) has argued that specific, difficult, challenging goals lead to higher levels of task performance than easy goals, no goals, or "do your best" goals. Locke and Latham (1990) reviewed 201 studies involving over 40,000 subjects. Of these studies, 91% supported Locke's initial hypothesis. These results were found by using approximately 90 different tasks in both laboratory and field settings, highlighting the robustness and generalizability of these findings.

Locke and Latham (2002, 2006) have more recently confirmed these findings.

A second core aspect of Locke's goal-setting theory is that there is a linear relationship between degree of goal difficulty and performance. The only exception is when subjects reach the limits of their ability at high goal-difficulty levels; in such cases, performance levels off. Three separate meta-analyses have reviewed the empirical studies testing the goal difficulty–performance relationship (Chidester & Grigsby, 1984; Mento et al., 1987; Tubbs, 1986). Results from these meta-analyses have revealed effect sizes ranging from 0.52 to 0.82. In addition, of the 192 studies reviewed, 175 (91%) provided support for harder goals producing higher levels of task performance than easy goals. Thus, the goal difficulty–specificity relationships found in industrial settings provide one of the most consistent and robust effects in the social science literature.

Goal Setting in Sport and Exercise

Although considerable research has been conducted on goal setting in industrial and organizational settings, sport and exercise psychology researchers have studied the topic for only 20 to 25 years. A systematic and concerted effort to study this relationship began with the publication of Locke and Latham's (1985) article on the application of goal setting to sports. Following the emphasis in industrial psychology, goal-setting research in sport and exercise settings has focused on the areas of goal specificity, goal difficulty, and goal proximity.

These areas have been investigated using a variety of skilled and physical fitness tasks such as sit-ups, basketball free throws, lacrosse ground balls, circuit training, and swimming different distances. Although there have been some inconsistent results, the vast majority of studies have revealed that goal setting can help physical and athletic performance (see Burton & Weiss, 2008; Weinberg, 1992, for reviews). Weinberg (1994) argued that some of the earlier inconsistent findings were at least in part due to methodological and design considerations including spontaneous goal setting in control groups, participant motivation and commitment, task characteristics, and competition among participants. Studies conducted in the past 15 years have improved on these methodological shortcomings and have revealed stronger goal setting–performance relationships (see Burton & Weiss, 2008, for a review).

Research to assess the perceived effectiveness of goal setting has also been conducted by surveying sport psychology consultants working with U.S. Olympic athletes. Results revealed that goal setting was one of the most often used psychological interventions in both individual athlete–coach and group consultations (Gould, Tammen, Murphy, & May, 1989; Sullivan & Nashman, 1998). In addition, results from Orlick and Partington's (1988) study of Canadian Olympic athletes and extensive questionnaire research (Burton, Pickering, Weinberg, Yukelson, & Weigand, 2010) demonstrate the extensive use of goal setting as athletes reported daily goal setting as part of their regular training regimen.

Overall, it seems that goal setting is an extremely powerful technique for enhancing performance. For example, several intervention studies conducted across athletic seasons revealed that setting specific, obtainable, moderately difficult goals led to higher levels of performance than equivalent control conditions (Kingston & Hardy, 1997; Swain & Jones, 1995; Weinberg, Stitcher, & Richardson, 1994). In addition, other studies using athlete populations (e.g., Burton et al., 2010; Burton, Weinberg, Yukelson, & Weigand, 1998; Filby, Maynard, & Graydon, 1999; Weinberg, Burke, & Jackson, 1997; Weinberg, Burton, Yukelson, & Weigand, 2000) as well as a meta-analysis (Kyllo & Landers, 1995) and an exhaustive review (Burton & Weiss, 2008) have demonstrated that there are certain consistencies in the goal-setting literature in sport and exercise settings. These consistencies are as follows:

- Almost all athletes use some type of goal setting to enhance performance and find these goals to be moderately to highly effective.
- Athletes using multiple goal strategies exhibit the best performances.
- Athletes and coaches are not systematic in writing down their goals.
- The primary reason for setting goals is to provide direction and focus.
- Major barriers to achieving goals include lack of time, stress, fatigue, academic pressures, and social relationships.
- Goals should be moderately difficult, challenging, and realistic.
- Athletes should focus on process- as opposed to product-related goals.
- Athletes should use both short-term and long-term goals.
- Goal commitment and acceptance are important in keeping motivation high over time.
- Action plans facilitate the effective implementation of goal-setting strategies.

Thus, it is clear from the research and professional practice literature that goal setting can be effective in enhancing performance. However, these studies have revealed that goal setting is not a foolproof method that can be easily implemented without careful thought and planning. As a result, individuals who attempt to implement goal-setting programs in sport and exercise settings should have a firm understanding of the goal-setting process.

Why Goal Setting Is Effective

Locke et al. (1981) put forth the mechanistic explanation regarding the effectiveness of goals in enhancing performance. They argued that goals influence performance in four distinct ways: (a) directing attention, (b) mobilizing effort, (c) enhancing persistence, and (d) developing new learning strategies. Each of these mechanisms is briefly discussed next.

One way that goals can influence performance is by directing an individual's attention to the task and the relevant cues in the athletic or exercise environment. In fact, college and Olympic athletes have reported that the most important reason they set goals is to focus attention on the task at hand (Burton et al., 2010; Weinberg et al., 2000). For example, if a basketball player sets a goal of improving his field goal percentage, foul shot percentage, and assists, then undoubtedly he would focus his attention in these specific game areas. In essence, the basketball player's attention is focused on important elements of his game that need to be improved.

In addition to focusing attention, goals increase effort and persistence by providing feedback in relation to progress. For example, a long-distance runner may not feel like putting in the required mileage day after day or may become bored with the repetitive routine of training. By setting short-terms goals and seeing progress toward long-term goals, motivation can be maintained on a day-by-day basis as well as over time. Similarly, losing 60 pounds might seem like an impossible task for an obese person who has been overweight much of his or her life. However, by setting a goal of losing 2 pounds a week and charting this subgoal accomplishment, the individual can stay motivated and persist with the weight loss program for the time required.

The final mechanism by which goals can influence performance is through the development of relevant learning strategies. That is, when goals are set, strategies can be put in place by coaches or athletes to help reach the goal. This is an area in which both coaches and athletes should be especially diligent and detailed in designing strategies to meet goals. For example, if a basketball player had a goal of improving her free throw percentage from 70% to 75%, she might invoke the strategy of shooting an extra 100 free throws each day, changing her preshot routine, or changing her mechanics of shooting. In any case, new strategies are developed to help the player attain her free throw shooting goal.

Goal-Setting Principles

It is apparent from the theoretical and empirical research reviewed previously that goal setting can enhance performance and personal growth in sport and exercise environments. The key is to structure goal-setting programs so that they are consistent with the basic principles derived from the organizational and sport psychology literature as well as from professional practice knowledge of sport and exercise psychologists working in field settings (Weinberg, 2010). Keep in mind that the success of any motivational technique is dependent on the interaction of the individuals and the situation in which the individuals are placed (Dweck, 1986). For example, goal effectiveness is maximized when goal orientations and specific types of goals are matched (Giannini, Weinberg, & Jackson, 1988). Thus, task-oriented individuals are most motivated by goals that focus on self-improvement, whereas ego-oriented individuals are most motivated by goals that focus on winning and losing (Pierce & Burton, 1998). The goal-setting principles listed in Exhibit 3.1 and discussed subsequently should be considered within this context.

SET SPECIFIC, MEASURABLE GOALS

One of the most consistent findings from the goal-setting literature is that specific goals produce higher levels of task performance than no goals or general "do your best" goals (Burton & Weiss, 2008; Weinberg & Weigand, 1993). Athletes often hear coaches and teachers tell participants simply to "go out and do your best," but the vagueness inherent in "do your best" makes it hard to determine whether goals have been met. Although "do your best" instructions can be motivating, they are not

---

EXHIBIT 3.1

Goal-Setting Principles

---

1. Set specific goals.
2. Set realistic but challenging goals.
3. Set both long- and short-term goals.
4. Set goals for practice and competition.
5. "Ink it, don't think it."
6. Develop goal achievement strategies.
7. Set performance and process goals.
8. Set individual and team goals.
9. Provide support for goals.
10. Provide for goal evaluation.

---

as powerful in enhancing motivation and performance as is encouraging participants to achieve a specific goal. Furthermore, in identifying specific goals, it is important that goals be measurable in behavioral terms. For example, telling a tennis player to improve her first serve percentage would not be as helpful as telling her that you want her to improve her percentage from 50% to 60% by tossing the ball out in front. This gives the player a specific goal to shoot for and a way to determine whether she achieved the goal. To take an exercise example, it does not help much to tell people taking a weight-training class that the goal is to become stronger. Rather, a specific goal of increasing the amount they can bench press by 25% over the next 3 months would be more useful. Finally, specific goals should emphasize both quantity and quality if possible. For example, a goal might be to improve the number of good shots on goal (in soccer) by 20%.

SET REALISTIC BUT CHALLENGING OR MODERATELY DIFFICULT GOALS

Another of the consistent findings from the research literature is that goals should be challenging and difficult, yet attainable (Burton & Naylor, 2002; Burton, Naylor, & Holliday, 2001; Locke & Latham, 1990). Goals that are too easy do not present a challenge to the individual, which leads to less than maximum effort. This, in turn, might result in being satisfied with a mediocre performance instead of extending oneself to reach one's potential. Conversely, setting goals that are too difficult and unrealistic will often result in failure. This can lead to frustration, lowered self-confidence and motivation, and decreased performance. For example, many high school and college athletes have goals and aspirations of becoming professional athletes. Unfortunately, less than 1% will likely ever reach this goal (Coakley, 2009), and thus the vast majority of these athletes are doomed to failure and possible motivational problems. This is not to say that athletes should not strive to aspire for a professional career. Rather, a realistic look at one's abilities and chances of success is needed within the context of that dream goal of becoming a professional athlete. Thus, the secret is to find a balance between setting oneself up for failure and pushing oneself to strive for success. In this middle ground reside challenging, realistic, attainable goals.

Those who have been athletes, coaches, and teachers understand that striking this balance between goal difficulty and achievability is no easy task. For example, it is critical for sport psychologists and coaches to know the capabilities and motivation of athletes in attempting to help them set realistic goals. Sometimes this is a trial-and-error process. But a good rule of thumb is to set more immediate goals no more than 5% above current performance over the past few weeks. In addition, the individual should be fairly confident that the goal is achievable. So if a runner has a best time of 5:00 minutes for the mile, a short-term goal might be approximately 4:50 in 3 months. If this seems too difficult (or too easy), the goal can be adjusted upward or downward. As a general rule, as athletes' performances get closer to the limits of their abilities, performance improvements of as little as 1% can be significant. For example, a mile runner whose best time the past few weeks had been 4:00 might find cutting 2 to 3 seconds to be a significant and challenging goal. Thus, sport and exercise professionals can help athletes in goal setting by supporting athletes in the goal-setting process, offering concrete suggestions for challenging goals. If it becomes apparent that the goals are too easy or too hard or the athletes meet their goals, realistic and challenging goals should be established.

SET BOTH SHORT- AND LONG-TERM GOALS

In working with sport and exercise participants, the focus tends to be on long-term or seasonal goals such as winning the state championship or losing 30 pounds in 6 months. However, research has shown that both short- and long-term goals are necessary in keeping motivation and performance high over time (Weinberg, Burton, Yukelson, & Weigand, 1993; Weinberg et al., 2000). Short-term goals are important because they can provide feedback concerning progress toward the long-term goal. The feedback can serve a motivational function and allow the adjustment of goals either upward or downward, depending on the situation. Short-term goals by their nature allow sport and exercise participants to focus on improvement in smaller increments, which may make goals seem more attainable than would an otherwise seemingly impossible long-term goal.

For example, a swimmer getting ready for the Olympic Games calculated that he would have to cut 2 seconds off his time in the 200-meter backstroke if he was to win a medal in the upcoming games. Two seconds is an enormous amount of time in a short race, and the swimmer felt this to be impossible. But then instead of focusing on the long-term goal, he figured out how to break it up into manageable short-term goals. Specifically, the Olympics were 2 years away, so he figured that he would have to knock off 1 second per year. Furthermore, given that there are 12 months in a year, he figured he would have to knock off 0.08 seconds each month. Finally, because there are 4 weeks in a month, he would have to shave off 0.02 seconds each week. The swimmer felt he could do this! Thus, achieving short-term weekly goals of reducing his time by 0.02 seconds became his goal. The result was a gold medal in the backstroke for John Nabor.

Although short-term goals are obviously important, long-term goals are also necessary. Long-term goals provide the direction and final destination for sport and exercise participants and sometimes act as a dream goal. In essence, they keep the focus on where to end up. If progress toward this goal is not fast enough, or if it is ahead of schedule, then the long-term goal can be adjusted so that it is in tune with the new short-term goals. A good way to envision the interaction of short-term and long-term goals is to think of a staircase with the long-term goal at the top, the present level of performance at the bottom, and a sequence of progressively linked short-term goals connecting the top and the bottom of the stairs.

SET GOALS FOR PRACTICE AND COMPETITION

One of the mistakes that is often made in setting goals is focusing solely or predominantly on competition goals. This does not imply that setting competitive goals is inappropriate; rather, it suggests that practice goals should not be forgotten (Bell, 1983). With the emphasis placed on winning in most competitive sports, it is no wonder that competition goals that focus on competitive outcomes are predominant. However, for most sports, daily practices encompass much more time commitment than do competitions. This is especially the case in sports such as gymnastics, figure skating, and track and field, where usually there are only a few important meets; the rest of the time is spent on practice, practice, practice. Moreover, most athletes report that it is easier to "get up" and get motivated for a game or match, whereas additional motivation is needed for daily practice (Gould, 2010).

Practice goals should focus on both performance and nonperformance outcomes. In addition, practice goals should focus on the quantity or quality of skill mechanics and should push athletes past their comfort zone. Practice goals should be difficult enough to encourage athletes to strive to improve in some way every day. Some typical practice goals could include arriving at practice on time, giving teammates positive reinforcement and encouragement, displaying leadership behaviors, and achieving certain performance standards for specific drills. For example, a basketball player might set a goal of hitting 10 consecutive free throws at the end of practice. This practice goal can serve several purposes. First, it will help the player focus on his free throw shooting and possibly developing different strategies to improve his free throw shooting percentage (e.g., preshot routine). In addition, as the player gets closer to hitting 10 in a row, the pressure starts to build because the player certainly does not want to miss after making eight or nine in a row and then have to start all over. This creates a sense of pressure that will help transfer to the pressure of real game situations. Finally, research indicates that practice goals are as important as competition goals (Filby et al., 1999). But competition goals are also valuable, particularly when they are focused on doing the things that lead to winning, rather than solely on outcomes such as winning. Thus, swimmers might set a competition goal of executing their turns correctly using a cue word such "push-off" or "head up" to ensure proper turning. (See Chapter 5 in this volume for more information about self-talk.)

"INK IT, DON'T THINK IT"

Several sport psychologists (e.g., Burton & Raedeke, 2008; Gould, 2010; Weinberg et al., 2000) have emphasized the importance of writing down and recording goals. Not only should goals be written down, they also should be recorded in a place where they can be easily seen. This can be done in a number of ways, such as by putting goals (as well as goal progress) on a bulletin board outside a swimming pool with a graph recording the number of miles that each swimmer has completed each week. Athletes can write their goals on a 3 × 5 card before each practice. The key is not simply that the goals are written down but that goals are available and remain salient to each individual, that is, that the goals garner goal commitment (see Burton & Weiss, 2008, for a review). Often coaches will go through elaborate goal-setting procedures with their athletes at the beginning of the season, writing down all sorts of goals that are placed in a drawer, never to be looked at again. Particularly in working with individuals with little goal-setting experience, it is useful to set a limited number of goals, choosing those of the highest priority. Coaches or sport and exercise psychologists should set and record the highest-priority goals, then find a highly visible spot to keep them fresh in the participant's mind. Some athletes post goals in their lockers or on their bedroom mirrors.

DEVELOP GOAL ACHIEVEMENT STRATEGIES

Locke (1968), in his seminal work, proposed that one of the mechanisms underlying the effectiveness of goals in enhancing performance is the development of relevant learning strategies. Unfortunately, this aspect of goal setting is often neglected, as goals are set without a solid series of strategies for achieving these them. Setting goals without also setting appropriate strategies for achieving them is like setting a goal to drive from New York City to Los Angeles in 4 days but forgetting to bring a map.

A good example of an athlete who was systematic in planning to reach his goals was Michael Johnson, Olympic gold medalist in the 200 and 400 meters.

> You must understand, I am not by nature a daydreamer. I try to control those parts of my life that can be controlled, to plan everything that I want to happen down to the most insignificant

detail. I "traffic" in a world where fractions of a second separate success and failure, so I'd visualized the 1996 Olympics down to the millisecond. I'd crafted a decade of dreams into ambitions, refined ambitions into goals, and finally hammered goals into plans. (Johnson, 1996, p. xiv)

Many athletes and exercisers are great in setting goals but lack specific action plans for reaching them. For example, if someone who has been sedentary for a long time wants to start exercising, she might set a goal of walking for 15 minutes five times a week. Specific plans might include when to walk, where to walk, with whom to walk, how fast to walk, and even what to do about child care. The point is that specific action plans can really help in achieving goals. Thus, an athlete who sets a goal of running a 10-km race in under 40 minutes will also benefit from planning such things as how many miles a day to train, how fast a pace to train and race, how to gain improved biomechanics, how to maintain proper mental focus when running, and whether to train with a partner. Imagining the goal can be a powerful tool in enhancing goal commitment and achievement (Burton & Weiss, 2008).

PRIORITIZE PROCESS, PERFORMANCE, AND OUTCOME GOALS

It is extremely important for individuals to set goals that are based on their own levels of performance, rather than solely on the outcome of winning and losing. Unfortunately, given the emphasis society places on competition and winning, it is often difficult not to focus on the final score and outcome of the competition. The ironic thing about this focus on outcome goals is that sport psychologists working with elite athletes have found that the best way to win a championship or gold medal is to focus on performance or process goals (Kingston & Hardy, 1997; Orlick & Partington, 1988; Weinberg, 2010). Too much emphasis placed on outcome goals (i.e., winning) at the time of the competition can increase competitive anxiety. This can result in the athlete focusing on the consequences of success or failure ("What will my coach and friends think about me if I lose?") instead of on the task at hand.

Once again, the key point is not that outcome goals are inappropriate; rather, problems arise when individuals focus on outcome goals to the exclusion of performance goals (one's performance in relation to a standard such as high-jumping 6 feet 4 inches) and process goals (how one performs a skill such as jumping explosively for extra height). In fact, as most coaches will confirm, if athletes meet process and performance goals, then the outcome goal of winning will usually take care of itself. For example, if a basketball team meets its goals in the areas of effort, assists, field goal percentage, rebounds, and foul shot percentage, then the team's chances of winning will go up dramatically. Some research

(Weinberg et al., 1993) indicates that fun (along with performance and outcome goals) was given by collegiate athletes as one of their top three goals. Mixing in some fun in the practices and games can help keep motivation high and enhance persistence over the long haul.

SET INDIVIDUAL AND TEAM GOALS

Coaches of team sports often ask, "Should I have my players set individual goals in addition to team goals?" It depends on the nature of the individual goals. That is, there is a place for individual goals within a team sport, as long as the individual goals do not conflict with team goals (Weinberg et al., 2000). Thus, a hockey player's goal of scoring 30 goals throughout the season has the potential to be in conflict with team goals if the player becomes more concerned with scoring goals than helping the team win. In basketball, even a point guard's goal of increasing her assists per game could backfire if she turns down good opportunities for her own shots in favor of passing the ball. However, in many instances, athletes' meeting their individual goals can help ensure the success of the team. In fact, researchers have found that team goals enhance performance as effectively as individual goals if they foster individual goal setting (Locke & Latham, 1990). Thus, sport psychology consultants should be cautious when athletes set individual goals and ensure that they contribute to overall team goals.

Team goals without individual goals can result in reduced effort by individuals. This phenomenon is known as *social loafing* (Hardy & Latané, 1988). This performance problem plagues teams because athletes working together on a task tend to exert less individual effort and perform at a lower level than when they try to do the task themselves. They often feel that they can loaf because other teammates will take up the slack. Holding players accountable is important even in a team sport in which it is often difficult to determine individual contributions during the game. Although contributions cannot always be identified in real time, half-time talks or review of game film can help individual athletes evaluate their progress toward both team and individual goals.

Research by Brawley, Carron, and Widmeyer (1992) and Widmeyer and DuCharme (1997) revealed the widespread use of group or team goals both in practice and in competition. Dawson, Bray, and Widmeyer (2002) found four types of goals evident in sports teams: team members' goals for themselves, individual members' goals for the team, team or group goals, and the group goals for individual team members. They identified six principles of effective team goal setting:

1. Establish long-term goals first.
2. Establish clear paths of short-term goals en route to long-term goals.

3. Involve all members of the team in establishing team goals.
4. Monitor progress toward team goals.
5. Reward progress made toward team goals.
6. Foster collective team confidence or efficacy concerning team goals.

PROVIDE SUPPORT FOR GOALS

The psychological literature has provided strong evidence for the notion that social support is an important factor in keeping people motivated and persistent, especially when there are obstacles preventing goal attainment (Cohen, 1988; Weinberg & Gould, 2011). Similarly, research (Hardy, Richman, & Rosenfeld, 1991) has reinforced the critical role that significant others can play in helping individuals achieve their goals. For example, in fitness settings, Raglin (2001) showed that spouse support is an important factor affecting exercise adherence. As a result, exercise programs aimed at increasing fitness and losing weight often involve spouses in the program by informing them of the participant's goals and ways in which the spouse can support the participant's achievement of these goals. Similarly, volleyball coaches who are trying to emphasize performance goals with their athletes may encourage their athletes to enlist the help of teammates, parents, teachers, and friends in providing support for these performance goals.

GET FEEDBACK ON GOAL PROGRESS

Locke and Latham (1990) found that in 17 of 18 studies, goals plus feedback produced significantly higher performance than goals alone and that 21 of 22 studies found that a combination of goals and feedback was significantly better than feedback alone. Furthermore, adding feedback to goals raised performance by approximately 17% (Mento et al., 1987). An outside person such as a coach or exercise leader can provide feedback, or feedback can be provided by the athlete or exerciser. For example, a gymnast may need specific feedback from the coach because it is often hard to assess progress on the basis of subjective judging in competitions. Gymnasts might also monitor thoughts, feelings, and performance by keeping performance logs. Self-monitoring can be done after every practice, and progress toward goals can be achieved by comparing the logs with the goals. In addition, reasons for not achieving goals may be found in the log, and thus appropriate changes can be made.

EVALUATE GOAL PROGRESS

Goal evaluation may be the most important step in the goal-setting process (Locke & Latham, 1990). Although feedback provides athletes

TABLE 3.1

Goal Evaluation Card

Stroke	Specific goal	Strategy	Short-term goal	Target date
Serve	Improve first serve percentage from 50% to 60%	Hit an extra 50 serves in practice	Improve first serve percentage to 55% over the next three matches	Achieve 60% first serve by end of the season

and exercisers information on how they are doing (e.g., keeping their head still while hitting a tennis ball) or what to adjust (e.g., predicting a certain play based on the defense in football), evaluation provides specific information on how individuals are progressing toward their goals (e.g., averaging 10 points a game in basketball when the goal was 12 points per game). See Table 3.1 for an example. Periodically evaluating goals can help individuals know when to reevaluate their goals. If a runner, for example, was injured and her mile time increased from 5:00 to 5:10, then her goal of 4:45 could be readjusted to 5:00. Conversely, if the runner had already reached her stated goal, then it might be readjusted to 4:35. The main point is that goals are starting places and not ending places, and athletes and exercisers should reevaluate their goals regularly. That does not mean that goals should be changed daily just because of fluctuations in performance. For example, Weinberg et al. (2000) found that coaches varied widely in how often they reevaluated their goals, ranging from daily to monthly to yearly. However, Burton and Raedeke (2008) argued that goals should be maintained for at least a week before adjusting them. The frequent evaluation will tend to keep individuals' motivation and confidence high.

REINFORCE GOAL ATTAINMENT

Reinforcing goal attainment (or significant progress toward achieving a goal) will help individuals continue that behavior (Smith, 2010). In addition, the reward should encourage the individual to start a new goal-setting process as the individual builds toward higher and more challenging goals. Oftentimes in the teaching of new skills, whether in sport or exercise settings, skills are broken down into smaller units so that individuals can more easily learn the movements. Rewards can be provided for individuals attaining each or some of these smaller goals as they move toward their larger goal of learning the entire skill. For example, the tennis serve is a complicated skill. Just getting a consistent ball toss is difficult for most beginners (even pros occasionally have trouble with this). Thus, achieving a consistent toss might very well deserve a reward.

EVALUATE GOAL BARRIERS

For most people, barriers crop up while they are trying to achieve goals. This is especially the case if the goals are long term in nature, as both internal and external barriers can get in the way. Research on Olympic athletes indicates that internal barriers, including lack of confidence, lack of physical ability (relative to the other Olympic athletes), goals that were too difficult, and increased pressure, and external barriers such as lack of time to train properly, lack of social support, work commitments, and family responsibilities all contributed to a lack of goal attainment (Weinberg et al., 2000). Of course, the specific barriers that affect individual athletes and exercisers may vary. For example, exercisers could have a variety of internal and external barriers, including lack of child care, no perceived time because of family or work responsibilities, lack of motivation, lack of money (to join a fitness facility), low self-esteem, and injury.

In all cases, barriers should be considered as well as strategies for overcoming the barriers. For example, a basketball player who sets a goal of improving rebounding might have a coach who emphasizes learning different offensive plays and defensive alignments, spending most practice time on these aspects. To overcome this barrier to attainment of the rebounding goal, an athlete might plan to stay after practice to work specifically on rebounding, watch great rebounders on tape to learn the fine points of rebounding, or talk to the coach about rebounding weak points and how to address them. Anticipating and overcoming goal barriers can greatly contribute to goal-setting success.

Special Cases of Goal Setting

Much of the chapter thus far has dealt with goal setting and athletes and exercisers. However, the focus in recent years has been on applying goal setting to different sport populations or subpopulations. Here, we examine goal setting in young athletes and in rehabilitation settings.

GOALS AND YOUNG ATHLETES

Research in the area of hope has led the way to goal-setting programs using this concept with young athletes. Specifically, Snyder (1994) examined why some people go after and achieve their goals, whereas others seem to be much less effective in doing so. Snyder argued that hope is not simply wishing for something to happen without working for it. Rather, hope involves the thinking process, whereby individuals have an overall perception that goals can be met, along with the skills to achieve these goals.

Building on this research, Gould et al. (2000) developed the Power 4W goal-setting system for helping young athletes learn to set goals and develop high levels of hope as part of a coaching life-skills program for athletes. The program is based on the finding that successful people in sports and life are positive, optimistic, and achievement oriented. Successful people on and off the field set goals, develop strategies for achieving goals, work hard to accomplish goals, and view difficulties and challenges as opportunities rather than as insurmountable obstacles (Snyder, 1994). The Power 4W system developed by Gould et al. (2000) for young athletes included the following aspects:

- *Wish power:* Identifying his or her dream goals (e.g., Charles wants to get a college scholarship to play football)
- *Want power:* Setting realistic short- and long-term goals that will help toward the accomplishment of the dream goal (e.g., Charles will lift weights, do conditioning in the off-season, and watch film to understand strategy)
- *Way power:* Developing multiple plans, paths, and strategies for achieving one's goals (e.g., Charles will lift weights three times per week, run 30 minutes five times a week, and study film 5 hours per week; he will do this with a friend/teammate to help him stay on target with his goals)
- *Will power:* Finding the determination, commitment, and discipline needed to work consistently toward one's goals and overcome obstacles that may arise (e.g., Charles will place a picture of the college football team where he wants to earn a scholarship on his bathroom mirror to remind him of his dream as well as changing his self-talk from negative to positive whenever he starts to doubt himself).

GOALS FOR INJURY REHABILITATION

Goal setting can be especially useful for athletes rehabilitating from injury (Brewer, 2007). For example, Theodorakis, Malliou, Papaioannou, Beneca, and Filactakidou (1996) found that setting personal performance goals with knee-injured participants facilitated performance, just as it did with uninjured individuals. Penpraze and Mutrie (1999) found that athletes who were assigned specific rehabilitation goals had greater understanding of and adherence to their injury rehabilitation protocols than did athletes who were given nonspecific rehabilitation goals. Furthermore, Evans and Hardy (2002) found that athletes who received a goal-setting intervention reported adhering better to their injury rehabilitation program than did athletes who were given social support or no treatment. It can be concluded that in combination with strategies designed to enhance self-efficacy, personal performance goals can be especially helpful in decreasing an athlete's recovery time.

Goal-setting strategies to use with injured athletes include setting a date to return to competition; determining the number of times per week to come to the training room for therapy; and deciding the number of range-of-motion, strength, and endurance exercises to do during recovery sessions. Highly motivated athletes tend to do more than is required during therapy, and they can reinjure themselves by over-doing it. Emphasize the need to stick to goal plans and not do more when they feel better on a given day.

Conclusion

This chapter focused on the effectiveness of setting goals in sport and exercise environments. A goal was defined as attaining a specific level of proficiency on a task, usually within a specified period of time, and a distinction was made between subjective and objective goals. Locke's theory of goal setting, which indicated that specific, difficult, challenging goals lead to higher levels of task performance than easy goals, no goals, or "do your best" goals, was presented. More recent research investigating the goal–performance relationship in sport and exercise settings has also found support for the effectiveness of goals, although the findings are not as robust as those in the industrial literature.

It has been hypothesized that goals directly influence behavior by orienting performer attention to important elements of the task, increasing effort and persistence, and facilitating the development of relevant learning strategies. Goals also can influence behavior indirectly through changes in cognitions (e.g., self-confidence) and anxiety and can be mediated by goal orientation (i.e., task- vs. ego-orientation). Basic goal-setting principles based on the literature were presented, including setting specific goals, setting realistic and challenging goals, setting both short- and long-term goals, setting performance goals, writing goals down, providing support for goals, and providing for goal evaluation. In addition, a seven-step process was discussed for setting goals most effectively. The effectiveness of any goal-setting program relies in large part on the interaction of the coach, exercise leader, or sport psychologist and on the motivations of the specific participants. Individual differences and environmental considerations should always be taken into account when setting goals.

References

Bell, K. F. (1983). *Championship thinking: The athlete's guide to winning performance in all sports.* Englewood Cliffs, NJ: Prentice-Hall.

Brawley, L., Carron, A., & Widmeyer, W. (1992). The nature of group goals in team sports: A phenomenological analysis. *The Sport Psychologist, 6,* 323–333.

Brewer, B. W. (2007). Psychology of sport injury rehabilitation. In G. Tenenbaum & R. Eklund (Eds.), *Handbook of sport psychology* (3rd ed., pp. 404–424). Hoboken, NJ: Wiley.

Burton, D., & Naylor, S. (2002). The Jekyll/Hyde nature of goals: Revisiting and updating goal setting in sport. In T. S. Horn (Ed.), *Advances in sport psychology* (2nd ed., pp. 459–499). Champaign, IL: Human Kinetics.

Burton, D., Naylor, S., & Holliday, B. (2001). Goal setting in sport: Investigating the goal effectiveness paradox. In R. N. Singer, H. H. Hausenblas, & C. M. Janelle (Eds.), *Handbook of sport psychology* (2nd ed., pp. 497–528). New York, NY: Wiley.

Burton, D., Pickering, M., Weinberg, R., Yukelson, D., & Weigand, D. (2010). The competitive goal effectiveness paradox revisited: Examining the goal practices of prospective Olympic athletes. *Journal of Applied Sport Psychology, 22,* 72–86. doi:10.1080/10413200903403232

Burton, D., & Raedeke, T. (2008). *Sport psychology for coaches.* Champaign, IL: Human Kinetics.

Burton, D., Weinberg, R. S., Yukelson, D., & Weigand, D. (1998). The goal effectiveness paradox in sport: Examining the goal practices of collegiate athletes. *The Sport Psychologist, 12,* 404–418.

Burton, D., & Weiss, C. (2008). The fundamental goal concept: The path to process and performance success. In T. Horn (Ed.), *Advances in sport psychology* (3rd ed., pp. 339–375). Champaign, IL: Human Kinetics.

Chidester, J. S., & Grigsby, W. C. (1984). A meta-analysis of the goal setting performance literature. In A. Pearce & R. B. Robinson (Eds.), *Proceedings of the 44th annual meeting of the Academy of Management* (pp. 202–206). Ada, OH: Academy of Management.

Coakley, J. (2009). *Sport in society. Issues and controversies* (9th ed.). St. Louis, MO: Times Mirror/Mosby College.

Cohen, S. (1988). Psychosocial models of the role of social support in the etiology of physical disease. *Health Psychology, 7,* 269–297. doi:10.1037/0278-6133.7.3.269

Dawson, K. A., Bray, S. R., & Widmeyer, W. N. (2002). Goal setting for intercollegiate sport teams and athletes. *Avante, 8*(2), 14–23.

Dweck, C. S. (1986). Motivational processes affecting learning. *American Psychologist, 41,* 1040–1048. doi:10.1037/0003-066X.41.10.1040

Evans, L., & Hardy, L. (2002). Injury rehabilitation: A goal-setting intervention study. *Research Quarterly for Exercise and Sport, 73,* 310–319.

Filby, C. D., Maynard, I. W., & Graydon, J. K. (1999). The effect of multiple-goal strategies on performance outcomes in training and competition. *Journal of Applied Sport Psychology, 11,* 230–246. doi:10.1080/10413209908404202

Garland, H. (1985). A cognitive mediation theory of task goals and human performance. *Motivation and Emotion, 9,* 345–367. doi:10.1007/BF00992205

Giannini, J., Weinberg, R. S., & Jackson, A. (1988). The effects of master, competitive and cooperative goals on the performance of simple and complex basketball skills. *Journal of Sport & Exercise Psychology, 10,* 408–417.

Gould, D. (2010). Goal setting for peak performance. In J. Williams (Ed.), *Applied sport psychology: Personal growth to peak performance* (6th ed., pp. 201–220). Mountain View, CA: Mayfield.

Gould, D., Danish, S., Fazio, R., Medberry, R., Collins, K., & Rolo, C. (2000). The power 4W success program. In D. Gould (Ed.), *Coaching academy playbook* (pp. 302–317). Morristown, NJ: National Football Foundation and College Hall of Fame.

Gould, D., Tammen, V., Murphy, S., & May, J. (1989). An examination of U.S. Olympic sport psychology consultants and the services they provide. *The Sport Psychologist, 3,* 300–312.

Hardy, C., & Latané, B. (1988). Social loafing in cheerleaders: Effect of team membership and competition. *Journal of Sport & Exercise Psychology, 10(1),* 109–114.

Hardy, C. V., Richman, J. M., & Rosenfeld, L. B. (1991). The role of social support in the life stress/injury relationship. *The Sport Psychologist, 5,* 128–139.

Harwood, C., Spray, C., & Keegan, R. (2008). Achievement goal theories in sport. In T. Horn (Ed.), *Advances in sport psychology* (3rd ed., pp. 157–185). Champaign, IL: Human Kinetics.

Johnson, M. (1996). *Slaying the dragon.* New York, NY: Harper-Collins.

Kennedy, S. (1998). *Winning at life (p. 25).* Bloomington, MN: Garborg's Inc.

Kingston, K., & Hardy, L. (1997). Effects of different types of goals on processes that support performance. *The Sport Psychologist, 11,* 277–293.

Klein, H. J., Wesson, J., Hollenbeck, J., & Alge, B. (1999). Commitment and the goal-setting process: Conceptual clarification and empirical synthesis. *Journal of Applied Psychology, 84,* 885–896. doi:10.1037/0021-9010.84.6.885

Kyllo, L. B., & Landers, D. M. (1995). Goal setting in sport and exercise: A research synthesis to solve the controversy. *Journal of Sport & Exercise Psychology, 17,* 117–137.

Locke, E. A. (1966). The relationship of intentions to level of performance. *Journal of Applied Psychology, 50,* 60–66. doi:10.1037/h0022937

Locke, E. A. (1968). Toward a theory of task motivation incentives. *Organizational Behavior & Human Performance, 3,* 157–189. doi:10.1016/0030-5073(68)90004-4

Locke, E. A. (1978). The ubiquity of the technique of goal setting in theories of and approaches to employee motivation. *Academy of Management Review, 3,* 594–601.

Locke, E. A., & Latham, G. P. (1985). The application of goal setting to sports. *Journal of Sport Psychology, 7,* 205–222.

Locke, E. A., & Latham, G. P. (1990). *A theory of goal setting and task performance.* Englewood Cliffs, NJ: Prentice-Hall.

Locke, E. A., & Latham, G. P. (2002). Building a practically useful theory of goal setting and task motivation: A 35-year odyssey. *American Psychologist, 57,* 705–717. doi:10.1037/0003-066X.57.9.705

Locke, E. A., & Latham, G. P. (2006). New directions in goal-setting theory. *Current Directions in Psychological Science, 15,* 265–268. doi:10.1111/j.1467-8721.2006.00449.x

Locke, E. A., Shaw, K. N., Saari, L. M., & Latham, G. P. (1981). Goal setting and task performance. *Psychological Bulletin, 90,* 125–152. doi:10.1037/0033-2909.90.1.125

Mento, A. J., Steel, R. P., & Karren, R. J. (1987). A meta-analytic study of the effects of goal setting on task performance: 1966–1984. *Organizational Behavior and Human Decision Processes, 39,* 52–83. doi:10.1016/0749-5978(87)90045-8

Nicholls, J. G. (1984a). Achievement motivation: Conception of ability, subjective experience, task choice and performance. *Psychological Review, 91,* 328–346. doi:10.1037/0033-295X.91.3.328

Nicholls, J. G. (1984b). Conception of ability and achievement motivation. In R. Ames & C. Ames (Eds.), *Research on motivation in education: Vol. 1. Student motivation* (pp. 39–73). New York, NY: Academic Press. 10.1037/0022-0663.76.5.909

Orlick, T., & Partington, J. (1988). Mental links to excellence. *The Sport Psychologist, 2,* 105–130.

Penpraze, P., & Mutrie, N. (1999). Effectiveness of goal setting in an injury rehabilitation program for increasing patient understanding and compliance. [Abstract]. *British Journal of Sports Medicine, 33,* 60.

Pierce, B. E., & Burton, D. (1998). Scoring a perfect 10: Investigating the impact of goal setting styles on a goal-setting program for female gymnasts. *The Sport Psychologist, 12,* 156–168.

Raglin, J. (2001). Factors in exercise adherence: Influence of spouse participation. *Quest, 53,* 356–361.

Smith, R. (2010). A positive approach to coaching effectiveness and performance enhancement. In J. Williams (Ed.). *Applied sport psychology: Personal growth to peak performance* (6th ed., pp. 42–58). New York, NY: McGraw-Hill.

Snyder, C. (1994). *The psychology of hope.* New York, NY: Free Press.

Sullivan, P. A., & Nashman, H. W. (1998). Self-perceptions of the role of USOC sport psychologists in working with Olympic athletes. *The Sport Psychologist, 12,* 95–103.

Swain, A., & Jones, G. (1995). Effects of goal setting interventions on selected basketball skills: A single subject design. *Research Quarterly for Exercise and Sport, 66,* 51–63.

Theodorakis, Y., Malliou, P., Papaioannou, A., Beneca, A., & Filactakidou, A. (1996). The effect of personal goals, self-efficacy, and self-satisfaction on injury rehabilitation. *Journal of Sport Rehabilitation, 5,* 214–233.

Tubbs, M. E. (1986). Goal setting: A meta-analytic examination of the empirical evidence. *Journal of Applied Psychology, 71,* 474–483. doi:10.1037/0021-9010.71.3.474

Weinberg, R. S. (1992). Goal setting and motor performance: A review and critique. In G. C. Roberts (Ed.), *Motivation in sport and exercise* (pp. 177–198). Champaign, IL: Human Kinetics.

Weinberg, R. S. (1994). Goal setting and performance in sport and exercise settings: A synthesis and critique. *Medicine & Science in Sports and Exercise, 26,* 469–477. doi:10.1249/00005768-199404000-00012

Weinberg, R. S. (2010). Goal setting for coaches: A primer. *Journal of Sport Psychology in Action, 1,* 57–66. doi:10.1080/21520704.2010.513411

Weinberg, R. S., Burke, K., & Jackson, A. W. (1997). Coaches' and players' perceptions of goal setting in junior tennis: An exploratory investigation. *The Sport Psychologist, 11,* 426–439.

Weinberg, R. S., Burton, D., Yukelson, D., & Weigand, D. (1993). Goal setting in competitive sport: An exploratory investigation of practices of collegiate athletes. *The Sport Psychologist, 7,* 275–289.

Weinberg, R. S., Burton, D., Yukelson, D., & Weigand, D. (2000). Perceived goal setting practices of Olympic athletes: An exploratory investigation. *The Sport Psychologist, 14,* 280–296.

Weinberg, R. S., & Gould, D. (2011*). Foundations of sport and exercise psychology* (5th ed.). Champaign, IL: Human Kinetics.

Weinberg, R. S., Stitcher, T., & Richardson, P. (1994). Effects of a seasonal goal setting program on lacrosse performance. *The Sport Psychologist, 8,* 166–177.

Weinberg, R. S., & Weigand, D. (1993). Goal setting in sport and exercise: A reaction to Locke. *Journal of Sport & Exercise Psychology, 15,* 88–95.

Widmeyer, W. N., & DuCharme, K. (1997). Team building through team goal setting. *Journal of Applied Sport Psychology, 9,* 61–72. doi:10.1080/10413209708415386

Daniel Gould, Dana K. Voelker,
Nicole Damarjian, and Christy Greenleaf

Imagery Training
for Peak Performance

4

Carolyn is a highly talented professional golfer. She plays well during practice rounds but does not seem to be able to play up to her potential during tournaments. In an effort to enhance her confidence, her coach recommends that she imagine herself executing each shot perfectly before she actually swings. Although skeptical, Carolyn tries this in her next tournament. She finds it difficult to control the "pictures" in her mind and sees herself making mistakes. Frustrated, Carolyn sees little immediate improvement in her game, decides that she is not good at imagery, and retreats to the driving range to hit balls.

Alan is the new basketball coach at Bacon Academy and decides that he will develop an imagery training program for his team. Every day, after 2 hours of hard practice, Alan has his team lie down and imagine themselves going through various plays outlined in practice. As the season progresses, Alan notices more and more resistance from some of his players with regard to the imagery training. He overhears them complain that they want to go home and eat supper after

http://dx.doi.org/10.1037/14251-004
Exploring Sport and Exercise Psychology, Third Edition, J. Van Raalte and
B. Brewer (Editors)

a workout, not sit in the dark and daydream. Besides, they have no idea why they are doing all this "mental stuff' anyway. Concerned about losing credibility with his team, Alan decides to drop the imagery program.

Lauren is an elite gymnast. Six weeks before the Olympic tryouts, she sprains her ankle on a dismount. The athletic trainer assures Lauren and her coach that the injury is minor and that with proper rest and rehabilitation she should be completely recovered in time for the try-outs. Two weeks later, Lauren returns to her normal practice schedule, but she continues to hesitate before her dismounts. Both her sport psychologist and coach encourage her to replay past successful dismounts in her mind to overcome the fear she has developed as a result of her recent fall. Lauren halfheartedly does as they suggest but is not truly committed to imagery training. She feels foolish and self-conscious in front of her teammates and insists that her ankle is still not fully recovered.

But doesn't imagery work? After all, Hank Aaron used it to become the then all-time home run leader in major league baseball, golf great Jack Nicklaus religiously did it before every shot, and what about all those Olympic athletes who report how useful imagery is in enhancing their performance? How can it be suggested that imagery does not work?

We believe in the power of imagery and its value as a psychological skill in enhancing sport performance. As we discuss in this chapter, research has clearly demonstrated the effectiveness of imagery as a sport psychological change mechanism. However, circumstances like those just described are not uncommon. Many well-meaning athletes, like Carolyn the golfer, assume that psychological skills such as imagery can be developed overnight to produce immediate performance improvements. When the expected results are not achieved, athletes may falsely conclude that imagery does not work. Other athletes, like Lauren the elite gymnast, do not fully understand what imagery is or how it can help them achieve their goals. They never truly commit to an imagery training program, and as a result they fail to gain performance benefits. This is why it is valuable for coaches like Alan to ensure that their teams understand what imagery is and how it can be used to enhance sport performance. This chapter is designed to provide a comprehensive and practical overview of imagery theory, research, and intervention.

What Is Imagery and How Can It Enhance Sport Performance

Imagery is defined as a process by which sensory experiences are stored in memory and internally recalled and performed in the absence of external stimuli (S. M. Murphy, 1994). Imagery involves the use of all senses, including sight, touch, taste, sound, smell, and bodily awareness. This is especially true in sports, where the feel of the movement is critical.

Assume, for example, that a swimmer is using imagery to mentally prepare for a conference meet in the next month. She imagines herself swimming confidently and strongly. She smells the chlorine of the pool as she waits for the race to begin. She sees herself dive into the water. She feels the power in her kick as she pushes herself past her competitors. She hears water splashing and her teammates cheering her on. By incorporating all of her appropriate senses, this athlete is able to imagine many aspects of her upcoming race more vividly.

With an appropriate training program, imagery skills can increase self-awareness, facilitate skill acquisition and maintenance, build self-confidence, control emotions, relieve pain, regulate arousal, and enhance preparation strategies (Martin, Moritz, & Hall, 1999; S. Murphy & Jowdy, 1992). However, before specific guidelines for setting up an imagery training program are outlined, it is important to summarize the theories that explain why and how imagery works, as well as to consider research examining the relationship between imagery and performance.

Theoretical Explanations for the Relationship Between Imagery and Performance

To use imagery effectively, sport psychologists and coaches must have an understanding of the mechanisms underlying the imagery–performance relationship. Traditionally, two main theories have been put forward within the sport psychology literature: psychoneuromuscular theory and symbolic learning theory. These theories, as well as information and motor process theories of imagery, psychological states notions, and applied models of imagery, are discussed here.

PSYCHONEUROMUSCULAR THEORY

Psychoneuromuscular theorists propose that imagery rehearsal duplicates the actual motor pattern being rehearsed, although the neuromotor activation is of smaller magnitude than in actual physical practice (Jacobson, 1932). The neuromuscular activation is thought to be sufficient to enhance motor schema in the motor cortex. Vealey and Greenleaf (1998) referred to this as *muscle memory*. For example, Suinn (1972) monitored muscle activity in the legs of skiers as they imagined a downhill run. He found that the electrical patterns in the muscles closely approximated those expected if the person had actually been skiing.

Unfortunately, not all research has replicated Suinn's (1972) results or shown support for psychoneuromuscular theory. In a meta-analysis of 60 mental practice studies, Feltz and Landers (1983) concluded that it is doubtful that imagery effects result in low-level muscular-impulse activity. More recent investigations have also failed to demonstrate strong support for psychoneuromuscular theory (e.g., Slade, Landers, & Martin, 2002; D. Smith, Collins, & Holmes, 2003). Furthermore, research in experimental psychology has suggested that the effects of imagery are more a function of higher level processes within the central nervous system than lower level muscular activity (Kohl & Roenker, 1983). The muscular responses found may merely be an effect mechanism rather than a cause of performance changes.

SYMBOLIC LEARNING THEORY

In contrast to psychoneuromuscular theory, symbolic learning theory contends that imagery effects are more often due to the opportunity to practice symbolic elements of a specific motor task than to the muscle activation itself (Sackett, 1935). More specifically, imagery functions by helping athletes develop a "mental blueprint" to guide overt performance. Support for symbolic learning theory has come from two areas of research. First, a number of studies have shown that imagery is more effective for tasks that have a high cognitive component as opposed to a high motor component (Ryan & Simons, 1981). Second, the notion that imagery has its greatest effects during the early stages of learning is compatible with motor learning theories contending that the early stages of learning are primarily cognitive.

INFORMATIONAL AND MOTOR PROCESS THEORIES OF IMAGERY

Although much of the imagery literature in sport psychology is based on psychoneuromuscular and symbolic learning theories, S. Murphy and Jowdy (1992) suggested that researchers look beyond traditional theories and investigate the relevance of imagery theories developed in other areas, such as cognitive and clinical psychology. Two such theories are Lang's (1977, 1979) bio-informational theory and Ahsen's (1984) triple-code model of imagery.

Lang's (1977, 1979) bio-informational theory is based on the assumption that an image is a functionally organized, finite set of propositions regarding the relationship and description of stimulus and response characteristics. Stimulus propositions describe the content of the scenario to be imagined, for example, the weather conditions of a particular tennis match or the pin position of a particularly difficult golf hole. Response propositions describe the imager's response to the imagined scenario, for example, a kinesthetic awareness of any muscular changes while performing. According to bio-informational theory (Lang, 1977, 1979), both stimulus and response propositions must be activated for imagery rehearsal to influence performance. Rather than conceptualizing an image as merely a stimulus in the athlete's mind to which he or she responds, this theory suggests that images also contain "response scenarios" that enable athletes to access the appropriate motor program and effectively alter athletic performance.

Similar to Lang's (1977, 1979) bio-informational theory, Ahsen's (1984) triple-code model of imagery also recognizes the primary importance of psychophysiological processes in the imagery process. However, Ahsen's theory goes one step further and incorporates the personal meaning that an image has for an individual. According to the triple-code model, there are three essential parts of imagery, including the image itself, the somatic response to the image, and the meaning of the image. For example, a sprinter imagines herself successfully qualifying for the 100-meter race in the 2012 Olympics. Her arousal level increases with the image of running in this event and having achieved her lifelong dream. In addition, she attaches a great sense of personal pride and satisfaction to the image of this accomplishment. Both the image itself and the somatic response to it are analogous to Lang's (1977, 1979) stimulus and response propositions. However, no other theory or model of imagery has addressed the importance of the meaning that an individual attaches to a particular image.

Although informational and motor process theories of imagery are intriguing, only a few studies have been conducted to test their major predictions. For example, Wilson, Smith, Burden, and Holmes (2010) found that making images more personal and having the participant (rather than the experimenter) generate the script resulted in greater electromyography activity and perceived imagery ability. The authors concluded that the results support bio-informational theory and emphasized the importance of making imagery more personally meaningful. Similarly, Cumming, Olphin, and Law (2007) found that imagery containing response propositions resulted in greater heart rate responses in athletes, thus providing initial support for Lang's (1977, 1979) bio-informational theory (see S. Murphy & Jowdy, 1992, and Suinn, 1993, for more detailed reviews of imagery theories).

PSYCHOLOGICAL STATES NOTION

Although most imagery theories focus on improving performance through information and motor control processes, imagery is also thought to influence athletic performance through its effect on other psychological states, such as self-efficacy or confidence, motivation, and anxiety. For example, in his classic theory of self-efficacy, Bandura (1977) proposed that an important source of efficacy information is the modeling of vicarious experiences and that imagery is an excellent way to reinforce modeled acts and mentally learn from others. Several studies have linked imagery use and levels of self-confidence (e.g., Callow, Hardy, & Hall, 1998; Moritz, Hall, Martin, & Vadocz, 1996). Moritz et al. (1996), for instance, found that highly confident athletes used more mastery and arousal control imagery than did athletes with lower confidence. More recent research suggests that imagery is predictive of confidence in both practice and competition (Hall et al., 2009), which may in turn improve athletic performance.

Imagery may also enhance performance by increasing intrinsic motivation. Martin and Hall (1995) found that beginner golfers in an imagery intervention practiced more and set higher goals, thus exhibiting higher levels of intrinsic motivation, than those in a control group. Harwood, Cumming, and Hall (2003) found that athletes with both high task (e.g., motivated by self-improvement) and high ego (e.g., motivated by beating others) orientations used imagery more often than those with low or moderate levels of task and ego orientations. Those who engage in mental strategies like imagery may already be motivated to enhance performance, thus contributing to imagery effectiveness.

Furthermore, widely used multimodal stress management techniques—such as Meichenbaum's (1985) stress management training, R. E. Smith's (1980) cognitive–affective stress management training, and Suinn's (1972) visuomotor behavioral rehearsal—all feature imagery as a means of reducing anxiety. A review of these programs shows that they have been successful in helping athletes control anxiety and enhance sport performance (Gould & Udry, 1994). Imagery thus influences important psychological states such as confidence, motivation, and anxiety, which in turn influence athletic performance.

APPLIED MODELS OF IMAGERY USE IN SPORT

Martin et al. (1999) developed an applied model of how imagery is used in sport (see Figure 4.1), including aspects of both bio-informational theory and the triple-code model, which was updated and modified in 2005 (Gregg, Hall, & Nederhof, 2005). Although this applied model does not attempt to explain the underlying mechanisms for why and how imagery affects performance, it provides a useful framework for imagery uses within sport. The model consists of four central components: (a) the sport situation, (b) the type of imagery used, (c) imagery ability, and (d) the outcomes of imagery use. In addition, five types of imagery are outlined based on Paivio's (1985) framework of imagery

FIGURE 4.1

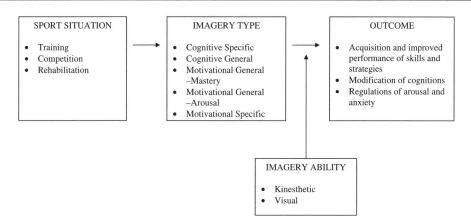

An applied model of mental imagery use in sport. From "Imagery Use in Sport: A Literature Review and Applied Model," by K. A. Martin, S. E. Moritz, and C. R. Hall, 1999, *The Sport Psychologist, 13*(3), p. 248. Copyright 1999 by Human Kinetics. Reprinted with permission.

functions. Cognitive-specific (CS) imagery involves an athlete imaging specific sport skills, such as a basketball free throw. The cognitive general (CG) type of imagery refers to imagery of competitive strategies, such as the use of a diamond defense in field hockey. Motivational general-mastery (MG-M) imagery involves imaging oneself coping effectively and mastering challenging situations, such as a tennis player imaging himself being confident and positive going into a tough match. The motivational general-arousal (MG-A) type of imagery refers to imagery focused on various arousal experiences associated with sport competition, such as anxiety and relaxation; for example, a shooter may imagine herself feeling physically calm and relaxed during her setup. Motivational-specific (MS) imagery focuses on imaging oneself working toward and achieving specific goals, such as a personal best time.

Martin et al. (1999) suggested three outcomes associated with imagery use based on previous research, including skill and strategy learning and performance, modifying cognitions, and regulating arousal and competitive anxiety. Based on a review of the imagery literature, they concluded that CS imagery is most effective for skill and strategy learning and performance and that MG-M and MS imagery are more effective for modifying cognitions. Finally, imagery, combined with other behavioral stress management strategies, is effective in regulating arousal and competition anxiety. Martin et al. also noted that imagery use is helpful in specific sport situations such as training, competition, and rehabilitation. Gregg et al. (2005) emphasized the importance of considering both the demands of the task and the desired outcomes in the design of imagery interventions programs and contended that Martin et al.'s model continues to be a valuable resource.

More recently, Holmes and Collins (2001) developed the PETTLEP model of imagery. The PETTLEP acronym symbolizes seven important components that should be considered when constructing a motor-based imagery program: physical, environment, task, timing, learning, emotion, and perspective. Based on cognitive psychology and neuroscience research, this model contends that the neurophysiological responses underlying both imagery and actual physical movement are the same, thus explaining the imagery–performance relationship. In the PETTLEP model, then, physical practice and imagery are viewed on a continuum. Imagery intervention programs that lie closer to the physical end of the continuum are predicted to be more effective than those closer to the imagery end of the continuum. Hence, the more one's imagery replicates actual performance by using the seven PETTLEP components as a guide, the more effective the imagery will be. For example, instead of lying down and imagining hitting a perfect golf swing, the PETTLEP model suggests that the golfer be outside, assume his stance, and hold his club while performing imagery. It is encouraging that studies have supported the contentions of the PETTLEP model. For example, in two studies conducted by D. Smith, Wright, Allsopp, and Westhead (2007), the use of PETTLEP model-based imagery (e.g., wearing the correct clothing and performing imaging in the actual environment) by field hockey players taking penalty shots and gymnasts executing a balance beam skill was found to be more effective than imagery interventions involving less specific imagery scripts.

Imagery Research

The research studies examining the relationship between imagery and athletic performance can be categorized into four main areas: (a) mental practice studies, (b) precompetition imagery intervention research, (c) imagery use studies, and (d) mediating variable studies.

MENTAL PRACTICE STUDIES

The majority of the mental practice studies are concerned with the effects of mental practice on the learning and performance of motor skills. In these studies, mental practice is typically defined as mental rehearsal of a given task or performance without any associated overt actions. Although mental practice may or may not include the use of imagery, the overlap between the two areas warrants a discussion of the findings.

The standard methodology used in the mental practice studies involves a between-subjects pretest–posttest design with four groups: physical practice only, mental practice only, both physical and mental practice, and no practice. For example, Rawlings, Rawlings, Chen, and Yilk (1972) examined the effects of mental practice on a pursuit rotor task. At the onset of the study, all participants were introduced to the task and received 25 practice trials. Following these trials, participants differed in their practice methods. Group 1 received physical practice only, Group 2 received no practice, and Group 3 received mental practice only (imagery and visualization). After an 8-day training period, all participants were retested on the pursuit rotor task for 25 more trials. The results showed that the mental practice group improved considerably over the course of the experiment, almost to the extent that the physical practice group did. In contrast, the no-practice group showed little, if any, improvement.

On the basis of a meta-analysis of 60 mental practice studies, Feltz and Landers (1983) suggested that mental practice is better than no practice at all. Furthermore, in a comprehensive review of the literature, Weinberg (1981) stated that

> mental practice combined and alternated with physical practice is more effective than either physical or mental practice alone. In addition, physical practice is superior to mental practice. Mental practice should not replace physical practice, but rather it can be used as a valuable addition to physical practice. (p. 203)

This literature supports the belief that the ideal training program combines physical and mental practice techniques.

PRECOMPETITION IMAGERY INTERVENTIONS

Unlike mental practice studies, precompetition imagery intervention studies involve the use of imagery or mental rehearsal immediately prior to performance. They examine the effectiveness of imagery in preparing an athlete who is about to perform. Unfortunately, studies in this area have generated more questions than answers.

For example, several studies have suggested that imagery rehearsal prior to performance can benefit performance on some tasks compared with a condition in which no imagery rehearsal is used (see S. Murphy & Jowdy, 1992, for a detailed review). Shelton and Mahoney (1978) found that 15 male weight lifters asked to use their favorite "psyching-up" strategy before a test of hand strength showed significantly greater improvement over baseline than did 15 male weight lifters asked to improve their performance but given a distracting cognitive task during preperformance. Unfortunately, this type of research is problematic, for two reasons. First, such designs do not specify the type of mental rehearsal that facilitates performance. Although each athlete may report having used imagery, this may mean different things to different athletes. Second, this research does little to improve understanding of how imagery interventions influence performance. It fails to address the important and often elusive question of what mechanisms underlie the imagery–performance relationship.

In addition to these problems, several studies have failed to find a positive relationship between imagery and performance. For example, Weinberg, Gould, Jackson, and Barnes (1980) examined three mental preparation strategies and their effects on a tennis serve task. Participants were divided into one of four conditions: (a) using imagery to prepare for serving, (b) making positive self-efficacy statements, (c) using attentional focus, and (d) a control condition in which participants were asked to prepare as they normally would. The results showed that none of the cognitive strategies increased performance over the control condition.

S. Murphy and Jowdy (1992) suggested that these mixed results may be due to a number of variables, including task, individual difference, and physiology. With regard to the task variables, imagery rehearsal may be a more effective strategy for some types of tasks than for others. Perhaps imagery rehearsal is more effective with predominantly cognitive as opposed to motor tasks, for example. It is also important to examine individual difference variables. Some individuals may, for instance, have a higher quality of imagery and thus experience greater improvements in performance. Finally, imagery may differentially influence certain physiological variables (e.g., electromyogram, electroencephalogram, heart rate). Although they show that an imagery–performance relationship often exists, the preperformance imagery intervention studies have been methodologically weak overall.

Some research in this area has included better intervention descriptions and manipulation checks. For example, Velentzas, Heinen, and Schack (2011) investigated the influence of an imagery-based routine on serve performance in volleyball. It was found that the imagery group served with greater accuracy and speed as compared with both a control group and a group that received physical training. In another study testing the PETTLEP imagery model, D. Smith et al. (2007) found that gymnasts who used internal perspective and kinesthetic imagery while in gymnastics attire on the balance beam improved as much as gymnasts who only physically practiced and more than both a control stretching group and a stimulus imagery group imagining the performance at home in street clothes. Finally, in an interesting 14-week case study intervention with an elite rugby player involving interviews, diaries, and the Sport Imagery Questionnaire, Evans, Jones, and Mullen (2004) found that the player reported more structure to his imagery use post-intervention. The respondent also indicated that he had greater imagery clarity; improved confidence; and better control of activation, anxiety, and motivation. Hence, the intervention was successful in helping him better control psychological processes.

IMAGERY USE STUDIES

Another area of imagery research has focused on the incidence of imagery use among athletes, including when, where, and why they use imagery. Athletes use imagery in conjunction with practice, competition, and rehabilitation (Martin et al., 1999), as well as in environments outside of practice and competition, such as school, home, and work (Salmon, Hall, & Haslam, 1994). Athletes tend to use imagery more often prior to competition than in association with practice situations (Barr & Hall, 1992; Hall, Rodgers, & Barr, 1990; K. J. Munroe, Giacobbi, Hall, & Weinberg, 2000; Salmon et al., 1994; Weinberg, Butt, Knight, Burke, & Jackson, 2003). K. Munroe, Hall, Simms, and Weinberg (1998) found that the imagery use of athletes from 10 sports differed across the duration of their respective competitive seasons. CG imagery and MS imagery were increasingly used as the competitive season progressed. Other changes in imagery use across the competitive season depended on the sport.

Similarly, K. J. Munroe et al. (2000) interviewed 14 athletes from seven sports to examine where, when, why, and what athletes image. Athletes reported using imagery both during and outside of practice as well as before, during, and after competition. Athletes in this study indicated that they found imagery to be most effective during practice and prior to competitive situations. Athletes reported a number of reasons for using imagery, many corresponding to the types of imagery described by Paivio (1985) and Martin et al. (1999). Specifically, they reported using imagery for skill development (CS), skill execution, and strategy development and execution (CG). They also reported using imagery to generate motivation related to performance and outcome (MS); to regulate excitement, control, and relaxation (MG-A); to enhance mental toughness, focus, and confidence (MG-G); and to get into flow states.

MEDIATING VARIABLES STUDIES

The final area of research to be discussed focuses on a variety of possible mediating variables and their influence on the imagery–performance relationship. Team cohesion is one situational variable that has been associated with greater imagery use (Short, Smiley, & Ross-Stewart, 2005).When considering individual characteristics, some researchers have examined the influence of imagery ability on performance. Imagery ability has been defined primarily by the level of vividness and controllability that athletes have over their imagery. Vividness refers to the clarity and reality in an athlete's image, whereas controllability refers to the athlete's ability to influence the content of the image. Several correlational studies have found that more successful performers have a higher quality of imagery (Highlen & Bennett, 1983; Meyers, Cooke, Cullen, & Liles, 1979). Athletes with greater imagery ability tend to use this psychological tool more often (Gregg, Hall, McGowan, & Hall, 2011).

Another possible mediating variable relates to the correctness of an athlete's imagery. For example, Woolfolk, Parrish, and Murphy (1985) used a golf putting task to determine the effects of imagery correctness on performance. The results showed that participants in the negative imagery condition performed significantly worse than participants in the positive imagery and control conditions.

A final mediating variable relates to imagery perspective. Some athletes imagine themselves from an internal perspective (i.e., they are inside their body actually experiencing the imagined sensations), whereas others imagine themselves from an external perspective (i.e., they are a spectator watching the performance). Although some researchers have found an internal perspective to be associated with higher levels of performance (Mahoney & Avener, 1977), others have found no difference in performance for those with internal versus external imagery perspectives (Mumford & Hall, 1985). Research by Hardy and colleagues (Hardy, 1997; Hardy & Callow, 1999; White & Hardy, 1998) suggests that an external imagery perspective is good for imaging tasks in which form is important; however, an internal imagery perspective is good for imaging open-skilled tasks where perception is important for performance. In addition, kinesthetic imagery is thought to be beneficial regardless of the imagery perspective used. Thus, considering individual differences and situational factors is critical in both the study and the application of imagery techniques.

Our brief review of the sport and motor performance imagery research shows that this area of investigation is not without problems. More carefully controlled and methodologically sound research is certainly needed (detailed recommendations for imagery researchers are provided by Short, Ross-Stewart, & Monsma, 2006). On a more positive note, when it is combined with physical practice, imagery has been shown to facilitate sport performance. However, this research also demonstrates that imagery does not work for all tasks, with all people, in all situations. Although improved research will clarify on what tasks, with whom, and in what situations imagery works best, it is clear that simply asking athletes to imagine themselves performing better will not guarantee beneficial effects. Sport psychology professionals and coaches must make informed imagery prescriptions that are guided by an understanding of imagery research and theory, feedback from athletes, and sport psychology guidelines identified for effective use.

Guidelines for Using Imagery

From the research conducted thus far, many practical applications have been suggested to help increase use of imagery as a performance enhancement tool. Similarly, some sport psychology professionals (Harris & Harris, 1984; Martens, 1987; Orlick, 1986, 1990; Vealey & Greenleaf, 1998) who have had extensive experience in using imagery rehearsal with athletes have developed a number of useful guidelines for those practitioners or athletes interested in implementing such techniques.

PRACTICE IMAGERY ON A REGULAR BASIS

Unfortunately, many coaches and athletes believe that psychological skills such as imagery do not require the same practice that physical skills require. For example, Carolyn, described at the beginning of this chapter, halfheartedly attempted to use imagery to enhance her golf game. She never truly committed to practicing imagery and became frustrated when she failed to realize immediate performance gains. Mental skills are like physical skills. Becoming proficient in the use of imagery requires a commitment throughout the training season. It is unrealistic to think that either a physical or mental skill will be effective in a competitive situation when it is never practiced at any other time. Ideally, imagery training should become an integral part of daily practice.

USE ALL SENSES TO ENHANCE IMAGE VIVIDNESS

The more senses incorporated into imagery, the more vivid and effective it will be (Harris & Harris, 1984; Orlick, 1986). Many athletes assume that imagery is synonymous with visualization. Although visualization can be an important component of imagery rehearsal, it is important to draw from senses other than sight to increase that quality of imagery, especially in physical activities like sports. For example, a skier may wish to familiarize herself with an upcoming race course. In addition to "seeing" the course, she also needs to experience the kinesthetic feeling of passing through a particularly tough gate, feeling the wind, and hearing the ski edges slash through the snow. This helps the athlete develop positive feelings as well as a sense of confidence when entering the upcoming event.

DEVELOP IMAGERY CONTROL

In addition to improving image clarity, it is important that athletes be able to control the content of their images. Is an athlete's image positive and self-enhancing or negative and self-defeating? Negative imagery can have a detrimental effect on performance. It is important to know the extent to which the individual athletes you are working with are able to influence the content of their imagery. For example, if a tennis player consistently imagines his serves going into the net, it may be important to provide specific exercises to strengthen his imagery control. Fortunately, with practice, most athletes can learn to control the content of their imagery.

USE BOTH INTERNAL AND EXTERNAL PERSPECTIVES

Some athletes imagine themselves from an inside-the-body perspective, actually experiencing the imagined sensations. Others imagine themselves from the perspective of watching their performances on a movie screen. It has been proposed that an internal imagery perspective is superior to an external imagery perspective because of the importance of kinesthetic awareness in sport performance (Mahoney & Avener, 1977). However, researchers have suggested that the use of external imagery for tasks in which form is important and internal imagery for tasks in which perception and decision making are important are effective (Hardy, 1997; Hardy & Callow, 1999; White & Hardy, 1998). For example, external imagery may enhance sport performance by building athletes' self-confidence. The best approach to imagery depends on the needs of the individual athlete and the demands of the specific sport.

FACILITATE IMAGERY THROUGH RELAXATION

Research suggests that imagery combined with relaxation is more effective than imagery alone (Weinberg, Seabourne, & Jackson, 1981). However, imagery can certainly be used without relaxation—for example, during competition (K. J. Munroe et al., 2000). It is thought that using relaxation strategies (e.g., passive progressive relaxation, deep breathing) prior to imagery rehearsal clears athletes' minds of possible distractions and, therefore, allows them to better concentrate on their imagery. The combination of relaxation and imagery training is especially helpful with athletes who are just developing their imagery skills. Unlike athletes who are highly proficient with imagery, less skilled imagers tend to be more easily distracted because their imagery skills are not yet automatic. The purpose of this chapter is not to review various relaxation techniques; however, readers can refer to Wilson and Taylor's chapter on intensity regulation and sport performance in this book (Chapter 6) for more specific relaxation strategies that may be used with imagery.

DEVELOP COPING STRATEGIES THROUGH IMAGERY

Although positive imagery is generally preferred over negative imagery, there are occasions when negative imagery can be helpful. If athletes always imagine themselves performing perfectly, then they are almost assured to set themselves up for failure. Therefore, it is important that they learn to cope with adversity as well as success. For example, a baseball player may wish to imagine himself striking out the first few times at bat, only to come back with a critical hit in the late innings. Coping imagery can help athletes turn a poor performance around. However, such imagery is not recommended for use just before a competitive event. Coping imagery may be best used in the off-season and should not be done too frequently. When athletes are preparing for an important competitive event, it seems best to have them imagine themselves performing successfully rather than unsuccessfully.

USE IMAGERY IN PRACTICE AND COMPETITION

Imagery rehearsal should be used in practice sessions as well as before competition. Imagery can help an athlete to get in the right zone both mentally and physically to optimize training. As an example, imagery can help direct an athlete's attention to specific practice goals. It can also help an athlete who may not be motivated to practice on a given day. Many athletes find it difficult to get up for practice in the off-season. Imagery of arousal-producing situations (e.g., losing to a rival) can be used to help motivate athletes to train hard for competitions that may be months away. Finally, the quality of imagery will improve if it is used daily in practice, and thus it will be of more help to athletes during the pressures of competition.

Imagery is not only helpful in preparing for practice but also should be used frequently during practice. For example, following a mistake, coaches can instruct athletes to mentally correct the problems through imagery before making the next attempts. Likewise, after performing correctly, athletes can take a moment to imagine the look and feel of the correct response. Similarly, when demonstrating, coaches should ask athletes to imagine the skill that was demonstrated before executing a response. Finally, when teaching new offensive or defensive plays to team-sport athletes, coaches should instruct athletes to visualize the correct flow of movement of the team's play. However, the effective use of imagery during practice does not typically mean that one stops play or instruction for a special 5- or 10-minute imagery session. Rather, coaches should repeatedly ask athletes to "imagine" for very short periods (3–10 seconds) as a part of normal coaching and instructional procedures.

USE DVDs OR AUDIOTAPES TO ENHANCE IMAGERY SKILLS

Some athletes find DVDs or audio recordings helpful to develop and reinforce constructive imagery. Although several audio recordings are on the market, athletes can make their own to help guide them through an imagery session. If athletes or sport psychology professionals create their own recordings, they can incorporate cues that are used during physical practice. For example, if a swimmer uses the cue word "punch" to instruct herself to explode off the turn, this cue could be used during imagery rehearsal.

DVDs can also be used to help athletes develop their imagery skills. "Highlight DVDs" can be made with clips of athletes' practices or competitions in which they have performed well. An athlete's favorite music can be added to serve as a cue to trigger excellent performance in the future. The U.S. women's ice hockey team combined season highlights interspersed with Muhammad Ali video clips to enhance imagery and create positive feelings of confidence prior to their gold medal winning game.

USE TRIGGERS OR CUES TO FACILITATE IMAGERY QUALITY

As mentioned above, triggers or cues are important components of imagery rehearsal. For some athletes, triggers are words or phrases that help them to focus on appropriate cues during imagery. Triggers may also include specific sensory experiences, such as how a given technique or movement feels kinesthetically. Triggers can involve any of the five senses. The key point is that whatever trigger or cue an athlete uses, it must be able to conjure up the appropriate image.

EMPHASIZE DYNAMIC KINESTHETIC IMAGERY

Another way to enhance the quality of imagery is to have athletes focus particular attention on the kinesthetic feel of the movement. Some athletes also find it useful to move during imagery rehearsal. For example, a sprinter may assume a starting position and then imagine blasting from the blocks en route to a record time. A golfer may stand at address and actually swing a golf club while imagining the ball traveling through the air and landing close to the hole. With dynamic imagery the actual movement of the activity often helps athletes to recall more clearly the sensations associated with their performance.

IMAGE IN REAL TIME

Research has shown that at times athletes find it helpful to slow down their play during imagery, particularly to analyze techniques or patterns of play, learn skills, or develop strategies (O & Hall, 2009). Sometimes they may find it useful to speed images up when imaging skills that have been mastered. However, because an athlete does not execute techniques in slow motion or at a faster-than-normal speed, the bulk of imagery should be in real time (i.e., the speed at which athletes actually perform). As a result, imagery practice will replicate the actual conditions of play.

USE IMAGERY LOGS

Imagery logs or notebooks can serve a variety of purposes. For instance, they can assist athletes in monitoring imagery practice and progress. Different imagery exercises can be recorded along with the extent to which athletes feel that exercises are helpful. Imagery logs can also be used to describe previous best performances in an effort to identify better triggers or cues for imagery rehearsal. Overall, imagery logs increase athletes' awareness with regard to the practice they devote to imagery as well as the effectiveness of this practice.

CONSIDER THE DEVELOPMENTAL LEVEL OF IMAGERY PARTICIPANTS

One important development in imagery research is the importance of understanding how athletes of different ages and skill levels use imagery. For example, Munroe-Chandler, Hall, Fisburne, and Stachan (2007) employed focus groups to study imagery use in athletes ranging from 7 to 14 years of age. They found that all groups studied used motivational and cognitive imagery in both training and competition. The youngest athletes (7–8 years of age), however, did not report using imagery immediately following competitions or out of practice. The younger athletes also reported less use of MG-A and MG-M imagery. Findings from another study suggest that youth sport participants may have little understanding of the psychological tools being employed. In a qualitative examination of youth athletes 10 to 15 years old, McCarthy, Jones, Harwood, and Olivier (2010) found that although mental imagery and goal setting were the better understood psychological skills (as compared with relaxation and self-talk), it is critical for practitioners to adapt their interventions to meet the age and developmental level of the participants. Other studies have shown that imagery use may be related to age and skill level. Gregg and Hall (2006) found that age predicted imagery use in golfers (8–87 years of age) and that the lower handicapped or more skilled golfers used all types of imagery more often than their less skilled counterparts. Hence, it may be especially important to encourage imagery use by less experienced, less skilled, and older athletes.

Developing an Imagery Training Program

Having established specific guidelines for using imagery, we now address how to best implement an imagery training program with athletes. Although no two imagery programs are alike, it is important to incorporate the four phases discussed here.

PHASE 1: AWARENESS, REALISTIC EXPECTATIONS, AND BASIC EDUCATION

Many coaches are eager to try all that imagery training has to offer. Unfortunately, their efforts are often undermined because many athletes do not understand what imagery is and how it can enhance performance. Consider the story of Alan at the beginning of this chapter. After attending a coaching education seminar, he decided to implement an imagery training program with his high school boys' basketball team. Although his intentions were good, he failed to educate his team on basic imagery principles and convince them of the importance of imagery training to their basketball success. As a result, his players questioned the purpose of all this "mental stuff" and never truly made a commitment to it during practice.

Before implementing any imagery training program, it is critical that sport psychology professionals and coaches explain what imagery is and address any possible misconceptions that athletes may have. For example, some athletes may look to imagery training as a quick-and-easy solution to complex performance problems. This thinking is consistent with the desire for instant gratification so prevalent in many parts of the world. In reality, however, developing and refining imagery skills require the same systematic practice as physical skills.

Another common misconception that many athletes have is that imagery training is not useful. The claims of athletes in the popular press and from a growing body of research indicate that imagery training helps athletes achieve their potential. Although imagery training certainly cannot solve all problems, it has helped many athletes reach higher levels of performance.

Finally, because the media attention surrounding sport psychology is often associated with elite performers, many falsely assume that mental skills such as imagery are only for top-ranked amateur or professional athletes. In reality, imagery training can help athletes of all ability levels to achieve their potential. Imagery rehearsal can be used in conjunction with physical training to enhance skill acquisition in any athlete.

Overall, athletes must be aware of the importance of imagery for performance success if they are to develop a commitment to a training program (Martens, 1987). However, sport psychology professionals and coaches must avoid unrealistic expectations about the effectiveness of imagery. Promises of dramatic performance improvements will set up even the best-designed program for failure and undermine the credibility of imagery training.

Therefore, before implementing a program, sport psychology professionals and coaches should hold a brief introductory meeting to explain what imagery is and how it has helped other athletes in the past, especially those in the same sport as the athletes they are speaking to. For example, Alan could have conveyed to his basketball team how Bill Russell, one of the all-time best basketball players and winner of 11 National Basketball Association championships, used imagery to execute new plays and build self-confidence (Russell & Branch, 1979). Such stories can help to establish credibility and respect with athletes, demonstrate an understanding of the language of the sport, and show athletes how to relate imagery skills to their specific individual needs (Orlick & Partington, 1987; Partington & Orlick, 1987; Ravizza, 1988).

It is also important to stress in the introductory meeting the need to practice imagery on a regular basis. During preseason, many coaches and athletes are enthusiastic about the prospects of an imagery training program. Unfortunately, as the season progresses and time demands and pressures increase, imagery training is often reduced to a handful of brief meetings added on to an already demanding practice schedule. Coaches and athletes must view imagery training as an integral part of practice. Practicing sport psychology professionals should emphasize that imagery training will not take away from physical practice but will instead enhance it.

PHASE 2: IMAGERY SKILL EVALUATION AND DEVELOPMENT

Once athletes are aware of the value of imagery training, have realistic expectations, and have received basic education, their specific imagery skills should be evaluated and developed. There are several methods for evaluating imagery ability. One is to administer a psychological skills inventory, such as the Sport Imagery Questionnaire discussed by Vealey and Greenleaf (1998). This questionnaire was originally created by Martens (1982) to measure athletes' ability to experience each of the five senses as well as various emotional or mood states. Another way to evaluate imagery ability is to guide an athlete through an imagery exercise and, afterward, discuss the quality of the images. One should consider several aspects of the athlete's images in such an evaluation: (a) Were the images vivid and controllable? (b) Were they experienced from an internal or an external perspective? (c) Was the athlete able to feel the physical movements while imaging? (d) Were images under the athlete's control? It is important to remember that, just as individual athletes differ in physical ability, they will also differ in their ability to image.

Once sport psychology professionals recognize athletes' strengths and weaknesses with regard to imagery, they can determine what specific practice strategies are most appropriate. In general, imagery training is designed to enhance the vividness and controllability of an athlete's imagery. Martens (1987) recommended that a sport imagery training program consist of three steps: (a) sensory awareness training, (b) vividness training, and (c) controllability training.

Sensory Awareness Training

The first step in Martens's (1987) sport imagery training program is to have athletes become more aware of their sport experiences. The more athletes are consciously aware of what they see, hear, and feel, the more likely that they will be able to mentally recreate these experiences through imagery. For example, following a successful practice or competition, an athlete may wish to make note of the various sensations associated with that performance in an effort to identify specific cues that will enhance the quality of imagery in the future.

Vividness Training

After athletes have gained a greater sense of awareness with regard to their sport experiences, Martens (1987) suggested they should work to develop and refine the vividness of their images. This can be accomplished with a variety of exercises. For example, if athletes have very poor imagery skills, the sport psychology professional or coach might recommend that they start with a simple exercise, such as imagining the details of their bedroom or a piece of equipment associated with their sport (e.g., a football, running shoes). As their imagery skills develop, they can begin to imagine more complex skills associated with their sport performance using the PETTLEP model components to make their imagery script as realistic as possible. Also, athletes may find it helpful to practice in a relaxed environment, free of any possible distractions at first and then later in accordance with PETTLEP model guidelines move into more realistic environments. As discussed earlier, many athletes use relaxation techniques prior to imagery rehearsal to better focus their attention. There is no limit to the exercises that athletes can do to enhance the vividness of their images. It requires only a little imagination and creativity.

Controllability Training

The final step of Martens's (1987) sport imagery training program involves learning to control and manipulate images. Similar to vividness training, if athletes have poor imagery skills, it is important to begin with a simple exercise in a quiet setting before moving to a more complex, sport-specific exercise. Assume, for example, that a basketball player has difficulty controlling the content of his images. When he tries to imagine himself hitting a 3-point shot, he is unable to visualize the ball going into the basket. In this situation, a practicing sport psychology professional or coach may want to suggest that the athlete try a more simple exercise, such as simply imagining that he is dribbling the ball from a stationary position. As he becomes more proficient with this exercise, he can gradually work toward controlling images of more complex basketball skills (e.g., layups, 8-foot jumpshots, 16-foot jumpshots, then 3-point shots).

It is also important to remind athletes to be patient with themselves at first and not expect too much too soon. This is apparent from comments by Sylvie Bernier, former Olympic champion in springboard diving:

> It took me a long time to control my images and perfect my imagery, maybe a year, doing it every day. At first I couldn't see myself, I always saw everyone else, or I would see my dives

wrong all the time. I would get an image of hurting myself, or tripping on the board, or I would "see" something done really bad. As I continued to work at it, I got to the point where I could feel myself doing a perfect dive and hear the crowd yelling at the Olympics. But it took me a long time. (Orlick, 1990, p. 68)

Regardless of whether an athlete is working on sensory awareness, image vividness, or image control, imagery is a skill like any other, requiring consistent effort to attain a high level of proficiency.

Individuals differ in their ability to image. Therefore, it is critical that athletes be evaluated with regard to their imagery ability. Once athletes' strengths and weaknesses are recognized, an imagery program can be tailored to fit the individual needs of a team or athlete.

PHASE 3: USING IMAGERY

Once athletes have evaluated and developed their imagery skills, it is important that they be reminded to continue to use them on a regular basis. Coaches are in the best position to remind athletes to use imagery and can do so with any number of strategies. For example, Mike White, former University of Illinois football coach, made a large meeting room available to his team in the hotel on the nights before games. This "imagery room" was used on a voluntary basis, and players went to this dark, quiet place to mentally prepare themselves. Coaches can also incorporate the use of imagery in instructional settings by having athletes visualize demonstrations, correct mistakes, and learn new offensive and defensive strategies. Knowledge of Martin et al.'s (1999) applied model of imagery, with its five types of imagery and focus on the outcomes desired and the types of situations athletes are performing in, can serve as an excellent guide for coaches to go beyond saying simply imagine doing a skill. Coach support and involvement, then, are valuable for imagery training programs. Finally, players should spend time visualizing themselves performing successfully and achieving their goals. They should also be encouraged to focus on the seven components of the PETTLEP model to help themselves design the most effective motor imagery programs.

PHASE 4: IMAGERY EVALUATION, ADJUSTMENT, AND REFINEMENT

The final steps in any successful imagery training program involve determining whether the program is meeting its objectives (Weinberg & Williams, 1998) and identifying adjustments and refinements needed to enhance the program. It is valuable to start by evaluating current imagery ability levels and assigning appropriate exercises for each player. Midway through the season, athletes' imagery ability could be reevaluated (e.g., with Martens's, 1982, Sport Imagery Questionnaire) to determine what, if any, progress has been made. For athletes who have shown little improvement, individual meetings could be set up to identify possible problems. Depending on the individual situation, a new strategy might be developed. Athletes who are improving would simply be encouraged to continue with their current strategies, to log imagery effectiveness, and to explore new ways of using imagery.

If an imagery training program is meeting its objectives, athletes can continue with confidence. However, if the program is not meeting its objectives, it is critical to determine why. What are the obstacles, and how can they be overcome? Without critically examining an imagery training program, some athletes may falsely conclude that they are poor imagers when, in fact, they were using inappropriate strategies to develop their imagery skills. Program evaluations provide important feedback as to what strategies are effective and for whom they are effective. In addition, they provide an opportunity to alter ineffective strategies.

In summary, no two imagery training programs are identical. Each is designed to meet the unique characteristics and needs of an athlete or team. However, an individual training program should include each of the four phases outlined above. For any training program to be effective, the athletes must understand that imagery is a skill that requires consistent effort over time to develop. Further, during the training process, progress must be evaluated and adjustments made to ensure that the program is meeting its desired objectives.

Summary

Imagery, a process by which sensory experiences are stored in memory and internally recalled and performed in the absence of external stimuli, is a powerful performance enhancement technique studied and used by practicing sport psychology professionals. Several imagery theories and models focus on explaining how imagery influences performance, as well as how athletes can use imagery. Based on research and practical experience, several guidelines were suggested to help practitioners or athletes interested in implementing imagery rehearsal to enhance sport performance. In implementing an imagery training program, it is important to incorporate the four specific phases we have outlined in this chapter. Finally, we have addressed several common problems involving the implementation of an imagery training program and made specific suggests about how to best handle these potential obstacles. Imagery is like any physical skill in that it requires systematic practice. Individual athletes will differ in their ability to image and, therefore, must be encouraged to remain patient. Imagery is not a magical cure for performance woes. It is, however, an effective tool that—when combined with practice and commitment—can help athletes reach their personal and athletic potentials.

References

Ahsen, A. (1984). ISM: The triple code model for imagery and psychophysiology. *Journal of Mental Imagery, 8,* 15–42.

Bandura, A. (1977). Self-efficacy: Toward a unifying theory of behavioral change. *Psychological Review, 84,* 191–215. doi:10.1037/0033-295X.84.2.191

Barr, K., & Hall, C. (1992). The use of imagery by rowers. *International Journal of Sport Psychology, 23,* 243–261.

Callow, N., Hardy, L., & Hall, C. (1998). The effect of a motivational-mastery imagery intervention on the sport confidence of three elite badminton players. *Journal of Applied Sport Psychology, 10,* S135.

Cumming, J., Olphin, T., & Law, M. (2007). Self-reported psychological states and physiological responses to different types of motivational general imagery. *Journal of Sport & Exercise Psychology, 29,* 629–644.

Evans, L., Jones, L., & Mullen, R. (2004). An imagery intervention during the competitive season with an elite rugby union player. *The Sport Psychologist, 18,* 252–271.

Feltz, D. L., & Landers, D. M. (1983). The effects of mental practice on motor skill learning and performance: A meta-analysis. *Journal of Sport Psychology, 5,* 25–57.

Gould, D., & Udry, E. (1994). Psychological skills for enhancing performance: Arousal regulation strategies. *Medicine & Science in Sports and Exercise, 26,* 478–485. doi:10.1249/00005768-199404000-00013

Gregg, M., & Hall, C. (2006). The relationship of skill level and age to the use of imagery by golfers. *Journal of Applied Sport Psychology, 18,* 363–375. doi:10.1080/10413200600944140

Gregg, M., Hall, C., McGowan, E., & Hall, N. (2011). The relationship between imagery ability and imagery use among athletes. *Journal of Applied Sport Psychology, 23,* 129–141. doi:10.1080/10413200.2010.544279

Gregg, M., Hall, C., & Nederhof, E. (2005). The imagery ability, imagery use, and performance relationship. *The Sport Psychologist, 19,* 93–99.

Hall, C. R., Munroe-Chandler, K. J., Cumming, J., Law, B., Ramsey, R., & Murphy, L. (2009). Imagery and observational learning use and their relationship to sport confidence. *Journal of Sports Sciences, 27,* 327–337. doi:10.1080/02640410802549769

Hall, C. R., Rodgers, W. M., & Barr, K. A. (1990). The use of imagery by athletes in selected sports. *The Sport Psychologist, 4,* 1–10.

Hardy, L. (1997). Three myths about applied consultancy work. *Journal of Applied Sport Psychology, 9,* 277–294. doi:10.1080/10413209708406487

Hardy, L., & Callow, N. (1999). Efficacy of external and internal visual imagery perspectives for the enhancement of performance on tasks in which form is important. *Journal of Sport & Exercise Psychology, 21,* 95–112.

Harris, D. V., & Harris, B. L. (1984). *The athlete's guide to sport psychology: Mental training for physical people.* New York, NY: Leisure Press.

Harwood, C., Cumming, J., & Hall, C. (2003). Imagery use in elite youth sport participants: Reinforcing the applied significance of achievement goal theory. *Research Quarterly for Exercise and Sport, 74,* 292–300.

Highlen, P. S., & Bennett, B. B. (1983). Elite divers and wrestlers: A comparison between open and closed-skilled athletes. *Journal of Sport Psychology, 5,* 390–409.

Holmes, P. S., & Collins, D. J. (2001). The PETTLEP approach to motor imagery: A functional equivalence model for sport psychologists. *Journal of Applied Sport Psychology, 13,* 60–83. doi:10.1080/10413200109339004

Jacobson, E. (1932). Electrophysiology of mental activities. *The American Journal of Psychology, 44,* 677–694. doi:10.2307/1414531

Kohl, R. M., & Roenker, D. L. (1983). Mechanism involvement during skill imagery. *Journal of Motor Behavior, 15,* 179–190.

Lang, P. J. (1977). Imagery in therapy: An information processing analysis of fear. *Behavior Therapy, 8,* 862–886. doi:10.1016/S0005-7894 (77)80157-3

Lang, P. J. (1979). A bio-information theory of emotional imagery. *Psychophysiology, 16,* 495–512. doi:10.1111/j.1469-8986.1979.tb01511.x

Mahoney, M. J., & Avener, M. (1977). Psychology of the elite athlete: An exploratory study. *Cognitive Therapy and Research, 3,* 361–366. doi:10.1007/BF01173634

Martens, R. (1982, September). *Imagery in sport.* Paper presented at the Medical and Scientific Aspects of Elitism in Sport Conference, Brisbane, Australia.

Martens, R. (1987). *Coaches guide to sport psychology.* Champaign, IL: Human Kinetics.

Martin, K. A., & Hall, C. R. (1995). Using mental imagery to enhance intrinsic motivation. *Journal of Sport & Exercise Psychology, 17,* 54–69.

Martin, K. A., Moritz, S. E., & Hall, C. R. (1999). Imagery use in sport: A literature review and applied model. *The Sport Psychologist, 13,* 245–268.

McCarthy, P. J., Jones, M. V., Harwood, C. G., & Olivier, S. (2010). What do young athletes implicitly understand about psychological skills? *Journal of Clinical Sport Psychology, 4,* 158–172.

Meichenbaum, D. (1985). *Stress inoculation training.* Elmsford, NY: Pergamon Press.

Meyers, A. W., Cooke, C. J., Cullen, J., & Liles, L. (1979). Psychological aspects of athletic competitors: A replication across sports. *Cognitive Therapy and Research, 3,* 361–366. doi:10.1007/BF01184450

Moritz, S. E., Hall, C. R., Martin, K. A., & Vadocz, E. (1996). What are confident athletes imaging? An examination of image content. *The Sport Psychologist, 10,* 171–179.

Mumford, B., & Hall, C. (1985). The effects of internal and external imagery on performing figures in figure skating. *Canadian Journal of Applied Sport Sciences, 10,* 171–177.

Munroe, K., Hall, C., Simms, S., & Weinberg, R. (1998). The influence of type of sport and time of season on athletes' use of imagery. *The Sport Psychologist, 12,* 440–449.

Munroe, K. J., Giacobbi, P. R., Hall, C., & Weinberg, R. (2000). The four W's of imagery use: Where, when, why, and what. *The Sport Psychologist, 14,* 119–137.

Munroe-Chandler, K. J., Hall, C. R., Fisburne, G. J., & Stachan, L. (2007). Where, when, and why young athletes use imagery: An examination of developmental differences. *Research Quarterly for Exercise and Sport, 78,* 103–116. doi:10.5641/193250307X13082490460580

Murphy, S., & Jowdy, D. (1992). Imagery and mental rehearsal. In T. Horn (Ed.), *Advances in sport psychology* (pp. 221–250). Champaign, IL: Human Kinetics.

Murphy, S. M. (1994). Imagery interventions in sport. *Medicine & Science in Sports and Exercise, 26,* 486–494. doi:10.1249/00005768-199404000-00014

O, J., & Hall, C. (2009). A quantitative analysis of athletes' voluntary use of slow motion, real time, and fast motion images. *Journal of Applied Sport Psychology, 21,* 15–30. doi:10.1080/10413200802541892

Orlick, T. (1986). *Psyching for sport: Mental training for athletes.* Champaign, IL: Leisure Press.

Orlick, T. (1990). *In pursuit of excellence: How to win in sport and life through mental training.* Champaign, IL: Leisure Press.

Orlick, T., & Partington, J. (1987). The sport psychology consultant: Analysis of critical components as viewed by Canadian athletes. *The Sport Psychologist, 1,* 4–7.

Paivio, A. (1985). Cognitive and motivational functions of imagery in human performance. *Canadian Journal of Applied Sport Sciences, 10,* 22S–28S.

Partington, J., & Orlick, T. (1987). The sport psychology consultant: Olympic coaches' views. *The Sport Psychologist, 1,* 95–102.

Ravizza, K. (1988). Gaining entry with athletic personnel for season-long consulting. *The Sport Psychologist, 2,* 243–254.

Rawlings, E. I., Rawlings, I. L., Chen, C. S., & Yilk, M. D. (1972). The facilitating effects of mental rehearsal in the acquisition of rotary pursuit tracking. *Psychonomic Science, 26,* 71–73.

Russell, B., & Branch, T. (1979). *Second wind.* New York, NY: Ballantine Books.

Ryan, E. D., & Simons, J. (1981). Cognitive demand imagery and frequency of mental practice as factors influencing the acquisition of mental skills. *Journal of Sport Psychology, 15,* 1–15.

Sackett, R. S. (1935). The influences of symbolic rehearsal upon the retention of a maze habit. *Journal of General Psychology, 13,* 113–130. doi:10.1080/00221309.1935.9917869

Salmon, J., Hall, C., & Haslam, I. (1994). The use of imagery by soccer players. *Journal of Applied Sport Psychology, 6,* 116–133. doi:10.1080/10413209408406469

Shelton, T. O., & Mahoney, M. J. (1978). The content and effect of "psyching-up" strategies in weight lifters. *Cognitive Therapy and Research, 2,* 275–284. doi:10.1007/BF01185789

Short, S. E., Ross-Stewart, L., & Monsma, E. V. (2006). Onwards with the evolution of imagery research in sport psychology. *Athletic Insight: The Online Journal of Sport Psychology, 8,* 1–15.

Short, S. E., Smiley, M., & Ross-Stewart, L. (2005). Relationship between efficacy beliefs and imagery use in coaches. *The Sport Psychologist, 19,* 380–394.

Slade, J. M., Landers, D. M., & Martin, P. E. (2002). Muscular activity during real and imagined movements: A test of inflow explanations. *Journal of Sport & Exercise Psychology, 24,* 151–167.

Smith, D., Collins, D., & Holmes, P. (2003). Impact and mechanism of mental practice effects on strength. *International Journal of Sport and Exercise Psychology, 1,* 293–306. doi:10.1080/1612197X.2003.9671720

Smith, D., Wright, C., Allsopp, A., & Westhead, H. (2007). It's all in the mind: PETTLEP-based imagery in sports performance. *Journal of Applied Sport Psychology, 19,* 80–92. doi:10.1080/10413200600944132

Smith, R. E. (1980). A cognitive–affective approach to stress management training for athletes. In C. Nadeau, W. Halliwell, K. Newell, & G. C. Roberts (Eds.), *Psychology of motor behavior and sport* (pp. 54–72). Champaign, IL: Human Kinetics.

Suinn, R. (1972). Removing emotional obstacles to learning and performance by visuomotor behavioral rehearsal. *Behavior Therapy, 3,* 308–310. doi:10.1016/S0005-7894(72)80096-0

Suinn, R. (1993). Imagery. In R. N. Singer, M. Murphey, & L. K. Tennant (Eds.), *Handbook of research on sport psychology* (pp. 492–510). New York, NY: Macmillan.

Vealey, R., & Greenleaf, C. (1998). Seeing is believing: Understanding and using imagery in sport. In J. M. Williams (Ed.), *Applied sport psychology: Personal growth to peak performance* (3rd ed., pp. 237–269). Mountain View, CA: Mayfield.

Velentzas, K., Heinen, T., & Schack, T. (2011). Routine integration strategies and their effects on volleyball serve performance and players' movement mental representation. *Journal of Applied Sport Psychology, 23,* 209–222. doi:10.1080/10413200.2010.546826

Weinberg, R., Butt, J., Knight, B., Burke, K. L., & Jackson, A. (2003). The relationship between the use and effectiveness of imagery: An exploratory investigation. *Journal of Applied Sport Psychology, 15,* 26–40. doi:10.1080/10413200305398

Weinberg, R. S. (1981). The relationship between mental preparation strategies and motor performance: A review and critique. *Quest, 33,* 195–213. doi:10.1080/00336297.1981.10483754

Weinberg, R. S., Gould, D., Jackson, A., & Barnes, P. (1980). Influence of cognitive strategies on tennis serves of players of high and low ability. *Perceptual and Motor Skills, 50,* 663–666. doi:10.2466/pms.1980.50.2.663

Weinberg, R. S., Seabourne, T. G., & Jackson, A. (1981). Effects of visuo-motor behavior rehearsal, relaxation, and imagery on karate performance. *Journal of Sport Psychology, 3,* 228–238.

Weinberg, R. S., & Williams, J. M. (1998). Integrating and implementing a psychological skills training program. In J. M. Williams (Ed.), *Applied sport psychology: Personal growth to peak performance* (3rd ed., pp. 329–358). Mountain View, CA: Mayfield.

White, A., & Hardy, L. (1998). An in-depth analysis of the uses of imagery by high-level slalom canoeists and artistic gymnasts. *The Sport Psychologist, 12,* 387–403.

Wilson, C., Smith, D., Burden, A., & Holmes, P. (2010). Participant-generated imagery scripts produce greater EMG activity and imagery ability. *European Journal of Sport Science, 10,* 417–425. doi:10.1080/17461391003770491

Woolfolk, R., Parrish, W., & Murphy, S. M. (1985). The effects of positive and negative imagery on motor skill performance. *Cognitive Therapy and Research, 9,* 335–341. doi:10.1007/BF01183852

Aidan Moran

Cognitive Strategies in Sport Psychology

5

A lthough sport is played with the body, it is won mainly in the mind. For example, Xavi Hernández, the famous Spanish soccer player who won both the 2010 Fédération Internationale de Football Association (FIFA) World Cup and the 2011 Union of European Football Association Champions League medals, said, when he joined FCBarcelona, that "the first thing they teach is: Think, think, think" (cited in Lowe, 2011, pp. 6–7). But what exactly should athletes pay attention to and think about in striving for optimal performance in competitive situations? Answers to such questions about cognitive strategies in sport may be found in the field of *cognitive sport psychology*, the scientific study of mental processes in athletes (Moran, 2009).

As the term *cognition* (which is derived from the Latin word *cognoscere*, to know) denotes the activity or process of knowing, cognitive psychology involves the systematic attempt to investigate how people acquire, store, and use their knowledge of the world and of themselves and others.

http://dx.doi.org/10.1037/14251-005
Exploring Sport and Exercise Psychology, Third Edition, J. Van Raalte and B. Brewer (Editors)

According to Dozois and Beck (2011), the roots of this latter discipline may be traced back to the philosopher Immanuel Kant (1781/1929), who postulated that the mind creates representations of the world and uses these cognitive templates to filter and interpret events and experiences. Typical cognitive processes include attention ("the process of concentrating on specific features of the environment, or on certain thoughts or activities"; Goldstein, 2008, p. 100) and thinking (or the "internal processes involved in making sense of the environment, and deciding what action might be appropriate"; Eysenck & Keane, 2010, p. 1). In studying such processes, the discipline of cognitive psychology has become largely synonymous with that of cognitive neuroscience because of the shared assumption that in understanding how the mind works, we need to explore people's brain processes as well as their behavior and experience (Cacioppo & Decety, 2009).

Despite a rather shaky start (discussed in the next section of this chapter), recent years have witnessed a proliferation of research interest in cognitive sport psychology. To illustrate, papers have been published on decision making (Dosseville, Laborde, & Raab, 2011), working memory (Furley & Memmert, 2010), pattern perception (Gorman, Abernethy, & Farrow, 2011), expertise (Müller et al., 2009; Williams & Ford, 2008), self-talk (Hatzigeorgiadis, Zourbanos, Galanis, & Theodorakis, 2011), motor control (Toner & Moran, 2011), motor imagery (Moran, Guillot, MacIntyre, & Collet, 2012), and attentional (Causer, Holmes, Smith, & Williams, 2011) processes in sport. Such research has addressed some interesting theoretical questions—for example, whether the study of motor imagery processes in athletes can serve as a bridge between cognitive sport psychology and cognitive neuroscience (see Moran et al., 2012). However, its practical implications have not been clarified adequately. Accordingly, there are many gaps in our understanding of the efficacy of the various cognitive strategies athletes use to improve their performance. In particular, three key unresolved questions come to mind. First, what exactly should athletes pay attention to in attempting to achieve optimal performance? Second, what is the relationship between athletes' self-talk (i.e., what they "say to themselves out loud or internally and privately"; Van Raalte, 2010, p. 510) and skilled performance? Finally, how can athletes learn to think more effectively in order to avoid dwelling on setbacks, past mistakes, or missed opportunities in competitive sport situations? This chapter provides empirically based answers to questions concerning cognitive self-regulation strategies in sport. The answers are urgently required by practitioners because an important goal of applied sport psychology is to help athletes to think effectively (Newburg, 1992). Indeed, some psychologists (e.g., Kirschenbaum, 1984) have claimed that all mental training is essentially an exercise in cognitive self-regulation.

The chapter begins with an outline of paradigm changes that have led cognitive psychologists to abandon their traditional indifference to sport in favor of a more enthusiastic attitude. Next, key underlying principles and strategies used in achieving optimal attentional focus in sport performance are discussed. The relationship between self-talk and sport performance is explored. Finally, practical tips for effective thought management are presented.

Studying Cognitive Processes in Sport: A Tale of Two Paradigms

For the layperson, thinking and action lie at opposite ends of the behavioral spectrum. Reflecting this view, traditional information processing psychology (see Lachman, Lachman, & Butterfield, 1979) regarded the mind's cognitive and motor systems as functionally independent. Accordingly, actions were held to be "the uninteresting end-result of cognitive processing . . . the aftermath of cognition" (Freedman, Dale, & Farmer, 2011, p. 1). Influenced by the latter assumption, and ignoring William James's (1890) famous dictum that "my thinking is first and last and always for the sake of my doing," cognitive psychologists largely ignored the domain of sport in their quest to understand how the mind works (Moran, 2009). Even today, the subject indices of leading textbooks in this field (e.g., Eysenck & Keane, 2010; Gobet, Chassy, & Bilalic, 2011; Goldstein, 2011; Matlin, 2009; Reisberg, 2010) contain few, if any, references to terms such as *sport* or *athlete*. Fortunately, this indifference among cognitive researchers to the mental processes of athletes has been replaced by enthusiasm over the past few years as a result of two key paradigm shifts, one in cognitive psychology and another in cognitive neuroscience. First, cognitive psychologists discovered that the information processing approach could not explain adequately how cognition, perception, and action interface with each other (Barsalou, 2008). This discovery led to alternative theoretical approaches such as *embodied cognition*—the idea that cognitive representations are "grounded in, and simulated through, sensorimotor activity" (Slepian, Weisbuch, Rule, & Ambady, 2011, p. 26). According to embodiment theory, many of the brain circuits that are responsible for abstract thinking are linked to those that process sensory experience. Empirical support for this approach comes from the *functional equivalence* hypothesis (Jeannerod, 1994) or the finding that cognitive simulation processes (e.g., mental imagery) share certain representations, neural structures, and theoretical mechanisms with like-modality perception and with motor preparation and execution (e.g., imagined and executed actions activate many common brain areas; see Moran et al., 2012). The second paradigm shift is more subtle and has occurred in cognitive neuroscience. Specifically, whereas researchers in this latter field traditionally studied mental processes by exploring cognitive *deficits* in *clinical* populations (e.g., patients with brain damage), they are now beginning to investigate the neural substrates of cognition in action by focusing on highly skilled participants such as athletes (Aglioti, Cesari, Romani, & Urgesi, 2008) and dancers (e.g., Bläsing et al., 2012) drawn from *elite* populations. This gradual change from a deficit-based approach to a strength-based approach to the study of cognitive processes has led to an upsurge of neuroimaging research on sport expertise (e.g., see Wei & Luo, 2010). Taken together, these twin paradigm shifts have led many psychologists and neuroscientists to regard competitive sport as a natural laboratory in which to study basic cognitive processes such as attention, imagery, and expertise in the performance of complex skills and movements under severe time constraints and in rapidly changing environments.

Having sketched the paradigm changes that have shaped cognitive psychologists' newfound enthusiasm for sport, let us now consider three questions that lie at the heart of the cognitive strategies reviewed in this chapter.

Attentional Focus: What Should Athletes Concentrate on to Achieve Optimal Performance

The ability to concentrate, or pay attention to the task at hand while ignoring distractions (Moran, 1996), is a crucial prerequisite of successful performance in sport. For example, Alex Ferguson (Manchester United), one of the most successful team managers in the world, proclaimed that in soccer, "without question, at the top level, concentration is a big part of a player's game—whether they're a keeper or outfield" (cited in Northcroft, 2009, p. 12). In studying cognitive processes, psychology researchers use metaphors to explain new phenomena in terms of familiar ones. Of the various metaphors of attention postulated since the 1950s, the spotlight approach (Posner, 1980) is probably the most influential in cognitive sport psychology. According to this metaphor, concentration resembles a mental spotlight that we shine at things that are important to us at a given moment. These targets of our concentration beam may be external (i.e., located in the world around us) or internal (i.e., located in the private domain of our own thoughts and feelings; for a more technical account, see Chun, Golomb, & Turk-Browne, 2011). For example, aiming a tennis serve at one's opponent's backhand involves an external focus of attention, whereas concentrating on the rhythm of one's service action involves an internal focus of attention.

Although the spotlight metaphor has several weaknesses (e.g., it neglects emotional influences on attentional processes), it has two important practical implications in sport and exercise psychology. First, it shows that concentration is never truly "lost" because a mental spotlight is always shining somewhere—either externally or internally. In addition, it suggests that whenever this beam is focused on the "wrong" target (i.e., something irrelevant to the task at hand or that lies outside of personal control), distraction results and performance is likely to deteriorate. For example, Roger Federer's victory over Robin Söderling in the final of the 2009 French Open tennis championship was jeopardized by the sudden appearance of a spectator who jumped onto the court and approached him. Clearly upset by this external distraction, Federer lost the next three points and admitted afterwards, "it definitely threw me out of my rhythm" (cited in Sarkar, 2009). Fortunately for Federer, he regained his concentration and won the match.

So, what exactly should athletes focus on to do their best when it matters most? The information provided below and highlighted in Figure 5.1 describes principles of and practical strategies for achieving effective concentration in sport (see also Kremer & Moran, 2012; Moran, 1996, 2012).

DECIDE TO CONCENTRATE

Athletes must decide to concentrate—it won't happen by chance. The first principle of effective concentration in sport is the idea that athletes have to make a *deliberate* decision to invest mental effort in some aspect of their performance. Put simply, they have to *prepare* to concentrate rather than hope that it will happen by chance. A useful practical strategy for implementing this principle is to establish an imaginary "switch on" zone before a competitive performance. For example, leaving the locker room before a competition may prompt an athlete to mentally engage his or her concentration system. This strategy was favored by Martin Corry, the former England and British and Irish Lions rugby star. As he revealed, "I used to like switching the dressing room light off to signify the end of our preparations and the start of something new" (Corry, 2007, p. 3).

In addition to effortful concentration, sport psychology consultants and athletes might consider a mindfulness approach to competition. Mindfulness is an attentional focusing strategy that originated in the Buddhist meditative tradition (Erisman & Roemer, 2010). According to one of its leading proponents, Kabat-Zinn (2005), mindfulness involves "an openhearted, moment-to-moment, non-judgmental awareness" (p. 24) of oneself and of the world. Evidence is accumulating to suggest

FIGURE 5.1

1. Athletes must *decide* to concentrate—it won't happen by chance

2. Athletes should be single-minded—focusing on only *one thought* at a time

3. Athletes' minds are *focused* when they are doing exactly what they are thinking

4. Athletes *lose* their concentration when they focus on factors that are outside their control

5. Athletes should focus *outward* when they become anxious

Concentration principles. From *Sport and Exercise Psychology: A Critical Introduction* (2nd ed; p. 146), by A. P. Moran, 2012, London, England: Routledge. Copyright 2012 by Taylor & Francis. Reprinted with permission.

that mindfulness-based interventions are effective not only in reducing stress (Chiesa & Serretti, 2009) but also in improving certain cognitive abilities such as attention (Chiesa, Calati, & Serretti, 2011). Mindfulness has also been shown to elicit changes in the brain regions associated with learning and memory processes (Hölzel et al., 2011). On the basis of such evidence, it seems plausible that training in mindfulness could enhance sport and other types of performance (Tan, 2012). Mindfulness training differs from more active cognitive control techniques such as thought stopping (whereby a verbal cue such as "stop" is stated aloud every time an undesired thought is encountered) because it urges acceptance rather than attempted elimination of intrusive, unwanted thoughts and feelings. In short, mindfulness training purports to help sport performers to concentrate on the here and now.

Aherne, Moran, and Lonsdale (2011) investigated the effects of a 6-week, CD-based mindfulness training program on elite athletes' flow experiences in training. Participants (who were international athletes from a university "high performance center") were assigned either to a control group or an experimental group. Athletes in the experimental group received a 6-week program of mindfulness training exercises (e.g., somatic awareness activities involving breath control and yoga). Both groups completed a psychometric measure of flow. Results showed that the athletes who underwent the mindfulness training reported increases in their global flow experiences and on the flow dimensions of "clear goals" and "sense of control." These findings are interesting because these two dimensions may be related to the self-regulation of attention, which, according to Bishop et al. (2004), is a key component of mindfulness. Given the exploratory nature of this experiment, however, additional research using larger samples and more stringent controls is required before firm conclusions can be drawn regarding the efficacy of this cognitive strategy of mindfulness training for enhanced flow and sport performance.

FOCUS ON ONE THOUGHT

Athletes have to be single-minded—focusing on only one thought at a time. This "one thought" principle has some neurological plausibility because working memory, the cognitive system that regulates conscious awareness (Baddeley, 2012; Logie, 2011), is fragile and limited in duration. Indeed, Garavan (1998) suggested that the focus of attention in working memory is limited to a single item at a time. Endorsing this one-thought concentration strategy, the swimmer Michael Phelps, who has won more Olympic gold medals than any other athlete in history, offered his practical strategy whereby "you have to go one day at a time, one meet at a time, and one practice at a time" (cited in Walsh, 2008, p. 13).

Associative strategies in sport involve the use of a focusing technique whereby athletes learn to concentrate deliberately on bodily signals such as breathing, heartbeat, and kinesthetic sensations when competing in arduous endurance events. This rather counterintuitive strategy (concentrating on the source of one's pain and discomfort) came to scientific prominence as a result of a seminal study by Morgan and Pollock (1977). Briefly, these researchers discovered that elite marathon runners reported using associative cognitive strategies during races, whereas nonelite runners tended to prefer *dissociative* strategies—or those that involved attempting to *block out* sensations of pain and discomfort. For Morgan (1978), an athlete who dissociates "purposefully cuts himself off from the sensory feedback he normally receives from his body" (p. 39).

Early research on this topic showed that associative attentional strategies, when compared with dissociative equivalents, were related to faster performance in sports such as running and swimming. From such evidence, K. Masters and Ogles (1998) concluded that the "use of association is generally correlated with faster running performances, whereas the opposite is true for dissociation" (p. 267). A subsequent review by Brewer and Buman (2006) concluded that associative strategies are superior to dissociative ones in endurance events—especially for experienced athletes. More recently, Salmon, Hanneman, and Harwood (2010) conducted a review of 50 studies on association/dissociation published in sport and exercise psychology between 1977 and 2008. These studies included participants drawn mainly from running, strength/endurance activities, walking, stair-climbing, and cycling. Having pointed out that studies in this field have been hampered by some conceptual confusion (e.g., an overreliance on a rather simplistic dichotomous model of association/dissociation) and by certain methodological problems (e.g., the use of unvalidated measures of relevant constructs), Salmon et al. concluded that traditional notions of association/dissociation are somewhat arbitrary and offer only "modest utility and conceptual explanatory power" (p. 148) in accounting for variance among performers in sustained physical activity settings. In particular, the latter researchers proposed that the cognitive strategies of people performing endurance activities are more complex and variable than those postulated originally in Morgan and Pollock's (1977) dichotomous model of association/dissociation. Similar criticisms were offered by Lind, Welch, and Ekkekakis (2009) in their review of the effects of attentional focusing strategies on various indices of exercise performance. For example, they noted that there has been considerable variation among researchers in the definitions of association and dissociation over the years and that a "guiding theoretical framework" (Lind et al., 2009, p. 748) has yet to emerge in this field. Interestingly, as an alternative to the association/dissociation approach developed by Morgan and Pollock (1977), Salmon et al. (2010) suggested that a mindfulness model (discussed earlier) may be fruitful. It is not clear, however, if this change in theoretical approach will improve sport and exercise psychology practitioners' ability to advise athletes what exactly they should focus on in training or competitive situations.

COMBINE THINKING WITH DOING

Athletes' minds are focused when there is no difference between what they are doing and what they are thinking. The fusion of thinking and action in this third principle of effective concentration in sport is especially characteristic of peak performance experiences. For example, after Roger Bannister had run the first sub-4-minute mile in May 1954 in Oxford, England, he said, "There was no pain, only a great unity of movement and aim" (Bannister, 2004, p. 12). Similarly, when the golfer Pádraig Harrington had won the 2007 Open Championship at Carnoustie after a playoff against Sergio Garcia, he described his thoughts as he prepared for his final putt: "No conscious effort whatsoever went into that putt. There were no thoughts about 'this is for the Open' . . . I stroked it in" (cited in Jones, 2007, p. 12). For athletes, a useful way of implementing this principle is to focus on actions that are specific, relevant, and under their own control.

FOCUS ON ACTIONS UNDER YOUR CONTROL

Athletes lose their concentration when they focus on factors that are outside their control. The fourth concentration principle suggests that athletes are most likely to become distracted whenever they allow themselves to dwell on factors that are outside their control or irrelevant to the job at hand (see the review in Moran, 1996). To counteract this tendency, a useful practical strategy is for athletes to focus on actions that are under their control. For example, when golfer Paul McGinley faced a putt to win the 2002 Ryder Cup match for Europe against the United States, he revealed that he "became absorbed in the line of the putt . . . My only job at that moment in time was to set the ball off on the line that I had chosen. *That was the only thing I could control*" (cited in Clarke & Morris, 2005, p. 63, emphasis added).

FOCUS OUTWARD

Athletes should focus outward when they become anxious. The final building block of effective concentration is the proposition that when athletes get nervous, they should focus outward on actions, not inward on doubts. For example, an anxious tennis player who is receiving serve at match point down may deliberately focus on returning the ball to a specific target on his or her opponent's side of the net rather than wondering what will happen next. This switch to an external focus is necessary because anxiety tends to induce an internal focus of attention and causes athletes to "reinvest" (R. Masters & Maxwell, 2008) their cognitive resources by attempting to exert conscious control over skills that had previously been performed automatically. In such circumstances, a form of "paralysis by analysis" can occur in which skilled performance deteriorates suddenly because athletes think too much about the mechanics of what they are doing (R. Masters, 1992). Such an internal focus of attention is central to the ubiquitous experience of "choking" in sport—a phenomenon in which an athlete's normally expert level of performance deteriorates suddenly and significantly under conditions of perceived pressure (Kremer, Moran, Walker, & Craig, 2012). Among top golfers, a practical strategy for focusing externally in pressure situations where there is a danger of thinking too much about stroke mechanics is to engage one's caddie in conversation. For example, Rory McIlroy, who won the 2011 U.S. Open championship, revealed that "having a conversation about something completely different is probably the best thing for me as it takes my mind off it and stops me getting too involved in what I'm doing" (cited in *Irish Times*, 2011, p. 20).

The idea that athletes should adopt an external focus of attention under pressure is supported by laboratory studies. Specifically, Wulf (2007) and Wulf, Shea, and Lewthwaite (2010) reviewed research on focus of attention (i.e., external or internal), learning, and performance of various motor skills. They concluded that an external focus of attention (i.e., one that targets the effects of a given motor movement on the environment) is typically more effective in facilitating skill learning and performance than is an internal focus of attention (i.e., one that targets the movements of performers' body parts such as the hands or hips). For example, in sports such as basketball, volleyball, and soccer, coaching instructions that direct players' attention to the trajectory of the ball usually lead to increased movement accuracy than do instructions that focus attention on the hand or foot that produced the effect (Wulf et al., 2010). According to Wulf, the benefits of an external focus of attention are consistent across a variety of skills (e.g., balance tasks, golf, American football), levels of experience (i.e., whether the performers are experts or novices), and participant populations (including those with motor impairments).

Having considered the benefits to athletes of adopting a particular focus of attention, let us now examine the relationship between self-talk and performance in sport.

What Is the Relationship Between Self-Talk and Sport Performance

It has long been known that athletes talk to themselves regularly—either silently or out loud—when they train and compete. Such attempted cognitive self-regulation is typically conducted by athletes in an effort to improve their thinking and concentration in their quest for optimal performance. For example, the British Olympic athlete Paula Radcliffe reported counting her steps silently to herself during races in an effort to maintain her concentration. As she explained,

> When I count to 100 three times, it's a mile. It helps me to focus on the moment and not to think about how many miles I have to go. I concentrate on breathing and striding, and I go within myself. (cited in Kolata, 2007, p. 1)

Similarly, the former rugby player Michael Lynagh claimed that he had instructed himself silently as follows when preparing to kick the penalty that helped Australia to defeat England in the 1991 World Cup final: "Five steps back, three to the left, and kick through the ball" (cited in Brolly, 2007, p. 93).

The efficacy of self-talk in enhancing athletic performance has been demonstrated in observational studies (e.g., Van Raalte, Brewer, Rivera, & Petitpas, 1994), laboratory-based experiments (e.g., Van Raalte et al., 1995), intervention studies (e.g., Johnson, Hrycaiko, Johnson, & Hallas, 2004), and research using single-case designs (e.g., Hamilton, Scott, & McDougall, 2007). For example, Hamilton et al. (2007) showed that athletes who used *positive* self-talk consistently improved their cycling time-trial performance significantly more than did counterparts who used *negative* self-talk. More recently, a meta-analytic review by Hatzigeorgiadis et al. (2011) of 32 studies on this topic revealed a positive moderate effect of self-talk on athletic performance (namely, 0.48—almost half a standard deviation). More precise analysis showed that self-talk intervention programs were more effective for fine than for gross motor skills and for novel, as compared with well-learned, tasks. Turning to an applied setting, Taylor, Gould, and Rolo (2008) discovered that instructional self-talk (i.e., the covert use of specific cue words or phrases in an effort to improve one's performance) was one of the strongest predictors of successful Olympic performance among U.S. athletes. Given this evidence on the efficacy of self-talk, we now need to explore this cognitive strategy in more detail.

According to Hardy, Oliver, and Tod (2009a), the term *self-talk* refers to "those automatic statements reflective of, and deliberate techniques (e.g., thought stopping) athletes use to direct, sports-related thinking" (p. 38). It involves the use of vividly phrased cue words to help athletes to control their thoughts and to instruct and motivate themselves (Zinsser, Bunker, & Williams, 2010). In sport and exercise psychology, Hardy (2006) postulated that self-talk is a multidimensional construct with three main components: *overtness* (i.e., whether self-talk is expressed explicitly or covertly), *valence* (i.e., whether self-talk is positive or negative), and *functions* (e.g., either cognitive/instructional or motivational). Much research on self-talk in sport has focused on instructional and motivational self-talk. *Instructional* self-talk (as exemplified by Michael Lynagh above) refers to covert self-directed statements that are intended to enhance sport performance through the adoption of a task-relevant attentional focus. *Motivational* self-talk involves similar statements intended to facilitate performance by increasing effort and energy expenditure. For example, when tennis player Serena Williams defeated Daniela Hantuchova at Wimbledon in 2007, she repeated motivational phrases to herself such as "My good thoughts are powerful—only negative thoughts are weak" (cited in Martin, 2007, p. 5). Instructional and motivational self-talk appear to have different effects on skilled performance. For example, Kolovelonis, Goudas, and Dermitzaki (2011) found that whereas instructional self-talk is beneficial for the performance of tasks that require precision or timing, motivational self-talk is beneficial for the performance of tasks that require strength or endurance. A detailed analysis of the factors that mediate the effects of self-talk is provided by Hatzigeorgiadis et al. (2011). However, additional research is needed to identify definitively what self-talk is most effective for whom and under what circumstances.

Self-Talk and Thought Control in Athletes

The empirical review presented in the previous section suggests that positive self-talk enhances performance and that negative self-talk is detrimental to performance. Given such evidence, how can athletes learn to control what they think about and say to themselves? To answer this question, it may be valuable to consider principles and strategies developed in the field of cognitive therapy (for more detailed accounts of this field, see reviews by Beck, 2005; Clark & Beck, 2010; Dozois & Beck, 2011).

According to Clark and Beck (2010), cognitive therapy is a structured, collaborative, and problem-oriented form of psychotherapy that helps people (especially those with anxiety and depression) in modifying their maladaptive thoughts, attitudes, beliefs, and information process-ing biases (e.g., "If I fail to win an important match, then I'm a failure as a person" or "We must win this game"). At least three key principles underlie this form of therapy (Dozois & Beck, 2011). First, people's cog-nition is assumed to affect both their emotions and their behavior. Sec-ond, it is assumed that people can learn to monitor and modify much of their cognitive activity. There is some debate, however, about the degree to which people can modify automatic thoughts (i.e., those that are not accessible to conscious deliberation) directly. Third, cognitive therapists assume that by changing one's beliefs, one can achieve desired change in one's behavior and experience. In summary, the cornerstone of cog-nitive therapy is the proposition that people can learn to regard their thoughts as hypotheses rather than as facts. By testing the validity of these hypotheses empirically, people can "shift their cognitive apprais-als from ones that are unhealthy and maladaptive to ones that are more evidence-based and adaptive" (Dozois & Beck, 2011, p. 30).

Before any cognitive change is possible, however, people need to become more aware of their thinking habits and self-talk (Zinsser et al., 2010). In an effort to investigate athletes' awareness of their self-talk, Hardy, Roberts, and Hardy (2009b) evaluated the efficacy of two cognitive–behavioral intervention strategies—a thought awareness log book and an exercise requiring athletes to transfer paper clips from one pocket to another whenever they used a negative self-statement. Results showed that although both treatment groups demonstrated increased aware-ness of the *content* of their negative self-talk, the log book group showed greater awareness than the control group of the *use* of negative self-talk. Accordingly, Hardy et al. (2009b) recommended that log book mainte-nance may be a useful tool for increasing awareness of negative self-talk among athletes in applied settings.

Some applied sport psychology consultants have suggested that athletes augment their awareness of negative self-talk with the use of a thought control technique such as thought stopping. That is, they suggest that athletes who become aware of negative self-talk should actively try to suppress or stop this detrimental internal dia-logue. This approach may not be ideal, however. When working memory is overloaded due to anxiety or fatigue, attempts to suppress a thought may prove paradoxical or counterproductive—serving only to *increase* the prominence of the thought in consciousness (Wegner, 1994, 2009). In such circumstances, thought stopping may ironically elicit a *rebound* experience whereby the suppressed thought becomes even more prominent in consciousness than was the case previously. This tendency for a suppressed thought to come to mind more readily than a thought that is the focus of intentional concentration is called *hyperaccessibility* and is especially likely to occur under conditions of heavy mental load. Wegner's (1994) ironic processes model has attracted increasing attention from sport and exercise psychologists in recent years—especially with regard to ironies of action, where sport performers experience rebound effects as a result of using avoidant instructions (e.g., "Don't double-fault!" or "Don't get caught offside!") under pressure. For example, Woodman and Davis (2008) investigated the effects of ironic processes on golf performance. They discovered that when players were under pressure (e.g., when competing for a financial prize) and when thinking about *not* doing something (e.g., don't overshoot), they tended to commit ironic errors. Clearly, this finding raises doubts about the commonsense wisdom of asking anxious athletes not to worry about an important impending competitive event. In summary, for applied sport and exercise psychologists, the theory of ironic processes suggests that thought stopping should be used with great caution when trying to help athletes reduce their negative self-talk.

Practical Tips on Thought Management in Sport: Some Insights From Cognitive Therapy

In the previous section, three key assumptions underlying cognitive therapy were presented. Based on these assumptions, a number of practical strategies have been developed by cognitive therapists (e.g., Dozois & Beck, 2011) to counteract the common cognitive errors and processing biases that people (including athletes) display in everyday life. Some of the most pervasive of these errors and biases, along with suggested strategies for challenging them, are summarized next. Relatively little empirical research has been conducted in sport and exercise psychology on thinking flaws in athletes and how to overcome them. For a more detailed discussion of these issues, see Claspell (2010) and Zinsser et al. (2010).

> ∎ *Avoid all-or-nothing thinking:* Athletes need to become aware of the danger of interpreting sporting outcomes in a dichotomous manner—either as a total success or as a total failure. Such black-and-white thinking, which can cause athletes to label themselves as "chokers" or "losers," is unhelpful because it prevents rational analysis of the strengths and weaknesses of their performance. As Zinsser et al. (2010) noted, "labeling is disabling" (p. 325).

A possible solution? Athletes should be encouraged to pick and cite specific examples of aspects of their performances that went well, aspects of their performances that they need to improve for the future, and changes that they will make to their performance to reach their goals.

- *The peril of perfectionism:* Striving for perfection is admirable and may serve to motivate, but judging oneself harshly because one has not met expectations, has made mistakes, or is imperfect can be damaging psychologically. This idea is supported by a review of research on perfectionism in sport by Stoeber (2011). In this review, Stoeber postulated that perfectionism is a complex and multidimensional construct with two key components—perfectionistic strivings (e.g., setting exceedingly high standards for one's performance) and "perfectionistic concerns" (e.g., fear of making mistakes and of negative evaluations of one's performance by others). Furthermore, he argued that only perfectionistic concerns are associated with debilitating sporting outcomes such as competitive anxiety and fear of failure. In contrast, he concluded that perfectionistic strivings are often associated with "positive affect, functional motivational orientations, and higher performance" (p. 138). Clearly, additional research is required to test the validity of this distinction between perfectionistic strivings and concerns.

  A possible solution? Help athletes understand the costs and benefits of perfectionist beliefs. At a practical level, athletes can be encouraged to explore what happens when they replace perfectionist self-talk with more constructive phrases. For example, words like *must,* which suggest a requirement for precise performance, can be replaced with *like to,* which suggests a desire to achieve a goal. Similarly, replacing phrases like *have to* with *want to* may help to reduce pressure and lead to better performances. For further information on how certain habitually negative thoughts can be reframed constructively, see Zinsser et al. (2010).

- *The problem of personalization:* According to Dozois and Beck (2011), *personalization* involves the cognitive flaw of automatically attributing negative events to oneself rather than examining other possible causes of such outcomes. In sport, this faulty thinking habit is evident whenever athletes take failure personally. All athletes make mistakes—but not all athletes get caught up in self-blame as a result.

  A possible solution? Help athletes to understand the difference between controllable and uncontrollable outcomes and to look for alternative explanations for events rather than solely blaming themselves. Evidence shows that distinguishing between controllable and uncontrollable aspects of sport performance (sometimes called *attributional retraining*) can facilitate motivation. For example, competitive tennis players who make internal, unstable attributions (e.g., "I wasn't fit enough for this match, but I'll be ready next time") may be more likely to train hard to win future matches than athletes who make other types of attributions (Van Raalte, 1994). Sinnott and Biddle (1998) discovered that an attributional retraining intervention helped to improve the intrinsic motivation of a group of young athletes (ages 11–12 years) who had labeled themselves as being "poor" on a ball-dribbling task.

▪ *Dealing with disappointment:* It has long been assumed that athletes need to overcome disappointment by keeping things in perspective. One way of doing this is to remind sports performers that in a year's time, they probably will not even remember the silly mistake that preoccupies them at present. An intriguing challenge to the assumption that disappointment is inevitably problematic, however, comes from Andrews and Thompson (2009), who conducted an extensive review of research on the possible adaptive effects of depression. Briefly, these authors argued that there is a "bright side of being blue"—provided that the analysis and rumination to which depression gives rise can be channeled effectively into enhanced problem solving. For example, disappointment can be adaptive if it helps athletes to gain increased self-awareness and to work harder in preparation for future competitive challenges.

A possible solution? Help athletes to discover that disappointments are usually temporary and that they can serve as useful signposts for improvement. Athletes may want to develop the habit of identifying good things (e.g., lessons learned, such as changes in perspective or increased motivation to train) that come out of setbacks.

▪ *Watch out for wishful thinking:* Athletes have to learn to recognize and reduce a natural tendency to think about what might have been. Such wishful (or "counterfactual"; Rose & Olson, 1995) thinking cannot change anything and is a waste of time. Nevertheless, the proclivity to imagine how things could have turned out differently is ubiquitous in sport. Dray and Uphill (2009) investigated the prevalence, characteristics, and consequences of counterfactual thinking in a sample of 217 athletes. Results showed that counterfactual thoughts were experienced by a large majority (88%) of these athletes—especially when they failed to meet their performance expectations by a large margin. Furthermore, these athletes tended to spend the most time imagining how things could have been better rather than worse. Perhaps not surprisingly, the former type of counterfactual thinking was associated with negative emotional responses.

A possible solution? Athletes need to develop the skill of asking themselves what action stems from a particular thought. If they were in the same situation, what would they do differently? Top athletes rarely focus on the mistakes they have made. Instead, they concentrate on what they plan to do differently the next time. In general, athletes can benefit from asking themselves what aspects of the setback they can change in the future.

■ *Check for catastrophizing:* According to Dozois and Beck (2011), *catastrophizing* is a cognitive tendency to predict future calamity in one's life. In sport, this tendency may involve athletes over-generalizing from one specific setback (e.g., "I lost a match") to a series of global negative conclusions (e.g., "I'm a loser").

A possible solution? Athletes can challenge faulty thinking habits by looking for evidence that contradicts the "worst case" scenarios that they imagine. Using the technique of cognitive restructuring (see Clark & Beck, 2010), athletes can learn to evaluate the veracity of their reasoning and to generate alternative conclusions that are more adaptive and plausible than those that first come to mind. For example, Claspell (2010) suggested that athletes could be challenged with questions such as "What is your evidence to support your catastrophic assumption?" and instructions such as "Consider alternative explanations for why things in your life are occurring."

Summary

Mental processes (e.g., attention, thinking) have practical importance in sport and are receiving increased research attention from cognitive psychologists. Despite this upsurge of research interest, there are several gaps in our understanding of the efficacy of various cognitive strategies athletes use to improve their performance. In particular, we know relatively little about what athletes should pay attention to when striving for peak performance, exactly what factors mediate the self-talk–performance relationship, and how athletes can learn to think more effectively when confronted by the setbacks that are ubiquitous in competitive sport. Drawing on a variety of psychological principles and findings, this chapter offered practical tips for athletes with regard to each of the three problems discussed. Overall, key themes that emerged from this chapter are the importance of focusing on the controllable in competitive situations and the value of becoming aware of faulty thinking habits that can hamper sport performance.

References

Aglioti, S. M., Cesari, P., Romani, M., & Urgesi, C. (2008). Action anticipation and motor resonance in elite basketball players. *Nature Neuroscience, 11,* 1109–1116. doi:10.1038/nn.2182

Aherne, C., Moran, A., & Lonsdale, C. (2011). The effects of mindfulness training on athletes' flow: An initial investigation. *The Sport Psychologist, 25,* 177–189.

Andrews, P. W., & Thompson, J. A., Jr. (2009). The bright side of being blue: Depression as an adaptation for analyzing complex problems. *Psychological Review, 116,* 620–654. doi:10.1037/a0016242

Baddeley, A. (2012). Working memory: Theories, models, and controversies. *Annual Review of Psychology, 63,* 1–29. doi:10.1146/annurev-psych-120710-100422

Bannister, R. (2004, May 1). "Fear of failure haunted me right to the last second." *The Guardian,* p. 12 (Sport), pp. 12–13.

Barsalou, L. W. (2008). Grounded cognition. *Annual Review of Psychology, 59,* 617–645. doi:10.1146/annurev.psych.59.103006.093639

Beck, A. T. (2005). The current state of cognitive therapy: A 40-year retrospective. *Archives of General Psychiatry, 62,* 953–959. doi:10.1001/archpsyc.62.9.953

Bishop, S. R., Lau, M., Shapiro, S., Carlson, L. E., Anderson, N. D., Carmody, J., . . . Devins, G. (2004). Mindfulness: A proposed operational definition. *Clinical Psychology: Science and Practice, 11,* 230–241. doi:10.1093/clipsy.bph077

Bläsing, B., Calvo-Merino, B., Cross, E. S., Jola, C., Honisch, J., & Stevens, C. J. (2012). Neurocognitive control in dance perception and performance. *Acta Psychologica, 139,* 300–308. doi:10.1016/j.actpsy.2011.12.005

Brewer, B. W., & Buman, M. P. (2006). Attentional focus and endurance performance: Review and theoretical integration. *Kinesiologia Slovenica, 12,* 82–97.

Brolly, J. (2007, January 14). How to win Sam or Liam? Start as you aim to finish. *The Irish Mail on Sunday,* p. 93.

Cacioppo, J. T., & Decety, J. (2009). What are the brain mechanisms on which psychological processes are based? *Perspectives on Psychological Science, 4,* 10–18. doi:10.1111/j.1745-6924.2009.01094.x

Causer, J., Holmes, P. S., Smith, N. C., & Williams, A. M. (2011). Anxiety, movement kinematics, and visual attention in elite-level performers. *Emotion, 11,* 595–602. doi:10.1037/a0023225

Chiesa, A., Calati, R., & Serretti, A. (2011). Does mindfulness training improve cognitive abilities: A systematic review of neuropsychological findings. *Clinical Psychology Review, 31,* 449–464. doi:10.1016/j.cpr.2010.11.003

Chiesa, A., & Serretti, A. (2009). Mindfulness-based stress reduction for stress management in healthy people: A review and meta-analysis. *Journal of Alternative and Complementary Medicine, 15,* 593–600. doi:10.1089/acm.2008.0495

Chun, M. M., Golomb, J. D., & Turk-Browne, N. B. (2011). A taxonomy of external and internal attention. *Annual Review of Psychology, 62,* 73–101. doi:10.1146/annurev.psych.093008.100427

Clark, D. A., & Beck, A. T. (2010). Cognitive theory and therapy of anxiety and depression: Convergence with neurobiological findings. *Trends in Cognitive Sciences, 14,* 418–424. doi:10.1016/j.tics.2010.06.007

Clarke, D., & Morris, K. (2005). *Golf—The mind factor* (p. 63). London, England: Hodder & Stoughton.

Claspell, E. (2010). Cognitive-behavioral therapies. In S. J. Hanrahan & M. B. Andersen (Eds.), *Handbook of applied sport psychology: A comprehensive guide for students and practitioners* (pp. 131–140). Abingdon, Oxford, England: Routledge.

Corry, M. (2007, October 13). "Broccoli, foul focus drinks and hip-hop: How we will prepare for the big kick-off". *The Guardian* (Sport), p. 3.

Dosseville, F., Laborde, S., & Raab, M. (2011). Contextual and personal motor experience effects in judo referees' decisions. *The Sport Psychologist, 25,* 67–81.

Dozois, D. J. A., & Beck, A. T. (2011). Cognitive therapy. In J. D. Herbert & E. M. Forman (Eds.), *Acceptance and mindfulness in cognitive behavior therapy* (pp. 26–56). Hoboken, NJ: Wiley.

Dray, K., & Uphill, M. (2009). A survey of athletes' counterfactual thinking: Precursors, prevalence, and consequences. *Sport and Exercise Psychology Review, 5,* 16–26.

Erisman, S. M., & Roemer, L. (2010). A preliminary investigation of the effects of experimentally induced mindfulness on emotional responding to film clips. *Emotion, 10,* 72–82. doi:10.1037/a0017162

Eysenck, M. W., & Keane, M. T. (2010). *Cognitive psychology: A student's handbook* (6th ed.). Hove, East Sussex, England: Psychology Press.

Freedman, J. B., Dale, R., & Farmer, T. A. (2011). Hand in motion reveals mind in motion. *Frontiers in Psychology, 2:*59, 1–6. doi:10.3389/fpsyg.2011.00059

Furley, P. A., & Memmert, D. (2010). The role of working memory in sport. *International Review of Sport and Exercise Psychology, 3,* 171–194. doi:10.1080/1750984X.2010.526238

Garavan, H. (1998). Serial attention in working memory. *Memory & Cognition, 26,* 263–276. doi:10.3758/BF03201138

Gobet, F., Chassy, P., & Bilalic, M. (2011). *Foundations of cognitive psychology.* Maidenhead, Berkshire, England: McGraw-Hill.

Goldstein, E. B. (2008). *Cognitive psychology: Connecting mind, research, and everyday experience* (2nd ed.). Belmont, CA: Thompson/Wadsworth.

Goldstein, E. B. (2011). *Cognitive psychology: Connecting mind, research, and everyday experience* (3rd ed.). Belmont, CA: Wadsworth/Cengage.

Gorman, A. D., Abernethy, B., & Farrow, D. (2011). Investigating the anticipatory nature of pattern perception in sport. *Memory & Cognition, 39*, 894–901. doi:10.3758/s13421-010-0067-7

Hamilton, R. A., Scott, D., & MacDougall, M. P. (2007). Assessing the effectiveness of self-talk interventions on endurance performance. *Journal of Applied Sport Psychology, 19*, 226–239. doi:10.1080/10413200701230613

Hardy, J. (2006). Speaking clearly: A critical review of the self-talk literature. *Psychology of Sport and Exercise, 7*, 81–97. doi:10.1016/j.psychsport.2005.04.002

Hardy, J., Oliver, E., & Tod, D. (2009a). A framework for the study and application of self-talk within sport. In S. Mellalieu & S. Hanton (Eds.), *Advances in applied sport psychology: A review* (pp. 37–74). London, England: Routledge.

Hardy, J., Roberts, R., & Hardy, L. (2009b). Awareness and motivation to change negative self-talk. *The Sport Psychologist, 23*, 435–450.

Hatzigeorgiadis, A., Zourbanos, N., Galanis, E., & Theodorakis, Y. (2011). Self-talk and sports performance: A meta-analysis. *Perspectives on Psychological Science, 6*, 348–356. doi:10.1177/1745691611413136

Hölzel, B. K., Carmody, J., Vangel, M., Congleton, C., Yerramsetti, S. M., Gard, T., & Lazar, S. W. (2011). Mindfulness training leads to increases in regional brain gray matter density. *Psychiatry Research: Neuroimaging, 191*, 36–43. doi:10.1016/j.pscychresns.2010.08.006

Irish Times. (2011, June 21). McIlroy's talent finds its own rewards in finest fashion (pp. 20–21). Dublin, Ireland: Author.

James, W. (1890). *Principles of psychology*. New York, NY: Holt, Rinehart, & Winston. doi:10.1037/11059-000

Jeannerod, M. (1994). The representing brain: Neural correlates of motor intention and imagery. *Behavioral and Brain Sciences, 17*, 187–245. doi:10.1017/S0140525X00034026

Johnson, J., Hrycaiko, D. W., Johnson, G. V., & Hallas, J. M. (2004). Self-talk and female youth soccer performance. *The Sport Psychologist, 18*, 44–59.

Jones, M. (2007, December 23). Open minded. *Mad About Sport* (issue 9). *Sunday Tribune* [Suppl.].

Kabat-Zinn, J. (2005). *Coming to our senses: Healing ourselves and the world through mindfulness*. New York, NY: Hyperion.

Kant, I. (1929). *Critique of pure reason* (N. K. Smith, Trans.). London, England: Macmillan. (Original work published 1781)

Kirschenbaum, D. S. (1984). Self-regulation and sport psychology: Nurturing an emergent symbiosis. *Journal of Sport Psychology, 6*, 159–183.

Kolata, G. (2007, December 6). "I'm not really running, I'm not really running . . .". *The New York Times*. Retrieved from http://www.nytimes.com/2007/12/06/health/nutrition/06Best.html

Kolovelonis, A., Goudas, M., & Dermitzaki, I. (2011). The effects of instructional and motivational self-talk on students' motor task performance in physical education. *Psychology of Sport and Exercise, 12,* 153–158. doi:10.1016/j.psychsport.2010.09.002

Kremer, J., & Moran, A. (2012). *Pure sport: Practical sport psychology* (2nd ed). Hove, East Sussex, England: Routledge.

Kremer, J., Moran, A., Walker, G., & Craig, C. (2012). *Key concepts in sport psychology.* London, England: Sage.

Lachman, R., Lachman, J. C. L., & Butterfield, E. C. (1979). *Cognitive psychology and information processing.* Hillsdale, NJ: Erlbaum.

Lind, E., Welch, A. S., & Ekkekakis, P. (2009). Do 'mind over muscle' strategies work? Examining the effects of attentional association and dissociation on exertional, affective and physiological responses to exercise. *Sports Medicine, 39,* 743–764. doi:10.2165/11315120-000000000-00000

Logie, R. H. (2011). The functional organization and capacity limits of working memory. *Current Directions in Psychological Science, 20,* 240–245. doi:10.1177/0963721411415340

Lowe, S. (2011, February 11). "I'm a romantic, says Xavi, heart of the world's best team." *The Guardian* (Sport), pp. 6–7.

Martin, A. (2007, July 3). More than words: Book of Serena the answer to Williams' prayers." *The Guardian* (Sport), p. 5.

Masters, K. S., & Ogles, B. M. (1998). Associative and dissociative cognitive strategies in exercise and running: 20 years later, what do we know? *The Sport Psychologist, 12,* 253–270.

Masters, R. S. W. (1992). Knowledge, "knerves" and know-how: The role of explicit versus implicit knowledge in the breakdown of complex motor skill under pressure. *The British Journal of Psychology, 83,* 343–358. doi:10.1111/j.2044-8295.1992.tb02446.x

Masters, R. S. W., & Maxwell, J. P. (2008). The theory of reinvestment. *International Review of Sport and Exercise Psychology, 1*(2), 160–183. doi:10.1080/17509840802287218

Matlin, M. (2009). *Cognition* (7th ed.). New York, NY: Wiley.

Moran, A., Guillot, A., MacIntyre, T., & Collet, C. (2012). Re-imagining motor imagery: Building bridges between cognitive neuroscience and sport psychology. *British Journal of Psychology, 103,* 224–247. doi:10.1111/j.2044-8295.2011.02068.x

Moran, A. P. (1996). *The psychology of concentration in sport performers: A cognitive analysis.* Hove, East Sussex, England: Psychology Press.

Moran, A. P. (2009). Cognitive psychology in sport: Progress and prospects. *Psychology of Sport and Exercise, 10,* 420–426. doi:10.1016/j.psychsport.2009.02.010

Moran, A. P. (2012). *Sport and exercise psychology: A critical introduction* (2nd ed.). London, England: Routledge.

Morgan, W. P. (1978). The mind of the marathoner. *Psychology Today, 11*, 38–49.

Morgan, W. P., & Pollock, M. L. (1977). Psychologic characterization of the elite distance runner. *Annals of the New York Academy of Sciences, 301*, 382–403. doi:10.1111/j.1749-6632.1977.tb38215.x

Müller, S., Abernethy, B., Reece, J., Rose, M., Eid, M., McBan, R., . . . Abreu, C. (2009). An in-situ examination of the timing of information pick-up for interception by cricket batsmen of different skill levels. *Psychology of Sport and Exercise, 10*, 644–652. doi:10.1016/j.psychsport.2009.04.002

Newburg, D. (1992). Performance enhancement: Toward a working definition. *Contemporary Thought on Performance Enhancement, 1*, 10–25.

Northcroft, J. (2009, February 12–13). "They shall not pass." *Sunday Times* (Sport), p. 8.

Posner, M. I. (1980). Orienting of attention: The VIIth Sir Frederic Bartlett lecture. *The Quarterly Journal of Experimental Psychology, 32*, 3–25. doi:10.1080/00335558008248231

Reisberg, D. (2010). *Cognition* (4th ed.). New York, NY: Norton.

Rose, N., & Olson, J. (1995). *What might have been: The social psychology of counterfactual thinking.* Mahwah, NJ: Erlbaum.

Salmon, P., Hanneman, S., & Harwood, B. (2010). Associative/dissociative cognitive strategies in sustained physical activity: Literature review and proposal for a mindfulness-based conceptual model. *The Sport Psychologist, 24*, 127–156.

Sarkar, P. (2009). Open—Federer unnerved by spectator intrusion. *ESPN Tennis Online.* Retrieved from http://sports.espn.go.com/espn/wire?section=tennis&id=4239263

Sinnott, K., & Biddle, S. (1998). Changes in attributions, perceptions of success and intrinsic motivation after attributions in children's sport. *International Journal of Adolescence and Youth, 7*, 137–144. doi:10.1080/02673843.1998.9747818

Slepian, M. L., Weisbuch, M., Rule, N. O., & Ambady, N. (2011). Tough and tender: Embodied categorization of gender. *Psychological Science, 22*, 26–28. doi:10.1177/0956797610390388

Stoeber, J. (2011). The dual nature of perfectionism in sports: Relationships with emotion, motivation, and performance. *International Review of Sport and Exercise Psychology, 4*, 128–145. doi:10.1080/1750984X.2011.604789

Tan, C. (2012). *Search inside yourself: The unexpected path to achieving success, happiness (and world peace).* New York, NY: HarperOne.

Taylor, M. K., Gould, D., & Rolo, C. (2008). Performance strategies of US Olympians in practice and competition. *High Ability Studies, 19*, 19–36. doi:10.1080/13598130801980281

Toner, J., & Moran, A. (2011). The effects of conscious processing on golf putting proficiency and kinematics. *Journal of Sports Sciences, 29,* 673–683. doi:10.1080/02640414.2011.553964

Van Raalte, J. L. (1994). Sport performance attributions: A special case of self-serving bias? *Australian Journal of Science and Medicine in Sport, 26,* 45–48.

Van Raalte, J. L. (2010). Self-talk. In S. J. Hanrahan & M. B. Andersen (Eds.), *Handbook of applied sport psychology: A comprehensive guide for students and practitioners* (pp. 510–517). Abingdon, Oxford, England: Routledge.

Van Raalte, J. L., Brewer, B. W., Lewis, B. P., Linder, D. E., Wildman, G., & Kozimor, J. (1995). The effects of positive and negative self-talk on dart throwing performance. *Journal of Sport Behavior, 18,* 50–57.

Van Raalte, J. L., Brewer, B. W., Rivera, P. M., & Petitpas, A. J. (1994). The relationship between observable self-talk and competitive junior tennis players' match performance. *Journal of Sport & Exercise Psychology, 16,* 400–415.

Walsh, D. (2008, July 6). "Is this the world's greatest athlete?" *The Sunday Times* (Sport), 12–13.

Wegner, D. M. (1994). Ironic processes of mental control. *Psychological Review, 101,* 34–52. doi:10.1037/0033-295X.101.1.34

Wegner, D. M. (2009, July 3). How to think, say, or do precisely the worst thing for any occasion. *Science, 325,* 48–50. doi:10.1126/science.1167346

Wei, G., & Luo, J. (2010). Sport expert's motor imagery: Functional imaging of professional motor skills and simple motor skills. *Brain Research, 1341,* 52–62. doi:10.1016/j.brainres.2009.08.014

Williams, A. M., & Ford, P. R. (2008). Expertise and expert performance in sport. *International Review of Sport & Exercise Psychology, 1,* 4–18. doi: 10.1080/17509840701836867

Woodman, T., & Davis, P. A. (2008). The role of repression in the incidence of ironic errors. *The Sport Psychologist, 22,* 183–196.

Wulf, G. (2007). Attentional focus and motor learning: A review of 10 years of research. *Bewegung und Training, 1,* 4–14.

Wulf, G., Shea, C., & Lewthwaite, R. (2010). Motor skill learning and performance: A review of influential factors. *Medical Education, 44,* 75–84. doi:10.1080/17509840701836867

Zinsser, N., Bunker, L., & Williams, J. (2010). Cognitive techniques for building confidence and enhancing performance. In J. M. Williams (Ed.), *Applied sport psychology: From personal growth to peak performance* (6th ed., pp. 305–335). New York, NY: McGraw-Hill.

Gregory S. Wilson and Jim Taylor

Intensity Regulation and Sport Performance

6

n his book *The Four-Minute Mile,* Sir Roger Bannister (1989) wrote: "I am certain that one's feelings at the last minute before a race matter most. Confidence that has been supreme until that moment can be lost quite suddenly" (pp. 236–237). To put Bannister's comments into sport psychology terminology, precompetition intensity is strongly related to performance outcomes. Achieving an ideal level of intensity can allow athletes to perform their best.

This chapter provides an in-depth understanding of intensity, how it affects athletic performance, and what sport psychologists can do to help athletes attain an ideal level of intensity for competition. First, an explanation of the term *intensity* is offered and why this particular term is used in place of related terms such as *arousal* or *anxiety.* Second, the chapter provides a discussion of the latest theoretical formulations and empirical findings associated with intensity. Third, the nature of intensity as experienced by athletes is presented, with particular attention to the symptoms and

http://dx.doi.org/10.1037/14251-006
Exploring Sport and Exercise Psychology, Third Edition, J. Van Raalte and B. Brewer (Editors)

causes of over- and underintensity. Fourth, ideal intensity is examined, and examples are provided that illustrate various ways the sport psychologist can assist athletes in specifying an appropriate level of intensity for best performances. Finally, a variety of cognitive, physiological, and general interventions that can be used to regulate precompetition levels of intensity are presented.

What Is Intensity

The study of anxiety and its effects on sport performance has long been of great interest to sport psychologists (Smith, Smoll, Cumming, & Grossbard, 2006). Although the terms arousal, anxiety, and nervousness have often been used synonymously (Weinberg & Gould, 2011), it is important to distinguish among these terms before offering an explanation of the use of intensity when dealing with athletes. *Arousal* is a complex physiological process involving activation of the sympathetic nervous system that represents nonspecific physiological responses such as muscle tension, increased heart rate, and metabolic rates (Buckworth & Dishman, 2002; Robazza, Pellizzari, Bertollo, & Hanin, 2008). In sport, what is often referred to as an arousal response is actually a change in autonomic nervous system activity that can be viewed as a continuum ranging from total relaxation to extreme excitement (Cox, 2006). *Anxiety*, on the other hand, is a cognitive response that represents the way in which people interpret a specific situation and the emotions they associate with the interpretation (Schmidt & Wrisberg, 2008) and may be characterized by negative emotional states such as worry or apprehension (Weinberg & Gould, 2011). In addition to the cognitive component of anxiety, there is a somatic component, the perceived degree of arousal activation. Although increases in cognitive anxiety are often associated with increases in physiological arousal, this may not always be the case (Buckworth & Dishman, 2002).

Terms such as anxiety or nervousness are typically perceived negatively and as states to be avoided. Therefore, it is suggested that "intensity" be used when working with athletes. The term *intensity* does not carry negative connotations and is readily viewed by athletes as a positive and important contributor to optimal competitive performance (Wilson & Taylor, 2005).

In the realm of sport psychology, the definition of intensity has been a point of contention for decades because it is difficult to separate the physical (arousal) and mental (intensity) reactions to athletic competition (Cox, 2006; Landers & Arent, 2010; Spielberger, 1966). Theorists have suggested that intensity is best viewed as a multidimensional construct that includes emotional, cognitive, and physiological factors (Hanin, 2007; Hardy, Beattie, & Woodman, 2007). The combination of physiological activation, cognition, and emotional responses to sport competition is interpreted by athletes as intensity. Intensity may be experienced by athletes positively as increased confidence and motivation (Wilson & Taylor, 2005). However, athletes may also perceive heightened intensity levels negatively and experience increased muscle tension, increased heart and respiration rates, reduced reaction time, and cognitive worry (Balague, 2005; Eysenck & Calvo, 1992).

Theoretical and Empirical Perspectives on Intensity

The primary theoretical explanations for the relationship between intensity and athletic performance include the inverted-U hypothesis (Yerkes & Dodson, 1908), the individual zone of optimal functioning model (IZOF; Hanin, 2000, 2007), catastrophe theory (Hardy et al., 2007), and reversal theory (Apter, 1984; Kerr, 1997).

INVERTED-U HYPOTHESIS

The inverted-U hypothesis (Yerkes & Dodson, 1908) has been used as a popular explanation of the relationship between intensity and subsequent athletic performance (Raglin & Wilson, 2009). The original research did not focus on intensity and sport performance but, rather, explored the relationship between performance and stimulus intensity with rats involved in maze discrimination learning. As the rats' degree of learning difficulty increased, the optimal level of electrical stimulus for learning decreased (Cox, 2006). In other words, Yerkes and Dodson (1908) found that increases in intensity produced commensurate improvements in performance, but only up to a specified point, after which greater intensity inhibited performance (Raglin & Wilson, 2009). Hence, when performance was plotted against intensity, a curvilinear relationship in the shape of an inverted-U was depicted.

Oxendine (1970) popularized the basic principles of the inverted-U hypothesis and applied the concept to sport performance. Oxendine proposed that moderate levels of intensity were appropriate for most motor tasks, although the optimal level of intensity was dependent on the specific type of sport task to be performed. For example, gross motor activities involving speed and strength (e.g., shot put, weight lifting) would benefit from high levels of intensity for optimal sport performances, whereas low levels of intensity would predict success for athletic performances in which fine muscle movements, steadiness, coordination, and general concentration (e.g., golf putting, diving) were essential. Hence, Oxendine suggested that intensity is sport- and sport-task-specific.

Despite the intuitive appeal of the inverted-U hypothesis, there is only limited empirical research that supports its application to sport performance (Fazy & Hardy, 1988; Gould & Krane, 1992; Kleine, 1990; Neiss, 1988) and research examining the claim that optimal intensity is influenced by motor skill has not supported Oxendine's contention (Imlay, Carda, Stanbrough, & O'Connor, 1995; Krane & Williams, 1994). Possibly the most important criticism of the inverted-U hypothesis is that it implies that only moderate levels of intensity are appropriate for all athletes and does not account for individual differences in the way athletes respond to the stress of competition, even on similar tasks (Hassmén, Raglin, & Lundqvist, 2004; Raglin & Wilson, 2009). Because of this and other criticisms of the inverted-U hypothesis, Weinberg and Gould (2011) suggested that alternative explanations are needed to better address the complex relationship between intensity and sport performance.

INDIVIDUAL ZONE OF OPTIMAL FUNCTIONING MODEL

Partly in response to these concerns, Hanin (2000, 2007) developed the IZOF model. The original idea of individual differences in optimal levels of intensity among athletes stemmed from data gathered from elite Soviet athletes showing that they differed in the level of precompetition intensity experienced right before competing (Cratty & Hanin, 1980). The results of this work supported the idea that on an individual level, anxiety is a significant psychological factor in sport performance, but on a group level, associations predicted by the inverted-U hypothesis between intensity and sport performance were not found (Hanin, 2007; Raglin & Hanin, 2000). That is, regardless of the type of sport, some athletes performed best at very low levels of intensity, whereas others were successful at very high levels of intensity.

These findings represent a significant difference between the IZOF model and the inverted-U hypothesis. The inverted-U hypothesis suggests that successful performances may be obtained only when athletes perform under states of moderate intensity. In contrast, the IZOF model contends that athletes differ markedly in their individual level of optimal intensity (Hanin, 2007; Nieuwenhuys, Hanin, & Bakker, 2008; Raglin, Wise, & Morgan, 1990; Wilson & Raglin, 1997). Moreover, IZOF theory contends that the optimal intensity zone, rather than being a single discrete point, may range on a continuum from very low to very high depending on the unique characteristics of the individual athlete

(Robazza et al., 2008). Indeed, this model predicts that for athletes of similar skill who are competing in the same event, a large number will perform best when intensity levels are high (Harmison, 2006; Raglin & Turner, 1992; Raglin & Wilson, 2009). Hence, the optimal level of intensity is considered to be dependent on the individual (Hanin, 2007).

The optimal level of intensity for individual athletes was first determined through assessments of state anxiety approximately 1 hour prior to actual competitions throughout a competitive season until an outstanding or best performance occurred (Raglin & Wilson, 2009). Once the athlete achieved this level of performance, Hanin (2007) established an optimal zone by adding and subtracting one half a standard deviation from the intensity scores obtained by using the State–Trait Anxiety Inventory (Spielberger, Gorsuch, Lushene, Vagg, & Jacobs, 1983). However, this method proved to be a logistical challenge because following athletes throughout an entire competitive season is difficult and can be distracting to the athletes (Raglin & Hanin, 2000). As a result, Hanin (2007) developed a retrospective recall method for determining athletes' IZOFs by asking them to remember or "recall" how they felt immediately prior to their all-time best performance. By comparing these scores with their original values, Hanin (2007) was able to conclude that athletes were highly successful in recalling their intensity levels (correlations between predicted and actual precompetition anxiety up to 48 hours prior to competition have been found to range from .60 to .80), negating the need to follow athletes throughout entire seasons (Hanin, 1986; Morgan et al., 1987; Morgan, O'Connor, Sparling, & Pate, 1988; Raglin & Turner, 1992; Raglin & Wilson, 2009; Wilson, 1998; Wilson & Raglin, 1997; Wilson, Raglin, & Harger, 2000).

Although the IZOF model has received considerable support (Gould & Krane, 1992; Morgan, O'Connor, Sparling, & Pate, 1987; Nieuwenhuys et al., 2007; Raglin et al., 1990; Robazza et al., 2008; Wilson & Raglin, 1997), some aspects of the model have been questioned. A main criticism has been that the IZOF model is descriptive in nature and that it does not explain why some athletes perform better under certain levels of intensity, whereas others do not (Balague, 2005). Furthermore, the IZOF model is focused primarily on anxiety, but other variables (e.g., optimism, defensive pessimism, pessimism) have been hypothesized to affect optimal intensity levels in athletes (Wilson, 2010; Wilson, Raglin, & Pritchard, 2002; Wilson & Steinke, 2002). Hanin has recently extended the IZOF model to include other emotions beyond anxiety in an attempt to better understand this issue (Nieuwenhuys et al., 2007; Robazza et al., 2008). As a result, the current IZOF model is multidimensional. It incorporates somatic, cognitive, and self-confidence components of intensity and considers how these factors interact to influence sport performance (Cox, 2006; Landers & Arent, 2010).

CATASTROPHE THEORY

Using a mathematically based model, Hardy (1996) suggested that the combination of somatic and cognitive intensity along with self-confidence exerts an interactive three-dimensional influence on performance. Specifically, catastrophe theory predicts that athletes experience a complex interaction between physiological arousal and cognitive anxiety that influences individual performance levels (Hardy et al., 2007).

In performance situations where physiological arousal is high, cognitive anxiety can rise to a point at which catastrophic drops in performance will occur (Woodman & Hardy, 2001). Yet, in situations where physiological activation is low, increases in cognitive anxiety may serve to enhance performance by bringing athletes into their optimal intensity ranges (Cox, 2006; Woodman & Hardy, 2001).

Many of the basic assumptions of catastrophe theory have been criticized (Cohen, Pargman, & Tenenbaum, 2003; Krane, Joyce, & Rafeld, 1994; Mellalieu, Hanton, & Fletcher, 2006). For example, Arent and Landers (2003) found no support for a rapid drop-off in performance once physiological arousal levels peaked at 70% to 90% as predicted by catastrophe theory. Gill (1994) questioned whether the interactive effects of the cognitive, somatic, and self-confidence components are stable characteristics within an athlete or whether they are subject to situational influences. Gould and Tuffey (1996) suggested that more specific affective components of anxiety may exist. Woodman, Albinson, and Hardy (1997) conceded that the catastrophe model has not been able to explain why successful performances occur under conditions of high cognitive anxiety for certain athletes.

Hardy et al. (2007) proposed that two different cusp catastrophe models may exist that explain the relationship between performance and intensity. The first incorporates an interaction of cognitive anxiety and physiological arousal, whereas the second involves an interaction of cognitive anxiety and the degree of effort required for success by athletes. Other factors may also be involved in the intensity–performance relationship. For example, Woodman, Davis, Hardy, Callow, Glasscock, and Yuill-Proctor (2009) examined the effects of emotions of happiness, hope, and anger on sport performance and the influence these emotions have on the intensity–performance relationship. Anger was associated with enhanced gross muscular peak force performance, whereas hope was related to faster soccer-related reaction times. Interestingly, Woodman and colleagues noted that extraversion acted as a moderator of the anger–performance relationship. In other words, extraverts' peak force increased more than that of introverts when angry. Although the catastrophe model is difficult to test (Balague, 2005), research suggests that the catastrophe model may prove to be useful in helping to explain the complex relationships between intensity and performance.

REVERSAL THEORY

On the basis of research conducted by Apter (1984), reversal theory has been applied to sport settings (Kerr, 1997; Kerr, Wilson, Bowling, & Sheahan, 2005). Reversal theory takes into account athletes' interpretation of physical activation. For example, if athletes perceive high intensity levels to be positive, then such levels are in fact positive for performance. If athletes perceive high intensity levels as negative, then such intensity levels can have debilitating effects on performance. Hence, for successful performances to occur, athletes must view their intensity as positive rather than negative (Kerr, 1997).

Furthermore, reversal theory suggests that there are shifts in perceptions of intensity throughout the duration of a competition (Kerr et al., 2005). For example, an athlete may begin a competition feeling confident and motivated and interpret the accompanying intensity as beneficial. However, as the competition progresses and the athlete performs poorly, there can be a shift in perception of intensity such that the same level of intensity may be viewed negatively. For this reason, reversal theory suggests that perceptions of intensity are not static, but, rather, dynamic and constantly changing throughout a competition, and that many factors such as cognition may play a significant role in these changes (Kerr et al., 2005).

Although reversal theory is primarily a descriptive model with limited empirical support to date (Balague, 2005), Hanin (2007) noted that the role of changing emotions, as described by reversal theory, may be important in understanding individual perceptions of intensity by athletes. The factors identified by reversal theory may be worthy of consideration by researchers, practitioners, and athletes.

Understanding the Experience of Intensity

For sport psychologists to assist athletes effectively in identifying and attaining optimal levels of intensity, it is first necessary to gain a clear understanding of the experience of intensity for athletes. This experience includes the symptoms and causes of over- and underintensity.

SYMPTOMS OF OVERINTENSITY

As alluded to in the theoretical discussion above, intensity can be manifested physically, behaviorally, and psychologically (Hanin, 2007; Jones, 1995; Kerr et al., 2005). The most common symptoms of intensity are physical reactions that include extreme muscle tension, shaking muscles, difficulty breathing, and excessive perspiration (Landers & Arent, 2010). Other more subtle physical symptoms include stomach butterflies, fatigue, and a decrease in motor coordination. Behaviorally, symptoms of intensity may include mistakes during precompetition preparation, an increase in pace during competition, generalized agitation, an increase in performance-irrelevant or superstitious behaviors, tense body language, and a decrease in competitive performance (Eysenck & Calvo, 1992). Psychological symptoms of overintensity include negative self-talk (e.g., "I know I'll screw up"), irrational thinking (e.g., "If I perform poorly, everyone will hate me"), a shift from performance-relevant thoughts to negative or performance-irrelevant thoughts, an overnarrowing of concentration (Wilson & Taylor, 2005), and emotional feelings of fear and dread or a decrease in motivation (Robazza et al., 2008).

CAUSES OF OVERINTENSITY

Causes of overintensity have been characterized as psychological, social, and situational. They may include pressures to perform, competitive concerns and level of performance, personal relationships, and lifestyle demands (McKay, Niven, Lavallee, & White, 2008). Lack of confidence may also contribute to overintensity. For example, athletes who do not believe they will be successful in a competition, yet must perform regardless of these feelings, may perceive the situation as threatening and experience overintensity (Wilson & Taylor, 2005). These perceptions, in turn, interfere with athletes' ability to perform at their highest level. Hanin (2007) supported this view by suggesting that emotional reactions and intensity are influenced by athletes' appraisals of the likelihood of achieving their goals. In addition, Edwards and Hardy (1996) reported that athletes whose confidence increased perceived their anxiety to facilitate their competitive performances.

A severe manifestation of lack of confidence is irrational thinking, in which athletes develop extreme and often harmful cognitions about their performance. For example, a downhill ski racer inspecting the course comes to a difficult high-speed turn that she doubts she can negotiate. She sees a tree that would be in her path if she is unable to make the turn and thinks, "That tree has my name on it!"

Another psychological cause of overintensity involves focusing on the outcome of the competition rather than its process. Whether the outcome is positive (e.g., "If I win, people will expect me to always win") or negative (e.g., "If I lose, I will let the whole town down"), considering the consequences of a performance adds pressure and detracts from a proper competitive focus that allows for optimal performance.

Social causes of overintensity are derived primarily from expectations of significant others in the lives of athletes, including parents, coaches, friends, community, and media. Overintensity results from the perception that if athletes do not live up to the socially derived expectations, they will not be loved and supported, a direct threat to self-esteem (Krohne, 1980; Passer, 1982).

Environmental variables may exacerbate the overintensity reaction. Factors such as unfamiliarity with the situation, the occurrence of unexpected events, and worry over uncontrollable aspects of the competitive situation can cause overintensity by producing feelings of uncertainty and helplessness.

SYMPTOMS OF UNDERINTENSITY

Due to the inherent pressures associated with competition, underintensity is not a common occurrence (Williams & Harris, 1998). However, it may be evident in some athletes and in some competitive situations. As with overintensity, underintensity can manifest itself physically, behaviorally, and psychologically.

Physical symptoms of underintensity include decreased sympathetic nervous system activation, resulting in lower heart, respiration, and metabolic rates. These changes are exhibited in the form of low energy and feelings of lethargy. Behaviorally, underintensity can be seen as a decrease in pace during competition, generalized lethargy, "let-down" body language, a reduction in performance-relevant behaviors (e.g., routines), an oversensitivity to external distractions, and a decline in competitive performance. Psychological symptoms include a loss of motivation to compete, difficulty narrowing concentration, and a generalized feeling of "not being all there."

CAUSES OF UNDERINTENSITY

Unlike overintensity, underintensity is less influenced by social and situational factors and may be characterized primarily as having psychological and physical causes. Overconfidence is a significant psychological cause of underintensity. Athletes who are overconfident believe that they will win easily with little effort. A lack of interest in competing or motivation to compete or an absence of fun or enthusiasm will also produce underintensity. Athletes who lack the desire to perform will not feel the need to activate themselves physiologically. Social and situational contributors to underintensity include lack of emphasis by coaches or an unimportant game. Fatigue from overtraining or overcompeting, sleeping difficulties, and competitive stress are physical causes of underintensity. Other physical causes of underintensity include nutritional deficiencies and injuries. Athletes suffering from these physical causes have fewer physiological resources.

Identifying Ideal Intensity

As suggested above, there is no one ideal intensity level for all athletes. Rather, ideal intensity involves individual optimal levels of both physiological and cognitive activity for each athlete. In addition, ideal intensity is not something that athletes will automatically attain in all competitions. Intensity is determined by numerous personal, social, and situational variables, which an athlete may have little awareness of and even less control over (Schmidt & Wrisberg, 2008).

Hanin (1986, 2000) has suggested two methods for assessing ideal intensity. First, athletes can measure their level of intensity prior to each performance throughout a competitive season. Once they achieve a personal best performance, the level of intensity can be identified and a range of intensity can be established (Hanin, 1986; Raglin & Hanin, 2000). Second, athletes recall the level of intensity experienced immediately prior to their best performance, and a range or zone is developed through this retrospection (Hanin, 2000). Athletes who are in their ideal intensity zones are expected to perform well. Deviations from the optimal intensity zone may provide sport psychologists with information necessary for developing appropriate interventions (Hanin, 2007). However, simply being in one's optimal zone of intensity does not guarantee sport success. A variety of other factors, including psychological, emotional, environmental, and physical variables, can affect an athlete's level of performance (Hanin, 2007).

A tool such as the Intensity Identification form (see Figure 6.1) can help athletes identify their ideal intensity by having them answer such questions as the following: (a) Prior to and during a successful competition, how did your body feel, for example, heart pounding and sweating or calm and at ease? (b) What were your thoughts and emotions at the time, for example, positive and excited or neutral and calm? (c) What social influences were present or absent during successful performances, for example, family, coaches, friends? The same questions should be asked for poor performances. Athletes can then summarize the factors that are associated with their successful and unsuccessful performance. In rare instances, athletes may be unable to find a difference in intensity between successful and unsuccessful performances. In these cases, they should look for other psychological or physical factors that can account for the differences.

FIGURE 6.1

Directions: In the spaces below, indicate the psychological and situational factors that affect your intensity and the quality of your competitive performances. At the bottom, summarize the positive and negative performance factors that distinguish your best and worst performances.

	Best performances	Worst performances
Physical		
Feelings		
Thoughts		
Emotions		
Social		
Influences		
Competition		
Site		
Event		
Competitive		
Level		
Positive performance factors		
Negative performance factors		

Intensity Identification.

The purpose of identifying ideal intensity is to create an understanding in athletes of what their body feels like, what they are thinking and feeling, and with whom they are interacting when they perform well or perform poorly. The goal of intensity identification is to make athletes aware of these differences before they compete so that they can then take steps to reproduce the factors that are associated with good performance through the use of intensity regulation.

Intensity Regulation

Once athletes have identified their ideal and nonideal levels of intensity, they can learn how to shift their intensity to its ideal level as competition approaches. Intensity interventions can be implemented cognitively, physiologically, generally, and situationally, and at various times as the competition approaches (e.g., during training and precompetitive preparation).

COGNITIVE INTERVENTIONS FOR INTENSITY REGULATION

Cognitive Reappraisal

Overintensity is most often caused by negative, inaccurate, or extreme cognitive appraisal of a situation (Jones, 2003). Consequently, a good place to begin controlling overintensity is at its source, during the appraisal process (Kerr et al., 2005). Sport psychologists can assist athletes in rationally assessing the upcoming competition by discussing five appraisal areas (i.e., demands, resources, consequences, meaning, recognition of bodily reactions). Many athletes experience overintensity prior to competition and find a discussion of appraisal areas to be helpful in reducing irrational thinking. Furthermore, considering alternative ways of viewing the situation can help athletes to shift intensity to an ideal level (Jones, 2003).

Sport psychologists can also use this approach in addressing the social causes of overintensity. Assessing athletes' perceptions of others' expectations and then intervening when appropriate can diminish the negative effects of social influences, thus reducing overintensity and improving competitive performance.

All of these interventions have the effect of altering debilitating intensity in several ways. That is, they can offer athletes new perspectives that make competition less threatening. They can change the attitudes that cause overintensity. Finally, they can restructure the perceptions of the intensity symptoms so that athletes see them as positive and facilitating (Kerr, 1990).

Self-Talk

At a more direct level, negative, worrying, or irrational self-talk (e.g., "I know I will fail," "I am so scared," "I'm going to break every bone in my body") is typically found in athletes suffering from overintensity. Interventions based on cognitive restructuring techniques that include thought replacement and positive litanies can be helpful. For example, athletes might say "positive" when a negative thought occurs. Furthermore, they might replace negative thoughts with positive statements such as "I will try my hardest and play my best." Developing a series of positive self-statements (e.g., "I love to compete," "I am a great athlete," "I always think and talk positively") may also be useful. These strategies can increase athletes' awareness of unproductive thinking and show them how to develop a more positive way of thinking about future situations (Hardy, Hall, & Hardy, 2005; Jones, 2003).

Keywords

Athletes can also identify meaningful keywords to adjust their intensity levels (see Figure 6.2). Keywords such as *breathe, loose, calm,* and *easy* may help athletes reduce their intensity levels when necessary. Keywords like *charge, attack, commit,* and *believe* may be useful for increasing intensity levels. Some athletes find that writing keywords on index cards and placing them in visible settings like bedrooms, locker rooms, and weight rooms help them to familiarize themselves with and practice using their keywords. Some athletes have keywords in performance venues and on equipment so that they will see the keywords and remember to monitor and adjust their intensity during competition.

Familiarization

Hanin (2000) indicated that athletes' appraisals of their environments have a substantial impact on competitive performance. For instance, lack of knowledge of the physical environment in which athletes compete may contribute to overintensity. A good solution for this particular problem is to give athletes an opportunity to familiarize themselves with the competitive setting, ideally through practice or preliminary competition in the competitive arena. In the absence of direct experience practicing or competing in a venue, enabling athletes to attend another competition at the site, walking around, viewing video of the setting,

---

FIGURE 6.2

Directions: A variety of intensity keywords have been provided. In the spaces below, identify other intensity keywords you can use.

Psych down	Psych up
Breathe	Go for it
Loose	Charge
Relax	Attack
Calm	Positive
Easy	Hustle
Focus	Punch it
Trust	Commit
Cool down	Fire up

Intensity keywords.

and getting information from coaches and athletes with firsthand experiences at the site can be particularly helpful. Athletes may also want to pay attention to the setup of competition facilities as well as to expected media coverage, training and competitive schedules, transportation issues, audience location and responses, access to locker rooms, location of warm-up areas, accessibility and location of athletic trainers, and so forth. Combining this observational experience of the setting with mental imagery in the days before a competition can help athletes to manage their intensity levels.

Anticipating Unexpected Events

Another difficulty that causes overintensity is the occurrence of unexpected events prior to and during competitions. The most effective means of handling such problems is to prevent or minimize unexpected incidents. This does not mean that all problems can be prevented from arising during a competition. Rather, the goal is to prevent these problems from being unexpected, thereby causing overintensity.

Managing unexpected events may be achieved in two steps. First, athletes should identify things that can go wrong at a competition. Then, they can propose solutions to these occurrences (see Figure 6.3). When such difficulties inevitably arise, athletes will recognize that a problem has occurred and will have a plan for solving it, thus making it more likely that intensity will remain at an ideal level.

FIGURE 6.3

Directions: A variety of unexpected situations and how to deal with them have been provided. In the spaces below, identify specific unexpected situations that you may encounter and how to deal with them.

Unexpected	Plan
Late arrival to competition	Have shortened precompetitive routine
Forget clothing or accessory	Pack extra gear
Broken equipment	Have backup equipment properly prepared
No place to practice	Have alternative physical warm-up routine
Bad weather or conditions	Stay relaxed and focused; stay warmed up
Change in schedule	Repeat precompetitive routine
Different opponent	Stay calm; reassess strategy

Expect the unexpected.

Focusing on Controllable Events

Athletes, like other people, spend considerable time worrying about things over which they have little control (Bandura, 1986). This is a fruitless endeavor because they not only lack influence over those things but also they may negatively affect their intensity levels by worrying. Much of what occurs in the competitive sports world is outside of the control of athletes. Moreover, only one thing is truly within their control—themselves. As a result, athletes should focus primarily on themselves when preparing for competition; specifically, they should focus on what they need to do to perform their best.

Sport psychologists can play a meaningful role in helping athletes to maintain focus on controllable factors. When a sport psychologist hears athletes worrying about things outside of their control, athletes should be asked several questions. First, is this something that is within your control? If it is, athletes should be asked what they can do to address the problem and should develop a plan to do so. If it is not within their control, they should be asked what in the situation they can control, and they should focus on the controllable (see Figure 6.4).

FIGURE 6.4

Directions: A variety of controllable and uncontrollable factors have been provided. In the spaces below, identify specific controllable and uncontrollable factors that you may encounter.

Controllable	Uncontrollable
Your behavior	Others' attitudes, thoughts, emotions, behavior
Physical condition	Competitors' performances
Motivation/effort	Coaches
Attitude	Family
Thoughts	Officials
Emotions	Opponent selection
Equipment	Competition conditions
Preparation	Weather
Performance	

Control or not to control.

PHYSIOLOGICAL INTERVENTIONS FOR INTENSITY REGULATION

Because of the situational and social aspects of competition, many athletes will experience intensity levels outside of their optimal range despite the athletes' best efforts. Consequently sport psychologists should be familiar with simple and practical physiological techniques they may use prior to and during competition that will enable athletes to attain ideal intensity.

Breathing

Perhaps the simplest yet the most important technique that can reduce overintensity is breathing (Williams, 2010). Often, athletes who are in a state of overintensity will take quick, choppy breaths. Fast, shallow breathing reduces the amount of oxygen entering the bloodstream and may cause fatigue, reduced coordination, and muscle tension, all of which can impair performance. By taking deep, slow, rhythmic breaths, athletes can replenish their oxygen supply and reduce overintensity, thus enabling them to perform better.

Breathing also has psychological ramifications. A significant problem with overintensity is that athletes tend to become focused on the negative symptoms such as muscle tension and stomach butterflies. By taking slow, deep breaths, athletes alleviate some of these symptoms, thereby increasing self-confidence and general feelings of well-being. In addition, focusing on breathing distracts from some of the negative feelings associated with overintensity.

Muscle Relaxation

One of the most uncomfortable manifestations of overintensity is muscle tension (Williams, 2010). Tight muscles inhibit coordination, interfere with quality performance, and increase the likelihood of injury. One strategy to counter muscle tension is passive relaxation, a procedure that involves deep breathing and muscle relaxation (see Figure 6.5; Balague, 2005). Another technique that directly affects this symptom of overintensity is called progressive relaxation (Jacobson, 1938). This procedure involves tightening and relaxing major muscle groups (see Figure 6.6).

Progressive relaxation has value for athletes at two levels. First, athletes are often so accustomed to being tense that they are simply not aware of their level of muscle tension and how it affects their competitive performances. The process of tightening and relaxing muscles teaches athletes to discriminate between the states of tension and relaxation. Once this recognition occurs, athletes often become more sensitive to

Imagine there are drain plugs on the bottom of your feet. When you open them, all the tension will drain out of your body and you will become very, very relaxed. Take a slow, deep breath.

Now, undo those plugs. Feel the tension begin to drain out of your body. Down from the top of your head, past your forehead, your face and neck; you're becoming more and more relaxed. The tension drains out of your jaw and down past your neck. Now your face and your neck are warm and relaxed and comfortable. Take a slow, deep breath.

The tension continues to drain out of your upper body, past your hands and forearms, and out of your upper arms and shoulders. Now your hands, arms, and shoulders are warm and relaxed and comfortable. Take a slow, deep breath.

The tension continues to drain out of your upper body, past your chest and upper back, down past your stomach and lower back, and your upper body is becoming more and more relaxed. There is no more tension left in your upper body. Now your entire upper body is warm and relaxed and comfortable. Take a slow, deep breath.

The tension continues to drain out of your lower body, past your buttocks and down past your thighs, and your knees. Your lower body is becoming more and more relaxed. The tension drains out of your calves. There is almost no more tension left in your body and the last bit of tension drains past your ankles, the balls of your feet, and your toes. Now do a brief survey of your body from head to toe to ensure that there is no more tension left in your body. Your entire body is warm and relaxed and comfortable. Now replace the plugs so that no tension can get back in. Take a slow, deep breath. Feel the calm and relaxation envelop you. Enjoy that feeling, and remember what it feels like to be completely relaxed.

Passive relaxation script.

their body's signals and better able to respond effectively to nonideal levels of intensity (Williams, 2010).

As with any technique, the muscle awareness and control that develop from progressive relaxation take practice. Coaches and sport psychologists can facilitate relaxation skill development by making relaxation a part of practice. For example, they might encourage athletes to practice relaxing quickly during breaks in intense action to reach optimal levels of intensity or might offer relaxation sessions at the end of practice as an enjoyable and beneficial part of the cool-down process.

Biofeedback

Biofeedback allows athletes to learn how to control specific autonomic responses such as respiration, blood pressure, muscle tension, and brain activity. Similar to progressive relaxation techniques, biofeedback enables athletes to address physiological symptoms associated with

FIGURE 6.6

Progressive relaxation involves tightening and relaxing major muscle groups. This is so that you can contrast the feelings of muscle tension and relaxation. You will focus on four major muscle groups: legs and buttocks, chest and back, arms and shoulders, face and neck. To start, tense the muscles in your legs and buttocks for 5 seconds, then release. Take a long, slow, deep breath. Feel the difference between the tension and relaxation. Repeat this process in your legs and buttocks.

Tense the muscles in your chest and back for 5 seconds, then release. Take a long, slow, deep breath. Feel the difference between the tension and the relaxation. Try to relax for twice as long as you tensed. Repeat this process in your chest and back.

Tense the muscles in your arms and shoulders for 5 seconds, then release. Take a long, slow, deep breath. Relax for a full 10 seconds. Feel the difference between the tension and relaxation. Repeat this process in your arms and shoulders.

Tense the muscles in your face and neck for 5 seconds, then release for a slow relaxing 10 seconds. Take a long, slow, deep breath. Feel the difference between the tension and the relaxation. Repeat this process in your face and neck.

Tense the muscles in your entire body for five seconds, then release. Take a long, slow, deep breath and relax for 10 seconds. Feel the difference between the tension and the relaxation. Repeat this process in your entire body.

Now do a mental checklist to make sure that every muscle is relaxed. Your feet are relaxed, calves, thighs, buttocks, stomach, back, chest, arms, shoulders, neck, and face. Every muscle in your body is completely relaxed. If an area is not yet fully relaxed, try tensing the area again for 5 seconds and then relaxing for 10 seconds until your whole body is fully relaxed.

Progressive relaxation script.

---

overintensity to bring on feelings of relaxation and reduce intensity levels. Research has found biofeedback to be effective in eliciting relaxation responses in both athletes and nonathletic populations (Blumenstein, Bar-Eli, & Tenenbaum, 1995). Singer (2004) examined the effect of biofeedback on performance anxiety in dancers and found that overall anxiety levels decreased following 20 sessions of biofeedback training. Blumenstein and colleagues (1995) reported an increase in relaxation with biofeedback use. However, only moderate improvements in athletic performance were reported. Davis and Sime (2005) suggested that confidence enhancement and not anxiety reduction may be the greater benefit of biofeedback. Clearly, further research on the type, dose, electrode placement, waveform suppressed and enhanced, and other relevant variables is needed before clear advice can be given about biofeedback and its relationship to intensity management. Some research is reportedly being conducted by professional teams with regard to these variables, but it is not being published in scientific journals as these teams strive to gain particular advantages for their players.

Smiling

This physiological intervention is so basic that its effectiveness is surprising. The technique is smiling, and although much of the evidence supporting its efficacy is anecdotal (Weinberg & Gould, 2011), the simple act of smiling may effectively reduce elevated intensity levels for some athletes (Wilson & Taylor, 2005). A case study provides an interesting example of how smiling may affect behavior. Several years ago a sport psychologist was working with a professional tennis player, who became frustrated and angry during an on-court practice session as she struggled to improve a weak part of her game. The tennis player became so tense that she simply could not perform. Purely on a whim, the sport psychologist told her to smile. As you can imagine, smiling was the last thing she wanted to do, and she expressed that quite emphatically. However, with persistence, and to appease her sport psychologist, she formed a big smile. The sport psychologist told her to hold the smile. Within 2 minutes, a remarkable transformation occurred. As she held the smile, the tension in her shoulders disappeared, the wrinkle in her brow went away, and her body, which had been hunched and closed, began to rise and open up. She went on to have a productive practice in which she was able to overcome her earlier difficulties (Wilson & Taylor, 2005).

The sport psychologist hypothesized that smiling had such a dramatic effect because people are conditioned to associate smiling with happiness and feeling good. Moreover, it is difficult to think and feel in a way that is contrary to what the body is expressing. As such, it is difficult to be frustrated, angry, and tense when smiling.

Physical Activity

Intensity is influenced by the amount of physiological activity experienced by an athlete. As a result, one of the most direct ways to increase intensity is simply through vigorous physical activity. The type of physical activity depends on the particular sport, but any form of running, jumping, or active movement will be sufficient. Increasing such physiological factors as heart, respiration, and metabolic rate can increase intensity and reduce overintensity.

High-Energy Body Language

Internal physiological activity can be effectively activated with external physiological activity such as high-energy body language (Cox, 2006). For example, athletes who pump their fist, slap their thighs, and give high fives to their teammates are all using this technique to increase their intensity. Athletes in many sports use high-energy body language to maintain ideal intensity.

GENERAL INTERVENTIONS FOR INTENSITY REGULATION

In addition to the cognitive and physiological techniques just described, a number of general performance enhancement strategies are beneficial to many aspects of mental preparation for athletes. Some of these interventions are discussed next in terms of how they can be used to regulate intensity and affect athletes both cognitively and physiologically.

Mental Imagery

Research has demonstrated that the use of mental imagery can assist athletes in achieving optimal intensity levels prior to competition or practice settings (Bernier & Fournier, 2010; Hale & Seiser, 2005). High-energy images of intense competition, strong effort, and success raise physiological activity. Calming images of relaxing scenes, peace, and tranquillity reduce intensity. The use of imagery in sport and exercise psychology is further discussed in Chapter 4 of this volume.

Music

Music can have profound emotional and physiological effects on people (Karageorghis et al., 2009). Music can cause people to feel happy, sad, inspired, or angry (Kreutz, Ott, Teichmann, Osawa, & Vaitl, 2007). Music can also excite or relax people (Karageorghis et al., 2009). Although this relationship has not been studied empirically in the sports world, it is common to see athletes using music as a way to help regulate their intensity before competition (Williams, 2010). Athletes who need to increase their intensity should probably listen to high-energy music (Karageorghis et al., 2009). In contrast, those who need to lower their intensity should listen to relaxing music.

SITUATIONAL INTERVENTIONS FOR INTENSITY REGULATION

Situational strategies are those that help athletes to manage intensity levels by addressing environmental and preparatory factors. Factors such as time, setting, and preparation prior to competition can affect intensity. Athletes who are able to identify and gain control over the most disruptive situational contributors to over- or underintensity are more likely to perform at optimal intensity levels.

Precompetition Management

On the day of the competition, the time that athletes spend before they compete is a crucial period of competitive mental preparation. Athletes should have three goals before they compete. Their equipment should be ideally prepared. Their body should be properly warmed up to their ideal level of intensity. Finally, athletes should be mentally prepared, most notably with ideal levels of intensity, confidence, and focus. Sport psychologists can assist in this total preparation by asking athletes, or having athletes ask themselves, four simple questions (see Figure 6.7) relating to the precompetitive environment.

Where to Spend Time at the Competition Site?

Where athletes can best accomplish their precompetitive preparation depends largely on their attentional style (Williams, Nideffer, Wilson, Sagal, & Peper, 2010). Athletes who are overly sensitive to external distractions should isolate themselves from the typical activity of the competition site. This will reduce the likelihood that environmental distractions such as other competitors, coaches, and officials will interfere with their precompetitive preparations. In contrast, athletes who are

---

FIGURE 6.7

Directions: Respond to each question below as it relates to your precompetitive preparation. Then apply this information to your precompetitive routine.

Where should you stay in the competition site?

What do you need to do to be totally prepared?

Who can assist you with your preparation?

Who and what can interfere with your preparation?

Precompetitive management plan.

overly sensitive to internal distractions should stay around the activity of the competition site. By doing so, athletes will be drawn out of their internal focus by the activity and will be less likely to dwell on negative or irrelevant thoughts that will inhibit their precompetitive preparation.

What Is Needed to be Totally Prepared?

Athletes who have the proper equipment and are physically and mentally prepared are more likely to perform optimally. Specific methods can be developed to ensure total preparation. Developing precompetitive routines (discussed in more detail below) can enable athletes to combine preparation strategies into a cohesive plan that is most effective for the particular athlete and competition.

Who Can Assist in Preparation?

Smith (2010) reported that coaches who provide frequent positive reinforcement and social support have teams that perform at high levels. Thus, Smith's findings suggest that certain coaches and possibly others such as parents or teammates might be helpful in precompetitive preparation by providing support or resources that will facilitate precompetitive preparation.

Who and What Can Interfere With Preparation?

Unfortunately, not all coaches and other people at the competition site are helpful. Indeed, some coaches, teammates, family, friends, and fans may serve as a distraction or adversely affect intensity levels. Such people can act to distract athletes from relevant precompetitive focus and inhibit their precompetitive efforts (Magill, 2011; Williams et al., 2010). Avoiding or developing plans to manage individuals who adversely affect precompetition preparation can be a useful strategy.

Precompetitive Routines

Precompetitive routines are an effective means of controlling intensity and enhancing the consistency and quality of performances (Balague, 2005; Schack & Whitmarsh, 2005). Routines are valuable for many reasons. They increase the likelihood of completion of key aspects of precompetitive preparation and serve to enhance the familiarity of a new situation, since the routines themselves are familiar to athletes. Routines may increase feelings of control over the competitive environment and by extension may raise confidence and reduce intensity. As a result, routines are an important part of precompetitive preparation and are useful to athletes in attaining and maintaining ideal intensity.

Routines Versus Rituals

The goal of routines is to prepare athletes for competition. Everything done in a precompetitive routine should serve a specific and necessary function in the preparation for competition (Bertollo, Saltarelli, & Robazza, 2009). That is, routines should be flexible and adapted to the unique aspects of each competitive situation. Rituals and superstitions, in contrast, tend to be rigid and do not serve a specific purpose in preparation for competition. Athletes may come to believe that particular rituals or superstitions must be done or they will not perform well. For example, an athlete may feel that he needs to have a lucky piece of equipment put on in a particular way to compete effectively. Although routines, superstitions, and rituals may appear to be similar, athletes control their routines, but rituals and superstitions control athletes.

What to Put in a Precompetitive Routine?

Each athlete's precompetitive routine should comprise the key factors that positively influence competitive performance. These factors differ for each individual but may include (a) meals, (b) physical warm-up, (c) equipment, (d) technical warm-up, and (e) mental preparation. Athletes can develop precompetitive routines and then modify them based on comfort with the routine and performance results. Team sport athletes, as opposed to individual sport athletes, also generally have team precompetitive routines (e.g., a football offensive unit running plays). Team sport athletes must integrate their personal precompetitive routines with team requirements to meet both individual and team precompetitive needs.

Early Morning Routine

For many athletes, precompetitive preparation begins as soon as they awaken in the morning. This early morning preparation sets the tone for the day and ensures that the athletes are physically and mentally ready for later preparation. Some athletes use mental imagery to rehearse their performance in the upcoming competition before they get out of bed. Others begin their routines by preparing equipment or physically warming up. Overall, the purpose of the precompetition routine is to begin the process of attaining ideal intensity when the competition begins. Routines set the stage for the competitive performance by generating positive feelings and focus.

Arrival at the Competition Site

A similar preparation process should be conducted on arrival at the competition site to further the athlete's readiness for competition. This can include putting on equipment, mental imagery, and other physical and psychological techniques. A more vigorous physical warm-up is also often necessary to continue the shift toward ideal intensity. For technical sports such as tennis, golf, and baseball, this phase is generally accompanied by technical warm-up in which proper technique is rehearsed and reinforced. Initial physical and technical warm-up should be slow and gentle. Once the initial warm-up is completed, the preparation should be rehearsed with increasing focus and intensity aimed at simulating competitive conditions. This priming effect makes it more likely that athletes will have attained their ideal focus and intensity when the competition begins.

Final Preparation Routine

This last stage of the athlete's precompetitive routine ensures that complete readiness is attained just prior to the competition. Any adjustments that may be needed to an athlete's equipment should be made to ensure confidence that no later problems will arise. As with the previous routines, emphasis needs to be placed on fine-tuning the athlete both mentally and physically, which may mean increasing or decreasing intensity to reach the optimal range. The goal of precompetitive preparation is to help athletes become mentally and physically ready to perform their best. The manner in which each of these factors is accomplished is what makes a routine personal. Once athletes have established the basic components of their routines, they may choose to modify the routines to fully satisfy their individual needs and styles (see Figure 6.8).

Summary

As competition approaches, the level of intensity experienced by athletes becomes key in influencing performance. However, athletes differ in their optimal levels of intensity. Some athletes perform best when very relaxed, and others perform best when intensity levels are high. Moreover, intensity is not sport specific; athletes in the same sport can exhibit differences in their optimal levels of intensity.

Overintensity is often characterized by muscle tension, difficulty breathing, negative self-talk, loss of coordination, and feelings of fear and dread. Common causes of overintensity may include a lack of confidence; extreme or inaccurate cognitive appraisals of the competition; and unfa-

FIGURE 6.8

Directions: List the precompetition activities that will help you prepare to perform your very best.

Early Morning

1. Physical:

2. Mental:

Arrival at Competition Site

1. Physical:

2. Mental:

Prior to Competition

1. Equipment:

2. Physical:

3. Mental:

Precompetitive routine.

miliar, unexpected, or uncontrollable events before the competition. Conversely, underintensity is typically the result of overconfidence, lack of motivation, fatigue, and high ability combined with low demands by the athlete. Athletes often experience underintensity as feelings of lethargy and low energy, an absence of alertness and interest, and problems in narrowing concentration prior to and during a competition.

Athletes can assess their intensity levels when they are performing well versus poorly to identify their ideal intensity levels. Overintensity can be lessened cognitively by building self-confidence, countering inaccurate or extreme thinking, rationally assessing upcoming competition, making unfamiliar situations seem more familiar, planning for unexpected events, and focusing on controllable events. Intensity can also be regulated physiologically through such methods as controlled breathing, progressive relaxation techniques, smiling, exercise, and high-energy thinking and talking. General techniques to regulate intensity include mental imagery, keywords, and listening to music. Finally, situational interventions that can be used to regulate intensity include precompetition management and precompetitive routines.

Optimizing an athlete's intensity level involves a complex balancing of personality, emotional, and physiological needs. Both overintensity and underintensity can occur before or during competition. Athletes who can recognize and reach their optimal level of intensity are well positioned to perform successfully more of the time.

References

Apter, M. J. (1984). Reversal theory and personality: A review. *Journal of Research in Personality, 18,* 265–288. doi:10.1016/0092-6566(84)90013-8

Arent, S. M., & Landers, D. (2003). Arousal, anxiety, and performance. A reexamination of the inverted-U hypothesis. *Research Quarterly for Exercise and Sport, 74,* 436–444.

Balague, G. (2005). Anxiety: From pumped to panicked. In S. Murphy (Ed.), *The sport psychology handbook* (pp. 73–91). Champaign, IL: Human Kinetics.

Bandura, A. (1986). *Social foundations of thought and action.* Englewood Cliffs, NJ: Prentice-Hall.

Bannister, R. (1989). *The four-minute mile.* New York, NY: Lyons & Burford.

Bernier, M., & Fournier, J. F. (2010). Functions of mental imagery in expert golfers. *Journal of Sport and Exercise Psychology, 11,* 444–452. doi:10.1016/j.psychsport.2010.05.006

Bertollo, M., Saltarelli, B., & Robazza, C. (2009). Mental preparation strategies of elite modern pentathletes. *Psychology of Sport and Exercise, 10,* 244–254. doi:10.1016/j.psychsport.2008.09.003

Blumenstein, B., Bar-Eli, M., & Tenenbaum, G. (1995). The augmenting role of biofeedback: Effects of autogenic, imagery, and music training on physiological indices and athletic performance. *Journal of Sports Sciences, 13,* 343–354. doi:10.1080/02640419508732248

Buckworth, J., & Dishman, R. K. (2002). *Exercise psychology.* Champaign, IL: Human Kinetics.

Cohen, A., Pargman, D., & Tenenbaum, G. (2003). Critical elaboration and empirical investigation of the cusp catastrophe model: A lesson for practitioners. *Journal of Applied Sport Psychology, 15,* 144–159. doi:10.1080/10413200305393

Cox, R. H. (2006). *Sport psychology: Concepts and applications* (6th ed.). Boston, MA: McGraw-Hill.

Cratty, B. J., & Hanin, Y. L. (1980). *The athlete in the sports team.* Denver, CO: Love.

Davis, P. A., & Sime, W. E. (2005). Toward a psychophysiology of performance: Sport psychology principles dealing with athletes.

International Journal of Stress Management, 12, 363–378. doi:10.1037/1072-5245.12.4.363

Edwards, T., & Hardy, L. (1996). The interactive effects of intensity and direction of cognitive and somatic anxiety and self-confidence upon performance. *Journal of Sport & Exercise Psychology, 18,* 296–312.

Eysenck, M. W., & Calvo, M. S. (1992). Anxiety and performance: The processing efficiency theory. *Cognition and Emotion, 6,* 409–434. doi:10.1080/02699939208409696

Fazy, J., & Hardy, L. (1988) *The inverted-U hypothesis: A catastrophe for sport?* (Bass Monograph 1). Leeds, England: White Line Press.

Gill, D. L. (1994). A sport and exercise psychology perspective on stress. *Quest, 46,* 20–27. doi:10.1080/00336297.1994.10484108

Gould, D., & Krane, V. (1992). The arousal–athletic performance relationship: Current status and future directions. In T. S. Horn (Ed.), *Advances in sport psychology* (pp. 119–142). Champaign, IL: Human Kinetics.

Gould, D., & Tuffey, S. (1996). Zones of optimal functioning research: A review and critique. *Anxiety, Stress, and Coping, 9,* 53–68. doi:10.1080/10615809608249392

Hale, B. D., & Seiser, L. (2005). Mental imagery. In J. Taylor & G. S. Wilson (Eds.), *Applying sport psychology: Four perspectives* (pp. 117–135). Champaign, IL: Human Kinetics.

Hanin, Y. (1986). State–trait research in sports in the USSR. In C. D. Spielberger & R. Diaz-Guerrero (Eds.), *Cross-cultural anxiety* (Vol. 3, pp. 45–64). Washington, DC: Hemisphere.

Hanin, Y. L. (2000). Individual zones of optimal functioning (IZOF) model: Emotions-performance relationships in sport. In Y. L. Hanin (Ed.), *Emotions in sport* (pp. 65–89). Champaign, IL: Human Kinetics.

Hanin, Y. L. (2007). Emotions in sport: Current issues and perspectives. In G. Tenenbaum & R. C. Eklund (Eds.), *Handbook of sport psychology* (3rd ed., pp. 31–58). Hoboken, NJ: Wiley. doi:10.1002/9781118270011.ch2

Hardy, L. (1996). Testing the predictions of the cusp catastrophe model of anxiety and performance. *The Sport Psychologist, 10,* 140–156.

Hardy, L., Beattie, S., & Woodman, T. (2007). Anxiety-induced performance catastrophes: Investigating effort required as an asymmetry factor. *British Journal of Psychology, 98,* 15–31. doi:10.1348/000712606X103428

Hardy, J., Hall, C., & Hardy, L. (2005). Quantifying athlete self-talk. *Journal of Sports Sciences, 23,* 905–917. doi:10.1080/02640410500130706

Harmison, R. J. (2006). Peak performance in sport: Identifying ideal performance states and developing athletes' psychological skills. *Professional Psychology: Research and Practice, 37,* 233–243. doi:10.1037/0735-7028.37.3.233

Hassmén, P., Raglin, J. S., & Lundqvist, C. (2004). Intra-individual variability in state anxiety and self-confidence in elite golfers. *Journal of Sport Behavior, 27,* 277–290.

Imlay, G. J., Carda, R. D., Stanbrough, M. E., & O'Connor, P. J. (1995). Anxiety and performance: A test of optimal function theory. *International Journal of Sport Psychology, 26*, 295–306.

Jacobson, E. (1938). *Progressive relaxation.* Chicago, IL: University of Chicago Press.

Jones, G. (1995). Competitive anxiety in sport. In S. J. H. Biddle (Ed.), European perspectives on exercise and sport psychology (pp. 128–153). Leeds, England: Human Kinetics.

Jones, M. V. (2003). Controlling emotions in sport. *The Sport Psychologist, 17*, 471–486.

Karageorghis, C. I., Mouzourides, D. A., Priest, D. L., Sasso, T. A., Morrish, D. J., & Walley, C. L. (2009). Psychophysical and ergogenic effects of synchronous music during treadmill walking. *Journal of Sport & Exercise Psychology, 31*, 18–36.

Kerr, J. H. (1990). Stress and sport: Reversal theory. In G. Jones & L. Hardy (Eds.), *Stress and performance in sport* (pp. 107–131). Chichester, West Sussex, England: Wiley.

Kerr, J. H. (1997). *Motivation and emotion in sport: Reversal theory.* East Sussex, United Kingdom: Psychology Press Ltd.

Kerr, J. H., Wilson, G. V., Bowling, A., & Sheahan, J. P. (2005). Game outcome and elite Japanese women's field hockey player's experience of emotions and stress. *Psychology of Sport and Exercise, 6*, 251–263. doi:10.1016/j.psychsport.2003.11.002

Kleine, D. (1990). Anxiety and sports performance: A meta-analysis. *Anxiety Research, 2*, 113–131. doi:10.1080/08917779008249330

Krane, V., Joyce, D., & Rafeld, J. (1994). Competitive anxiety, situational criticality, and softball performance. *The Sport Psychologist, 8*, 58–72.

Krane, V., & Williams, J. M. (1994). Cognitive anxiety, somatic anxiety and confidence in track and field athletes: The impact of gender, competitive level, and task characteristics. *International Journal of Sport Psychology, 25*, 203–217.

Kreutz, G., Ott, U., Teichmann, D., Osawa, P., & Vaitl, D. (2007). Using music to induce emotions: Influences of musical preference and absorption. *Psychology of Music, 36*, 101–126. doi:10.1177/0305735607082623

Landers, D. M., & Arent, S. M. (2010). Arousal–performance relationship. In J. M. Williams (Ed.), *Applied sport psychology* (6th ed., pp. 221–246). Boston, MA: McGraw-Hill.

Magill, R. A. (2011). *Motor learning: Concepts and applications* (9th ed.). Boston, MA: McGraw-Hill.

McKay, J., Niven, A. G., Lavallee, D., & White, A. (2008). Sources of strain among elite UK track athletes. *The Sport Psychologist, 22*, 143–163.

Mellalieu, S. D., Hanton, S., & Fletcher, D. (2006). A competitive anxiety review: Recent directions in sport psychology research. In S. Hanton

& S. D. Mellalieu (Eds.), *Literature reviews in sport psychology* (pp. 1–45). New York, NY: Nova.

Morgan, W. P., O'Connor, P. J., Ellickson, K. A., & Bradley, P. W. (1988). Personality structure, mood states, and performance in elite male distance runners. *International Journal of Sport Psychology, 19*, 247–263.

Morgan, W. P., O'Connor, P. J., Sparling, P. B., & Pate, R. R. (1987). Psychological characteristics of elite female distance runners. *International Journal of Sports Medicine, 8*, S124–S131. doi:10.1055/s-2008-1025717

Neiss, R. (1988). Reconceptualizing arousal: Psychological states in motor performance. *Psychological Bulletin, 103*, 345–366. doi:10.1037/0033-2909.103.3.345

Nieuwenhuys, A., Hanin, Y. L., & Bakker, F. C. (2008). Performance-related experiences and coping during races: A case of an elite sailor. *Psychology of Sport and Exercise, 9*(1), 61–76. doi:10.1016/j.psychsport.2006.12.007

Oxendine, J. B. (1970). Emotional arousal and motor performance. *Quest, 13*, 23–32. doi:10.1080/00336297.1970.10519673

Raglin, J. S., & Hanin, Y. L. (2000). Competitive anxiety. In Y. L. Hanin (Ed.), *Emotions in sport* (pp. 93–111). Champaign, IL: Human Kinetics.

Raglin, J. S., & Turner, P. E. (1992). Predicted, actual and optimal precompetition anxiety in adolescent track and field athletes. *Scandinavian Journal of Medicine & Science in Sports, 2*, 148–152. doi:10.1111/j.1600-0838.1992.tb00336.x

Raglin, J. S., & Wilson, G. S. (2009). Psychological characteristics of athletes and their responses to sport-related stressors. In M. Maughan (Ed.), *The Olympic textbook of science in sport* (pp. 272–282). West Sussex, England: Blackwell.

Raglin, J. S., Wise, K., & Morgan, W. P. (1990). Predicted and actual pre-competition anxiety in high school girl swimmers. *Journal of Swimming Research, 6*, 5–8.

Robazza, C., Pellizzari, M., Bertollo, M., & Hanin, Y. (2008). Functional impact of emotions on athletic performance: Comparing the IZOF model and the directional perception approach. *Journal of Sports Sciences, 26*, 1033–1047. doi:10.1080/02640410802027352

Schack, T., & Whitmarsh, B. (2005). Routines. In J. Taylor & G. S. Wilson (Eds.), *Applying sport psychology: Four perspectives* (pp. 137–150). Champaign, IL: Human Kinetics.

Schmidt, R. A., & Wrisberg, C. A. (2008). *Motor learning and performance* (4th ed.). Champaign, IL: Human Kinetics.

Singer, K. (2004). The effect of neurofeedback on performance anxiety in dancers. *Journal of Dance Medicine & Science, 8*, 78–81.

Smith, R. E. (2010). A positive approach to coaching effectiveness and performance enhancement. In J. M. Williams (Ed.), *Applied sport psychology* (6th ed., pp. 42–58). Boston, MA: McGraw-Hill.

Smith, R. E., Smoll, F. L., Cumming, S. P., & Grossbard, J. R. (2006). Measurement of multidimensional sport performance anxiety in children and adults: The Sport Anxiety Scale-2. *Journal of Sport & Exercise Psychology, 28,* 479–501.

Spielberger, C. D. (1966). Theory and research on anxiety. In C. D. Spielberger (Ed.), *Anxiety and behavior* (pp. 3–22). New York, NY: Academic Press.

Spielberger, C. D., Gorsuch, R. L., Lushene, P. E., Vagg, P. R., & Jacobs, G. A. (1983). *Manual for the State–Trait Anxiety Inventory.* Palo Alto, CA: Consulting Psychologist Press.

Weinberg, R. S., & Gould, D. (2011). *Foundations of sport and exercise psychology* (6th ed.). Champaign, IL: Human Kinetics.

Williams, J. M. (2010). Relaxation and energizing techniques of regulation of arousal. In J. M. Williams (Ed.), *Applied sport psychology* (6th ed., pp. 247–266). Boston, MA: McGraw-Hill.

Williams, J. M., & Harris, D. V. (1998). Relaxation and energizing techniques of regulation of arousal. In J. M. Williams (Ed.) *Applied sport psychology: Personal growth to peak performance* (3rd ed. pp. 219–236). Mountain View, CA: Mayfield.

Williams, J. M., Nideffer, R. M., Wilson, V. E., Sagal, M., & Peper, E. (2010). Concentration and strategies for controlling it. In J. M. Williams (Ed.), *Applied sport psychology* (6th ed., pp. 336–586). Boston, MA: McGraw-Hill.

Wilson, G. S. (1998). Gender differences in levels of precompetition and postcompetition anxiety response and individual ratings of performance in collegiate cross-country runners. *International Sports Journal, 1,* 49–56.

Wilson, G. S. (2010). Exercise and sport psychology. In G. Wilson (Ed.), *Exploring exercise science* (pp. 58–74). Boston, MA: McGraw-Hill.

Wilson, G. S., & Raglin, J. S. (1997). Optimal and predicted anxiety in 9–12-year-old track and field athletes. *Scandinavian Journal of Medicine & Science in Sports, 7,* 253–258. doi:10.1111/j.1600-0838.1997.tb00149.x

Wilson, G. S., Raglin, J. S., & Harger, G. J. (2000). A comparison of the STAI and CSAI-2 in five-day recalls of precompetition anxiety in collegiate track and field athletes. *Scandinavian Journal of Medicine & Science in Sports, 10,* 51–54. doi:10.1034/j.1600-0838.2000.010001051.x

Wilson, G. S., Raglin, J. S., & Pritchard, M. E. (2002). Optimism, pessimism, and precompetition anxiety in college athletes. *Personality and Individual Differences, 32,* 893–902. doi:10.1016/S0191-8869(01)00094-0

Wilson, G. S., & Steinke, J. S. (2002). Cognitive orientation, precompetition, and actual competition anxiety in collegiate softball players. *Research Quarterly for Exercise and Sport, 73,* 335–339.

Wilson, G. S., & Taylor, J. (2005). Intensity and athletic performance. In J. Taylor & G. S. Wilson (Eds.), *Applying sport psychology: Four perspectives* (pp. 33–49). Champaign, IL: Human Kinetics.

Woodman, T., Albinson, J. G., & Hardy, L. (1997). An investigation of the zones of optimal functioning hypothesis within a multidimensional framework. *Journal of Sport & Exercise Psychology, 19*, 131–141.

Woodman, T., Davis, P. A., Hardy, L., Callow, N., Glasscock, I., & Yuill-Proctor, J. (2009). Emotions and sport performance: An exploration of happiness, hope, and anger. *Journal of Sport & Exercise Psychology, 31*, 169–188.

Woodman, T., & Hardy, L. (2001). Stress and anxiety. In R. Singer, H. Hausenblas, & C. Janelle (Eds.), *Handbook of sport psychology* (2nd ed., pp. 290–318). New York, NY: Wiley.

Yerkes, R. M., & Dodson, J. D. (1908). The relation of strength of stimulus to rapidity of habit formation. *The Journal of Comparative Neurology and Psychology, 18*, 459–482. doi:10.1002/cne.920180503

Penny McCullagh, Diane Ste-Marie, and Barbi Law

Modeling 7
Is What You See, What You Get?

Watching others has long been recognized as an important technique for modifying individual and group behavior (see McCullagh & Weiss, 2002). Numerous empirical studies have been conducted from a variety of approaches (behavioral to neuropsychological), and researchers have begun to study how observational learning is used by athletes in realistic settings. To demonstrate the potential effectiveness of observational learning, we present three case studies, define observational learning, briefly review relevant theoretical and empirical approaches, and suggest potential solutions to our case studies.

We acknowledge the assistance of Angelica M. Villalpando from California State University East Bay and Nadine Steenhoek from Nipissing University for their assistance in gathering references for this chapter.

http://dx.doi.org/10.1037/14251-007

Exploring Sport and Exercise Psychology, Third Edition, J. Van Raalte and B. Brewer (Editors)

Case Studies

HOCKEY COACH

John has been coaching his daughter's team since she was 6 years old, and this year is the first year the team is in a competitive league. The team players (ages 9–10 years) have been having trouble getting the puck out of their defensive end. Although John has used a number of drills and verbal instructions during practice to teach the girls their positions and how to move the puck out of the zone, they are not executing these skills effectively during games. John wonders what else he can do to have the team learn proper positional and tactical play to accomplish this important component of the game.

SOCCER PLAYER

Sam, a soccer player, is in his first season playing on the senior boys' team at his high school. He trained hard all summer to be in peak shape to make the team. His season started well, but then during a regular season game, Sam collided with another player and injured his knee. Following a series of tests, Sam was told that he tore his anterior cruciate ligament (ACL) and must undergo surgery and 6 to 8 months of rehabilitation before he will be ready to return to soccer. Sam has never had a serious injury before and is uncertain what to expect. He is worried about how long the recovery process will take, how much pain will be involved, and whether he will be able to return to soccer at the same level of play.

BALLET DANCER

Taylor is a ballet dancer who has been training at a professional school since she was 14 years old. She moved away from her family to study at this prestigious academy while attending high school. Upon graduation, she moved into an apprentice position with a professional company. Taylor greatly admires one particular professional dancer and repeatedly watches all her videos. As for her own dancing, Taylor is becoming frustrated. She is not sure how she is doing because she is not getting constant corrections from a teacher, and many of her classes are in rooms without mirrors so that she does not have the benefit of viewing her performance daily.

What Is Modeling and How Does It Work

It is difficult to discuss the topic of observational learning (also called modeling) without reference to Bandura. His classic work in the 1960s on aggression (Bandura, 1965) clearly demonstrated the powerful impact of observation on behavioral outcomes, and his development of social learning, self-efficacy, and social cognitive theories (Bandura 1977, 1986, 1997) led him to acknowledge modeling "to be one of the most powerful means of transmitting values, attitudes and patterns of thought and behavior" (Bandura, 1986, p. 47). Over the years, a variety of terms have appeared in the literature to refer to this phenomenon, including *imitation, vicarious learning, identification, observational learning,* and *modeling,* to name a few. Greer, Dudek-Singer, and Gautreaux (2006) recently suggested that the diversity of terms used to examine observational learning effects has impeded progress, and in fact many studies have examined different types of behaviors. In this chapter, we refer to the process of observing others as *modeling* or *observational learning.* Because we are primarily interested in behaviors in sport, exercise, and other physical activity settings, we focus on how observation can change overt physical behavior (such as performance in sport) or psychological behaviors (such as anxiety and self-efficacy) in physical activity settings, with emphasis on visually presented information, recognizing that other modalities may also be important.

There has been further confusion in the literature beyond terminology with regard to the types of interventions used in experimental studies. Studies on imagery, one of the most popular techniques used by sport psychology practitioners, often confound observational learning with imagery interventions, without labeling them as such. Although similarities between observational learning and imagery have received attention in the literature for decades (e.g., Feltz & Landers, 1983; McCullagh, Weiss, & Ross, 1989), only a few researchers have attempted to separate the independent effects of imagery and observational learning, and several researchers have suggested that many studies labeled as imagery are actually observational learning studies (Martin, Moritz, & Hall, 1999; Ram, Riggs, Skaling, Landers, & McCullagh, 2007). The primary difference between the two techniques is the type of stimulus provided. In an observational learning study, the observer is presented with an external stimulus (typically visual, but other modalities, such as auditory, can also be used), and then the observer produces a self-generated behavior. In a strict imagery condition, participants would not receive an external stimulus but would be required to create their own image based on past experience. Many imagery studies include an external stimulus to help participants generate an image (see Martin et al., 1999), and it is likely that many participants in observational learning studies use imagery (even without prompting) to rehearse and commit to memory the behaviors they have just observed.

From a theoretical standpoint, there have been a variety of explanations for the effects of modeling that typically align with the approaches in vogue during a particular era. Early instinctual interpretations of imitation (e.g., Tarde, 1903) were replaced by associative theories (e.g., Allport, 1924), reinforcement theories (e.g., Miller & Dollard, 1941), and finally cognitive interpretations (e.g., Bandura, 1969, 1997; Sheffield, 1961), including self-regulation (Kirschenbaum, 1984; Zimmerman, 1996). Beyond the cognitive interpretations, others have taken a more dynamic approach (Scully & Newell, 1985). In recent years, the notion of mirror neurons, which both when performing a task and when observing the same task performed by another, has gained prominence in examining both imagery and observational learning, and these ideas have been extended to the sport domain (e.g., Holmes & Calmels, 2008). Holmes and Calmels (2008) suggested "that imagery may not be as efficacious as the literature would indicate . . . and propose observation-based approaches to offer more valid and effective techniques in sport psychology and motor control" (p. 433). For a more extensive review of theoretical approaches, see McCullagh, Law, and Ste-Marie (2012).

Whom Should You Watch

WATCHING OTHERS

Think about a typical situation where someone is attempting to teach a physical skill. One of the most common techniques is to demonstrate the skill. But who should do the demonstrating, and does the specific demonstrator matter?

There are at least two opposing ideas about why the person who demonstrates influences observer performance. Bandura's early conceptual approaches suggested that the amount of attention paid to the demonstration influenced subsequent performance. Accordingly, it was predicted that watching a model of high status would command more attention and thus lead to better performance than watching someone unimportant. This issue has received limited attention in the sport psychology literature (McCullagh, 1986). Despite having neither theoretical nor empirical support, the value of elite athletes as role models remains a popular notion (see Guest & Cox, 2009). In opposition to the idea of elite athletes as superior observational learning models, evidence in the literature suggests that when the observer feels similar to the model, performance will be enhanced (Gould & Weiss, 1981; McCullagh, 1987; Schunk, Hanson, & Cox, 1987).

In selecting a model, it is useful to consider both mastery and coping models. Mastery models are similar to correct models in that they demonstrate expert performance. In addition, they verbalize and emulate confident psychological behaviors. Coping models, on the other hand, are more like learning models. They have not yet achieved high-level performance, and as they are performing they verbalize and emulate low confidence and perhaps even fear of executing the skill in question and gradually progress to positive comments. Schunk (1987) demonstrated the effectiveness of coping models in educational settings, and the idea has been tested in swimming (Lewis, 1974; Weiss, McCullagh, Smith, & Berlant, 1998) and rehabilitation (Flint, 1993) settings. Coping models may be effective because research participants feel similar to the coping model, who is also working to achieve a higher level of performance.

WATCHING AND DOING WITH OTHERS

Peer learning, defined as the "acquisition of knowledge and skill through active helping and supporting among status equals or matched companions" (Topping, 2005, p. 631), is a broad term that encompasses several forms of learning in groups, such as cooperative learning and peer tutoring/monitoring/assessment/mentoring. Recently, the emphasis on peer learning has shifted from groups structured as peer teacher–learner to those where the peers are more closely matched in skill level and where both may benefit from the learning experience (Topping, 2005). Often these forms of peer learning occur in dyads; however, cooperative learning may involve small groups working toward shared goals, similar to a sport team. In the realm of sport and exercise, peer tutoring and cooperative learning are most commonly used.

Studies examining dyadic learning show that it has performance and affective benefits for both individuals within the dyad (Granados & Wulf, 2007). For example, Shea, Wulf, and Whitacre (1999) demonstrated that dyadic practice can help to train multiple individuals on a new task simultaneously by providing the opportunity both to perform physical practice trials and to observe those of the learning partner. This highlights the notion that dyadic practice may be a more efficient learning strategy than practicing alone, particularly for tasks where repeated physical performance may result in fatigue or increase the risk of injury.

Similarly, peer tutoring can produce physical performance benefits as well as improvements in psychological variables. For both boxing and swimming tasks, peer tutoring has been shown to increase performance scores (d'Arripe-Longueville, Gernigon, Huet, Cadopi, et al., 2002; d'Arripe-Longueville, Gernigon, Huet, Winnykamen, et al., 2002; Legrain, d'Arripe-Longueville, & Gernigon, 2003). In addition, groups receiving peer tutoring had higher levels of self-efficacy, enjoyment, and more personally controllable causal attributions than did groups who did not receive peer tutoring (Legrain et al., 2003). In contrast to other areas of observational learning research, it appears that gender differences are prevalent within dyadic learning. Legrain et al. (2003) noted that males benefited more from peer tutoring than females. Interestingly, when the tutors were of higher skill level than the learners, males benefited more than females, yet females benefited more when tutors were at the novice level (d'Arripe-Longueville, Gernigon, Huet, Cadopi, et al., 2002; d'Arripe-Longueville, Gernigon, Huet, Winnykamen, et al., 2002). These findings suggest that both skill level and gender of dyads are important.

WATCHING YOURSELF

At this point, it is clear that there are a variety of models that can be observed and that the similarity between the model and the observer can influence observational learning benefits. More specifically, greater gains are obtained from observation when the observer perceives the model to be similar as opposed to dissimilar. It is not surprising, then, that researchers turned to questions related to using the "self" as a model, with the reasoning that the self would be the ultimate model in terms of similarity and thus a more powerful model than one's peers or teachers (e.g., Dowrick & Dove, 1980). Furthermore, observation of self-generated actions may be more informative for an individual because of the greater functional similarity of the neural activity as opposed to watching other models or imaging (Holmes & Calmels, 2008). Thus, there are logical arguments for employing self-as-a-model.

The use of the self-as-a-model is typically accomplished via video, although other methods, such as a series of still pictures or audiotape, can be used as well. Although we do not cover the clinical roots of the use of the self-as-a-model and its more recent use in special populations and settings, we draw the reader's attention to a number of interesting articles on the topic (e.g., Bellini & Akullian, 2007; Buggey, 2007; Dowrick, 1999).

Video self-as-a-model techniques can be described under two broad categories: self-observation and self-modeling. *Self-observation* is perhaps the more common intervention and involves watching a video replay of one's performance. *Self-modeling* is a more effortful procedure, as it involves editing the content captured on video to include adaptive behavior only (Dowrick, 1999). Within self-modeling there are two further subclassifications that distinguish between a positive self-review and a feedforward technique. An example of the positive self-review technique involves reviewing video footage and selecting the best performance out of multiple attempts. The feedforward method capitalizes on the fact that there are behaviors that cannot yet be performed in a given sequence (Dowrick, 1999). In a feedforward method, the video is edited to eliminate performance errors and to make it appear that the athlete performed the skill correctly. When using a feedforward method, one should be cautious not to show a learner in a situation that could be dangerous.

Self-Observation

As Franks and Maile (1991) noted, there are intuitive benefits associated with using video observation of the self for motor skill learning. For instance, the video provides quick (i.e., immediate replay possible), precise, and complete details of the just executed movements. Moreover, the video can be paused at critical points in skill execution or played at slower or faster speeds for full analysis of the action. Such displays, then, are potentially informative sources in terms of identifying errors in movement dynamics or outcome, as well as correct performance qualities.

Researchers, however, have noted that not everyone benefits from self-observation. The benefits obtained from watching oneself on video, for example, are argued to interact with the learners' skill level (e.g., Rothstein & Arnold, 1976). Advanced and intermediate learners gain more from video self-observation than do novices when no verbal cueing is provided. Novice learners need to be guided to the relevant aspects of the performance to observe. Such results mimic those of Adams (1986) and McCullagh and Caird (1990), which indicated that observation of an unskilled model is only beneficial if it is supplemented with feedback. Along similar lines, Laguna (1996) found that learning was optimized when the observer was able to contrast the self-observed information with that of the correct model using a split-screen technique (see also Baudry, Leroy, & Chollet, 2006).

Thus, a clear recommendation to be made for video self-observation is to ensure that the observer can interpret the information being provided for future skill correction, whether that be through guided instruction, observation of a correct model, or the observer having sufficient knowledge of the skill. Indeed, skilled performers have been shown to gain much information from a self-observation video (e.g., Hars & Calmels, 2007). Other recommendations that have been made include (a) having the angle of viewing such that the observer can pick up key points in the movement pattern, (b) inserting a short delay between performance and observation, and (c) allowing the learner to control speed (i.e., slow motion, pause, rewind) of the visual display (Franks & Maile, 1991).

Self-Modeling

The research on self-modeling has shown a variety of effects. In terms of positive results, Dowrick's work has shown that self-modeling assists children with spina bifida in learning swimming skills (Dowrick & Dove, 1980) and assists other children with various physical disabilities in learning activities of daily living (Dowrick & Raeburn, 1995). Similarly, research by Clark and Ste-Marie's (2007) with regard to children learning swim strokes showed that a group receiving a self-modeling intervention had both performance superior to a control group that did not receive a video and enhanced learning over that of a self-observation group. Adults have also benefited more from self-modeling than peer modeling for learning swimming skills (Starek & McCullagh, 1999). In contrast, research that used self-modeling to improve the skill acquisition of figure skating jumps (Law & Ste-Marie, 2005), gymnastic beam skills (Winfrey & Weeks, 1993), and volleyball skills (Ram & McCullagh, 2003) has not shown clear learning advantages.

One of the reasons that self-modeling interventions have been found to be effective in some studies but not in others may be that the feedforward technique is more powerful than positive self-review (Dowrick, 1999). Much of the research that did not yield significant benefits used the positive self-review technique, whereas Dowrick and Dove's (1980), as well as Clark and Ste-Marie's (2007) research, incorporated feedforward videos.[1] More research is also needed to tease out whether factors such as type of skill, skill level, or duration of the intervention moderate the benefits of self-modeling. Certainly, the skill of swimming has been shown to profit from self-modeling, whether that

---

[1]Clark and Ste-Marie (2007) stated that the intervention used in their research was positive self-review self-modeling; however, if one reads the method section in detail, we argue the videotape is actually a feedforward video. Specifically, Clark and Ste-Marie indicated that

> the videos were evaluated by the first author to select out the child's best performance of the stroke. This may have been, for example, just the middle 2-m segment of the 10-m videoed. This 2-m segment would then be spliced together five times to create a 10-m best performance swim video. (p. 580)

As such, the video showed a behavior in the swimmer's repertoire (successful attainment of the swimming stroke for a short distance) that had not yet been attained in full sequence (i.e., same skillful swim stroke completed for a longer distance of 10 m).

be with children or adults, able-bodied or disabled individuals. Differences in observational learning benefits may be a function of type of model observed as well as skill classification (see Ashford, Bennett, & Davids, 2006).

Although the emphasis to this point has been on skill acquisition, self-modeling has also been used as an intervention to enhance motor performance in the competitive arena. Indeed, sport psychologists have described their use of positive self-review videos, often referred to as *highlight tapes,* for performance enhancement with elite athletes (e.g., Halliwell, 1990). Empirical research on the value of positive self-review videotapes, however, is limited. One example is Templin and Vernacchia's (1995) examination of positive self-review tapes, accompanied by inspirational music, to enhance field goal percentage in basketball (see also Leavitt, Young, & Connelly, 1989). The dearth of research on this topic identifies it as a fruitful area for future investigations.

The feedforward technique of self-modeling has also been used by researchers to explore athletic performance enhancement. Maile (1985, as cited in Franks & Maile, 1991) generated a video that made it look as though a powerlifter was lifting more weight than she could at that time. Her performance in competition improved by 26%, generating more than a twofold improvement over what would have been expected based on pure physiological changes from training. Another example (Ste-Marie, Rymal, Vertes, & Martini, 2011) provided feedforward videos to 22 gymnasts prior to their beam competition. Gymnastic beam performance scores were higher when the gymnasts viewed their self-modeling tape prior to competing than when they did not.

When self-modeling benefits are obtained for motor skill acquisition or motor performance, it raises the question of how this happens. Certainly, Bandura's (1997) argument that seeing oneself perform successfully "provides clear information on how to perform skills, and it strengthens beliefs in one's capabilities" (p. 94) incited a number of researchers to measure self-efficacy as a possible mediator for self-modeling benefits. Associated increases in self-efficacy as a result of a self-modeling intervention for motor skill acquisition, however, have not been consistently demonstrated (see Clark & Ste-Marie, 2007; Law & Ste-Marie, 2005; Ram & McCullagh, 2003; Starek & McCullagh, 1999; Winfrey & Weeks, 1993). Starek and McCullagh (1999) argued that other self-regulatory processes, beyond self-evaluation, could be mediating self-modeling benefits.

In accordance with this proposition, Clark and Ste-Marie (2007) examined the possible contributions of self-regulatory beliefs and processes to self-modeling benefits using Zimmerman's (2000) social cognitive perspective of self-regulation. Of specific interest to Clark and Ste-Marie were self-efficacy beliefs, intrinsic motivation, and the learners' reflections on their satisfaction with progress. As noted previously, no differences were found for self-efficacy between the self-modeling and control group. However, those who had received the self-modeling intervention showed greater increases in intrinsic motivation and self-satisfaction. Such research suggests that examining a broader set of self-regulatory processes to explain self-modeling effects is warranted.

How Do Athletes Use Modeling

Researchers studying applications of observational learning in sport have begun to explore how and why athletes use observation as a learning and performance enhancement tool (Cumming, Clark, Ste-Marie, McCullagh, & Hall, 2005; Hars & Calmels, 2007; Rymal, Martini, & Ste-Marie, 2010). Rymal et al. (2010) interviewed competitive divers following a self-modeling intervention. Divers reported using video for imagery, technical analysis of movements, and for modification of affect (see Hars & Calmels, 2007). Cumming et al. (2005) created the Functions of Observational Learning Questionnaire (FOLQ) and identified three functions that observation serves for athletes: a skill function, a strategy function, and a performance function. The skill function involves observing the self or others to learn new sport skills or to refine current skills. The strategy function refers to observing in order to learn new strategies, game plays, and routines or to refine those already in the athlete's repertoire. The performance function refers to observing in order to learn or refine the athlete's ability to regulate mental states, such as to maintain confidence, stay positive, and regulate arousal and anxiety levels.

Subsequent research using the FOLQ as a measurement tool has shown that athletes consistently employ the skill function most frequently, followed by the strategy and performance functions (e.g., Hall et al., 2009; Hancock, Rymal, & Ste-Marie, 2011). The pattern of observational learning use varies minimally according to gender (Cumming et al., 2005; Hall et al., 2009; Wesch, Law, & Hall, 2007). The most consistent sport-type difference appears to be that team sport athletes use the strategy function more than individual sport athletes (Hall et al., 2009; Wesch et al., 2007). Independent sport athletes make greater use of the skill and performance functions than athletes in interactive sports (Cumming et al., 2005; Law & Hall, 2009a). Greater use of the functions of observational learning is associated with enhanced confidence and self-efficacy among both experienced (Hall et al., 2009) and novice level (Law & Hall, 2009b) athletes. Hars and Calmels (2007) explored the skill function of observational learning with a specific skill by asking a sample of elite youth gymnasts to think aloud while observing video feedback of their uneven bar performance during practice. Based on the verbal reports, Hars and Calmels (2007) identified four purposes for engaging in observation: to improve self-assessment, to increase technical execution, to enhance imagery, and to facilitate visual perception. Although these findings present an overview of how observation is used by athletes, more research is needed to explore the antecedents and consequences involved when employing each of these functions.

Hancock et al. (2011) extended the examination of the functions of observational learning beyond athletes to include both coaches and sport officials. All three groups employed the skill function most frequently, followed by the strategy and performance functions. However, coaches made greater use of the skill and strategy functions than did the other two groups. Officials made greater use of the performance function than did coaches. These results suggest that within a team sport context, coaches and officials use observation in ways that are somewhat similar to those of athletes. Further research in this area may help to identify functions of observational learning specific to each of these groups and to explore the contextual factors underlying these differences.

Modeling in Rehabilitation

Much rehabilitation research has focused on the use of coping models to increase compliance with physical therapist–prescribed exercises and to change perceptions of pain and self-efficacy within the athletic injury domain. Flint's doctoral dissertation (as cited in Flint, 1993) examined modeling effects in rehabilitation. Female basketball players recovering from knee surgery were shown a series of coping model videos. Athletes who viewed the models showed motivation to adhere to their rehabilitation programs and were knowledgeable about their needs. Maddison, Prapavessis, and Clatworthy (2006) examined the effects of viewing a coping model on both pre- and postoperative outcomes for patients undergoing ACL surgery. Participants who viewed the coping model reported lower perceptions of preoperative expected pain, greater self-efficacy at discharge from hospital, and higher functional outcome scores than did participants in a traditional treatment control group.

In clinical populations, coping models have also shown promise for enhancing patients' rehabilitation experiences. Often individuals diagnosed with chronic heart failure or other chronic disease (e.g., chronic obstructive pulmonary disease) are prescribed exercise as part of their disease management and rehabilitation but become anxious about increased heart rate and breathing rate associated with exercise, as they are symptoms they also associate with their medical conditions (see Maddison, Prapavessis, Armstrong, & Hill 2008; Ng, Yuen, Tam, Yew, & Lam, 1999).

Qualitative research has suggested that live models, and in particular, peer models, within the rehabilitation setting can help individuals with spinal cord injuries and neurological diseases learn skills and cope with their disabilities (Standal & Jespersen, 2008). Research on the mirror neuron system has shown that when one is observing movements, this system becomes activated (Ertelt et al., 2007). This suggests that modeling may even be used to supplement physical practice or as an efficiency strategy to reduce the amount of physical practice required to relearn skills following injury or disease onset. In their review of research related to stroke rehabilitation methods, Garrison, Winstein, and Aziz-Zadeh (2010) suggested that methods based on the mirror neuron system, including observation and imitation, may serve as effective adjuncts to traditional physical therapy.

Although the use of self-observation and self-modeling is prevalent within the sport literature, the use of the self-as-a-model has received scant attention within rehabilitation contexts. Given the early success of other models and the potential for employing self-observation as well as self-modeling techniques, we certainly encourage exploration of the self-as-a-model techniques for enhancing physical and psychological rehabilitation outcomes. From a psychological perspective, self-as-a-model techniques may provide important motivation and aid in goal setting throughout the often long road to regaining strength and function.

Modeling in Exercise

The vast literature on exercise adherence and compliance clearly acknowledges the important role of others in influencing attitudes and physical activity behavior, although modeling and observational learning are not generally explicitly acknowledged (e.g., Carron, Hausenblas, & Mack, 1996; Lox, Ginis, & Petruzzello, 2010). It is quite likely that these "important others" may serve as exercise role models as well. Carron et al. (1996) demonstrated that physical activity contexts that involve exercising with others are both preferred and, as shown in a meta-analysis, more effective in promoting adherence than exercising alone (Burke, Carron, Eys, Ntoumanis, & Estabrooks, 2006). There is also a wealth of research examining the role of exercise leaders (i.e., expert models) and their effect on exercisers' attitudes (Edmunds, Ntoumanis, & Duda, 2008; Lamarche & Gammage, 2010; Loughead & Carron, 2004). If we look more closely at the ways in which the group is used to increase exercise adherence, we can find definite examples of cooperative learning, peer models, and coping models that present a parallel to how modeling is used to facilitate motor skill learning and performance.

Studies examining the effects of modeling in exercise are not often labeled as "modeling" studies; nevertheless, they involve some form of modeling intervention. A notable exception is research by McAuley, Courneya, Rudolph, and Lox (1994), who explicitly outlined several ways in which vicarious experience through modeling enhances self-efficacy beliefs and subsequent exercise adherence. Suggested methods include modeling situations commonly referred to as peer models, mastery models, coping models, participant modeling, and working in dyads. Other researchers have called for the use of similar strategies for enhancing self-efficacy and physical activity levels among older adults (Lee, Arthur, & Avis, 2008). Indeed, Bandura (2004) described the potential of modeling as a method of health promotion. Other studies that include modeling as either the sole focus or as part of an intervention have found positive effects on exercise behavior (e.g., Dorgo, Robinson, & Bader, 2009).

Research examining youth physical activity behavior has explored whether parental role modeling of physical activity translates to more active children and adolescents. The research results here are mixed (Sallis, Prochaska, & Taylor, 2000; Van Der Horst, Paw, Twisk, & Van Mechelen, 2007), with both supportive (e.g., Bois, Sarrazin, Brustad, Trouilloud, & Cury, 2005; Freedson & Evenson, 1991) and contradictory (e.g., Brustad, 1993; Kimiecik & Horn, 1998; Trost et al., 2003) findings. What this research seems to suggest is that modeling behavior alone may not be sufficient for promoting physical activity; parents may also need to model the cognitions and affective responses associated with the behavior and to provide tangible forms of social support to influence youth physical activity.

Studies in the exercise psychology literature have examined the effects of observing others on affective responses. Martin Ginis, Prapavessis, and Haase (2008) had inactive women watch an exercise video of either a model dressed in attire that revealed her thin and toned body (i.e., physique-salient condition) or the same model dressed in loose attire that concealed her physique (i.e., physique nonsalient condition). Interestingly, they found that regardless of which video they watched, participants who reported a higher negative discrepancy between their bodies and the model's also reported higher levels of social physique anxiety and poorer body satisfaction and body evaluations after exercising to the video.

Other exercise psychology researchers have examined how exercise in front of a mirror influences self-efficacy beliefs. Observing yourself in real time through a mirror could be considered modeling in the form of self-observation. Some research has found that moderately active women report decreased self-efficacy when exercising in mirrored environments (Katula, McAuley, Mihalko, & Bane, 1998), although others have found no effect of mirrors on sedentary women's self-efficacy beliefs (Martin Ginis, Jung, & Gauvin, 2003). Conversely, highly active women reported increased self-efficacy when exercising in mirrored environments (Katula & McAuley, 2001) and no difference in affect when performing resistance training in mirrored as opposed to nonmirrored environments (Chmelo, Hall, Miller, & Sanders, 2009). In these studies, and sedentary women who exercised in mirrored environments reported decreased positive feeling states associated with exercise (Focht & Hausenblas, 2003, 2004; Martin Ginis, Burke, & Gauvin, 2007). Certainly, this has implications for the design of physical activity facilities and health promotion intervention strategies.

Solutions to Case Studies

At the beginning of the chapter, we presented three case studies. In this section, we describe how modeling interventions might aid the athlete, coach, and performer described in those cases.

HOCKEY COACH

John had been frustrated with the poor performance of his daughter's hockey team, particularly with regard to their inability to move the puck out of their defensive end. John decided to enlist a parent to videotape the games. He went through the video after each game and selected three game plays that he reviewed with the girls at the next off-ice session. Initially, two of the game plays illustrated the girls making errors in positioning or tactics (self-observation technique), and the third illustrated the best positional and tactical play of the game that resulted in the puck moving out of the defensive end (self-modeling, positive self-review technique). During the off-ice session, John played the first video sequence that showed the girls' unsuccessful attempt and verbally cued them to look at key factors related to the video sequence as it was played. On the second review of the first sequence, he paused the video at key time points and instructed the girls on where they should have been during the play. On the third viewing of the first sequence, he allowed the girls to watch the play as it unfolded and to think about where they should have been on the ice. He followed the same sequence for the second video sequence. Finally, for the third video sequence, he showed the positive self-review game play, verbally cued the girls to focus on two important elements of the play that were properly executed, and praised them in their success in effectively moving the puck out of the defensive zone. He had them view this video sequence two more times, each time highlighting two other important elements in the game play. Just eight weeks into the season, the team advanced so well on this component of game play that John found he was able to select three positive self-review videos for each off-ice training session. On the basis of this success, John began to think ahead to the next critical component of the girls' game that could be improved through the self-as-a model technique of observational learning.

SOCCER PLAYER

Sam tore his ACL during a regular season soccer game and was very concerned about his impending knee surgery and how the 6- to 8-month rehabilitation process would affect his return to play. Sam and his parents met with a sport psychology consultant about what to do to help him cope with his injury and his anxiety about not recovering fast enough to play next season. The consultant suggested that modeling could help Sam to learn from the experiences of someone else who has overcome the same situation. Working with his physical therapist and three of her clients who were recovering from similar injuries (i.e., coping models), the sport psychology consultant created a series of coping model videos. Early in the rehabilitation process, Sam viewed a video of a coping model working through discomfort and completing the prescribed rehabilitation exercises. As he progressed through the rehabilitation process, the consultant provided him with another video showing the progress of the coping model in terms of physical functioning. The model expressed confidence in his recovery and demonstrated his return to sport-related training. The final video shown in the series depicted a player who returned to sport successfully after ACL reconstructive surgery. The model was shown playing in a game situation and talking about how he managed the anxiety and built confidence to get back on the field. Throughout the rehabilitation process, Sam also watched game tapes of himself (i.e., self-observation) and of his teammates and imagined that he was playing to stay "fresh" in terms of the plays and decision making in different situations. He also continued to attend practices and games and stayed involved with the team. Sam successfully completed physical therapy and said that the videos helped to make him feel more confident about being able to overcome this challenge. He told his physical therapist that he would love to be a model for other videos to help athletes in the same situation, and he has encouraged his injured teammates to use the videos.

BALLET DANCER

Taylor was concerned about her development as a dancer after starting as an apprentice at a professional dance company. She met with a sport psychology consultant to discuss her concerns. Taylor's frustrations seem to have developed when she moved from her relatively high-ranking position in the ballet school setting to an entry-level position with a professional company. The consultant decided to use modeling to help Taylor with her current low level of confidence. First, she got copies of Taylor's performances over the past 3 years. She edited the videos to show a progression so that Taylor could easily see her improvement. As they viewed the videos, they could see that improvements in performance came in gradual small steps, reinforcing the idea that performance cannot be expected to increase dramatically. Second, the consultant encouraged Taylor not only to watch her idol but also to watch a host of other dancers who might not be as expert, explaining that Taylor might be able to identify and learn from younger dancers who have not yet achieved the level of her hero. Finally, she encouraged Taylor to train at a dance studio with mirrors whenever she could so that she could check her own performances.

Summary

Although observational learning or modeling has not received major attention in the sport and exercise psychology literature, there is a growing body of literature that examines how people acquire skills and behaviors through observation. Perhaps modeling has been somewhat ignored because people have an inherent belief in learning styles. Numerous dichotomous learning styles have been suggested, such as linear vs. holistic, impulsive vs. reflective, reasoning vs. insight, and visual vs. verbal (Riener & Willingham, 2010). However, a review of the research (Pashler, McDaniel, Rohrer, & Bjork, 2008) suggests that although individuals stated preferences for how material was presented to them in learning situations, most studies did not have experimental designs adequate for determining the effect of preferred learning style on subsequent learning. Those studies that did employ appropriate methods included several that directly contradicted meshing hypotheses that method of presentation should match the learner's preference (e.g., visual preferences should receive visual presentations). Thus, visual presentation through the form of modeling can likely contribute in some way to any learning situation, and there may certainly be a need for further examination of learning styles within the observational learning setting.

References

Adams, J. A. (1986). The use of the model's knowledge of results to increase the observer's performance. *Journal of Human Movement Studies, 12,* 89–98.

Allport, F. H. (1924). *Social psychology.* Boston, MA: Houghton Mifflin Company.

Ashford, D., Bennett, S. J., & Davids, K. (2006). Observational modeling effects for movement dynamics and movement outcome measures across differing task constraints: A meta-analysis. *Journal of Motor Behavior, 38,* 185–205. doi:10.3200/JMBR.38.3.185-205

Bandura, A. (1965). Influence of model's reinforcement contingencies on the acquisition of imitative responses. *Journal of Personality and Social Psychology, 1,* 589–595. doi:10.1037/h0022070

Bandura, A. (1969). *Principles of behavior modification.* New York, NY: Holt, Reinhart, & Winston.

Bandura, A. (1977). Self-efficacy: Toward a unifying theory of behavioral change. *Psychological Review, 84,* 191–215. doi:10.1037/0033-295X.84.2.191

Bandura, A. (1986). *Social foundations of thought and action: A social cognitive theory.* Englewood Cliffs, NJ: Prentice-Hall.

Bandura, A. (1997). *Self-efficacy: The exercise of control.* New York, NY: Freeman.

Bandura, A. (2004). Health promotion by social cognitive means. *Health Education & Behavior, 31,* 143–164. doi:10.1177/1090198104263660

Baudry, L., Leroy, D., & Chollet, D. (2006). The effect of combined self- and expert modeling on the performance of the double leg circle on the pommel horse. *Journal of Sports Sciences, 24,* 1055–1063. doi:10.1080/02640410500432243

Bellini, S., & Akullian, J. (2007). A meta-analysis of video modeling and video self-modeling interventions for children and adolescents with autism spectrum disorder. *Exceptional Children, 73,* 264–287.

Bois, J. E., Sarrazin, P. G., Brustad, R. J., Trouilloud, D. O., & Cury, F. (2005). Elementary schoolchildren's perceived competence and physical activity involvement: The influence of parents' role modelling behaviours and perceptions of their child's competence. *Psychology of Sport and Exercise, 6,* 381–397. doi:10.1016/j.psychsport.2004.03.003

Brustad, R. J. (1993). Who will go out and play? Parental and psychological influences on children's attraction to physical activity. *Pediatric Exercise Science, 5,* 210–223.

Buggey, T. (2007). A picture is worth: Video self-modeling applications at school and home. *Journal of Positive Behavior Interventions, 9,* 151–158. doi:10.1177/10983007070090030301

Burke, S. M., Carron, A. V., Eys, M. A., Ntoumanis, N., & Estabrooks, P. A. (2006). Group versus individual approach? A meta-analysis of the effectiveness of interventions to promote physical activity. *Sport and Exercise Psychology Review, 2,* 19–35.

Carron, A., Hausenblas, H., & Mack, D. (1996). Social influence and exercise: A meta-analysis. *Journal of Sport & Exercise Psychology, 18,* 1–16.

Chmelo, E. A., Hall, E. E., Miller, P. C., & Sanders, K. N. (2009). Mirrors and resistance exercise: Do they influence affective responses? *Journal of Health Psychology, 14,* 1067–1074. doi:10.1177/1359105309342300

Clark, S. E., & Ste-Marie, D. M. (2007). The impact of self-as-a-model interventions on children's self regulation of learning and swimming performance. *Journal of Sports Sciences, 25,* 577–586. doi:10.1080/02640410600947090

Cumming, J., Clark, S. E., Ste-Marie, D. M., McCullagh, P., & Hall, C. (2005). The Functions of Observational Learning Questionnaire (FOLQ). *Psychology of Sport and Exercise, 6,* 517–537. doi:10.1016/j.psychsport.2004.03.006

d'Arripe-Longueville, F., Gernigon, C., Huet, M., Cadopi, M., & Winnykamen, F. (2002). Peer tutoring in a physical education setting: Influence of tutor skill level on novice learners' motivation and performance. *Journal of Teaching in Physical Education, 22,* 105–123.

d'Arripe-Longueville, F., Gernigon, C., Huet, M., Winnykamen, F., & Cadopi, M. (2002). Peer-assisted learning in the physical activity domain: Dyad type and gender differences. *Journal of Sport & Exercise Psychology, 24,* 219–238.

Dorgo, S., Robinson, K. M., & Bader, J. (2009). The effectiveness of a peer-mentored older adult fitness program on perceived physical, mental, and social function. *Journal of the American Academy of Nurse Practitioners, 21,* 116–122. doi:10.1111/j.1745-7599.2008.00393.x

Dowrick, P. W. (1999). A review of self modeling and related interventions. *Applied and Preventive Psychology, 8,* 23–39. doi:10.1016/S0962-1849(99)80009-2

Dowrick, P. W., & Dove, C. (1980). The use of self-modeling to improve the swimming performance of spina bifida children. *Journal of Applied Behavior Analysis, 13,* 51–56. doi:10.1901/jaba.1980.13-51

Dowrick, P. W., & Raeburn, J. M. (1995). Self-modeling: Rapid skill training for children with physical disabilities. *Journal of Developmental and Physical Disabilities, 7,* 25–37. doi:10.1007/BF02578712

Edmunds, J., Ntoumanis, N., & Duda, J. L. (2008). Testing a self-determination theory-based teaching style intervention in the exercise domain. *European Journal of Social Psychology, 38,* 375–388. doi:10.1002/ejsp.463

Ertelt, D., Small, S., Solodkin, A., Dettmers, C., McNamara, A., Binkofski, F., & Buccino, G. (2007). Action observation has a positive impact on rehabilitation of motor deficits after stroke. *NeuroImage, 36*(Suppl. 2), T164–173. doi:10.1016/j.neuroimage.2007.03.043

Feltz, D. L., & Landers, D. M. (1983). The effects of mental practice on motor skill learning and performance: A meta-analysis. *Journal of Sport Psychology, 5,* 25–57.

Flint, F. A. (1993). Seeing helps believing: Modeling in injury rehabilitation. In D. Pargam (Ed.), *Psychological bases of sport injuries* (pp. 221–234). Morgantown, WV: Fitness Information Technology.

Focht, B., & Hausenblas, H. (2003). State anxiety responses to acute exercise in women with high social physique anxiety. *Journal of Sport & Exercise Psychology, 25,* 123–144.

Focht, B., & Hausenblas, H. (2004). Perceived evaluative threat and state anxiety during exercise in women with social physique anxiety. *Journal of Applied Sport Psychology, 16,* 361–368. doi:10.1080/10413200490517968

Franks, I. M., & Maile, L. J. (1991). The use of video in sport skill acquisition. In P. W. Dowrick (Ed.), *Practical guide to using video in the behavioral sciences* (pp. 231–243). New York, NY: Wiley.

Freedson, P. S., & Evenson, S. (1991). Familial aggregation in physical activity. *Research Quarterly for Exercise and Sport, 62,* 384–389.

Garrison, K. A., Winstein, C. J., & Aziz-Zadeh, L. (2010). The mirror neuron system: A neural substrate for methods in stroke rehabilitation. *Neurorehabilitation and Neural Repair, 24,* 404. doi:10.1177/1545968309354536

Gould, D. R., & Weiss, M. R. (1981). The effect of model similarity and model talk on self-efficacy and muscular endurance. *Journal of Sport Psychology, 3,* 17–29.

Granados, C., & Wulf, G. (2007). Enhancing motor learning through dyad practice: Contributions of observation and dialogue. *Research Quarterly for Exercise and Sport, 78,* 197–203. doi:10.5641/193250307X13082490460940

Greer, R. D., Dudek-Singer, J., & Gautreaux, G. (2006). Observational learning. *International Journal of Psychology, 41,* 486–499. doi:10.1080/00207590500492435

Guest, A. M., & Cox, S. (2009). Using athletes as role models? Conceptual and empirical perspectives from a sample of elite women soccer players. *International Journal of Sports Science & Coaching, 4,* 567–581. doi:10.1260/174795409790291385

Hall, C. R., Munroe-Chandler, K. J., Cumming, J., Law, B., Ramsey, R., & Murphy, L. (2009). Imagery and observational learning use and their relationship to sport confidence. *Journal of Sports Sciences, 27,* 327–337. doi:10.1080/02640410802549769

Halliwell, W. (1990). Providing sport psychology consultant services in professional hockey. *The Sport Psychologist, 4,* 369–377.

Hancock, D. J., Rymal, A. M., & Ste-Marie, D. M. (2011). A triadic comparison of the use of observational learning amongst team sport athletes, coaches, and officials. *Psychology of Sport and Exercise, 12,* 236–241. doi:10.1016/j.psychsport.2010.11.002

Hars, M., & Calmels, C. (2007). Observation of elite gymnastic performance: Processes and perceived functions of observation. *Psychology of Sport and Exercise, 8,* 337–354. doi:10.1016/j.psychsport.2006.06.004

Holmes, P., & Calmels, C. (2008). A neuroscientific review of imagery and observation use in sport. *Journal of Motor Behavior, 40,* 433–445. doi:10.3200/JMBR.40.5.433-445

Katula, J. A., & McAuley, E. (2001). The mirror does not lie: Acute exercise and self-efficacy. *International Journal of Behavioral Medicine, 8,* 319–326. doi:10.1207/s15327558ijbm0804_6

Katula, J. A., McAuley, E., Mihalko, S. L., & Bane, S. M. (1998). Mirror, mirror on the wall . . . Exercise environment influences on self-efficacy. *Journal of Social Behavior & Personality, 13,* 319–332.

Kimiecik, J. C., & Horn, T. (1998). Parental beliefs and children's moderate-to-vigorous physical activity. *Research Quarterly for Exercise and Sport, 69,* 163–175.

Kirschenbaum, D. S. (1984). Self-regulation and sport psychology: Nurturing an emerging symbiosis. *Journal of Sport Psychology, 6,* 159–183.

Laguna, P. L. (1996). The effects of model demonstration strategies on motor skill acquisition and performance. *Journal of Human Movement Studies, 30,* 55–79.

Lamarche, L., & Gammage, K. (2010). The effects of leader gender on self-presentational concerns in exercise. *Psychology & Health, 25,* 769–781. doi:10.1080/08870440902866886

Law, B., & Hall, C. (2009a). Observational learning use and self-efficacy beliefs in adult sport novices. *Psychology of Sport and Exercise, 10,* 263–270. doi:10.1016/j.psychsport.2008.08.003

Law, B., & Hall, C. (2009b). The relationships among skill level, age, and golfers' observational learning use. *The Sport Psychologist, 23,* 42–58.

Law, B., & Ste-Marie, D. M. (2005). Effects of self-modeling on figure skating jump performance and psychological variables. *European Journal of Sport Science, 5,* 143–152. doi:10.1080/17461390500159273

Leavitt, J., Young, J., & Connelly, D. (1989). The effects of videotape highlights on state self-confidence. *Journal of Applied Research in Coaching and Athletics, 4,* 225–232.

Lee, L. L., Arthur, A., & Avis, M. (2008). Using self-efficacy theory to develop interventions that help older people overcome psychological barriers to physical activity: A discussion paper. *International Journal of Nursing Studies, 45,* 1690–1699. doi:10.1016/j.ijnurstu.2008.02.012

Legrain, P., d'Arripe-Longueville, F., & Gernigon, C. (2003). Peer tutoring in a sport setting: Are there any benefits for tutors? *The Sport Psychologist, 17,* 77–94.

Lewis, S. (1974). A comparison of behavior therapy techniques in the reduction of fearful avoidance behavior. *Behavior Therapy, 5,* 648–655.

Loughead, T. M., & Carron, A. V. (2004). The mediating role of cohesion in the leader behavior–satisfaction relationship. *Psychology of Sport and Exercise, 5,* 355–371. doi:10.1016/S1469-0292(03)00033-5

Lox, C., Ginis, K. M., & Petruzzello, S. J. (2010). *The psychology of exercise: Integrating theory and practice* (3rd ed.). Scottsdale, AZ: Holcomb Hathaway.

Maddison, R., Prapavessis, H., Armstrong, G. P., & Hill, C. (2008). A modeling intervention in heart failure. *Annals of Behavioral Medicine, 36,* 64–69. doi:10.1007/s12160-008-9050-y

Maddison, R., Prapavessis, H., & Clatworthy, M. (2006). Modeling and rehabilitation following anterior cruciate ligament reconstruction. *Annals of Behavioral Medicine, 31,* 89–98. doi:10.1207/s15324796abm3101_13

Martin, K. A., Moritz, S. E., & Hall, C. R. (1999). Imagery use in sport: A literature review and applied model. *The Sport Psychologist, 13,* 245–268.

Martin Ginis, K. A., Burke, S. M., & Gauvin, L. (2007). Exercising with others exacerbates the negative effects of mirrored environments on sedentary women's feeling states. *Psychology & Health, 22,* 945–962. doi:10.1080/14768320601070571

Martin Ginis, K. A., Jung, M. E., & Gauvin, L. (2003). To see or not to see: Effects of exercising in mirrored environments on sedentary women's feeling states and self-efficacy. *Health Psychology, 22,* 354–361. doi:10.1037/0278-6133.22.4.354

Martin Ginis, K. A., Prapavessis, H., & Haase, A. M. (2008). The effects of physique-salient and physique non-salient exercise videos on women's body image, self-presentational concerns, and exercise motivation. *Body Image, 5,* 164–172. doi:10.1016/j.bodyim.2007.11.005

McAuley, E., Courneya, K. S., Rudolph, D. L., & Lox, C. L. (1994). Enhancing exercise adherence in middle-aged males and females. *Preventive Medicine, 23,* 498–506. doi:10.1006/pmed.1994.1068

McCullagh, P. (1986). Model status as a determinant of observational learning and performance. *Journal of Sport Psychology, 8,* 319–331.

McCullagh, P. (1987). Model similarity effects on motor performance. *Journal of Sport Psychology, 9,* 249–260.

McCullagh, P., & Caird, J. K. (1990). Correct and learning models and the use of model knowledge of results in the acquisition and retention of a motor skill. *Journal of Human Movement Studies, 18,* 107–116.

McCullagh, P., Law, B., & Ste-Marie, D. (2012). Modeling and performance. In S. Murphy (Ed.), *The Oxford handbook of sport and performance psychology* (pp. 250–272). New York, NY: Oxford University Press.

McCullagh, P., & Weiss, M. R. (2002). Observational learning: The forgotten psychological method in sport psychology. In J. L. Van Raalte & B. W. Brewer (Eds.), *Exploring sport and exercise psychology* (2nd ed., pp. 131–149). Washington, DC: American Psychological Association. doi:10.1037/10465-007

McCullagh, P., Weiss, M. R., & Ross, D. (1989). Modeling considerations in motor skill acquisition and performance. In K. B. Pandolf (Ed.). *Exercise and Sport Sciences Reviews* (Vol. 17, pp. 475–513). Baltimore, MD: Williams & Wilkins.

Miller, N. E., & Dollard, J. (1941). *Social learning and imitation.* New Haven, CT: Yale University Press.

Ng, Y., Yuen, J., Tam, S. F., Yew, W. W., & Lam, W. K. (1999). Effects of video modeling on self-efficacy and exercise performance of COPD patients. *Social Behavior and Personality, 27,* 475–486. doi:10.2224/sbp.1999.27.5.475

Pashler, H., McDaniel, M., Rohrer, D., & Bjork, R. (2008). Learning styles: Concepts and evidence. *Psychological Science in the Public Interest, 9,* 105–119. doi:10.1111/j.1539-6053.2009.01038.x

Ram, N., & McCullagh, P. (2003). Self-modeling: Influence on psychological responses and physical performance. *The Sport Psychologist, 17,* 220–241.

Ram, N., Riggs, S. M., Skaling, S., Landers, D. M., & McCullagh, P. (2007). A comparison of modelling and imagery in the acquisition and retention of motor skills. *Journal of Sports Sciences, 25,* 587–597. doi:10.1080/02640410600947132

Riener, C., & Willingham, D. (2010, September–October). The myth of learning styles. *Change: The Magazine of Higher Education.* Retrieved from http://www.changemag.org

Rothstein, A. L., & Arnold, R. K. (1976). Bridging the gap: Application of research on videotape feedback and bowling. *Motor Skills: Theory Into Practice, 1,* 35–62.

Rymal, A., Martini, R., & Ste-Marie, D. M. (2010). Self-regulatory processes employed during self-modeling: A qualitative analysis. *The Sport Psychologist, 24,* 1–15.

Sallis, J. F., Prochaska, J. J., & Taylor, W. C. (2000). A review of correlates of physical activity of children and adolescents. *Medicine and Science in Sports and Exercise, 32,* 963. doi:10.1097/00005768-200005000-00014

Schunk, D. H. (1987). Peer models and children's behavioral change. *Review of Educational Research, 57,* 149–174.

Schunk, D. H., Hanson, A. R., & Cox, P. D. (1987). Peer-model attributes and children's achievement behaviors. *Journal of Educational Psychology, 79,* 54–61.

Scully, D. M., & Newell, K. M. (1985). Observation and the acquisition of motor skills: Towards a visual perception perspective. *Journal of Human Movement Studies, 11,* 169–186.

Shea, C. H., Wulf, G., & Whitacre, C. (1999). Enhancing training efficiency and effectiveness through the use of dyad training. *Journal of Motor Behavior, 31,* 119–125. doi:10.1080/00222899909600983

Sheffield, F. N. (1961). Theoretical considerations in the learning of complex sequential tasks from demonstration and practice. In A. A. Lumsdaine (Ed.), *Student response in programmed instruction* (pp. 13–32). Washington, DC: National Research Council, National Academy of Sciences.

Standal, Ø. F., & Jespersen, E. (2008). Peers as resources for learning: A situated learning approach to adapted physical education. *Adapted Physical Activity Quarterly, 25,* 208–227.

Starek, J., & McCullagh, P. (1999). The effect of self-modeling on the performance of beginning swimmers. *The Sport Psychologist, 13,* 269–287.

Ste-Marie, D. M., Rymal, A., Vertes, K., & Martini, R. (2011). Self-modeling and competitive beam performance enhancement examined within a self-regulation perspective. *Journal of Applied Sport Psychology, 23,* 292–307. doi:10.1080/10413200.2011.558049

Tarde, G. (1903). *The laws of imitation.* New York, NY: Holt.

Templin, D. P., & Vernacchia, R. A. (1995). The effect of highlight music videotapes upon games performance of intercollegiate volleyball players. *The Sport Psychologist, 9,* 41–50.

Topping, K. J. (2005). Trends in peer learning. *Educational Psychology, 25,* 631–645. doi:10.1080/01443410500345172

Trost, S. G., Sallis, J. F., Pate, R. R., Freedson, P. S., Taylor, W. C., & Dowda, M. (2003). Evaluating a model of parental influence on youth physical activity. *American Journal of Preventive Medicine, 25,* 277–282. doi:10.1016/S0749-3797(03)00217-4

Van Der Horst, K., Paw, M. J., Twisk, J. W., & Van Mechelen, W. (2007). A brief review on correlates of physical activity and sedentariness in youth. *Medicine and Science in Sports and Exercise, 39,* 1241. doi:10.1249/mss.0b013e318059bf35

Weiss, M. R., McCullagh, P., Smith, A. L., & Berlant, A. T. (1998). Observational learning and the fearful child: Influence of peer models on swim skill performance and psychological responses. *Research Quarterly for Exercise and Sport, 69,* 380–394.

Wesch, N. N., Law, B., & Hall, C. R. (2007). The use of observational learning by athletes. *Journal of Sport Behavior, 30,* 219–231.

Winfrey, M. L., & Weeks, D. M. (1993). Effects of self-modeling on self-efficacy and balance beam performance. *Perceptual and Motor Skills, 77,* 907–913. doi:10.2466/pms.1993.77.3.907

Zimmerman, B. J. (1996). Enhancing student academic and health functioning: A self-regulatory perspective. *School Psychology Quarterly, 11,* 47–66. doi:10.1037/h0088920

Zimmerman, B. J. (2000). Attaining self-regulation: A social cognitive perspective. In M. Boekaerts, P. R. Pintrich, & M. Zeidner (Eds.), *Handbook of self-regulation* (pp. 13–39). San Diego, CA: Academic Press. doi:10.1016/B978-012109890-2/50031-7

PROMOTING WELL-BEING | II

Beth C. Bock, Sarah E. Linke, Melissa A. Napolitano,
Matthew M. Clark, Ronnesia B. Gaskins, and Bess H. Marcus

Exercise Initiation, Adoption, and Maintenance in Adults
Theoretical Models and Empirical Support

8

I n this chapter, we focus on the promotion of physical activity in the general population. We discuss the health benefits of regular physical activity and present data on the prevalence of sedentary lifestyle. Historically, the lack of theory-driven interventions has been a limitation in exercise promotion efforts, but this is changing. We present a summary of useful theoretical models for exercise adoption and adherence. For the practitioner, we provide information on exercise interventions that are based on some of these theories. Finally, we identify important issues that need to be addressed in exercise promotion.

Health Benefits of Physical Activity

Physical activity and cardiorespiratory fitness are associated with decreased morbidity and mortality in both men and women (Blair et al., 1989; Kokkinos & Myers, 2010;

http://dx.doi.org/10.1037/14251-008
Exploring Sport and Exercise Psychology, Third Edition, J. Van Raalte and
B. Brewer (Editors)

Paffenbarger et al., 1993). Research conducted over the past 50 years has demonstrated that active individuals who engage in regular moderate-intensity physical activity are less likely to develop coronary heart disease than their sedentary peers, and if they do develop coronary heart disease, it occurs at a later age and tends to be less severe (Berlin & Colditz, 1990; Sofi, Capalbo, Cesari, Abbate, & Gensini, 2008). The health risk differentials are relatively small when comparing moderate- with vigorous-intensity physical activity. Thus, most guidelines have focused on promoting moderate-intensity physical activity (Briffa et al., 2006; Donnelly et al., 2009; U.S. Department of Health and Human Services [USDHHS], 2008).

Epidemiological studies demonstrate that physical activity also provides weight control benefits; provides protection against other diseases, such as certain cancers and Type 2 diabetes mellitus; and improves bone and joint health (USDHHS, 1996; Vogel et al., 2009). Physical activity is recommended as an adjunctive treatment to diet for controlling non-insulin-dependent diabetes and managing weight (Levine et al., 2005; Thompson, Cook, Clark, Bardia, & Levine, 2007). There is growing evidence that regular physical activity is associated with reduced incidence of colon and breast cancers and, to a lesser extent, of endometrial, lung, and prostate cancers (Friedenreich, Neilson, & Lynch, 2010; Newton & Galvão, 2008). Regular physical activity also helps maintain healthy joints and may control symptoms of osteoarthritis. Weight-bearing exercise in particular builds bone mass in childhood and early adolescence and maintains bone mass in adulthood (USDHHS, 1996; Vogel et al., 2009).

Regular physical activity also offers psychological benefits, such as improvements in anxiety, depression, and self-concept (Blumenthal et al., 1999; Dunn Trivedi, & O'Neal, 2001; Peluso & Guerra de Andrade 2005; Scully, Kremer, Meade, Graham, & Dudgeon, 1998). Sedentary adults who begin regular exercise report significantly reduced depressive symptoms in as little as 10 weeks (Annesi, 2005). Furthermore, physical activity can improve overall health status, functional capacity, and quality of life in cancer survivors (e.g., San Juan, Wolin, & Lucia, 2011; Spence, Heesch, & Brown, 2010).

Current Status of Physical Activity

The U.S. Centers for Disease Control and Prevention (CDC) and the American College of Sports Medicine (ACSM; Pate et al., 1995) have recommended that every adult accumulate at least 30 minutes of moderate-intensity physical activity (e.g., brisk walking) on most, preferably all, days of the week. More recent guidelines (USDHHS, 2008) specify that greater health benefits can be obtained by engaging in at least 300 minutes/week of physical activity. In addition to aerobic activity, the 2008 guidelines recommend that adults participate in muscle-strengthening activities on 2 or more days/week. The 2020 Healthy People guidelines suggest that youth and adults (over age 9) engage in 60 minutes/day of aerobic activity, muscle-strengthening activity 3 days/week, and weekly activities that combine both forms of exercise.

Responses to the 2008 National Health Interview Survey have shown that only 31% of U.S. adults meet recommendations for leisure-time physical activity (CDC, 2006; Pleis, Lucas, & Ward, 2009). The groups least likely to meet recommendations included women (29% of men vs. 23% of women), ethnic minorities (20% African American and 19% Hispanic vs. 28% White), the less educated (12% among those with < 12 years education vs. 37% with > 12 years education) and older adults (22% of those 65 years and older vs. 36% among those 18–44 years old) (Carlson, Fulton, Schoenborn, & Loustalot, 2010; Pleis et al., 2009). Individuals with disabilities are more sedentary than their healthy counterparts (Christensen, Holt, & Wilson, 2010; USDHHS, 2010). Surprisingly, leisure-time physical activity has a direct relationship with degree of urbanization: Even when analyses are adjusted for age, education, and income, 43% of residents in rural areas reported no physical activity versus 35% in central metropolitan areas (Pleis et al., 2009). Even among individuals who begin an exercise program, approximately half will stop within 6 months (Crain, Martinson, Sherwood, & O'Connor, 2010; Dishman, 1988; USDHHS, 1996). Therefore, there is a great need for the development of effective interventions that promote the adoption and maintenance of a physically active lifestyle.

Theoretical Models Used in Exercise Research

Psychological theories can significantly contribute to the knowledge base for guiding the development of new interventions to promote the adoption and maintenance of physical activity. Researchers base their questions on their theoretical frame of reference. In the past, many researchers sought to identify an "exercise personality," that is, an individual who would be more likely to be physically active (Feltz, 1992). Researchers examined profiles of athletes based on standard personality profiles. However, such research generally lacked a theoretical rationale, and few conclusive results were drawn using these atheoretical approaches (Feltz, 1992). More recently, researchers have examined cognitive, behavioral, and environmental models. In this section, we describe several of these useful models of physical activity adoption and maintenance.

HEALTH BELIEF MODEL

The health belief model (Becker & Maiman, 1975; Rosenstock, 1974) proposes that the likelihood that an individual will engage in preventive health behaviors (e.g., physical activity) primarily on two appraisals: (a) the individual's perception of a potential illness's severity and (b) his or her perceived susceptibility to that illness. In considering these two factors, the individual weighs the benefits (pros) against the costs (cons) related to taking action. If an individual believes the potential illness is serious, that he or she is at risk, and that the pros of taking action outweigh the cons, the individual is likely to adopt the target health behavior. Other factors such as demographic characteristics (e.g., age, ethnicity, gender), psychosocial variables (e.g., socioeconomic status, peer influence), and cues in the environment (e.g., media campaigns) can also influence individuals' decisions about whether to engage in specific health behaviors. For example, younger persons may feel less susceptible to the types of diseases linked to inactivity, such as cardiovascular disease (CDC, 2007) and certain types of cancer (Friedenreich & Orenstein, 2002), which tend to occur later in life. Therefore, interventions targeting younger populations should focus on their preexisting perceived vulnerabilities (e.g., body-image issues) or target other aspects of the health belief equation.

THEORY OF REASONED ACTION AND THEORY OF PLANNED BEHAVIOR

The theory of reasoned action, developed by Ajzen and Fishbein (1980), is based on the premise that people generally do behaviors that they intend to do. In this model, intentions are the product of individuals' attitudes toward a particular behavior and their perceptions of what is normative regarding the behavior (subjective norm). The subjective norm is a product of beliefs about others' opinions and the individual's own motivation to comply with others' opinions. Attitudes are determined by beliefs about the outcome of the behavior and the value placed on that outcome. For example, Susan, a sedentary individual, may believe that other people think she should be physically active, and she may wish to do what others want her to do. This results in a positive subjective norm for physical activity. In addition, she may believe that she will lose weight if she engages in regular physical activity. Because Susan values these results highly, she forms a positive attitude toward physical activity, which should, in turn, create a positive intention for Susan to become physically active.

Ajzen and Fishbein (1980) observed that the theory of reasoned action was most useful in predicting behaviors that were entirely subject to volitional control. However, most behaviors involve a degree of practical constraint outside of individual control. The theory of planned behavior (Ajzen, 1985) incorporates subjective norm and attitudes and adds the notion of perceived behavioral control (people's perception of their ability to perform the behavior) as a predictor of behavioral outcome. Perceived behavioral control in this model is similar to Bandura's (1997) construct of self-efficacy. The theory of planned behavior postulates that if people believe they do not have the resources or opportunities to perform a behavior, attitudes and subjective norms may not be enough to influence the intention to perform that behavior.

SOCIAL-COGNITIVE THEORY

Social-cognitive theory (SCT; Bandura, 1986, 2001) is an integration of operant conditioning, social learning theory, and cognitive psychology. SCT proposes that personal, behavioral, and environmental factors operate as reciprocal interacting determinants of each other (reciprocal determinism). Personal factors including cognitions, emotions, and physiology are also important in this theory. Bandura (1977) was one of the first to state that learning may occur as a result of direct reinforcement of a behavior or as a result of observing the consequences that others experience. Because individuals learn through the consequences of their own behavior and by observation of others, modeling is an efficient method of learning. Thus, according to this model, researchers should examine the role of modeling in exercise. (See Chapter 7, this volume, for more on modeling in sport and exercise).

Two cognitive processes, outcome expectations and self-efficacy, have been identified as important components of SCT. Outcome expectations are beliefs about the effects of a behavior. Individuals may expect improvement in health status, to receive social approval, or to experience self-satisfaction as an outcome of exercising (e.g., Williams, Anderson, & Winett, 2005). Outcomes can be classified as immediate benefits, such as a lower stress level, or long-term benefits, such as improvements in body composition. Self-efficacy is a judgment of one's ability to perform a behavior successfully (Bandura, 1997). People's perception that they can perform a behavior successfully increases the likelihood that they will engage in that behavior. Self-efficacy is behavior specific; thus, self-efficacy for physical activity (Marcus, Selby, Niaura, & Rossi, 1992) is different from self-efficacy for smoking cessation or weight management. Self-efficacy judgments have been found to predict physical activity level (Bock et al., 1997; Dalle Grave, Calugi, Centis, El Ghoch, & Marchesini, 2011; Sullum, Clark, & King, 2000).

Intervention studies have shown that increases in self-efficacy are associated with increased physical activity (Pinto, Clark, Cruess, Szymanski, & Pera, 1999). Self-efficacy has also been shown to interact with outcome expectations (Sears & Stanton, 2001) and increases in self-esteem (i.e., perceptions of attractiveness, physical conditioning, and strength) to predict physical activity behavior (McAuley, Blissmer, Katula, Duncan, & Mihalko, 2000).

DECISION THEORY

Decisional balance is based on the theoretical model developed by Janis and Mann (1977) and is the individual's perception and evaluation of the relative costs (cons) and benefits (pros) associated with exercise participation. These strategies have been adapted and applied to exercise adoption (Marcus, Rakowski, & Rossi, 1992) by using a decisional balance sheet: The individual documents the anticipated consequences of physical activity participation in terms of gains and losses to self and others and approval or disapproval from others and from the self. This procedure may promote an awareness of the benefits and costs of physical activity participation that are salient to the individual (Wankel, 1984). Decisional balance has frequently been used as a component of effective interventions (Massoudi et al., 2010; Napolitano et al., 2008).

TRANSTHEORETICAL MODEL

The transtheoretical model (TTM) incorporates aspects of both SCT and decision theory (Prochaska, DiClemente, & Norcross, 1992; Prochaska & Velicer, 1997). In this model, individuals progress through a series of stages of behavior change: precontemplation, contemplation, preparation, action, and maintenance. Precontemplators are not physically active and do not intend to become physically active in the next 6 months. Contemplators do not currently engage in physical activity but intend to start in the next 6 months. Those in preparation are physically active but not at a level sufficient to meet the guidelines (e.g., ACSM, 1990; USDHHS, 2008). Action is the stage for individuals who regularly engage in physical activity but have done so for less than 6 months. Maintenance includes individuals who have had a physically active lifestyle for 6 months or longer (Marcus, Rossi, Selby, Niaura, & Abrams, 1992). Movement across the stages is thought to be cyclic, not linear, as many do not succeed in their efforts at establishing and maintaining lifestyle changes (Prochaska et al., 1992). Most intervention programs are designed for individuals in the preparation stage. However, few individuals are in that stage. Marcus, Rossi, et al. (1992), in a sample of 1,172 participants in a work site health promotion project, classified 24% in precontemplation, 33% in contemplation, 10% in preparation, 11% in action, and 22% in maintenance. This pattern is similar to the distribution of stages of change for other behaviors.

Research has demonstrated that when there is a mismatch between stage of change and intervention strategy, attrition is high (Spencer, Adams, Malone, Roy, & Yost, 2006). Therefore, matching treatment strategies to an individual's stage of change is one strategy to improve adherence and reduce attrition.

The TTM also incorporates a number of cognitive and behavioral processes. While the stages of change document *when* people change, the processes of change describe *how* people change. Processes are divided into two categories: cognitive and behavioral. The degree of use of the specific processes of change varies across the stages of change. Use of the cognitive processes tends to peak in the preparation stage, while use of the behavioral processes tends to peak in the action stage. The Processes of Change questionnaire is a 40-item measure of these processes for physical activity (Marcus, Rossi, et al., 1992), and a sample item from each process is listed in Exhibit 8.1. Change over time on the Processes of Change questionnaire has been shown to predict success in attaining and maintaining a program of regular physical activity (Dunn et al., 1997, 1999; Spencer et al., 2006).

Also related to stage of change is a cost–benefit analysis called decisional balance, which was discussed in the Decision Theory section. When individuals are considering a lifestyle change, they weigh the benefits (pros) of that behavior against the costs (cons) of that behavior.

EXHIBIT 8.1

Exercise Processes of Change

Cognitive Processes

Consciousness raising: I recall information people have personally given me on the benefits of exercise.
Dramatic relief: Warnings about health hazards of inactivity move me emotionally.
Environmental reevaluation: I feel I would be a better role model for others if I exercised regularly.
Self-reevaluation: I am considering that regular exercise would make me a healthier, happier person to be around.
Social liberation: I find society changing in ways that make it easier for the exerciser.

Behavioral Processes

Counterconditioning: Instead of remaining inactive, I engage in some physical activity.
Helping relationships: I have someone on whom I can depend when I am having problems with exercising.
Reinforcement management: I reward myself when I exercise.
Self-liberation: I tell myself I am able to keep exercising if I want to.
Stimulus control: I put things around my home to remind me of exercising.

Across multiple behaviors, the cons are usually stronger than the pros in the precontemplation and contemplation stages (Prochaska et al., 1994). Typically, the crossover in strength of pros versus cons occurs in the preparation stage, and the pros are greater than the cons in the action and maintenance stages (Prochaska et al., 1994). Decisional balance has been predictive of exercise participation across diverse groups (Cardinal et al., 2009; Napolitano et al., 2008).

RELAPSE PREVENTION MODEL

The problem of relapse is an important challenge in health behaviors (Brownell, Marlatt, Lichtenstein, & Wilson, 1986). Relapse rates from physical activity programs are high. Approximately 50% of physical activity program participants drop out during the first 6 months of enrollment (Crain et al., 2010; Dishman, 1988; USDHHS, 1996). It has been suggested (Marcus et al., 2000) that the relapse prevention model, which has been applied to physical activity, can be a useful framework for understanding the process from lapse to relapse (Amati et al., 2007; Stetson et al., 2005).

The goal of relapse prevention is to help individuals anticipate problems and cope effectively in high-risk situations. Negative emotions, physiological factors, limited coping skills, limited social support, low motivation, high-risk situations, and stress all appear to predict relapse (Kayman, Bruvold, & Stern, 1990; Stetson et al., 2005). The principles of the relapse prevention model include identifying high-risk situations for relapse (e.g., change in season, change in work hours) and related problem-solving solutions for these high-risk situations (e.g., "When it starts to snow, I'll shift from outdoor walks to walking in the mall"). When individuals do experience a lapse (a few days of not participating in their planned activity), they need to challenge the abstinence violation effect (AVE), which applies to a range of behaviors. Simply stated, the AVE is the belief that once one has slipped, one is doomed. Therefore, individuals who have lapsed may see themselves as failures and give up exercising.

SELF-DETERMINATION THEORY

Self-determination theory (SDT) focuses on social and environmental conditions that are related to self-motivation and psychological development (Deci & Ryan, 1985; Ryan & Deci, 2000). SDT emphasizes that the social environment can optimize individuals' development, performance, and well-being. Intrinsic and extrinsic motivation, two factors that influence individuals' behavior in everyday experiences, are core SDT constructs. Intrinsic motivation influences the tendency to seek out new experiences and challenges, explore, learn, and develop one's capacities. A subtheory within SDT, cognitive evaluation theory, seeks to describe social and environmental factors related to intrinsic motivation, including choice, opportunities for self-direction, discovery of intrinsically interesting activities, and opportunities to demonstrate competence and autonomy, across a range of behaviors and situations. Extrinsic motivation refers to performing an activity for the purpose of a separate outcome, such as an external reward or praise (Ryan & Deci, 2000). Social influences that facilitate or hinder behavioral change are an important component of extrinsic motivation. A meta-analysis revealed that three out of six papers evaluating the relationship between intrinsic motivation and physical activity reported a significant independent effect of intrinsic motivation on physical activity (Rhodes, Fiala, & Conner, 2009). Furthermore, a study examining the association between physical activity and motivation among older adults reported that greater amounts of intrinsic and self-determined extrinsic motivation are associated with higher physical activity levels (Dacey, Baltzell, & Zaichkowsky, 2008).

MOTIVATIONAL INTERVIEWING

Motivational interviewing (MI) is a clinical and theoretical approach that was developed in the addictions field to assist individuals in working through their ambivalence toward making behavior changes (Miller & Rollnick, 1991). In this model, motivation is viewed not as a personality trait but rather as a state or eagerness of readiness similar to the TTM (Prochaska & DiClemente, 1983). The counselor's task in using MI is to assist individuals finding, utilizing, and adhering to specific behavior change strategies (Miller, 1983, 1985). Miller and Rollnick (1991) identified eight important building blocks that counselors can use to facilitate behavior change: (a) give advice, (b) remove barriers, (c) provide choice, (d) decrease desirability, (e) practice empathy, (f) provide feedback, (g) clarify goals, and (h) active helping.

The effectiveness of MI principles in helping people to change exercise behavior was demonstrated in a study that compared the effectiveness of two communication styles ("negotiation" vs. "direct advice") with that of a no-intervention control. Participants were 1,658 men and women ages 45 to 64. Posttreatment, both communication groups significantly increased their level of physical activity. However, the negotiation group increased their physical activity behavior 10% more than did the control group, highlighting the benefits of MI-based interventions for improving physical activity (Hillsdon, Thorogood, White, Foster, & Diamond, 2000). More recent studies of MI and physical activity have incorporated other mediums of intervention delivery, such as print materials, in accommodating individual differences and improving treatment efficacy (Black et al., 2010). For example, in one study, participants ($N = 1,629$) were recruited through primary care and randomized to receive either four tailored print letters, four MI telephone calls, two each of MI telephone calls and print letters, or no information. Results indicated that participants in MI only or MI combination groups were significantly more likely than controls to increase physical activity at the end of treatment (3 months) and at 6 and 9 months follow-up (van Keulen et al., 2011). Thus, MI appears to be a robust strategy for improving physical activity.

ECOLOGICAL MODELS

Ecological models take into consideration that individuals do not live within a vacuum but rather within environments and that the people, places, and things around them influence their health behaviors. Four core assumptions are critical to the application of social ecological principles to physical activity behavior change: (a) there is a dynamic interplay between environmental and personal factors, each of which influences health behavior; (b) environments are multidimensional and complex; (c) persons are multidimensional and complex, and interventions should be designed to address both the individual and the groups with which the individual is affiliated; and (d) people–environment transactions exert multiple levels of influence, such that people may modify their settings to be more healthful (e.g., buy a treadmill), and social features of settings influence individuals (e.g., a lunchtime walking club). Within this framework, Stokols (2000; Stokols, Allen, & Bellingham, 1996) has suggested that both person-focused and environment-focused strategies can be applied to physical activity. For example, person-focused strategies might include preventive screening programs, individual counseling, or participation in a lifestyle intervention. Environmental strategies include both geographic (e.g., mixed-use communities) and sociocultural (e.g., changing organization development to make the integration of physical activity part of the culture) aspects. Finally, some have suggested that a new, transdisciplinary paradigm is needed to address the current rate of physical inactivity (Baranowski, Cullen, Nicklas, Thompson, & Baranowski, 2003; Grzywacz & Fuqua, 2000; King, Stokols, Talen, Brassington, & Killingsworth, 2002). Social ecological models are relevant to physical activity promotion and form a cohesive conceptual approach for this area.

Some challenges naturally exist in the application of the social ecological models to physical activity due to the complexity of addressing multiple levels of influence, including regional (e.g., neighborhoods), structural (e.g., the physical environment), and institutional (e.g., government, work site, family; Baranowski et al., 2003), on health behaviors. More research is needed to disentangle the critical components necessary for making a true public health impact on physical inactivity. However, using this model for the design, implementation, and measurement of physical activity interventions seems very promising (Vrazel, Saunders, & Wilcox, 2008).

CONCLUSIONS ABOUT MODELS

Physical activity researchers are increasingly applying theoretical models to guide their investigations, but numerous questions remain. Most models were initially developed for or first applied to other behaviors. Physical activity may differ from other behaviors in important ways that may require modification of existing models. In addition, much of the early research was conducted on majority populations. Although diverse populations are increasingly included in research studies, exactly how these models apply to other demographic groups is still unclear. Finally, studies have typically examined one model rather than directly comparing different models, which prevents definitive conclusions about relative efficacy from being drawn.

Many of the models reviewed contain common theoretical elements or constructs. The health belief model examines the individual's perception of risks associated with a sedentary lifestyle and the perceived benefits of engaging in physical activity. Similarly, SCT examines the interaction of social and personal factors (beliefs, emotions, and physiology). Intrinsic and extrinsic motivation can also be conceptualized in the context of other theories; for example, each might influence benefits and barriers toward being active (health belief model) and can be related to personal factors (SCT). Intrinsic motivation, in particular, may be related to aspects of SCT: Individuals with high self-efficacy are also often more intrinsically motivated to participate in physical activity than are individuals with lower self-efficacy (Lloyd & Little, 2010). In decision theory, these comparisons can be reduced to a simpler two-factor structure comparing the benefits with the costs of being physically active. Similarly, the relapse prevention model focuses on cognitive processes that enhance or inhibit a long-term active lifestyle. In addition, the theory of planned behavior incorporates people's beliefs about physical activity and confidence in their ability to be physically active. The TTM incorporates many components of the previously described models, including perceived benefits and costs, self-confidence, and strategies for change, into a model of a series of stages of change. MI also incorporates aspects of the other theoretical models, including the

TTM. Finally, ecological models encompass many of the person factors that make up the other models and incorporate environmental factors that other models do not address. Further research is needed to highlight differences among these models.

Intervention Applications

In this section, we describe some practical strategies for interventions based on some of the theories we have reviewed, particularly the TTM.

One concept that has been popular for years in psychotherapy is that of patient–treatment matching. The notion that treatments should be matched to the specific characteristics and needs of the patient has also gained popularity in smoking cessation and obesity treatments. This concept has been slow to reach the arena of physical activity interventions, in part because sedentary lifestyle was not recognized as a significant public health problem until the mid-1990s (Fletcher et al., 1992; King et al., 1992; Pate et al., 1995; USDHHS, 1996). When one looks at the large percentage of sedentary people in the population and the high dropout rate from programmed exercise (e.g., Crain et al., 2010), the time seems right to consider patient treatment matching for the promotion of physical activity.

The underlying theme of the TTM is that interventions need to use differing strategies to match the level of readiness of the individual. That is, interventions that approach the individual with messages that are sensitive to where the person is (on various variables and constructs) will be more efficacious than a one-size-fits-all approach. To illustrate the utility of this model for physical activity, we will describe a few studies that were conducted to address the lack of success prior interventions had in recruiting and retaining individuals who were sedentary but thinking about becoming physically active (i.e., contemplators).

The "Imagine Action" campaign was a community-wide program designed to increase participation in physical activity (Marcus, Banspach, et al., 1992). Participants were 610 adults who enrolled through their work sites or in response to advertisements. The 6-week intervention consisted of stage-matched self-help manuals: resource materials that described a wide variety of free and low-cost light, moderate, and vigorous physical activity options in the local community; and weekly "fun walks" and "activity nights." The content of the manuals was based on key issues in the exercise adherence literature and was informed by the TTM and SCT. The emphasis of each manual was matched to the participant's stage of readiness for adopting physical activity. For example, the manual for contemplators was called *What's in It for You* and focused primarily on encouraging the reader to consider the benefits and costs (i.e., pros and cons) of becoming more active. Since those in contemplation are *considering* becoming more active but are not ready to take action, it was considered most important to help them shift their view of the relative benefits and barriers to activity rather than recommend activities they could undertake immediately. This manual therefore emphasized considering the benefits (e.g., weight control) and barriers (e.g., takes too much time) of becoming more active, the social benefits of activity (e.g., meet people in a class, walk with significant other), and ways of rewarding oneself for increasing activity (e.g., buying self flowers as a reward for increasing from 1 to 2 walks per week). Likewise, the manual for those in the preparation stage was called *Ready for Action* and focused more on setting short-term and longer term activity goals (e.g., walking for 30 minutes five times per week), rewarding oneself for activity, managing time to fit activities into a busy schedule (e.g., ride exercise bicycle or walk on treadmill while watching the news or other television), and developing the details of a walking program. The program also contained a manual for those who had been regularly active for only a short time called *Keeping It Going,* which focused on troubleshooting situations that might lead to relapse (e.g., injury, boredom), goal setting, cross-training to prevent boredom, and gaining social support (e.g., finding people to be active with or people supportive of one's active lifestyle).

Following the intervention, 30% of those in contemplation and 61% of those in preparation at baseline progressed to the action stage, and an additional 31% who had been in contemplation progressed to preparation. These findings demonstrate that a low-cost, relatively low-intensity intervention can produce significant improvement in stages of exercise adoption.

The above study was not a controlled trial, however. Several more recent studies have used stage-matched manuals (Bock, Marcus, & Bock, 1998; Marcus, Bock, et al., 1998; Marcus, Emmons, et al., 1998), individually tailored materials (Marcus, Lewis, et al., 2007), and web-delivered interventions (Marcus, Napolitano, et al., 2007) that tailor their content to the individual's characteristics relevant to physical activity adoption. These characteristics can include stage of readiness, self-efficacy, decision making, and behavioral and cognitive processes relevant to physical activity adoption, among others. Several additional studies have been conducted that build on this work and demonstrate the efficacy of this approach (Dunn et al., 1999; Marcus, Lewis, et al., 2007; Marcus, Napolitano, et al., 2007; Marshall, Bauman, et al., 2003; Marshall, Leslie, et al., 2003; Napolitano et al., 2003).

Future Directions

In earlier sections of this chapter, we highlighted issues that merit further investigation. However, several specific challenges confront both clinicians and researchers working in physical activity promotion. One critically important challenge is disseminating interventions to the large population of sedentary individuals. Although practitioners can assist many individuals on a one-on-one or group basis, their reach remains limited, especially to those with disproportionately low physical activity levels and increased health burden (Bryan et al., 2011; Pekmezi, Marquez, & Marcus-Blank, 2010). Combining brief face-to-face contacts with different physical activity promotion mediums (e.g., telephone calls, mailed print materials, and newer technologies such as texting and web-based applications) appears to promote delivery and dissemination of programs (Marcus, Ciccolo, & Sciamanna, 2009; Marshall, Owen, & Bauman, 2004). Furthermore, pedometers have shown promise as quality control and objective measures of physical activity as well as adjunct intervention tools that help to increase physical activity (Bravata et al., 2007).

National guidelines that recommend accumulating moderate bouts of activity need to be used in physical activity programs for individuals, groups, work sites, and communities (USDHHS, 2008). Physical activity opportunities and programs should be tailored to individuals' level of readiness to consider, prepare for, initiate, and maintain increases in physical activity. In particular, creative efforts are needed to establish programs that appeal to the large proportion of sedentary and underactive segments of the population. Further tailoring of programs to meet the diverse needs of various racial, ethnic, and socioeconomic groups is also critical. We still have much to learn in terms of which variables to use for tailoring (e.g., literacy level, setting of intervention, self-efficacy), how many variables to assess, and how the variables combine additively or synergistically to influence behavior change (Carroll et al., 2010; Wanner, Martin-Diener, Braun-Fahrländer, Bauer, & Martin, 2009).

In recent years, there has been an increasing interest in filling the gap in evidence-based translation of research into physical activity health promotion practice (Dzewaltowski, Estabrooks, & Glasgow, 2004; Owen, Glanz, Sallis, & Kelder, 2006). Many people prefer to engage in physical activity on their own or with friends but not in a formal class-based program. However, these people may need guidance and support from professional or lay individuals to initiate and maintain a physically active lifestyle (Williams, Matthews, Rutt, Napolitano, & Marcus, 2008). Therefore, information about how to be physically active on one's own at home, work, or in the community is needed. In addition, policies that address barriers to becoming physically active in these types of settings, including establishing transdisciplinary community health promotion partnerships to help build walkable neighborhoods and parks and reduce the impact of crime, are necessary (Brownson, Hoehner, Day, Forsyth, & Sallis, 2009; Sallis et al., 2006). Work site health promotion and educational programs can be successful because they can reach people who may not ordinarily seek out information or opportunities for being physically active. However, these programs could be enhanced by offering a variety of physical activities, maximizing convenience, permitting employees to exercise on company time or allowing flexible time schedules, and using incentives judiciously (see reviews by Bopp & Fallon, 2008; Dishman, Oldenburg, O'Neal, & Shepard, 1998).

The rise in the popularity of social networking applications such as Facebook has fueled an interest in understanding the efficacy of social networking in helping with physical activity health promotion. We have yet to understand the implications of social networking for physical activity health, the extent to which such technologies worsen health through increases in sedentary behavior (van Uffelen et al., 2010), and the ways in which their popularity can be channeled toward physical activity promotion (Christakis & Fowler, 2007). These and other targeted approaches may be particularly desirable for older adults; parents of young children; individuals who have difficulty with transportation due to disabilities, finances, or other reasons; ethnic minority populations; and those affected by chronic diseases, such as obesity and diabetes, which are widespread among the U.S. adult population.

Summary

The studies reviewed in this chapter highlight the importance of including theoretical approaches and techniques to enhance success in physical activity interventions. However, many opportunities remain for using these approaches, particularly in clinical and community populations. In addition, it is essential that studies begin to incorporate strong theoretical foundations along with innovative interventions, such as tailoring programs to individual characteristics and finding avenues for reaching people who may not avail themselves of traditional programs. These approaches show great promise for continuing to target and modify the public health burden of physical inactivity.

References

Ajzen, I. (1985). From intentions to actions: A theory of focus on these important subgroups. In J. Kuhl & J. Beckman (Eds.), *Action-control: From cognition to behavior* (pp. 11–39). Heidelberg, Germany: Springer.

Ajzen, I., & Fishbein, M. (1980). *Understanding attitudes and predicting social behavior.* Englewood Cliffs, NJ: Prentice-Hall.

Amati, F., Barthassat, V., Miganne, G., Hausman, I., Monnin, D. G., Costanza, M. C., & Golay, A. (2007). Enhancing regular physical activity and relapse prevention through a 1-day therapeutic patient education workshop: A pilot study. *Patient Education and Counseling, 68,* 70–78. doi:10.1016/j.pec.2007.05.004

American College of Sports Medicine. (1990). Position statement on the recommended quantity and quality of exercise for developing and maintaining cardiorespiratory and muscular fitness in healthy adults. *Medicine and Science in Sports and Exercise, 22,* 265–274.

Annesi, J. J. (2005). Changes in depressed mood associated with 10 weeks of moderate cardio-vascular exercise in formerly sedentary adults. *Psychological Reports, 96,* 855–862. doi:10.2466/pr0.96.3.855-862

Bandura, A. (1977). Self-efficacy: Toward a unifying theory of behavior change. *Psychological Review, 84,* 191–215. doi:10.1037/0033-295X. 84.2.191

Bandura, A. (1986). *Social foundations of thought and action: A social cognitive theory.* Englewood Cliffs, NJ: Prentice Hall.

Bandura, A. (1997). *Self-efficacy: The exercise of control.* New York, NY: Freeman.

Bandura, A. (2001). Social cognitive theory: An agentic perspective. *Annual Review of Psychology, 52,* 1–26. doi:10.1146/annurev.psych.52.1.1

Baranowski, T., Cullen, K. W., Nicklas, T., Thompson, D., & Baranowski, J. (2003). Are current health behavioral change models helpful in guiding prevention of weight gain efforts? *Obesity Research, 11*(Suppl. 10), 23S–43S. doi:10.1038/oby.2003.222

Becker, M. H., & Maiman, L. A. (1975). Sociobehavioral determinants of compliance with health care and medical care recommendations. *Medical Care, 13,* 10–24. doi:10.1097/00005650-197501000-00002

Berlin, J. A., & Colditz, G. A. (1990). A meta-analysis of physical activity in the prevention of coronary heart disease. *American Journal of Epidemiology, 132,* 612–628.

Black, M. M., Hager, E. R., Le, K., Anliker, J., Arteaga, S. S., Diclemente, C., . . . Wang, Y. (2010). Challenge! Health promotion/obesity prevention mentorship model among urban, Black adolescents. *Pediatrics, 126,* 280–288. doi:10.1542/peds.2009-1832

Blair, S. N., Kohl, H. W., III, Paffenbarger, R. S., Jr., Clark, D. G., Cooper, K. H., & Gibbons, L. W. (1989). Physical fitness and all cause mortality: A prospective study of healthy men and women. *JAMA, 262,* 2395–2401. doi:10.1001/jama.1989.03430170057028

Blumenthal, J. A., Babyak, M. A., Moore, K. A., Craighead, W. E., Herman, S., Khatri, P., . . . Krishnan K. R. (1999). Effects of exercise training on older patients with major depression. *Archives of Internal Medicine, 159,* 2349–2356. doi:10.1001/archinte.159.19.2349

Bock, B. C., Albrecht, A. E., Traficante, R. M., Clark, M. M., Pinto, B. M., Tilkemeier, P., & Marcus, B. H. (1997). Predictors of exercise adherence following participation in a cardiac rehabilitation program. *International Journal of Behavioral Medicine, 4,* 60–75. doi:10.1207/s15327558ijbm0401_4

Bock, B. C., Marcus, B. H., & Bock, F. R. (1998, May–June). *Six month exercise maintenance following an intervention tailored via computer expert system.* Paper presented at the 15th annual meeting of the American College of Sports Medicine, Orlando, FL.

Bopp, M., & Fallon, E. (2008). Community-based interventions to promote increased physical activity: A primer. *Applied Health Economics and Health Policy, 6,* 173–187. doi:10.1007/BF03256132

Bravata, D. M., Smith-Spangler, C., Sundaram, V., Gienger, A. L., Lin, N., Lewis, R., . . . Sirard, J. R. (2007). Using pedometers to increase physical activity and improve health: A systematic review. *JAMA, 298,* 2296–2304. doi:10.1001/jama.298.19.2296

Briffa, T. G., Maiorana, A., Sheerin, N. J., Stubbs, A. G., Oldenburg, B. F., Sammel, N. L., Allan, R. M., & National Heart Foundation of Australia. (2006). Physical activity for people with cardiovascular disease: Recommendations of the National Heart Foundation of Australia. *The Medical Journal of Australia, 184,* 71–75.

Brownell, K. D., Marlatt, G. A., Lichtenstein, E., & Wilson, G. T. (1986). Understanding and preventing relapse. *American Psychologist, 41,* 765–782. doi:10.1037/0003-066X.41.7.765

Brownson, R. C., Hoehner, C. M., Day, K., Forsyth, A., & Sallis, J. F. (2009). Measuring the built environment for physical activity: state of the science. *American Journal of Preventive Medicine, 36,* S99–123.e12.

Bryan, A. D., Nilsson, R., Tompkins, S. A., Magnan, R. E., Marcus, B. H., & Hutchison, K. E. (2011). The big picture of individual differences in physical activity behavior change: A transdisciplinary approach. *Psychology of Sport and Exercise, 12,* 20–26. doi:10.1016/j.psychsport.2010.05.002

Cardinal, B. J., Lee, J. Y., Kim, Y. H., Lee, H., Li, K. K., & Si, Q. (2009). Behavioral, demographic, psychosocial, and sociocultural concomitants of stage of change for physical activity behavior in a mixed-culture sample. *American Journal of Health Promotion, 23,* 274–278. doi:10.4278/ajhp.06051667

Carlson, S. A., Fulton, J. E., Schoenborn, C. A., & Loustalot, F. (2010). Trend and prevalence estimates based on the 2008 Physical Activity Guidelines for Americans. *American Journal of Preventive Medicine, 39,* 305–313. doi:10.1016/j.amepre.2010.06.006

Carroll, J. K., Lewis, B. A., Marcus, B. H., Lehman, E. B., Shaffer, M. L., & Sciamanna, C. N. (2010). Computerized tailored physical activity reports. A randomized controlled trial. *American Journal of Preventive Medicine, 39,* 148–156. doi:10.1016/j.amepre.2010.04.005

Centers for Disease Control and Prevention. (2006). Trends in strength training—United States, 1998–2004. *Morbidity and Mortality Weekly Report, 55,* 769–772.

Centers for Disease Control and Prevention. (2007). Prevalence of regular physical activity among adults—United States, 2001 and 2005. *Morbidity and Mortality Weekly Report, 56,* 1209–1212.

Christakis, N. A., & Fowler, J. H. (2007). The spread of obesity in a large social network over 32 years. *The New England Journal of Medicine, 357,* 370–379. doi:10.1056/NEJMsa066082

Christensen, K. M., Holt, J. M., & Wilson, J. F. (2010). Effects of perceived neighborhood characteristics and use of community facilities on physical activity of adults with and without disabilities. *Preventing Chronic Disease, 7*(5), A105.

Crain, A. L., Martinson, B. C., Sherwood, N., & O'Connor, P. J. (2010). The long and winding road to physical activity maintenance. *American Journal of Health Behavior, 34,* 764–775. doi:10.5993/AJHB.34.6.11

Dacey, M., Baltzell, A., & Zaichkowsky, L. (2008). Older adults' intrinsic and extrinsic motivation toward physical activity. *American Journal of Health Behavior, 32,* 570–582. doi:10.5993/AJHB.32.6.2

Dalle Grave, R., Calugi, S., Centis, E., El Ghoch, M., & Marchesini, G. (2011). Cognitive–behavioral strategies to increase the adherence to exercise in the management of obesity. *Journal of Obesity, 2011,* 11 pages. Online publication. doi:10.1155/2011/348293

Deci, E. L., & Ryan, R. M. (1985). *Intrinsic motivation and self-determination in human behavior.* New York, NY: Plenum.

Dishman, R. K. (1988). Overview. In R. Dishman (Ed.), *Exercise adherence* (pp. 1–9). Champaign, IL: Human Kinetics.

Dishman, R. K., Oldenburg, B., O'Neal, H., & Shepard, R. J. (1998). Worksite physical activity interventions. *American Journal of Preventive Medicine, 15,* 344–361. doi:10.1016/S0749-3797(98)00077-4

Donnelly, J. E., Blair, S. N., Jakicic, J. M., Manore, M. M., Rankin, J. W., Smith, B. K., & American College of Sports Medicine. (2009). American College of Sports Medicine Position Stand. Appropriate physical activity intervention strategies for weight loss and prevention of weight regain for adults. *Medicine and Science in Sports & Exercise, 41,* 459–471. doi:10.1249/MSS.0b013e3181949333

Dunn, A. L., Marcus, B. H., Kampert, J. B., Garcia, M. E., Kohl, H. W., III, & Blair, S. N. (1997). Reduction in cardiovascular disease risk factors: 6-month results from Project Active. *Preventive Medicine, 26*, 883–892. doi:10.1006/pmed.1997.0218

Dunn, A. L., Marcus, B. H., Kampert, J. B., Garcia, M. E., Kohl, H. W., III, & Blair, S. N. (1999). Comparison of lifestyle and structured interventions to increase physical activity and cardiorespiratory fitness: A randomized trial. *JAMA, 281*, 327–334. doi:10.1001/jama.281.4.327

Dunn, A. L., Trivedi, M. H., & O'Neal, H. A. (2001). Physical activity dose–response effects on outcomes of depression and anxiety. *Medicine and Science in Sports and Exercise, 33*(Suppl. 6), 587–597. doi:10.1097/00005768-200106001-00027

Dzewaltowski, D. A., Estabrooks, P. A., & Glasgow, R. E. (2004). The future of physical activity behavior change research: What is needed to improve translation of research into health promotion practice? *Exercise and Sport Sciences Reviews, 32*(2), 57–63. doi:10.1097/00003677-200404000-00004

Feltz, D. L. (1992). The nature of sport psychology. In T. S. Horn (Ed.), *Advances in sport psychology* (pp. 3–11). Champaign, IL: Human Kinetics.

Fletcher, G. F., Blair, S. N., Blumenthal, J., Caspersen, C., Chaitman, B., Epstein, S., . . . Pina, I. L. (1992). Statement on exercise: Benefits and recommendations for physical activity programs for all Americans: A statement for health professionals by the Committee on Exercise and Cardiac Rehabilitation of the Council on Clinical Cardiology, American Heart Association. *Circulation, 86*, 340–344. doi:10.1161/01.CIR.86.1.340

Friedenreich, C. M., Neilson, H. K., & Lynch, B. M. (2010). State of the epidemiological evidence on physical activity and cancer prevention. *European Journal of Cancer, 46*, 2593–2604. doi:10.1016/j.ejca.2010.07.028

Friedenreich, C. M., & Orenstein, M. R. (2002). Physical activity and cancer prevention: Etiologic evidence and biological mechanisms. *Journal of Nutrition, 132*, 3456S–3464S.

Grzywacz, J. G., & Fuqua, J. (2000). The social ecology of health: Leverage points and linkages. *Behavioral Medicine, 26*, 101–115. doi:10.1080/08964280009595758

Hillsdon, M., Thorogood, M., White, I., Foster, C., & Diamond, A. (2000). Brief negotiation vs. direct advice: A randomized controlled trial of physical activity promotion in primary care. *Medicine and Science in Sports and Exercise, 32*, S252.

Janis, I. L., & Mann, L. (1977). *Decision making: A psychological analysis of conflict, choice and commitment.* New York, NY: Free Press.

Kayman, S., Bruvold, W., & Stern, J. S. (1990). Maintenance and relapse after weight loss in women: Behavioral aspects. *The American Journal of Clinical Nutrition, 52*, 800–807.

King, A. C., Blair, S. N., Bild, D. E., Dishman, R. K., Dubbert, P. M., Marcus, B. H., . . . Yeager, K. K. (1992). Determinants of physical activity and interventions in adults. *Medicine and Science in Sports & Exercise, 24,* 221–236. doi:10.1249/00005768-199206001-00005

King, A. C., Stokols, D., Talen, E., Brassington, G. S., & Killingsworth, R. (2002). Theoretical approaches to the promotion of physical activity: Forging a transdisciplinary paradigm. *American Journal of Preventive Medicine, 23*(Suppl. 2), S15–S25. doi:10.1016/S0749-3797(02)00470-1

Kokkinos, P., & Myers, J. (2010). Exercise and physical activity: Clinical outcomes and applications. *Circulation, 122,* 1637–1648. doi:10.1161/CIRCULATIONAHA.110.948349

Levine, J. A., Lanningham-Foster, L. M., McCrady, S. K., Krizan, A. C., Olson, L. R., Kane, P. H., . . . Clark, M. M. (2005, January 28). Inter-individual variation in posture allocation: Possible role in human obesity. *Science, 307,* 584–586. doi:10.1126/science.1106561

Lloyd, K. M., & Little, D. E. (2010). Keeping women active: An examination of the impacts of self-efficacy, intrinsic motivation, and leadership on women's persistence in physical activity. *Women & Health, 50,* 652–669. doi:10.1080/03630242.2010.520250

Marcus, B. H., Banspach, S. W., Lefebvre, R. C., Rossi, J. S., Carleton, R. A., & Abrams, D. B. (1992). Using the stages of change model to increase the adoption of physical activity among community participants. *American Journal of Health Promotion, 6,* 424–429. doi:10.4278/0890-1171-6.6.424

Marcus, B. H., Bock, B. C., Pinto, B. M., Forsyth, L., Roberts, M., & Traficante, R. (1998). Efficacy of individualized, motivationally tailored physical activity intervention. *Annals of Behavioral Medicine, 20,* 174–180. doi:10.1007/BF02884958

Marcus, B. H., Ciccolo, J. T., & Sciamanna, C. N. (2009). Using electronic/computer interventions to promote physical activity. *British Journal of Sports Medicine, 43,* 102–105. doi:10.1136/bjsm.2008.053744

Marcus, B. H., Dubbert, P. M., Forsyth, L. H., McKenzie, T. L., Stone, E. J., Dunn, A. L., & Blair, S. N. (2000). Physical activity behavior change: Issues in adoption and maintenance. *Health Psychology, 19*(Suppl. 1), 32–41. doi:10.1037/0278-6133.19.Suppl1.32

Marcus, B. H., Emmons, K. M., Simkin-Silverman, L. R., Linnan, L. A., Taylor, E. R., Bock, B. C., . . . Abrams, D. B. (1998). Evaluation of motivationally tailored vs. standard self-help physical activity interventions at the workplace. *American Journal of Health Promotion, 12,* 246–253. doi:10.4278/0890-1171-12.4.246

Marcus, B. H., Lewis, B. A., Williams, D. M., Whiteley, J. A., Albrecht, A. E., Jakicic, J. M., . . . Bock, B. C. (2007). Step into Motion: A randomized trial examining the relative efficacy of Internet vs. print-based physical activity interventions. *Contemporary Clinical Trials, 28,* 737–747. doi:10.1016/j.cct.2007.04.003

Marcus, B. H., Napolitano, M. A., King, A. C., Lewis, B. A., Whiteley, J. A., Albrecht, A., . . . Papandonatos, G. D. (2007). Telephone versus print delivery of an individualized motivationally tailored physical activity intervention: Project STRIDE. *Health Psychology, 26,* 401–409. doi:10.1037/0278-6133.26.4.401

Marcus, B. H., Rakowski, W., & Rossi, J. S. (1992). Assessing motivational readiness and decision-making for exercise. *Health Psychology, 11,* 257–261. doi:10.1037/0278-6133.11.4.257

Marcus, B. H., Rossi, J. S., Selby, V. C., Niaura, R. S., & Abrams, D. B. (1992). The stages and processes of exercise adoption and maintenance in a worksite sample. *Health Psychology, 11,* 386–395. doi:10.1037/0278-6133.11.6.386

Marcus, B. H., Selby, V. C., Niaura, R. S., & Rossi, J. S. (1992). Self-efficacy and the stages of exercise behavior change. *Research Quarterly for Exercise and Sport, 63,* 60–66.

Marshall, A. L., Bauman, A. E., Owen, N., Booth, M. L., Crawford, D., & Marcus, B. H. (2003). Population-based randomized trial of a stage-based and mailed print media physical activity intervention. *Annals of Behavioral Medicine, 25,* 194–202. doi:10.1207/S15324796ABM2503_05

Marshall, A. L., Leslie, E. R., Bauman, A. E., Marcus, B. H., & Owen, N. (2003). Print versus website physical activity programs: A randomized trial. *American Journal of Preventive Medicine, 25*(2), 88–94. doi:10.1016/S0749-3797(03)00111-9

Marshall, A. L., Owen, N., & Bauman, A. E. (2004). Mediated approaches for influencing physical activity: Update of the evidence on mass media, print, telephone and website delivery of interventions. *Journal of Science and Medicine in Sport, 7*(Suppl. 1), 74–80. doi:10.1016/S1440-2440(04)80281-0

Massoudi, B. L., Olmsted, M. G., Zhang, Y., Carpenter, R. A., Barlow, C. E., & Huber, R. (2010). A web-based intervention to support increased physical activity among at-risk adults. *Journal of Biomedical Informatics, 43*(Suppl. 5), S41–S45. doi:10.1016/j.jbi.2010.07.012

McAuley, E., Blissmer, B., Katula, J., Duncan, T. E., & Mihalko, S. L. (2000). Physical activity, self-esteem, and self-efficacy relationships in older adults: A randomized controlled trial. *Annals of Behavioral Medicine, 22,* 131–139. doi:10.1007/BF02895777

Miller, W. R. (1983). Motivational interviewing with problem drinkers. *Behavioural Psychotherapy, 11,* 147–172. doi:10.1017/S0141347300006583

Miller, W. R. (1985). Motivation for treatment: A review with special emphasis on alcoholism. *Psychological Bulletin, 98,* 84–107. doi:10.1037/0033-2909.98.1.84

Miller, W. R., & Rollnick, S. (1991). *Motivational interviewing: Preparing people to change addictive behavior.* New York, NY: Guilford Press.

Napolitano, M. A., Fotheringham, M., Tate, D., Sciamanna, C., Leslie, E., Owen, N., . . . Marcus, B. H. (2003). Evaluation of an Internet-based physical activity intervention: A preliminary investigation. *Annals of Behavioral Medicine, 25*(2), 92–99. doi:10.1207/S15324796ABM2502_04

Napolitano, M. A., Papandonatos, G. D., Lewis, B. A., Whiteley, J. A., Williams, D. M., King, A. C., . . . Marcus, B. H. (2008). Mediators of physical activity behavior change: A multivariate approach. *Health Psychology, 27,* 409–418. doi:10.1037/0278-6133.27.4.409

Newton, R. U., & Galvão, D. A. (2008). Exercise in prevention and management of cancer. *Current Treatment Options in Oncology, 9,* 135–146. doi:10.1007/s11864-008-0065-1

Owen, N., Glanz, K., Sallis, J. F., & Kelder, S. H. (2006). Evidence-based approaches to dissemination and diffusion of physical activity interventions. *American Journal of Preventive Medicine, 31*(Suppl. 4), 35–44. doi:10.1016/j.amepre.2006.06.008

Paffenbarger, R. S., Hyde, R. T., Wing, A. L., Lee, I. M., Jung, D. L., & Kambert, J. B. (1993). The association of changes in physical-activity level and other lifestyle characteristics with mortality among men. *The New England Journal of Medicine, 328,* 538–545. doi:10.1056/NEJM199302253280804

Pate, R. R., Pratt, M., Blair, S. N., Haskell, W. L., Macera, C. A., Bouchard, C., . . . Wilmore, J. H. (1995). Physical activity and public health: A recommendation from the Centers for Disease Control and Prevention and the American College of Sports Medicine. *JAMA, 273,* 402–407. doi:10.1001/jama.1995.03520290054029

Pekmezi, D., Marquez, B., & Marcus-Blank, J. (2010). Health promotion in Latinos. *American Journal of Lifestyle Medicine, 4,* 151–165. doi:10.1177/1559827609351223

Peluso, M. A., & Guerra de Andrade, L. H. (2005). Physical activity and mental health: The association between exercise and mood. *Clinics* [Journal online], *60*(1), 61–70. doi:10.1590/S1807-59322005000100012

Pinto, B. M., Clark, M. M., Cruess, D. G., Szymanski, L., & Pera, V. (1999). Changes in self-efficacy and decisional balance for exercise among obese women in a weight management program. *Obesity Research, 7,* 288–292. doi:10.1002/j.1550-8528.1999.tb00408.x

Pleis, J. R., Lucas, J. W., & Ward, B. W. (2009). Summary health statistics for U.S. adults: National Health Interview Survey, 2008. *Vital and Health Statistics, Series 10 (242),* 1–157.

Prochaska, J. O., & DiClemente, C. C. (1983). Stages and processes of self-change of smoking: Toward an integrative model of change. *Journal of Consulting and Clinical Psychology, 51,* 390–395. doi:10.1037/0022-006X.51.3.390

Prochaska, J. O., DiClemente, C. C., & Norcross, J. C. (1992). In search of how people change. *American Psychologist, 47,* 1102–1114. doi:10.1037/0003-066X.47.9.1102

Prochaska, J. O., & Velicer, W. F. (1997). The transtheoretical model of health behavior change. *American Journal of Health Promotion, 12,* 38–48. doi:10.4278/0890-1171-12.1.38

Prochaska, J. O., Velicer, W. F., Rossi, J. S., Goldstein, M. G., Marcus, B. H., Rakowski, W., . . . Rossi, S. R. (1994). Stages of change and decisional balance for twelve problem behaviors. *Health Psychology, 13,* 39–46. doi:10.1037/0278-6133.13.1.39

Rhodes, R. E., Fiala, B., & Conner, M. (2009). A review and meta-analysis of affective judgments and physical activity in adult populations. *Annals of Behavioral Medicine, 38,* 180–204. doi:10.1007/s12160-009-9147-y

Rosenstock, I. M. (1974). Historical origins of the health belief model. *Health Education Monographs, 2,* 328–335.

Ryan, R. M., & Deci, E. L. (2000). Self-determination theory and the facilitation of intrinsic motivation, social development, and well-being. *American Psychologist, 55,* 68–78. doi:10.1037/0003-066X.55.1.68

Sallis, J. F., Cervero, R. B., Ascher, W., Henderson, K. A., Kraft, M. K., & Kerr, J. (2006). An ecological approach to creating active living communities. *Annual Review of Public Health, 27,* 297–322. doi:10.1146/annurev.publhealth.27.021405.102100

San Juan, A. F., Wolin, K., & Lucia, A. (2011). Physical activity and pediatric cancer survivorship. *Fortschritte der Krebsforschung. Progres Dans les Recherches Sur le Cancer [Recent Results in Cancer Research], 186,* 319–347. doi:10.1007/978-3-642-04231-7_14

Scully, D., Kremer, J., Meade, M. M., Graham, R., & Dudgeon, K. (1998). Physical exercise and psychological well being: A critical review. *British Journal of Sports Medicine, 32,* 111–120. doi:10.1136/bjsm.32.2.111

Sears, S. R., & Stanton, A. L. (2001). Expectancy-value constructs and expectancy violation as predictors of exercise adherence in previously sedentary women. *Health Psychology, 20,* 326–333. doi:10.1037/0278-6133.20.5.326

Sofi, F., Capalbo, A., Cesari, F., Abbate, R., & Gensini, G. (2008). Physical activity during leisure time and primary prevention of coronary heart disease: An updated meta-analysis of cohort studies. *European Journal of Cardiovascular Prevention and Rehabilitation, 15,* 247–257. doi:10.1097/HJR.0b013e3282f232ac

Spence, R. R., Heesch, K. C., & Brown, W. J. (2010). Exercise and cancer rehabilitation: A systematic review. *Cancer Treatment Reviews, 36,* 185–194. doi:10.1016/j.ctrv.2009.11.003

Spencer, L., Adams, T. B., Malone, S., Roy, L., & Yost, E. (2006). Applying the transtheoretical model to exercise: A systematic and comprehensive review of the literature. *Health Promotion Practice, 7,* 428–443. doi:10.1177/1524839905278900

Stetson, B. A., Beacham, A., Frommelt, S., Boutelle, K., Cole, J., Ziegler, C., & Looney, S. (2005). Exercise slips in high-risk situations and activity patterns in long-term exercisers: An application of the relapse prevention model. *Annals of Behavioral Medicine, 30,* 25–35. doi:10.1207/s15324796abm3001_4

Stokols, D. (2000). Social ecology and behavioral medicine: Implications for training, practice, and policy. *Behavioral Medicine, 26,* 129–138. doi:10.1080/08964280009595760

Stokols, D., Allen, J., & Bellingham, R. L. (1996). The social ecology of health promotion: Implications for research and practice. *American Journal of Health Promotion, 10,* 247–251. doi:10.4278/0890-1171-10.4.247

Sullum, J., Clark, M. M., & King, T. K. (2000). Predictors of exercise relapse in a college population. *Journal of American College Health, 48,* 175–180. doi:10.1080/07448480009595693

Thompson, W. G., Cook, D. A., Clark, M. M., Bardia, A., & Levine, J. A. (2007). Treatment of obesity. *Mayo Clinic Proceedings, 82,* 93–101.

U.S. Department of Health and Human Services. (2008). *2008 physical activity guidelines for Americans.* Retrieved from http://www.health.gov/paguidelines/guidelines/default.aspx#toc.

U.S. Department of Health and Human Services. (2010). *Healthy people 2010. Objectives for improving health: disability and secondary conditions* (2nd ed.). Washington, DC: USDHHS. (Original work published 2000)

U.S. Department of Health and Human Services, Centers for Disease Control & Prevention, National Center for Chronic Disease Prevention and Health Promotion. (1996). *Physical activity and health: A report of the Surgeon-General.* Retrieved from http://www.cdc.gov/nccdphp/sgr/summary.htm.

van Keulen, H. M., Mesters, I., Ausems, M., van Breukelen, G., Campbell, M., Resnicow, K., . . . de Vries, H. (2011). Tailored print communication and telephone motivational interviewing are equally successful in improving multiple lifestyle behaviors in a randomized controlled trial. *Annals of Behavioral Medicine, 41*(1), 104–118. doi:10.1007/s12160-010-9231-3

van Uffelen, J. G., Wong, J., Chau, J. Y., van der Ploeg, H. P., Riphagen, I., Gilson, N. D., . . .Brown, W. J. (2010). Occupational sitting and health risks: A systematic review. *American Journal of Preventive Medicine, 39,* 379–388. doi:10.1016/j.amepre.2010.05.024

Vogel, T., Brechat, P. H., Leprêtre, P. M., Kaltenbach, G., Berthel, M., & Lonsdorfer, J. (2009). Health benefits of physical activity: The evidence. *International Journal of Clinical Practice, 63,* 303–320. doi:10.1111/j.1742-1241.2008.01957.x

Vrazel, J., Saunders, R. P., & Wilcox, S. (2008). An overview and proposed framework of social–environmental influences on the physical-activity behavior of women. *American Journal of Health Promotion, 23,* 2–12. doi:10.4278/ajhp.06070999

Wankel, L. M. (1984). Decision-making and social support strategies for increasing exercise involvement. *Journal of Cardiac Rehabilitation, 4,* 124–135.

Wanner, M., Martin-Diener, E., Braun-Fahrländer, C., Bauer, G., & Martin, B. W. (2009). Effectiveness of active-online, an individually tailored physical activity intervention, in a real-life setting: Randomized controlled trial. *Journal of Medical Internet Research, 11*(3), e23. doi:10.2196/jmir.1179

Williams, D. M., Anderson, E. S., & Winett, R. A. (2005). A review of the outcome expectancy construct in physical activity research. *Annals of Behavioral Medicine, 29*(1), 70–79. doi:10.1207/s15324796abm2901_10

Williams, D. M., Matthews, C. E., Rutt, C., Napolitano, M. A., & Marcus, B. H. (2008). Interventions to increase walking behavior. *Medicine and Science in Sports and Exercise, 40,* S567–S573. doi:10.1249/MSS.0b013e31817c7006

David A. Dzewaltowski

Promotion of Physical Activity in Communities
Public Health Psychology of Physical Activity

9

Practice professionals, policymakers, and scientists worldwide have recognized that daily physical activity is central to decreasing the risk for chronic disease and increasing quality and years of life across the life span. The World Health Organization (WHO) recognized that physical inactivity is the fourth leading risk factor for global mortality and developed recommendations to guide efforts to promote physical activity worldwide (WHO, 2010). Healthy People 2020, a program housed within the U.S. Department of Health and Human Services (USDHHS), includes objectives for increasing the proportion of adults and children who meet current U.S. federal guidelines for aerobic physical activity and muscle-strengthening activity (USDHHS, 2010). For example, Healthy People 2020 objectives include increasing the proportion of adults who engaged in physical activity in 2008—the 44% of adults who engaged in aerobic physical activity of at least moderate intensity for at least 150 minutes per week, or of vigorous intensity for 75 minutes per week, or an equivalent

http://dx.doi.org/10.1037/14251-009
Exploring Sport and Exercise Psychology, Third Edition, J. Van Raalte and B. Brewer (Editors)

combination, and increasing the 22% of adults who performed muscle-strengthening activities on 2 or more days of the week—by 10%. These objectives are based on data from the National Health Interview Survey, which has been used to monitor health in the United States since 1957. Objective physical activity data collected by accelerometer from a representative sample in the United States suggest that the actual proportion of the population meeting the aerobic physical activity guidelines is less than 5% (Troiano et al., 2008). Goals for a 10% improvement in physical activity have been set for children and adolescents as well. The public health challenge, therefore, is to implement strategies that can successfully achieve a 10% improvement in 2008 baseline U.S. physical activity data by 2020 (USDHHS, 2010).

This chapter describes the field of public health psychology of physical activity to direct research and practice efforts toward achieving an increase in the prevalence of physical activity. A definition of public health psychology of physical activity is provided. Then an evidence-based approach to public health research and practice is described. Example intervention studies directed toward increasing physical activity using the evidence-based public health approach are summarized. This chapter concludes with a discussion of the competencies necessary for public health psychology of physical activity research and practice.

Definition of Public Health Psychology of Physical Activity

Much of the focus in the research and practice of sport and exercise psychology is about helping individuals improve their performance in sport or adherence to exercise programs. Sometimes sport and exercise psychology focuses on improving the performance of a team or exercise class. However, it is rare for sport and exercise psychology to focus on improving physical activity in communities and large populations. This may be due to the historical tradition of the field, rather than to the direction that sport and exercise psychology is moving toward in the future.

Psychologists and kinesiologists have identified the need to join in an effort to target multiple levels of influence (e.g., individuals, specific behavior settings, communities, states, national policy) to improve physical activity and public health (Dzewaltowski, 1997; Sallis & Owen, 1997; Spence & Lee, 2003). Some in psychology have proposed a new subdiscipline of psychology called *public health psychology*, which, in collaboration with other disciplines, would contribute to improving public health (Hepworth, 2004). Within kinesiology, several leaders and organizations (e.g., American College of Sports Medicine) have been influential in influencing public health physical activity guidelines and practice (e.g., Pate et al., 1995; Physical Activity Guidelines Advisory Committee, 2008).

Public health psychology of physical activity is the scientific study of human behavior that affects the physical activity of communities and the practical application of that knowledge to improve the prevalence of physical activity in targeted populations. This chapter's definition of public health psychology of physical activity draws on definitions from several related fields to identify a field that integrates research and practice. *Public health* is defined as the science of protecting and improving the health of communities through education, promotion of healthy lifestyles, and research on disease and injury prevention (Association of Schools of Public Health, 2011). Within the discipline of psychology, a focus on bringing psychology expertise to the public health issue has been viewed as including the following key elements: (a) examination of psychological processes, (b) inclusion of epidemiology methods with rigorous sampling and statistical modeling, and (c) extension of traditional psychological empirical methods to evaluate the effectiveness of interventions in public health outcomes (Wardle, 2000). Within the discipline of kinesiology, *sport and exercise psychology* has been defined as "that branch of kinesiology that involves the scientific study of human behavior in sport and exercise as well as the practical application of that knowledge in physical activity settings" (Gill, 2008, p. 7). The term *sport and exercise psychology* within kinesiology represents a behavioral science approach to human behavior in physical activity. *Physical activity* is defined as any bodily movement produced by the contraction of skeletal muscles that increases energy expenditure above a basal level (USDHHS, 1996). *Exercise* is a subcategory of physical activity that is planned, structured, and repetitive and that has a goal of improving or maintaining one or more components of physical fitness (Caspersen, Powell, & Christenson, 1985). The target behavior for public health is any physical activity in addition to exercise, which may include movement for tasks such as transportation (e.g., walking, biking) and work.

The opportunity for kinesiology within public health is to go beyond psychological processes and draw on multiple perspectives to target all levels of influence on human behavior. Although there is a strong precedent for public health psychology of physical activity, a public health approach that focuses on the population rather than the individual requires a metatheoretical shift. This shift is necessary; models of health behavior change that focus primarily on individuals in isolation are doomed to fail because they overlook powerful physical and social environmental influences.

TABLE 9.1

Focus of Public Health Psychology of Physical Activity Compared With Traditional Sport and Exercise Psychology

Target	Public health	Sport and exercise psychology
Outcomes	Population	Individual
Intervention target	Primary and secondary prevention	Treatment and prevention
Behavior	Physical activity	Exercise
Intervention level	Multilevel (policy, community, delivery setting, group, individual)	Individual or small group
Delivery agent	Typical staff/technology	PhD or master's expertise
Primary funding	Institutional support from government and private human service agencies	Private with some institutional support

Public health prevention strategies are intended to be inexpensive and often are designed to be delivered by community partner organization staff or volunteers with little academic training in behavior change or through mass media and other technology, rather than in a one-on-one setting or small group by a highly trained PhD or MS in sport and exercise psychology. Public health services are often funded by human service institutions (e.g., governmental agencies, not-for-profit foundations) rather than individual clients, because interventions are intended to affect whole populations. Key components of a public health psychology of physical activity approach are presented in Table 9.1. These components are contrasted with a sport and exercise psychology approach to interventions in terms of outcome, intervention target, behavior, intervention level, and delivery agent.

Evidence-Based Approach to Public Health Research and Practice

Implicit in public health psychology of physical activity is the adoption of an evidence-based public health approach. *Evidence-based public health* has been defined as the development, implementation, and evaluation of effective programs and policies in public health through application of principles of scientific reasoning, including systematic uses of data and information systems, and appropriate use of behavioral science theory and program planning models (Brownson, Gurney, & Land, 1999). Additional components of evidence-based public health include (a) making decisions on the basis of the best available, peer-reviewed evidence; (b) using data and information systems; (c) applying program-planning frameworks; (d) engaging the community in decision making; (e) conducting sound evaluation; and (f) disseminating what is learned (Brownson, Fielding, & Maylahn, 2009). Simply put, evidence-based public health is about helping communities integrate evidence-based interventions with their community preferences to improve the health of the population (Kohatsu, Robinson, & Torner, 2004).

The first step in evidence-based public health is to develop the best available evidence. Sallis, Owen, and Fotheringham (2000) proposed that behavioral medicine researchers and practitioners work to increase behavior change through five behavioral epidemiology phases: (a) establish links between physical activity and health, (b) develop measures of physical activity, (c) identify influences on physical activity, (d) evaluate interventions to change physical activity, and (e) translate physical activity behavior change intervention research into practice. For public health psychology of physical activity following an evidence-based public health approach, these phases may be effective in establishing the evidence for individual behavior change, but they do not highlight the larger practical public health challenge of working within communities. After the evidence for behavior change is established, public heath psychology of physical activity practitioners should help communities use local data and information systems, apply program-planning frameworks, engage in community-led decision making, conduct sound evaluation, and disseminate what is learned back to community partners to inform their future decision making.

RE-AIM Framework

One method for effectively integrating evidence-based interventions for physical activity into communities is by employing the RE-AIM (reach, efficacy, adoption, implementation, and maintenance; http://www.re-aim.org) framework (Dzewaltowski, Estabrooks, & Glasgow, 2004; Glasgow, Vogt, & Boles, 1999) in the planning and evaluation of physical activity promotion initiatives. As described in Table 9.2, the RE-AIM framework includes both individual level targets (i.e., reach, efficacy) and public health targets (i.e., adoption, implementation). Furthermore, the RE-AIM framework includes the larger goal of sustaining the delivery of intervention programs and maintaining individual behavior change over time to influence the populational prevalence of physical activity.

TABLE 9.2

RE-AIM Dimension Questions for Planning and Evaluating Public Health Physical Activity Promotion Programs

Dimension (level)	Question	Example
Reach (individual)	What percentage of the audience participated and how representative were the participants of the larger target population in the community?	What percentage of elementary school students participated in the physical activity promotion program, and were they similar in gender, ethnicity, and socioeconomic status to students enrolled at the school?
Efficacy/effectiveness (individual)	What impact did the intervention have on participants' physical activity and sedentary behavior and what were negative, unintended consequences?	Did adults attending the work site physical activity promotion program participate in more physical activity and less sedentary behavior than nonparticipants? Did their involvement help or limit their work productivity?
Adoption (setting)	What percentage of delivery settings and physical activity promotion leaders within these settings agreed to deliver the program, and how representative were they?	What percentage of 4th-grade teachers within the school district agreed to deliver the physical activity program, and were these teachers similar in years of experience to all 4th-grade teachers in the school district?
Implementation (setting)	To what extent were the critical elements of the physical activity promotion intervention implemented as intended?	Did nutrition education teachers delivering the obesity prevention program deliver both the six nutrition education lessons and the six physical activity lessons? Promotion of lessons during the fall semester?
Maintenance (setting)	To what extent did the various physical activity promotion program critical elements continue or become institutionalized or part of routine organizational practices and policies after the initial program or grant period expired?	Did the preschool program continue to offer daily physical activity sessions 6 months after the conclusion of the federal grant to prevent childhood obesity?
Maintenance (individual)	What were the effects of the promotion program on meeting physical activity guidelines for 6 or more months after completion of the intervention?	Did adults continue to meet physical activity guidelines 6 months after completing the group lifestyle intervention program?

REACH

Defined as the number or proportion of individuals in a target audience who are willing to participate in a physical activity promotion effort, *reach* also includes assessment of the representativeness of the participants relative to the target population. Physical activity programs may often be successful on a small scale in recruiting highly motivated people who may already be somewhat physically active. For example, an exercise facility at a work site may offer several structured exercise classes to 25 participants and routinely achieve 100% participation. From a small group perspective, the classes may be perceived as being successful, contributing to public health outcomes. However, programs with a broad reach are able to recruit a large percentage of the target population, especially those who are most in need (e.g., the sedentary, those of low economic status, ethnic and racial minorities). A corporate wellness program that offers 10 exercise classes to 25 people may reach 250 middle- and upper level managers but not affect the physical activity of the other 5,000 employees. Reach in this case would be only 250 out of 5,000, or 5%. A program that does not reach a representative group of the target population may actually increase physical activity disparities. For example, middle- and upper level managers may increase their physical activity, whereas no change may occur with other employees, few of whom may have been meeting public health physical activity guidelines.

EFFICACY

The impact of an intervention on physical activity, including any negative effects (e.g., injuries, body image) and economic outcomes, is considered to be the efficacy of a program. *Efficacy* is a measure of how the physical activity intervention program works under ideal conditions. In contrast, *effectiveness* is a measure of how the program works in real-world settings with local community challenges. Effective physical activity intervention programs improve physical activity in the target population in the face of community challenges, are cost-effective, and have no or minimal negative impact. Although it may be possible to increase activity with one-on-one interventions delivered by costly doctoral level experts, this type of intervention will never influence public health outcomes because community resources are not sufficient to provide them in large numbers. Furthermore, physical activity programs may be shown to have efficacy but may not be effective due to negative outcomes when delivered in a community to a representative group. For example, a program that works with most adolescent girls might adversely affect a subgroup who experience body image concerns and increased risk of developing eating disorders.

ADOPTION

The number or proportion of community settings or staff willing to initiate delivery of the physical activity promotion program represents program *adoption*. Adoption can be measured as the absolute number of settings or staff that agree to deliver the program, the percentage of settings or staff that agree to deliver the program, and the representativeness of the sample of settings and staff. Many intervention programs are designed to be delivered under ideal conditions by highly trained staff. These programs are less likely to be adopted by community settings such as schools, work sites, and fitness centers because these settings do not typically have sufficient financial resources available to implement such programs.

IMPLEMENTATION

It is necessary for staff to implement and deliver intervention programs according to protocol. *Implementation* can be assessed as delivery as intended, time for delivery, and cost. Implementation can also be examined as the target audience's use of the intervention strategies. Often programs may have efficacy under ideal conditions but are not easily implemented. It is possible that a program that is less effective in promoting physical activity under ideal conditions than another program will have greater public health impact in a community because the program can easily be adopted by settings, reach more of the target audience, and be implemented following guidelines.

MAINTENANCE

At the setting level, the extent to which a program is continued or sustained over time is an important indicator of long-term public health impact. Programs must be easily maintained. At the individual level, *maintenance* is defined as maintaining physical activity behavior change or meeting public health physical activity guidelines for more than 6 months after intervention. Experienced public health professionals often have the experience of leading an effective effort to promote physical activity only to see the program end when staff change or grant funding runs out. Although there may be initial excitement in the community due to a program's success, the actual public health impact can be small if the prevalence of physical activity in the community is not sustained.

SUMMARY

Public health psychology of physical activity seeks to increase the percentage of adults and children meeting physical activity guidelines by translating research evidence into practice. The challenge for public health psychology of physical activity practitioners is to launch proven intervention strategies in real-world settings. The practice of public health psychology of physical activity involves helping communities and organizations use limited resources to adopt and implement evidence-based policies and programs that create and sustain physical activity.

Example Studies

There are several evidence-based programs and strategies that serve as effective examples of ways to promote physical activity in communities. Each of the following examples targets primary and secondary prevention to promote physical activity. Multilevel interventions (e.g., community, school, group, individual) are used, and community members are employed as service delivery agents. The first group of example programs, involving rigorous school randomized trials, show the effectiveness of multilevel interventions in increasing physical activity when these programs implement theory-based strategies and engage the community in tailoring these strategies to unique community needs. The second group of programs address how to engage community members systematically and build their capacity to lead their public health physical activity promotional efforts. Specifically, the second group of programs define a train-the-trainer model in which the role of the public health psychology of physical activity expert is to train others to implement public health physical activity promotion initiatives.

The Lifestyle Education for Activity Program (LEAP) was designed to increase physical activity in ninth-grade girls by building the capacity of individuals already within the school to deliver the LEAP program. A group of school personnel called the LEAP team was led by a LEAP champion, who was usually a teacher for girls' physical education classes. The LEAP teams provided workshops, demonstrations, on-site training, consultation, and instructional materials to change the content of physical and health education to meet the preferences of girls and to provide a supportive school environment. Girls in intervention schools reported greater vigorous physical activity than girls in control schools (Pate et al., 2005).

The El Paso Coordinated Approach to Child Health (CATCH) used a similar staff capacity-building approach with a collaboration between public health physical activity experts and school staff. CATCH intervention schools had a smaller increase in the percentage of overweight children and children at risk for overweight than did control schools (Coleman et al., 2005).

Finally, the Trial of Activity for Adolescent Girls (TAAG) did not have positive effects when research staff played a major role in delivering the intervention in 2005. However, there was a significant increase in physical activity in 2006 when the intervention was delivered by school staff, perhaps because the program champions better tailored the programs to the unique needs of their schools, communities, and girls (Webber et al., 2008).

LEAP, El Paso CATCH, and TAAG all effectively increased physical activity and enhanced the capacity of individuals within the targeted populations to lead evidence-based intervention delivery. However, no specific protocol was used to explicitly determine how capacity building and implementation occurred. Without a specific staff training and implementation intervention protocol, there is an inability to replicate these studies and disseminate a training model. Healthy Places (Dzewaltowski et al., 2009), the YMCA after-school learning collaboratives study (Wiecha, Nelson, Roth, Glashagel, & Vaughan, 2010), Healthy Opportunities for Physical Activity and Nutrition (HOP'N) after-school (Dzewaltowski et al., 2010), and the Healthy Options for Nutrition Environments in Schools (ONES) project (Coleman, Shordon, Pomichowski, Caparosa, & Dzewaltowski, 2011) have all demonstrated promise for a research–practice intervention model. These programs differ from the first group of studies in that they specify a protocol for a staff training intervention that defines the public health psychology of physical activity experts' and other experts' contact with community members. By targeting the development of the staff training level of intervention, progress is made toward identification of a multilevel intervention that can be adopted, implemented, and sustained widely.

The Healthy Youth Places (HYP) intervention targeted increased fruit and vegetable consumption and physical activity through building the environmental change skills and efficacy of adults and youth (see Figure 9.1). HYP included a four-time yearly group training for adult school site leaders led by public health psychology of physical activity experts, environmental change skill curriculum based on social cognitive theory, and youth-led fruit and vegetable consumption and physical activity environment change teams. Sixteen schools were randomized to either implement the HYP program or not. Participants ($N = 1,582$) were assessed on fruit and vegetable consumption and physical activity and hypothesized HYP program mediators (e.g., proxy efficacy) at the end of sixth grade (baseline), seventh grade (Postintervention Year 1), and eighth grade (Postintervention Year 2). Over the 2-year intervention period, school site coordinators (similar to program champions) attended a learning community led by public health psychology of physical activity experts who then trained youth to lead evidence-based environmental change initiatives. After the intervention, HYP schools did not change in

FIGURE 9.1

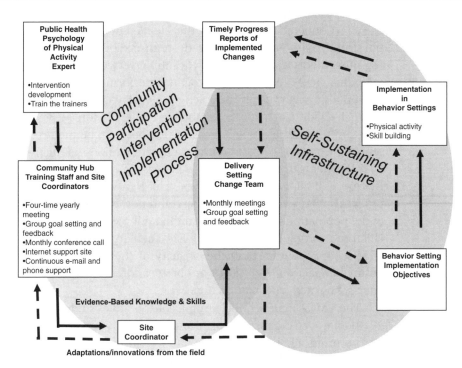

Table 9.1. Public health promotion of physical activity training model. From "Healthy Youth Places: A Randomized Controlled Trial to Determine the Effectiveness of Facilitating Adult and Youth Leaders to Promote Physical Activity and Fruit and Vegetable Consumption in Middle Schools," by D. A. Dzewaltowski, P. A. Estabrooks, G. Welk, J. Hill, G. Milliken, K. Karteroliotis, and J. A. Johnston. *Health Education Behavior, 36,* p. 587. Copyright 2009 by Sage. Adapted with permission.

fruit and vegetable consumption but did significantly change in physical activity compared with control schools. Youth proxy efficacy to influence school physical activity environments mediated the program effects. Building the skills and efficacy of adults and youth to lead school environmental change following theory-based strategies showed promise as an effective method for promoting youth physical activity (Dzewaltowski et al., 2009).

Using a similar training model, the HOP'N after-school project was a 3-year study in which after-school programs were assessed across a baseline year, randomly assigned to receive the program or to a control condition, then assessed for two subsequent intervention years (Dzewaltowski et al., 2010). HOP'N included an intervention team facilitated by public health psychology of physical activity experts who delivered a three-time yearly training for after-school staff, after-school staff who delivered daily physical activity for 30 minutes following CATCH guidelines and a daily healthful snack, and a community human services agency (Cooperative Extension) that delivered a weekly nutrition and physical activity curriculum based on an ecologically informed social cognitive theory approach (HOP'N Club). Overweight or obese children attending HOP'N after-school programs performed 5.92 minutes more moderate to vigorous physical activity per day after intervention than did such children at control sites and were offered more active recreation program time. While this increase may appear to be modest, it represents a mean change of an entire target population that likely receives health benefits from any consistent increase in caloric expenditure. Furthermore, if all overweight or obese children who attend after-school programs were exposed to the intervention, the shift in the distribution of the population would likely result in an increase in the percentage of children meeting public health physical activity guidelines. The HOP'N after-school program built the capacity of the community and had a positive impact on overweight or obese children's physical activity and after-school active recreation time.

The YMCA after-school learning collaboratives study (Wiecha et al., 2010) improved organizational infrastructure, physical environment, and staff to promote physical activity and nutrition by tailoring the break-through series (BTS) learning collaborative model for organizational change, which was initially developed by the Institute for Healthcare Improvement (2010). The BTS model is similar to the HYP and HOP'N after-school interventions in that it involves a continuous group-based learning community that works to implement evidence-based practices. The BTS model begins with the development of a set of quality practice guidelines or program outcomes. The physical activity guidelines for the YMCA study were to (a) include moderate, fun physical activity for every child every day (30-minute after-school programs, 60-minute holi-day and vacation programs); (b) include vigorous, fun physical activity as an option three times a week for 20 minutes each time; and (c) strongly encourage staff to participate in physical activity with the children. An intervention team led the organization (here the YMCA) through a data-driven decision-making model that involved collecting important bench-mark data, implementing organization and program changes, evaluating their successes to define best practices, and using these learning experiences to build new programs and practices. These program-based experiments followed a *plan, do, study, act* format. The project demonstrated initial qualitative and quantitative success (Wiecha et al., 2010). For example, weekly servings of fresh fruit and vegetables increased, and weekly servings of desserts and foods with added sugars decreased (Mozaffarian et al., 2010). For physical activity, there were greater increases in average level of physical activity and minutes of moderate and vigorous physical activity as measured by accelerometer compared with control sites (Gortmaker et al., 2012).

Another study using continuous training and the plan, do, study, act format was Healthy ONES (Coleman et al., 2011). Healthy ONES was designed to determine the effects of changing low-income public school nutrition environments and policies on child obesity. Using stakeholder input, and following a modified plan, do, study, act cycle with school staff, the morning snack recess environment in intervention schools was changed to provide a fresh fruit snack provided by cafeteria staff and served by students and to offer physical activity. A unique observation system was developed to monitor outside foods and beverages during recess. Five observations were made per semester for each recess period at each intervention and control school in the spring semester of 2008 (baseline) and the fall and spring semesters of the two following intervention years. In addition, the System for Observing Play and Leisure in Youth (SOPLAY) was used to observe the physical activity levels of students in one intervention and one control school. After baseline, control schools increased and intervention schools decreased average number of snack items per student during recess. SOPLAY results indicated that moderate to vigorous physical activity was significantly higher during recess in the intervention school (73%) than in the control school (47%). This was especially pronounced for boys (80%) as opposed to girls (43%). Therefore, modifying the elementary school recess environment by using a capacity-building intervention showed promise in the promotion of physical activity.

Healthy Places, HOP'N after-school, the YMCA after-school learning collaboratives study, and Healthy ONES all followed a specific process using public health experts to train community setting staff to attain quality outcomes to promote healthful behavior. Staff capacity was increased to use theory-based principles in the design and implementation of programs to promote physical activity. These studies illustrate that leading community change to influence the prevalence of physical activity in the population is an emerging area of study and practice for the public health psychology of physical activity.

Public Health Psychology of Physical Activity Practice

Using public health psychology of physical activity content to influence the prevalence of physical activity in a community requires that practitioners have expertise in both exercise psychology and public health. One step in creating an entry-level definition of competencies in this area has been defined by the National Society for Physical Activity Practitioners in Public Health and the American College of Sports Medicine. These organizations are working in partnership for certification in Physical Activity in Public Health Specialist (PAPHS). Certified PAPHS practitioners are able to review and provide advice on the design and implementation of physical activity initiatives. The PAPHS certification requires a bachelor's degree in a health-related field and 1,200 hours in settings that promote physical activity. Specific competencies that must be demonstrated by examination include an understanding of (a) partnerships, (b) data and scientific information, (c) interventions, (d) organizational structure, and (e) exercise science in a public health setting. Future certification at the master's and doctoral levels, perhaps for those with expertise in the psychology of physical activity (e.g., someone with a doctorate or master's degree in the area) and with knowledge of public health (e.g., with a master's degree in public health) would be well situated to move the field forward and to help communities increase the prevalence of physical activity.

Conclusion

The public health psychology of physical activity field seeks to increase the percentage of adults and children meeting physical activity guidelines by translating research evidence into practice in communities. The challenge for practitioners is to translate evidence-based intervention strategies into practice in communities with unique local challenges. Interventions that include public health psychology of physical activity experts as part of intervention training teams and that build the capacity of community members have been successful. Interventions that lead communities to use their limited resources to implement evidence-based policies and programs across numerous community settings over time can contribute to increasing populational physical activity.

References

Association of Schools of Public Health. (2011). *What is public health?* Retrieved from http://www.whatispublichealth.org/

Brownson, R. C., Fielding, J. E., & Maylahn, C. M. (2009). Evidence-based public health: A fundamental concept for public health practice.

Annual Review of Public Health, 30, 175–201. doi:10.1146/annurev. publhealth.031308.100134

Brownson, R. C., Gurney, J. G., & Land, G. H. (1999). Evidence-based decision making in public health. *Journal of Public Health Management and Practice, 5,* 86–97.

Caspersen, C. J., Powell, K. E., & Christenson, G. M. (1985). Physical activity, exercise, and physical fitness: Definitions and distinctions for health-related research. *Public Health Reports, 100,* 126–131.

Coleman, K. J., Shordon, M., Pomichowski, M. E., Caparosa, S. L., & Dzewaltowski, D. A. (2011). Decreasing unhealthy snacks and increasing physical activity during elementary morning recess. *Medicine and Science in Sports and Exercise, 43,* 24–25. doi:10.1249/01. MSS.0000402742.19945.ff

Coleman, K. J., Tiller, C. L., Sanchez, J., Heath, E. M., Sy, O., Milliken, G., & Dzewaltowski, D. A. (2005). Prevention of the epidemic increase in child risk of overweight in low-income schools: The El Paso coordinated approach to child health. *Archives of Pediatrics & Adolescent Medicine, 159,* 217–224. doi:10.1001/archpedi.159.3.217

Dzewaltowski, D. A. (1997). The ecology of physical activity and sport: Merging science and practice. *Journal of Applied Sport Psychology, 9,* 254–276. doi:10.1080/10413209708406486

Dzewaltowski, D. A., Estabrooks, P. A., Welk, G., Hill, J., Milliken, G., Karteroliotis, K., & Johnston, J. A. (2009). Healthy youth places: A randomized controlled trial to determine the effectiveness of facilitating adult and youth leaders to promote physical activity and fruit and vegetable consumption in middle schools. *Health Education & Behavior, 36,* 583–600. doi:10.1177/1090198108314619

Dzewaltowski, D. A., Estabrooks, P. A., Glasgow, R. E., (2004). The future of physical activity behavior change research: What is needed to improve translation of research into health promotion practice? *Exercise and Sport Science Reviews, 32,* 57–63.

Dzewaltowski, D. A., Rosenkranz, R. R., Geller, K. S., Coleman, K. J., Welk, G. J., Hastmann, T. J., & Milliken, G. A. (2010). HOP'N after-school project: An obesity prevention randomized controlled trial. *The International Journal of Behavioral Nutrition and Physical Activity, 7,* 90. doi:10.1186/1479-5868-7-90

Gill, D. L. (2008). *Psychological dynamics of sport and exercise* (3rd ed.). Champaign, IL: Human Kinetics.

Glasgow, R. E., Vogt, T. M., & Boles, S. M. (1999). Evaluating the public health impact of health promotion interventions: The RE-AIM framework. *American Journal of Public Health, 89,* 1322–1327.

Gortmaker, S. L., Lee, R. M., Mozaffarian, R. S., Sobal, A. M., Nelson, T. F., Roth, B. A., & Wiecha, J. L. (2012). Impact of an after-school intervention on increases in children's physical activity. *Medicine and Science in Sports and Exercise, 44,* 450–457. doi:10.1249/MSS.0b013e3182300128

Hepworth, J. (2004). Public health psychology: A conceptual and practical framework. *Journal of Health Psychology, 9,* 41–54. doi:10.1177/1359105304036101

Institute for Healthcare Improvement. (2010). *Science of improvement: How to improve?* Retrieved from http://www.ihi.org/knowledge/Pages/HowtoImprove/ScienceofImprovementHowtoImprove.aspx

Kohatsu, N. D., Robinson, J. G., & Torner, J. C. (2004). Evidence-based public health: An evolving concept. *American Journal of Preventive Medicine, 27,* 417–421.

Mozaffarian, R. S., Wiecha, J. L., Roth, B. A., Nelson, T. F., Lee, R. M., & Gortmaker, S. L. (2010). Impact of an organizational intervention designed to improve snack and beverage quality in YMCA after-school programs. *American Journal of Public Health, 100,* 925–932. doi:10.2105/AJPH.2008.158907

Pate, R. R., Pratt, M., Blair, S. N., Haskell, W. L., Macera, C. A. Bouchard, C., . . .Wilmore, J. H. (1995). Physical activity and public health. A recommendation from the Centers for Disease Control and Prevention and the American College of Sports Medicine, *Journal of the American Medical Association, 273,* 402–407.

Pate, R. R., Ward, D. S., Saunders, R. P., Felton, G., Dishman, R. K., & Dowda, M. (2005). Promotion of physical activity among high-school girls: A randomized controlled trial. *American Journal of Public Health, 95,* 1582–1587. doi:10.2105/AJPH.2004.045807

Physical Activity Guidelines Advisory Committee. (2008). *Physical Activity Guidelines Advisory Committee report.* Washington, DC: U.S. Department of Health and Human Services. Retrieved from http://www.health.gov/paguidelines/report/

Sallis, J. F., & Owen, N. (1997). Ecological models. In K. Glanz, F. M. Lewis, & B. K. Rimer (Eds.), *Health behavior and health education: Theory, research, and practice* (2nd ed., pp. 403–424). San Francisco, CA: Jossey-Bass.

Sallis, J. F., Owen, N., & Fotheringham, M. J. (2000). Behavioral epidemiology: A systematic framework to classify phases of research on health promotion and disease prevention. *Annals of Behavioral Medicine, 22,* 294–298. doi:10.1007/BF02895665

Spence, J. C., & Lee, R. E. (2003). Toward a comprehensive model of physical activity. *Psychology of Sport and Exercise, 4*(1), 7–24. doi:10.1016/S1469-0292(02)00014-6

Troiano, R. P., Berrigan, D., Dodd, K. W., Masse, L. C., Tilert, T., & McDowell, M. (2008). Physical activity in the United States measured by accelerometer. *Medicine and Science in Sports and Exercise, 40,* 181–188.

U.S. Department of Health and Human Services. (2010). *Healthy people 2020: The road ahead.* Retrieved from http://www.health.gov/healthypeople/url/

U.S. Department of Health and Human Services, Centers for Disease Control and Prevention, National Center for Chronic Disease Prevention and Health Promotion. (1996). *Physical activity and health: A report of the Surgeon General.* Retrieved from http://www.cdc.gov/nccdphp/sgr/pdf/sgrfull.pdf

Wardle, J. (2000). Public health psychology: Expanding the horizons of health psychology. *British Journal of Health Psychology, 5,* 329–336. doi:10.1348/135910700168955

Webber, L. S., Catellier, D. J., Lytle, L. A., Murray, D. M., Pratt, C. A., Young, D., . . . Pate, R. R. (2008). Promoting physical activity in middle school girls: Trial of activity for adolescent girls. *American Journal of Preventive Medicine, 34,* 173–184. doi:10.1016/j.amepre.2007.11.018

Wiecha, J. L., Nelson, T. F., Roth, B. A., Glashagel, J., & Vaughan, L. (2010). Disseminating health promotion practices in after-school programs through YMCA learning collaboratives. *American Journal of Health Promotion, 24,* 190–198. doi:10.4278/ajhp.08022216

World Health Organization. (2010). *Global recommendations on physical activity for health.* Geneva, Switzerland: WHO Press.

Kate F. Hays and Wesley E. Sime

Clinical Applications of Exercise Therapy for Mental Health

10

To those who participate regularly, the psychological benefits of exercise are readily apparent. Over the past 3 decades, a growing body of scientific evidence has shown that exercise is effective in the prevention and treatment of various psychological disorders (Folkins & Sime, 1981; Liu & Spaulding, 2010; Petruzzello, Landers, & Salazar, 1993). It is a concern, therefore, that so few therapists feel competent or comfortable using exercise as therapy or engaging in exercise or walk/talk therapy (McEntee & Halgin, 1996). However, the future holds some promise for expansion of these services as the concept of exercise therapy becomes better known and understood.

Physicians and mental health professionals often recommend exercise for their patients. It is not surprising, though, that when a physician or therapist prescribes a treatment—like exercise—without providing supervision or proper guidance, patients either do not follow through at all or do not maintain a regular program of exercise over the long term

http://dx.doi.org/10.1037/14251-010
Exploring Sport and Exercise Psychology, Third Edition, J. Van Raalte and B. Brewer (Editors)

(Goldstein et al., 1999). To achieve effective maintenance of exercise (especially among sedentary middle-aged and older adults), intensive, sustained interventions are necessary, even when prescribed by physicians. Such programs have been successful when the activities are individually prescribed and motivationally tailored to the unique history and personal life experience of each participant (Marcus et al., 1998).

In some situations, however, prescribing exercise may be counterproductive. For example, after failing to meet the goals of an exercise program, a client might feel more guilt, remorse, and a depressing sense of worthlessness than previously experienced. Exercise therapy may be difficult—or even contraindicated—whether for medical reasons or personal preference. It is therefore critical for the therapist to understand the scientific and therapeutic basis for exercise and to approach the prescription process based on a combination of research, clinical practice, and patient preference (Goodheart, Kazdin, & Sternberg, 2006).

This chapter offers recommendations for the clinical application of exercise therapy for mental health. It discusses what exercise therapy is and how it has been used effectively. Theory and research explaining the relationship between exercise and mental health are presented. Specific information is offered, indicating for whom exercise therapy is effective. The chapter concludes with practical suggestions for the clinical application of exercise therapy.

What Is Exercise Therapy, and How Has It Been Used Effectively

In order to define exercise therapy, it is important to understand each element—exercise and therapy—separately. *Exercise* is organized, focused physical activity that involves a certain amount of exertion. It is distinguished from movement, which may be random. Exercise is also distinct from organized "sport" or "sports" in being noncompetitive. It consists of either passive or active muscle exertion involving small or large areas of body muscle mass, sometimes taxing either or both anaerobic and aerobic metabolic systems. Exercise may be "prescribed," or it may include a wide variety of self-directed, enjoyable, play-type, recreational, or leisure activities, ones that are inherently satisfying or autotelic (Csikszentmihalyi, 1990). Hiking, biking, and cross-country skiing, for example, may create the opportunity to enjoy scenic vistas while enduring the physical challenge of both exertion and weather, thus assisting in the development of psychological hardiness (Dienstbier, 1991; Rejeski, Thompson, Brubaker, & Miller, 1992).

Therapy involves a set of procedures aimed at facilitating return to normal functioning in a patient or client who has experienced some form of injury, temporary disorder, or permanent disability. In the present context, therapy in its broadest form refers to treatment intended to rehabilitate or improve a client's mental or psychological functioning.

Types of Exercise Therapy

In light of these definitions, when exercise is described as therapeutic or reference is made to exercise therapy, what is meant? Three different categories can be considered: (a) exercise itself may be the central element or form of (psycho)therapy; (b) exercise may be adjunctive to psychotherapy; and (c) exercise may be the medium in which the psychotherapy occurs. In this chapter, we focus primarily on the latter two categories.

EXERCISE AS THERAPY

Exercise can be described as "therapeutic" in recognition that it is good for a person's well-being and relieves psychological distress. The most commonly researched forms of exercise in relation to well-being include rhythmic aerobic activities such as running, brisk walking, cycling, or swimming (Sachs, 1984). Less strenuous forms of exercise, such as hatha yoga, water aerobics, and qigong, may have similar positive effects on mood state (Johansson, Hassmen, & Jouper, 2008; Ross & Thomas, 2010; Wei, Kilpatrick, Naquin, & Cole, 2010). In fact, some recent studies suggest that, at least in nonclinical populations, yoga may provide more beneficial effects on mood and anxiety than metabolically matched walking (Streeter et al., 2010).

Beyond its therapeutic nature, exercise has at times been prescribed as a type of therapy. In a now-classic study comparing running with verbal therapy for the relief of depression, Greist et al. (1979) pointed out that "depressive cognitions and affect seldom emerge during running, and when they do, they are virtually impossible to maintain" (p. 45).

Although varying in quality, numerous studies have addressed the effectiveness of exercise in reducing the two most frequent mental health conditions: anxiety and depression. Blumenthal and colleagues have conducted a number of experiments in which exercise was compared with psychotropic medication among older people with moderate clinical depression (e.g., Babyak et al., 2000; Blumenthal et al., 1999; Hoffman et al., 2011). Reviews of the effect of exercise as a treatment for clinical depression regularly have indicated positive effects, although methodological limitations have also been noted (e.g., Mead et al., 2009). In a systematic review of 40 studies of patients with a chronic medical illness, exercise training significantly decreased levels of anxiety, particularly for exercise sessions of more than 30 minutes (Herring, O'Connor, & Dishman, 2010).

The therapeutic potency of exercise with a wide variety of psychopathological conditions continues to be explored, even among people with severe mental illness. In two separate, well-designed studies, for example, physical exercise improved mood and quality of life among hospitalized psychiatric patients, including those with schizophrenia (Acil, Dogan, & Dogan, 2008; Haworth & Young, 2009). A critical review of the literature noted both an increasing trend toward using exercise for patients with psychosis as well as improved mental health outcomes among those patients (Ellis, Crone, Davey, & Grogan, 2007).

Elevating exercise to the status of a specific form of therapy may have selectively important clinical utility. It can be argued that the biochemical mechanisms that occur with exercise that are *psycho*therapeutic may be similar or even superior to those underlying the effectiveness of psychotropic medications. Furthermore, some patients or clients may be averse to verbal psychotherapy or reluctant to express themselves openly. As yet, however, there is no data-based consensus as to which type of exercise would be most effective for which type of psychopathology, nor is there a specification of ideal dose or appropriate prescriber.

EXERCISE AS AN ADJUNCT TO PSYCHOTHERAPY

As information about the mental benefits of exercise proliferates, increasing numbers of psychotherapists recognize that these mental benefits may be useful to their clients. Qualitative research during the 1980s suggested that a multimodal approach, in which exercise is encouraged in conjunction with psychotherapy, might offer greater success than either intervention used alone (Sime & Sansteadt, 1987). In a study of cancer survivors, home-based, moderate intensity exercise, when added to group psychotherapy, increased patients' sense of well-being and decreased their fatigue (Courneya et al., 2003).

Results from a convenience sample of psychotherapists (Hays, 1999) indicated that psychotherapists used exercise adjunctively in the following ways: The therapist might serve as a provider of information, a supporter of its (psycho)therapeutic benefits, or a "coach" with regard to issues of exercise initiation or maintenance. Eleven years later (Hays, 2010), with different technology, a similar survey showed a fourfold increase in response rate, greater awareness of the research connections between exercise and mental health, and a consciousness among psychotherapists of the value of specific exercise recommendations for particular mental health issues or benefits.

EXERCISE DURING PSYCHOTHERAPY

Psychotherapy occurring while the therapist and client are physically active was popularized by Kostrubala (1977) at the peak of the first running boom. Although the range of types of exercise has been somewhat limited (typically, walking or running), therapists who used this method suggested markedly beneficial effects on mood, sense of well-being, and self-esteem (Hays, 1994, 1999; Johnsgard, 2004).

In an online survey of 200 psychotherapists interested in issues of exercise and mental health (Hays, 2010), approximately one fifth reported exercising with clients at selected times and for selected reasons. Two thirds of these respondents suggested exercise as valuable in initiating the "exercise habit," particularly useful for clients who are moving into the preparation or action stages of (exercise) change (Prochaska, Norcross, & DiClemente, 1995). Exercising with a client can serve as a method of in vivo desensitization (e.g., working out together at a gym), although as noted below, boundary and privacy issues need to be thoroughly addressed in public spaces. Exercise with clients can break an emotional impasse, and 40% described it as an opportunity to "bypass an impasse." Nearly half described exercise as a synergistic medium for psychotherapy that can help manage agitation, anxiety, or interpersonal tension; facilitate catharsis; or (especially with children or adolescents) develop rapport via a different relational mode. Anecdotal reports suggest that the combination of exercise and psychotherapy can lead to exploration of less conscious issues and increase the availability of affect expression, creativity, or insight. The mood improvement associated with exercise can give clients the emotional freedom to engage in cognitive restructuring (Hays, 1994). More than half of psychotherapists surveyed reported that exercise during therapy helped clients become more open in subsequent therapy. The predominant mode (80%) of exercise was walk–talk therapy. Run–talk therapy was conducted by 10%, and 40% used noncompetitive exercise, such as throwing a softball or shooting basketball hoops.

How Exercise Therapy Differs From Other Therapies

Exercise therapy has its own characteristics and demands: It is an active, as opposed to passive, treatment and one that has risks as well as benefits. Exercise therapy differs from other forms of rehabilitation in which the active ingredient is a drug, a form of radiation therapy, or a palliative physical therapy intervention such as heat, stimulation, massage, or ultrasound. During passive interventions, the client is the recipient in the process. By contrast, treatment applications using exercise engage the client actively in the treatment process, as evidenced by effort, strain, minor discomfort, and increased metabolism. To follow the exercise prescription, the client must (a) overcome inertia to initiate motion; (b) make choices regarding activity, location, and time; and (c) continue the effort, with resultant feelings of "hurts so good" as well as the sense of relief and accomplishment at completion.

Because exercise incurs a certain degree of accommodation and strain or potential discomfort, it is not surprising that exercise programs in healthy as well as clinical populations show 50% losses after 6 months (Dishman, 2003). On the other hand, all therapies are fraught with similar problems of adherence, compliance, and recidivism (DiMatteo, Giordani, Lepper, & Croghan, 2002). By following proper guidelines for clinical applications, it is possible to improve on the recidivism rate to achieve the desired psychological benefits.

Theory and Research

EPIDEMIOLOGICAL RESEARCH ON THE EFFECTS OF EXERCISE

There is clearly a significant association between exercise and several psychological measures of mental health, based on research with large populations. Among both adolescents and adults, exercise has been inversely related to anxiety, depression, hostility, and stress (Russell, 2002). The influence of exercise habits on the incidence of depression rates, in particular, is noteworthy. Clients who exercise are healthier and more emotionally stable, thus allowing a reduction in rates of suicide, the worst possible psychological outcome of depression (Craft & Perna, 2004; Paffenbarger, Lee, & Leung, 1994).

The most compelling epidemiological research supporting exercise benefits has concerned the impact of exercise in regard to age-related cognitive decline in older adults. Several research teams (Abbott et al., 2004; Larson et al., 2006) conducted cross-sectional studies each with several thousand participants (2,257 men and 1,740 men and women, respectively) and found the levels of dementia to be significantly lower among the more active populations over the age of 65. Similarly, assessment of physical activity levels in middle age was used to predict the risk of dementia 20 or more years later (Rovio et al., 2005). Those with leisure-time physical activities lasting 20 to 30 minutes and occurring at least twice per week showed significantly reduced dementia later in life (between 65 and 79 years of age), even after adjusting for sex, education, medical condition, vascular risk factors, smoking, and drinking.

Another prospective observational study reviewed both self-report and maximal oxygen uptake (VO_2 max measures) of fitness over a 6-year period among 349 individuals over age 55 years. Measures of cognitive decline were significantly associated with the level of fitness as measured by the more objective and reliable index of VO_2, but not with the self-report measures of level of activity (Barnes, Yaffe, Satariano, & Tager, 2003). The authors concluded that only aerobic levels of activity were likely reflected in the VO_2 measures; therefore, these more intense activity levels were likely associated with less diminished cognitive capacity.

The positive impact of exercise has not been uniform. For example, not all studies have found lower levels of negative affect or depression among previously sedentary community participants (Gauvin, Rejeski, Norris, & Lutes, 1997). In spite of physiological changes in fitness levels through exercise, some work site studies have noted a lack of improvement in mood state (Grønningsæter, Hyten, Skauli, & Christensen, 1992; Puetz, O'Connor, & Dishman, 2006).

CLINICAL EFFECTS OF EXERCISE THERAPY

Exercise therapy has been found to be effective with a broad spectrum of individuals, many of whom have serious mental illness (Carless & Douglas, 2008; Tetlie, Heimsnes, & Almvik, 2009; Trivedi et al., 2011). Institutionalized patients in Norway showed substantial improvements in mood and affect following an exercise program (Martinsen, 1994). Psychiatric patients randomly assigned to a running program were significantly less depressed than those assigned to nonrunning groups (Acil et al., 2008). Young adult women participating in aerobic training reported a significant decrease in depressive symptoms relative to weight lifting and control groups (Balkin, Tietjen-Smith, Caldwell, & Shen, 2007).

Others have found that the combination of exercise and talk therapy was more effective than an equivalent experience in cognitive therapy alone (i.e., the exercise was determined to be an essential element in the improvement of psychological functioning; Ellis et al., 2007; Haworth & Young, 2009; Trivedi et al., 2011). For example, Trivedi and colleagues (2011) found that exercise offered substantial benefit as an augmentation treatment for major depressive disorder in a treatment with exercise augmentation for depression study. In a well-documented research report, even modest exercise was shown to combat depression as effectively as antidepressant medication, when maintained as a regular, ongoing life activity (Babyak et al., 2000). The reduction in depression was about the same with the administration of the antidepressant or exercise, either alone or in combination. At 6-month follow-up the benefits persisted, especially for members of the exercise group who maintained this habit. Interestingly, the long-term improvements in mood were significantly greater for the group that received exercise only. In addition, there were lower depression relapse rates for the exercise-only group than for either the groups on antidepressants or those exercising in combination with antidepressants. Ironically, it appears that the concurrent use of medication with exercise may undermine the psychological benefits of exercise alone (Babyak et al., 2000; Martinsen & Stanghelle, 1997). Attributing recovery to oneself as opposed to a pill may have a sustained salutary effect (Blumenthal et al., 1999).

In general, the psychiatric community has come to view exercise as a valuable adjunct to mental health therapy (Steptoe, Kearsley, & Walters, 1993; Tetlie et al., 2009), especially in the reduction of anxiety in nonclinical populations (D. R. Brown, Morgan, & Raglin, 1993; Herring et al., 2010) and in treatment for depression (Babyak et al., 2000; Lehofer, Klebel, Gersdorf, & Zapotoczke, 1992; Ryan, 2008; Trivedi et al., 2011). Review articles (with meta-analyses) have supported the effectiveness of exercise as a part of a comprehensive treatment program, although issues with experimental design continue to be a limiting factor (Colcombe & Kramer, 2003). In one well-controlled intervention study, a cognitive behavioral stress management program was initiated while clients were in the midst of a heavy training program (rowing), with encouraging results (Perna, Antoni, Kumar, Cruess, & Schneiderman, 1998). A significant reduction in depression, fatigue, and cortisol, together with an increase in adaptation to heavy training, occurred among those receiving psychological (cognitive–behavioral) intervention along with exercise.

Although there appears to be more potential benefit than risk associated with exercise therapy, caution must be used in drawing conclusions from the accumulated available data. Multiple problems have been identified with these studies with regard to research design. That is, many researchers have conducted studies that fail to conceal randomization, lack experimental control, do not mask outcome, and use community volunteers as research participants, among other shortcomings (Lawlor & Hopker, 2001). Issues of participant adherence are especially challenging in this literature (Dishman, 2003).

Because there is ample evidence supporting the use of exercise for its psychological benefit, it is next useful to examine the possible mechanisms that account for these benefits. Exercise works. Why?

Why Is Exercise Beneficial for Mental Health

The mechanisms responsible for the mental health benefits may be physiological and/or psychological. Potential "body-based" explanations range from straightforward physiological effects (thermogenic changes) to biochemical changes in one or more of several neurotransmitters and/or receptors in the autonomic nervous system. Psychological explanations include distraction, self-esteem/self-mastery, and interpersonal relationships.

PHYSIOLOGICAL EXPLANATIONS

The Thermogenic Hypothesis

Exercise has been shown to increase tolerance for both heat and cold, thereby influencing emotional stability (Dienstbier, LaGuardia, & Wilcox, 1987; Lowry, Lightman, & Nutt, 2009). The elevation in core temperature during and after moderate to intense exercise is related to simultaneous decreases in muscle tension (deVries, Beckman, Huber, & Dieckmeir, 1968). This theory is supported by the fact that the physiological process of modulating core temperature is known to influence emotion substantially (Koltyn & Morgan, 1993). Reduction in gamma motor activity is a key physiological mechanism accounting for the reductions in muscle tension and state anxiety that occur following exercise and passive heating (Morgan, 1988). Temperature may also be related to changes in brain wave laterality, thus linking exercise to mental health (Petruzzello et al., 1993). Although temperature accounts for a small percentage of variance in anxiety and for the changes in electroencephalogram laterality, there are more direct benefits from electroencephalogram brain wave changes (Robbins, 2000). Increments in cognitive functioning have been documented through functional magnetic resonance imaging (Colcombe et al., 2004). The thermogenic hypothesis appears to be related to a reduction in anxiety, but no data are available regarding effects on depression—and it is not clear why the temperature change during exercise makes a difference.

Neurotransmitter Hypotheses

A variety of brain chemicals have been identified as contributing to the interaction of exercise and mental health. Recent research suggests that exercise raises or adjusts serotonin, dopamine, and norepinephrine, as well as having an impact on chemicals (e.g., brain-derived neurotrophic factor [BDNF]; insulin-like growth factor; vascular endothelial growth factor [VEGF]; fibroblast growth factor-2) that allow for the construction of new connections and neurons (Johnsgard, 2004; Ratey, 2008).

The most popular description of neurotransmitter effects relates to endorphins. Lobstein and Rasmussen (1991) found that endurance training changed resting plasma beta-endorphins and improved nonclinical depression in healthy middle-aged men. Daniel, Martin, and

Carter (1992) used naltrexone, the opiate receptor antagonist, and a placebo in a randomized double-blind crossover design to demonstrate that high-intensity exercise reduced levels of depression. When naltrexone was given before the exercise (to neutralize endorphins), there was no change in level of depression, thus supporting the endorphin hypothesis. An increase in endorphin levels is also associated with a reduction in stress reactivity effects (McCubbin, Cheung, Montgomery, Bulbulian, & Wilson, 1992) and with reduced sensitivity to pain (Haier, Quaid, & Mills, 1981). Although this theory is an interesting explanation for exercise beneficence, considerable controversy continues, particularly regarding the challenge of measuring brain endorphins.

Deficiencies in norepinephrine and serotonin systems are associated with the onset of depression and anxiety (Johnsgard, 2004). Adaptive changes in serotonin receptor functioning appear to play an important role in mediating the action of various antidepressant medications (Dey, 1994; Dey, Singh, & Dey, 1992). Exercise increases the sensitivity of serotonin receptors, making these naturally produced chemicals more potent in reducing depression. The role of exercise in decreasing sympathetic and increasing parasympathetic activity is also associated with a simultaneous improvement in emotional stability (Perna et al., 1998).

BDNF is one of a family of brain proteins designed to build and maintain the infrastructure of the brain itself (Ratey, 2008), particularly in the hippocampus (Mata, Thompson, & Gotlib, 2010). This chemical is thought to protect against stress-induced neuronal damage; it has also been shown to be a mediator or moderator in reducing depressive symptoms (Gomez-Pinilla, Vaynman, & Ying, 2008; Vaynman, Ying, & Gomez-Pinilla, 2004). BDNF appears directly related to learning, whether in terms of rate of learning or retention. Aerobic exercise increases BDNF production. It has been described as "a crucial biological link between thought, emotions, and movement" (Ratey, 2008, p. 40).

Gamma-aminobutyric acid (GABA) is another factor being considered as an explanation for the positive effect of exercise on mood and tension (Berchtold, Kesslak, & Cotman, 2002; Streeter et al., 2010). GABA helps to regulate nerve activity, thereby reducing mood and anxiety disorders. A further transmitter being explored with regard to its role in relation to exercise and mental health is VEGF (Vaynman et al., 2004).

PSYCHOLOGICAL EXPLANATIONS

A number of psychological explanations may account for the "affective beneficence" (Morgan, 1985) of exercise. A meta-analytic review of the effects of exercise on mood state among elderly people, for example, found that exercise was associated with both enhanced positive mood and reduced negative mood (Arent, Landers, & Etnier, 2000).

In a meta-analysis of controlled studies of the effects of exercise on self-esteem and physical self-perception, 78% of the studies noted positive changes in some aspects of physical self-esteem or self-concept (Fox, 2000). In clinical research, after a 16-week aerobic exercise training program, subjects with major depression showed significantly improved self-esteem, equivalent to that obtained with medication or a combination of exercise and medication (Blumenthal et al., 1999).

Exercise has also been associated with decreases in stress reactivity. Exercise may be experienced as a coping strategy (e.g., "time out"), and it may be an "inoculator" that can assist people in responding more effectively to psychosocial stressors (Landers & Arent, 2001).

The regulation of social distance through exercise can be an important psychological contributor as well. People who are clinically depressed often decrease contact with others. Exercise that involves interaction with others may be a way of decreasing social isolation, whether that social support is the necessary ingredient or the mediator of other factors (Dunn, Trivedi, & O'Neal, 2001). Other people, especially women overwhelmed by "people demands," may find that exercise justifies being intentionally alone, providing the opportunity for reflection, self-nurturance, or differentiation (Hays, 1999).

INTERACTIVE EXPLANATIONS

There is no one answer to the question of why exercise is beneficial to mental health; for any particular individual, exercise may have a combination of effects. Noting his improved mood with exercise, for example, a depressed man may begin feeling more hopeful. Claiming "legitimate" time to herself for exercise may embolden a woman with low self-esteem to assert herself at work. A woman who uses the diaphragmatic breathing that she learned through yoga class to stave off panic attacks may come to feel more in control of her mind and body. Much research remains to be done to understand the Homeric principle of a "sound mind in a sound body."

Optimal Types of Exercise for Mental Health Benefits

Given that exercise is beneficial for mental health, what is most helpful and for whom? How much exercise, to feel how much better? Are there short-term positive effects as well as benefits that accrue only if exercise is continued over the long term? Many variables can be considered, such as type of exercise: frequency, intensity, and time (duration); the appropriate exercise parameters in regard to specific levels of mental health or illness; and the dose–response interaction.

Aerobic activities such as running and swimming compare favorably with anaerobic (strength-training) exercise (Folkins & Sime, 1981), although yoga, water aerobics, and qigong have the same potential for mental health benefits (Berger & Owen, 1992; Bing, Kilpatrick, Naquin, & Cole, 2010; Johansson et al., 2008; Ross & Thomas, 2010; Streeter et al., 2010). Other studies note that benefits from weight training in reducing anxiety, depression, and hostility are high (Ströhle, 2009).

Hansen, Stevens, and Coast (2001) compared acute (i.e., immediate) effects of three different bouts of exercise on mood states among female college students. Vigor improved, while fatigue decreased, after just 10 minutes of bicycle ergometer exercise. In a landmark study addressing the dose–response relationship of exercise in relation to clinical depression, Dunn, Trivedi, Kampert, Clark, and Chambliss (2005) compared the effects of exercise of differing intensity and duration. Over 12 weeks, they found that exercise intensity (7.0 kcal/kg/week vs. 17.5 kcal/kg/week) but not frequency (3 days/week vs. 5 days/week) resulted in decreases in depression rating among the exercise participants. This suggests that a greater intensity of exercise and frequency of at least three sessions per week may be most beneficial in decreasing mild to moderate clinical depression.

A comparison of antidepressant medication and exercise with regard to depression showed that exercise was as effective as medication in decreasing moderate clinical depression in an elderly community sample. At 10-month follow-up, the exercise group showed better long-term continuation of benefits and lower recidivism rates than did the medication group (Babyak et al., 2000). Similarly, college students who had been exercising independently for more than 6 months demonstrated higher intrinsic motivation and well-being than those exercising for less than 6 months (Maltby & Day, 2001).

Berger (1994) developed a taxonomy to describe relevant types of physical activity most likely to result in positive mental benefits. She concluded that the four primary components are exercise that involves abdominal, rhythmical breathing; the absence of interpersonal competition; a closed or predictable environment; and repetitive and rhythmical movement. At least among nonclinical populations, research supports the mental benefits of nonaerobic and less strenuous exercise, if it includes abdominal, rhythmical breathing (e.g., Berger & Owen, 1992; Bing et al., 2010; Johansson et al., 2008; Ross & Thomas, 2010).

Some research advocates the benefit of one or another type of exercise. Overall, personal preference and enjoyment of the activity may be the critical factor for mental health benefit, rather than any single modality of exertion (Wankel, 1993). At present it appears that Berger's (1994) taxonomy is a helpful guide and that for mental benefit exercise should be a minimum of three times per week, of moderate intensity, of at least 20 minutes duration, and developed as a life habit.

Particular Populations That Benefit From Exercise Therapy

DEPRESSION, ANXIETY, LOW SELF-ESTEEM, AND EATING DISORDERS

Clients with mild to moderate depression are good candidates for treatment with exercise, whether independently or in conjunction with psychotherapy or medication. Exercise initiation may be challenging, however, as many patients have difficulty overcoming the inertia associated with depression. Feedback from depressed clients who have successfully started exercising indicates that it is useful for practitioners to help clients to find a fitness center or other appropriate place to exercise; set goals; identify and modify negative thinking; and provide personal support, encouragement, and accountability (Seime & Vickers, 2006).

Exercise therapy is also an effective treatment for patients suffering from various forms of anxiety disorders (e.g., test anxiety, social phobia, panic attack). Exercise can serve as a means of interoceptive exposure (Antony, 2011) that brings about some of the physical sensations of panic attack in a controlled environment, allowing clients with panic disorders to reinterpret their symptoms in a constructive manner (Orwin, 1973).

The complex interaction of body image, self-esteem, and weight management suggests that exercise recommendations need to take into account a variety of socialized perceptions before exercise recommendations are confirmed, particularly for those with low self-esteem, body issues, or eating disorders (Furnham, Badmin, & Sneade, 2002; Martin, Sinden, & Fleming, 2000). On the one hand, exercise may be an active and effective treatment, for example with binge eating disorder (Levine, Marcus, & Moulton, 1996). On the other hand, exercise itself is sometimes used as a method of restriction in anorexia or purging in bulimia (Peñas-Lledó, Vaz Leal, & Waller, 2002). Paying attention to the role of gender socialization and cognition in designing, recommending, or implementing programs is a useful strategy (Martin Ginis, Burke, & Gauvin, 2007).

SPECIAL POPULATIONS IN NEED OF EXERCISE THERAPY

Three other populations deserve special attention in regard to exercise therapy: young adults, older people, and those with disabilities. Given the developmental adaptations that young adults face, many are especially vulnerable to anxiety, depression, and low self-esteem. Aerobic exercise (running) was shown to be an efficacious treatment with psychiatric institutionalized adolescents (S. W. Brown, Welsh, Labbe, Gitulli, & Kulkarni, 1992; Carless & Douglas, 2008; Tetlie et al., 2009) as well as with outpatient clients (Norris, Carroll, & Cochrane, 1992). Reductions were seen in depression, anxiety, hostility, confused thinking, and fatigue. Adolescents and adults with diagnoses of hyperactivity or attention-deficit disorder also should be good candidates for exercise therapy (Shipman, 1984).

With an aging population, increasingly, research has been conducted regarding both the cognitive and affective benefits of exercise among older people. In a meta-analysis, Colcombe and Kramer (2003) reviewed 18 studies from 1996 to 2001 of participants ages 55 to 80. Introduction of a fitness program resulted in positive effects on cognition, especially for executive control, that is, planning, scheduling, working memory, and multitasking. Even better results were obtained when strength and flexibility exercises were added to the aerobic activities for these participants. Exercise periods longer than 30 minutes were more effective than those of shorter duration in increasing the volume of gray matter, as measured by magnetic resonance imaging. These findings were corroborated in a more recent study (Erickson et al., 2010) indicating that elderly community dwellers who walked 4 miles per week showed a twofold benefit in gray matter volume compared with those with less physical activity; this in turn was associated with a reduced risk of cognitive impairment.

The research on exercise in older people is especially relevant with regard to women, who, on average, live longer than men, are twice as likely to be diagnosed with depression, and are more likely to be treated for depression through pharmacology. The inclusion of regular physical activity is likely to prevent, reduce, or ameliorate cognitive and emotional (as well as physical) decline (Erickson et al., 2007; Wilson, Arnold, Schneider, Li, & Bennett, 2007) through the complex interaction of hormonal changes, depression, chronic stress, and exercise.

Maintenance or improvement in cognitive functioning can be useful in three interactive ways: intellectual processing, social interaction, and physical activity (Hertzog, Kramer, Wilson, & Lindenberger, 2008). The synaptic plasticity brought on by exercise builds brain health; improves the ability to learn and remember; and has been shown to reduce both depression and inflammation, which are causal factors in neurodegeneration associated with aging (Cotman, Berchtold, & Christie, 2007). Furthermore, when exercise is introduced to help reduce pulmonary symptoms, there is a notable improvement in overall cognitive function (Emery, Shermer, Hauck, Hsiao, & MacIntyre, 2003). A meta-analysis involving more than 2,000 subjects in 30 separate trials showed that exercise increased fitness, physical function, cognitive function, and positive behavior in those who already had some dementia and other cognitive impairments (Heyn, Abreu, & Ottenbacher, 2004).

People with disabilities also benefit psychologically from exercise programs (Shephard, 1991). Wheelchair-bound students, for example, who were able to exercise on an arm crank bicycle ergometer showed a significant decrease in anxiety (D. R. Brown et al., 1993). The development of equipment initially designed for road races and elite sports featuring highly skilled wheelchair athletes may serve as a precedent for creating more opportunities for housebound people with paraplegia.

The populations that might benefit the most from exercise therapy have been identified, and the practical applications of exercise therapy in a clinical setting are now considered.

Recommendations for the Clinical Application of Exercise Therapy

How might exercise therapy be incorporated into one's clinical practice? The recommendations that follow should be tailored to (a) the practitioner's level and type of training, especially in regard to exercise sciences; (b) local practices and practice regulations; and (c) client interest and preference. It will be useful to keep in mind the varieties of exercise therapy noted above (i.e., exercise as therapy, exercise as adjunct to psychotherapy, and exercise during psychotherapy).

1. In taking the client's history, include questions about current exercise habits. Find out what the client does regularly in work or leisure that might be conducive to the addition of more vigorous activity (e.g., if the job requires trips to different floors in the building, consider taking the stairs instead of the elevator). Then begin to explore both positive and negative past experiences: Identify or increase opportunities for positive experiences with exercise and problem-solve regarding obstacles to activity. Exercise that is experienced as enjoyable is critical to the long-term continuation of an exercise program (Wankel, 1993).

2. During one of the early counseling sessions, suggest to the client that it might be interesting and enjoyable to continue talking while going for a walk in the nearby vicinity. As noted above, walking during therapy can have many benefits. The duration of this initial walk/talk might be 10 to 20 minutes, depending on the condition of the client and on the attractive elements of the environment versus its distracting qualities. If walking in this setting tends to facilitate the client's interaction, then continue as long as possible. However, if the walk in this setting tends to be intimidating or distracting to the client, then return to the counseling office after a short while.

3. Explain to the client that the purpose of the walk/talk is to demonstrate the invigorating aspects of exercise and the refreshing aspects of recovery from exercise. You also can give the client a brief explanation of the reasons (theories) underlying the potential benefits of exercise, noting the aesthetic and kinesthetic experiences associated with movement as well as the synergistic effects. You can encourage the client to self-rate mood on a 1-to-10 scale both before and after the walk/talk time. Experientially, the client may come to a better understanding of the mood-altering benefits of the activity.

4. Use the walking experience as an opportunity for greater emotional–cognitive catharsis on the part of the client. The exercise can be considered as a catalyst to help clear the clutter and to free associate to achieve dreamlike thinking that is ordinarily ignored. In addition, it can be viewed as an opportunity for introspection and the creation of more lucid thinking. Note the ways the client responds to this rationale and note the questions or comments he or she volunteers in the midst of walking conversation. For some clients, side-by-side conversation (in contrast to face-to-face therapy) seems to elicit more candor; the movement, together with the informal nature of the activity, seems to break down barriers and to facilitate greater emotional release (Kendzierski & Johnson, 1993). Note that the most intense exercise (e.g., marathon running) is, in fact, associated with much greater candor and catharsis and more dramatic changes in cognitive orientation than one would ordinarily see in walk/talk therapy (Acevedo, Dzewaltowski, Gill, & Noble, 1992). Selectively, therapist and client may choose to run together during therapy (Hays, 1994). However, most therapists and most clients are not prepared for such vigorous activity during therapy.

5. Recognize individual differences in ability and motivation. Not every client is endowed with a burning desire to begin or stay

involved in exercise, nor do all clients see physical activity as the province of psychotherapy. Some clients may be unwilling to try this approach with you but may be willing to try exercising on their own. A good-quality pedometer can be an excellent method for self-reinforcement. Sometimes clients respond to stories about other people who have overcome their problems by exercising. Kenneth Cooper, the physician who invented the term *aerobics,* told the story of a man with heart disease who was so despondent that he wanted to die. Because his heart was weak, he decided, logically, that the best way to commit suicide without embarrassing his family would be to run around the block as fast as he could until he killed himself. After several futile attempts at causing a fatal heart attack in this manner, he discovered to his surprise that he was beginning to feel better. Eventually, he chose to live instead of to die.

6. Take advantage of environmental factors as natural reinforcers: Encourage the client to walk on the beach, over hills, through wooded areas, and down streets to make exercise more pleasurable. In bad weather, the client might exercise in an enclosed stairway, in a mall, or at home. Dealing with excuses is a critical issue (Kendzierski & Johnson, 1993). Encourage the client to obtain comfortable and attractive clothing (shorts, sweats, shoes) gradually as rewards or added incentives for the accomplishment of continuing the exercise program. Help the client notice that wearing comfortable, casual clothing makes it easier to include exercise as a natural part of daily activities of living (Fahlberg, Fahlberg, & Gates, 1992). The accompaniment of a favored radio show or iPod mix may serve as further incentive (Plante, Gustafson, Brecht, Imberi, & Sanchez, 2011).

7. Consider options to make exercise functional, especially when the client cannot afford home exercise equipment or health club membership fees. Cost-effective exercise options include commuting to and from work by walking, jogging, or biking; hiking to a remote scenic area; or doing hard physical work (shoveling snow, moving cartons, or doing lawn/gardening work). Commuting exercise is perhaps the most functional because it contains the inherent rewards of saving money otherwise spent on bus fare, gas, or parking and may appeal to the client's "green" consciousness. If the commuting distance is not reasonable for biking or jogging, the client might take a bus or other form of mass transportation one way and drive partway, thus saving on parking and avoiding traffic congestion.

8. Have clients consider a broad spectrum of activities. Some may involve socializing with others; some may be physically

challenging, requiring conditioning for full enjoyment. Older, retired adults, for example, may train for handling the physical demands of social or square dancing by walking or climbing stairs. If a client complains that one form of exercise is uncomfortable, urge him or her to switch to other parallel activities. The multiple station workout (e.g., alternating between stationary bicycle, rowing machine, mini-tramp, stair climber) is helpful in avoiding boredom and fatigue localized to one muscle area. During home exercise, radio, television, or iPod can relieve boredom or serve as immediate reinforcement for having started the exercise program for that day. For some clients, the music or TV used in health club programs may serve as an essential distractor or motivator.

9. Set standards for frequency, intensity, and duration on the basis of level of conditioning, tolerance for discomfort, and length of time since beginning the exercise program. Your own skill set may include exercise physiology or knowledge of motivational principles. If so, help the client set reasonable goals and be prepared to adjust the workload (e.g., to increase the frequency, intensity, or duration as needed). If you are not trained or experienced in exercise physiology, it is advisable to seek the assistance of a local specialist who can supervise the ongoing prescription process. Above all, be aware of the risks of too much activity at one extreme and the lack of benefit with too little exercise at the other.

10. Facilitate social supports for exercise. Initially, try to facilitate activities that bring the client into positive interaction with others while also gaining benefits from exercise. Be aware that this may—or may not—include friends and family. If friends and family offer little support or actually disdain exercise, the client will have a bigger hurdle to overcome in maintaining exercise. Also consider encouraging the client to exercise as a role model for his or her children or another family member.

11. Help the client set up self-behavior modification strategies to reinforce the activity. For example, the client might form a pact with you whereby he or she will watch TV only when exercising on a bicycle ergometer, mini-trampoline, stair-stepper, or treadmill. Alternatively, the client might agree to not watch more than 1 hour of TV without engaging in at least 10 to 20 minutes of exercise. The TV becomes the reinforcer for the exercise behavior, in a self-generated behavior modification system. Set up a log and a system of accountability for the client so he or she can review progress in accomplishments (e.g., distance walked; consecutive days; changes in mood, alertness,

and fatigue; relief from joint or muscle pain). The system of record keeping can provide reinforcement for success in continuing the training regime and in discovering the correlation with psychological changes that might occur.

12. Anticipate recidivism and let the client know that it is likely to occur. Nearly everyone who engages in exercise will also experience periodic lapses from exercise due to job, family, illness, injury, or changes in routine. Planning ahead serves to defuse the devastating effects of failure (i.e., guilt, remorse, low self-esteem). Help clients anticipate the problem, plan for the adjustment, and welcome the return to activity following a lapse. To prevent future relapse, seek to identify the client's immediate rewards for exercise. They may include (a) a break from the hassles of the day; (b) an opportunity to enjoy the outdoors; (c) a chance to talk with you, or with a friend, about problems; (d) the refreshing sensation of the cool air or warm shower, depending on the existing weather conditions; and (e) a pleasant and satisfying meal or the fluid replacement of a favorite nonalcoholic drink.

13. Evaluate progress in mood state and overall state of well-being. Several psychological scales or inventories offer a snapshot of current functioning, such as (a) the Profile of Mood States (McNair, Lorr, & Droppleman, 1971), (b) the Beck Depression Inventory (Beck, Ward, Mendelson, Mock, & Erbaugh, 1961), (c) the State–Trait Anxiety Scale (Spielberger, 1983), and (d) the Tennessee Self-Concept Scale (Fitts, 1964). Clients can keep a log of relevant health habits: They may become aware of positive and reinforcing changes, such as more rapid sleep onset and more restful, nightlong sleep patterns (Bliwise, King, Harris, & Haskell, 1992). Fluids and healthy foods such as fruits and vegetables may taste better following a vigorous bout of exercise, a shower, and an extended recovery period. These aesthetic rewards of exercise can be powerful immediate reinforcers.

    Research on participants' prediction of enjoyment of exercise (i.e., yoga, Pilates, weight training, aerobic exercise) noted that they routinely underestimated enjoyment (Ruby, Dunn, Perrino, Gillis, & Viel, 2011). This "affective forecasting bias" may occur if people focus on the beginning of a workout, which may feel effortful or unpleasant. A "meditational model" addressing expectations of overall enjoyment may result in increased intention to exercise. Reviewing clients' progress at 2- to 4-week intervals can allow for refocus, reframing, and redirection, if needed.

14. Follow ethical practices involving responsibility to and communication with other health care professionals. It is important

to obtain medical clearance for exercise and to establish regular communication with other health care professionals (e.g., primary physician, physical therapist, psychiatrist, counselor) regarding progress and concerns. Observe other ethical guidelines per professional licensing requirements. Maintain clearly established boundaries. Remember, as the therapist, your responsibility is to get clients to start exercising and set well-founded goals, to participate with them on occasion during the counseling session while maintaining strict ethical boundaries, and to highlight the potential benefits of exercise to the client. You are not, however, responsible for clients' motivation or their personal social agenda.

Be certain that you are able to articulate your purposes and your methods. Because some of these activities may be outside of the traditional in-office focus on the psyche, risk management suggests that practitioners should be knowledgeable about the types, use, and benefits of physical activity to mental health.

Contraindications and Pitfalls to Be Avoided in Exercise Therapy

The issues detailed here should be seriously considered, to avoid frustration and disappointment with difficult client problems—and to aid in the prevention of unwarranted lawsuits.

1. Don't expect everyone to appreciate the benefits of exercise. Many happy, healthy, well-functioning individuals with no mental health problems do not exercise in a manner that fits the definition of vigorous exercise; some individuals seem to be "allergic" to activity and may never develop an appreciation for the benefits of exercise.
2. Don't expect the program to supersede other lifestyle patterns. Sometimes, no matter how much brainstorming you do with a client, exercise will not fit into his or her life at this time. Relevant tools from motivational interviewing (Miller & Rollnick, 2002) or the transtheoretical model (Prochaska et al., 1995) may be helpful—if not now, then at a later time.
3. Some clients may expect rapid changes in how they feel soon after the onset of activity. Help them appreciate the aesthetic aspects of the activity at the beginning and gradually increase

the prescriptive workload to achieve a reasonable physiological training effect, as well as enduring mood elevation. This is especially important for treating depression. Be aware that, for most people, the antianxiety effects of exercise last 2 to 4 hours and the antidepressant effects for 12 to 24 hours. With this prescriptive information in mind, for anxiety you should recommend exercise (of shorter duration and lower intensity) at frequent intervals throughout the day. For depression, exercising daily but with somewhat greater intensity should be effective. You can encourage your client to maintain a record indicating the amount and duration of impact on symptoms.

4. Some clients will take exercise to an extreme the same way that they have behaved with other life experiences (e.g., workaholic, alcoholic). Other personality variables, such as the Type A behavior pattern, have been associated with overdoing the exercise prescription, due to poor perception of appropriate exercise intensity (Hassmen, Stähl, & Borg, 1993). Be cautious in the use of exercise for clients with eating disorders. Exercise may produce more opiatelike endorphins than the client can handle, which can be addictive. Purging via exercise is one form of bulimia.

5. Do not let the exercise prescription preclude the need for traditional psychotherapy. Some clients tend to avoid the real problem; exercise can be a risky substitute for necessary counseling about other issues not resolved by exercise. Remember that, like medication, exercise is generally a method of obtaining immediate (and temporary) symptom relief. As such, medication and exercise both allow the person to get through a particularly difficult period of pain or discomfort (either physical or emotional), after which time insight-oriented or problem-solving counseling may be needed to prevent escalating problems.

6. Treatment with exercise can create risks, in spite of the therapeutic intention. Outdoor activity (walking or running) amidst vehicular traffic can be a problem if the therapist or client does not maintain awareness of his or her surroundings. Parks and trails are not always easily accessible from clinical offices. In addition, a client could use the exercise intervention as a way to avoid emotional content rather than confront or embrace it. Some clients may not recognize the professional boundaries of the client–therapist relationship. The change of venue implies a boundary crossing; privacy and confidentiality may need to be addressed beforehand. It is important to make sure that the exercise circumstances uphold professionalism in the form of clothing, behavior, physical contact, transference, and consent

(Hays, 1994). Documentation, consultation, and recognition of individual differences mean that adjustments may well need to be made with each client.

Conclusion

In this chapter, exercise has been considered as a viable, adjunctive therapy in the treatment of a broad array of psychological disorders as well as other medical disorders with underlying psychological etiology. Evidence has been presented supporting the effectiveness of various modalities of exercise treatment among diverse populations across a wide range of disorders. Although most of the evidence is positive in regard to exercise, the exact mechanism of beneficence (cognitive or physiological) is not completely understood. The dosage of exercise needed to achieve benefits may differ greatly across individuals; the type of exercise prescribed should take personal preference and accessibility (opportunity to be active) into account as the primary determinants.

The benefits of exercise will occur only if clients find a way to become actively involved in vigorous motion as often as possible with as much enjoyment and satisfaction as possible. In addition, for some clients it seems desirable that some parts of an exercise program be functional, that is, that the product of the activity be rewarding (e.g., commuting to work, chopping wood, dancing, hiking in a scenic area). A number of recommendations, contraindications, and concerns have been noted. The exercise therapist is encouraged to be bold in the use of innovative strategies but cautious where there are extenuating circumstances that might be risky for the client.

References

Abbott, R. D., White, L. R., Ross, G. W., Masaki, K. H., Curb, J. D., & Petrovitch, H. (2004). Walking and dementia in physically capable elderly men. *Journal of the American Medical Association, 292,* 1447–1453. doi:10.1001/jama.292.12.1447

Acevedo, E., Dzewaltowski, D., Gill, D., & Noble, J. (1992). Cognitive orientations of ultramarathoners. *The Sport Psychologist, 6,* 242–252.

Acil, A. A., Dogan, S., & Dogan, O. (2008). The effects of physical exercises to mental state and quality of life in patients with schizophrenia. *Journal of Psychiatric and Mental Health Nursing, 15,* 808–815. doi:10.1111/j.1365-2850.2008.01317.x

Antony, M. M. (2011). Recent advances in the treatment of anxiety disorders. *Canadian Psychology/Psychologie canadienne, 52,* 1–9. doi:10.1037/a0022237

Arent, S. M., Landers, D. M., & Etnier, L. L. (2000). The effects of exercise on mood in older adults: A meta-analytic review. *Journal of Aging and Physical Activity, 8,* 407–430.

Babyak, M., Blumenthal, J. A., Herman, S., Khatri, P., Doraiswamy, M., Moore, K., & Ranga Krishnan, K. (2000). Exercise treatment for major depression: Maintenance of therapeutic benefit at 10 months. *Psychosomatic Medicine, 62,* 633–638.

Balkin, R. S., Tietjen-Smith, T., Caldwell, C., & Shen, Y.-P. (2007). The utilization of exercise to decrease depressive symptoms in young adult women. *AdultSpan Journal, 6,* 30–35. doi:10.1002/j.2161-0029.2007.tb00027.x

Barnes, D. E., Yaffe, K., Satariano, W. A., & Tager, I. B. (2003). A longitudinal study of cardiorespiratory fitness and cognitive function in healthy older adults. *Journal of the American Geriatrics Society, 51,* 459–465. doi:10.1046/j.1532-5415.2003.51153.x

Beck, A. T., Ward, C. H., Mendelson, M., Mock, J., & Erbaugh, J. (1961). An inventory for measuring depression. *Archives of General Psychiatry, 4,* 561–571. doi:10.1001/archpsyc.1961.01710120031004

Berchtold, N. C., Kesslak, J. P., & Cotman, C. W. (2002). Hippocampal brain-derived neurotrophic factor gene regulation by exercise and the medial septum. *Journal of Neuroscience Research, 68,* 511–521. doi:10.1002/jnr.10256

Berger, B. G. (1994). Coping with stress: The effectiveness of exercise and other techniques. *Quest, 46,* 100–119. doi:10.1080/00336297.1994.10484112

Berger, B. G., & Owen, D. R. (1992). Mood alteration with yoga and swimming: Aerobic exercise may not be necessary. *Perceptual and Motor Skills, 75,* 1331–1343. doi:10.2466/pms.1992.75.3f.1331

Bing, W., Kilpatrick, M., Naquin, M., & Cole, D. (2010). Psychological perceptions to walking, water aerobics and yoga in college students. *American Journal of Health Studies, 21,* 142–147.

Bliwise, D. L., King, A., Harris, R., & Haskell, W. (1992). Prevalence of self-reported poor sleep in a healthy population aged 50 to 65. *Social Science & Medicine, 34*(1), 49–55. doi:10.1016/0277-9536(92)90066-Y

Blumenthal, J. A., Babyak, M. A., Moore, K. A., Craighead, W. E., Herman, S., Khatri, P., & Krishman, R. (1999). Effects of exercise training on older patients with major depression. *Archives of Internal Medicine, 159*? 2349–2356.

Brown, D. R., Morgan, W., & Raglin, J. (1993). Effects of exercise and rest on the state anxiety and blood pressure of physically challenged college students. *The Journal of Sports Medicine and Physical Fitness, 33,* 300–305. doi:10.1016/S1469-0292(02)00018-3

Brown, S. W., Welsh, M., Labbe, E., Gitulli, W., & Kulkarni, P. (1992). Aerobic exercise and the psychological treatment of adolescents. *Perceptual and Motor Skills, 74,* 555–560. doi:10.2466/pms.1992.74.2.555

Carless, D., & Douglas, K. (2008). The role of sport and exercise in recovery from serious mental illness: Two case studies. *International Journal of Men's Health, 7,* 137–156. doi:10.3149/jmh.0702.137

Colcombe, S., & Kramer, A. F. (2003). Fitness effects on the cognitive function of older adults: A meta-analytic study. *Psychological Science, 14,* 125–130. doi:10.1111/1467-9280.t01-1-01430

Colcombe, S. J., Kramer, A. F., Erickson, K. I., Scalf, P., McAuley, E., Cohen, N. J., & Elavsky, S. (2004). Cardiovascular fitness, cortical plasticity, and aging. *Proceedings of the National Academy of Sciences of the United States of America, 101,* 3316–3321. doi:10.1073/pnas.0400266101

Cotman, C. W., Berchtold, N. C., & Christie, L. A. (2007). Exercise builds brain health: Key roles of growth factor cascades and inflammation. *Trends in Neurosciences, 30,* 464–472. doi:10.1016/j.tins.2007.06.011

Courneya, K. S., Friedenreich, C. M., Sela, R. A., Quinney, H. A., Rhodes, R. E., & Handman, M. (2003). The group psychotherapy and home-based physical exercise (group-hope) trial in cancer survivors: Physical fitness and quality of life outcomes. *Psycho-Oncology, 12,* 357–374. doi:10.1002/pon.658

Craft, L. L., & Perna, F. M. (2004). The benefits of exercise for the clinically depressed. *Journal of Clinical Psychiatry, 6,* 104–111.

Csikszentmihalyi, M. (1990). *Flow: The psychology of optimal experience.* New York, NY: Harper.

Daniel, M., Martin, A., & Carter, J. (1992). Opiate receptor blockade by naltrexone and mood state after acute physical activity. *British Journal of Sports Medicine, 26,* 111–115. doi:10.1136/bjsm.26.2.111

deVries, H. A., Beckman, P., Huber, H., & Dieckmeir, L. (1968). Electromyographic evaluation of the effects of sauna on the neuromuscular system. *The Journal of Sports Medicine and Physical Fitness, 8,* 61–69.

Dey, S. (1994). Physical exercise as novel anti-depressant agent: Possible role of serotonin receptor subtypes. *Psychological Behavior, 55,* 323–329. doi:10.1016/0031-9384(94)90141-4

Dey, S., Singh, R., & Dey, P. (1992). Exercise training: Significance of regional alterations in serotonin metabolism of rat brain in relation to anti-depressant effect of exercise. *Physiology & Behavior, 52,* 1095–1099. doi:10.1016/0031-9384(92)90465-E

Dienstbier, R. A. (1991). Behavioral correlates of sympathoadrenal reactivity: The toughness model. *Medicine & Science in Sports and Exercise, 23,* 846–852. doi:10.1249/00005768-199107000-00013

Dienstbier, R. A., LaGuardia, R. L., & Wilcox, N. S. (1987). The tolerance of cold and heat: Beyond (cold hands–warm heart). *Motivation and Emotion, 11,* 269–295. doi:10.1007/BF01001414

DiMatteo, M. R., Giordani, P. J., Lepper, H. S., & Croghan, T. W. (2002). Patient adherence and medical treatment outcomes: A meta-analysis. *Medical Care, 40,* 794–811. doi:10.1097/00005650-200209000-00009

Dishman, R. K. (2003). The impact of behavior on quality of life. *Quality of Life Research, 12*(Suppl. 1), 43–49. doi:10.1023/A:1023517303411

Dunn, A. L., Trivedi, M. H., Kampert, J. B., Clark, C. G., & Chambliss, H. O. (2005). Exercise treatment for depression: Efficacy and dose response. *American Journal of Preventive Medicine, 28,* 1–8. doi:10.1016/j.amepre.2004.09.003

Dunn, A. L., Trivedi, M. H., & O'Neal, H. A. (2001). Physical activity dose-response effects on outcomes of depression and anxiety. *Medicine and Science in Sports and Exercise, 33,* S587-S597. doi:0.1097/00005768-200106001-00027

Ellis, N., Crone, D., Davey, R., & Grogan, S. (2007). Exercise interventions as an adjunct therapy for psychosis: A critical review. *British Journal of Clinical Psychology, 46,* 95–111. doi:10.1348/014466506X122995

Emery, C. F., Shermer, R. L., Hauck, E. R., Hsiao, E. T., & MacIntyre, N. R. (2003). Cognitive and psychological outcomes of exercise in a 1-year follow-up study of patients with chronic obstructive pulmonary disease. *Health Psychology, 22,* 598–604. doi:10.1037/0278-6133.22.6.598

Erickson, K. I., Colcombe, S. J., Elavsky, S., McAuley, E., Korol, D. L., Scalf, P. E., & Kramer, A. F. (2007). Interactive effects of fitness and hormone treatment on brain health in postmenopausal women. *Neurobiology of Aging, 28,* 179–185. doi:10.1016/j.neurobiolaging.2005.11.016

Erickson, K. I., Raji, C. A., Lopez, O. L., Becker, J. T., Rosano, C., Newman, A. B., & Kuller, L. H. (2010). Physical activity predicts gray matter volume in late adulthood. *Neurology, 75,* 1415–1422. doi:10.1212/WNL.0b013e3181f88359

Fahlberg, L. L., Fahlberg, L. A., & Gates, W. K. (1992). Exercise and existence: Exercise behavior from an existential–phenomenological perspective. *The Sport Psychologist, 6,* 172–191.

Fitts, W. H. (1964). *Tennessee Self-Concept Scale.* Nashville, TN: Counselor Recordings and Tests.

Folkins, C. H., & Sime, W. E. (1981). Physical fitness training and mental health. *American Psychologist, 36,* 373–389. doi:10.1037/0003-066X.36.4.373

Fox, K. R. (2000). Self-esteem, self-perceptions and exercise. *International Journal of Sport Psychology, 31,* 228–240.

Furnham, A., Badmin, N., & Sneade, I. (2002). Body image dissatisfaction: Gender differences in eating attitudes, self-esteem, and reasons for exercise. *The Journal of Psychology, 136,* 581–596. doi:10.1080/00223980209604820

Gauvin, L., Rejeski, W. J., Norris, J. L., & Lutes, L. (1997). The curse of inactivity: Failure of acute exercise to enhance feeling states in a community sample of sedentary adults. *Journal of Health Psychology,* *2,* 509–523. doi:10.1177/135910539700200408

Goldstein, M. G., Pinto, B., Marcus, B., Lyn, H., Jett, A., Rakowski, W., & Tennstedt, F. (1999). Position based physical activity counseling for middle-aged and older adults: A randomized trial. *Annals of Behavioral Medicine, 21,* 40–47. doi:10.1007/BF02895032

Gomez-Pinilla, F., Vaynman, S., & Ying, Z. (2008). Brain-derived neuro-trophic factor functions as a metabotrophin to mediate the effects of exercise on cognition. *European Journal of Neuroscience, 28,* 2278–2287. doi:10.1111/j.1460-9568.2008.06524.x

Goodheart, C. D., Kazdin, A. E., & Sternberg, R. J. (Eds.). (2006). *Evidence-based psychotherapy: Where practice and research meet.* Washington, DC: American Psychological Association. doi:10.1037/11423-000

Greist, J. H., Klein, M. H., Eischens, R. R., Faris, J., Gurman, A. S., & Morgan, W. P. (1979). Running as treatment for depression. *Comprehensive Psychiatry, 20,* 41–54. doi:10.1016/0010-440X(79)90058-0

Grønningsæter, H., Hyten, K., Skauli, G., & Christensen, C. (1992). Improved health and coping by physical exercise or cognitive behavioral stress management training in a work environment. *Psychology & Health, 7,* 147–163. doi:10.1080/08870449208520016

Haier, R. J., Quaid, B. A., & Mills, J. S. (1981). Naloxone alters pain perceptions after jogging. *Psychiatry Research, 5,* 231–232. doi:10.1016/0165-1781(81)90052-4

Hansen, C. J., Stevens, L. C., Coast, J. R. (2001). Exercise duration and mood state: How much is enough to feel better? *Health Psychology, 20,* 267–275. doi:10.1037/0278-6133.20.4.267

Hassmen, P., Stähl, R., & Borg, G. (1993). Psychophysiological responses to exercise in type A/B men. *Psychosomatic Medicine, 55,* 178–184.

Haworth, J., & Young, C. (2009). The effects of an "exercise and education" program on exercise self-efficacy and level of independent activity in adults with acquired neurological pathologies: An exploratory, randomized study. *Clinical Rehabilitation, 23,* 371–383. doi:10.1177/0269215508101728

Hays, K. F. (1994). Running therapy: Special characteristics and therapeutic issues of concern. *Psychotherapy: Theory, Research, Practice, Training, 31,* 725–734. doi:10.1037/0033-3204.31.4.725

Hays, K. F. (1999). *Working it out: Using exercise in psychotherapy.* Washington, DC: American Psychological Association. doi:10.1037/10333-000

Hays, K. F. (2010, October). Exercise and psychotherapy: Mental benefits and therapists' perspectives. In K. F. Hays (Chair), *Exercise and quality of life: A 25 year, integrative review of research and practice.* Symposium conducted at the annual conference of the Association for Applied Sport Psychology, Providence, RI.

Herring, M. P., O'Connor, P. J., & Dishman, R. K. (2010). The effect of exercise training on anxiety symptoms among patients: A systematic review. *Archives of Internal Medicine, 170,* 321–331. doi:10.1001/archinternmed.2009.530

Hertzog, C., Kramer, A. F., Wilson, R. S., & Lindenberger, U. (2008). Enrichment effects on adult cognitive development. Can the functional capacity of older adults be preserved and enhanced? *Psychological Science in the Public Interest, 9,* 1–65.

Heyn, P., Abreu, B. C., & Ottenbacher, K. J. (2004). The effects of exercise training on elderly persons with cognitive impairment and dementia: A meta-analysis. *Archives of Physical Medicine and Rehabilitation, 85,* 1694–1704. doi:10.1016/j.apmr.2004.03.019

Hoffman, B. M., Babyak, M. A., Craighead, W. E., Sherwood, A., Doraiswamy, P. M., Coons, M. J., & Blumenthal, J. A. (2011). Exercise and pharmacotherapy in patients with major depression: One-year follow-up of the SMILE study. *Psychosomatic Medicine, 73,* 127–133. doi:10.1097/PSY.0b013e31820433a5

Johansson, M., Hassmen, P., & Jouper, J. (2008). Acute effects of qigong exercise on mood and anxiety. *International Journal of Stress Management, 15,* 199–207. doi:10.1037/1072-5245.15.2.199

Johnsgard, K. W. (2004). *Conquering depression and anxiety through exercise.* Amherst, NY: Prometheus.

Kendzierski, D., & Johnson, W. (1993). Excuses, excuses, excuses: A cognitive behavioral approach to exercise implementation. *Journal of Sport & Exercise Psychology, 15,* 207–219.

Koltyn, K., & Morgan, W. P. (1993). The influence of wearing a wet suit on core temperature and anxiety responses during underwater exercise [Abstract]. *Medicine and Science in Sports and Exercise, 25,* S-45. doi:10.1249/00005768-199305001-00250

Kostrubala, T. (1977). *The joy of running.* New York, NY: Pocket.

Landers, D. M., & Arent, S. M. (2001). Physical activity and mental health. In R. N. Singer, H. A. Hausenblas, & C. M. Janelle (Eds.), *Handbook of sport psychology* (2nd ed.) (pp. 740–765). New York, NY: Wiley.

Larson, E. B., Wang, L., Bowen, J. D., McCormick, W. C., Teri, L., Crane, P., & Kukull, W. (2006). Exercise is associated with reduced risk for incident dementia among persons 65 years of age or older. *Annals of Internal Medicine, 144,* 73–81. doi:10.1111/j.1600-0838.2006.00572.x

Lawlor, D. A., & Hopker, S. W. (2001). The effectiveness of exercise as an intervention in the management of depression: Systematic review and meta-regression analysis of randomised controlled trials. *British Medical Journal, 322,* 763–770. doi:10.1136/bmj.322.7289.763

Lehofer, M., Klebel, H., Gersdorf, C. H., & Zapotoczke, H. G. (1992). Running in motion therapy for depression. *Psychiatria Danubina, 4,* 149–152.

Levine, M. D., Marcus, M. D., & Moulton, P. (1996). Exercise in the treatment of binge eating disorder. *International Journal of Eating Disorders,*

19, 171–177. doi:10.1002/(SICI)1098-108X(199603)19:2<171::AID-EAT7>3.0.CO;2-K

Liu, N. H., & Spaulding, W. D. (2010). Pilot study of health-focused day program on improving health behaviors, clinical functioning, and perceived wellness in individuals with severe mental illness. *Psychological Services, 7,* 233–241. doi:10.1037/a0021426

Lobstein, D. D., & Rasmussen, C. (1991). Decreases in resting plasma beta-endorphine and depression scores after endurance training. *The Journal of Sports Medicine and Physical Fitness, 31,* 543–551.

Lowry, C. A., Lightman, S. L., & Nutt, D. J. (2009). That warm fuzzy feeling: Brain serotonergic neurons and the regulation of emotion. *Journal of Psychopharmacology, 23,* 392–400. doi:10.1177/0269881108099956

Maltby, J., & Day, L. (2001). The relationship between exercise motives and psychological well-being. *The Journal of Psychology, 135,* 651–660. doi:10.1080/00223980109603726

Marcus, B., Bock, B., Pinto, B., Forsyth, L., Roberts, M., & Traficante, R. (1998). Efficacy of an individualized, motivationally-tailored physical activity intervention. *Annals of Behavioral Medicine, 20,* 174–180. doi:10.1007/BF02884958

Martin, K., Sinden, A., & Fleming, J. (2000). Inactivity may be hazardous to your image: The effects of exercise participation on impression formation. *Journal of Sport & Exercise Psychology, 22,* 283–291.

Martin Ginis, K. A., Burke, S. M., & Gauvin, L. (2007). Exercising with others exacerbates the negative effects of mirrored environments on sedentary women's feeling states. *Psychology & Health, 22,* 945–962. doi:10.1080/14768320601070571

Martinsen, E. W. (1994). Physical activity and depression: Clinical experience. *Acta Psychiatrica Scandinavica, 89*(Suppl.), 23–27. doi:10.1111/j.1600-0447.1994.tb05797.x

Martinsen, E. W., & Stanghelle, J. K. (1997). Drug therapy and physical activity. In W. P. Morgan (Ed.), *Physical activity and mental health* (pp. 81–90). Washington, DC: Taylor & Francis.

Mata, J., Thompson, R. J., & Gotlib, I. H. (2010). BDNF genotype moderates the relation between physical activity and depressive symptoms. *Health Psychology, 29,* 130–133. doi:10.1037/a0017261

McCubbin, J. A., Cheung, R., Montgomery, T. B., Bulbulian, R., & Wilson, J. F. (1992). Aerobic fitness and opiodergic inhibition of cardiovascular stress reactivity. *Psychophysiology, 29,* 687–697.

McEntee, D. J., & Halgin, R. (1996). Therapists' attitudes about addressing the world of exercise in psychotherapy. *Journal of Clinical Psychology, 52,* 48–60. doi:10.1002/(SICI)1097-4679(199601)52:1<48::AID-JCLP7>3.0.CO;2-S

McNair, D. M., Lorr, N., & Droppleman, L. F. (1971). *Manual for the Profile of Mood States.* San Diego, CA: Educational and Industrial Testing Service.

Mead, G. E., Morley, W., Campbell, P., Greig, C. A., McMurdo, M., & Lawlor, D. A. (2009). Exercise for depression. *Cochrane Database of Systematic Reviews, 4,* CD004366. doi:10.1016/j.mhpa.2009.06.001

Miller, W. R., & Rollnick, S. (2002). *Motivational interviewing: Preparing people for change.* New York, NY: Guilford Press.

Morgan, W. P. (1985). Affective beneficence of vigorous physical activity. *Medicine & Science in Sports & Exercise, 17,* 94–100. doi:10.1249/00005768-198502000-00015

Morgan, W. P. (1988). Exercise and mental health. In R. K. Dishman (Ed.), *Exercise adherence: Its impact on public health* (pp. 9–121). Champaign, IL: Human Kinetics.

Norris, R., Carroll, D., & Cochrane, R. (1992). The effects of physical activity and exercise training on psychological stress and well-being in an adolescent population. *Journal of Psychosomatic Research, 36,* 55–65. doi:10.1016/0022-3999(92)90114-H

Orwin, A. (1973). "The running treatment": A preliminary communication on a new use for an old therapy (physical activity) in the agoraphobic syndrome. *The British Journal of Psychiatry, 122,* 175–179. doi:10.1192/bjp.122.2.175

Paffenbarger, R. S., Jr., Lee, I. M., & Leung, R. (1994). Physical activity and personal characteristics associated with depression and suicide in American college men. *Acta Psychiatrica Scandanavia, S 377,* 16–22.

Peñas-Lledó, E., Vaz Leal, F. J., & Waller, G. (2002). Excessive exercise in anorexia nervosa and bulimia nervosa: Relation to eating characteristics and general psychopathology. *International Journal of Eating Disorders, 31,* 370–375. doi:10.1002/eat.10042

Perna, F. M., Antoni, M., Kumar, M., Cruess, D., & Schneiderman, N. (1998). Cognitive, cognitive–behavioral intervention effects on mood and cortisol during exercise training. *Annals of Behavioral Medicine, 20,* 92–98. doi:10.1007/BF02884454

Petruzzello, S. J., Landers, D. M., & Salazar, W. (1993). Exercise and anxiety reduction: Examination of temperature as an explanation for effective change. *Journal of Sport & Exercise Psychology, 15,* 63–76.

Plante, T. G., Gustafson, C., Brecht, C., Imberi, J., & Sanchez, J. (2011). Exercising with an iPod, friend, or neither: Which is better for psychological benefits? *American Journal of Health Behavior, 35,* 199–208. doi:10.5993/AJHB.35.2.7

Prochaska, J. O., Norcross, J., & DiClemente, C. (1995). *Changing for good.* New York, NY: Harper.

Puetz, T. W., O'Connor, P. J., & Dishman, R. K. (2006). Effects of chronic exercise on feelings of energy and fatigue: A quantitative synthesis. *Psychological Bulletin, 123,* 866–876. doi:10.1037/0033-2909.132.6.866

Ratey, J. J. (2008). *Spark: The revolutionary new science of exercise and the brain.* New York, NY: Little, Brown.

Rejeski, W. J., Thompson, A., Brubaker, P., & Miller, H. (1992). Acute exercise: Buffering psychosocial stress responses in women. *Health Psychology, 11,* 355–362. doi:10.1037/0278-6133.11.6.355

Robbins, J. (2000). *The symphony of the brain.* New York, NY: Atlantic Monthly Press.

Ross, A., & Thomas, S. (2010). The health benefits of yoga and exercise: A review of comparison studies. *The Journal of Alternative and Complementary Medicine, 16,* 3–12. doi:10.1089/acm.2009.0044

Rovio, S., Kareholt, I., Helkala, E. L., Viitanen, M., Winblad, B., Tuomilenhto, J., . . . Kivipelto, M. (2005). Leisure time physical activity at midlife and the risk of dementia and Alzheimer's disease. *Lancet Neurology, 4,* 705–711. doi:10.1016/S1474-4422(05)70198-8

Ruby, M. B., Dunn, E., Perrino, A., Gillis, R., & Viel, S. (2011). The invisible benefits of exercise. *Health Psychology, 30,* 67–74. doi:10.1037/a0021859

Russell, W. (2002). Comparison of self-esteem, body satisfaction, and social physique anxiety across males of different exercise frequency and racial background. *Journal of Sport Behavior, 25,* 74–90.

Ryan, M. (2008). The anti-depressant effects of physical activity: Mediating self-esteem and self-efficacy mechanisms. *Psychology & Health, 23,* 279–307. doi:10.1080/14768320601185502

Sachs, M. L. (1984). Psychological well-being and vigorous physical activity. In J. M. Silva, III, & R. S. Weinberg (Eds.), *Psychological foundations of sport* (pp. 435–444). Champaign, IL: Human Kinetics.

Seime, R., & Vickers, K. (2006). The challenges of treating depression with exercise: From evidence to practice. *Clinical Psychology: Science and Practice, 13,* 194–197. doi:10.1111/j.1468-2850.2006.00022.x

Shephard, R. J. (1991). Benefits of sports and physical activity for the disabled: Implications for the individual and for society. *Scandinavian Journal of Rehabilitation Medicine, 23,* 51–59.

Shipman, W. M. (1984). Emotional and behavioral effects of long-distance running on children. In M. Sachs & G. Buffone (Eds.), *Running as therapy: An integrated approach* (pp. 125–137). Lincoln: University of Nebraska Press.

Sime, W. E., & Sansteadt, M. (1987). Running therapy in the treatment of depression: Implications for prevention. In R. F. Munoz (Ed.), *Depression prevention* (pp. 125–138). New York, NY: Hemisphere.

Spielberger, C. D. (1983). *Manual for the State–Trait Anxiety Inventory (Form Y).* Palo Alto, CA: Consulting Psychologists Press.

Steptoe, A., Kearsley, M., & Walters, N. (1993). Acute mood responses to maximal and sub-maximal exercise in active and inactive men. *Psychology & Health, 8,* 89–99. doi:10.1080/08870449308403169

Streeter, C. C., Whitfield, T. H., Owen, L., Rein, T., Karri, S. K., Yakhkind, A., . . . Jensen, J. E. (2010). Effects of yoga versus walking on mood, anxiety, and brain GABA levels: A randomized controlled MRS study.

The Journal of Alternative and Complementary Medicine, 16, 1145–1152. doi:10.1089/acm.2010.0007

Ströhle, A. (2009). Physical activity, exercise, depression and anxiety disorders. *Journal of Neural Transmission, 116,* 777–784. doi:10.1007/s00702-008-0092-x

Tetlie, T., Heimsnes, M. C., & Almvik, R. (2009). Using exercise to treat patients with severe mental illness. How and why? *Journal of Psychosocial Nursing and Mental Health Services, 47,* 33–40. doi:10.3928/02793695-20090201-14

Trivedi, M. H., Greer, T. L., Church, T. S., Carmody, T. J., Grannemann, B. D., Galper, D. I., & Blair, S. N. (2011). Exercise as an augmentation treatment for nonremitted major depressive disorder: A randomized, parallel dose comparison. *Journal of Clinical Psychiatry, 72?* 677–684. doi:10.4088/JCP.10m06743

Vaynman, S., Ying, Z., & Gomez-Pinilla, F. (2004). Hippocampal BDNF mediates the efficacy of exercise on synaptic plasticity and cognition. *European Journal of Neuroscience, 20,* 2580–2590. doi:10.1111/j.1460-9568.2004.03720.x

Wankel, L. (1993). The importance of enjoyment to adherence and psychological benefits from physical activity. *International Journal of Sport Psychology, 24,* 151–169.

Wei, B., Kilpatrick, M., Naquin, M., & Cole, D. (2010). Psychological perceptions to walking, water aerobics and yoga in college students. *American Journal of Health Studies, 3/4,* 142–147.

Wilson, R. S., Arnold, S. E., Schneider, J. A., Li, Y., & Bennett, D. A. (2007). Chronic distress, age-related neuropathology, and late life dementia. *Psychosomatic Medicine, 69,* 47–53. doi:10.1097/01.psy.0000250264.25017.21

Albert J. Petitpas and Taunya Marie Tinsley

Counseling Interventions in Applied Sport Psychology

11

More than 25 years ago, the Advisory Board on Sport Psychology, United States Olympic Committee (1983), published a document that outlined three types of sport psychology activities: clinical, educational, and research. *Clinical* interventions were described as those assisting athletes who exhibited severe emotional problems such as depression, panic, and interpersonal conflicts. *Educational* interventions were said to focus on teaching psychological skills, such as relaxation, imagery, and attention control to enhance athletes' sport performance. The third category, *research,* was seen not as a form of intervention but as an important activity to enhance the work of both clinical and educational practitioners. Although these guidelines were developed to show the range of activities deemed necessary for the provision of comprehensive sport psychology services to Olympic athletes, they inadvertently spawned a turf war between professionals trained in psychology and those trained in the sport sciences. Even today, questions about appropriate training, practitioner competencies, and the use of the term *sport psychologist* persist (Berger, 2010).

http://dx.doi.org/10.1037/14251-011
Exploring Sport and Exercise Psychology, Third Edition, J. Van Raalte and B. Brewer (Editors)
Copyright © 2014 by the American Psychological Association. All rights reserved.

Most sport psychologists identify with either psychology or sport science. Professionals who enter the field with a preparation in counseling psychology often find themselves misclassified as clinical specialists. By training, counseling psychologists focus on individuals' strengths and adaptive strategies across the life span, a focus that has more in common with educational sport psychology (Petitpas, Buntrock, Van Raalte, & Brewer, 1995; Petitpas, Danish, & Giges, 1999). The purpose of this chapter is to examine counseling-based interventions with athletes. Specifically, (a) a definition of counseling-based interventions is discussed, (b) the role of sport in human development is explored, (c) several examples of counseling-based interventions are outlined, and (d) suggestions for working with athletes from a counseling perspective are offered.

Defining Counseling Interventions

Differences between clinical and counseling psychologists have become less clear over the past several decades (Society of Counseling Psychology, 2011). In most cases, both clinical and counseling psychologists are trained to provide counseling and psychotherapy, are eligible to hold licensure in every state in the United States as "licensed psychologist," and are able to practice independently as health care providers. Typically, counseling psychologists have a psychoeducational and developmental focus that emphasizes growth and enhancement in normal populations, although many counseling psychology programs also train individuals to diagnose and treat pathology (Danish, Petitpas, & Hale, 1993).

According to the Society of Counseling Psychology (2011), Division 17 of the American Psychological Association (APA), differences between clinical and counseling psychology can be understood by examining the history and traditions of each subspecialty. Clinical derives from the Greek word for bed, *kline*, which refers to providing bedside care to the ill patient, whereas counseling derives from the Latin word *consulere*, which means to advise or consult. Historically, clinical psychologists focused on mental illness and learning disabilities, while counseling psychologists provided career guidance. In fact, it was in 1951 when APA's Division of Personnel and Guidance Psychologists changed its name to the Division of Counseling Psychology. At that time, Division 17 changed from an exclusive focus on career issues to an emphasis on positive well-being throughout the life span. This emphasis on identifying and building on individuals' strengths and adaptive strategies was reaffirmed at the Third National Conference for Counseling Psychology in 1987 (Weiner, 2003).

Traditional counseling psychologists have been described as career development or lifework planning specialists, system change agents, psychoeducators, and primary prevention specialists (Hansen, 1981). These work roles are consistent with Shertzer and Stone's (1966) description of counseling as "an interaction process which facilitates meaningful understanding of self and environment and results in the establishment and/or clarification of goals and values for future behavior" (p. 26). For the purpose of this chapter, counseling interventions with athletes are those that focus on individual strengths, development, decision making, and lifework planning across the life span.

Positive psychology has gained considerable momentum during the past decade, and research has shown that interventions that build gratitude and increase awareness of self-positives and character strengths can increase happiness and decrease depression (Seligman & Csikszentmihalyi, 2000; Seligman, Steen, Park, & Peterson, 2005). What remains unclear is how positive psychology interventions differ from a traditional counseling psychology. Is positive psychology a new focus in psychology or simply an up-named version of traditional counseling psychology? Whatever the answer, there was and still is considerable merit in conducting positive asset searches with athlete clients, building on their strengths, and assisting them in planning for life transitions. Consistent with the mantra of positive youth development, "problem free does not mean prepared for the future" (Pittman, 1991), and both positive and traditional counseling psychology strive to identify strengths and assist individuals in acquiring the skills necessary to function and prosper throughout the life span.

Sport psychology practice has also evolved from an exclusive focus on improving sport skills to a broader concern for the impact of sport on human development and the use of sport in enhancing personal competence (Danish et al., 1993). Within this broader view of sport psychology, counseling interventions have been added to the traditional educational and clinical activities, resulting in a new model of sport psychology consultation. Counseling interventions not only assist athletes through the use of various psychoeducational strategies but also use the sport experience as an opportunity to help individuals acquire life skills and facilitate their development through the life cycle.

Sport and Human Development

If counseling interventions focus on growth across the life span, then an understanding of the role of sport in human development is important in planning interventions for athletes. The legitimacy of sport as a cocurricular activity is based on the premise that sport participation prepares students for adult roles. Many coaches, parents, and educators believe that sport teaches young people how to live by rules, work hard to achieve goals, and play and interact with others (Danish et al., 1993; Ewing, Seefeldt, & Brown, 1996; Petitpas, Cornelius, Van Raalte, & Jones, 2005). Nonetheless, the efficacy of sport as a vehicle in enhancing development and "building character" has not been substantiated, and several authors have argued that the increased competitive nature of sport and the emphasis on winning have a deleterious effect on the psychosocial development of young athletes (Ewing et al., 1996; Petitpas & Champagne, 2000). In any event, sport participation is highly valued by youth and provides them with numerous opportunities to learn about themselves (Danish et al., 1993).

Building on the works of Freud and Hartmann, White (1959) proposed that individuals were motivated by independent energies that allowed the ego to go beyond the confines of instinctual drives. Using considerable experimental and physiological evidence, White argued that all living things were motivated by a need to master the environment and to move freely in the world. He labeled this drive *effectance* and defined *personal competence* as individuals' abilities to interact successfully with the environment in a manner that allows them not only to maintain themselves but also to grow and flourish (White, 1963). Therefore, rather than simply acting to satisfy basic needs, individuals gain feelings of efficacy when they are able to have an effect on their environment.

White (1963) believed that infants begin the process of cognitive and motor learning by engaging in simple behaviors such as holding crib toys. By the time infants start to crawl, they have had numerous interactions with their environments that begin to shape their beliefs about what they can and cannot do. These beliefs form the basis for self-efficacy. As children continue to grow, they construct views of their worlds based on what they have learned about their abilities and begin to develop primitive estimates of their levels of personal competence. Without some level of self-efficacy, it is doubtful that young children would have the desire or readiness necessary to imitate the complex behaviors exhibited by older role models.

As children begin school, they interact with larger numbers of their peers and have increased opportunities to engage in social comparisons. Through this process, they receive feedback about their competencies and begin to make judgments about themselves that affect the range and type of activities that they will attempt (White, 1963). For young people, these social comparisons are most likely to be made around physical abilities. When a group of children come together to engage in a sport activity, they typically identify the two best players as captains and then the captains take turns selecting their teammates from the remaining group members (Petitpas & Champagne, 2000). This selection process provides concrete feedback about how one stacks up against his or her peers. The captains and early selections receive frequent reinforcement for their athletic involvement. Those chosen last are left to evaluate their status among their peers according to their interpretation of the situation. Those who are several years younger may continue to participate in hope of becoming a "captain" among their age peers in the future. Some will view their selection status as a challenge to work hard and prove their competency or as motivation to participate in other sport activities that are better suited for their physical abilities. Unfortunately, an increasing number of young people will simply discontinue their sport involvement (Gould, 1987).

According to Erikson (1959), children who experience success and achieve adequate levels of self-efficacy during latency develop a sense of industry. Children who are not able to meet their effectance needs develop feelings of inferiority and are less likely to take risks or explore new opportunities. Much of organized sport is based on competition and a "survival of the fittest" mentality. As individuals progress through the various levels of competition and winning takes on more importance, playing time and opportunities to prove oneself are often reserved for the more skillful performers. Athletes are required to devote more time and energy to sport in efforts to maintain their level of achievement. By the time most athletes reach high school, however, the external rewards associated with athletic success have taken on larger importance and correlate with a number of positive psychosocial traits. Typically, successful high school athletes experience strong feelings of accomplishment and begin to develop a sense of identity based on their sports achievements (Petitpas & France, 2010).

Although the literature suggests that there are many benefits to sports participation, including higher school grades, increased self-esteem, and better interpersonal skills, there is danger that too much emphasis on sport may be detrimental, particularly for older teenagers (Petitpas & Champagne, 2000). As students move into late adolescence, their developmental tasks shift from gaining a sense of industry and competence to a search for a personal identity. According to developmental theorists (Erikson, 1959; Marcia, Waterman, Matteson, Archer, & Orlofsky, 1993), identity development requires two activities. First, individuals must engage in exploratory behavior investigate the merits of various careers, lifestyles, and other alternatives of adult life. Second, they must make a commitment to those occupational and ideological alternatives that are most consistent with their values, needs, interests, and skills. It is the first of these two tasks, exploratory behavior, which may not be compatible with a sport system that demands conformity and requires such large amounts of time and effort.

Research has shown that an exclusive focus on sport may leave some athletes vulnerable to several psychosocial problems (Brewer, 1993). There is evidence that the dream of a professional sports career, coupled with the personal, social, and even financial rewards that come from athletic successes, often results in an overemphasis on sports involvement at the expense of the exploratory behavior that is necessary for optimal educational, career, and personal development (Petitpas & France, 2010). Individuals develop coping skills and resources that allow them to become self-sufficient and better able to handle life challenges through exploratory behavior (Jordaan, 1963). Ironically, high school and college sports often promote compliance and conformity rather than leadership (Ewing et al., 1996). Therefore, instead of developing independence, many athletes relinquish their ability to make decisions and blindly adhere to team rules and coaching mandates (LeUnes & Nation, 1982).

Danish (1983) suggested that athletes may use selective optimization, a process in which they give exclusive attention to their sport at the expense of all other interests. This concept is closely linked to a developmental status called *identity foreclosure* (Marcia, 1966). Foreclosure occurs when individuals make commitments to roles without engaging in exploratory behavior. On the surface, identity foreclosed individuals appear to be psychosocially mature (Marcia et al., 1993). They have low levels of anxiety and confusion and are clearly committed to a role. However, this seemingly healthy presentation may mask a lack of self-awareness and a failure to develop adequate coping resources (Marcia et al., 1993; Petitpas & France, 2010). Problems associated with foreclosed commitments to sport roles are most likely to surface when the athletic identity is threatened (Baillie & Danish, 1992; Brewer, 1993).

Several studies have shown that the strength and exclusivity of an athletic identity are related to negative consequences when athletes disengage from sport roles because of retirement, injury, or the selection process (Brewer, 1993; Kleiber & Brock, 1992). Unfortunately, the sport system does little to assist athletes in preparing for threats to their identities and often promotes the attitude that only a "110%" level of commitment to sport is acceptable (Petitpas & Danish, 1995).

Little has been written on the impact of athletic participation on later developmental tasks. Heyman (1987) suggested that athletes may not be experienced in developing meaningful interpersonal relationships and therefore may have difficulty resolving the "intimacy versus isolation" crisis of young adulthood. Although there is no empirical support for this notion with athlete samples, foreclosed men have been shown to engage in stereotyped or pseudo-intimate dating relationships (Marcia et al., 1993).

Most formal athletic careers end before individuals reach middle or later adulthood and are faced with the "generativity versus stagnation" crisis of this stage. Heyman (1987) suggested that retired athletes who have not developed another source of meaning or enjoyment in life would be prone to stagnation. This hypothesis has not been empirically tested. Nevertheless, assisting athletes in expanding their self-concepts and identities beyond athletics may be helpful in preparing them for later adult transitions (Pearson & Petitpas, 1990).

From the above developmental perspective, counseling interventions should, therefore, be geared toward creating environments where athletes can learn about themselves through exploratory behavior, develop coping skills, prepare for future events, and have fun. If sport is structured in a manner that allows young people to master skills and engage in exploratory behavior, they are likely to become more self-aware and better prepared for the future (Petitpas et al., 2005). Counseling strategies that target not only athletes but all components of the athletic system, including coaches, parents, and athletic administrators, are in the best position to promote youth development.

Counseling-Based Interventions With Athletes

An examination of athletes' transitions provides a useful framework for understanding developmental processes that underlie counseling interventions with this population (Pearson & Petitpas, 1990). Athletes go through a series of normative transitions as they move through their sport life cycle. For example, National Basketball Association (NBA) players typically progress from youth sport, to high school, to college, and to the NBA before they retire from sport. Each of these transitions can be anticipated and counseling services provided. In addition, athletes may experience unexpected events (e.g., injury) or "nonevents" (e.g., not making the starting team) that may require attention (Danish et al., 1993; Pearson & Petitpas, 1990).

Although it may be possible to extrapolate from transitional theory and identify athletes who might be most susceptible to problems during transitions, getting at-risk athletes to participate in prevention programs is often difficult (Pearson & Petitpas, 1990). Therefore, a well-designed counseling program should contain several types of interventions.

In designing counseling programs for athletes, linking the timing of the transitional experience to an appropriate intervention is helpful (Danish et al., 1993). These interventions can occur before, during, or after a transition. Interventions that assist athletes in preparing for upcoming events by identifying transferable skills or developing new coping or life skills are called enhancement strategies. During a transition, interventions can buffer the impact of a transition by assisting athletes in mobilizing their personal and support resources. Other counseling-related strategies can be used to assist athletes in coping with the aftermath of a transition (Danish et al., 1993). More information about other expected and unexpected transitions of athletes is available elsewhere (Baillie & Danish, 1992; Petitpas, Brewer, & Van Raalte, 2009).

To illustrate the link between developmental theory and counseling-based interventions, two approaches to service delivery will be examined. First, a framework for assisting athletes in managing the psychological aspects often associated with a significant sport injury is presented. Then, The First Tee, a program that uses involvement with sport as a vehicle to teach life skills to disadvantaged youth, is described.

COUNSELING ATHLETES WITH INJURIES

Incurring a physical injury can be a stressor for most individuals. For athletes, who derive significant portions of their self-worth from sports, a serious injury can be a threat to their basic identity (Brewer, Van Raalte, & Linder, 1993). Several studies have shown a relationship between the strength and exclusivity of one's identification with sport and negative reactions in athletes who experience injury (Brewer, 1993; Kleiber & Brock, 1992). However, attempts to equate reactions to sport injury to stage models of grief and loss have received little empirical support (Brewer, 1994). Two longitudinal studies revealed that athletes experienced mood disturbance following severe injury but that emotional distress diminished when athletes perceived they were making progress toward recovery (McDonald & Hardy, 1990; Smith, Scott, O'Fallon, & Young, 1990).

In planning counseling interventions for injured athletes, commitment to sport roles should be considered as one of several factors that can affect psychological adjustment. If this commitment suggests identity foreclosure, differentiating between situational and psychological types of foreclosure will facilitate treatment planning. As described by Henry and Renaud (1972), psychological foreclosure is an intrapsychic defense mechanism whereby individuals ward off threats to their self-worth by avoiding any situations that might challenge their identity. This contrasts markedly with situationally foreclosed individuals, whose commitment to an athletic identity is due to a lack of exposure to new options or possibilities, not because it is their main defensive structure. Many of these differences can be seen in the extended case study presented by Brewer and Petitpas (2005).

Other factors to consider when planning counseling interventions for injured athletes include the individual's coping skills, life stress, family life cycle dynamics, secondary gain, sources and types of support, injury characteristics, and a range of situational variables (Brewer & Petitpas, 2005; Hardy & Crace, 1993; Petitpas & Danish, 1995; Smith, Scott, & Wiese, 1990; Wiese-Bjornstal & Smith, 1993). The complexity of the sport injury situation requires counselors to put considerable time and energy into understanding athletes and their injury experience.

The goal in counseling athletes with injuries is to assist them in identifying and developing resources to cope more effectively with the injury process. Although several counseling models for athletes with injuries offer suggestions for *what* to do (e.g., Smith, Scott, O'Fallon, et al., 1990; Smith, Scott, & Wiese, 1990; Wiese-Bjornstal & Smith, 1993), there is little attention given to how to intervene with injured athletes (Brewer & Petitpas, 2005; Petitpas & Danish, 1995). Some guidelines for *how* to intervene with athletes with injuries are described below.

The first step in the counseling process for athletes with injuries is to build rapport and develop a working alliance. Although several definitions of the working alliance are available in the counseling literature, they all describe some form of collaborative relationship between the counselor and the client in which they work together to help the client manage a specific concern (Osachuk & Cairns, 1995). The primary function of a working alliance is to create a climate of trust and an emotional bond, in which the client and counselor come to a clear agreement about treatment goals and the tasks necessary to achieve them (Bordin, 1979). Without a trusting relationship and agreement on goals, it is doubtful that clients will adhere to the prescribed treatment plan or put forth the effort required to achieve their desired outcomes (Locke & Latham 2002).

The key to establishing rapport and an effective working alliance is attending to the client's agenda and striving to understand the situation from the client's point of view. Counselors should use basic listening and attending skills to assess clients' beliefs about their injuries, emotional reactions, and expectations. As described by Meichenbaum and Turk (1987), the following three areas need to be explored:

1. the personal meanings that clients ascribe to their injuries;
2. clients' worries, fears, or concerns about their injuries; and
3. clients' expectations about treatment and their health care providers.

To acquire this information, counselors need to display acceptance, genuineness, and empathy toward their client; listen attentively; and probe for the messages that may be under the surface of the client's initial responses.

Many athletes display confusion, anxiety, and doubt during the initial time period following a serious injury, so it is important to be patient and avoid the urge to offer a quick "fix" (Petitpas & Danish, 1995). Some athletes may use potentially harmful strategies in coping with the injury (e.g., withdrawing from teammates, abusing alcohol). It is helpful to examine what these strategies are doing for the athlete and then explore other options that might give the athlete the same benefits without the potential costs. Premature confrontations may cause athletes to lose face and jeopardize the therapeutic relationship (Brewer & Petitpas, 2005; Petitpas & Danish, 1995).

Counselors should ensure that athletes with injuries are provided with specific information about the nature of the injury, the medical procedures to be used, any possible side effects, and the goals of rehabilitation (Petitpas & Cornelius, 2004). This type of information helps prepare athletes with injuries for what lies ahead and may help them to anticipate possible plateaus or setbacks in rehabilitation and to eliminate some of the "surprises" that could happen during rehabilitation.

Collaborating with athletes with injuries in identifying coping resources can help athletes feel more in control and more responsible for rehabilitation outcomes. Using coping skills that athletes with injuries are already familiar with may help them feel more confident in their ability to influence their recovery. If athletes with injuries lack appropriate coping resources, counselors can teach them new skills (see Danish & Hale, 1981; Meichenbaum, 1985).

Once coping skills are identified or learned, counselors and athletes with injuries should collaborate to develop goal ladders for the rehabilitation process and strategies to address any roadblocks to goal attainment. Counselors are also typically involved in working with athletes with injury support systems (e.g., family, sports medicine personnel, coaches) to ensure a good rehabilitation and smooth return to competition. These suggested techniques are described in more detail elsewhere (Brewer & Petitpas, 2005; Petitpas & Danish, 1995).

Although the interventions described above take place after an injury has occurred, the focus of these counseling strategies is on coping skill identification and acquisition, not pathology. In addition, the quality of the working alliance between the counselor and the athlete facilitates skill acquisition and is often critical to treatment adherence and positive outcomes.

THE FIRST TEE

As stated earlier, one of the important roles played by counseling psychologists is that of psychoeducators who assist individuals in identifying strengths, learning important life skills, and preparing for the future. This psychoeducational approach is evident in a number of sport-based youth development initiatives (e.g., Going for the Goal, Play It Smart) where counseling psychologists have created life skill enhancement programs that assist children in acquiring important skills and have provided training in basic listening and relationship-building skills to caring adult mentors. The First Tee is a youth development organization that illustrates how a counseling intervention can be used to enhance personal development.

The First Tee was created in 1997 by the World Golf Foundation to "bring golf to youth that otherwise would not be exposed to the game and its positive values" (The First Tee, 2006, p. 2). Although The First Tee's initial mission was to provide greater access to golf by developing more golf learning centers across the United States, the program developers quickly realized the power of golf to enhance youth development. As a result, in 1998, a small group of counseling and sport psychologists were brought together to create The First Tee Life Skills Experience. Currently, The First Tee operates more than 250 learning facilities across the United States and in five additional countries.

The current mission of The First Tee is "to impact the lives of young people by providing learning facilities and educational programs that promote character development and life-enhancing values through the game of golf" (The First Tee, 2006, p. 1). Inherent in this mission statement is the belief that golf provides an ideal context for youth development. Golf requires not only physical skills but also considerable amounts of decision making and self-management. In addition, there are no officials or referees in golf, so participants call penalties on themselves and abide by the etiquette of golf that calls for respect for the course, environment, and other participants.

The First Tee Life Skills Experience program provides a solid context for enhancing positive youth development. The First Tee golf program "is a voluntary activity that provides challenge and fun, requires commitment and effort over time, and has clear rules" (The First Tee, 2006, p. 3). To ensure that participants (i.e., boys and girls ages 5–18) experience the type of context that is most conducive to youth development, adult mentors are trained to introduce golf skills and life skills seamlessly in a manner that creates a mastery climate in which young people are provided structured opportunities for self-discovery.

Adult mentors participate in The First Tee coach program, a structured training program that has three levels and continuing education requirements. It typically takes an individual at least 2 years to fulfill all the experiences required to become a coach for The First Tee program. To ensure that mentors are developing quality relationships with participants and that the curriculum is implemented in a relatively consistent manner across all sites, The First Tee program begins with a set of four building blocks that serve as the cornerstones for the delivery of the life skill core lessons. The activity-based building block is based on the belief that a learning environment that emphasizes more "doing versus telling" and introduces golf and life skills in a "fun and seamless" fashion is more likely to hold the interest of participants as they engage in self-discovery. The mastery-driven building block involves the creation of an environment that focuses on self-improvements rather than social comparisons. As a result, The First Tee coaches strive to "balance process and outcomes" by emphasizing the importance of paying attention to the specific behaviors (process) that are likely to lead to the individual's desired outcomes. For example participants who want to make their high school golf team (outcome) may recognize that maintaining balance (process) is a key to an effective golf swing. The First Tee coaches could assist young golfers by creating fun activities that focus on balance and by providing feedback on their ability to maintain balance, not necessarily focusing on the outcome of the specific shots. The First Tee refers to this strategy as "intention equals attention." Empower youth is the third building block, and this segment of training focuses on helping The First Tee coaches learn strategies for remaining "youth centered" in their interactions by striving to understand participants' experiences of situations from their perspectives. The belief is that by using appropriate listening and relationship-building skills, The First Tee coaches will empower youth and become mentors rather than simply instructors of the golf swing. The final building block is continuous learning, which supports self-evaluation and feedback to participants through "coachable moments" and good/better/how self- and peer assessments.

The First Tee has a structured curriculum, The First Tee Life Skills Experience program, that is divided into levels (i.e., par, birdie, eagle, ace) and introduced through a set of core lessons. The 22 primary core lessons are organized in a progression and address four general areas: interpersonal skills, goal setting, self-management skills, and resilience skills.

Although The First Tee curriculum provides a comprehensive life skills experience, it is the quality of the relationships built by The First Tee coaches that correlates with participants' abilities to apply these life skills successfully at home, at school, and in their communities (Petitpas, Cornelius, & Van Raalte, 2008). Consistent with a traditional counseling approach, The First Tee coaches are trained in basic listening and relationship-building skills, focus on participants' strengths, and assist participants in planning for the future.

Special Considerations in Counseling Athletes

Athletes have a culture of their own with special issues and unique developmental needs (Cole & Tinsley, 2009; Harris, Altekruse, & Engels, 2003; Jolly, 2008; Stambulova & Alfermann, 2009). As such, it is important for sport psychology practitioners not only to be aware of their own cultural influences but also to do their best to increase their awareness and knowledge of their athlete client's cultural background. International status, race, ethnicity, gender, and religion can all affect athletes' goals and objectives for participating and competing in sports (Cole, 2006; Cole & Tinsley, 2009; Steinfeldt, Reed, & Steinfeldt, 2010; Tinsley, 2005). Athletes, like other minority groups, can also face oppression, prejudice, and discrimination (Baucom & Lantz, 2001; Simons, Bosworth, Fujita, & Jensen, 2007; Steinfeldt, Reed, & Steinfeldt, 2010).

By extending the principles of multicultural counseling and the cross-cultural psychology approach to include the athlete population, practitioners may be in a better position to respond to the developmental needs of athletes and enhance the quality of services they provide (Pinkerton, 2009; Stambulova & Alfermann, 2009; Tinsley, 2005; Ward, Sandstedt, Cox, & Beck, 2005). As with many cultural groups, athletes face a multitude of complex demands, stressors, and challenges that may extend outside the issues normally addressed by traditional counseling and psychological services (Etzel, 2009; Tinsley, 2005; Ward et al., 2005). To this point, the American Counseling Association recognized a need for specialized training more than 25 years ago and published a set of sport counseling competencies (Nejedlo, Arrendondo, & Benjamin, 1985). More recently, Tinsley (2005) developed multicultural sports-counseling competencies consisting of four dimensions for professional counselors, and Ward et al. (2005) identified 17 essential competencies for psychologists working with athletes.

The competencies described by Tinsley (2005) and Ward et al. (2005) can be categorized within the domains of attitudes/beliefs, knowledge, and skills that promote counseling awareness and sensitivity within the sport culture. More specifically, the Ward et al. competencies were designed to assist counseling professionals not trained in sport psychology to identify areas where further education, training, and experiences are needed to ensure effective and ethical service delivery. They stated that developing and having "competencies will (a) help psychologists and students not trained in sport psychology identify areas in which they need further education, training, or experiences in order to competently work with athlete clients; (b) further define the specialty of athlete-counseling; and (c) assist athlete clients, as well as non-athlete clients, to distinguish among available psychological services" (Ward et al., 2005, p. 321).

Psychologists, who are accustomed to working with clients in clinical settings, often find that consultation work with athletes is different from their traditional practice (Danish et al., 1993). As described earlier, the sport system can be so narrowly focused that it becomes a closed system, where nonparticipants are seen as outsiders. Many athletes and coaches have reservations about working with "shrinks," whose lack of understanding of the sport environment can result in behaviors that are intrusive and potentially harmful to performance (Orlick & Partington, 1987; Van Raalte, Brewer, Brewer, & Linder, 1992).

To gain access to the sport system, sport and exercise psychology consultants must demonstrate a general understanding of the sport environment and an appreciation for what athletes go through during practices and competitions (Danish et al., 1993). Psychology-trained consultants with a basic understanding of the sport sciences and experience as an athlete have clear advantages over their non-sport-oriented colleagues in gaining entry to the sports world. However, all sport and exercise psychology consultants can enhance their knowledge and expertise related to sport by reading relevant literature, attending professional meetings related to sport psychology, talking to athletes and coaches, assisting with sport teams, becoming involved in sport and exercise themselves as participants, and observing the athletes and teams with whom they would like to work. It is critical to become familiar with the culture, rules, and language of sport to be effective. For example, many athletes are action oriented. Therefore, consultants who provide concrete information that is sport-specific are likely to be more effective than those who use more abstract, insight-oriented interventions (Danish et al., 1993). In addition, boundaries are not as clearly defined as they are in traditional clinical practice. Contacts with clients are more extensive, and attendance at practices and games is often an expectation (Orlick & Partington, 1987). Although this extended contact is helpful in giving consultants opportunities for observing their clients perform, it is time-consuming. In addition, consultants may be expected to travel with teams, have meals and share lodging with team members, and participate in team social functions. For psychologists, balancing relationship expectations with appropriate clinical boundaries is often a difficult challenge (Andersen, Van Raalte, & Brewer, 2001).

Confidentiality is another common concern in working with athletes. Most often, the initial contact for consultation services will come from a coach, parent, or sport administrator who wants help for a team or an individual athlete. These individuals often assume that because they are responsible for these athletes, they should have access to records and be informed about what happens during counseling. It is important to clarify who will have access to records and who will be informed about the counseling relationship before consultations begin. In cases where a sport administrator hires a sport and exercise psychologist to work with a team, the sport and exercise psychologist must clearly define the nature of the consultation with the coach, as well as the sport administrator. The most effective consultants appear to be those who work through coaches and know when to assist and when to stay in the background (Giges, Petitpas, & Vernacchia, 2004; Orlick & Partington, 1987).

Conclusion

The purpose of this chapter has been to examine counseling interventions with athletes. Counseling-based approaches can be used to enhance both sport performance and athletes' abilities to transfer skills that they acquired through sport to other life domains. Sport and exercise psychologists who understand the world of sport are in a better position to gain access to consulting with this unique population.

References

Andersen, M. B., Van Raalte, J. L., & Brewer, B. W. (2001). Sport psychology service delivery: Staying ethical while keeping loose. *Professional Psychology: Research and Practice, 32,* 12–18. doi:10.1037/0735-7028.32.1.12

Baillie, P. H. F., & Danish, S. J. (1992). Understanding the career transition of athletes. *The Sport Psychologist, 6,* 77–98.

Baucom, C., & Lantz, C. D. (2001). Faculty attitudes toward male division II student-athletes. *Journal of Sport Behavior, 24,* 265–276.

Berger, B. (2010, October). *Celebrating 25 years of AASP: Looking back and looking at the present as we chart our future.* Presidential address at the annual meeting of the Association for Applied Sport Psychology, Providence, RI.

Bordin, E. (1979). The generalizability of the psychoanalytic concept of the working alliance. *Psychotherapy: Theory, Research, & Practice, 16,* 252–260. doi:10.1037/h0085885

Brewer, B. W. (1993). Self-identity and specific vulnerability to depressed mood. *Journal of Personality, 61,* 343–364. doi:10.1111/j.1467-6494.1993.tb00284.x

Brewer, B. W. (1994). Review and critique of models of psychological adjustment to athletic injury. *Journal of Applied Sport Psychology, 6,* 87–100. doi:10.1080/10413209408406467

Brewer, B. W., & Petitpas, A. J. (2005). Returning to self: The anxieties of coming back after injury. In M. Andersen (Ed.), *Sport psychology in practice* (pp. 93–108). Champaign, IL: Human Kinetics.

Brewer, B. W., Van Raalte, J. L., & Linder, D. E. (1993). Athletic identity: Hercules' muscles or Achilles heel? *International Journal of Sport Psychology, 24,* 237–254.

Cole, K. W. (2006). An examination of school counselors' knowledge and perceptions of recruited student-athletes. (Doctoral dissertation, University of Iowa). *Dissertation Abstracts International: Section A, The Humanities and Social Sciences, 67,* 2891.

Cole, K. W., & Tinsley, T. M. (2009). Sports counseling. In American Counseling Association (Ed.), *The ACA encyclopedia of counseling* (pp. 522–524). Alexandria, VA: American Counseling Association.

Danish, S. J. (1983). Musings about personal competence: The contributions of sport, health, and fitness. *American Journal of Community Psychology, 11*, 221–240. doi:10.1007/BF00893365

Danish, S. J., & Hale, B. D. (1981). Toward an understanding of the practice of sport psychology. *Journal of Sport Psychology, 3*, 90–99.

Danish, S. J., Petitpas, A. J., & Hale, B. D. (1993). Life development interventions for athletes: Life skills through sports. *The Counseling Psychologist, 21*, 352–385. doi:10.1177/0011000093213002

Erikson, E. H. (1959). Identity and the life cycle. *Psychological Issues, 1*, 1–171.

Etzel, E. F. (2009). *Counseling and psychological services for college student-athletes.* Morgantown, WV: Fitness Information Technology.

Ewing, M. E., Seefeldt, V. D., & Brown, T. P. (1996). Role of organized sport in the education and health of American children and youth. In A. Poinsett (Ed.), *The role of sports in youth development* (pp. 1–157). New York, NY: Carnegie Corporation.

The First Tee. (2006). *The First Tee Coach Program: Overview and requirements* (3rd ed.). St. Augustine, FL: Author.

Giges, B., Petitpas, A. J., & Vernacchia, R. (2004). Helping coaches meet their own needs: Challenges for the sport psychology consultant. *The Sport Psychologist, 18*, 430–444.

Gould, D. (1987). Promoting positive sport experiences in children. In J. R. May & M. J. Asken (Eds.), *Sport psychology: The psychological health of the athlete* (pp. 77–98). New York, NY: PMA.

Hansen, F. K. (1981). Primary prevention and counseling psychology: Rhetoric or reality? *The Counseling Psychologist, 9*, 57–60. doi:10.1177/001100008100900212

Hardy, C. J., & Crace, R. K. (1993). The dimensions of social support when dealing with sport injuries. In D. Pargman (Ed.), *Psychological bases of sport injuries* (pp. 121–144). Morgantown, WV: Fitness Information Technology.

Harris, H. L., Altekruse, M. K., & Engels, D. W. (2003). Helping freshman student-athletes adjust to college life using psychoeducational groups. *Journal for Specialists in Group Work, 28*, 64–81. doi:10.1177/019339202250079

Henry, M., & Renaud, H. (1972). Examined and unexamined lives. *Research Reporter, 7*, 5.

Heyman, S. R. (1987). Counseling and psychotherapy with athletes: Special considerations. In J. R. May & M. J. Asken (Eds.), *Sport psychology: The psychological health of the athlete* (pp. 135–156). New York, NY: PMA.

Jolly, J. C. (2008). Raising the question # 9: Is the student-athlete population unique? And why should we care? *Communication Education, 57,* 145–151. doi:10.1080/03634520701613676

Jordaan, J. P. (1963). Exploratory behavior: The formulation of self and occupational concepts. In D. E. Super, R. Starishevsky, N. Matlin, & J. P. Jordaan (Eds.), *Career development: Self-concept theory* (pp. 46–57). New York, NY: CEEB Research Monographs.

Kleiber, D. A., & Brock, S. C. (1992). The effect of career-ending injuries on the subsequent well-being of elite college athletes. *Sociology of Sport Journal, 9,* 70–75.

LeUnes, A., & Nation, J. R. (1982). Saturday's heroes: A psychological portrait of college football players. *Journal of Sport Behavior, 5,* 139–149.

Locke, E. A., & Latham, G. (2002). Building a practically useful theory of goal setting and task motivation: A 35-year odyssey. *American Psychologist, 57,* 705–717. doi:10.1037/0003-066X.57.9.705

Marcia, J. E. (1966). Development and validation of ego-identity status. *Journal of Personality and Social Psychology, 3,* 551–558. doi:10.1037/h0023281

Marcia, J. E., Waterman, A. S., Matteson, D. R., Archer, S. L., & Orlofsky, J. L. (1993). *Ego identity: A handbook for psychosocial research.* New York, NY: Springer-Verlag. doi:10.1007/978-1-4613-8330-7

McDonald, S. A., & Hardy, C. J. (1990). Affective response patterns of the injured athlete: An exploratory analysis. *The Sport Psychologist, 4,* 261–274.

Meichenbaum, D. (1985). *Stress inoculation training.* Elmsford, NY: Pergamon Press.

Meichenbaum, D., & Turk, D. (1987). Facilitating treatment adherence: A practitioner's guidebook. New York, NY: Plenum Press.

Nejedlo, R. J., Arrendondo, P., & Benjamin, L. (1985). *Imagine: A visionary model for the counselors of tomorrow.* DeKalb, IL: George's Printing.

Orlick, T., & Partington, J. (1987). The sport psychology consultant: Analysis of critical components as viewed by Canadian Olympic athletes. *The Sport Psychologist, 1,* 4–17.

Osachuk, T., & Cairns, S. (1995). Relationship issues. In D. Martin & A. Moore (Eds.), *First steps in the art of intervention: A guidebook for trainees in the helping professions* (pp. 19–43). Pacific Grove, CA: Brooks-Cole.

Pearson, R., & Petitpas, A. (1990). Transitions of athletes: Developmental and preventive perspectives. *Journal of Counseling & Development, 69,* 7–10. doi:10.1002/j.1556-6676.1990.tb01445.x

Petitpas, A., Brewer, B., & Van Raalte, J. (2009). Transitions of the student-athlete: Theoretical, empirical, and practical perspectives. In E. F. Etzel (Ed.), *Counseling and psychological services for college student-athletes* (pp. 283–302). Morgantown, WV: Fitness Information Technology.

Petitpas, A., & Danish, S. (1995). Psychological care for injured athletes. In S. Murphy (Ed.), *Sport psychology interventions* (pp. 255–282). Champaign, IL: Human Kinetics.

Petitpas, A., & France, T. (2010). Identity foreclosure in sport. In S. J. Hanrahan & M. B. Andersen (Eds.), *Handbook of applied sport psychology* (pp. 282–291). New York, NY: Routledge.

Petitpas, A. J., Buntrock, C. L., Van Raalte, J. L., & Brewer, B. W. (1995). Counseling athletes: A new specialty in counselor education. *Counselor Education and Supervision, 34,* 212–219. doi:10.1002/j.1556-6978.1995.tb00243.x

Petitpas, A. J., & Champagne, D. (2000). Sport and social competence. In S. J. Danish & T. P. Gullotta (Eds.), *Developing competent youth and strong communities through after-school programming* (pp. 115–137). Washington, DC: CWLA Press.

Petitpas, A. J., & Cornelius, A. (2004). Practitioner–client relationships: Building working alliances. In G. S. Kolt & M. Andersen (Eds.), *Psychology in the physical and manual therapies* (pp. 57–70). Edinburgh, Scotland: Churchill Livingston. doi:10.1016/B978-0-443-07352-6.50010-5

Petitpas, A. J., Cornelius, A., & Van Raalte, J. (2008). Youth development through sport: It's all about relationships. In N. L. Holt (Ed.), *Positive youth development through sport* (pp. 61–70). New York, NY: Routledge.

Petitpas, A. J., Cornelius, A. E., Van Raalte, J. L., & Jones, T. (2005). A framework for planning youth sport programs that foster psychosocial development. *The Sport Psychologist, 19,* 63–80.

Petitpas, A. J., Danish, S. J., & Giges, B. (1999). The sport psychologist–athlete relationship: Implications for training. *The Sport Psychologist, 13,* 344–357.

Pinkerton, R. (2009). Forward. In E. F. Etzel (Ed.), *Counseling and psychological services for college student-athletes* (pp. viii–xi). Morgantown, WV: Fitness Information Technology.

Pittman, K. J. (1991). Promoting youth development: Strengthening the role of youth-serving and community organizations. *Report prepared for the U.S. Department of Agriculture Extension Services.* Washington, DC: Center for Youth Development and Policy Research.

Seligman, M. E. P., & Csikszentmihalyi, M. (2000). Positive psychology: An introduction. *American Psychologist, 55,* 5–14. doi:10.1037/0003-066X.55.1.5

Seligman, M. E. P., Steen, T. A., Park, N., & Peterson, C. (2005). Positive psychology progress: Empirical validation of interventions. *American Psychologist, 60,* 410–421. doi:10.1037/0003-066X.60.5.410

Shertzer, B., & Stone, S. (1966). *Fundamentals of counseling.* Boston, MA: Houghton Mifflin.

Simons, H. D., Bosworth, C., Fujita, S., & Jensen, M. (2007). The athlete stigma in higher education. *College Student Journal, 41,* 251–273.

Smith, A. M., Scott, S. G., O'Fallon, W. M., & Young, M. L. (1990). Emotional responses of athletes to injury. *Mayo Clinic Proceedings, 65,* 38–50. doi:10.1016/S0025-6196(12)62108-9

Smith, A. M., Scott, S. G., & Wiese, D. M. (1990). The psychological effects of sports injuries: Coping. *Sports Medicine, 9,* 352–369. doi:10.2165/00007256-199009060-00004

Society of Counseling Psychology. (2011). Counseling vs. clinical. Retrieved from http://www.div17.org/students_differences.html

Stambulova, N. B., & Alfermann, D. (2009). Putting culture into context: Cultural and cross-cultural perspectives in career development and transition research and practice. *International Journal of Sport and Exercise Psychology, 7,* 292–308. doi:10.1080/1612197X.2009.9671911

Steinfeldt, J., Reed, C., & Steinfeldt, M. C. (2010). Racial and athletic identity of African American football players at historically Black colleges and universities and predominantly White institutions. *Journal of Black Psychology, 36*(1), 3–24. doi:10.1177/0095798409353894

Tinsley, T. M. (2005). The self-reported multicultural sports counseling competencies among professional school counselors and Play It Smart academic coaches (Doctoral dissertation, Duquesne University). *Dissertation Abstracts International, 66*(11), 3942. (UMI No. 3199518)

United States Olympic Committee. (1983). USOC establishes guidelines for sport psychology services. *Journal of Sport Psychology, 5,* 4–7.

Van Raalte, J. L., Brewer, B. W., Brewer, D. D., & Linder, D. E. (1992). NCAA Division II college football players' perceptions of an athlete who consults a sport psychologist. *Journal of Sport & Exercise Psychology, 14,* 273–282.

Ward, D. G., Sandstedt, S. D., Cox, R. H., & Beck, N. C. (2005). Athlete-counseling competencies for U.S. psychologists working with athletes. *The Sport Psychologist, 19,* 318–334.

Weiner, I. (2003). *Handbook of psychology* (Vol. 1–12). Hoboken, NJ: Wiley. doi:10.1002/0471264385

White, R. W. (1959). Motivation reconsidered: The concept of competence. *Psychological Review, 66,* 297–333. doi:10.1037/h0040934

White, R. W. (1963). *Ego and reality in psychoanalytic theory: A proposal regarding independent ego energies* (Psychological Issues, Vol 3., No. 3, Monograph 11). New York, NY: International Universities Press.

Wiese-Bjornstal, D. M., & Smith, A. M. (1993). Counseling strategies for enhanced recovery of injured athletes within a team approach. In D. Pargman (Ed.), *Psychological bases of sport injuries* (pp. 149–182). Morgantown, WV: Fitness Information Technology.

Tanya Forneris, Kathryn A. Conley, Steven J. Danish,
and Lauren M. Stoller

Teaching Life Skills Through Sport

Community-Based Programs to Enhance Adolescent Development

12

S port has the capacity to enhance competence and promote development throughout the life span (Danish, Petitpas, & Hale, 1993). As a result, many sport psychologists are as concerned about "life" development as they are about athletic development. The parallels between sport and the challenges encountered throughout life are numerous; thus, it is not surprising that the effects of life-skills-oriented sport psychology interventions extend beyond the playing arena. Said another way, the learning that takes place in sport can generalize to "real life."

In this chapter, we focus on how sport can be an environment for teaching life skills to athletes of all ages. Because we have adopted a life skills perspective, our aims may differ from those of other sport psychology orientations. We begin by reviewing the literature on the use of life skills within sport. We then delineate the framework we have used to develop and implement our sport-based life skills intervention program (Sports United to Promote Education and Recreation, or SUPER) with a brief overview of

http://dx.doi.org/10.1037/14251-012
Exploring Sport and Exercise Psychology, Third Edition, J. Van Raalte and
B. Brewer (Editors)

how this framework has evolved to include aspects of self-determination theory (Deci & Ryan, 2002). Following the discussion of the framework, we examine ways of delivering and evaluating life skills programs in various community settings.

An Overview of Life Skills

There are multiple definitions of *life skills*. For example, the World Health Organization (1999) defined life skills as "abilities for adaptive and positive behaviour that enable individuals to deal effectively with the demands and challenges of everyday life" (p. 1). More specifically, the World Health Organization identified life skills as a group of cognitive, personal, and interpersonal abilities that help individuals make informed decisions, solve problems, think critically and creatively, communicate effectively, and build healthy relationships. Danish, Forneris, Hodge, and Heke (2004) defined life skills as

> those skills that enable individuals to succeed in the different environments in which they live such as school, home and in their neighborhoods. Life skills can be behavioral (communicating effectively with peers and adults) or cognitive (making effective decisions) and interpersonal (being assertive) or intrapersonal (setting goals). (p. 40)

Gould and Carson (2008) defined *sport-based life skills* as "those internal personal assets, characteristics and skills such as goal setting, emotional control, self-esteem, and hard work ethic that can be facilitated or developed in sport and are transferred for use in non-sport settings" (p. 60).

Research on Life Skills in Sport

Research has shown that youth develop a number of life skills through sport, such as goal setting, communication, time management, teamwork, responsibility, relationship building, respect, and leadership (Camiré, Trudel, & Forneris, 2009; Holt, Tamminem, Tink, & Black, 2009; Holt, Tink, Mandigo, & Fox, 2008; Jones & Lavallee, 2009), and may even develop values such as perseverance and honesty (Camiré & Trudel, 2010). In addition, research has shown that youth have positive experiences in sport when they are surrounded by caring and supportive coaches who demand a strong work ethic, provide constructive feedback, and communicate effectively and with whom youth can develop meaningful relationships (Collins, Gould, Lauer, & Chung, 2009; Fraser-Thomas, & Côté, 2009; Fraser-Thomas, Côté, & Deakin, 2008; Gould, Collins, Lauer, & Chung, 2007).

Biddle, Brown, and Lavallee (2008) conducted a review of life-skills-based interventions to determine the impact these programs have on positive youth development. They examined 11 life skills interventions that targeted youth (ages 10–18). Despite similarities in target population and intervention goals, the research studies differed in a number of aspects, including sample size, research design, and measures used. Biddle et al. separated the studies in their review by research design. Of the 11 interventions reviewed, five were experimental designs, three were nonexperimental pre–post designs, and three were longitudinal designs. Biddle et al. concluded that the five studies using experimental designs provided evidence that teaching life skills can lead to increased knowledge of various life skills—such as goal setting, problem solving, and positive thinking—and to increased self-efficacy with regard to using these skills. Results from some of these studies also indicated that life skills programs can lead to enhanced self-esteem, intrinsic motivation, and self-determined motivation (Goudas, Dermitzaki, Leondari, & Danish, 2006; Goudas & Giannoudis, 2008; Heke & Hodge, 2001; Kolovelonis, Goudas, Dimitriou, & Gerodimos, 2006; Papacharisis, Goudas, Danish, & Theodorakis, 2005). Four of these five experimental studies were based on the implementation of the SUPER program, a life skills program developed by Danish (2002b), described in detail in the section of this chapter titled Sports United to Promote Education and Recreation.

The results of the three nonexperimental pre–post designs demonstrated that participating in a life skills program can lead to increased community engagement, higher academic achievement, an increased sense of belongingness, as well as the development of respect and trust, social interest, social responsibility, and goal knowledge (Brunelle, Danish, & Forneris, 2007; Petitpas, Van Raalte, Cornelius, & Presbrey, 2004). In one study, these gains were maintained for 6 months (Brunelle et al., 2007). Similarly, the results from the two longitudinal studies demonstrated that life skills programming led to the development of various life skills, improved school attendance, and decreased misbehavior. Notably, Biddle et al. (2008) observed that a key factor in the development of life skills and positive developmental outcomes within youth settings is the formation of a positive relationship between the program leaders and youth participants.

Delineating a Framework for Life Skills

Two constructs serve as the basis for the conceptual framework of life skills programming: life development intervention (LDI; Danish & D'Augelli, 1980; Danish, D'Augelli, & Ginsberg, 1984; Danish & Forneris, 2008;

Danish et al., 1993) and self-determination theory (SDT; Deci & Ryan, 2000, 2002, 2008). LDI is based on a life-span human development perspective. A core feature of LDI is an emphasis on continuous growth and change with particular attention paid to critical life events (Danish & D'Augelli, 1980). Some refer to these events as *crises,* but it should be noted that the word *crisis* is not synonymous with disaster. Indeed, the origin of the word *crisis* is Greek and means decision. As defined in *The Random House Dictionary of the English Language* (1987), crisis is "a stage in a sequence of events at which the trend of all future events, especially for better or for worse, is determined; turning point." Critical life events may result in stress and impaired functioning or little or no change in life circumstances or may serve as a catalyst for growth (Danish & Forneris, 2008).

SDT is one of the most commonly used models of motivation, optimal growth, and psychological well-being in psychology (e.g., Deci & Ryan, 2002; Gagné, Ryan, & Bargmann, 2003; Hagger & Chatzisarantis, 2007; Reinboth & Duda, 2006; Reis, Sheldon, Gable, Roscoe, & Ryan, 2000; Richer, Blanchard, & Vallerand, 2002). Deci and Ryan (2000) described the psychological needs of autonomy, competence, and relatedness as central to well-being and fulfillment for all individuals regardless of age, gender, or culture (see also Ryan & Deci, 2002). Hodge, Danish, and Martin (2012) noted that by integrating aspects of SDT with the LDI model, the life skills conceptual framework is strengthened. That is, life skills programs focused on autonomy, competence, and relatedness—the three basic psychological needs identified in SDT—are especially effective for people experiencing critical life events.

Sports United to Promote Education and Recreation

SUPER (Danish, 2002b) uses the context of sport as a training ground for life. Participants are taught to use a variety of physical and mental skills to improve their athletic performance, to recognize situations both in and out of sports requiring these skills, and then to apply them in sport and nonsport settings. The overall goal of the SUPER program is to have participants recognize that there is a relationship between performance excellence in sport and personal excellence in life and that life skills can enhance both sport and personal performance. SUPER is a peer-led series of 18 modules taught like sports clinics. Participants are involved in three sets of activities: learning the physical skills related to a specific sport, learning life skills related to sports in general, and playing the sport. SUPER is patterned after the nationally known, award-winning Going for the Goal program (Danish, 2002a). Going for the

Goal is the 1996 winner of the Lela Rowland Prevention Award given by the National Mental Health Association and has been honored by the U.S. Department of Health and Human Services.

The leaders of the SUPER program are older student-athletes (e.g., high school, university). The rationale for using a peer-led approach is to create what Seidman and Rappaport (1974) called an *educational pyramid*. Such a pyramid starts with the life skills center staff, who develop the intervention and then train the SUPER student-athlete leaders who implement the intervention. The SUPER leaders then teach the SUPER program to youth, completing the pyramid. There are a number of advantages to this implementation strategy. First, successful older peers serve as concrete images of what younger adolescents can become. Therefore, because SUPER leaders have often grown up in the same neighborhoods, attended the same schools, and confronted similar roadblocks as the SUPER participants, they serve as important role models and thus are in an ideal position to be effective teachers (Danish, 1997). A second goal is to extend the educational pyramid into community organizations by training on-site community professionals to select and train SUPER leaders and oversee the program's implementation, thereby increasing program opportunities and sustainability.

The SUPER program has been implemented and evaluated in a number of contexts and countries. For example, Danish and his colleagues (Brunelle et al., 2007; Danish, 2001) applied this model to golf in their collaboration with The First Tee, a national golf and life skills enrichment academy for underserved adolescents. Results from an evaluation of The First Tee indicated that the program had a significant positive impact on adolescents' prosocial values. Papacharisis et al. (2005) applied an abbreviated (eight-session) version of the SUPER program to soccer and volleyball with Greek school children ages 10 to 12. Two pretest–posttest comparison group design evaluations were conducted. In both studies, measures included assessments of physical skills; knowledge of the SUPER program; and self-beliefs about the ability to set goals, problem solve, and think positively. The results of both studies indicated that students who received the intervention endorsed higher self-beliefs for personal goal setting, problem solving, and positive thinking than did those on the control teams. In addition, students in the intervention group demonstrated an increase in program knowledge and improvement in physical skills compared with students in the control condition.

The SUPER program was also adapted and implemented with an indigenous population in New Zealand. The *Hokowhitu* program (Heke, 2001) is a sport-based intervention program designed by New Zealand Maori for New Zealand Maori using Maori language and culture in program development, implementation, and evaluation. The Hokowhitu program sought to use sport to teach life skills such as decision making, time management, task-related discipline, and goal setting.

The Hokowhitu program involved ten 2-hour workshops taught by eight *Tuakana*, senior high school students ages 16 to 18. Although the Tuakana benefited from being involved with the Hokowhitu program, the main recipients of the Hokowhitu program were 25 *Teina*, students ages 10 to 13. The Hokowhitu program also recruited life skills coaches or *Kaiwhakawaiwai*, who were employed by the Raukawa Trust Board to train the Tuakana in communication, group management, and the teaching skills necessary for running the Hokowhitu program. The Kaiwhakawaiwai remained on site while the Hokowhitu program was being taught, but the Tuakana were encouraged to teach the Kaiwhakawaiwai intervention independently. Throughout the 10 sessions, sport was used as the metaphor for teaching life skills. The Hokowhitu program was conducted and evaluated at an intermediate school by the Ministry of Education of New Zealand. Those in the ministry concluded that the program benefited youth as a result of the use of the preferred learning styles and protocols of Maori. They also noted that student self-esteem, attitude, and focus increased markedly and greater confidence was shown in planning for future career choices.

Papacharisis et al. (2005) adapted the SUPER program (Danish, 2002b) for use with youth ($M = 11.5$ years) volleyball ($n = 40$) and soccer ($n = 32$) players. The experimental group was taught life skills at the beginning of each training session for 8 weeks. The results of the study indicated that students who received the intervention had higher self-beliefs for personal goal setting, problem solving, and positive thinking than did those in the control group. In addition, the intervention group demonstrated an increase in program knowledge and improvement in physical skills compared with the control group.

Goudas et al. (2006) extended Papacharisis et al.'s (2005) work with students in middle school physical education classes ($n = 73$, $M = 12.32$ years). As in the previous studies, the researchers found that the experimental group improved significantly more than the control group in self-beliefs for personal goal setting, problem solving, and positive thinking and maintained the positive changes over a 1-month follow up period. Kolovelonis et al. (2006) expanded on Goudas et al.'s (2006) study by examining the intrinsic and extrinsic motivation (labeled *self-determination*) of the same 73 students and found that higher positive scores in life skills knowledge and self-belief correlated with greater self-determination. Further, Goudas and Giannoudis (2008) examined the effect of a 17-session version of the SUPER program with middle school physical education classes. Life skills were taught to participants ($n = 130$, ages 12–14 years) prior to starting team sport activities. Results were similar to those of Papacharisis et al. (2005), although the only significant change in self-beliefs occurred for negative thinking.

Forneris (2011) collaborated with a local Nepalese nongovernment organization to implement a physical-activity-based life skills program in Nepal. This program was adapted from SUPER and focused on five life skills (goal setting, communication, teamwork, confidence, and leadership). A pilot version of the program was implemented in 2007 with sixth- through eighth-grade students in four government (public) schools. More specifically, each grade participated in one life skills session per day for a period of 3 weeks for a total of 15 sessions. The education system in Nepal is based primarily on rote learning, and therefore there is very little active participation on the part of the students. Because of this structure, the little experience students have participating in physical activity games, and the limited exposure to the concept of life skills, the program was structured so that the youth were exposed to each of the five life skills repetitively throughout the 3-week program. It was believed that this structure would lead to a greater understanding of the life skills and would provide increased opportunity to practice each of the skills. The program was implemented by teams of Canadian and Nepalese university students. Each school had a team of two Canadian university students and one Nepalese university student who had a prior relationship with the school.

To examine the impact of the pilot program, interviews were conducted with the Canadian university students and the Nepalese leaders, and school principals completed open-ended questionnaires. Results from the study indicated that all involved believed the program to be very important for both the development of Nepalese youth as well as the development of the country. One principal wrote,

> If the students have an opportunity to do the program like this
> regularly it will be helpful for their life and study . . . I think
> Nepali youth need to continue to develop into healthy adults.
> The youth are the backbone of the country.

All of the participants reported that the program had a positive effect on youth, particularly for increasing confidence, developing initiative, and goal setting. One program leader shared, "It has injected in them a notion of many good things like goal-setting, confidence building, and leadership development."

To enhance the sustainability of such life skills programs in Nepal, the program was implemented again the following year in three of the four schools. The goal of this implementation was to have the youth engage in the program for a second time to continue to enhance their life skills development and to establish life skills clubs at the schools. Between six and eight youths from Grades 7 and 8 who had participated in the life skills programming and were interested in becoming leaders, formed life skills clubs at their schools. These clubs were then responsible for organizing life skills activities at their schools throughout the school year. The life skills club was overseen by the Nepalese leader who had implemented the physical-activity-based life skills program with the Canadian students. Results from a qualitative study that examined the impact of these life skills clubs indicated that the youth increased their confidence, leadership, and ability to work well with others. For example, one youth shared, "I have developed self-confidence and I have guts to speak in front of other people. I learnt that I can be successful if I work jointly with others." Another stated, "Before, I did not have control over the class when playing games but after Life Skill training I have good leadership skill and confident to control over junior classes." These life skills clubs continue to organize life skill activities in their schools. To enhance the sustainability and impact of life skills programming in Nepal, a workshop for teachers from the government schools was conducted. The 3-day teacher training workshop focused on helping teachers learn about how they can integrate life skills activities into their curriculum and teach social and personal responsibility to their students.

Delivering Life Skills Programs in Community Settings

Effective delivery of life skills programming includes awareness of and adaptation to the needs of a particular community. However, the more an intervention is adapted or becomes removed from those who designed it, the more likely it is to lose some (if not all) of its essence. Several steps can be taken to increase the likelihood that much of a program's essence will be maintained.

When making contact with teams, organizations, schools, or community groups, it is important that local personnel are identified to serve as a coordinating group for their community. This coordinating group can become an essential part of what Seidman and Rappaport (1974) called an educational pyramid, which may also be seen as a leadership pyramid. Providing life skills and leadership opportunities at all levels maximizes the positive effect that these skills can have for all participants in the program. Moreover, involving various constituencies within a community expands community capacity through a radiating process.

As part of this process, local groups are encouraged to find local private sector support to implement programming. Having private sector support enhances the community's sense of control. To obtain support from the private sector, the following guidelines have proved to be helpful. First, a program curriculum must be developed, printed, and available for dissemination so that interested private sector sponsors can see how the program operates. Second, it is critical when establishing relationships with other systems, either in the public or private sector, that a credible local person assist in developing contacts and serve as a champion for the program. Third, the cost of the dissemination must be reasonable and specific, as determined, for example, by use-per-person cost. In this way, a local organization can sponsor or cosponsor a program and, if the cost is reasonable, make an ongoing commitment. Finally, programs that have the potential to enhance life skills are much more likely to be supported by private businesses because they see these skills as essential for future employees (Danish, 1997).

A typical educational pyramid consists of four levels: (a) the staff who know the program and are skilled in training others; (b) the community, organization, and/or school personnel who receive training, practice teaching skills, and coordinate the program in their respective settings; (c) peer leaders who are selected by their organizations, schools, or communities and serve as positive role models; and (d) younger students who are recipients of and participants in the program. Educating, training, and involving other interested and available constituents enhance the commitment of the community to the program. With such a commitment, there is a greater likelihood that the communities and schools will involve themselves and their students more completely in the program, which increases the chances that the program will be successful and sustainable.

Once the community is organized and staff who know the program and are skilled in training others are ready, peer leaders should be identified and trained. Peer leaders are especially effective at teaching skills because they are able to use their own experiences and successes as examples. If the role of the leader were to impart information, a more knowledgeable messenger such as a classroom teacher would be the most appropriate choice. However, because life skills are being taught, the more similar the teachers and students are in their life experiences and skill level, the more the students will learn (Danish, 1997). In other words, when teaching life skills to adolescents, a coping model is preferred over a mastery model. During the training, the peer leaders learn the concepts taught in the program and how to apply them to their own lives. In addition, they learn how to teach these skills to younger students, the program's ultimate audience. Leaders are also taught how to work with groups, organize a class or lecture, encourage discussion, be good listeners, teach skills, facilitate the transfer of skills, communicate effectively, give feedback, and manage groups of peers and adults. They are given guidelines on what to say and how long each activity should take. A critical program component is for peer leaders to gain experience sharing their personal experiences with the students.

Over the course of the training, many peer leaders come to realize that they have been entrusted with influencing the future of students who are just a few years their junior. The students have positive role models in those who teach and supervise them and have an opportunity to take their first steps in the direction of becoming community leaders themselves. According to DePree's (1989) definition, *leaders* are people who facilitate others (individuals, families, organizations and/or communities) in reaching their potential by (a) helping them identify goals related to their potential, (b) instilling in them the confidence to reach these goals, (c) teaching them to develop and implement a plan to attain these goals, and (d) encouraging them to share with others in their community what they have learned. In other words, leaders have the requisite life skills necessary to succeed and the commitment and vision to use their skills and knowledge to help others succeed.

Evaluating Life Skills Programs in Community Settings

There is undoubtedly a great need for positive youth development programs, including programs that focus on developing life skills. However, community-based programs often struggle to gain acceptance and widespread adoption. Funding available for community programs is often insufficient to allow for a comprehensive and rigorous evaluation. In addition, individuals within community organizations who implement programs do not always have the experience needed to implement a rigorous evaluation. Furthermore, when researchers are the primary developers and implementers of a program, they often do not work closely enough with community organizations to translate research findings into practice. However, a number of steps can be taken to promote rigorous program evaluation that will allow for the continued improvement, acceptance, and widespread adoption of life-skills-based programs in community settings.

The Reach, Efficacy/Effectiveness, Adoption, Implementation, and Maintenance (RE-AIM) framework is an evaluation model that stresses the use of a multidimensional approach to program evaluation (Dzewaltowski, Glasgow, Klesges, Estabrooks, & Brock, 2004; Glasgow, Vogt, & Boles, 2004). Each of these RE-AIM components helps to ensure that the evaluation carried out is feasible yet comprehensive. In addition, the framework incorporates both process and outcome evaluation components. Process evaluation complements outcome evaluation and focuses on describing and assessing the implementation of the program. More specifically, process evaluation examines aspects such as how well the intervention was delivered, who received the program, whether the program was delivered as planned, and whether the program reached the target population (Dehar, Casswell, & Duigan, 1993; McGraw et al., 1994). Outcome evaluation assesses the immediate effects of the program on its participants (e.g., pre-to-post changes in life skills knowledge or behavior; Wurzbach, 2004).

The Reach dimension of the RE-AIM framework examines the percentage of potentially eligible participants who participated or were excluded and how representative these individuals are within the community or setting in which the program is being implemented. To determine the Reach dimension, demographic information and participation rates are collected.

The Efficacy/Effectiveness dimension examines the impact of the intervention on process intermediate and primary outcomes and on both positive and negative (unintended) outcomes for all participants who started the program. This dimension involves the use of outcome measures such as quantitative self-report and/or observational measures and/or qualitative interviews designed to capture changes in behavior, knowledge, and attitudes. It is important to recognize that a criticism of program evaluation research is that evaluation focuses on outcomes that were not specifically addressed in the program (Durlak & Wells, 1997). Therefore, it is critical that the outcomes measured in the program evaluation are those outcomes that the program was designed to impact, and these outcomes should be determined while the program is being developed.

The Adoption dimension examines what percentage of settings and intervention agents within these settings (e.g., teams, schools, educators) participated and how representative they were. Therefore, the Adoption dimension collects demographic as well as operational data about the various sites that adopted, did not adopt, or were excluded from receiving the program.

The Implementation dimension examines the extent to which the various intervention components were delivered as intended. As a result, the Implementation dimension focuses on the process evaluation and involves fidelity checks (e.g., number of sessions implemented, sessions implemented as designed, leader and participant attendance) and participants' receptivity and enjoyment of the program. Measures within the implementation dimension can involve having independent observers randomly observe sessions, having instructors complete surveys after each session has been taught, or tracking the number of participants and conditions under which the program is implemented (e.g., determining whether the school or community cooperative is providing enough time and space needed to effectively implement the program).

Finally, the Maintenance dimension examines the extent to which a program or policy becomes institutionalized and the long-term effects of a program on outcomes (e.g., 6 months or 1 year postprogram).

Therefore, the Maintenance dimension involves collecting data at the individual level and at the setting level. At the individual level, the data collection may be very similar to the process used in the Efficacy/Effectiveness dimension. It is important to measure those outcomes examined under the Efficacy/Effectiveness dimension longitudinally. However, it is also important at this stage of evaluation to examine the intended long-term outcomes (e.g., transfer of life skills, quality of life) of the program. As with immediate program outcomes, these intended long-term outcomes should be delineated at the design phase of the program. At the level of setting, data pertaining to how sustainable the program has been within the organization(s) in which the program was implemented are collected. Specifics may include whether the program is still being implemented, how much of the program is being implemented as it was originally designed, the number of resources being allocated for program sustainability, and number of staff members trained since the initial program implementation.

Conclusion

Life skills programs, particularly those that are sport based, have the potential to reach millions of youth. Providing opportunities for more adolescents to experience programs that teach both sport and life skills will require recruiting and training new coaches and retraining current coaches to teach these programs. It will require expanding a community's capacity to offer such programs by reaching out to its largest and most untapped, yet valuable, resource—the youth themselves. Collaborating with national organizations, including professional sports organizations, to disseminate effective programs will be necessary if sport psychologists wish to expand the number of adolescents they reach and enhance the impact on those they do reach. Finally, they need to recognize that sport is a common means of communication; it extends beyond the limits of language and national boundaries. For this reason, using sport to teach life skills may be an effective means of helping youth around the world to develop skills that will help them become successful and perhaps even leaders of the future.

References

Biddle, S., Brown, H., & Lavallee, D. (2008). *The development of life skills in children through golf.* Loughborough, England: The Institute of Youth Sport.

Brunelle, J., Danish, S. J., & Forneris, T. (2007). The impact of a sport-based life skill program on adolescent prosocial values. *Applied Developmental Science, 11,* 43–55.

Camiré, M., & Trudel, P. (2010). High school athletes' perspectives on character development through sport participation. *Physical Education and Sport Pedagogy, 15,* 193–207. doi:10.1080/17408980902877617

Camiré, M., Trudel, P., & Forneris, T. (2009). High school athletes' perspectives on support, communication, negotiation and life skill development. *Qualitative Research in Sport and Exercise, 1,* 72–88. doi: 10.1080/19398440802673275

Collins, K., Gould, D., Lauer, L., & Chung, Y. (2009). Coaching life skills through football: Philosophical beliefs of outstanding high school football coaches. *International Journal of Coaching Science, 3,* 29–54.

Danish, S. J. (1997). Going for the Goal: A life skills program for adolescents. In T. Gullotta & G. Albee (Eds.), *Primary prevention works* (pp. 291–312). Newbury Park, CA: Sage. doi:10.4135/9781452243801.n13

Danish, S. J. (2001). The first tee: Teaching youth to succeed in golf and life. In P. R. Thomas (Ed.), *Optimizing performance in golf* (pp. 67–74). Brisbane: Australian Academic Press.

Danish, S. J. (2002a). *Going for the goal: Leader manual* (4th ed.). Richmond: Virginia Commonwealth University, Life Skills Associates.

Danish, S. J. (2002b). *SUPER (Sports United to Promote Education and Recreation) program: Leader manual and student activity book* (3rd ed.). Richmond: Virginia Commonwealth University, Life Skills Center.

Danish, S. J., & D'Augelli, A. (1980). Promoting competence and enhancing development through life development intervention. In L. A. Bond & J. C. Rosen (Eds.), *Primary prevention of psychopathology* (Vol. 4, pp. 105–129). Hanover, NH: University Press of New England.

Danish, S. J., D'Augelli, A., & Ginsberg, M. (1984). Life development intervention: Promotion of mental health through the development of competence. In S. Brown & R. Lent (Eds.), *Handbook of counseling psychology* (pp. 520–544). New York, NY: Wiley.

Danish, S. J., & Forneris, T. (2008). Promoting positive development and competency across the lifespan. In S. D. Brown & R. W. Lent (Eds.), *Handbook of counseling psychology* (4th ed., pp. 500–517). Hoboken, NJ: Wiley.

Danish, S. J., Forneris, T., Hodge, K., & Heke, I. (2004). Enhancing youth development through sport. *World Leisure Journal, 46,* 38–49. doi:10.1080/04419057.2004.9674365

Danish, S. J., Petitpas, A. J., & Hale, B. D. (1993). Life development intervention for athletes: Life skills through sports. *The Counseling Psychologist, 21,* 352–385. doi:10.1177/0011000093213002

Deci, E. L., & Ryan, R. (2008). Facilitating optimal motivation and psychological well-being across life's domains. *Canadian Psychology, 49,* 14–23. doi:10.1037/0708-5591.49.1.14

Deci, E. L., & Ryan, R. M. (2000). The "what" and "why" of goal pursuits: Human needs and the self-determination of behavior. *Psychological Inquiry, 11,* 227–268. doi:10.1207/S15327965PLI1104_01

Deci, E. L., & Ryan, R. M. (Eds.). (2002). *Handbook of self-determination research.* Rochester, NY: University of Rochester Press.

Dehar, M., Casswell, S., & Duigan, P. (1993). Formative and process evaluation of health promotion and disease prevention programs. *Evaluation Review, 17,* 204–220. doi:10.1177/0193841X9301700205

DePree, M. (1989). *Leadership is an art.* New York, NY: Doubleday.

Durlak, J. A., & Wells, A. M. (1997). Primary prevention mental health programs for children and adolescents: A meta-analytic review. *American Journal of Community Psychology, 25,* 115–152. doi:10.1023/A:1024654026646

Dzewaltowski, D. A., Glasgow, R. E., Klesges, L. M., Estabrooks, P. A., & Brock, E. (2004). RE-AIM: Evidence-based standards and a web resource to improve translation of research into practice. *Annals of Behavioral Medicine, 28,* 75–80. doi:10.1207/s15324796abm2802_1

Forneris, T. (2011). *The impact of school-based life skills programming in Nepal.* Manuscript submitted for publication.

Fraser-Thomas, J., & Côté, J. (2009). Understanding adolescents' positive and negative developmental experiences in sport. *The Sport Psychologist, 23,* 3–23.

Fraser-Thomas, J., Côté, J., & Deakin, J. (2008). Understanding dropout and prolonged engagement in adolescent competitive sport. *Psychology of Sport and Exercise, 9,* 645–662. doi:10.1016/j.psychsport.2007.08.003

Gagné, M., Ryan, R., & Bargmann, K. (2003). Autonomy support and need satisfaction in the motivation and well-being of gymnasts. *Journal of Applied Sport Psychology, 15,* 372–390. doi:10.1080/714044203

Glasgow, R. E., Vogt, T. M., & Boles, S. M. (1999). Evaluating the public health impact of health promotion interventions: The RE-AIM framework. *American Journal of Public Health, 89,* 1322–1327. doi:10.2105/AJPH.89.9.1322

Goudas, M., Dermitzaki, I., Leondari, A., & Danish, S. J. (2006). The effectiveness of teaching a life skills program in a physical education context. *European Journal of Psychology of Education, 21,* 429–438. doi:10.1007/BF03173512

Goudas, M., & Giannoudis, G. (2008). A team-sports-based life-skills program in a physical education context. *Learning and Instruction, 18,* 528–536. doi:10.1016/j.learninstruc.2007.11.002

Gould, D., & Carson, S. (2008). Personal development through sport. In O. Bar-Or & H. Hebestreit (Eds.), *The encyclopedia of sports medicine—The child and adolescent athlete* (pp. 287–301). Oxford, England: Blackwell Science.

Gould, D., Collins, K., Lauer, L., & Chung, Y. (2007). Coaching life skills through football: A study of award winning high school coaches. *Journal of Applied Sport Psychology, 19*, 16–37. doi:10.1080/10413200601113786

Hagger, M. S., & Chatzisarantis, N. L. D. (Eds.). (2007). *Intrinsic motivation and self-determination in exercise and sport.* Champaign, IL: Human Kinetics.

Heke, I. (2001). *The Hokowhitu Program: Designing a sporting intervention to address alcohol and substance abuse in adolescent Maori.* Unpublished manuscript, School of Physical Education, University of Otago, Dunedin, New Zealand.

Heke, I., & Hodge, K. (2001). *The Hokowhitu Programme: Pilot test.* Otago. Dunedin, New Zealand: University of Otago, Raukawa Trust Board and School of Physical Education..

Hodge, K., Danish, S. J., & Martin, J. (2012) Developing a conceptual framework for life skills interventions. *The Counseling Psychologist,* Advance online publication. doi:10.1177/0011000012462073

Holt, N. L., Tamminem, K. A., Tink, L. N., & Black, D. E. (2009). An interpretive analysis of life skills associated with sport participation. *Qualitative Research in Sport and Exercise, 1*, 160–175. doi:10.1080/19398440902909017

Holt, N. L., Tink, L. N., Mandigo, J. L., & Fox, K. L. (2008). Do youth learn life skills through their involvement in high school sport? A case study. *Canadian Journal of Education, 31*, 281–304.

Jones, M., & Lavallee, D. (2009). Exploring perceived life skills development and participation in sport. *Qualitative Research in Sport and Exercise, 1*, 36–50. doi:10.1080/19398440802567931

Kolovelonis, A., Goudas, M., Dimitriou, E., & Gerodimos, V. (2006). The effect of a life skills training program on students' self-determination. *Inquiries in Sport & Physical Education, 4*, 379–389.

McGraw, S. A., Stone, E. J., Osganian, S. K., Elder, J. P., Perry, C. L., Johnson, C. C., . . . Luepker, R. V. (1994). Design of process evaluation within the Child and Adolescent Trial for Cardiovascular Health (CATCH). *Health Education Quarterly, 21*, S5–S26.

Papacharisis, V., Goudas, M., Danish, S. J., & Theodorakis, Y. (2005). The effectiveness of teaching a life skills program in a sport context. *Journal of Applied Sport Psychology, 17*, 247–254. doi:10.1080/10413200591010139

Petitpas, A. J., Van Raalte, J. L., Cornelius, A. E., & Presbrey, J. (2004). A life skills development program for high school student athletes. *Journal of Primary Prevention, 24*, 325–334. doi:10.1023/B:JOPP.0000018053.94080.f3

The Random House Dictionary of the English Language (2nd ed.). (1987). New York, NY: Random House.

Reinboth, M., & Duda, J. (2006). Perceived motivational climate, need satisfaction, and indices of well-being in team sports: A longitudinal perspective. *Psychology of Sport and Exercise, 7,* 269–286. doi:10.1016/j.psychsport.2005.06.002

Reis, H. T., Sheldon, K. M., Gable, S. L., Roscoe, R., & Ryan, R. (2000). Daily well-being: The role of autonomy, competence, and relatedness. *Personality and Social Psychology Bulletin, 26,* 419–435. doi:10.1177/0146167200266002

Richer, F. S., Blanchard, C., & Vallerand, R. J. (2002). A motivational model of work turnover. *Journal of Applied Social Psychology, 32,* 2089–2113. doi:10.1111/j.1559-1816.2002.tb02065.x

Seidman, E., & Rappaport, J. (1974). The educational pyramid: A paradigm for training, research, and manpower utilization in community psychology. *American Journal of Community Psychology, 2,* 119–130. doi:10.1007/BF00878039

World Health Organization. (1999). *Partners in life skills education.* Geneva, Switzerland: Author.

Wurzbach, M. E. (2004). *Community health education and promotion: A guide to program design and evaluation* (2nd ed.). Toronto, Ontario, Canada: Jones & Bartlett.

CLINICAL ISSUES

Selen Razon and Gershon Tenenbaum

Measurement in Sport and Exercise Psychology

13

M easurement in sport and exercise psychology is a broad topic that includes measurement of psychological factors related to sport performance; of exercise adherence and related constructs; of team-related factors; of cognitive, affective, and self-assessment of athletes; and more (Tenenbaum, Eklund, & Kamata, 2012). There is not one "best" way to assess athletes and exercisers for performance enhancement, clinical concerns, or research purposes. Rather, the theoretical orientation of the practitioner and/or researcher guides the assessment and subsequent plan of action that is developed (see Chapter 2, this volume).

The purpose of this chapter is to highlight key aspects of measurement in sport and exercise psychology. We begin with a brief history of measurement in sport and exercise psychology, followed by an overview of methods for capturing psychological processes in athletes. Next, we discuss cultural, ethical, and other issues related to measurement within sport and exercise psychology settings. We conclude

http://dx.doi.org/10.1037/14251-013
Exploring Sport and Exercise Psychology, Third Edition, J. Van Raalte and B. Brewer (Editors)

with a presentation of tools for measuring psychological factors relevant to sport and exercise psychology (e.g., psychological skills, motivation, cognitive and perceptual processes, self-perception, affect, mood and emotion, perceived effort, team-related attributes, physical activity outcomes).

History of Measurement in Sport and Exercise Psychology

In the 1930s, Coleman Griffith designed surveys and questionnaires to measure a set of psychological attributes (e.g., attitudes, perceptions, personality) in athletes and coaches. This early sport psychology assessment work was followed by the design of the Athletic Motivation Inventory by Tutko, Lyon, and Ogilvie in 1969. Although both of these early attempts at measurement were positive developments in the field, they failed to meet the established psychometric standards of their time.

During the 1960s and 1970s, the "sport personality debate" emerged, focusing on the issue of whether there was an ideal personality for elite sport performance. The debate was decided when it became evident that the standardized personality tests were limited in their ability to accurately predict sport performance outcomes from elite athlete personality types (for reviews, see Mahoney & Epstein, 1981; Straub, 1978). By 1976, psychological testing of athletes was widespread to the point that the National Football League Players Association voted against the psychological testing of its members. This decision was largely due to the misuse of psychological tests and test results (Heil & Henschen, 1996).

Rather than focusing on testing to determine an athletic personality ideal in the 1970s, W. P. Morgan and his colleagues (W. P. Morgan, Brown, Raglin, O'Connor, & Ellickson, 1987; W. P. Morgan & Pollock, 1977) examined the mood and performance of athletes using the Profile of Mood States (McNair, Lorr, & Droppleman, 1971). W. P. Morgan et al. (1987) found that the best performers tended to report experiencing higher than average drive and below average anxiety, irritation, tiredness, and uncertainty.

Throughout the 1980s and into the 1990s, a number of sport-specific measurement tools, including the Competitive State Anxiety Inventory—II (Martens, Burton, Vealey, Bump, & Smith, 1982; Martens, Vealey, & Burton, 1990) and the Psychological Skills Inventory for Sports (Mahoney, Gabriel, & Perkins, 1987), were developed. By 1990, there were enough sport and exercise psychology tests to fill a book. Ostrow (1990) collected and presented 175 tests designed to measure aggression, anxiety, attention, attitudes toward sport and exercise, attributions, body image, cognitive strategies, cohesion, confidence, imagery, leadership, life adjustment, locus of control, motivation, sex roles, and more. These sport and exercise psychology tools were well received by applied sport psychologists because of their face validity and unique fit to sport settings. However, as improved rigor was brought to these sport-specific instruments, the psychometric integrity of some was called into question (Dewey, Brawley, & Allard, 1989; Vallerand, 1983). Tenenbaum and Bar-Eli's (1995) review concluded that sport psychology lagged behind other disciplines and did not use the most up-to-date measurement protocols. Andersen, McCullagh, and Wilson (2007) criticized the arbitrary metrics used in many sport and exercise inventories.

Zhu (2012) noted that the psychometric quality of sport and exercise psychology measurement would be significantly improved by (a) enhanced measurement training in sport and exercise psychology curricula, (b) the promotion of measurement-specific research in the field, (c) interdisciplinary thinking and research, (d) the adoption of systematic approaches directed at avoiding the use of poorly constructed measurement tools, and (e) the development of new measurement tools of high validity and reliability. Some of the ideas suggested are coming to fruition. For example, Tenenbaum et al.'s (2012) text on measurement in sport and exercise psychology may facilitate training and research on measurement-related issues in the field. Psychophysiological assessments tools including biofeedback and neurofeedback are being developed and used in sport settings for the assessment of psychological skills central to sport performance (see Beauchamp, Harvey, & Beauchamp, 2012). Sport psychology consultants are also using neuropsychological assessment tools for symptom recognition and management for athletes with concussions (see Kontos, Collins, & Russo, 2004).

Measurement in sport and exercise psychology is related to the development of measurement within the psychological and educational domains (Zhu, 2012). According to Zhu (2012), the most relevant developments in psychological and educational testing include computerized adaptive testing, cognitively based diagnostic assessment, and the technological revolution.

COMPUTERIZED ADAPTIVE TESTING

Adaptive tests allow test items to be administered on the basis of the examinee's performance on previously administered items. The concept of adaptive tests was developed during World Wars I and II when the military needed more efficient procedures than interviews for ordering the workforce into available occupations and improving training and selection. Initial algorithms and software for computerized adaptive tests were designed in 1970 and 1980s (Wainer et al., 1990; Weiss, 1983). Currently, computerized adaptive testing is used in educational realms to help determine proficiency and skill level on such exams as the Graduate Record Examination and the Test of English as a Foreign Language (Parshall, Spray, Kalohn, & Davey, 2003).

COGNITIVELY BASED DIAGNOSTIC ASSESSMENT

For a long time, measurement practice was focused on measuring the product rather than the process. Starting in the late 1980s, however, greater efforts have been made to integrate cognitive processes such as level of knowledge, learning, memory, mental representations, and schemas into measurement systems. The motive behind this initiative was to learn how and why individuals score in a particular way. Cognitively based diagnostic assessments typically are based on the latest theories from the field of cognitive psychology, current statistical models, and up-to-date technology (Leighton & Gierl, 2007; Tatsuoka, 2009).

COMPUTERS, THE INTERNET, AND THE TECHNOLOGICAL REVOLUTION

Technology has facilitated measurement in three main ways: (a) improved measurement efficiency by computerizing existing measurement tools, (b) measurement of new constructs in an all-inclusive manner through innovative formats (i.e., simulation), and (c) incorporation of measurement within instruction and/or intervention (Bennett, 2008). Advances in technology are expected to further the measurement process by allowing direct measurement of more complex concepts and abilities (Quellmalz & Pellegrino, 2009; Tucker, 2009).

SUMMARY

Historically, measurement has not been a strength of the field of sport and exercise psychology. However, increased attention, rigor, and collaboration among researchers in various fields of study have led to improvements. Some particularly promising collaborations are found in such areas as concussion assessment and psychophysiological testing.

Methods for Capturing Psychological Processes in Athletes

INTROSPECTION

Most sport and exercise psychology measures are introspective in nature, gauging a skill or quality within a person (Tenenbaum et al., 2012). To gather introspective data, practitioners or researchers speak directly to exercisers, athletes, team members, coaches, and sports organizations or administer questionnaires on such topics as self-concept, self-perception, self-efficacy, effort perception, motivation for sport and exercise, affect, mood, emotions, burnout, coping, team cohesion, team communication, and leadership. To the extent that introspective measures reflect subjective perceptions, results from introspective measures should be interpreted cautiously. Specifically, practitioners, clinicians, and researchers could use introspective data for purposes of description (i.e. diagnosis), prediction (i.e., prognosis), and process monitoring (i.e., recording changes due to intervention). This said, one should be cognizant of the fact that individuals differ in the ways they perceive the world and themselves. Respondents' preconceptions and biases are an inherent part of introspective data.

OBSERVATION

During observation, a phenomenon of interest is observed in its natural environment. Typically, efforts are made to observe and describe aspects of a setting without influencing the setting. The observer's role can range from complete observation to complete participation. During a complete observation, sport and exercise psychology practitioners might observe team practices as outsiders. In such circumstances, they are not members of the population that is being observed and have no past experience with the setting in which the observation is taking place. An example of complete observation would be the use of the Coaching Behavior Assessment System (CBAS; Smith, Smoll, & Hunt, 1977), which involves the assessment of 12 categories of coaching behavior. With the role of complete observer comes the benefit of separating oneself from the phenomenon under investigation and making comparisons to other settings.

A complete participant in sport and exercise psychology is someone who becomes immersed in the field setting and fully participates in the events under investigation. An example of a complete participant is an exercise psychologist interested in measuring the effect of recreational settings (e.g., cycling clubs, running groups, walking squads) on exercise participation. As a complete participant, the practitioner becomes a club member and attempts to understand how the social dynamics in the club and interactions among club members are related to exercise behaviors. A benefit that comes with being a complete participant is the opportunity to see and understand the events from the perspective of other participants.

It is important to note that in the majority of field settings, the observer may start in one role and shift to another. For example, a sport and exercise psychologist may start as a complete observer interested in effective coaching styles, observing coaches and their players. Over time, the observer may take on some tasks that are typically completed by an assistant coach, thus gradually increasing participation with the team and shifting into the role of partial participant. In another situation, a sport and exercise psychologist interested in the effects of parental involvement on youth sport participation may assume a participant role by enrolling in a program designed for young athletes' parents. Over time, the psychologist may gradually withdraw from the group to become an observer. Some observations are actually collaborations between the observer and the observed. For example, a coach might ask a sport and exercise psychology consultant to observe practice and then provide feedback to help improve coaching and training.

Observations can be documented in a number of ways, such as through field notes, time sampling, checklists, and video recordings. Each of these approaches has strengths and weaknesses. Use of a combination of assessment tools has proven to be particularly effective in many circumstances (for a review, see Tenenbaum & Driscoll, 2005).

INTERVIEWS

The purpose of an interview is to gather pertinent information from the interviewee's views and narratives (Patton, 2002). Interviews go beyond regular observations in that practitioners ask specific questions to interviewees, allowing meaning to be attached to answers. Interviews range from open-ended and unstructured to structured and standardized clinical intake and research-focused protocols. Detailed interview guides can be useful to ensure consistency of questioning across multiple interviewers and interviewees for research purposes. However, an overly detailed and structured approach may include leading probes and jeopardize the validity of the collected data (Shank, 2002) or may lead to missing important information that might otherwise have been covered in less structured formats.

Think-aloud interviews are interviewee driven and can help identify cognitive processes that emerge during task execution (Ericsson & Simon, 1993). During such interviews, interviewees are typically asked to "think aloud" while performing a task (e.g., executing a move, solving a problem, developing a strategy). The interviews are typically recorded and analyzed (for a review, see Eccles, 2012). Think-aloud interviews tend to provide more specific data than retrospective reports because people often find it easier to speak their current thoughts aloud than to fully and accurately recall their past thoughts and feelings. Further, retrospective reports often include people's beliefs and interpretations of what occurred and may not fully reflect their actual experiences. When one is using think-aloud interviews, it may be useful to provide some training because it can take time some people a while to become comfortable with speaking their thoughts aloud.

Focus group interviews typically involve six to nine people who are asked to discuss specific topics of interest (Greenbaum 1997, 2000; D. L. Morgan, 1988, 1998; D. L. Morgan & Krueger, 1997). During focus group sessions, participants listen to others and can expand on their own answers in relation to the discussion. Focus groups that include interviewees who know one another can be challenging for the interviewer. In these circumstances, some interviewees may be influenced to articulate beliefs and attitudes that are consistent with the expectations of others in the group rather than those that are a true reflection of their own beliefs (for a review, see Tenenbaum & Driscoll, 2005).

Special Measurement Considerations

CULTURAL ISSUES

J. C. Watson, Etzel, and Vosloo (2012) noted that it is important for sport and exercise psychologists to understand the cultural background of the people or populations they are assessing. Understanding one's own and other cultures requires going beyond socioeconomic status, country of origin, and religious background (Cohen, 2009) to consideration of such issues as social identity and relatedness to social groups organized around race, sexual orientation, ability, and age (Dadlani, Overtree, & Perry-Jenkins, 2012). Because no measures are culture free, efforts should be made to (a) use measurements with minimal cultural biases, (b) take into account the original population the measurement was developed for, and (c) be aware of the shortcomings of the measurement tools used (Etzel, Yura, & Perna, 1998). Extra care should be taken when using measurement tools that are not specifically created for the population being assessed (C. B. Fisher, 2003). It may be best to adopt a combination of several measures rather than relying solely on self-report measures (for reviews, see Fiske, 2002; Heine, Lehman, Peng, & Greenholtz, 2002).

Researchers in cultural sport psychology have clarified the intricate definitions of sport psychological terms including *motivation, emotion, cognition, self,* and *identity* in various cultural contexts (Ryba, Schinke, & Stambulova, 2012). The major tenet of cultural sport psychology is that it is culture that makes up one's psyche and gives meaning to behaviors; therefore, understanding psychological functioning requires understanding cultural meaning. Krane and Baird (2005) noted that "it is impossible to comprehend athletes' mental states and behaviors without understanding the social norms and culture that encompass them" (p. 88).

ETHICAL ISSUES

Ethical guidelines provide guidance related to the construction, administration, interpretation, and application of the results of measurement tools. For example, it is ethical for sport and exercise psychology practitioners to use appropriate measurement tools (see J. C. Watson et al., 2012), the most adequate measurement for the attributes and populations being assessed. This means that tools with demonstrated reliability and validity with the population being tested are a good choice. Measurement tools used in conjunction with broad unsubstantiated claims (e.g., this measure identifies the "best mentally strong players") are a poor choice. The specific tool selected may depend in part on the knowledge, skills, and training of the sport and exercise psychologist because some questionnaires require test administrators to have special training.

Those who are assessed have the right to privacy and confidentiality. That is, the data collected will be managed in such a way as to ensure the privacy and confidentiality of the people who are assessed. In sport and exercise psychology, maintaining privacy and confidentiality might include the use of pseudonyms and the omission of information related to team, year of season, and the player's nationality (for a review, see Kristiansen, Roberts, & Sisjord, 2011). Issues of confidentiality in sport and exercise psychology can be complicated by the assessment of children whose legal rights are more limited than those of adults and by the fame of some athletes. That is, there may be more pressure and interest in confidential results of assessments with famous athletes than with other populations.

Ethical standards hold that all people must be assessed of their own free will and must have the option to stop being measured at any time and at no cost (American Psychological Association, 2010, Standard 3.10,

Informed Consent). It is not ethical to force individuals to participate in a measurement process. Many sport and exercise practitioners use signed informed consent and/or assent forms at the start of the assessment process to make sure that those being assessed understand (a) the rationale for use of measurement, (b) pertinent costs, (c) interests of third parties (e.g., coaches, trainers, managers) in the measurement process, (d) the amount of time required for the assessment and feedback process, (e) the limits of confidentiality (M. A. Fisher, 2009), and (f) the storage plan for the data.

Common Measures of Psychological Variables in Sport and Exercise Psychology

Sport and exercise psychologists use numerous measures. Although it is beyond the scope of this chapter to present and discuss all of them, some of the most widely used assessment tools designed to measure psychological skills, motivation, cognitive and perceptual processes, the self, affect, mood, emotion, perceived effort, team factors, and physical activity are presented in the subsections that follow. See Tenenbaum et al. (2012) for a more thorough review of these and other measures.

MEASUREMENT OF PSYCHOLOGICAL SKILLS

Psychological skills include a number of mental skills (e.g., imagery, relaxation, goal setting, self-talk) that are critical to athletes' optimal performance (Weinberg & Forlenza, 2012). Measures have been developed to assess athletes' psychological skills, most of which involve retrospective reports of general psychological skill use and abilities. Unfortunately, many of these measures are limited by the arbitrary metrics that they use (Andersen et al., 2007).

Measures designed to assess psychological skills such as mental preparation, focus, confidence, emotional control, goal setting, motivation for achievement, self-talk, imagery, and relaxation include the Psychological Skills Inventory for Sports (Mahoney et al.,1987), the Athletic Coping Skills Inventory—28 (Smith, Schutz, Smoll, & Ptacek, 1995), and the Test of Performance Strategies (Thomas, Murphy, & Hardy, 1999). To more precisely measure psychological skills, instruments have been developed to assess particular skills such as imagery and self-talk. For example, the Movement Imagery Questionnaire—Revised (MIQ–R; Hall & Martin, 1997), Vividness of Movement Imagery Questionnaire

(VMIQ; Isaac, Marks, & Russell, 1986), and Vividness of Visual Imagery Questionnaire (Roberts, Callow, Hardy, Markland, & Bringer, 2008) all measure athletes' ability to use imagery. The Sport Imagery Questionnaire (Hall, Mack, Paivio, & Hausenblas, 2007) evaluates the frequency of use for various types of imagery. These measures have adequate reliability. However, the MIQ–R may be the imagery measure of choice because of its ease of administration. When working with teams with limited physical space, the VMIQ could be the most appropriate because unlike the MIQ–R, the VMIQ does not require test takers to perform any physical movement during the test. Ideally, the VMIQ and the MIQ–R can be used in conjunction and in a complementary fashion because these measure different aspects of imagery ability (Hall & Martin, 1997).

Questionnaires designed to measure self-talk generally involve retrospective recall of self-talk during past performances. These measures have good reliability. However, the extent to which they fully assess athletes' self-talk during particular performances is unclear. Actual self-talk used during sport performance can be hard to accurately recall. Some of the more widely used self-talk questionnaires include (a) the Self-Talk Use Questionnaire (J. Hardy, Hall, & Hardy, 2005), which measures the frequency and the type (positive, negative) of self-talk; (b) the Functions of Self-Talk Questionnaire (Theodorakis, Hatzigeorgiadis, & Chroni, 2008), which gauges the functions inherent in self-talk use and the reasons prompting the athlete to use self-talk (e.g., focusing); and (c) the Self-Talk Questionnaire (Zervas, Stavrou, & Psychountaki, 2007), which assesses the extent to which self-talk is related to learning, performance, focus, and confidence in sport.

Psychological skills assessment tools can be used to measure specific variables at one point in time and to measure the effectiveness of psychological skills interventions when providing applied services to athletes and teams or when assessing psychological skills for research purposes. Such outcome assessments can be carried out using pretest–posttest or other designs, providing useful data about (a) the psychological skills of athletes, (b) the effects of psychological interventions, and (c) guiding the development of future interventions. To support the collection of outcome data, the American Psychological Association created PracticeOUTCOMES: Measures for Psychologists, a database providing information about outcome measures useful for practitioners (Nordal, 2012).

MEASUREMENT OF MOTIVATION

Motivation is "the hypothetical construct used to describe the internal and/or external forces that produce the initiation, intensity, and persistence of behavior" (Vallerand & Thill, 1993, p. 18). *Intrinsic motivation* refers to the type of motivation experienced when one participates in an activity for its own sake and for the satisfaction associated with participating in it (Deci & Ryan, 1985, 2000). Tennis players who are motivated by the feeling of hitting the ball with a racquet and chasing down drop shots are examples of intrinsically motivated athletes. *Extrinsic motivation* refers to being motivated to participate in activities to gain something positive or avoid something negative (Deci & Ryan, 2000). Tennis players who strive only to expand on trophies and tournaments won are extrinsically motivated. Intrinsic motivation and extrinsic motivation are not mutually exclusive. A combination of intrinsic (e.g., enjoyment) and extrinsic (e.g., winning prizes, losing weight) motivational factors may factor into participation in sport and exercise. Finally, *amotivation* (Deci & Ryan, 1985) represents the lack of motivation, either intrinsic or extrinsic (Vallerand, 1997). Amotivation may help predict or explain some people's relative lack of persistence in sport and exercise settings.

A number of general measures of motivation in sport and exercise have been developed. These measures focus on specific populations or aspects of motivational processes. In addition to the questionnaires described in the paragraph that follows, information pertaining to motivation may be gathered from athletes' or exercisers' significant others, training partners, athletic trainers, and coaches (see Reiss & Havercamp, 1998).

The Situation Motivation Scale (Guay, Vallerand, & Blanchard, 2000) and the Sport Motivation Scale (Brière, Vallerand, Blais, & Pelletier, 1995) are used to assess intrinsic, extrinsic, and amotivation in athletes from different age groups and cultures. The Pictorial Motivation Scale (Reid, Vallerand, Poulin, & Crocker, 2009) is used with people with intellectual disability to assess reasons for participating in sport and exercise. The Behavioral Regulation in Sport Questionnaire (Lonsdale, Hodge, & Rose, 2008) is specifically designed to assess the motivation of elite athletes. Sport and exercise psychologists generally use motivation scales that have been validated with the population being studied and best match their assessment question of interest.

MEASUREMENT OF COGNITIVE AND PERCEPTUAL PROCESSES

The term *cognition* means "to know" or "to recognize." Cognitive processes include perception, recognition, attention, memory, language, knowledge, expertise, judgment, decision making, and reasoning. Thus, cognitive and perceptual processes are more than just knowing and represent a range of skills that enable people to engage mentally with the environment. A number of measures have been developed to assess these capacities. Generally, these measures are used in a complementary fashion as more than one assessment may be needed to best describe cognitive and perceptual capacities.

Anticipation in sport is the cognitive ability to predict the intentions of others, typically through bodily and other environmental cues. *Temporal occlusion methods* expose athletes to selected game-related video sequences gauging athletes' ability to pick up on relevant bodily cues and anticipate upcoming events (see A. M. Williams & Abernethy, 2012). The *spatial occlusion paradigm* is used to identify cues athletes rely on when anticipating opponents' moves in the field. Spatial occlusion resembles temporal occlusion, but in spatial occlusion, specific cues from video sequences are occluded for the full period of the test (see Abernethy & Russell, 1987; Müller, Abernethy, & Forrow, 2006; A. M. Williams & Davids, 1998). *Eye movement recording* captures athletes' gaze patterns, often through head-mounted corneal reflection systems. These systems identify the position of the pupil and the reflection of a light source off the surface of the cornea in a video image of the eye. The relative positions of the signals from these two sources are used to compute the point of gaze associated with the optics (for a review, see A. M. Williams, Janelle, & Davids, 2004). Finally, *verbal reports* are helpful in identifying thought processes during performances (Ericsson & Simon, 1993). Verbal reports require individuals to verbally express their thoughts aloud as they perform tasks.

Sport-and-exercise-psychology-specific measures of attention, orientation, executive functioning, and memory have not been created. Therefore, sport and exercise psychologists interested in assessing these variables use mainstream psychological measures such as the California Verbal Learning Test (Delis, Kramer, Kaplan, & Ober, 1987) and the Digit Span Test (Wechsler, 1997) to measure *memory capacity;* the Flanker Test (Eriksen & Schultz, 1979) to measure *executive functioning,* that is, higher order cognitive capacity that governs others functions, including planning, scheduling, and working memory (Etnier & Chang, 2009); and the Stroop Test (Stroop, 1935) to measure *attention and orientation.* The Mini-Mental Status Exam (Folstein, Folstein, & McHugh, 1975) can be used to measure cognitive impairment and a range of cognitive abilities, including orientation, attention, arithmetic abilities, memory, and language.

MEASUREMENT OF THE SELF

Self can be defined as a psychological construct that promotes conscious reflection on the individual's roles, descriptions, and assumed identities (Leary & Tangney, 2003). Self is a dynamic notion that is formed through interactions with others (Harter, 1999). In sport and exercise settings, *self-concept* (i.e., the way individuals describe themselves), *possible selves* (i.e., self-perceptions that are geared toward the future, such as the attractive, fit, hoped for self and the feared unhealthy self), and *self-efficacy* (i.e., beliefs individuals hold pertaining to how well they can accomplish specific tasks) are frequently measured (Zaccaro, Blair, Peterson, & Zananis, 1995). Results of self-measurement can be used to assess individual states and the effects of interventions.

To measure self-concept related to physical abilities in adult, adolescent, and youth populations, sport and exercise psychologists often use the Physical Self-Perception Profile (Fox, 1990; Fox & Corbin, 1989), the Self-Description Questionnaire III (Marsh & O'Neill, 1984), and the Children and Youth Physical Self-Perception Profile (Whitehead, 1995), respectively. Self-schemata pertaining to exercise behavior and overall interest in and commitment to exercise may be assessed through the Self-Schemata Measure (Markus, 1977), which requires test takers to endorse statements related to the self from a designated list. Possible selves can be assessed by the Close-Ended Possible Selves Measure (Markus & Nurius, 1986), which requires respondents to report on the number of positive and negative possible selves that they endorse from a provided list, and by the Open-Ended Possible Selves Measure (Cross & Markus, 1991; Dunkel, Kelts, & Coon, 2006). Possible selves can also be explored in depth by providing test takers with a blank sheet that includes lines to describe their hoped-for selves and another sheet to describe their feared possible selves (Cross & Markus, 1991). To explore the relationship between possible selves and exercise behavior, respondents may be asked to choose from their list of possible selves and the self that is most closely associated with the current level of exercise behavior and/or to answer specific closed-ended questions associated with the most important exercise-related self (for a review, see Whaley, 2003).

Self-efficacy with regard to exercise can be assessed by scales such as the Self-Efficacy for Exercise Scale (Resnick & Jenkins, 2000) and the Self-Efficacy to Regulate Exercise (Bandura, 2006), which gauge individuals' beliefs in their capacity to consistently participate in exercise despite perceived barriers. It is important to note that several barrier scales include relatively few items and thus may not assess relevant barriers. Self-efficacy with regard to carrying out a specific physical activity task can be measured using specific self-efficacy scales such as the Task-Specific Self-Efficacy Scale (Bandura, 2006) and the Tai Chi Exercise Self-Efficacy (Taylor-Piliae & Froelicher, 2004). These scales are most suitable for evaluating self-efficacy beliefs associated with a particular behavior. General measures of self-efficacy may not fully reflect the strength of an individual's self-efficacy beliefs for a specific task.

MEASUREMENT OF AFFECT, MOOD, AND EMOTION

Affect, mood, and emotion are related but distinct concepts. Roughly defined, the term *affect* represents mental states that result from the experience of feelings (Coan & Allen, 2007). Individuals experience core affects (e.g., pleasure, displeasure, tension, relaxation, energy, tiredness) continually, but the type and the degree of affect fluctuate over time (Ekkekakis, 2012). *Mood states* reflect the sum of affective states (D. Watson & Clark, 1997). Relative to affect, mood states endure longer and are felt less intensely (Ekman & Davidson, 1994). *Emotion* is a subjective feeling state that triggers the body for immediate vigorous reaction, a reaction that is both psychological and physiological in nature (*The Merriam-Webster Dictionary*, 2005). Anxiety is one of the most frequently measured emotions in sport settings (Janelle & Naugle, 2012).

Because affective states are important determinants of behavior, it can be useful to measure the fluctuation of affective states over time (Ekkekakis, 2012). For example, participating in exercise is known to decrease feelings of fatigue (Puetz, O'Connor, & Dishman, 2006) and to increase feelings of strength and vitality (Reed & Ones, 2006). People are more likely to continue to participate in exercise if they experience pleasure during exercise (Kwan & Bryan, 2010; D. M. Williams et al., 2008). With regard to sport performance, frequent and accurate assessment of affect and emotions can be used to identify optimal levels of emotion, precursors to optimal sport performance (Kamata, Tenenbaum, & Hanin, 2002).

Sport-and-exercise-specific measures of affect include the Exercise-Induced Feeling Inventory (Gauvin & Rejeski, 1993), the Subjective Exercise Experience Scale (McAuley & Courneya, 1994), and the Physical Activity Affect Scale (Lox, Jackson, Tuholski, Wasley, & Treasure, 2000). General measures of affect used in sport and exercise psychology include the Positive and Negative Affect Schedule (D. Watson, Clark, & Tellegen, 1988) and the Activation–Deactivation Adjective Checklist (Thayer, 1989). Specific measures of affect were developed on the basis of the premise that physical activity behaviors elicit specific affective responses best captured by specific measures of affect. Criticisms associated with these scales include their less than ideal fit with the latest theoretical frameworks and their development based primarily on data from select groups of young, healthy, active college students. The affect of elderly, disabled, physically inactive, and chronically ill populations may not be best captured using these scales (Ekkekakis, 2012). The Positive and Negative Affect Schedule is one of the most widely used measures of affect, but it has been criticized for its lack of items gauging *fatigue* and *serenity* (D. Watson & Clark, 1997), both of which are of particular interest to exercise psychology (Ekkekakis, 2012).

For easy administration, some researchers have developed shorter affect scales, such as the Self-Assessment Manikin (Bradley & Lang, 1994; Lang, 1980), the Affect Grid (Russell, Weiss, & Mendelsohn, 1989), the Feeling Scale (C. J. Hardy & Rejeski, 1989), and the Felt

Arousal Scale (Svebak & Murgatroyd, 1985). Because most of the extremely short measures are single-item scales, administration of these measures typically takes seconds, something that can be a strength when trying to assess fleeting emotions.

To measure mood, sport and exercise psychologists often use the Profile of Mood States (POMS; McNair et al., 1971). The POMS was initially developed for use with clinical populations; hence some caution may be needed when interpreting scores with nonclinical and physically active populations. Another practical consideration with the POMS is that its subscales measure primarily negative mood characteristics (i.e., tension, depression, anger, fatigue, confusion). Those examining depression may consider the Beck Depression Inventory (BDI; Beck, Steer, & Garbin, 1988) and the Hamilton Rating Scale for Depression (HRSD; Hamilton, 1960). A self-administered instrument, the BDI is easy to score and relatively inexpensive (Sharp & Lipsky, 2002). As for the HRSD, it is important to note that the HRSD is not a diagnostic tool but rather is designed for rating the severity of symptoms in individuals with major depression (Berrios & Bulbena-Villarasa, 1990; Hedlund & Viewig, 1979). Unlike the BDI, the HRSD is interviewer administered and scored. To reduce the bias that may be associated with the interviewer-administered format, a structured interview guide for the questionnaire has been made available (J. B. W. Williams, 1988). The most widely used measure of emotion in sport settings is the State–Trait Anxiety Inventory (STAI; Spielberger, 1983; Spielberger, Gorsuch, & Lushene, 1970). The STAI helps distinguish feelings of anxiety from depression. The STAI is fairly cost-effective and is best used with those attempting to perform high-stress or anxiety-prone tasks. The STAI was recognized for its cultural sensitivity and can be effectively used with any individuals regardless of their race, gender, and spiritual beliefs (for a review, see Tilton, 2008).

MEASUREMENT OF PERCEIVED EFFORT

Perceived effort represents an ensemble of perceptions inherent in effort expenditure. Perceived exertion, fatigue, and motivation are central to the effort experience and to the behaviors associated with exercise, such as adherence and intensity (Razon, Hutchinson, & Tenenbaum, 2012). Measures of effort perception are built on the assumption that individuals can accurately estimate and clearly express their perception of effort. However, this assumption may not always hold true. It can be difficult for people to report their effort perceptions while they are exerting effort. In some circumstances, social desirability may affect reporting. That is, people may inaccurately report their effort perceptions in an effort to appear fit and physically capable. Informing test takers that their real perceptions are needed and providing them with the opportunity to ask questions and practice using scales can mitigate the impact of some measurement limitations and challenges (Maresh & Noble, 1984; Noble & Robertson, 1996).

Borg's 15-point scale (Borg, 1971) and Borg's Category Ratio–10 (Borg, 1982) are widely used to measure perceived exertion in sport and exercise settings. The anchors for the 15-point scale range from 6 (*least effort*) to 20 (*very very hard*). The anchors for the 10-point scale range from 0 (*nothing at all*) to 10 (*very very hard, maximal*). Both scales can be used for description and monitoring purposes. When used descriptively, the scales help evaluate perceived effort. When used for monitoring, the scales assess the intensity of exercise training.

Scales to measure exertion have been developed for use with specific populations. For example, the Braille Rating of Perceived Exertion Scale (Buckley, Eston, & Sim, 2000) has been developed for people who are visually impaired. Measures of perceived exertion that include images as well as numbers and words, such as the Cart and Load Effort Rating Scale (Eston, Parfitt, Campbell, & Lamb, 2000) and the Pictorial Children's Effort Rating Table (Yelling, Lamb, & Swaine, 2002), can be used with adolescents and children. Finally, the Children's OMNI Scale of Perceived Exertion has been tailored to number of specific activities, including the OMNI—Bike for cycling (Robertson et al., 2000), OMNI—RES for resistance training (Robertson et al., 2003), OMNI—Step for stepping exercise (Robertson et al., 2005), and OMNI—Walk/Run for walking and running (Utter, Robertson, Nieman, & Kang, 2002).

TEAM-RELATED MEASURES

Numerous factors affect team performance and team members' satisfaction with the team experience. In team settings, it may be useful to identify teams' current needs and potential areas for improvement by administering a team needs assessment. Such assessments are often designed by practitioners and researchers to learn about teams' past experiences, current abilities and interests, and future goals. Specific topics, such as cohesion, sport performance, leadership, and prosocial and antisocial behaviors, may be presented or offered for further consideration or discussion.

Cohesion, "a dynamic processes which is reflected in the tendency for a group to stick together and remain united in the pursuit of its instrumental objectives and/or for the satisfaction of member affective needs" (Carron, Brawley, & Widmeyer, 1998, p. 213), has long been considered an essential aspect of group processes (Golembiewski, 1962; Lott & Lott, 1965). Team cohesion may be related to and affected by *leadership.* Leadership refers to "the behavioral process of influencing individuals and groups toward set goals" (Barrow, 1977, p. 232). In sport settings, leadership is a much sought after quality, and coach leadership is particularly emphasized (Chelladurai, 2012). Team cohesion and leadership both affect and may be affected by team members' prosocial and antisocial behaviors. *Prosocial* behavior refers to any behavior carried out with the intent to help or benefit others (Eisenberg & Fabes, 1998). Letting opponents borrow equipment and congratulating teammates are examples of prosocial behaviors in sport (Kavussanu & Boardley, 2012). *Antisocial* behaviors are those carried out with the intent to hurt or inconvenience others (Kavussanu, 2006; Sage, Kavussanu, & Duda, 2006). Examples of antisocial behaviors in sport are purposefully attempting to injure an opponent, violating the rules, and cheating (Kavussanu & Boardley, 2012).

Several sport-specific questionnaires have been developed to measure team cohesion. These include the Group Environment Questionnaire (Carron, Widmeyer, & Brawley, 1985), the Youth Sport Environment Questionnaire (Eys, Loughead, Bray & Carron, 2009), and the Physical Activity Group Environment Questionnaire (Estabrooks & Carron, 2000). The Youth Sport Environment Questionnaire and the Physical Activity Group Environment Questionnaire address the two main limitations associated with Group Environment Questionnaire, its low readability, and its negatively phrased item structures. As a result, the Youth Sport Environment Questionnaire and the Physical Activity Group Environment Questionnaire are effectively used when assessing team cohesion in youth and cohesion in physical activity groups of elderly people (Carron, Eys, & Martin, 2012; Estabrooks & Carron, 2000; Eys, Carron, Bray, & Brawley, 2007).

Leadership has proven to be a particularly difficult construct to measure, in part because leadership is affected by both personal and environmental factors (Amorose & Horn, 2000; Chelladurai, 2012). The Revised Leadership Scale for Sports (Zhang, Jensen, & Mann, 1997) measures designated leaders' (i.e., coaches') behaviors. The CBAS (Smith, Smoll, & Curtis, 1978) gauges leadership behaviors as well as athletes' and coaches' recollection of coach behaviors. The Coaching Behavior Questionnaire (Kenow & Williams, 1992) measures athletes' perception of a number of coaches' characteristics including their ability to communicate, composure, emotional control, arousal levels, and confidence. In contrast to this general measure of coach behavior, the Coaching Feedback Questionnaire (Amorose & Horn, 2000) measures athletes' perceptions of the feedback provided by the coach. The CBAS remains the most frequently used measure of coaching behavior (Smith, Smoll, & Curtis, 2007). The CBAS provides a comprehensive account of the quality and frequency of the feedback provided by the coach during both practice and competitive events (Smith et al., 2007). Practitioners should make informed decisions as to whether a general (i.e., Revised Leadership Scale for Sports) or specific (i.e., CBAS, Coaching Behavior Questionnaire, and Coaching Feedback Questionnaire) measure is most appropriate to use in a given situations.

The measurement of prosocial and antisocial behavior in sport and exercise psychology has received limited attention, although sport-related scandals do cause public attention to be paid to this topic. The Fair Play in Physical Education Questionnaire (Hassandra, Hatzigeorgiadis, & Goudas, 2005) is used to evaluate moral approach (Lee, Whitehead, & Ntoumanis, 2007) and sportpersonship behaviors (Vallerand, Brière, Blanchard, & Provencher, 1997) in the physical education context. The Prosocial and Antisocial Behavior in Sport Scale (Kavussanu & Boardley, 2009) provides test takers with prosocial and antisocial scenarios. Test takers articulate what they would do were they in the situation in question. Because these measures involve self-report, potential biases associated with social desirability (Arnold & Feldman, 1981) and retrospective recollection (for a review, see Hodge & Lonsdale, 2011) may occur. Video recordings can be used during training and contests to allow for later analysis of real behaviors. When reviewing video, practitioners may be able to identify the events that precede and follow prosocial and antisocial behaviors to determine their causes and consequences (see Kirker, Tenenbaum, & Mattson, 2000).

MEASUREMENT OF PHYSICAL ACTIVITY

Physical activity refers to any physical movement produced by muscles and leading to energy expenditure (Caspersen, 1989). *Exercise* is a type of physical activity that is recurrent, scheduled, structured, and helps to improve or maintain physical fitness and health (Montoye, Kemper, Saris, & Washburn, 1996). Measurement of physical activity and its outcomes is crucial when attempting to develop or evaluate the success of physical activity programs such as strength-training programs for athletes and flexibility programs for older adults (Nigg, Jordan, & Atkins, 2012). A number of strategies can be used to measure exercise behavior, including direct observation, diaries and logs, questionnaires, and physical activity monitoring tools. Direct observation allows for assessment of exercise but can be subject to error. People often alter their behavior when being observed. Furthermore, direct observations can be taxing on the observer's time and may require more than one observer to fully capture a behavior in its entirety. Diaries and logs require individuals to keep regular records of physical activity. Information recorded in diaries might include the intensity, context, and affective responses to the activity (Woods, Sivarajan-Froelicher, Underhill-Motzer, & Bridges, 2005). The quality of information collected through diaries and logs depends on the collaboration and meticulousness of the participant keeping these records. Physical activity questionnaires such as the Yale Physical Activity Survey (Dipietro, Caspersen, Ostfeld, & Nadel, 1993), and the Community Healthy Activities Model Program for Seniors (Stewart et al., 1997) can provide practitioners with extensive data on individuals' reported levels of physical activity. Physical activity monitoring tools such as pedometers and accelerometers are less vulnerable to social desirability biases but can fall prey to technical difficulties when used in field settings. Testing of physiological markers through assays and processes such as those that involve the use of doubly labeled water are more expensive and often require exercisers to make visits to the lab, but they may ultimately prove effective for assessing key aspects of exercise behavior.

Summary and Conclusion

Measurement is an essential procedure for accurately describing phenomena and fully understanding people's motivations, cognitions, affect, and behaviors. Measurement is essential not only for sound research and new knowledge gain but also for evidence-based and responsible practice. Throughout this chapter, we emphasized that to best capture athletic and exercise behaviors, multiple methods (e.g., introspection, observation, interview) should be used. Measurement tools must be reliable, valid, and sensitive to the culture within which they are administered. Following these guidelines and those of ethical measurement practice is appropriate for all sport and exercise psychologists, who may then incorporate the findings from assessment tools into ongoing programs of research or interventions to serve athletes, coaches, and teams.

References

Abernethy, B., & Russell, D. G. (1987). Expert–novice differences in an applied selective attention task. *Journal of Sport Psychology, 9,* 326–345.

American Psychological Association. (2010). *Ethical principles of psychologists and code of conduct (2002, Amended June 1, 2010).* Retrieved from http://www.apa.org/ethics/code/index.aspx

Amorose, A. J., & Horn, T. S. (2000). Intrinsic motivation: Relationships with collegiate athletes gender, scholarship status, and perceptions of their coaches behavior. *Journal of Sport & Exercise Psychology, 22,* 63–84.

Andersen, M. B., McCullagh, P., & Wilson, G. J. (2007). But what do the numbers really tell us? Arbitrary metrics and effect size reporting in sport psychology research. *Journal of Sport & Exercise Psychology, 29,* 664–672.

Arnold, H. J., & Feldman, D. C. (1981). Social desirability response bias in self-repot choice situations. *Academy of Management Journal, 24,* 377–385. doi:10.2307/255848

Bandura, A. (2006). Guide for constructing self-efficacy scales. In F. Pajares & T. Urdan (Eds.), *Self-efficacy beliefs of adolescents* (pp. 307–337). Greenwich, CT: Information Age.

Barrow, J. C. (1977). The variables of leadership: A review and conceptual framework. *Academy of Management Review, 2,* 231–251.

Beauchamp, M. K., Harvey, R. H., & Beauchamp, P. H. (2012). An integrated biofeedback and psychological skill training program for Canada's Olympic short-track speed skating team. *Journal of Clinical Sport Psychology, 6,* 67–84.

Beck, A. T., Steer, R. A., & Garbin, M. G. (1988). Psychometric properties of the Beck Depression Inventory: Twenty-five years of evaluation. *Clinical Psychology Review, 8,* 77–100. doi:10.1016/0272-7358(88)90050-5

Bennett, R. E. (2008). *Technology for large-scale assessment* (Report No. RM-08-10). Princeton, NJ: Educational Testing Service.

Berrios, G. E., & Bulbena-Villarasa, A. (1990). The Hamilton Depression Scale and the numerical description of the symptoms of depression. In P. Bech & A. Coppen (Eds.), *The Hamilton scales* (pp. 80–92). Berlin, Germany: Springer-Verlag. doi:10.1007/978-3-642-75373-2_10

Borg, G. A. (1971). The perception of physical performance. In R. J. Shephard (Ed.), *Frontiers of fitness* (pp. 280–294). Springfield, IL: Charles C Thomas.

Borg, G. A. (1982). Psychological bases of perceived exertion. *Medicine and Science in Sports and Exercise, 14,* 377–381. doi:10.1249/00005768-198205000-00012

Bradley, M. M., & Lang, P. J. (1994). Measuring emotion: The self-assessment manikin and the semantic differential. *Journal of Behavior Therapy and Experimental Psychiatry, 25,* 49–59. doi:10.1016/0005-7916(94)90063-9

Brière, N. M., Vallerand, R. J., Blais, M. R., & Pelletier, L. G. (1995). Developpement et validation d'une mesure de motivation intrinseque, extrinseque et d'amotivation en contexte sportif: l'Echelle de motivation dans les sports (EMS) [Development and validation of the French form of the Sport Motivation Scale]. *International Journal of Sport Psychology, 26,* 465–489.

Buckley, J. P., Eston, R. G., & Sim, J. (2000). Ratings of perceived exertion in braille: Validity and reliability in production mode. *British Journal of Sports Medicine, 34,* 297–302. doi:10.1136/bjsm.34.4.297

Carron, A. V., Brawley, L. R., & Widmeyer, W. N. (2002). *The Group Environment Questionnaire: Test manual.* Morgantown, WV: Fitness Information Technology.

Carron, A. V., Eys, M. A., & Martin, L. J. (2012). Cohesion. In G. Tenenbaum., R. C. Eklund, & A. Kamata (Eds.), *Measurement in sport and exercise psychology* (pp. 411–421).Champaign, IL: Human Kinetics.

Carron, A. V., Widmeyer, W. N., & Brawley, L. R. (1985). The development of an instrument to assess cohesion in sport teams: The group environment questionnaire. *Journal of Sport Psychology, 7,* 244–266.

Caspersen, C. J. (1989). Physical activity epidemiology: concepts, methods, and applications to exercise science. *Exercise and Sport Sciences Reviews, 17,* 423–473.

Chelladurai, P. (2012). Models and measurement of leadership in sport. In G. Tenenbaum., R. C. Eklund, & A. Kamata (Eds.), *Measurement in sport and exercise psychology* (pp. 433–442). Champaign, IL: Human Kinetics.

Coan, J. A., & Allen, J. J. B. (Eds.). (2007). *Handbook of emotion elicitation and assessment.* New York, NY: Oxford University Press.

Cohen, A. B. (2009). Many forms of culture. *American Psychologist, 64,* 194–204. doi:10.1037/a0015308

Cross, S. E., & Markus, H. (1991). Possible selves across the life span. *Human Development, 34,* 230–255. doi:10.1159/000277058

Dadlani, M. B., Overtree, C., & Perry-Jenkins, M. (2012). Culture at the center: A reformulation of diagnostic assessment. *Professional Psychology: Research and Practice, 43,* 175–182. doi:10.1037/a0028152

Deci, E. L., & Ryan, R. M. (1985). *Intrinsic motivation and self-determination in human behavior.* New York, NY: Plenum Press.

Deci, E. L., & Ryan, R. M. (2000). The "what" and "why" of goal pursuits: Human needs and the self-determination of behavior. *Psychological Inquiry, 11,* 227–268. doi:10.1207/S15327965PLI1104_01

Delis, D. C., Kramer, J. H., Kaplan, E., & Ober, B. A. (1987). *The California Verbal Learning Test.* New York, NY: The Psychological Corporation.

Dewey, D., Brawley, L., & Allard, F. (1989). Do the TAIS attentional-style scales predict how information is processed? *Journal of Sport & Exercise Psychology, 11,* 171–186.

Dipietro, L., Caspersen, C. J., Ostfeld, A. M., & Nadel, E. R. (1993). A survey for assessing physical activity among older adults. *Medicine & Science in Sports & Exercise, 25,* 628–642. doi:10.1249/00005768-199305000-00016

Dunkel, C. S., Kelts, D., & Coon, B. (2006). Possible selves as mechanisms of change in therapy. In C. Dunkel & J. Kerpelman (Eds.), *Possible selves: Theory, research and application* (pp. 187–204). Hauppauge, NY: NOVA Science.

Eccles, D. W. (2012). Verbal reports of cognitive processes. In G. Tenenbaum, R. C. Eklund, & A. Kamata (Eds.), *Measurement in sport and exercise psychology* (pp. 103–117). Champaign, IL: Human Kinetics.

Eisenberg, N., & Fabes, R. A. (1998). Prosocial development. In W. Damon (Series Ed.) & N. Eisenberg (Vol. Ed.), *Handbook of child psychology: Vol. 3. Social, emotional, and personality development* (5th ed., pp. 701–778). New York, NY: Wiley.

Ekkekakis, P. (2012). Affect, mood, and emotion. In G. Tenenbaum., R. C. Eklund, & A. Kamata (Eds.), *Measurement in sport and exercise psychology* (pp. 321–332).Champaign, IL: Human Kinetics.

Ekman, P., & Davidson, R. J. (Eds.). (1994). *The nature of emotion: Fundamental questions.* New York, NY: Oxford University Press.

Emotion. (2005). In *The Merriam-Webster Dictionary* (5th ed.). Springfield, MA: Merriam-Webster.

Ericsson, K. A., & Simon, H. A. (1993). *Protocol analysis.* Cambridge, MA: MIT Press.

Eriksen, C. W., & Schultz, D. W. (1979). Information processing in visual search: A continuous flow conception and experimental results. *Perception & Psychophysics, 25,* 249–263. doi:10.3758/BF03198804

Estabrooks, P. A., & Carron, A. V. (2000). The physical activity group environment questionnaire: An instrument for the assessment of cohesion in exercise classes. *Group Dynamics, 4,* 230–243. doi:10.1037/1089-2699.4.3.230

Eston, R. G., Parfitt, G., Campbell, L., & Lamb, K. L. (2000). Reliability of effort perception for regulating exercise intensity in children using the Cart and Load Effort Rating (CALER) Scale. *Pediatric Exercise Science, 12,* 388–397.

Etnier, J. L., & Chang, Y. (2009). The effect of physical activity on executive function: A brief commentary on definitions, measurement issues, and the current state of the literature. *Journal of Sport & Exercise Psychology, 31,* 469–483.

Etzel, E., Yura, M., & Perna, F. (1998). Ethics and testing in applied sport psychology. In J. Duda (Ed.), *Advances in measurement in sport and exercise psychology* (pp. 423–432). Morgantown, WV: Fitness Information Technology.

Eys, M. A., Carron, A. V., Bray, S. R., & Brawley, L. R. (2007). Item wording and internal consistency of a measure of cohesion: The Group Environment Questionnaire. *Journal of Sport & Exercise Psychology, 29,* 395–402.

Eys, M. A., Loughead, T., Bray, S. R., & Carron, A. V. (2009). Development of a cohesion questionnaire for youth: The Youth Sport Environment Questionnaire. *Journal of Sport & Exercise Psychology, 31,* 390–408.

Fisher, C. B. (2003). *Decoding the ethics code: A practical guide for psychologists.* Thousand Oaks, CA: Sage.

Fisher, M. A. (2009). Ethics-based training for nonclinical staff in mental health settings. *Professional Psychology: Research and Practice, 40,* 459–466. doi:10.1037/a0016642

Fiske, A. P. (2002). Using individualism and collectivism to compare cultures—A critique of the validity and measurement of the constructs: Comment on Oyserman et al. (2002). *Psychological Bulletin, 128,* 78–88. doi:10.1037/0033-2909.128.1.78

Folstein, M. F., Folstein, S. E., & McHugh, P. R. (1975). Mini-mental state: A practical method for grading the cognitive state of patients for the clinician. *Journal of Psychiatric Research, 12,* 189–198. doi:10.1016/0022-3956(75)90026-6

Fox, K. R. (1990). *The Physical Self-Perception Profile manual.* DeKalb: Northern Illinois University, Office for Health Promotion.

Fox, K. R., & Corbin, C. B. (1989). The Physical Self-Perception Profile: Development and preliminary validation. *Journal of Sport & Exercise Psychology, 11,* 408–430.

Gauvin, L., & Rejeski, W. J. (1993). The exercise-induced feeling inventory: Development and initial validation. *Journal of Sport & Exercise Psychology, 15,* 403–423.

Golembiewski, R. T. (1962). *The small group: An analysis of research concepts and operations.* Chicago, IL: University of Chicago Press.

Greenbaum, T. L. (1997). *The handbook for focus group research.* Thousand Oaks, CA: Sage.

Greenbaum, T. L. (2000). *Moderating focus groups: A practical guide for group facilitation.* Thousand Oaks, CA: Sage.

Guay, F., Vallerand, R. J., & Blanchard, C. (2000). On the assessment of situational intrinsic and extrinsic motivation: The Situational Motivation Scale (SIMS). *Motivation and Emotion, 24,* 175–213. doi:10.1023/A:1005614228250

Hall, C. R., Mack, D. E., Paivio, A., & Hausenblas, H. A. (2007). Imagery use by athletes: Development of the Sport Imagery Questionnaire. In D. Smith & M. Bar-Eli (Eds.), *Readings in sport and exercise psychology* (pp. 258–264). Champaign, IL: Human Kinetics.

Hall, C. R., & Martin, K. A. (1997). Measuring movement imagery abilities: A revision of the movement imagery questionnaire. *Journal of Mental Imagery, 21,* 143–154.

Hamilton, M. (1960). A rating scale for depression. *Journal of Neurology, Neurosurgery & Psychiatry, 23,* 56–62. doi:10.1136/jnnp.23.1.56

Hardy, C. J., & Rejeski, W. J. (1989). Not what, but how one feels: The measurement of affect during exercise. *Journal of Sport & Exercise Psychology, 11,* 304–317.

Hardy, J., Hall, C. R., & Hardy, L. (2005). Quantifying athlete self-talk. *Journal of Sports Sciences, 23,* 905–917. doi:10.1080/02640410500130706

Harter, S. (1999). *The construction of the self: A developmental perspective.* New York, NY: Guilford Press.

Hassandra, M., Hatzigeorgiadis, A., & Goudas, M. (2005). Confirmatory factor analysis of the Fair Play in Physical Education Questionnaire.

In *Proceedings of the 8th European Conference of Psychological Assessment* (pp. 82–83). Budapest: Hungarian Psychological Association.

Hedlund, J. L., & Viewig, B. W. (1979). The Hamilton Rating Scale for Depression: A comprehensive review. *Journal of Operational Psychiatry, 10,* 149–165.

Heil, J., & Henschen, K. (1996). Assessment in sport and exercise psychology. In J. L. Van Raalte & B. W. Brewer (Eds.), *Exploring sport and exercise psychology* (pp. 229–255). Washington, DC: American Psychological Association. doi:10.1037/10186-010

Heine, S. J., Lehman, D. R., Peng, K., & Greenholtz, J. (2002). What's wrong with cross-cultural comparisons of subjective Likert scales? The reference-group effect. *Journal of Personality and Social Psychology, 82,* 903–918. doi:10.1037/effect0022-3514.82.6.903

Hodge, K., & Lonsdale, C. (2011). Prosocial and antisocial behavior in sport: The role of coaching style, autonomous vs. controlled motivation, and moral disengagement. *Journal of Sport & Exercise Psychology, 33,* 527–547.

Isaac, A., Marks, D., & Russell, D. (1986). An instrument for assessing imagery of movement: The Vividness of Movement Imagery Questionnaire (VMIQ). *Journal of Mental Imagery, 10,* 23–30.

Janelle, C. M., & Naugle, K. M. (2012). Emotional reactivity. In G. Tenenbaum., R. C. Eklund, & A. Kamata (Eds.), *Measurement in sport and exercise psychology* (pp. 333–348).Champaign, IL: Human Kinetics.

Kamata, A., Tenenbaum, G., & Hanin, Y. L. (2002). Individual zone of optimal functioning (IZOF): A probabilistic estimation. *Journal of Sport & Exercise Psychology, 24,* 189–208.

Kavussanu, M. (2006). Motivational predictors of prosocial and antisocial behavior in football. *Journal of Sports Sciences, 24,* 575–588.

Kavussanu, M., & Boardley, I. D. (2009). The prosocial and antisocial behavior in sport scale. *Journal of Sport & Exercise Psychology, 31,* 97–117.

Kavussanu, M., & Boardley, I. D. (2012). Moral behavior. In G. Tenenbaum., R. C. Eklund, & A. Kamata (Eds.), *Measurement in sport and exercise psychology* (pp. 443–454).Champaign, IL: Human Kinetics.

Kenow, L. J., & Williams, J. M. (1992). Relationship between anxiety, self-confidence, and evaluation of coaching behaviors. *The Sport Psychologist, 6,* 344–357.

Kirker, B., Tenenbaum, G., & Mattson, J. (2000). An investigation of the dynamics of aggression: Direct observations in ice hockey and basketball. *Research Quarterly for Exercise and Sport, 71,* 373–386.

Kontos, A. P., Collins, M., & Russo, S. A. (2004). An introduction to sports concussion for the sport psychology consultant. *Journal of Applied Sport Psychology, 16,* 220–235. doi:10.1080/10413200490485568

Krane, V., & Baird, S. M. (2005). Using ethnography in applied sport psychology. *Journal of Applied Sport Psychology, 17,* 87–107. doi:10.1080/10413200590932371

Kristiansen, E. E., Roberts, G. C., & Sisjord, M. K. (2011). Coping with negative media content: The experiences of professional football goalkeepers. *International Journal of Sport and Exercise Psychology, 9,* 295–307. doi:10.1080/1612197X.2011.623451

Kwan, B. M., & Bryan, A. D. (2010). Affective response to exercise as a component of exercise motivation: Attitudes, norms, self-efficacy, and temporal stability of intentions. *Psychology of Sport and Exercise, 11,* 71–79. doi:10.1016/j.psychsport.2009.05.010

Lang, P. J. (1980). Behavioral treatment and bio-behavioral assessment: Computer applications. In J. B. Sidowski, J. H. Johnson, & T. A. Williams (Eds.), *Technology in mental health care delivery systems* (pp. 119–137). Norwood, NJ: Ablex.

Leary, M. R., & Tangney, J. P. (2003). The self as an organizing construct in the behavioral and social sciences. In M. R. Leary & J. P. Tangney (Eds.), *Handbook of self and identity* (pp. 3–14). New York, NY: Guilford Press.

Lee, M. J., Whitehead, J., & Ntoumanis, N. (2007). Development of the Attitudes to Moral Decisions in Youth Sport Questionnaire. *Psychology of Sport and Exercise, 8,* 369–392. doi:10.1016/j.psychsport.2006.12.002

Leighton, J. P., & Gierl, M. J. (Eds.) (2007). *Cognitive diagnostic assessment for education: Theory and applications.* Cambridge, England: Cambridge University Press. doi:10.1017/CBO9780511611186

Lonsdale, C., Hodge, K., & Rose, E. A. (2008). The Behavioral Regulation in Sport Questionnaire (BRSQ): Instrument development and initial validity evidence. *Journal of Sport & Exercise Psychology, 30,* 323–355.

Lott, A. J., & Lott, B. E. (1965). Group cohesiveness as interpersonal attraction: A review of relationships with antecedent and consequent variables. *Psychological Bulletin, 64,* 259–309. doi:10.1037/h0022386

Lox, C. L., Jackson, S., Tuholski, S. W., Wasley, D., & Treasure, D. C. (2000). Revisiting the measurement of exercise induced feeling states: The Physical Activity Affect Scale (PAAS). *Measurement in Physical Education and Exercise Science, 4,* 79–95. doi:10.1207/S15327841Mpee0402_4

Mahoney, M. J., & Epstein, M. L. (1981). The assessment of cognition in athletes. In T. V. Merluzzi, C. R. Glass, & M. Genest (Eds.), *Cognitive assessment* (pp. 435–451). New York, NY: Guilford Press.

Mahoney, M. J., Gabriel, T. J., & Perkins, T. S. (1987). Psychological skills and exceptional athletic performance. *The Sport Psychologist, 1,* 181–199.

Maresh, C., & Noble, B. J. (1984). Utilization of perceived exertion ratings during exercise testing and training. In L. K. Hall (Ed.), *Cardiac rehabilitation: Exercise testing and prescription* (pp. 155–173). Great Neck, NY: Spectrum.

Markus, H. (1977). Self-schemata and processing information about the self. *Journal of Personality and Social Psychology, 35,* 63–78. doi:10.1037/0022-3514.35.2.63

Markus, H., & Nurius, P. (1986). Possible selves. *American Psychologist, 41,* 954–969. doi:10.1037/0003-066X.41.9.954

Marsh, H. W., & O'Neill, R. (1984). Self-Description Questionnaire III: The construct validity of multidimensional self-concept ratings by late adolescents. *Journal of Educational Measurement, 21,* 153–174. doi:10.1111/j.1745-3984.1984.tb00227.x

Martens, R., Burton, D., Vealey, R. S., Bump, L. A., & Smith, D. (1982). *Cognitive and somatic dimensions of competitive anxiety.* Paper presented at the meeting of the North American Society for the Psychology of Sport and Physical Activity, University of Maryland, College Park.

Martens, R., Vealey, R. S., & Burton, D. (1990). *Competitive anxiety in sport.* Champaign, IL: Human Kinetics.

McAuley, E., & Courneya, K. S. (1994). The Subjective Exercise Experiences Scale (SEES): Development and preliminary validation. *Journal of Sport & Exercise Psychology, 16,* 163–177.

McNair, D. M., Lorr, M., & Droppleman, L. F. (1971). *Profile of mood states.* San Diego, CA: Educational and Industrial Testing Services.

Montoye, H. J., Kemper, H. C. G., Saris, W. H. M., & Washburn, R. A. (1996). Questionnaires and interviews. In H. J. Montoye, H. C. G. Kemper, & W. H. M. Saris (Eds.), *Measuring physical activity and energy expenditure* (pp. 42–71). Champaign, IL: Human Kinetics.

Morgan, D. L. (1988). *Focus groups as qualitative research.* Thousand Oaks: Sage.

Morgan, D. L. (1998). *The focus group guide book.* Thousand Oaks, CA: Sage.

Morgan, D. L., & Krueger, R. A. (1997). *The focus group kit.* Thousand Oaks, CA: Sage.

Morgan, W. P., Brown, D. R., Raglin, J. S., O'Connor, P. J., & Ellickson, K. A. (1987). Psychological monitoring of overtraining and staleness. *British Journal of Sports Medicine, 21,* 107–114. doi:10.1136/bjsm.21.3.107

Morgan, W. P., & Pollock, M. L. (1977). Psychological characterization of the elite distance runner. *Annals of the New York Academy of Sciences, 301,* 382–403. doi:10.1111/j.1749-6632.1977.tb38215.x

Müller, S., Abernethy, B., & Farrow, D. (2006). How do world-class cricket batsmen anticipate a bowler's intention? *The Quarterly Journal of Experimental Psychology: Human Experimental Psychology, 59,* 2162–2186. doi:10.1080/02643290600576595

Nigg, C. R., Jordan, P. J., & Atkins, A. (2012). Behavioral measurement of physical activity. In G. Tenenbaum, R. C. Eklund, & A. Kamata (Eds.), *Measurement in sport and exercise psychology* (pp. 455–462). Champaign, IL: Human Kinetics.

Noble, B. J., & Robertson, R. J. (1996). *Perceived exertion.* Champaign, IL: Human Kinetics.

Nordal, K. C. (2012, January). Outcomes measurement benefits psychology. *Monitor on Psychology, 43*(1), 51.

Ostrow, A. C. (Ed.). (1990). *Directory of psychological tests in sport and exercise sciences.* Morgantown, WV: Fitness Information Technology.

Parshall, C. G., Spray, J. A., Kalohn, J. C., & Davey, T. (2003). Practical considerations in computer-based testing: Book review. *Applied Psychological Measurement, 27,* 78–80.

Patton, M. Q. (2002). *Qualitative research and evaluation methods.* Thousand Oaks, CA: Sage.

Puetz, T. W., O'Connor, P. J., & Dishman, R. K. (2006). Effects of chronic exercise on feelings of energy and fatigue: A quantitative synthesis. *Psychological Bulletin, 132,* 866–876. doi:10.1037/0033-2909.132.6.866

Quellmalz, E. S., & Pellegrino, J. W. (2009, January 2). Technology and testing. *Science, 323,* 75–79. doi:10.1126/science.1168046

Razon, S., Hutchinson, J., & Tenenbaum, G. (2012). Effort perception. In G. Tenenbaum., R. C. Eklund, & A. Kamata (Eds.), *Measurement in sport and exercise psychology* (pp. 265–277). Champaign, IL: Human Kinetics.

Reed, J., & Ones, D. S. (2006). The effect of acute aerobic exercise on positive activated affect: A meta-analysis. *Psychology of Sport and Exercise, 7,* 477–514. doi:10.1016/j.psychsport.2005.11.003

Reid, G., Vallerand, R. J., Poulin, C., & Crocker, P. (2009). The development and validation of the pictorial motivation scale in physical activity. *Motivation and Emotion, 33,* 161–172. doi:10.1007/s11031-008-9117-x

Reiss, S., & Havercamp, S. M. (1998). Toward a comprehensive assessment of fundamental motivation: Factor structure of the Reiss Profiles. *Psychological Assessment, 10,* 97–106. doi:10.1037/1040-3590.10.2.97

Resnick, B., & Jenkins, L. S. (2000). Testing the reliability and validity of the self-efficacy for exercise scale. *Nursing Research, 49,* 154–159. doi:10.1097/00006199-200005000-00007

Roberts, R., Callow, N., Hardy, L., Markland, D., & Bringer, J. (2008). Movement imagery ability: Development and assessment of a revised version of the vividness of movement imagery questionnaire. *Journal of Sport & Exercise Psychology, 30,* 200–221.

Robertson, R. J., Goss, F. L., Andreacci, J. L., Dube, J. J., Rutkowski, J. J., Frazee, K. W., & Snee, B. M. (2005). Validation of the children's OMNI-Resistance Exercise Scale of perceived exertion. *Medicine and Science in Sports and Exercise, 37,* 819–826. doi:10.1249/01. MSS.0000162619.33236.F1

Robertson, R. J., Goss, F. L., Boer, N. F., Peoples, J. A., Foreman, A., Dabayebeh, I. M., . . . Thompkins, T. (2000). Children's OMNI Scale of Perceived Exertion: Mixed gender and race validation. *Medicine & Science in Sports & Exercise, 32,* 452–458. doi:10.1097/00005768-200002000-00029

Robertson, R. J., Goss, F. L., Rutkowski, J., Lenz, B., Dixon, C., Timmer, J., & Andreacci, J. L. (2003).Concurrent validation of the OMNI Perceived Exertion Scale for Resistance Exercise. *Medicine and Science in Sports and Exercise, 35, 3,* 33–341.

Russell, J. A., Weiss, A., & Mendelsohn, G. A. (1989). Affect Grid: A single-item scale of pleasure and arousal. *Journal of Personality and Social Psychology, 57,* 493–502. doi:10.1037/0022-3514.57.3.493

Ryba, T. V., Schinke, R. J., & Stambulova, N. B. (2012). Cultural sport psychology: Special measurement considerations. In G. Tenenbaum, R. C. Eklund, & A. Kamata (Eds.), *Measurement in sport and exercise psychology* (pp. 143–152). Champaign, IL: Human Kinetics.

Sage, L., Kavussanu, M., & Duda, J. L. (2006). Goal orientations and moral identity as predictors of prosocial and antisocial functioning in male association football players. *Journal of Sports Sciences, 24,* 455–466. doi:10.1080/02640410500244531

Shank, G. D. (2002). *Qualitative research: A personal skills approach.* Upper Saddle River, NJ: Merrill Prentice Hall.

Sharp, L. K., & Lipsky, M. S. (2002). Screening for depression across the lifespan: A review of measures for use in primary care settings. *American Family Physician, 66,* 1001–1008.

Smith, R. E., Schutz, R. W., Smoll, F. L., & Ptacek, J. T. (1995). Development and validation of a multidimensional measure of sport-specific psychological skills: The Athletic Coping Skills Inventory—28. *Journal of Sport & Exercise Psychology, 17,* 379–398.

Smith, R. E., Smoll, F. L., & Curtis, B. (1978). Coaching behaviors in little league baseball. In F. L. Smoll & R. E. Smith (Eds.), *Psychological perspectives in youth sports* (pp. 173–201). Washington, DC: Hemisphere.

Smith, R. E., Smoll, F. L., & Curtis, B. (2007). Coach effectiveness training: A cognitive–behavioral approach to enhancing relationship skills in youth sport coaches. In R. E. Smith, F. L. Smoll, & B. Curtis (Eds.), *Essential readings in sport and exercise psychology* (pp. 393–400). Champaign, IL: Human Kinetics.

Smith, R. E., Smoll, F. L., & Hunt, E. (1977). A system for the behavioral assessment of athletic coaches. *Research Quarterly, 48,* 401–407.

Spielberger, C. D. (1983). *Manual for the State–Trait Anxiety Inventory (Form Y).* Palo Alto, CA: Consulting Psychologists Press.

Spielberger, C. D., Gorsuch, R. L., & Lushene, R. L. (1970). *Manual for the State–Trait Anxiety Inventory.* Palo Alto, CA: Consulting Psychologists Press.

Stewart, A. L., Mills, K. M., Sepsis, P. G., King, A. C., McLellan, B. Y., Roitz, K., & Ritter, P. L. (1997). Evaluation of CHAMPS, a physical activity promotion program for older adults. *Annals of Behavioral Medicine, 19,* 353–361. doi:10.1007/BF02895154

Straub, W. F. (Ed.). (1978). *Sport psychology: An analysis of athlete behavior.* Ithaca, NY: Mouvement.

Stroop, J. R. (1935). Studies of interference in serial verbal reactions. *Journal of Experimental Psychology, 18,* 643–662. doi:10.1037/h0054651

Svebak, S., & Murgatroyd, S. (1985). Metamotivational dominance: A multimethod validation of reversal theory constructs. *Journal of Personality and Social Psychology, 48,* 107–116. doi:10.1037/0022-3514.48.1.107

Tatsuoka, K. K. (2009). *Cognitive assessment: An introduction to the rule space method.* New York, NY: Routledge/Taylor & Francis Group.

Taylor-Piliae, R. E., & Froelicher, E. S. (2004). Measurement properties of tai chi exercise self-efficacy among ethnic Chinese with coronary heart disease risk factors: A pilot study. *European Journal of Cardiovascular Nursing, 3,* 287–294. doi:10.1016/j.ejcnurse.2004.09.001

Tenenbaum, G., & Bar-Eli, M. (1995). Contemporary issues in exercise and sport psychology research. In S. J. H. Biddle (Ed.), *European perspectives on sport and exercise psychology* (pp. 292–323). Champaign, IL: Human Kinetics.

Tenenbaum, G., & Driscoll, M. P. (2005). *Methods of research in sport science: Quantitative and qualitative approaches.* Oxford, England: Meyer & Meyer Sport.

Tenenbaum, G., Eklund, R. C., & Kamata, A. (Eds.). (2012). *Measurement in sport and exercise psychology.* Champaign, IL: Human Kinetics.

Thayer, R. E. (1989). *The biopsychology of mood and arousal.* New York, NY: Oxford University Press.

Theodorakis, Y., Hatzigeorgiadis, A., & Chroni, S. (2008). Self-talk: It works, but how? Development and preliminary validation of the functions of Self-Talk Questionnaire. *Measurement in Physical Education and Exercise Science, 12,* 10–30. doi:10.1080/10913670701715158

Thomas, P. R., Murphy, S. M., & Hardy, L. (1999). Test of performance strategies: Development and preliminary validation of a comprehensive measure of athletes' psychological skills. *Journal of Sports Sciences, 17,* 697–711. doi:10.1080/026404199365560

Tilton, S. R. (2008). Review of the State–Trait Anxiety Inventory (STAI). *News Notes, 48,* 1–3.

Tucker, B. (2009). *Beyond the bubble: Technology and the future of student assessment.* Washington, DC: Education Sector.

Tutko, T. A., Lyon, L. P., & Ogilvie, B. C. (1969). *Athletic motivation inventory.* San Jose, CA: Institute for the Study of Athletic Motivation.

Utter, A. C., Robertson, R. J., Nieman, D. C., & Kang, J. (2002). Children's OMNI Scale of Perceived Exertion: Walking/running evaluation. *Medicine & Science in Sports and Exercise, 34,* 139–144.

Vallerand, R. J. (1983). Attention and decision making: A test of the predictive validity of the Test of Attentional and Interpersonal Style (TAIS) in a sport setting. *Journal of Sport Psychology, 3,* 149–165.

Vallerand, R. J. (1997). Toward a hierarchical model of intrinsic and extrinsic motivation. In M. P. Zanna (Ed.), *Advances in experimental social psychology* (pp. 271–360). San Diego, CA: Academic Press. doi:10.1016/S0065-2601(08)60019-2

Vallerand, R. J., Brière, N. M., Blanchard, C., & Provencher, P. (1997). Development and validation of the Multidimensional Sportspersonship Orientations Scale. *Journal of Sport & Exercise Psychology, 19,* 197–206.

Vallerand, R. J., & Thill, E. (Eds.). (1993). *Introduction a la psychologie de la motivation* [Introduction to the psychology of motivation]. Laval, Quebec, Canada: Etudes Vivantes.

Wainer, H., Dorans, N. J., Green, B. F., Steinberg, L., Flaugher, R., Mislevy, R. J., & Thissen, D. (1990). *Computerized adaptive testing: A primer.* Hillsdale, NJ: Erlbaum.

Watson, D., & Clark, L. A. (1997). Measurement and mismeasurement of mood: Recurrent and emergent issues. *Journal of Personality Assessment, 68,* 267–296. doi:10.1207/s15327752jpa6802_4

Watson, D., Clark, L. A., & Tellegen, A. (1988). Development and validation of brief measures of positive and negative affect: The PANAS scales. *Journal of Personality and Social Psychology, 54,* 1063–1070. doi:10.1037/0022-3514.54.6.1063

Watson, J. C., Etzel, E. F., & Vosloo, J. (2012). Ethics: Assessment and measurement in sport and exercise psychology. In G. Tenenbaum., R. C. Eklund, & A. Kamata (Eds.), *Measurement in sport and exercise psychology* (pp. 169–176). Champaign, IL: Human Kinetics.

Wechsler, D. (1997). *Wechsler Adult Intelligence Scale—3rd edition (WAIS–3)* San Antonio, TX: Harcourt Assessment.

Weinberg, R., & Forlenza, S. (2012). Psychological skills. In G. Tenenbaum., R. C. Eklund, & A. Kamata (Eds.), *Measurement in sport and exercise psychology* (pp. 381–392). Champaign, IL: Human Kinetics.

Weiss, D. J. (1983). Latent trait test theory and computerized adaptive testing. In D. J Weiss (Ed.), *New horizons in testing* (pp. 257–283). New York, NY: Academic Press.

Whaley, D. E. (2003). Future-oriented self-perceptions and exercise behavior in middle-aged women. *Journal of Aging and Physical Activity, 11,* 1–17.

Whitehead, J. R. (1995). A study of children's physical self-perceptions using an adapted physical self-perception questionnaire. *Pediatric Exercise Science, 7,* 132–151.

Williams, A. M., & Abernethy, B. (2012). Anticipation and decision making: Skills, methods, and measures. In G. Tenenbaum, R. C. Eklund, & A. Kamata (Eds.), *Measurement in sport and exercise psychology* (pp. 191–202). Champaign, IL: Human Kinetics.

Williams, A. M., & Davids, K. (1998). Visual search strategy, selective attention, and expertise in soccer. *Research Quarterly for Exercise and Sport, 69,* 111–128.

Williams, A. M., Janelle, C. M., & Davids, K. (2004). Constraints on the search for visual information in sports. *International Journal of Sport and Exercise Psychology, 2,* 301–318. doi:10.1080/1612197X.2004.9671747

Williams, D. M., Dunsiger, S., Ciccolo, J. T., Lewis, B. A., Albrecht, A. E., & Marcus, B. H. (2008). Acute affective response to a moderate-intensity exercise stimulus predicts physical activity participation 6 and 12 months later. *Psychology of Sport and Exercise, 9,* 231–245. doi:10.1016/j.psychsport.2007.04.002

Williams, J. B. W. (1988). A structured interview guide for the Hamilton Depression Rating Scale. *Archives of General Psychiatry, 45,* 742–747. doi:10.1001/archpsyc.1988.01800320058007

Woods, S., Sivarajan-Froelicher, E., Underhill-Motzer, S., & Bridges, E. (Eds.). (2005). *Cardiac nursing* (5th ed.). Philadelphia, PA: Lippincott Williams & Wilkins.

Yelling, M., Lamb, K. L., & Swaine, I. L. (2002). Validity of a pictorial perceived exertion scale for effort estimation and effort production during stepping exercise in adolescent children. *European Physical Education Review, 8,* 157–175. doi:10.1177/1356336X020082007

Zaccaro, S., Blair, V., Peterson, C., & Zananis, M. (1995). Collective efficacy. In J. E. Maddux (Ed.), *Self-efficacy, adaptation, and adjustment: Theory, research, and application* (pp. 305–328). New York, NY: Plenum Press. doi:10.1007/978-1-4419-6868-5_11

Zervas, Y., Stavrou, N. A., & Psychountaki, M. (2007). Development and validation of the Self-Talk Questionnaire (S-TQ) for sports. *Journal of Applied Sport Psychology, 19,* 142–159. doi:10.1080/10413200601185156

Zhang, J., Jensen, B. E., & Mann, B. L. (1997). Modification and revision of the leadership scale for sport. *Journal of Sport Behavior, 20,* 105–122.

Zhu, W. (2012). Measurement practice in sport and exercise psychology: A historical, comparative, and psychometric view. In G. Tenenbaum, R. C. Eklund, & A. Kamata (Eds.), *Measurement in sport and exercise psychology* (pp. 9–21). Champaign, IL: Human Kinetics.

Britton W. Brewer and Trent A. Petrie

Psychopathology in Sport and Exercise

14

It may seem unusual to discuss psychopathology in association with sport and exercise because sport success is related to lower levels of psychopathology (Morgan, 1985) and exercise may be used as therapy for depression and other disorders (for a review, see Chapter 7, this volume). Yet, the reality is that sport and exercise participants, as human beings, experience psychopathology and related concerns (Heyman, 1986), and factors associated with sport and exercise may increase the risk (Auerbach, 1994; Beisser, 1977; Heyman, 1986). For example, the physical contact that exists in sports such as football, rugby, and soccer, as well as the emphasis on physical appearance that may be found in the sport environments of gymnastics, diving, and beach volleyball, may contribute to the occurrence of cognitive impairments (Matser, Kessels, Jordan, Lezak, & Troost, 1998) and eating disorders (Petrie & Greenleaf, 2012), respectively, among athletes. For some disorders (e.g., developmental coordination disorder, bulimia nervosa), pathological symptoms may include sport and exercise behaviors, such as poor sport performance and excessive

http://dx.doi.org/10.1037/14251-014
Exploring Sport and Exercise Psychology, Third Edition, J. Van Raalte and B. Brewer (Editors)
Copyright © 2014 by the American Psychological Association.
All rights reserved.

exercise (American Psychiatric Association, 2000). The existence of the International Society for Sport Psychiatry (founded in 1994) and the *Journal of Clinical Sport Psychology* (launched in 2007) bears witness to the relevance of psychopathology to sport.

Case studies and anecdotal reports have documented the occurrence of a wide variety of mental disorders in sport and exercise participants (Beisser, 1977; Ogilvie & Tutko, 1966). Examples of disorders experienced by top-level athletes include bipolar disorder (Berger, 2010; Visser, 2010), borderline personality disorder (Marchant & Gibbs, 2004), dissociative identity disorder ("Walker Reveals Struggles," 2008), major depression (Caplan, 2008; "Everything Was Negative. Dark," 2004), obsessive–compulsive disorder (Garber, 2007), panic disorder (Hales, 1993), seasonal affective disorder (Rosen, Smokler, Carrier, Shafer, & McKeag, 1996), schizoaffective disorder ("Maine Issue," 1997), and Tourette's syndrome (Page, 1990), and such disorders have been linked directly to the suicides of athletes from a wide range of sports (Torre, 2011). In nationwide surveys of clinical and counseling psychologists (Petrie & Diehl, 1995; Petrie, Diehl, & Watkins, 1995), the primary areas of psychopathology addressed in individual therapy with athlete clients were reported to be anxiety/stress, depressive disorders, eating disorders, and substance-related disorders.

Athletes and exercisers do experience a wide range of psychopathological conditions (for a review, see Reardon & Factor, 2010), so professionals who work in sport and exercise settings need to have a basic understanding and knowledge of mental health disorders and treatment. Such a recommendation is supported by professional organizations' certification criteria (e.g., Association for Applied Sport Psychology, n.d.) and recent descriptions of integrated sport psychology training programs (Petrie & Harmison, 2012) and underscored by research showing that performance enhancement interventions are less effective for athletes experiencing psychological difficulties (Wolanin & Schwanhausser, 2010). Thus, the main purposes of this chapter are to highlight areas of psychopathology that are particularly relevant to sport and exercise, to review empirical research on the epidemiology of psychopathology in sport and exercise populations, and to provide recommendations for diagnosis and treatment of psychopathology in the context of sport and exercise.

Psychopathology Relevant to Sport and Exercise

Although sport and exercise participants may experience a variety of mental disorders, certain ones may be exacerbated by the sport and exercise contexts. In this section, we discuss the epidemiology and treatment issues associated with eating disorders, substance-related disorders, psychological factors affecting physical condition (i.e., psychosocial antecedents of sport injury), and adjustment reactions (e.g., to sport injury). In addition, we highlight other disorders and subclinical syndromes (i.e., conditions in which impairment of behavioral, cognitive, or affective functioning is evident but insufficient to satisfy diagnostic criteria) that may be associated with sport and exercise participation but have been investigated less thoroughly.

EATING DISORDERS

For anorexia nervosa and bulimia nervosa, lifetime prevalence rates are higher among adult women (0.5%–0.9% and 1%–3%, respectively) than men (0.05%–0.3% and 0.1%–0.5%, respectively; American Psychiatric Association, 2000; Hudson, Hiripi, Pope, & Kessler, 2007). For both disorders, research in the United States and Europe has shown that rates are higher among adolescents than among young to middle-aged adults (Currin, Schmidt, Treasure, & Jick, 2005) and have remained stable across the 1990s (Currin et al., 2005) and into the 2000s (Crowther, Armey, Luce, Dalton, & Leahey, 2008; Keel, Heatherton, Dorer, Joiner, & Zalta, 2006). Rates of subclinical disorders are higher than clinical for both men and women (Crowther et al., 2008; Isomaa, Tsomaa, Marttunen, Kaltiala-Heino, & Bjorkqvist, 2009; Keel et al., 2006) and may exceed 35% with college student samples (Cohen & Petrie, 2005).

For collegiate and international elite athletes, prevalence rates may be slightly higher than in the general population. For example, rates of anorexia nervosa are estimated to be between 0% and 6.7% (female athletes) and 0% (male athletes), bulimia nervosa between 0% and 12.1% (women) and 0% to 7.5% (men), and eating disorder not otherwise specified between 2% and 13.4% (female athletes) and 0% to 9.7% (male athletes; Greenleaf, Petrie, Carter, & Reel, 2009; Johnson, Powers, & Dick, 1999; Petrie, Greenleaf, Reel, & Carter, 2008; Sundgot-Borgen & Torstveit, 2004); rates may be highest among athletes who participate in sports in which weight, body size and shape, and appearance are emphasized (e.g., gymnastics, cross-country). Subclinical eating disorder rates are higher, ranging from 19% of male collegiate athletes to almost 26% of female collegiate athletes (Greenleaf et al., 2009; Johnson et al., 1999; Petrie et al., 2008). Furthermore, athletes primarily use exercise (2 or more hours/day: 25.2% females and 37% males) and dieting or fasting (two or more times/year: 15.6% females and 14.2% males) to control or manage their weight; more extreme behaviors, such as self-induced vomiting, diuretics, and laxatives, are used much less frequently (e.g., Greenleaf et al., 2009; Petrie et al., 2008).

As a result of dietary restriction and reductions in energy availability, some female athletes will experience three interrelated conditions—disordered eating, amenorrhea, and osteoporosis—that constitute the *female athlete triad* (American College of Sports Medicine, 2007). The triad is associated with increased risk of injury (e.g., stress fractures), medical complications (e.g., infertility), and psychological problems (e.g., anxiety, depression; American College of Sports Medicine, 2007). Although prevalence rates of the triad are relatively low, ranging from 1.2% to 4.3% (e.g., Beals & Hill, 2006; Nichols, Rauh, Lawson, Ji, & Barkai, 2006; Torstveit & Sundgot-Borgen, 2005), rates associated with experiencing two of the three conditions, which still increase female athletes' risk of negative outcomes, can range from 5.4% to 27% (Beals & Hill, 2006; Hoch, Stavrakos, & Schimke, 2007; Nichols et al., 2006; Torstveit & Sundgot-Borgen, 2005).

Although the etiology of eating disorders is considered to be multidimensional, including familial, biological, personality, and genetic factors, sociocultural or environmental factors play a prominent role. Within sport, there are unique pressures that increase athletes' focus on how they look and how much they eat and thus their risk of developing a clinical eating disorder or engaging in a variety of disordered eating behaviors (Petrie & Greenleaf, 2012; Thompson & Sherman, 2010). First, some coaches and athletes believe that weight loss automatically leads to performance improvements. Although not supported by research, this belief may lead to subtle pressures and/or direct messages about diet, weight, and body size and shape being present within athletic teams. Second, in sports such as gymnastics, swimming and diving, and beach volleyball (for women), athletes are required to wear uniforms that are highly revealing and thus draw attention to their bodies. Third, people generally believe athletes in certain sports should have a specific body type and look. For example, gymnasts should be "tiny," runners "lanky," and football players "big." When athletes do not conform to these stereotypical images, they may be considered odd by teammates, judges, coaches, and/or fans. Fourth, on many teams and in many organizations, athletes are valued primarily for their performances; hence, health and well-being may become secondary to winning. In such situations, athletes may experience pressures to substantially increase training load and/or engage in other pathogenic weight loss behaviors in hopes of achieving their performance ideal. Fifth, within the sport environment, characteristics and traits such as exercising excessively, denying pain and discomfort, complying completely with requests, and pursuing perfection are valued and reinforced. Yet, these same characteristics may in reality be symptoms of disordered eating. Thus, what helps athletes be successful in sport also may increase their risk of developing an eating disorder. Whether singly or in combination, these pressures may lead athletes to become more body conscious and uncomfortable with how they look and to engage in more social comparison. Such scrutiny and evaluation and comparisons with others may increase the pressures athletes feel to take extreme measures to change their body shape and appearance, be it through caloric restriction or muscle enhancement. In fact, recent research (Anderson, Petrie, & Neumann, 2011) has shown a strong relationship between sport environment pressures and increases in dietary restraint and body dissatisfaction.

Because of these unique pressures, special consideration needs to be given to the prevention of eating disorders among athletes. Such prevention efforts might occur at the system level (Petrie & Greenleaf, 2012) by creating a "body-healthy" environment in which athletes' physical and psychological well-being are primary. To do so, coaches and other athletic department personnel can (a) deemphasize weight as a salient factor for performance improvements; (b) eliminate weigh-ins and weight requirements for athletes (if it is medically necessary to weigh athletes, such as when monitoring water loss during hot and humid practice conditions, medical personnel can do so privately); (c) become aware of and then change the unhealthy norms that may exist on a team about body, weight, eating, and appearance; (d) educate themselves about eating disorders to better understand how their behaviors may inadvertently have a negative influence and to recognize when some of their athletes may be struggling; and (e) use other professionals, such as nutritionists and sport psychologists, in training their athletes and thus not focus solely on weight loss as the means for achieving performance success but, rather, encourage healthy eating, developing mental toughness, and improving speed and conditioning. Because the scope of this chapter does not allow for a more detailed discussion of prevention and treatment issues, we refer readers to Thompson and Sherman (2010), Petrie and Greenleaf (2012), Petrie and Sherman (2000), and Stice, Shaw, and Marti (2007) for more information.

SUBSTANCE-RELATED DISORDERS

Although sport and exercise may connote images of clean living, health, and well-being, drug use by athletes is a serious concern. The issue of substance use is more complicated for sport and exercise participants than for other individuals because athletes may use drugs for both recreational and performance enhancement purposes (Martens, Dams-O'Connor, & Kilmer, 2007; Martens, Kilmer, & Beck, 2009). In addition to the legal and health (physical and mental) ramifications of drug use experienced by the general population, competitive athletes may face sanctions from their sports' governing bodies. The disqualification of athletes from sport events, such as the Olympic Games and Tour de France, for using performance-enhancing drugs bears witness to the potential negative sport-related consequences of substance use.

Alcohol and marijuana are the primary substances used recreationally by athletes (Selby, Weinstein, & Bird, 1990; Spence & Gauvin, 1996), and the prevalence of alcohol use for athletes, at least at the high school and college levels, is greater than that for nonathletes (Lisha & Sussman, 2010; Mays, DePadilla, Thompson, Kushner, & Windle, 2010; Musselman & Rutledge, 2010). For drugs other than alcohol, however, the available evidence suggests that the prevalence rates are lower for athletes than for nonathletes (Martens et al., 2007, 2009). These lower prevalence rates may be attributable to increases in drug testing of athletes and awareness of the health- and performance-compromising effects of many recreational drugs (Martens et al., 2007). Although athletes may curb their use of alcohol and recreational drugs during the competitive season (Martens, Dams-O'Connor, & Duffy-Paiment, 2006; Selby et al., 1990), athletes still binge drink and get drunk more often than nonathletes (Rainey, McKeown, Sargent, & Valois, 1996; Wechsler, Davenport, Dowdall, Grossman, & Zanakos, 1997).

In terms of anabolic steroid use, which is done to increase muscular size and strength, lifetime prevalence estimates range from 1.4% for eighth graders to 2.2% for high school seniors (National Institute on Drug Abuse, 2006); steroid use among athletes may range from 1% to 6% (National Institute on Drug Abuse, 2006), with prevalence being 3 to 5 times higher for male athletes than for female athletes (Gaa, Griffith, Cahill, & Tuttle, 1994; Kersey, 1996; Middleman & DuRant, 1996). Athletes also may use other banned substances to reduce pain (e.g., morphine), to increase energy and arousal (e.g., amphetamines), to promote relaxation or reduce arousal (e.g., beta blockers), or to control weight (e.g., diuretics) (Martens et al., 2007).

In summarizing the empirical and theoretical literature, Martens et al. (2007) identified excessive stress, sport-specific cultural and environmental factors, personality characteristics, and performance considerations as potential contributors to the use of recreational and performance enhancement drugs by athletes. Sport-specific cultural and environmental factors include the elevated social status of athletes (and the social opportunities accompanying that status), perceived social norms of heavy drinking among athlete peers, and the seasonal pattern of sport competition over the course of the year. Personality characteristics thought to influence substance use by athletes include impulsivity, sensation seeking, and competitiveness. Performance considerations include enhancing sport performance (e.g., heightening alertness, relaxing), reducing pain, and accelerating recovery from injury. Many of these reasons parallel explanations for drug use given by members of the general population but take into account the unique aspects of the sport environment.

Strategies for preventing drug use in sport have focused primarily on education, but few drug education programs have been subjected to controlled trials (Martens et al., 2009). Although comprehensive substance abuse prevention programs for athletes have been implemented (e.g., Goldberg et al., 1996; Grossman & Smiley, 1999), less well-developed programs suffer from a number of limitations, including a reliance on one-time lectures and a lack of follow-up (Petitpas & Van Raalte, 1992). Among the promising preventive approaches that have been tested experimentally, that do not rely exclusively on education, and that have shown favorable results is an Internet-based intervention in which athletes obtain personalized feedback on their drinking behavior in relation to national peer norms and risk status for negative alcohol-related consequences (Doumas & Haustveit, 2008; Doumas, Haustveit, & Coll, 2010).

Treatment for athletes with an identified substance-related disorder is likely to involve outpatient or inpatient modalities, depending on the severity of the problem (Carr & Murphy, 1995; Stainback, 1997). Although it is clear that scare tactics alone are not effective (Goldberg, Bents, Bosworth, Trevisan, & Elliot, 1991), intervention evaluation studies conducted with athletes are scarce, and there is not currently an empirical basis for recommending the use of one particular type of intervention over another (Martens et al., 2009).

PSYCHOLOGICAL FACTORS AFFECTING MEDICAL CONDITION

Because psychosocial factors such as coping resources, life stress, and social support may influence the occurrence of sport injury, it can be argued that the psychosocial antecedents of sport injury constitute "psychological factors affecting medical condition" (American Psychiatric Association, 2000, p. 731). Although early research investigating the relationship of psychological variables to sport injury was conducted primarily with high school and college football players and focused mainly on life stress as a predictor of injury, other sports and predictor variables have been considered more extensively in recent efforts. Empirical findings have provided consistent support for a theoretical model in which life stress and other psychosocial factors (e.g., social support, personality) exert direct and moderated effects on the occurrence of sport injury (for a review, see Petrie & Hamson-Utley, 2011), which has been estimated at 7 million per year in the United States (Conn, Annest, & Gilchrist, 2003).

Theoretically, psychological interventions can help reduce athletic injury by (a) assisting athletes in adapting to and recovering from the high-intensity training that is a typical part of sport and (b) reducing the presence and impact of negative psychosocial factors (e.g., life stress); increasing positive psychosocial factors (e.g., social support); changing psychological appraisals; and learning to reduce anxiety, worry, and stress responses that occur. Studies examining such interventions have shown that cognitive–behavioral stress management programs can be effective in reducing the rate of injuries in high-risk sports such as gymnastics, rugby, soccer, and rowing (for a review, see Petrie & Hamson-Utley, 2011).

ADJUSTMENT REACTIONS

During the course of their involvement in sport and exercise, participants may have to adjust to a number of personally challenging transitions (Pearson & Petitpas, 1990). For example, competitive athletes face the prospects of deselection (i.e., being cut from the team) and sport career termination, and both competitive athletes and exercisers may become injured and be unable to participate for a period of time. Psychological adjustment to injury is a topic of interest among researchers, who have examined the prevalence and correlates of postinjury emotional disturbance.

An estimated 5% to 24% of athletes report clinically meaningful levels of psychological distress, at least in the short term (i.e., 1–2 months), following injury (for a review, see Brewer, 2007). Research findings support a conceptualization in which personal and situational variables interact to influence cognitive, emotional, and behavioral responses to injury (Brewer, 2007). Thus, characteristics of the person (e.g., age, personality, psychological investment in sport) and the situation (e.g., injury severity, injury duration, life stress, social support) affect how the individual appraises the injury, reacts emotionally, and responds behaviorally. Managing affective responses to injury may be critical to physical rehabilitation because postinjury emotional disturbance has been associated with both poor adherence to sport injury rehabilitation regimens (Daly, Brewer, Van Raalte, Petitpas, & Sklar, 1995; Saez de Heredia, Ramirez, & Artaza, 2004) and poor rehabilitation outcome following sport injury (Brewer et al., 2000).

A variety of psychological treatments have been advocated for athletes with injuries, ranging from relaxation and imagery to counseling and psychotherapy (for a review, see Petitpas & Danish, 1995). Research has documented the beneficial effects of biofeedback, imagery, relaxation, and other cognitive–behavioral procedures on outcomes such as pain, reinjury anxiety, and physical rehabilitation parameters (for a review, see Brewer, 2010). Regardless of the particular intervention selected—which, of course, depends on the nature of the client's concerns and resources—Petitpas and Danish (1995) emphasized the importance of building rapport, educating injured athletes about their injury, helping injured athletes to develop coping skills, providing injured athletes with opportunities to practice their newly acquired coping skills, and evaluating the effectiveness of the intervention.

VARIOUS DISORDERS AND SUBCLINICAL SYNDROMES

Dose–Response Reactions

Sport and exercise participants engage in physical activity presumably to prepare for competition or to enhance their fitness and well-being. Sometimes, however, the amount or dose of physical training can be excessive and counterproductive. Competitive athletes who engage in high-volume training regimens are at risk of becoming overtrained, a condition characterized by diminished performance and a variety of symptoms, including disturbances in mood, sleep, and appetite (for a review, see Kellman, 2010). Because the symptoms of overtraining may mimic those of depressive disorders and chronic fatigue syndrome, careful evaluation is needed to rule out alternative causes of the symptoms (Puffer & McShane, 1991). Contemporary approaches to prevention and treatment of overtraining focus on monitoring athletes' states of recovery and stress and initiating substantial recovery efforts for athletes who become overtrained (Kellman, 2010).

Although many individuals struggle to establish a regular exercise habit, some exercisers and recreational athletes have the opposite problem in that they become dependent on their involvement in physical activity and persist in their participation past the point at which physical and mental health benefits are gained. Although research on exercise dependence has been fraught with definitional and measurement issues, commonly identified characteristics of the condition include prioritizing exercise over other important activities and relationships, engaging in exercise despite the presence of exercise-related physical health problems (e.g., injury, pain), and experiencing withdrawal symptoms (e.g., mood disturbance) when restricted from participation in physical activity (Hausenblas & Downs, 2002). Comorbidity with eating disorders (de Coverley Veale, 1987) and general psychopathology (White-Welkley, Higbie, Fried, Koenig, & Price, 1998) is a strong possibility among individuals with exercise dependence. Although little information is available regarding treatment, Morrow (1988) developed a cognitive–behavioral intervention for exercise dependence in which clients are reinforced for gradually relinquishing exercise time to other activities after being assessed and trained in coping skills.

Anxiety Reactions

Anxiety is a central aspect of sport participation (Hackfort & Spielberger, 1989); in fact, some athletes experience precompetitive anxiety to an extent that it interferes with performance (for a review, see Chapter 4, this volume). For the most part, the anxiety associated with sport involvement, even when it has an adverse effect on performance, is subclinical and can be addressed through performance enhancement interventions. In rare cases, however, the level of anxiety experienced is more severe and warrants clinical attention (e.g., Farkas, 1989). Silva (1994) identified a sport-specific condition in which anxiety is "isolated on an *element* of a total performance" (p. 104). As examples of this condition, termed *sport performance phobia*, Silva cited the behavior of a tennis player who was afraid to come to the net and a baseball catcher who developed an inability to throw the ball back to the pitcher despite being able to throw the ball to second base. Phobias and other extreme anxiety reactions should be addressed by sport and exercise psychology practitioners with clinical training.

Another sport- and exercise-related phenomenon with an anxiety component is muscle dysmorphia, a variant of body dysmorphic disorder. Muscle dysmorphia involves (a) a pathological preoccupation with one's body (viewing it as insufficiently lean, muscular, and large); (b) obsessive–compulsive involvement with dieting, weight lifting, and related activities; and (c) severe impairment of social and occupational functioning (e.g., giving up other activities so that one can work out; H. G. Pope, Gruber, Choi, Olivardia, & Phillips, 1997). In addition to anxiety, muscle dysmorphia may be associated with depression, poor self-concept, and suicidal ideology (McFarland & Kaminski, 2009; C. G. Pope et al., 2005). Muscle dysmorphia is more prevalent among men than women, and although there are no epidemiological studies regarding its prevalence, Olivardia (2001) estimated that hundreds of thousands of men experience some symptoms associated with the disorder. Among athletes, bodybuilders and weight lifters appear to be most at risk (e.g., Baghurst & Lirgg, 2009). Etiological factors in muscle dysmorphia are thought to include physical (i.e., body mass, anabolic androgenic steroid use), perceptual (i.e., body distortion), cognitive–affective (i.e., self-esteem, negative affect, ideal body internalization, body dissatisfaction), dispositional (i.e., perfectionism, health locus of control), and social (i.e., media influences) variables (Grieve, 2007; Rohman, 2009).

Personality Disorders

A number of forces in competitive sport may contribute to the development and maintenance of personality disorders in athletes. For example, the coddling and adulation received by gifted athletes may help to foster narcissistic personality disorder (Andersen, Denson, Brewer, & Van Raalte, 1994; House, 1989). Similarly, reinforcement of qualities such as toughness and aggressiveness in the sport environment may increase the likelihood of problem behavior among athletes with antisocial personality disorder (Andersen et al., 1994). Another factor that may exacerbate or contribute to the development of personality disorders in athletes is the dysfunctional performance-contingent social support that athletes receive in many circumstances (House, 1989). Although there have been no empirical investigations on the prevalence and treatment of personality disorders in athletic populations, anecdotal evidence suggests that athletes with personality disorders may not respond well to performance enhancement interventions and likely require clinical attention (Andersen et al., 1994; Marchant & Gibbs, 2004).

Pathological Gambling

Along with substance abuse and violence, gambling is an athlete behavior that has received considerable media attention. Athlete gambling behavior has increasingly become a topic of interest to researchers over the past two decades. Findings from epidemiological studies have suggested that (a) a majority of athletes in National Collegiate Athletic Association Division I football and basketball programs engage in some form of gambling (e.g., casino gambling, slot machines, playing cards for money, betting on sports) while in college (Cross & Vollano, 1999; Ellenbogen, Jacobs, Derevensky, Gupta, & Paskus, 2008), (b) approximately 25% of National Collegiate Athletic Association Division I football players bet on college sporting events (Cullen & Latessa, 1996), and (c) the extent of gambling behavior is at a problematic or pathological level for a considerable percentage (4%–12% for males and 0.4%–3.5% for females) of American intercollegiate athletes (Ellenbogen et al., 2008; Weinstock, Whelan, Meyers, & Watson, 2007). Because pathological gambling can exact tolls on the personal adjustment and sport participation eligibility of athletes as well as adversely affect the integrity of sport, further research is needed to identify the prevalence, causes, and concomitants of and optimal treatments for pathological gambling among athletes.

Sport Concussion

Over the past three decades, recognition of the frequency and serious aftereffects of mild head injury has grown dramatically (Moser, 2007), spawning the field of sports neuropsychology (Echemendia, 2006). Although some athletes who experience concussions have symptoms that resolve quickly, athletes who incur postconcussion syndrome may encounter persistent disruptions in cognitive (e.g., attention, concentration, processing speed), affective (e.g., irritability, depression), and physical (e.g., headaches, fatigue) domains that hinder academic or occupational functioning and overall psychological adjustment. As awareness of sport concussion has expanded, standard procedures for preseason (baseline) and postconcussion neurocognitive testing, concussion management, and return to play have been implemented in many sport settings (for more information, see McCrory et al., 2009).

Attention-Deficit/Hyperactivity Disorder

The attentional, behavioral, and social difficulties faced by people with attention-deficit/hyperactivity disorder (ADHD) can spill over into the realm of sport. As noted in a review by Lullo and Van Puymbroeck (2006), there is evidence that although children with ADHD perform below average in gross motor skills and physical fitness, they can experience improvements in outcomes such as sportspersonlike behavior, sport performance, interest in sport, and enjoyment of sport as result of reinforcement-based behavioral intervention (with and in some cases without medication). Recent research suggesting that physical activity may in itself exert a favorable effect on executive functioning (Gapin & Etnier, 2010b) and symptoms of inattention and hyperactivity (Gapin & Etnier, 2010a) is consistent with anecdotal reports that the prevalence of ADHD is higher among athletes than among nonathletes because athletes may be attracted to physical activity as a means of coping with their disorder (Burton, 2000). Because of their stimulant properties, common medications used to treat ADHD have been banned by some sport governing bodies, thereby necessitating a delicate process of determining when to use and not use prescribed medications to optimize progress toward the therapeutic and athletic aims of child and adult athletes with ADHD (Heil, Hartman, Robinson, & Teegarden, 2002).

Depression

Despite its high prevalence (for a mental disorder) in the general population (American Psychiatric Association, 2000), depression has been the subject of few epidemiological studies with athletes. Recent findings on college students, however, suggest that female athletes experience higher levels of depression than male athletes (Storch, Storch, Killiany, & Roberti, 2005; Yang et al., 2007) and both male and female nonathletes (Storch et al., 2005). Male athletes appear to have levels of depression that are similar to those of female nonathletes (Storch et al., 2005) and similar to (Storch et al., 2005) or lower than those of male nonathletes (Proctor & Boan-Lenzo, 2010; Yang et al., 2007). The reasons for these gender-specific athlete–nonathlete differences are not completely clear and warrant further exploration. Maniar and Sommers-Flanagan (2009) identified the unforgiving nature of the sport culture, injury, sport retirement, and performance-related stressors as unique contributors to depression in athletes and noted that the array of potential treatments for depression generally applied to nonathletes can also be applied to athletes, taking into account, of course, an athlete's individual circumstances.

Recommendations for Diagnosis and Treatment

For sport and exercise participants with diagnosable psychopathology, appropriate treatment can improve their quality of life and enhance their sport performance or involvement in exercise. In the absence of empirical data suggesting otherwise, diagnosis and treatment of psychopathology in sport and exercise participants should be the same as with nonparticipants. Circumstances specific to sport and exercise, however, should be taken into consideration. Accordingly, the following recommendations for diagnosis and treatment of psychopathology in the context of sport and exercise are offered.

1. Practitioners should recognize that some athletes' attitudes and behaviors that may appear to be pathological actually have adaptive value in sport and may be considered normal in the sport subculture. For example, detachment and lack of social conformity might assist ultramarathon runners in training and competition, which can be solitary activities (Folkins & Wieselberg-Bell, 1981), whereas extreme levels of perfectionism can help athletes reach the highest level in their sport. Thus, practitioners need to carefully monitor their own attitudes and reactions to ensure that labeling and bias do not occur. In addition, they may need to educate themselves about the general sport culture as well as specific competitive or exercise milieus prior to working with athletes and exercisers.

2. Practitioners should be sensitive to forces outside of the individual that may be particularly influential in producing apparently pathological behavior. For example, the constant scrutiny faced by athletes both on and off the field may produce feelings of paranoia and anxiety (House, 1989) or may contribute to disordered eating attitudes and behaviors (Petrie & Greenleaf, 2012). Likewise, a variety of sport-induced stressors such as pressure from coaches, restriction of social interaction, travel, and pain or injury (Petrie et al., 1997; Wrisberg, Johnson, & Brooks, 1997) may adversely affect athletes' mental state. Furthermore,

characteristics such as aggressiveness and single-minded devotion to sport may be reinforced by coaches and teammates (Heyman, 1986). Thus, it is important to consider both the athlete and the sport environment when assessing the behavior of sport and exercise participants. Both personal and situational factors should be assessed thoroughly before concluding that a problem resides within the individual.

3. Practitioners should be aware that athletes in particular may be reluctant to seek treatment of a psychological nature. Research has shown that relative to college student-nonathletes, college student-athletes have underused university mental health services (e.g., Bergandi & Wittig, 1984) and expressed less favorable attitudes toward seeking psychological assistance (Watson, 2005). Athletes may be hesitant to seek counseling for several reasons, including personal attributes (e.g., self-reliance), limited time, closed or protected sport environments, high visibility as an athlete, and potential loss of status or negative evaluation by others (Ferrante, Etzel, & Lantz, 1996). Although athletes may be receptive to working with a sport psychologist for performance enhancement (Van Raalte, Brewer, Brewer, & Linder, 1992), the idea of consulting a mental health practitioner for psychotherapy may be met with resistance. Because entering treatment for psychopathology may have negative ramifications for athletes' sport participation, they may be especially concerned about confidentiality. Practitioners should be attuned to this possibility and should make every effort to alleviate athlete-clients' concerns.

4. Practitioners should recognize that although sport may seem to be "just a game," many athletes are heavily invested in sport as a source of self-identity and self-worth (Brewer, Van Raalte, & Linder, 1993). Strong self-identification with sport involvement may benefit athletes in terms of developing a sense of self and enhancing motivation for training and competition but may leave athletes vulnerable to psychological distress when they experience transitions such as deselection, injury, and sport career termination (Brewer, 1993; Pearson & Petitpas, 1990). In extreme cases, threats to athletic self-identity may precipitate suicide (Petitpas & Danish, 1995; Smith & Milliner, 1994). Accordingly, the high degree of self-investment in sport participation possessed by some athletes should be acknowledged by practitioners and not dismissed as preoccupation with a frivolous activity. Furthermore, during transitional times when athletic identity is disrupted, practitioners may work with athletes to establish support networks among friends and teammates and to develop other roles (e.g., student, worker, romantic partner) with which the athletes may also identify.

5. Practitioners should be aware that although many athletic organizations may not ordinarily be receptive to psychological interventions, psychologists may be sought in crisis situations such as a player death or a suicide attempt or threat (Vernacchia, Reardon, & Templin, 1997). In such situations, sport psychologists with crisis intervention skills can provide counseling and consultation to help athletes, coaches, and administrators deal with the immediate and long-term consequences of the crisis (Buchko, 2005) and perhaps increase receptiveness to additional assistance in the future.

6. In keeping with ethical guidelines, practitioners should provide referrals for their sport and exercise participant-clients who have presenting problems that are outside their realm of competence. Referral is clearly needed when the client's problem is centered on a technical aspect of sport performance or when the client requests a performance enhancement intervention and the practitioner lacks sport- or exercise-specific knowledge. Referral also may be necessary when the client presents with psychopathology for which the practitioner has not received training or when supervision or consultation is not available. Thus, during the intake and early sessions, practitioners must thoroughly assess all areas of the athlete's life and functioning to determine the extent to which the problem is clinical in nature or performance related (Taylor & Schneider, 1992). For a review of referral processes in sport and exercise psychology, see Chapter 12, this volume.

Summary and Conclusions

In this chapter, we reviewed the major categories of psychopathology that have been identified and studied with sport and exercise participants. In addition, we provided recommendations for treatment and prevention as warranted by current research. Several points become clear from this review. First, athletes do experience psychopathology, such as eating disorders and substance abuse, at rates equal to and sometimes greater than the general population. Second, psychopathology specific to or exacerbated by sport or exercise involvement also exists. Third, although empirical reports have appeared in the literature with increasing frequency, research examining psychopathology in sport and exercise participants has been lacking, and, thus, comments concerning this area are tentative. Additional epidemiological, longitudinal, and well-controlled studies need to be conducted to expand the knowledge base. Finally, when treating psychopathology, it is essential that circumstances specific to sport and exercise be taken into consideration.

References

American College of Sports Medicine. (2007). The female athlete triad. *Medicine and Science in Sports and Exercise, 39,* 1867–1882. doi:10.1249/mss.0b013e318149f111

American Psychiatric Association. (2000). *Diagnostic and statistical manual of mental disorders* (4th ed., text revision). Washington, DC: Author.

Andersen, M. B., Denson, E. L., Brewer, B. W., & Van Raalte, J. L. (1994). Disorders of personality and mood in athletes: Recognition and referral. *Journal of Applied Sport Psychology, 6,* 168–184. doi:10.1080/10413209408406292

Anderson, C. M., Petrie, T., & Neumann, C. (2011). Psychosocial correlates of bulimic symptomatology among NCAA Division I female collegiate gymnasts and swimmers/divers. *Journal of Sport & Exercise Psychology, 33,* 483–505.

Association for Applied Sport Psychology. (n.d.). *Become a certified consultant.* Retrieved from http://appliedsportpsych.org/Consultants/become-certified

Auerbach, J. (1994). *Psychopathology in the world of men's sports.* Unpublished doctoral dissertation, Institute for Graduate Clinical Psychology, Widener University, Chester, PA.

Baghurst, T., & Lirgg, C. (2009). Characteristics of muscle dysmorphia in male football, weight training, and competitive natural and non-natural bodybuilding samples. *Body Image, 6,* 221–227. doi:10.1016/j.bodyim.2009.03.002

Beals, K. A., & Hill, A. K. (2006). The prevalence of disordered eating, menstrual dysfunction, and low bone mineral density among US collegiate athletes. *International Journal of Sport Nutrition and Exercise Metabolism, 16,* 1–23.

Beisser, A. R. (1977). *The madness in sports* (2nd ed.). Bowie, MD: Charles Press.

Bergandi, T., & Wittig, A. (1984). Availability of and attitudes toward counseling services for the collegiate athlete. *Journal of College Student Personnel, 25,* 557–558.

Berger, K. (2010, November 22). West deals with bipolar disorder, gets back on track. *CBS Sports.com.* Retrieved from http://www.cbssports.com/print/nba/story/14337635/west-deals-with-bipolar-gets-back on track

Brewer, B. W. (1993). Self-identity and specific vulnerability to depressed mood. *Journal of Personality, 61,* 343–364. doi:10.1111/j.1467-6494.1993.tb00284.x

Brewer, B. W. (2007). Psychology of sport injury rehabilitation. In G. Tenenbaum & R. C. Eklund (Eds.), *Handbook of sport psychology* (3rd ed., pp. 404–424). New York, NY: Wiley.

Brewer, B. W. (2010). The role of psychological factors in sport injury rehabilitation. *International Review of Sport and Exercise Psychology, 3,* 40–61. doi:10.1080/17509840903301207

Brewer, B. W., Van Raalte, J. L., Cornelius, A. E., Petitpas, A. J., Sklar, J. H., Pohlman, M. H., . . . Ditmar, T. D. (2000). Psychological factors, rehabilitation adherence, and rehabilitation outcome following anterior cruciate ligament reconstruction. *Rehabilitation Psychology, 45,* 20–37. doi:10.1037/0090-5550.45.1.20

Brewer, B. W., Van Raalte, J. L., & Linder, D. E. (1993). Athletic identity: Hercules' muscles or Achilles heel? *International Journal of Sport Psychology, 24,* 237–254.

Buchko, K. J. (2005). Team consultation following an athlete's suicide: A crisis intervention model. *The Sport Psychologist, 19,* 288–302.

Burton, R. W. (2000). Mental illness in athletes. In D. Begel & R. W. Burton (Eds.), *Sport psychiatry* (pp. 61–81). New York, NY: Norton.

Caplan, A. (2008, August 7). Mentally ill still subject to contempt: When an Eagle admitted he suffers from depression, the bashing began. *Philly.com.* Retrieved from http://articles.philly.com/2008-08-07/news/25258066_1_mental-illness-training-camp-mental-health-treatment

Carr, C. M., & Murphy, S. M. (1995). Alcohol and drugs in sport. In S. M. Murphy (Ed.), *Sport psychology interventions* (pp. 283–306). Champaign, IL: Human Kinetics.

Cohen, D. L., & Petrie, T. A. (2005). An examination of psychosocial correlates of disordered eating among undergraduate women. *Sex Roles, 52,* 29–42. doi:10.1007/s11199-005-1191-x

Conn, J. M., Annest, J. L., & Gilchrist, J. (2003). Sports and recreation related injury episodes in the US population 1997-1999. *Injury Prevention, 9,* 117–123. doi:10.1136/ip.9.2.117

Cross, M. E., & Vollano, A. G. (1999). *The extent and nature and gambling among college student athletes.* Ann Arbor, MI: University of Michigan, Department of Athletics.

Crowther, J. H., Armey, M., Luce, K., Dalton, G., & Leahey, T. (2008). The point prevalence of bulimic disorders from 1990 to 2004. *The International Journal of Eating Disorders, 41,* 491–497. doi:10.1002/eat.20537

Cullen, F. T., & Latessa, E. J. (1996). *The extent and sources of NCAA rule infractions: A national self-report study of student-athletes.* Cincinnati, OH: University of Cincinnati, Division of Criminal Justice.

Currin, L., Schmidt, U., Treasure, J., & Jick, H. (2005). Time trends in eating disorder incidence. *The British Journal of Psychiatry, 186,* 132–135. doi:10.1192/bjp.186.2.132

Daly, J. M., Brewer, B. W., Van Raalte, J. L., Petitpas, A. J., & Sklar, J. H. (1995). Cognitive appraisal, emotional adjustment, and adherence to sport injury rehabilitation. *Journal of Sport Rehabilitation, 4,* 23–30.

de Coverley Veale, D. M. W. (1987). Exercise dependence. *British Journal of Addiction, 82,* 735–740. doi:10.1111/j.1360-0443.1987.tb01539.x

Doumas, D. M., & Haustveit, T. (2008). Reducing heavy drinking among first year intercollegiate athletes: Evaluation of a web-based personalized feedback program. *The Sport Psychologist, 22,* 212–228.

Doumas, D. M., Haustveit, T., & Coll, K. M. (2010). Reducing heavy drinking among first year intercollegiate athletes: A randomized controlled trial of web-based normative feedback. *Journal of Applied Sport Psychology, 22,* 247–261. doi:10.1080/10413201003666454

Echemendia, R. (Ed.). (2006). *Sports neuropsychology: Assessment and management of traumatic brain injury.* New York, NY: Guilford Press.

Ellenbogen, S., Jacobs, D., Derevensky, J., Gupta, R., & Paskus, T. (2008). Gambling behavior among college student-athletes. *Journal of Applied Sport Psychology, 20,* 349–362. doi:10.1080/10413200802056685

Everything was negative. Dark. (2004, October 28). *ESPN.com: WNBA.* Retrieved from http://sports.espn.go.com/espn/print?id=1911836&type=news

Farkas, G. (1989). Exposure and response prevention in the treatment of an okeanophobic triathlete. *The Sport Psychologist, 3,* 189–195.

Ferrante, A. P., Etzel, E., & Lantz, C. (1996). Counseling college student-athletes: The problem, the need 1996. In E. Etzel, A. P. Ferrante, & J. W. Pinkney (Eds.), *Counseling college student-athletes: Issues and interventions* (2nd ed., pp. 3–26). Morgantown, WV: Fitness Information Technology.

Folkins, C. H., & Wieselberg-Bell, N. (1981). A personality profile of ultramarathon runners: A little deviance may go a long way. *Journal of Sport Behavior, 4,* 119–127.

Gaa, G. L., Griffith, E. H., Cahill, B. R., & Tuttle, L. D. (1994). Prevalence of anabolic steroid use among Illinois high school students. *Journal of Athletic Training, 29,* 216–222.

Gapin, J., & Etnier, J. L. (2010a). Parental perceptions of the effects of exercise on behavior in children and adolescents with AD/HD [Abstract]. *Journal of Sport & Exercise Psychology, 32*(suppl.), S165.

Gapin, J., & Etnier, J. L. (2010b). The relationship between physical activity and executive function performance in children with attention-deficit hyperactivity disorder. *Journal of Sport & Exercise Psychology, 32,* 753–763.

Garber, G. (2007, February 26). Draper's tale of two sports is one for the movies. *ESPN.com: Golf.* Retrieved from http://sports.espn.go.com/espn/print?id=2780719&type=story

Goldberg, L., Bents, R., Bosworth, E., Trevisan, L., & Elliot, D. L. (1991). Anabolic steroid education and adolescents: Do scare tactics work? *Pediatrics, 87,* 283–286.

Goldberg, L., Elliot, D., Clarke, G. N., MacKinnon, D., P., Moe, E., Zoref, L., . . . Lapin, A. (1996). Effects of a multidimensional anabolic steroid prevention intervention: The adolescents training and learning to avoid steroids (ATLAS) program. *JAMA, 276,* 1555–1562. doi:10.1001/jama.1996.03540190027025

Greenleaf, C., Petrie, T. A., Carter, R., & Reel, J. J. (2009). Female collegiate athletes: Prevalence of eating disorders and disordered eating behaviors. *Journal of American College Health, 57,* 489–496. doi:10.3200/JACH.57.5.489-496

Grieve, F. G. (2007). A conceptual model of factors contributing to the development of muscle dysmorphia. *Eating Disorders: The Journal of Treatment & Prevention, 15,* 63–80. doi:10.1080/10640260601044535

Grossman, S. J., & Smiley, E. B. (1999). APPLE: Description and evaluation of a substance abuse education and prevention program for collegiate athletics. *The Journal of Primary Prevention, 20,* 51–59. doi:10.1023/A:1021354318923

Hackfort, D., & Spielberger, C. D. (Eds.). (1989). *Anxiety in sports: An international perspective.* New York, NY: Hemisphere.

Hales, D. (1993, December 19). When panic strikes. *Parade Magazine,* pp. 12–13.

Hausenblas, H. A., & Downs, D. S. (2002). Exercise dependence: A systematic review. *Psychology of Sport and Exercise, 3,* 89–123. doi:10.1016/S1469-0292(00)00015-7

Heil, J., Hartman, D., Robinson, G., & Teegarden, L. (2002). Attention-deficit hyperactivity disorder in athletes. *Olympic Coach, 12*(2), 5–7.

Heyman, S. R. (1986). Psychological problem patterns found with athletes. *Clinical Psychologist, 39,* 68–71.

Hoch, A. Z., Stavrakos, D. E., & Schimke, J. E. (2007). Prevalence of female athlete triad characteristics in a club triathlon team. *Archives of Physical Medicine and Rehabilitation, 88,* 681–682. doi:10.1016/j.apmr.2007.02.035

House, T. (1989). *The jock's itch: The fast-track private world of the professional ballplayer.* Chicago, IL: Contemporary Books.

Hudson, J. I., Hiripi, E., Pope, H. G., & Kessler, R. C. (2007). The prevalence and correlates of eating disorders in the National Comorbidity Survey replication. *Biological Psychiatry, 61,* 348–358. doi:10.1016/j.biopsych.2006.03.040

Isomaa, R., Tsomaa, A., Marttunen, M., Kaltiala-Heino, R., & Bjorkqvist, K. (2009). The prevalence, incidence and development of eating disorders in Finnish adolescents—A two-step 3-year follow-up study. *European Eating Disorders Review, 17,* 199–207. doi:10.1002/erv.919

Johnson, C., Powers, P. S., & Dick, R. (1999). Athletes and eating disorders: The National Collegiate Athletic Association study. *International Journal of Eating Disorders, 26,* 179–188. doi:10.1002/(SICI)1098-108X(199909)26:2<179::AID-EAT7>3.0.CO;2-Z

Keel, P. K., Heatherton, T., Dorer, D., Joiner, T., & Zalta, A. (2006). Point prevalence of bulimia nervosa in 1982, 1992, and 2002. *Psychological Medicine, 36,* 119–127. doi:10.1017/S0033291705006148

Kellman, M. (2010). Overtraining and recovery. In S. J. Hanrahan & M. B. Andersen (Eds.), *Routledge handbook of applied sport psychology: A comprehensive guide for students and practitioners* (pp. 292–302). New York, NY: Routledge.

Kersey, R. D. (1996). Anabolic-androgenic steroid use among California community college student-athletes. *Journal of Athletic Training, 31,* 237–241.

Lisha, N. E., & Sussman, S. (2010). Relationship of high school and college sports participation with alcohol, tobacco, and illicit drug use: A review. *Addictive Behaviors, 35,* 399–407. doi:10.1016/j.addbeh.2009.12.032

Lullo, C., & Van Puymbroeck, M. (2006). Research update: Sports for children with ADHD. *Parks & Recreation, 41*(12), 20–23.

Maine issue is health. (1997, August 20). *Union-News,* p. D16.

Maniar, S., & Sommers-Flanagan, J. (2009). Clinical depression and college student-athletes. In E. Etzel (Ed.), *Counseling and psychological services for college student-athletes* (pp. 323–348). Morgantown, WV: Fitness Information Technology.

Marchant, D., & Gibbs, P. (2004). Ethical considerations in treating borderline personality in sport: A case example. *The Sport Psychologist, 18,* 317–323.

Martens, M. P., Dams-O'Connor, K., & Duffy-Paiment, C. (2006). Comparing off-season with in-season alcohol consumption among intercollegiate athletes. *Journal of Sport & Exercise Psychology, 28,* 502–510.

Martens, M. P., Dams-O'Connor, K., & Kilmer, J. R. (2007). Alcohol and drug use among athletes: Prevalence, etiology, and interventions. In G. Tenenbaum & R. C. Eklund (Eds.), *Handbook of sport psychology* (3rd ed., pp. 859–878). New York, NY: Wiley. doi:10.1002/9781118270011.ch39

Martens, M. P., Kilmer, J. R., & Beck, N. (2009). Alcohol and drug use among college athletes. In E. F. Etzel (Ed.), *Counseling and psychological services for college student-athletes* (pp. 451–475). Morgantown, WV: Fitness Information Technology.

Matser, J. T., Kessels, A. G. H., Jordan, B. D., Lezak, M. D., & Troost, J. (1998). Chronic traumatic brain injury in professional soccer players. *Neurology, 51,* 791–796. doi:10.1212/WNL.51.3.791

Mays, D., DePadilla, L., Thompson, N. J., Kushner, H., & Windle, M. (2010). Sports participation and problem alcohol use: A multi-wave national sample of adolescents. *American Journal of Preventive Medicine, 38,* 491–498. doi:10.1016/j.amepre.2010.01.023

McCrory, P., Meeuwisse, W., Johnston, K., Dvorak, J., Aubry, M., Molloy, M., & Cantu, R. (2009) Consensus statement on concussion in sport 3rd International Conference on Concussion in Sport held in Zurich, November 2008. *Clinical Journal of Sports Medicine, 19,* 185–200.

McFarland, M. B., & Kaminski, P. L. (2009). Men, muscles, and mood: The relationship between self-concept, dysphoria, and body image disturbances. *Eating Behaviors, 10,* 68–70. doi:10.1016/j.eatbeh.2008.10.007

Middleman, A. B., & DuRant, R. H. (1996). Anabolic steroid use and associated health risk behaviors. *Sports Medicine, 21,* 251–255. doi:10.2165/00007256-199621040-00001

Morgan, W. P. (1985). Selected psychological factors limiting performance: A mental health model. In D. H. Clarke & H. M. Eckert (Eds.), *Limits of human performance* (pp. 70–80). Champaign, IL: Human Kinetics.

Morrow, J. (1988, October). *A cognitive-behavioral interaction for reducing exercise addiction.* Paper presented at the meeting of the Association for the Advancement of Applied Sport Psychology, Nashua, NH.

Moser, R. S. (2007). The growing public health concern of sports concussion: The new psychology practice frontier. *Professional Psychology: Research and Practice, 38,* 699–704. doi:10.1037/0735-7028.38.6.699

Musselman, J. R. B., & Rutledge, P. C. (2010). The incongruous alcohol–activity association: Physical activity and alcohol consumption in college students. *Psychology of Sport and Exercise, 11,* 609–618. doi:10.1016/j.psychsport.2010.07.005

National Institute on Drug Abuse. (2006). *Anabolic steroid abuse.* Bethesda, MD: National Institutes of Health. Retrieved from http://www.nida.nih.gov/researchreports/steroids/anabolicsteroids2.html#scope

Nichols, J. F., Rauh, M. J., Lawson, M. J., Ji, M., & Barkai, H. S. (2006). Prevalence of the female athlete triad syndrome among high school athletes. *Archives of Pediatrics & Adolescent Medicine, 160,* 137–142. doi:10.1001/archpedi.160.2.137

Ogilvie, B. C., & Tutko, T. A. (1966). *Problem athletes and how to handle them.* London, England: Pelham.

Olivardia, R. (2001). Mirror, mirror on the wall, who's the largest of them all? The features and phenomenology of muscle dysmorphia. *Harvard Review of Psychiatry, 9,* 254–259.

Page, P. (1990). Tourette syndrome in athletics: A case study and review. *Athletic Training, 25,* 254–259.

Pearson, R. E., & Petitpas, A. J. (1990). Transitions of athletes: Pitfalls and prevention. *Journal of Counseling & Development, 69,* 7–10. doi:10.1002/j.1556-6676.1990.tb01445.x

Petitpas, A., & Danish, S. J. (1995). Caring for injured athletes. In S. M. Murphy (Ed.), *Sport psychology interventions* (pp. 255–281). Champaign, IL: Human Kinetics.

Petitpas, A. J., & Van Raalte, J. L. (1992, Spring). Planning alcohol education programs for intercollegiate student-athletes. *The Academic Athletic Journal,* 12–25.

Petrie, T. A., & Diehl, N. S. (1995). Sport psychology in the profession of psychology. *Professional Psychology: Research and Practice, 26,* 288–291. doi:10.1037/0735-7028.26.3.288

Petrie, T. A., Diehl, N. S., & Watkins, C. E., Jr. (1995). Sport psychology: An emerging domain in the counseling psychology profession? *The Counseling Psychologist, 23,* 535–545. doi:10.1177/0011000095233010

Petrie, T. A., Falkstein, D. L., Varnado, J. L., Austin, L. J., Harmison, R. J., Jenkins, M., & Harvey, P. (1997). The occurrence of negative life events in male and female college-student athletes [Abstract]. *Journal of Applied Sport Psychology, 9*(Suppl.), S144.

Petrie, T. A., & Greenleaf, C. (2012). Eating disorders in sport. In S. Murphy (Ed.), *Oxford handbook of sport and performance psychology* (pp. 635–659). New York, NY: Oxford University Press. doi:10.1002/9781118270011.ch16

Petrie, T. A., Greenleaf, C., Reel, J., & Carter, J. (2008). Prevalence of eating disorders and disordered eating behaviors among male collegiate athletes. *Psychology of Men & Masculinity, 9,* 267–277. doi:10.1037/a0013178

Petrie, T. A., & Hamson-Utley, J. (2011). Psychosocial antecedents of and responses to athletic injury. In T. Morris & P. Terry (Eds.), *The new sport and exercise psychology companion* (pp. 531–552). Morgantown, WV: Fitness Information Technology.

Petrie, T. A., & Harmison, R. (2012). Sport psychology in the field of counseling psychology. In E. Altmaier & J. I. Hanson (Eds.), *Oxford handbook of counseling psychology* (pp. 780–806). New York, NY: Oxford University Press.

Petrie, T. A., & Sherman, R. (2000). Counseling athletes with eating disorders: A case example. In M. Andersen (Ed.), *Doing sport psychology* (pp. 121–137). Champaign, IL: Human Kinetics.

Pope, C. G., Pope, H. G., Menard, W., Fay, C., Olivardia, R., & Phillips, K. A. (2005). Clinical features of muscle dysmorphia among males with body dysmorphic disorder. *Body Image, 2,* 395–400. doi:10.1016/j.bodyim.2005.09.001

Pope, H. G., Gruber, A. J., Choi, P., Olivardia, R., & Phillips, K. A. (1997). Muscle dysmorphia: An underrecognized form of body dysmorphic disorder. *Psychosomatics, 38,* 548–557. doi:10.1016/S0033-3182(97)71400-2

Proctor, S. L., & Boan-Lenzo, C. (2010). Prevalence of depressive symptoms in male intercollegiate student-athletes and nonathletes. *Journal of Clinical Sport Psychology, 4,* 204–220.

Puffer, J. C., & McShane, J. M. (1991). Depression and chronic fatigue in the college student-athlete. *Primary Care, 18,* 297–308.

Rainey, C. J., McKeown, R. E., Sargent, R. G., & Valois, R. F. (1996). Patterns of tobacco and alcohol use among sedentary, exercising, nonathletic, and athletic youth. *The Journal of School Health, 66,* 27–32. doi:10.1111/j.1746-1561.1996.tb06254.x

Reardon, C. L., & Factor, R. M. (2010). Sport psychiatry: A systematic review of diagnosis and medical treatment of mental illness in athletes. *Sports Medicine, 40,* 961–980. doi:10.2165/11536580-000000000-00000

Rohman, L. (2009). The relationship between anabolic androgenic steroids and muscle dysmorphia. *Eating Disorders: The Journal of Treatment & Prevention, 17,* 187–199. doi:10.1080/10640260902848477

Rosen, L. W., Smokler, C., Carrier, D., Shafer, C. L., & McKeag, D. B. (1996). Seasonal mood disturbances in collegiate hockey players. *Journal of Athletic Training, 31,* 225–228.

Saez de Heredia, A. R., Ramirez, A., & Artaza, J. (2004). The effect of psychological response on recovery of sport injury. *Research in Sports Medicine, 12,* 15–31. doi:10.1080/15438620490280567

Selby, R., Weinstein, H. M., & Bird, T. S. (1990). The health of university athletes: Attitudes, behaviors, and stressors. *Journal of American College Health, 39,* 11–18. doi:10.1080/07448481.1990.9936208

Silva, J. M., III. (1994). Sport performance phobias. *International Journal of Sport Psychology, 25,* 100–118.

Smith, A. M., & Milliner, E. K. (1994). Injured athletes and the risk of suicide. *Journal of Athletic Training, 29,* 337–341.

Spence, J. C., & Gauvin, L. (1996). Drug and alcohol use by Canadian university athletes: A national survey. *Journal of Drug Education, 26,* 275–287.

Stainback, R. D. (1997). *Alcohol and sport.* Champaign, IL: Human Kinetics.

Stice, E., Shaw, H., & Marti, C. (2007). A meta-analytic review of eating disorder prevention programs: Encouraging findings. *Annual Review of Clinical Psychology, 3,* 207–231. doi:10.1146/annurev.clinpsy.3.022806.091447

Storch, E. A., Storch, J. B., Killiany, E. M., & Roberti, J. W. (2005). Self-reported psychopathology in athletes: A comparison of intercollegiate student-athletes and non-athletes. *Journal of Sport Behavior, 28,* 86–98.

Sundgot-Borgen, J., & Torstveit, M. K. (2004). Prevalence of eating disorders in elite athletes is higher than in the general population. *Clinical Journal of Sport Medicine, 14*, 25–32. doi:10.1097/00042752-200401000-00005

Taylor, J., & Schneider, B. A. (1992). The sport-clinical intake protocol: A comprehensive interviewing instrument for applied sport psychology. *Professional Psychology: Research and Practice, 23*, 318–325. doi:10.1037/0735-7028.23.4.318

Thompson, R., & Sherman, R. (2010). *Eating disorders in sport.* New York, NY: Routledge.

Torre, P. S. (2011, August 15). Dangerous minds. *Sports Illustrated,* 12–13.

Torstveit, M. K., & Sundgot-Borgen, J. (2005). The female athlete triad exists in both elite athletes and controls. *Medicine and Science in Sports and Exercise, 37*, 1449–1459. doi:10.1249/01.mss.0000177678.73041.38

Van Raalte, J. L., Brewer, B. W., Brewer, D. D., & Linder, D. E. (1992). NCAA Division II college football players' perceptions of an athlete who consults a sport psychologist. *Journal of Sport & Exercise Psychology, 14*, 273–282.

Vernacchia, R. A., Reardon, J. P., & Templin, D. P. (1997). Sudden death in sport: Managing the aftermath. *The Sport Psychologist, 11*, 223–235.

Visser, L. (2010, May 12). Ten years after leaving field, Haley on more solid ground. *CBS Sports.com.* Retrieved from http://www.cbssports.com/columns/story/12777033

Walker reveals struggles with mental disorder in just-released book. (2008, April 14). *ESPN.com: NFL.* Retrieved from http://sports.espn.go.com/espn/print?id=3346240&type=story

Watson, J. C. (2005). College student-athletes' attitudes toward help-seeking behavior and expectations of counseling services. *Journal of College Student Development, 46*, 442–449. doi:10.1353/csd.2005.0044

Wechsler, H., Davenport, A. E., Dowdall, G. W., Grossman, S. J., & Zanakos, S. I. (1997). Binge drinking, tobacco, and illicit drug use and involvement in college athletics: A survey of students at 140 American colleges. *Journal of American College Health, 45*, 195–200. doi:10.1080/07448481.1997.9936884

Weinstock, J., Whelan, J. P., Meyers, A. W., & Watson, J. M. (2007). Gambling behavior of student-athletes and a student cohort: What are the odds? *Journal of Gambling Studies, 23*, 13–24.

White-Welkley, J. E., Higbie, E. J., Fried, A. L., Koenig, L. J., & Price, L. R. (1998). Exercise patterns, injury incidence, eating habits, aerobic fitness and psychopathology among non-competitive females [Abstract]. *Medicine and Science in Sports and Exercise, 30*(Suppl.), S118. doi:10.1097/00005768-199805001-00670

Wolanin, A. T., & Schwanhausser, L. A. (2010). Psychological functioning as a moderator of the MAC approach to performance enhancement. *Journal of Clinical Sport Psychology, 4,* 312–322.

Wrisberg, C. A., Johnson, M. S., & Brooks, G. (1997). The life experience of collegiate athletes: A phenomenological investigation [Abstract]. *Journal of Applied Sport Psychology, 9*(Suppl.), S76.

Yang, J., Peek-Asa, C., Corlette, J. D., Cheng, G., Foster, D. T., & Albright, J. (2007). Prevalence of and risk factors associated with symptoms of depression in competitive collegiate student-athletes. *Clinical Journal of Sport Medicine, 17,* 481–487. doi:10.1097/JSM.0b013e31815aed6b

Judy L. Van Raalte and Mark B. Andersen

Referral Processes in Sport Psychology

15

The purpose of this chapter is to address some of the complexities of referral processes in sport psychology. First, we describe why referrals should be considered in sport settings. Next, we discuss when and to whom referrals might be made. Finally, we explore key factors that enhance the effectiveness of referrals and increase the likelihood of sport psychologists receiving referrals. We begin with three case examples.

- *Case 1.* Jayden was the kind of football player who put all he had into every game. He had an impressive training regimen in the off season and worked all summer to be ready to be a starter in the fall. Jayden's season began as well as he had hoped, but he contacted the team's sport psychologist to gain an additional edge. Jayden said he wanted to work with the sport psychologist on his intensity because his balance and focus were off after he had "knocked heads" during a game a few days ago.
- *Case 2.* Coach was thrilled to have Abigail join the squad, and Abigail lived up to her promise. When Abigail played

http://dx.doi.org/10.1037/14251-015
Exploring Sport and Exercise Psychology, Third Edition, J. Van Raalte and B. Brewer (Editors)

well, the team was unstoppable. Recently, however, she has been unpredictable. If something goes wrong in a practice or a game, she can fly into a rage and has trouble recovering her cool. Abigail's teammates have started calling her "the head case." Coach knows that something more is needed to get Abigail back on track and has decided to refer her to a sport psychologist.

▪ *Case 3.* Chris has been working diligently with the athletic trainer for his knee pain issues. He also started meeting with the sport psychologist for performance enhancement. Rather than improving, Chris has started to struggle on the field. Chris told the sport psychologist that the knee pain is a serious problem but that competition and training are necessary to cope with the emotional pain caused by family problems.

Athletes begin working with sport psychologists for a variety of reasons. As illustrated in the case examples, consultation often begins with a focus on performance enhancement. Athletes may also contact a sport psychology consultant or be referred for other concerns such as coach or teammate conflicts, career issues, and injury. Over the course of consultation, the sport psychologist may come to believe that issues other than performance enhancement, such as family difficulties, physical injury, or psychopathology, are of central concern to the athlete. When these issues are outside the sport psychologist's areas of expertise or when the sport psychologist feels frustrated and is not making progress with a client, a referral may be in order (Corey, 2009; Sharp & Hodge, 2011).

The issue of referral has received limited attention within the sport psychology service delivery literature. Most of the referral information provided is based on the incorporation of clinical and counseling models of service delivery into mainstream sport and exercise psychology (e.g., Gayman & Crossman, 2006; Lesyk, 1998; Sharp & Hodge, 2011). Some consideration, however, has been given to referral being a delicate and potentially risky process (Petrie & Sherman, 2000; Tod & Andersen, 2010).

The structure of the referral can set the stage for the quality and efficacy of the therapeutic relationship that follows (Watson, McDonnell, & Bhaumik, 2005). When working with athletes, referrals to clinical or counseling psychologists are sometimes complicated by the stigma associated with mental problems and the derogation of those who seek help from mental health practitioners (Corrigan, 2004). Research has indicated that male college students and older male sports fans derogate an athlete who consults a sport psychologist or a psychiatrist relative to an athlete who attempts to resolve the same problem by working with his coach (Linder, Brewer, Van Raalte, & DeLange, 1991). Although college student-athletes differ in their attitudes related to stigma and mental health help seeking (Steinfeldt & Steinfeldt, 2011) and do not tend to derogate a fellow athlete who consults a sport psychologist, they do have a negative regard for an athlete who consults a psychiatrist (Van Raalte, Brewer, Brewer, & Linder, 1992). Thus, fear of derogation may leave athletes hesitant to accept referrals to mental health professionals.

Why Refer

Athletes, in general, probably exhibit a somewhat narrower range and frequency of mental disorders than are found in the population at large as a result of a natural selection process. That is, maintaining an athlete's schedule and regimen is generally more than a chronically incapacitated depressed individual or a person with a borderline personality disorder can handle for any significant length of time. The reported general good mental health of athletes (Raglin, 2001) may also be due, in part, to involvement in regular exercise. Various forms of physical activity have been found to be effective in treating depression and other psychological disorders (e.g., Ströhle, 2009). Nevertheless, mental health issues do occur in athletic populations (Brewer, 2009; Storch, Storch, Killiany, & Roberti, 2005; see also Chapter 14, this volume). Depending on the specific knowledge, competencies, and supervision resources available to the sport psychologist, referral may be in the best interest of the athlete to effectively address psychological problems such as anxiety, anger management, eating disorders, substance abuse, gambling problems, and other clinical disorders. Ethical guidelines for the practice of sport psychology around the world (e.g., Association of Applied Sport Psychology, 2011; British Association of Sport and Exercise Sciences, 2000; International Society of Sport Psychology, 2011) require sport psychologists to have or obtain the training, experience, consultation, or supervision necessary to ensure the competence of their services or to make referrals to ensure safe and suitable treatment for athletes.

In addition to psychological issues, it may also be appropriate for sport psychologists to consider referral when concerns arise about physical causes for psychological symptoms. Some of the more common physical concerns, interpersonal and intrapersonal issues, psychopathology, and related issues that a sport psychologist might encounter and make referrals for are detailed in the sections that follow.

PHYSICAL ISSUES

Sport psychologists should make every effort to gain knowledge of the technical and physical aspects of sport and exercise activities. Such knowledge helps them to recognize when a problem might be physical and to make referrals to sports medicine personnel and coaches. For example, the football player described in Case 1 at the beginning of this chapter who had "knocked heads" and was experiencing problems with balance and focus might be a candidate for concussion screening.

Knowledge of the technical aspects of the sport helps the sport psychologist better judge when an athlete's problems need the attention of the coach more than that of the sport psychologist. An example from our casebooks illustrates this point. A goalkeeper was seeing Judy L. Van Raalte and started work on imagery. On checking with the athlete about the quality, viewpoint, and sport specific details of her mental images, Van Raalte learned that she was getting rid of the ball as quickly as she could after a save. Van Raalte was pretty sure that she should have been looking at the field and strategically distributing the ball to her players. Because this issue was a coaching point, it was suggested that the athlete discuss ideal techniques with her coach. This discussion resulted in improved play for the athlete, enhanced the athlete's relationship with her coach, and gave the coach a favorable impression of the sport psychologist. Sport psychologists who cross the line into coaching, interfering in the technical area of athletes' sport performances are likely to be perceived as rivals by coaches and may not last long in the field.

Sport psychologists working in competitive sport may encounter athletes who are encouraged to "play through the pain." In some cases, athletes may be sent to a sport psychologist because they are not "tough" enough. That is, the coach may believe that athletes are "wimping out" or that psychological factors are causing recurrent injuries (as described for Chris in Case 3 at the beginning of the chapter). Before working with an athlete on specific techniques (e.g., pain management, concentration), the sport psychologist should refer the athlete to a sports medicine provider to make sure that additional athletic involvement will not cause physical damage. This referral itself can pose problems. The coach should be informed of any referral to sports medicine personnel. If this is not done, the coach may feel that an "end around" has been pulled. On the other hand, the sport psychologist cannot ethically reveal that a referral has been made without the express consent of the athlete. Referral for a thorough checkout framed as "just covering all the bases" may prove effective in putting both the athlete and the coach at ease.

As relationships between sport psychologists and athletes develop, athletes may begin to feel comfortable voicing dissatisfaction with training schedules and techniques. Athletes may discuss technical problems with their training that they believe are contributing to poor performances. Naturally, athletes should talk to their coaches about technical issues, but some athletes are uncomfortable around their coaches and are rather fearful of coaches' reactions. Sport psychologists can help athletes develop strategies to facilitate dialogue. Although encouraging athletes to talk to their coaches is not a referral in the strictest sense, it is getting athletes to the appropriate resource (see Chapter 16, this volume).

PERSONAL AND INTERPERSONAL ISSUES

Helping athletes cope with interpersonal issues may be within sport psychologists' realms of expertise, depending on their training. For those trained in exercise science or research psychology or for those hired to work in performance enhancement only, the structure of the consultation setting necessitates referral for interpersonal concerns. For example, if sport psychologists are hired to provide primarily performance enhancement services, they may decide to refer athletes to other sources for longer term consultation on issues such as aggression and sexuality concerns.

Aggression is an accepted part of many sport cultures (Mensch & Miller, 2007). As with Abigail in Case 2 at the beginning of the chapter, some athletes' aggression may become problematic. Difficulties can arise when athletes are so aggressive that they are unable to compete within the rules and/or are extremely aggressive off the field. For athletes who have been using alcohol, anabolic-androgenic steroids, or other illegal drugs, the situation becomes even more complicated. A sport psychologist may have success helping athletes manage their aggression if the athletes have a history of reasonable anger and aggression control. Athletes with more problematic histories may require more extensive treatment and may be good candidates for referral (Mensch & Miller, 2007).

The sexual activities of athletes are often considered newsworthy, although little research has been conducted on their actual sexual behavior (for exceptions to this rule, see Habel, Dittus, De Rosa, Chung, & Kerndt, 2010; Taliaferro, Rienzo, & Donovan, 2010). Like the rest of the population, athletes confront a number of issues concerning relationships, sexuality, and gender roles. Sport psychologists working primarily in the performance enhancement area still may come across sexuality issues with their athlete clients. It is common for an athlete after a month or two of building up trust with the sport psychologist to then reveal some very personal information. In some cases, sexuality issues may be part of that information. In most cases, being a gay, lesbian, or bisexual athlete is not the problem. Many of the problems these athletes face have to do with homophobia in sport and society. Sport psychologists not familiar or comfortable with sexual orientation and sexual identity issues need to refer (see also Griffin, 1998; Kauer & Krane, 2010).

PSYCHOPATHOLOGY

Sport psychologists should be familiar with symptoms associated with various psychopathologies so that they can appropriately treat or refer athletes (Andersen, Denson, Brewer, & Van Raalte, 1994). In this volume, Chapter 14 provides a discussion of some of the more common disorders that sport psychologists may encounter (e.g., adjustment reactions, anxiety disorders, eating disorders, pathological gambling, personality disorders). Depending on the specific knowledge and competencies of the sport psychologist, a variety of psychological problems may be detected that require referral.

SPORT-PSYCHOLOGIST-RELATED ISSUES

The effectiveness of consultation depends in part on the fit between sport psychologist and athlete. Sport psychologists who recognize the importance of culture, ethnicity, gender, language, racism, sexism, and/ or discrimination in the consultation process tend to be more effective (Kitchener, 2000). They should be willing to refer an athlete to another practitioner who may be a better match in terms of sociocultural factors that are important to the athlete.

When to Refer

A central issue in deciding whether to make a referral is the determination of the limits of one's competence. Do sport psychologists understand their limits of competency and make appropriate referrals? Research by Gayman and Crossman (2006) indicates that some sport psychologists make referrals to mental health professionals, but others never make such referrals. For sport psychology practitioners, knowing exactly when to make a referral can be difficult. Even careful self-assessment of one's abilities can have limited utility because blind spots in knowledge and training are, by definition, difficult to see.

One of the best ways to determine if a referral is in order may be through supervision (see Andersen, Van Raalte, & Brewer, 2000; Andersen, Van Raalte, & Harris, 2000; Tod, 2010; Van Raalte & Andersen, 2000). The first objective of supervision is the care and welfare of the athlete-client. The second objective, however, is the development of the sport psychologist as a competent practitioner. Through the help of their supervisors, sport psychologists can explore what they know and what they do not know to understand their boundaries of competence. When one is armed with such knowledge, decisions about whether to refer become easier to make.

Supervision can also serve a third, educational function. An athlete's problem may be just beyond the competence of a sport psychologist. With proper supervision and study, however, the practitioner may proceed with treating the athlete. This process of learning through supervision and study is one in which professional growth can occur. Supervision is not only for neophyte practitioners; it is a career-long process. Even seasoned practitioners can learn and expand their boundaries of competence through peer supervision with colleagues.

In addition to issues related to expertise, referrals may also need to be made when a sport psychologist is no longer able to work with an athlete. This situation may happen as a result of the sport psychologist relocating, being overly busy, or being committed to work or travel with another team or athlete. It might also happen when a sport psychologist is released from work with a sport organization, and therefore, a referral to another sport psychologist may be in order (Moore, 2003).

To Whom Should Athletes Be Referred

Once they have gathered information about the typical problems that may require referral and know the limits of their competence, it is then incumbent on sport psychologists to develop a referral network. A sport psychology referral network is a group of people with expertise in a variety of areas to whom athletes can be referred. Ideally, the professionals in the referral network have knowledge of sports and experience working with athletes. At the least, they should be interested in learning about sport and exercise and open to working with an athletic population.

Establishing a referral network takes time and motivation. First, professionals in the local area should be identified (Andersen, 2001). These individuals might include coaches, exercise physiologists, sports medicine experts, physical therapists, athletic trainers, psychologists, psychiatrists, social workers, and other sport psychologists. Selecting both male and female professionals of various theoretical orientations and professional backgrounds can be useful. Second, an effort should be made to develop a relationship with these professionals. Meeting for lunch and talking on a regular basis can facilitate the process of getting to know each other. Referrals are smoother if the referral is a fit for both the person being referred and the referral source (Watson et al., 2005). Athletes seem to find this team approach in which various sport professionals work together to be appealing (Andersen, 1992). Third, the referral network should be evaluated and modified on an ongoing basis to provide the best service for athletes. Having a broad group of practitioners available allows the sport psychologist to have some flexibility in this process. Sport psychologists must invest time and energy in developing and maintaining referral networks, but they also benefit as they become the recipients of referrals from other network practitioners (Wright & Keegan, 2011).

When developing a referral network, sport psychologists should keep in mind some of the specific concerns that athletes may have. Athletes who compete for sport organizations that pay for their sport psychology services may wonder who will know about and pay for services if they are referred to outside practitioners. It is possible that the sport organization will cover the costs of outside referrals but only if the sport organization is informed. Obviously, informing the organization brings up concerns related to confidentiality. In addition to confidentiality and financial concerns, athletes generally have limited time because of the demands of training and work or school. It is useful to select local practitioners who have some availability in their schedules and at least some of whom provide services on a sliding scale basis. For student-athletes attending colleges or universities, there are usually "free" on-campus services available. Developing a relationship with these providers increases the likelihood that athletes will follow through on referrals made.

The Referral Process

There is no one way to make the perfect referral. There are, however, steps that can be taken to make it more likely that referrals will be effective (Corey, 2009). These steps include preparing for referral, explaining why the referral is being made, describing what is generally involved in working with practitioner to whom you are referring, being sensitive to athletes' concerns, and being open to alternate strategies if the athlete is not interested in being referred. Each step is discussed in more detail in the subsections that follow.

PREPARE FOR REFERRAL

The referral process is often smoother if preparation for referral begins at the first athlete meeting. At this meeting, athletes can be informed that during the course of their work with the sport psychologist, referral to other practitioners is possible. Because a lot of information is covered in the initial session, many sport psychologists have developed written handouts reiterating important details about the consultation process for athletes to read and take home with them (Moore, 2003).

Referrals are often made after the athlete and sport psychologist have worked together for several meetings. After building rapport, the sport psychologist is generally better prepared to manage the timing of a referral, making the referral process proceed more smoothly. For some athletes and sport psychologists, the perfect moment for a referral may never appear. In these circumstances, a referral should still be made, even if under less than ideal conditions.

EXPLAIN WHY THE REFERRAL IS BEING MADE

If it becomes evident that the athlete should be referred, explain why (Heil, 1993). Athletes may be more receptive to the referral if it is explained in terms of their sport using performance enhancement language rather than in terms of pathology. If referral networks have been cultivated, it also is possible for sport psychologists to match athletes with compatible, competent practitioners. Although it may be tempting to tell the athlete that the new practitioner is outstanding and will provide needed solutions, it is also important to provide realistic information (Bobele & Conran, 1988). Creating false expectations will make it more difficult for other practitioners to work effectively with the athlete.

DESCRIBE WHAT WORKING WITH THE REFERRAL SOURCE IS LIKE

It is helpful if information is provided to athletes about what is generally involved in working with the practitioner to whom they are being referred (Heil, 1993). This approach is particularly important for athletes who are being referred to mental health practitioners. Although athletes do not seem to differ from nonathletes in their expectations about counseling (Miller & Moore, 1993), there are clearly misconceptions that exist about mental health treatments. It may be helpful to inform athletes about various forms of payment available (e.g., insurance, sliding scale, pro bono), but the mental health practitioner should set the specific fee.

BE SENSITIVE TO ATHLETES' CONCERNS

Some athletes consider referrals to be extremely embarrassing, an indication that that they are "head cases." Being sensitive to athletes' feelings and presenting referrals in a manner that allows them to maintain their dignity and save face can help athletes feel supported and make it more likely that they will pursue referrals (Brewer, Petitpas, & Van Raalte, 1999). Other athletes may be afraid that if they pursue the referral, the practitioner may take away what made them "great" performers (Tod & Andersen, 2010). Still other athletes may not want to pursue the referral but may feel that they must do so because of a fear of negative repercussions from coaches, parents, or teammates.

In some cases, it may be helpful to suggest a referral and then to step away from the topic for a time until athletes can come to better terms with their feelings.

For some athletes who are uncomfortable with the idea of meeting with another practitioner, it may be possible to refer "in." That is, bring the practitioner in to work together with the athlete and the sport psychologist (Andersen, 1992). This approach has the advantage of being convenient for the athlete and alleviating some athlete concerns about rejection and fears that if they pursue the referral they will be abandoned by their sport psychologist (for an example of an athlete who was resistant to talking to someone else and toward the referral process, see Tod & Andersen, 2010). It requires considerable work on the part of the sport psychologist and the other practitioner to minimize the athlete's risk of treatment confusion (American Psychological Association, 2010). When referring in is not feasible, athletes can be provided with the information needed to schedule an appointment with the practitioner. Some athletes may prefer to have the sport psychologist help schedule the first appointment when the referral is made.

BE OPEN TO ALTERNATE STRATEGIES IF THE ATHLETE IS NOT INTERESTED IN BEING REFERRED

Sport psychologists may want to schedule follow-up meetings to see how the referral worked. If the athlete decides not to follow through on the referral, the sport psychologist should then discuss alternate strategies for dealing with the problem (Heil, 1993). Sport psychologists should not hesitate to reintroduce the idea of referral at a later date (Heil, 1993).

How to Receive Referrals

Many sports medicine practitioners are not aware of sport psychology practitioners to whom they can refer their clients (Hemmings & Povey, 2002). Sport psychologists who are part of a referral network are likely not only to make referrals but also to be the recipients of referrals. Because referral to a sport psychologist can be a delicate process, it can be useful for sport psychologists to educate relevant others, including athletic trainers, coaches, physical therapists, strength and conditioning staff, family members, and teammates about sport psychology and effective ways to make referrals.

Whether teaching other practitioners how to make referrals for sport psychology services or making referrals to outside services, all might benefit from remembering the acronym REFER (Van Raalte, 2010):

- R-ecognize that a referral is needed.
- E-xplain the referral process.
- F-ocus on feelings. Discuss the referral in a clear, caring, and supportive manner.
- E-xit if emotions are too intense. You can return to the topic when things calm down.
- R-epeat (and follow-up) as needed. It often takes more than one suggestion for a referral to be accepted and acted on.

Sport psychologists who are teaching others to make referrals for sport psychology services might highlight the role of sport psychology in performance enhancement, injury rehabilitation, and helping athletes with personal issues. In some instances, discussion of the widespread use of sport psychology services by high profile athletes may be appropriate to mention (Heaney, 2006).

Conclusion

Referral comes in many varieties. Some referrals, such as sending an athlete to a sport nutritionist to learn how to eat correctly during heavy training, are relatively easy. Referring an athlete to a psychiatrist because it appears medication could be of some benefit requires a delicate touch. The referral process centers in large part on issues of competence. Routinely assessing one's own skills, participating in ongoing supervision, and continuing to develop referral networks to cover areas of athlete concerns outside one's competencies are important steps to take. We hope that this chapter has helped clarify some of the varieties of referral that are necessary to best serve the people that sport psychologists work for: the athletes and coaches.

References

American Psychological Association. (2010). *Ethical principles of psychologists and code of conduct (2002, Amended June 1, 2010).* Retrieved from http://www.apa.org/ethics/code/index.aspx

Andersen, M. B. (1992). Sport psychology and procrustean categories: An appeal for synthesis and expansion of service. *Association for the Advancement of Applied Sport Psychology Newsletter, 7*(3), 8–9.

Andersen, M. B. (2001). When to refer athletes for counseling or psychotherapy. In J. M. Williams (Ed.), *Applied sport psychology: Personal growth to peak performance* (4th ed., pp. 401–415). Mountain View, CA: Mayfield.

Andersen, M. B., Denson, E. L., Brewer, B. W., & Van Raalte, J. L. (1994). Disorders of personality and mood in athletes: Recognition and referral. *Journal of Applied Sport Psychology, 6,* 168–184. doi:10.1080/10413209408406292

Andersen, M. B., Van Raalte, J. L., & Brewer, B. W. (2000). When applied sport psychology consultants and graduate students are impaired: Ethical and legal issues in training and supervision. *Journal of Applied Sport Psychology, 12,* 134–150. doi:10.1080/10413200008404219

Andersen, M. B., Van Raalte, J. L., & Harris, G. (2000). Supervision II: A case study. In M. B. Andersen (Ed.), *Doing sport psychology* (pp. 167–179). Champaign, IL: Human Kinetics.

Association for Applied Sport Psychology. (2011). *AASP ethical principles and standards.* Retrieved from http://www.appliedsportpsych.org/about/ethics/code

Bobele, M., & Conran, T. J. (1988). Referrals for family therapy: Pitfalls and guidelines. *Elementary School Guidance & Counseling, 22,* 192–198.

Brewer, B. W. (2009). *Sport psychology: Olympic handbook of sports medicine.* Oxford, England: Wiley-Blackwell.

Brewer, B. W., Petitpas, A. J., & Van Raalte, J. L. (1999). Referral of injured athletes for counseling and psychotherapy. In R. Ray & D. M. Wiese-Bjornstal (Eds.), *Counseling in sports medicine* (pp. 127–141). Champaign, IL: Human Kinetics.

British Association of Sport and Exercise Sciences. (2011). *Code of conduct.* Retrieved from http://www.bases.org.uk/pdf/Code%20of%20Conduct.pdf

Corey, G. (2009). *Theory and practice of counseling and psychotherapy* (8th ed.). Belmont, CA: Brooks/Cole.

Corrigan, P. (2004). How stigma interferes with mental health care. *American Psychologist, 59,* 614–625. doi:10.1037/0003-066X.59.7.614

Gayman, A. M., & Crossman, J. (2006). Referral practices: Are sport psychology consultants out of their league? *Athletic Insight: The Online Journal of Sport Psychology, 8,* 1–12.

Griffin, P. (1998). *Strong women, deep closets: Lesbians and homophobia in sport.* Champaign, IL: Human Kinetics.

Habel, M. A., Dittus, P. J., De Rosa, C. J., Chung, E. Q., & Kerndt, P. R. (2010). Daily participation in sports and students' sexual activity. *Perspectives on Sexual and Reproductive Health, 42,* 244–250. doi:10.1363/4224410

Heaney, C. A. (2006). Recommendations for successfully integrating sport psychology into athletic therapy. *Athletic Therapy Today, 11,* 60–62.

Heil, J. (1993). *Psychology of sport injury.* Champaign, IL: Human Kinetics.

Hemmings, B., & Povey, L. (2002). Views of chartered physiotherapists on the psychological content of their practice: A preliminary study in the United Kingdom. *British Journal of Sports Medicine, 36,* 61–64. doi:10.1136/bjsm.36.1.61

International Society of Sport Psychology. (2011). *Code of ethics.* Retrieved from http://www.issponline.org

Kauer, K., & Krane, V. (2010). Diverse sexual and gender identities in sport. In S. J. Hanrahan & M. B. Andersen (Eds.), *Routledge handbook of applied sport psychology: A comprehensive guide for students and practitioners* (pp. 414–422). New York, NY: Routledge.

Kitchener, K. S. (2000). *Foundations of ethical practice, research, and teaching in psychology.* Washington, DC: American Psychological Association.

Lesyk, J. L. (1998). *Developing sport psychology within your clinical practice: A practical guide for mental health professionals.* San Francisco, CA: Jossey-Bass.

Linder, D. E., Brewer, B. W., Van Raalte, J. L., & DeLange, N. (1991). A negative halo for athletes who consult sport psychologists: Replication and extension. *Journal of Sport & Exercise Psychology, 13,* 133–148.

Mensch, J. M., & Miller, G. M. (2007). *The athletic trainer's guide to psychosocial intervention and referral.* Thorofare, NJ: SLACK.

Miller, M. J., & Moore, K. K. (1993). Athletes' and nonathletes' expectations about counseling. *Journal of College Student Development, 34,* 267–270.

Moore, Z. E. (2003). Ethical dilemmas in sport psychology: Discussion and recommendations for practice. *Professional Psychology: Research and Practice, 34,* 601–610. doi:10.1037/0735-7028.34.6.601

Petrie, T. A., & Sherman, R. T. (2000). Counseling athletes with eating disorders: A case example. In M. B. Andersen (Ed.), *Doing sport psychology* (pp. 121–137). Champaign, IL: Human Kinetics.

Raglin, J. S. (2001). Psychological factors in sport performance: The mental health model revisited. *Sports Medicine), 31,* 875–890. doi:10.2165/00007256-200131120-00004

Sharp, L., & Hodge, K. (2011). Sport psychology consulting effectiveness: The sport psychology consultant's perspective. *Journal of Applied Sport Psychology, 23,* 360–376. doi:10.1080/10413200.2011.583619

Steinfeldt, J. A., & Steinfeldt, M. C. (2011). Profile of masculine norms and help-seeking stigma in college football. *Sport, Exercise, and Performance Psychology, 1,* 58–71.

Storch, E. A., Storch, J. B., Killiany, E. M., & Roberti, J. W. (2005). Self-reported psychopathology in athletes: A comparison of intercollegiate student-athletes and non-athletes. *Journal of Sport Behavior, 28,* 86–98.

Ströhle, A. (2009). Physical activity, exercise, depression and anxiety disorders. *Journal of Neural Transmission, 116,* 777–784. doi:10.1007/s00702-008-0092-x

Taliaferro, L. A., Rienzo, B. A., & Donovan, K. A. (2010). Relationships between youth sport participation and selected health risk behaviors from 1999 to 2007. *The Journal of School Health, 80,* 399–410. doi:10.1111/j.1746-1561.2010.00520.x

Tod, D. (2010). Training and professional development in applied sport psychology. In S. J. Hanrahan & M. B. Andersen (Eds.), *Routledge handbook of applied sport psychology: A comprehensive guide for students and practitioners* (pp. 205–213). New York, NY: Routledge.

Tod, D., & Andersen, M. B. (2010). When to refer athletes for counseling or psychotherapy. In J. M. Williams (Ed.), *Applied sport psychology: Personal growth to peak performance* (6th ed., pp. 443–462). Boston, MA: McGraw Hill.

Van Raalte, J. L. (2010). Referring clients to other professionals. In S. J. Hanrahan & M. B. Andersen (Eds.), *Routledge handbook of applied sport psychology: A comprehensive guide for students and practitioners* (pp. 205–213). New York, NY: Routledge.

Van Raalte, J. L., & Andersen, M. B. (2000). Supervision I: From models to doing. In M. B. Andersen (Ed.), *Doing sport psychology* (pp. 153–165). Champaign, IL: Human Kinetics.

Van Raalte, J. L., Brewer, B. W., Brewer, D. D., & Linder, D. E. (1992). NCAA Division II college football players' perceptions of an athlete who consults a sport psychologist. *Journal of Sport & Exercise Psychology, 14,* 273–282.

Watson, J. M., McDonnell, V., & Bhaumik, S. (2005). Valuing people: Evaluating referral systems. A study of a multidisciplinary single point of referral system to dedicated adult learning disability health services in Leicester, UK. *British Journal of Developmental Disabilities, 51,* 155–170. doi:10.1179/096979505799103696

Wright, L., & Keegan, R. (2011). Initial consultation guidelines for one-to-one sport psychology consulting. *The Sport and Exercise Scientist, 12,* 11–14.

WORKING WITH SPECIFIC POPULATIONS | IV

Ronald E. Smith and Frank L. Smoll

Psychological Interventions in Youth Sports

16

A thletic competition for children is a firmly established part of American society. In the United States, it is estimated that about 60.3 million youngsters 6 to 18 years of age participate in agency-sponsored youth sports, such as Little League Baseball, the American Youth Soccer Organization, and the Boys and Girls Clubs (National Council of Youth Sports, 2008). Additionally, about 7.5 million youth (4.4 million boys, 3.1 million girls) participate in high school sports (National Federation of State High School Associations, 2010). Nearly 70% of Canadian youth participate in organized sport at least occasionally during the school year (Canadian Heritage, 2003). A similar participation level exists in Australia (Australian Bureau of Statistics, 2007).

Preparation of this chapter and much of the research reported herein was supported by Grant 1529 from the William T. Grant Foundation. The research program was also supported by Grant RO1 MH24248 from the National Institute of Mental Health.

Correspondence concerning this chapter should be addressed to Ronald E. Smith, Department of Psychology, Box 351525, University of Washington, Seattle, WA 98195-1525. E-mail: resmith@uw.edu

http://dx.doi.org/10.1037/14251-016
Exploring Sport and Exercise Psychology, Third Edition, J. Van Raalte and B. Brewer (Editors)

Sport scientists as well as popular writers have noted that the sport environment provides socialization opportunities and places adaptive demands on participants that parallel those of other important life settings (Martens, 1978; Smoll & Smith, 2002). For these reasons, organized athletic experiences are regarded as potentially important in child and adolescent development. Those who favor youth sports emphasize that many aspects of the experience contribute to personal development. Proponents generally view youth sports as miniature life situations in which participants can learn to cope with several of the important realities of life. Within sport, youngsters can compete and cooperate with others, they can learn risk taking and self-control, and they can deal with success and failure. Important attitudes are formed about achievement, authority, moral standards, and persistence in the face of adversity (M. R. Weiss, 2003). In addition, advocates point out, lifelong patterns of physical activity that promote health and fitness can be initiated through involvement in youth sports. On the positive side, sport participation is associated with a host of desirable physical and psychological effects in children and adolescents, including cardiovascular health, respiratory health, bone health, reduced weight gain, positive mental health, a sense of mastery, and a positive body image. Organized sport involvement also appears to serve as a protective factor against obesity, eating disorders, teen pregnancy, depression, and suicide (for a review, see Rosewater, 2010).

Despite the salutary effects of sport participation, concerns have been expressed about excessive physical and psychological demands placed on young people and that some sport programs exist primarily for the self-serving needs of coaches and parents. Annual dropout rates (defined as total withdrawal from sport participation) of 30% to 40% have been found (e.g., Barnett, Smoll, & Smith, 1992; Gould, 1987). By age 13, more than two thirds of participants have left sport programs (Ewing & Seefeldt, 1996), many young athletes claiming that adult-produced pressures have taken away the fun of participating. Critics also point to findings indicating that a "win at all costs" mentality and the sanctioning of aggressive behavior may have negative consequences on moral development (Bredemeier, 2003). Researchers have found that child and adolescent athletes sometimes exhibit lower levels of moral reasoning than do nonathletes and show greater acceptance of cheating and aggression as legitimate. Such findings challenge the dictum that "sports build character," and many critics have suggested that children and youth would benefit far more if adults simply left them alone to participate in their own games and activities.

A realistic appraisal of youth sports indicates that participation does not automatically result in either beneficial or detrimental effects for all children (Fredricks & Eccles, 2006). We believe that the sport environment affords a strong potential for achieving desirable objectives. The question is not whether youth sports should continue to exist, for they are here to stay. The real issue is how the programs can be effectively structured and conducted in ways that ensure attainment of positive outcomes. In this chapter, we focus on methods developed by sport psychologists to influence the effects of sport participation in a positive direction through interventions directed at coaches, parents, and athletes.

The Athletic Triangle: Coaches, Parents, and Athletes

The coach–parent–athlete triad has been referred to as the *athletic triangle* (Smith, Smoll, & Smith, 1989). The members of this social system interact with one another in complex ways, and the nature of those interactions can have significant consequences for the psychological development of the child (Davis & Jowett, 2010; M. R. Weiss, 2003). The coach–athlete relationship influences the child during important developmental periods, and the nature of the interpersonal transactions between coach and athlete have been shown to affect such variables as enjoyment of the activity, attraction toward coach and teammates, self-esteem, performance anxiety, team cohesion, and sport attrition (Fisher, Mancini, Hirsch, Proulx, & Staurowsky, 1982; Smith & Smoll, 2011; Westre & Weiss, 1991).

Parental influences on children's socialization into sport and on psychosocial consequences once involved have also been documented (Brustad, 2003; Greendorfer, Lewko, & Rosengren, 2002). Although there is a paucity of research on observed parental behaviors and their consequences, the negative impact they can have on child athletes is all too obvious. Parental misbehavior at competitive events has become such a problem that in some programs parents are barred from attending games. Other programs have resorted to playing games during the morning or afternoon so that parents cannot easily attend. If the quality of supervision is a critical issue in youth sports, so also is the manner in which some misguided parents can undermine the laudable goals of youth sports and thereby detract from the benefits that athletic experiences should provide for children. Assisting parents in ensuring that sports will be a positive influence on their relationship with their child is a worthy target for sport psychology intervention.

The young athlete is a third point of intervention in the athletic triangle. Psychology has developed an impressive and effective arsenal of techniques to enhance human performance and well-being. The fact that children engage in youth sports during a formative period of their lives provides a window of opportunity for sport psychology interventions designed to foster the personal development of the athlete and to facilitate the development of life skills that generalize from sports to other areas of life.

In the sections to follow, we provide practical guidelines for the practitioner who wishes to work in the area of youth sports. It will become readily apparent that some promising and empirically validated intervention strategies already exist but also that there is great opportunity for research and innovative approaches to enhancing the youth sport environment.

Coach-Based Interventions

Most athletes have their first sport experiences in programs staffed by volunteer coaches. Although many of these coaches are fairly well versed in the technical aspects of the sport, they rarely have had any formal training in creating a healthy psychological environment for youngsters. Moreover, through the mass media, these coaches are frequently exposed to college or professional coaches who model aggressive behaviors and a winning-is-everything philosophy that is highly inappropriate in a recreational and skill development context. Because the vast majority of youth coaches have desirable motives for coaching (Martens & Gould, 1979; Smith, Smoll, & Curtis, 1978), one can assume that their limitations result primarily from a lack of information on how to create a supportive interpersonal climate. Several educational programs have therefore been developed for the purpose of positively affecting coaching practices and thereby increasing the likelihood that youngsters will have positive sport experiences.

Five of the most prominent training programs currently available in the United States include curricular components designed to influence the manner in which coaches interact with young athletes: the American Sport Education Program (http://www.asep.com), the Mastery Approach to Coaching (MAC; http://www.y-e-sports.com), the National Youth Sports Coaches Association program (http://www.nays.org), a program offered by the Positive Coaching Alliance (http://www.positivecoach. org), and the Program for Athletic Coaches' Education (http://www.edu. msu.edu/ysi/). The national coaching associations of Australia (http:// www.athletics.com.au) and Canada (http://www.coach.ca) have also developed formal programs that provide training in sport psychology as well as other areas, such as sport pedagogy (teaching sport skills and strategies), sport physiology (conditioning, weight training, and nutrition), and sports medicine (injury prevention, care, and rehabilitation).

Of the widely used programs, however, the MAC is the only one that has been subjected to systematic evaluation to determine its influence on coaches' behaviors and the effects of such behaviors on youngsters' psychosocial development. We therefore describe the coach training program, developed over more than 30 years within our Youth Enrichment in Sports project (see http://www.Y-E-Sports.com), as an illustration of an empirical approach to the development and evaluation of intervention strategies in the youth sport arena.

DEVELOPING A COACH TRAINING PROGRAM

Our work was guided by a fundamental assumption that a training program should be based on scientific evidence rather than on intuition and/or what we "know" on the basis of informal observation. An empirical foundation for coaching guidelines not only enhances the validity and potential value of the program but also increases its credibility in the eyes of consumers. We now describe our approach to generating an empirical database for our training program.

Theoretical Model and Research Paradigm

Recognition of the potential impact of youth coaches on athletes' psychological welfare prompted several scientific questions that we felt were worth pursuing. For example, what do coaches do, and how frequently do they engage in such behaviors as encouragement, punishment, instruction, and organization? How are such behaviors related to children's reactions to their organized athletic experiences? Answers to such questions provide not only a first step in describing the behavioral ecology of one aspect of the youth sport setting but also an empirical basis for the development of psychologically oriented intervention programs.

To begin to answer such questions, we carried out a systematic program of basic research over a period of several years. The project was guided by a mediational model of coach–athlete interactions, the basic elements of which are represented as follows:

Coach Behaviors → Athlete Perception and Recall → Athletes' Evaluative Reactions

This model stipulates that the ultimate effects of coaching behaviors are mediated by the meaning that athletes attribute to them. In other words, what athletes remember about their coach's behaviors and how they interpret these actions affect the way that athletes evaluate their sport experiences. Furthermore, a complex of cognitive and affective processes is involved at this mediational level. Athletes' perceptions and reactions are likely to be affected not only by coaches' behaviors but also by other factors, such as athletes' age; what they expect of coaches (normative beliefs and expectations); and certain personality variables, such as self-esteem and anxiety. In recognition of this, the basic three-element model has been expanded to reflect these factors (Smoll & Smith, 1989). The expanded model specifies a number of situational factors as well as coach and athlete characteristics that could influence coach behaviors and the perceptions and reactions of athletes to them. Using this model as a starting point, we have sought to determine how observed coaching behaviors, athletes' perception and recall of the coach's behaviors, and athletes' attitudes are related to one another. We have also explored the manner in which athlete and coach characteristics might serve to affect these relations.

Measurement of Coaching Behaviors

To measure leadership behaviors, we developed the Coaching Behavior Assessment System (CBAS) to permit the direct observation and coding of coaches' actions during practices and games (Smith, Smoll, & Hunt, 1977). The CBAS contains 12 categories divided into two major classes of behaviors. *Reactive* (elicited) behaviors are responses to immediately preceding athlete or team behaviors, whereas *spontaneous* (emitted) behaviors are initiated by the coach and are not a response to a discernible preceding event. Reactive behaviors are responses to either desirable performance or effort (reinforcement, nonreinforcement), mistakes and errors (mistake-contingent encouragement, mistake-contingent technical instruction, punishment, punitive technical instruction, ignoring mistakes), or misbehaviors on the part of athletes (keeping control). The spontaneous class includes general technical instruction, general encouragement, organization, and general communication. The system thus involves basic interactions between the situation and the coach's behavior. Use of the CBAS in observing and coding coaching behaviors in a variety of sports indicates that the scoring system is sufficiently comprehensive to incorporate the vast majority of overt leader behaviors, that high interrater reliability can be obtained, and that individual differences in behavioral patterns can be discerned (Smith, Smoll, & Christensen, 1996).

Coaching Behaviors and Children's Evaluative Reactions

Following development of the CBAS, a field study was conducted to establish relations between coaching behaviors and several athlete variables specified in the conceptual model (Smith et al., 1978). Observed behaviors of 51 baseball coaches during 202 complete games were coded, and 542 children who played for the coaches were interviewed and administered questionnaires after the season ended.

At the level of overt behavior, three independent behavioral dimensions were identified through factor analysis: supportiveness (consisting of reinforcement and mistake-contingent encouragement), instructiveness (general technical instruction and mistake-contingent technical instruction vs. general communication and general encouragement), and punitiveness (punishment and punitive technical instruction vs. organizational behaviors). Relations between coaches' scores on these behavioral dimensions and player measures indicated that players responded most favorably to coaches who engaged in higher rates and percentages of supportive and instructional behaviors. Players on teams whose coaches created a supportive environment also liked their team-mates more. A somewhat surprising finding was that the team's won–lost record was essentially unrelated to how well the players liked the coach and how much they wanted to play for the coach in the future. It is worth noting, however, that winning assumed greater importance beyond age 12, although it continued to be a less important attitudinal determinant than coach behaviors.

Another important issue concerns the degree of accuracy with which coaches perceive their own behaviors. Correlations between CBAS-observed behaviors and coaches' ratings of how frequently they performed the behaviors were generally low and nonsignificant. The only significant correlation occurred for punishment. Children's ratings on the same perceived behavior scales correlated much more highly with CBAS measures than did the coaches' ratings. It thus appears that coaches have limited awareness of how frequently they engage in particular forms of behavior and that athletes are more accurate perceivers of actual coach behaviors.

Finally, analysis of the children's attraction responses toward the coaches revealed a significant interaction between coach supportiveness (the tendency to reinforce desirable performance and effort and to respond to mistakes with encouragement) and athletes' level of self-esteem (Smith & Smoll, 1990). Specifically, the low-self-esteem children were especially responsive to variations in supportiveness in a manner consistent with a self-enhancement model of self-esteem. This finding is consistent with the results of other studies which, collectively, suggest that self-enhancement motivation causes people who are low in self-esteem to be especially responsive to variations in supportiveness because of their greater need for positive feedback from others (Tesser, 1988).

From Basic Research to Intervention

The research results provided clear directions for the development of specific behavioral guidelines for a training program. The program developed in the late 1970s was called Coach Effectiveness Training. For reasons described in this section, the program was recently renamed Mastery Approach to Coaching.

From its inception, both our basic research and the intervention program have been guided primarily by social cognitive theory, a cognitive–behavioral approach to understanding the role of situational, psychological, and environmental factors in behavior (Mischel, 1973; Smith, 2006). More recently, we have incorporated another cognitive–behavioral theory, achievement goal theory (Duda, 2005), into our research and intervention program. Achievement goal theory has had a major influence on sport psychology over the past two decades. Achievement goal theory focuses on understanding the function and the meaning of goal-directed actions on the basis of how participants define success and how they judge whether they have demonstrated competence. The two central constructs in the theory are individual goal orientations that guide achievement perceptions and behavior and the motivational climate created within adult-controlled achievement settings. In a mastery motivational climate, success is defined in terms of giving maximum effort, enjoyment of the activity, and personal improvement. Mistakes are viewed as opportunities to improve performance and are not punished. An ego-oriented climate defines success in social comparison terms, emphasizing outperforming others, winning. Those who perform best get special attention. Poor performance elicits criticism and punishment.

A large body of research indicates that in sports, as in other achievement settings, mastery achievement goals and a mastery-oriented motivational climate are associated with salutary effects on athletes. Although mastery and ego orientations are not mutually exclusive, compared with primarily ego-oriented students and athletes, those high in mastery orientation report higher feelings of competence, greater enjoyment of the activity, and higher intrinsic motivation and effort. A mastery orientation (particularly in combination with a low ego orientation) is also related to lower levels of cognitive trait anxiety and preevent state anxiety. Finally, a mastery goal orientation is related to a variety of adaptive achievement behaviors, such as exerting consistent effort, persistence in the face of setbacks, and sustained and improved performance. Although an ego orientation has at times been linked to high levels of achievement, it also has a number of less desirable correlates, such as inconsistent effort, higher levels of performance anxiety, reduced persistence or withdrawal in the face of failure, decreased intrinsic motivation for sport involvement, and a willingness to use deception and illegal methods to win (Duda, 2005; McArdle & Duda, 2002; Roberts, Treasure, & Conroy, 2007).

A mastery motivational climate counters the win-at-all-costs philosophy that is all too common in youth sports. In such a climate, students and athletes tend to adopt adaptive achievement strategies such as selecting challenging tasks, giving maximum effort, persisting in the face of setbacks, and taking pride in personal improvement (McArdle & Duda, 2002). In youth sports, a mastery climate relates far more strongly to athletes' liking of their coach than does the team's won–lost record (Cumming, Smoll, Smith, & Grossbard, 2007). Coach-initiated mastery climate is positively related to increases in mastery goal orientation and decreases in ego orientation (Smith, Smoll, & Cumming, 2009). In contrast, an ego-involving climate promotes social comparison as a basis for success judgments. When coaches create an ego climate, they tend to give differential attention and positive reinforcement to athletes who are most competent and instrumental to winning, and skill development is deemed more important to winning than to personal improvement and self-realization. They are also more likely to respond to mistakes and poor performance with punitive responses, behaviors associated with athletes' increases in ego goal orientation (Smith, Smoll, & Cumming, 2009). Several studies conducted in physical education classes have shown that motivational climate is a stronger predictor of such outcomes as intrinsic motivation and voluntary activity participation than is students' achievement goal orientation (Roberts et al., 2007).

In recent years, the Coach Effectiveness Training program, which from its inception presented guidelines consistent with a mastery climate, has incorporated achievement goal concepts in an explicit fashion, with the stated goal of helping coaches develop a mastery climate. The Coach Effectiveness Training program was renamed Mastery Approach to Coaching to highlight this emphasis.

Behavioral Guidelines in the Mastery Approach to Coaching

A set of five core principles underlies the behavioral coaching guidelines communicated in the MAC program (Smoll & Smith, 2010). A most important first principle, consistent with a mastery climate, is that *winning* is defined not in terms of won–lost records but in terms of giving maximum effort and making improvements. The explicit and primary focus is on having fun, deriving satisfaction from being on the team, learning sport skills, and developing increased self-esteem. This philosophy is designed to maximize young athletes' enjoyment of sport and their chances of deriving the benefits of participation, partly as a result of combating competitive anxiety. The focus on controllable effort rather than uncontrollable outcome also promotes separation of the athlete's feelings of self-worth from the game outcome, which serves to help overcome fear of failure.

Our second principle, derived from social-cognitive learning theory, emphasizes a *positive approach* to coaching. In such an approach, coach–athlete interactions are characterized by the liberal use of positive reinforcement, encouragement, and sound technical instruction that help create high levels of interpersonal attraction between coaches and athletes. Punitive behaviors are strongly discouraged because they have been shown to create a negative team climate and to promote fear of failure. We emphasize that reinforcement should not be restricted to the learning and performance of sport skills. Rather, it should also be liberally applied to strengthen desirable psychosocial behaviors (e.g., teamwork, leadership, sportsmanship). Coaches are urged to reinforce effort as much as they do results. This guideline has direct relevance to developing a healthy philosophy of winning and a reduction in performance anxiety.

The MAC includes several positive approach guidelines pertaining to the appropriate use of technical instruction. For example, when giving instruction, we encourage coaches to emphasize the good things that will happen if athletes execute correctly rather than focusing on the negative things that will occur if they do not. This approach motivates athletes to make desirable things happen (i.e., develop a positive achievement orientation) rather than building fear of making mistakes.

The third coaching principle is to establish norms that emphasize athletes' mutual obligations to help and support one another. Such norms increase social support and attraction among teammates and thereby enhance cohesion and commitment to the team. Such norms are most likely to develop when coaches (a) model supportive behaviors and (b) reinforce athletes' behaviors that promote team unity. We also instruct coaches in how to develop a *we're-in-this-together* group norm. This norm can play an important role in building team cohesion among teammates, particularly if the coach frequently reinforces relevant bench behaviors of attention and mutual supportiveness.

A fourth principle is that compliance with team roles and responsibilities is most effectively achieved by involving athletes in decisions regarding team rules and reinforcing compliance with them rather than by using punitive measures to punish noncompliance. We believe that coaches should recognize that youngsters want clearly defined limits and structure.

The positive approach also applies to promoting compliance with team rules. One of the most effective ways of eliminating negative behaviors (and avoiding the negative side effects of punishment) is to strengthen incompatible positive behaviors. Thus, coaches are encouraged not to take rule compliance for granted but to acknowledge instances of compliance with the rules. By using positive reinforcement to strengthen desirable behaviors, coaches can often avoid having to deal with misbehaviors on the part of athletes.

Finally, MAC coaches are urged to obtain behavioral feedback and to engage in self-monitoring to increase awareness of their own behaviors and to encourage compliance with the positive approach guidelines. This is based on our finding that coaches have limited awareness of their own behavior patterns.

Training Procedures

In a MAC workshop, which lasts approximately 75 minutes, behavioral guidelines are presented both verbally and in a manual given to the coaches (Smoll & Smith, 2008). The written material supplements the guidelines with concrete suggestions for communicating effectively with young athletes, gaining their respect, and relating effectively to their parents. The importance of sensitivity and being responsive to individual differences among athletes is also stressed. The manual serves to (a) help keep the workshop organized, (b) facilitate coaches' understanding of the information, (c) eliminate the need for coaches to take notes, and (d) give coaches a tangible resource to refer to in the future. Also, animated PowerPoint content slides and cartoons illustrating important points are used to facilitate ease of comprehension and retention as well as to add to the organizational quality of the session. A detailed outline of the MAC intervention together with video segments from a workshop can be found on the Youth Enrichment in Sports website (http://www.y-e-sports.com).

The MAC also includes discussion of coach–parent relationships and provides instructions for organizing and conducting a sport orientation meeting with parents. Some purposes of the meeting are to inform parents about their responsibilities for contributing to the success of the sport program and to guide them toward working cooperatively with the coach (see Smith & Smoll, 2002).

Program Evaluation: Assessing the Efficacy of the Mastery Approach to Coaching

Sweeping conclusions are often drawn about the efficacy of intervention programs in the absence of anything approximating acceptable scientific evidence. Scientific accountability requires evidence that interventions produce the effects they are intended to produce (Luiselli & Reed, 2011; McHugh & Barlow, 2010). We therefore felt it was important not only to develop an empirical foundation for our intervention but also to measure its effects on coaches and the youngsters who play for them.

We have focused on six important outcome questions in our program evaluation studies. First, does the training program affect the behaviors of the trained coaches in a manner consistent with the behavioral guidelines? Second, the program is designed to help coaches create a mastery-oriented environment that would be expected to increase children's positive reactions to coach, teammates, and their sport experience. How does the program affect children's reactions to their athletic experience? Third, does exposure to a positive interpersonal environment created by trained coaches result in an increase in general self-esteem, particularly among low-self-esteem children?

Fourth, does coach training help reduce performance anxiety among young athletes? Fifth, does the mastery climate recommended in the program change children's achievement goal orientations? Do children become more mastery oriented in their definitions of achievement? And, finally, do positive changes in the first five outcomes increase the likelihood that young athletes will choose to return to the sport program? This last question is one of great practical importance because, as noted earlier, nearly 70% of children drop out of sports by age 13, and nonparticipation is associated with a host of negative consequences, including obesity, delinquency, and teen pregnancy (Brustad & Parker, 2005; Rosewater, 2010). Clearly, one goal should be to keep youngsters engaged in physical activity as they enter the adolescent years.

Positive findings regarding all six of these questions have been established in a series of outcome studies in which experimental groups of youth baseball and basketball coaches exposed to the training program were compared with untreated, control groups of coaches (Smith & Smoll, 2011). Trained coaches differed in both observed behaviors and in athlete-perceived behaviors in a manner consistent with the behavioral guidelines. Experimental group coaches were more reinforcing and encouraging, gave more technical instruction, and were less punitive and controlling than control group coaches. In turn, athletes who played for the trained coaches perceived their teams' motivational climate to be more mastery oriented, became more mastery oriented in their sport and academic achievement goals, enjoyed their experiences more, and liked their coach and teammates more. They also demonstrated significant increases in general self-esteem and significant decreases in performance anxiety over the course of the season (Smith, Smoll, & Barnett, 1995; Smith, Smoll, & Curtis, 1979; Smoll, Smith, Barnett, & Everett, 1993; Smoll, Smith, & Cumming, 2007b).

Finally, a study of attrition showed a dropout rate of 26% among children who played for control group coaches, a figure that is quite consistent with previous reports of attrition in youth sport programs (Gould, 1987). In contrast, only 5% of the children who had played for trained coaches failed to return to the program the next season (Barnett et al., 1992). These positive psychosocial outcomes are all the more noteworthy in light of the fact that experimental and control groups did not differ in average won–lost percentages in any of the studies.

The MAC program was initially presented only in live workshops. However, to expand program reach, developers sought other means of dissemination (McHugh & Barlow, 2010). Sousa, Smith, and Cruz (2008) found that MAC behavioral guidelines could be successfully taught through DVD presentation. The MAC workshop has now been transformed into a 66-minute DVD with an accompanying written manual (Smoll & Smith, 2009a). However, the effects of this version of the MAC intervention have yet to be determined.

RELATED THEORETICAL DEVELOPMENTS

In recent years there has been a surge of interest in coach–athlete relationships. Two noteworthy theoretical developments seem particularly relevant to the MAC as well as to other coach training programs. One is Fry and Gano-Overway's (2010) concept of the *caring climate* in which coaches create a setting in which athletes feel welcomed, safe, protected, valued, and respected. Their prescription for creating such an environment involves the use of positive reinforcement, encouragement, and creation of a mastery motivational climate that encourages intrinsic enjoyment of the activity. These prescriptions are highly consistent with MAC principles and behavioral guidelines. Fry and Gano-Overway have provided a measure of caring climate and have shown that such a setting is related to athletes' enjoyment of the coach, teammates, and the sport experience and to more caring behaviors toward their coaches and teammates. A summer camp intervention demonstrated that camp counselors can be trained to provide a caring environment and that this has positive effects on camp goers (Newton et al., 2007).

In a somewhat related development, Jowett (2007) applied concepts from attachment theory to the coach–athlete dyadic relationship. Three types of psychological attachment can exist within this framework: *secure* attachment in which athletes feel safe and cared for by a coach who will be responsive to any needs for assistance, *anxious* attachment in which athletes want the coach's support but worry about the coach's responsiveness in times of need, and *avoidant* attachment in which athletes experience discomfort with closeness and try to achieve independence from the coach. The latter two attachment forms are called *insecure* attachments. In a study of young adult athletes, Davis and Jowett (2010) showed that secure attachment to the coach is related to sport satisfaction, which is largely mediated by relationship satisfaction. Anxious and avoidant attachment are negatively related to relationship and sport satisfaction. We would expect these findings to apply to child athletes as well.

The goals of the MAC program are clearly consistent with creating a caring environment for young athletes and fostering secure attachment relationships between young athletes and their coaches because a mastery climate fosters both outcomes (Carr, 2009). However, the attachment and caring environment measures have yet to be used in outcome studies of the MAC intervention. In a more general sense, the melding of concepts, methods, and measures from diverse theoretical models is emphasized in the *translational approach* that is being promoted heavily within contemporary psychological and medical science (Smith & Smoll, 2011; Tashiro & Mortensen, 2006), and such an approach can only enrich the knowledge base and the intervention methods inspired by it.

Parent-Based Interventions

Mass media reports abound concerning parental influences that can potentially undermine the best-intentioned youth sport program. We hear on an increasingly frequent basis about sport parents engaging in objectionable and, at times, criminally violent actions toward coaches, young athletes, and sport officials. Consider the following examples (Smoll & Smith, 2005):

- In Massachusetts, a coach died after he was beaten unconscious following a hockey practice by a father who was upset about rough play in a scrimmage. The assailant was convicted of involuntary manslaughter.
- At a Philadelphia-area youth football game, a player's father brandished a .357 magnum during a dispute with a coach over his son's playing time.
- A Long Island, New York, soccer mom angered over being dropped from the team e-mail list for game-day directions was arrested after slamming a metal folding chair across the face of her daughter's coach. The woman was charged with second-degree reckless endangerment.

Fortunately, such incidents are not the norm. Yet, in their own dramatic fashion they illustrate pervasive problems that have caused some programs to take steps to protect the welfare of youth sport participants, coaches, and officials. The importance of parents in the youth sport experience cannot be overemphasized. Research has shown that parents play an important role in the socialization of children into sports and influence the psychosocial outcomes of sport experiences, including self-concept development and enjoyment of the activity (Brustad, 2003; Brustad & Parker, 2005). Thus, a potentially influential focus of interventions is on parents.

Several books have been written for the youth sport parent (e.g., Smoll & Smith, 2005; Thompson, 2008). Workshops for parents similar to those developed for coaches can be another vehicle for reaching parents and influencing the ways in which they interact with their child athletes. In the MAC, we provide coaches with guidelines for conducting an educational session with the parents of the athletes they are coaching (Smith & Smoll, 2002).

MASTERY APPROACH TO PARENTING IN SPORTS

More recently, we developed a Mastery Approach to Parenting in Sports (MAPS) intervention designed to parallel the MAC intervention and help parents create a mastery-oriented motivational climate for their children (Smoll & Smith, 2009b). Ideally used in combination with the MAC, the MAPS is designed to get coaches and parents "on the same page" and working cooperatively to create a growth-inducing sport environment. We now summarize some of the topics addressed in this intervention.

Objectives of Youth Sports

As noted previously, there are many possible benefits of participating in youth sports. Some of them are physical, such as acquiring sport skills and increasing health and fitness. Others are psychological, such as developing leadership skills, self-discipline, respect for authority, competitiveness, cooperativeness, sportsmanship, and self-confidence. Youth sports are also an important social activity in which children can make new friends and acquaintances and become part of an ever-expanding social network. Furthermore, the involvement of parents in the athletic enterprise can serve to bring families closer together and strengthen family unity. Finally, of course, youth sports are (or should be) just plain *fun!*

The basic right of the young athlete to have fun in participating should not be neglected. One of the quickest ways to reduce fun is for adults to begin treating children as if they were professional athletes. Coaches and parents alike need to keep in mind that young athletes are not miniature adults. They are children, and they have the right to play as children. Youth sports are first and foremost a play activity, and youngsters deserve to enjoy sports in their own way. In essence, it is important that programs remain *child centered* and do not become adult dominated.

What about *winning?* The common notion in sports equates success with victory. However, with a winning-is-everything philosophy, young athletes may lose opportunities to develop their skills, to enjoy participation, and to grow socially and emotionally. Well-informed parents realize that success is not equivalent to winning games, and failure is not the same as losing. Rather, the most important kind of success comes from striving to win and giving maximum effort. The only thing athletes can control is the amount of effort they give. They have incomplete control over the outcome that is achieved. Athletes at all levels of competition should be taught that they are never "losers" if they give maximum effort in striving for excellence. This philosophy of success is relevant to parents as well as coaches. In fact, it may be more important for parents to understand its meaning. They can apply it to many areas of their child's life in addition to sport.

We believe that most of the negative consequences of youth sports occur when adults erroneously impose a professional win-at-all-costs model on what should be a recreational and educational experience for youngsters. When excessive emphasis is placed on winning, it is easy to lose sight of the needs and interests of the young athlete. Indeed, when young athletes are asked what they want out of their youth sport experience, the developmental model comes out ahead. A survey of more than 100,000 youth sport participants in the state of Michigan indicated that young athletes most often participated in sports for the following reasons: (a) to have fun, (b) to improve their skills and learn new skills, (c) to be with their friends or make new friends, and (d) to succeed or win (Universities Study Committee, 1978). In a report based on data derived from a national survey of approximately 8,000 boys and girls, these same items were included in lists of the 10 most frequently selected reasons why youngsters play nonschool and interscholastic sports (Seefeldt, Ewing, & Walk, 1992). These goals should be communicated to parents, and they should be cautioned that none of these outcomes is achieved automatically through participation in sports. Coaches, parents, and sport administrators should be part of a team trying to accomplish common goals. By working together to reduce chances of misunderstanding and problems, the objectives that children have can be attained. In this regard, parents should be encouraged to view their involvement in youth sports as an integral part of their child-rearing responsibilities.

Parents' Responsibilities and Challenges

When a child enters a sport program, parents automatically take on some obligations. Some parents do not realize this at first and are surprised to find what is expected of them. Others never realize their responsibilities and miss opportunities to help their children grow through sports, or they may actually do things that interfere with their children's development.

To begin, parents must realize that children have a right to choose not to participate. Although parents might choose to encourage participation, children should not be pressured, intimidated, or bribed into playing. Athletes who feel "entrapped" report less enjoyment and lower intrinsic motivation and benefits of being involved in sports and are more likely to drop out of sports (W. M. Weiss & Weiss, 2006). In fulfilling their responsibility, parents should counsel their children, giving consideration to the sport selected and the level of competition at which the children want to play. And, of course, parents should respect their children's decisions.

Parents can enjoy their children's participation more if they acquire an understanding and appreciation of the sport. This includes knowledge of basic rules, skills, and strategies. Coaches can serve as valuable resources by answering parents' questions and by referring parents to appropriate websites, community and school libraries, or bookstores for educational materials (e.g., books, magazines, videos, video clips). In addition, coaches should devote part of an early season practice to a lecture/demonstration of the fundamentals of the sport, and parents having little background in the sport should be encouraged to attend this session.

Parents often assume an extremely active role in youth sports, and in some instances their influence becomes an important source of children's stress (Brustad, 2003; Smith, Smoll, & Passer, 2002). What might constitute the underlying basis of parent-induced stress? One factor is what we have come to refer to as the *reversed dependency phenomenon*. Some parents come to focus on youth sport to such an extent that they evaluate their own self-worth in terms of how successful their son or daughter is. The father who is a "frustrated jock" may seek to experience through his child the success he never knew as an athlete. Or the parent who was a star may be resentful and rejecting if the child does not attain similar achievements. Some parents thus become "winners" or "losers" through their children, and the pressure placed on the children to excel can be extreme. A child *must* succeed or the parent's self-image is threatened. Much more is at stake than a mere game, and the child of such a parent carries a heavy burden. When parental love and approval depend on adequacy of performance, sports are bound to be stressful.

Youth sport consultants may be able to counteract this tendency by explaining the identification process to parents. They can tell parents that if they place excessive pressure on children, they can decrease the potential that sports can have for enjoyment and personal growth. Further, children who experience high levels of stress are more likely to drop out of sport. A key to reducing parent-produced stress is to impress on parents that youth sport programs are for young athletes and that children and youth are not adults. Parents and children benefit when parents acknowledge the right of each child to develop athletic potential in an atmosphere that emphasizes participation, personal growth, and fun.

Commitments and Affirmations

To contribute to the success of a sport program, parents must be willing and able to commit themselves in many different ways. The following questions serve as important reminders of the scope of parents' responsibilities, questions to which parents must honestly answer yes to each one:

1. Can the parents share their son or daughter? This requires putting the child in the coach's charge and trusting the coach to guide the sport experience. It involves accepting the coach's authority and the fact that the coach may gain some of the admiration and affection that the child once directed solely at the parent. This commitment does not mean that parents cannot have input, but the coach is the boss! If parents are going to undermine the coach's leadership, it is best for all concerned not to have their child join the program.

2. Can the parents accept their child's disappointments? Every child athlete experiences "the thrill of victory and the agony of defeat" as part of the competition process. In addition to enjoying triumphs, parents are called on to support their children when they are disappointed and hurt. This may mean not being embarrassed, ashamed, or angry when their son or daughter cries after losing a contest. When an apparent disappointment occurs, parents should be able to help their children learn from the experience. By doing this without denying the validity of their child's feelings, parents can help their children see the positive side of the situation and thus change their children's disappointment into self-acceptance.

3. Can the parents give their children enough time? Parents need to decide how much time they can devote to their children's sport activities. Conflicts arise when they are very busy yet are also interested and want to encourage their children. The best advice to give parents is to deal honestly with the time commitment issue and not to promise more time than they can actually deliver. Parents should ask their children about their sport experiences and make every effort to watch some of their games.

Conduct at Sport Events

The most noticeable parent problem is misbehavior at games. As part of their responsibilities, parents should watch their children compete in sports. But their behavior must meet acceptable standards. In addition to acknowledging some obviously inappropriate actions (e.g., using profanity, drinking alcohol, throwing objects), the following rules for parental behavior (dos and don'ts) have been recommended:

1. Do remain in the spectator area during the event.
2. Don't interfere with the coach. Parents must be willing to relinquish the responsibility for their child to the coach for the duration of the practice or game.
3. Do express interest, encouragement, and support to your child. Be sure to cheer good effort as well as good performance. Communicate repeatedly that giving total effort is all you expect.
4. Don't shout instructions or criticisms to the children.
5. Do lend a hand when a coach or official asks for help.
6. Don't make abusive comments to athletes, parents, officials, or coaches of either team.

Good sportsmanship among spectators is a goal worth working for. Parents have the obligation not only to control their own behavior but also to remind others if necessary. When parents misbehave, it is the duty of other parents and league administrators to step in and correct the situation. The rule of thumb for all spectators is that nothing in their actions should interfere with any child's enjoyment of the sport.

PROGRAM EVALUATION

Compared with the MAC, evaluation research on the MAPS is in its infancy, and its efficacy remains to be demonstrated empirically. A study in which the MAC and MAPS were applied within the same sport program demonstrated a significant decrease in athletes' performance anxiety over the course of the season, but we were unable to establish the relative effects of the two interventions (Smoll, Smith, & Cumming, 2007a). To encourage research and to facilitate dissemination, the MAPS, like the MAC, has been converted to a self-instructional DVD format (Smoll & Smith, 2009b), and an outline of topics and video clips is available for viewing on the Youth Enrichment in Sports website (http://www.y-e-sports.com).

Athlete-Based Interventions

The third point in the athletic triangle is the young athlete. Some of the intervention programs directed at the athlete involve the application of psychological principles to enhance sport performance. Others are directed at psychosocial outcomes.

PERFORMANCE ENHANCEMENT INTERVENTIONS

Notable among the performance enhancement interventions is *behavioral coaching* (Martin & Hyrcaiko, 1983; Stokes & Luiselli, 2010), which involves teaching coaches to apply operant techniques, such as functional analysis and behavioral assessment of skill components, videotaped feedback, response-contingent reinforcement of response execution, the use of shaping procedures, self-monitoring and behavioral graphing of the skill acquisition process, and the systematic application of modeling procedures. More than a dozen studies have shown that operant techniques can be highly effective in facilitating skill acquisition and enhancing performance in a variety of sports and age levels (for reviews, see Smith et al., 1996; Stokes & Luiselli, 2010). Sport consultants who are conversant with the application of operant principles will find an eager audience of coaches who wish to be trained in these powerful performance enhancement techniques.

Imagery-based performance enhancement techniques have also been applied to child athlete populations. For example, Zhang, Ma, Orlick, and Zitzelberger (1992) tested the efficacy of a mental imagery program designed to increase the performance of promising Chinese table tennis players between the ages of 7 and 10. Children in the first condition received a comprehensive 22-week mental training program that included relaxation, video observation, and mental imagery sessions. A second treatment group received only the video observation component of the training. The third group was a no-treatment control condition. Results indicated that compared with the other two groups, the children who received the full mental training package significantly improved both the accuracy and technical quality of their table tennis forehand attack. In a more recent study, Copeland, Bonnell, Reider, and Burton (2009) tested an intensive 2-week mental skills program designed to develop relaxation-based stress management skills and team cohesion skills with adolescent luge athletes. The program was effective in reducing performance anxiety states prior to competition and in increasing team cohesion.

LIFE SKILLS AND MORAL DEVELOPMENT INTERVENTIONS

Another recent emphasis has been on training children in skills that not only enhance their sport performance but also extend as *life skills* to other areas of the child's life, such as academics and social interactions. For example, Orlick and McCaffrey (1991) described a psychological skills program for elementary school children that includes training in relaxation, imagery, focusing, and refocusing. The skills training was adapted to the child's level. For example, relaxation training was carried out while comparing tense muscles to uncooked spaghetti and relaxed muscles to limp cooked spaghetti.

One widely applied life skills program is Danish's (2002a) Going for the Goal program, in which young athletes are trained in specific goal-setting procedures designed to enhance their sport performance and to generalize to other settings. Promising results have been achieved in enhancing such skills. Another program with a wider set of life skills is Sports United to Promote Education and Recreation (Danish, 2002b) was applied within The First Tee, a national youth golf program. This program combined with a community service component had a significant impact on athletes' prosocial values, social responsibility, empathy, and social interest (Brunelle, Danish, & Forneris, 2007). This life skills approach carried out within the engaging sport context seems to hold considerable promise for promoting the development of important psychological skills. Such training could easily include generalization training to facilitate transfer of the skills to other life areas. Such training might be particularly useful in working with at-risk youth, who are typically resistant to life skills programs implemented within the school setting. Such youngsters might be more enthusiastic about a program designed and conducted within the realm of sport.

The finding that athletes often exhibit lower levels of moral reasoning and a greater acceptance of doing whatever it takes to win has suggested that psychological intervention may have salutary effects on moral development by counteracting these tendencies. Several studies have shown that explicit attention to moral training in sport and physical activity settings can promote significant advances in the moral reasoning maturity of children (Bredemeier, 2003). In one study, adult leaders described to young athletes how they themselves thought about and responded to moral issues involving themes of fairness, sharing, verbal and physical aggression, and distributive and retributive justice. They also used dialogue aimed at resolving interpersonal conflicts among the children as a vehicle for promoting moral growth. Children in a control condition participated in the normal camp program. By the end of the 6-week program, the children exposed to the intervention scored higher on measures of moral reasoning (Bredemeier, Weiss, Shields, & Shewchuk, 1986). Other research has shown that a mastery motivational climate promotes higher moral standards in young athletes than does an ego climate (McArdle & Duda, 2002). This is one way in which sports can provide a medium in which moral development is facilitated.

Conclusions and Future Directions

As we have seen, sport psychology interventions are a promising development that can enhance the well-being and psychosocial development of children and youth. This area constitutes an exciting arena for both psychological research and intervention. The researcher can discover the principles that govern the youth sport social system and that make a difference in the well-being of its members. Similarly, the practitioner is in a position to apply the principles and procedures of sport psychology in a manner that can better the lives of many young athletes, their coaches, and their parents. However, compared with interventions in other areas of psychology, many sport psychology interventions have not been empirically validated, and the ethical principles underlying evidence-based practice demand much greater emphasis in this area.

References

Australian Bureau of Statistics. (2007). *Participation in organized sports—2000, 2003, 2006.* Retrieved from: http://www.ausport.gov.au/information/scors/other_related_reports

Barnett, N. P., Smoll, F. L., & Smith, R. E. (1992). Effects of enhancing coach-athlete relationships on youth sport attrition. *The Sport Psychologist, 6,* 111–127.

Bredemeier, B. J. L. (2003). Moral community and youth sport in the new millennium. In R. M. Malina & M. A. Clark (Eds.), *Youth sports: Perspectives for a new century* (pp. 171–182). Monterey, CA: Coaches Choice.

Bredemeier, B. J. L., Weiss, M. R., Shields, D., & Shewchuk, R. M. (1986). Promoting moral growth in a summer sport camp: The implementation of theoretically grounded instructional strategies. *Journal of Moral Education, 15,* 212–220. doi:10.1080/0305724860150304

Brunelle, J., Danish, S. J., & Forneris, T. (2007). The impact of a sport-based life skills program on adolescent social values. *Applied Developmental Science, 11,* 43–55.

Brustad, R. J. (2003). Parental roles and involvement in youth sports: Psychosocial outcomes for children. In R. M. Malina & M. A. Clark (Eds.), *Youth sports: Perspectives for a new century* (pp. 127–138). Monterrey, CA: Coaches Choice.

Brustad, R. J., & Parker, M. (2005). Enhancing positive youth development through sport and physical activity. *Psychologica, 39,* 75–93.

Canadian Heritage. (2003). *Reconnecting Government With Sport Survey: Fact sheet.* Retrieved from http://www.pch.gc.ca/pgm/sc/info-fact/youth-eng.cfm

Carr, S. (2009). Implications of attachment theory for sport and physical activity research: Conceptual links with achievement goal and peer relationship models. *International Review of Sport and Exercise Psychology, 2,* 95–115. doi:10.1080/17509840902759173

Copeland, B., Bonnell, R. J., Reider, L., & Burton, D. (2009). Spawning sliding success: Evaluating a stress management and cohesion development program for young lugers. *Journal of Sport Behavior, 32,* 438–459.

Cumming, S. P., Smoll, F. L., Smith, R. E., & Grossbard, J. R. (2007). Is winning everything? The relative contributions of motivational climate and won–lost percentage in youth sports. *Journal of Applied Sport Psychology, 19,* 322–336. doi:10.1080/10413200701342640

Danish, S. J. (2002a). *Going for the goal: Leader manual.* Richmond, VA: Life Skills Associates.

Danish, S. J. (2002b). *SUPER (Sports United to Promote Education and Recreation): Leader manual.* Richmond, VA: Life Skills Associates.

Davis, L., & Jowett, S. (2010). Investigating the interpersonal dynam-ics between coaches and athletes based on fundamental principles of attachment. *Journal of Clinical Sport Psychology, 4,* 112–132.

Duda, J. L. (2005). Motivation in sport: The relevance of competence and achievement goals. In A. J. Elliot & C. S. Dweck (Eds.), *Handbook of competence and motivation* (pp. 318–335). New York, NY: Guilford Press.

Ewing, M. E., & Seefeldt, V. (1996). Patterns of participation and attri-tion in American agency-sponsored youth sports. In F. L. Smoll & R. E. Smith (Eds.), *Children and youth in sport: A biopsychosocial perspec-tive* (pp. 31–46). Boston, MA: McGraw-Hill.

Fisher, A. C., Mancini, V. H., Hirsch, R. L., Proulx, T. J., & Staurowsky, E. J. (1982). Coach–athlete interactions and team climate. *Journal of Sport Psychology, 4,* 388–404.

Fredricks, J. A., & Eccles, J. S. (2006). Is extracurricular partici-pation associated with beneficial outcomes? Concurrent and longitudinal relations. *Developmental Psychology, 42,* 698–713. doi:10.1037/0012-1649.42.4.698

Fry, M. D., & Gano-Overway, L. A. (2010). Exploring the contribution of the caring climate on the youth sport experience. *Journal of Applied Sport Psychology, 22,* 294–304. doi:10.1080/10413201003776352

Gould, D. (1987). Understanding attrition in children's sport. In D. Gould & M. R. Weiss (Eds.), *Advances in pediatric sport sciences* (pp. 61–85). Champaign, IL: Human Kinetics.

Greendorfer, S. L., Lewko, J. H., & Rosengren, K. S. (2002). Family and gender-based influences in sport socialization of children and ado-lescents. In F. L. Smoll & R. E. Smith (Eds.), *Children and youth in sport: A biopsychosocial perspective* (2nd ed., pp. 153–186). Dubuque, IA: Kendall/Hunt.

Jowett, S. (2007). Interdependence analysis and the 3 + 1Cs in the coach–athlete relationship. In S. Jowett & D. Lavalee (Eds.), *Social psychology in sport* (pp. 15–27). Champaign, IL: Human Kinetics.

Luiselli, J. K., & Reed, D. D. (2011). *Behavioral sport psychology: Evidence-based approaches to performance enhancement.* New York, NY: Springer. doi:10.1007/978-1-4614-0070-7

Martens, R. (1978). *Joy and sadness in children's sports.* Champaign, IL: Human Kinetics.

Martens, R., & Gould, D. (1979). Why do adults volunteer to coach children's sports? In G. C. Roberts & K. M. Newell (Eds.), *Psychology of motor behavior and sport—1978* (pp. 79–89). Champaign, IL: Human Kinetics.

Martin, G. L., & Hyrcaiko, D. (Eds.). (1983). *Behavior modification and coaching. Principles, procedures, and research.* Springfield, IL: Charles C Thomas.

McArdle, S., & Duda, J. K. (2002). Implications of the motivational climate in youth sports. In F. L. Smoll & R. E. Smith (Eds.), *Children and youth in sport: A biopsychosocial perspective* (2nd ed., pp. 409–434). Dubuque, IA: Kendall/Hunt.

McHugh, R. K., & Barlow, D. H. (2010). The dissemination and implementation of evidence-based psychological treatments: A review of current efforts. *American Psychologist, 65,* 73–84. doi:10.1037/a0018121

Mischel, W. (1973). Toward a cognitive social learning reconceptualization of personality. *Psychological Review, 80,* 252–283. doi:10.1037/h0035002

National Council of Youth Sports. (2008). *Report on trends and participation in organized youth sports.* Retrieved from http://www.ncys.org/publications/2008-sports-participation-study.php

National Federation of State High School Associations. (2010). *2009–2010 high school athletics participation survey.* Retrieved from http://www.nfhs.org/contact.aspx?id=3282&linkidentifier=id&itemid=3282

Newton, M., Watson, D. L., Gano-Overway, L., Fry, M., Kim, M., & Magyar, M. (2007). The role of a caring-based intervention in a physical domain. *The Urban Review, 39,* 281–299. doi:10.1007/s11256-007-0065-7

Orlick, T., & McCaffrey, N. (1991). Mental training with children for sport and life. *The Sport Psychologist, 5,* 322–334.

Roberts, G. C., Treasure, D. C., & Conroy, D. E. (2007). Understanding the dynamics of motivation in sport and physical activity: An achievement goal interpretation. In G. Tenenbaum & R. C. Eklund (Eds.), *Handbook of sport psychology* (3rd ed., pp. 1–30). New York, NY: Wiley. doi:10.1002/9781118270011.ch1

Rosewater, A. (2010). *Playing well: Organized sports and the health of children and youth.* Oakland, CA: Team-Up for Youth.

Seefeldt, V., Ewing, M. E., & Walk, S. (1992). *Overview of youth sport programs in the United States.* Washington, DC: Carnegie Council on Adolescent Development.

Smith, R. E. (2006). Understanding sport behavior: A cognitive–affective processing systems approach. *Journal of Applied Sport Psychology, 18,* 1–27. doi:10.1080/10413200500471293

Smith, R. E., & Smoll, F. L. (1990). Self-esteem and children's reactions to youth sport coaching behaviors: A field study of self-enhancement processes. *Developmental Psychology, 26,* 987–993. doi:10.1037/0012-1649.26.6.987

Smith, R. E., & Smoll, F. L. (2002). *Way to go, coach: A scientifically-proven approach to coaching effectiveness* (2nd ed.). Portola Valley, CA: Warde.

Smith, R. E., & Smoll, F. L. (2011). Cognitive–behavioral coach training: A translational approach to theory, research, and intervention. In J. K. Luiselli & D. D. Reed (Eds.), *Behavioral sport psychology: Evidence-based approaches to performance enhancement* (pp. 227–248). New York, NY: Springer. doi:10.1007/978-1-4614-0070-7_14

Smith, R. E., Smoll, F. L., & Barnett, N. (1995). Reduction of children's sport performance anxiety through social support and stress-reduction training for coaches. *Journal of Applied Developmental Psychology, 16,* 125–142. doi:10.1016/0193-3973(95)90020-9

Smith, R. E., Smoll, F. L., & Christensen, D. S. (1996). Behavioral assessment and interventions in youth sports: A review. *Behavior Modification, 20,* 3–44. doi:10.1177/01454455960201001

Smith, R. E., Smoll, F. L., & Cumming, S. P. (2009). Motivational climate and changes in young athletes' achievement goal orientations. *Motivation and Emotion, 33,* 173–183. doi:10.1007/s11031-009-9126-4

Smith, R. E., Smoll, F. L., & Curtis, B. (1978). Coaching behaviors in Little League Baseball. In F. L. Smoll & R. E. Smith (Eds.), *Psychological perspectives in youth sports* (pp. 173–201). Washington, DC: Hemisphere.

Smith, R. E., Smoll, F. L., & Curtis, B. (1979). Coach Effectiveness Training: A cognitive–behavioral approach to enhancing relationship skills in youth sport coaches. *Journal of Sport Psychology, 1,* 59–75.

Smith, R. E., Smoll, F. L., & Hunt, E. B. (1977). A system for the behavioral assessment of athletic coaches. *Research Quarterly, 48,* 401–407.

Smith, R. E., Smoll, F. L., & Passer, M. W. (2002). Competitive anxiety: Sources, consequences, and intervention strategies. In F. L. Smoll & R. E. Smith (Eds.), *Children and youth in sport: A biopsychosocial perspective* (2nd ed., pp. 501–536). Dubuque, IA: Kendall/Hunt.

Smith, R. E., Smoll, F. L., & Smith, N. J. (1989). *Parents' complete guide to youth sports.* Reston, VA: American Alliance for Health, Physical Education, Recreation, and Dance.

Smoll, F. L., & Smith, R. E. (1989). Leadership behaviors in sport: A theoretical model and research paradigm. *Journal of Applied Social Psychology, 19,* 1522–1551. doi:10.1111/j.1559-1816.1989.tb01462.x

Smoll, F. L., & Smith, R. E. (2002). The coach as a focus of research and intervention in youth sports. In F. L. Smoll & R. E. Smith (Eds.), *Children and youth in sport: A biopsychosocial perspective* (2nd ed., pp. 211–233). Dubuque, IA: Kendall/Hunt.

Smoll, F. L., & Smith, R. E. (2005). *Sports and your child: Developing champions in sports and in life.* Portola Valley, CA: Warde.

Smoll, F. L., & Smith, R. E. (2008). *Coaches who never lose: Making sure athletes win, no matter what the score* (3rd ed.). Portola Valley, CA: Warde.

Smoll, F. L., & Smith, R. E. (Producers). (2009a). *Mastery approach to coaching: A self-instruction program for youth sport coaches* [DVD]. Seattle, WA: Youth Enrichment in Sports.

Smoll, F. L., & Smith, R. E. (Producers). (2009b). *Mastery approach to parenting in sports: A self-instruction program for youth sport parents* [DVD]. Seattle, WA: Youth Enrichment in Sports.

Smoll, F. L., & Smith, R. E. (2010). Conducting psychologically oriented coach training programs: A social-cognitive approach. In J. M. Williams

(Ed.), *Applied sport psychology: Personal growth to peak performance* (6th ed., pp. 392–416). Boston, MA: McGraw-Hill.

Smoll, F. L., Smith, R. E., Barnett, N. P., & Everett, J. J. (1993). Enhancement of children's self-esteem through social support training for youth sport coaches. *Journal of Applied Psychology, 78,* 602–610. doi:10.1037/0021-9010.78.4.602

Smoll, F. L., Smith, R. E., & Cumming, S. P. (2007a). Effects of coach and parent training on performance anxiety in young athletes: A systemic approach. *Journal of Youth Development, 2,* Article 0701FA002. Retrieved from http://www.nae4ha.org/directory/jyd/index.html

Smoll, F. L., Smith, R. E., & Cumming, S. P. (2007b). Effects of a psychoeducational intervention for coaches on changes in child athletes' achievement goal orientations. *Journal of Clinical Sport Psychology, 1,* 23–46.

Sousa, C., Smith, R. E., & Cruz, J. (2008). An individualized behavioral goal setting program for coaches. *Journal of Clinical Sport Psychology, 2,* 258–277.

Stokes, J. V., & Luiselli, J. K. (2010). Functional analysis and behavioral coaching interventions to improve tackling skills of a high school football athlete. *Journal of Clinical Sport Psychology, 4,* 150–157.

Tashiro, T., & Mortensen, L. (2006). Translational research: How social psychology can improve psychotherapy. *American Psychologist, 61,* 959–966. doi:10.1037/0003-066X.61.9.959

Tesser, A. (1988). Toward a self-evaluative maintenance model of social behavior In L. Berkowitz (Ed.), *Advances in experimental social psychology* (Vol. 21, pp. 181–227). San Diego, CA: Academic Press. doi:10.1016/S0065-2601(08)60227-0

Thompson, J. (2008). *Positive sports parenting: How second goal parents raise winners in life through sports.* Portola Valley, CA: Balance Sports.

Universities Study Committee. (1978). *Joint legislative study on youth programs: Phase III. Agency sponsored sports.* East Lansing: Michigan Institute for the Study of Youth Sports.

Weiss, M. R. (2003). Social influences on children's psychosocial development in youth sports. In R. M. Malina & M. A. Clark (Eds.), *Youth sports: Perspectives for a new century* (pp. 109–126). Monterey, CA: Coaches Choice.

Weiss, W. M., & Weiss, M. R. (2006). A longitudinal analysis of commitment among competitive female gymnasts. *Psychology of Sport and Exercise, 7,* 309–323. doi:10.1016/j.psychsport.2005.08.010

Westre, K., & Weiss, M. (1991). The relationship between perceived coaching behaviors and group cohesion in high school football teams. *The Sport Psychologist, 5,* 41–54.

Zhang, L., Ma, Q., Orlick, T., & Zitzelberger, L. (1992). The effect of mental-imagery training on performance enhancement with 7–10-year-old children. *The Sport Psychologist, 6,* 230–241.

Scott B. Martin and Mark B. Andersen

Helping Intercollegiate Athletes In and Out of Sport

17

G errard was a sophomore football player at a highly competitive National Collegiate Athletic Association (NCAA) Division I university in the United States who was on a full scholarship. Although the university had a rich football tradition with years of winning success, last season's record of seven wins and five losses was viewed by many as extremely disappointing. The team had started off well this season, but if the coaching staff were going to keep their jobs, they would need big results.

Gerrard began the season as the starting tailback, a challenge that he embraced. He considered the university team to be a stepping stone to the professional ranks. Gerrard was looking forward to helping his family financially when he became a professional football player. To meet that goal, Gerrard started using anabolic-androgenic steroids to bulk up; to increase his strength, speed, and agility; and to recover more quickly from the intense weight training and practice schedule. As the pressure to perform on the field mounted, Gerrard's ability to focus on his schoolwork diminished, and he fell behind in his

http://dx.doi.org/10.1037/14251-017
Exploring Sport and Exercise Psychology, Third Edition, J. Van Raalte and
B. Brewer (Editors)

studies. He tried sleeping later in the mornings to get extra rest, but when his coaches found out that he was sleeping through classes, they chastised him in front of his teammates.

Some of Gerrard's friends noticed how upset he was and took him off campus to "relax." On the way, they were stopped by the campus police. In the car, the police found drug paraphernalia, including a hash pipe, a hypodermic needle, and an empty steroid container. Although the police let them go with only a warning, Gerrard was worried that the media, his coaches, and his family would find out. He did not want to lose his scholarship, put his coaches or teammates at risk, or embarrass his family. He was anxious and could not concentrate on the game. While running a routine play, he mishandled the ball and fell awkwardly, injuring his knee.

After the game, Gerrard was dejected about his performance and knee injury. The athletic trainer prescribed ice and rest for the next few days. The trainer also suggested that Gerrard speak to the athletic department's sport psychologist. Gerrard was resistant to the idea but when he found out that the sport psychologist was the person one of his teammates had said was "an OK guy," he decided to give sport psychology a try. The sport psychologist and Gerrard began meeting and working on Gerrard's worries about his performance, substance use, and other issues.

Gerrard's case illustrates the high-pressure environment that surrounds university athletes in the United States. The purpose of this chapter is to provide sport psychology consultants with the information they need to work effectively in university sport environments with intercollegiate athletes such as Gerrard. The chapter begins with an explanation of the distinctions among college and university programs and types of athletes. Next, we discuss developmental issues relevant to intercollegiate athletes. We then move to some of the specific pressures that are faced by intercollegiate athletes on and off the field, including academics, time management, injury, the media, and clinical mental health issues. The chapter concludes with a discussion of how practitioners can work effectively in intercollegiate sport environments.

Distinctions Among U.S. Intercollegiate Sport Programs

Colleges and universities with intercollegiate sport programs in the United States are primarily governed by one of the following three organizations: (a) the NCAA (http://www.ncaa.org/), (b) the National Association of Intercollegiate Athletics (NAIA; http://naia.cstv.com/), and (c) the National Junior College Athletic Association (NJCAA; http://www.njcaa. org/). Although there are other national intercollegiate athletic governing bodies, such as the National Christian College Athletic Association (http://www.thenccaa.org/) and the United States Collegiate Athletic Association (http://www.theuscaa.com/landing/index), that target smaller schools of like size and programs, in this chapter, we focus primarily on the NCAA, NAIA, and NJCAA. These three national organizations represent thousands of college and university sport programs and have standardized rules for the sports, athletes, and competitions that they govern. The oldest, largest, most established, and best-funded sanctioning organization is the NCAA, which currently represents over 1,200 institutions. Although the common perception is that intercollegiate sports generate a large amount of revenue for their schools, the money is mainly distributed among administrators, coaches, media outlets, and other entities. Only a few university sport programs break even; most have to rely on subsidies for coaches, training, competition venues, scholarships, equipment, travel, and personnel to operate the facilities and accommodate the athletes and staff (Berkowitz, 2008; Fulks, 2008; Sperber, 1990).

Intercollegiate athletic programs in the United States are generally divided into three divisions (Divisions I, II, and III). Athletes competing in Division I and Division II programs can receive scholarships for their athletic achievements. Division II institutions generally offer fewer athletic scholarships and/or more partial athletic scholarships than Division I schools. No athletic scholarships are awarded to Division III student-athletes; however, all students (including student-athletes) may be eligible for other forms of financial assistance and academic scholarships. In many Division I and Division II sports, a small number of athletic scholarships are available, and funding is divided among several student-athletes who must cover the remaining costs of their education.

Division I schools are often pressure cookers for athletes, especially those in American football, basketball, and baseball. Many schools also specialize in a few other sports (e.g., golf, swimming, tennis, volleyball), and pressures on athletes in those sports can be substantial. Because of the time-consuming nature, the intense mental and physical commitment, and the inordinate emphasis placed on winning, some believe that intercollegiate athletes should receive more than just athletic scholarships (Shanoff & Lipsyte, 2005).

Although Division II student-athletes may not experience the national exposure and pressure of Division I athletes, local and state-wide attention are often present. Division III sport programs generally receive less attention than Division I and Division II programs, but pressures to perform and media attention at the local and state level may still be extensive.

Distinctions Among Intercollegiate Athletes

A distinction in intercollegiate sports that is probably more important than the NJCAA, NAIA, or NCAA or Divisions I, II, and III is the difference between revenue and nonrevenue sports. The revenue-producing sports are usually football and men's basketball, with baseball a distant third. There are a few exceptions, but it is usually these programs that receive the most attention, acknowledgment, and money. Many coaches and athletes believe that revenue-producing sports financially support the athletics department; however, in the vast majority of cases, football and basketball programs operate in the red and are themselves a drain on university resources (Berkowitz, 2008; Fulks, 2008; Sperber, 1990). Unlike athletes on nonrevenue sports teams, those on high-profile, revenue-producing sports teams may have different backgrounds from other students on campus, often ones that may include a greater emphasis on athletic performance and less attention to academic skills. It is not surprising, then, that revenue-generating university sports teams often exhibit problems such as low graduation rates when it comes to education (see Coakley, 2009). Student-athletes and coaches in nonrevenue sports may feel resentment toward revenue-generating sports for getting more of the attention and money.

Another important distinction in university sports is between men's and women's sports. The passage of Title IX, Education Amendments in 1972 was designed to provide opportunities for women athletes (see http://www.dol.gov/oasam/regs/statutes/titleix.htm). Title IX helped increase the number of intercollegiate teams for women in the United States, but it did not completely resolve inequities in sport programs. Unintended consequences of Title IX include a reduction in the number of men's sports offered at some universities rather than an increase in opportunities for women athletes and an increase in male coaches of women's teams that has led to a reduction in women as coach role models (Jowett, Paull, Pensgaard, Hoegmo, & Riise, 2005). It is clear that issues of gender equity continue to affect intercollegiate athletics.

Developmental Issues

Transition to college or university life involves many physical, emotional, social, and intellectual changes (Oppenheimer, 1984). For example, intercollegiate student-athletes face academic pressures, developmental challenges, cultural adjustment, and sport-related concerns such as high training loads and team hazing. Furthermore, they often face decisions about complex and controversial issues such as body art, gambling, recreational drug use, steroids, and sexuality, all while under the media spotlight.

TRANSITION INTO TERTIARY EDUCATION INSTITUTIONS

Intercollegiate athletes usually range from 17 to 23 years of age. In Eriksonian terms, the developmental tasks they face concern identity and establishing intimate relationships (Erikson, 1968). In Erikson's formulations, student-athletes are in the process of forming pictures of who they are (ego identity) and may also be well on their way to making intimate lifelong links with others. Some student-athletes, however, may not develop strong identities (role confusion) or may become foreclosed (see Petitpas & France, 2010; see also Chapter 11, this volume, for more about identity development). Other student-athletes may end up in the usually unhappy state of isolation. Additional challenges experienced by college student-athletes include balancing sport and academic responsibilities (i.e., role strain), adapting to social challenges associated with their athlete status, maintaining a healthy competition weight and size, managing athletic successes and failures, dealing with physical injuries, and terminating sport careers (Parham, 1996; J. C. Watson, 2002; J. C. Watson & Kissinger, 2007).

The move to a university may also be a cultural transition, a change from star athlete to just a member of the team, from living at home to independent university living, from a rural location to an urban university, from an urban location to a rural university, and for some athletes from a home country to a new country and culture. The proportion of international scholarship athletes in many Division I and Division II programs is significant (Wilson & Wolverton, 2008). For example, during the 2005–2006 academic year, 30% of the male tennis players, 23% of male ice hockey players, 14% of female golfers, 13% of all skiers, and 10% of male soccer players were from outside the United States. Cultural transitions can affect adjustment to all aspects of college life, including sport performance; social life; academic outcomes; attitudes toward sport psychology services; responsiveness to support services available; and happiness or satisfaction with sport, school, and social experiences.

HAZING AND INITIATION INTO GROUPS

Assimilation into sports teams is fraught with challenges, including those imposed by teammates in the form of hazing behaviors and practices, such as being required to keep silent, carry unnecessary items, and wear embarrassing outfits; getting yelled, screamed, and cursed at; acting as a personal servant; being deprived of sleep; participating in drinking contests or games; shaving body hair; getting a tattoo or body piercing; engaging in or simulating sexual acts; being forced to shower with debris and feces; being stranded or kidnapped, transported, and abandoned; stealing objects or causing property damage; and being physically and psychologically assaulted (Allen & Madden, 2008; Hoover, 1999; McGlone, 2005). Although 44 states have hazing laws designed to prevent such behavior (http://www.stophazing.com), it is clear that hazing continues, and the vast majority of membership initiation practices and hazing incidents go unreported (Allen & Madden, 2008). Individuals involved in hazing activities can experience stress, anxiety, emotional trauma, physical injury, and even death (see Campo, Poulos, & Sipple, 2005). Prevalence of hazing in intercollegiate athletics has been found to be as high as 79% for NCAA college athletes. Male athletes have been found to be more likely than female athletes to be the victims of hazing in their college sports program and to have hazed others in the program (Allen & Madden, 2008; Campo et al., 2005). For those student-athletes who had experienced hazing incidents, approximately 50% reported that alcohol had been involved (NCAA, 2005). Sport psychologists who are aware of hazing-related issues may be well positioned to offer alternative positive team building activities to enhance cohesion (Van Raalte, Cornelius, Linder, & Brewer, 2007) and appropriate counseling and legal referrals for those student-athletes who have had negative hazing experiences.

SELF-EXPRESSION THROUGH BODY ART

Tattoos and body piercings are prevalent among college students, professional athletes, and actors (Koch, Roberts, Armstrong, & Owen, 2010). A Pew Research Center for the People and the Press (2007) report indicated that 36% of 18- to 25-year-olds have at least one tattoo. With respect to intercollegiate athletes, an assessment of students at one university showed that male athletes were significantly more likely to be tattooed than nonathletes (Mayers, Judelson, Moriarty, & Rundell, 2002). A potential risk of body art is infections and the transmission of blood-borne diseases that can cause health problems, which could ultimately have deleterious effects on athletic training and performance (Koch et al., 2010). In addition to these health issues, college students with tattoos as well as those with body piercings report other risky behaviors, such as gambling, alcohol and drug use, unsafe sexual activity, disordered eating, and suicidal ideation and attempts (see Schmidt & Armstrong, 2007).

GAMBLING

College-age individuals are the highest users of the Internet and the fastest growing sector of online gamblers (Brown, 2006; Rainie & Horrigan, 2005). Some reports indicate that college athletes have higher problem gambling rates than their nonathlete peers (Engwall, Hunter, & Steinberg, 2004), whereas others have found that college student-athletes are less likely to gamble than college nonathletes (NCAA Academic and Membership Affairs Staff, 2010). For both athletes and nonathletes, problem gambling and related behaviors such as alcohol use, tobacco and marijuana consumption, and disordered eating can threaten academic success, financial well-being, overall health, and by extension athletes' sport performance (Engwall et al., 2004; NCAA Academic and Membership Affairs Staff, 2010).

RECREATIONAL SUBSTANCE USE

An NCAA (2005) study indicated that more than 75% of intercollegiate athletes reported consuming alcohol during the previous year, often drinking six to 10 drinks or more in one sitting. Athletes were more likely than nonathletes to report heavy episodic drinking (Martens, Dams-O'Connor, & Beck, 2006), although alcohol consumption was lower during the athletes' competitive seasons. Student-athletes who use recreational substances such as alcohol, cocaine, marijuana, tobacco, and stimulants report that they use these substances to escape from pressures, socialize with others, and become accepted by peers (NCAA, 2005). However, athletes should be aware that those who consume alcohol while in training may experience performance decrements and sport-related injuries, with an injury incidence rate of over 50% in drinkers compared with less than 25% in nondrinkers (O'Brien & Lyons, 2000). The prevalence of injury in drinkers may be due partially to the hangover effect of alcohol consumption, which was also shown to reduce sport performance by more than 10%.

PERFORMANCE-ENHANCING SUBSTANCES

Intercollegiate athletes take performance-enhancing substances to improve performance, cope with pain and injury rehabilitation, manage weight and shape, increase strength and power, and for other physical and psychological reasons (Coakley, 2009). Anabolic-androgenic steroid use varies by gender and sport and is prevalent in men's water polo, football, and baseball and women's lacrosse and swimming (NCAA, 2001). Anabolic steroid use has been found to be related to greater binge drinking, a higher prevalence of alcohol-use disorders, greater marijuana and other drug use, and more high-risk behaviors than athletes who do not use steroids (McCabe, Brower, West, Nelson, & Wechsler, 2007). An NCAA (2005) study revealed the average usage rate had declined in all three divisions from its earlier 2001 investigation.

Painkillers are frequently used to treat and minimize pain and injury (often so that injured athletes can continue playing), whereas stimulants are used to enhance metabolism and weight loss, improve mood, increase aggressiveness, raise energy, and improve speed and quickness (NCAA, 2005). Painkiller, stimulant, and diet drug use is more prevalent in contact sports, such as American football and hockey, which require speed and aggression and may result in daily bumps and bruises, but the use really depends on the type of sport (NCAA, 2005). Sport psychologists who are aware of the attraction and risks associated with performance-enhancing substances, particularly those widely used in the sports they are working with, may be well positioned to address student-athlete issues and concerns with regard to these substances.

SEXUALITY

There is not an extensive literature on college athletes and sexual behavior. Some studies from the 1990s, however, revealed that compared with student nonathletes, student-athletes reported having significantly more sexual partners in a year's time (Butki, Andersen, & Heyman, 1996; Heyman, Varra, & Keahey, 1993). More recently, Gage (2008) found that male American football players scored higher on callous sexual attitudes and lower on attitudes toward women and had more sexual partners than their male tennis athlete and nonathlete peers. Both athletes and nonathletes also reported low frequencies of condom use, but male athletes reported even lower frequencies of condom use than their nonathlete peers (Kokotailo, Henry, Koscik, Fleming, & Landry, 1996). More partners and low condom use suggest that some athletes are involved in risky sexual behavior. A. Watson and Martin (1998) found that female athletes had twice the rate of sexually transmitted diseases compared with nonathletes. Sport psychologists working with intercollegiate student-athletes may want to consider offering psychoeducational programs on responsible sexual behavior for their athletes.

THE ERIKSONIAN CHALLENGES REVISITED

The psychosocial developmental challenges of the college athlete are to establish an identity and form intimate relationships. Erikson's stages of ego identity versus role confusion and intimacy versus isolation describe sources of struggle for many athletes in college. University athletic administrations may claim to strive to develop the whole person in their athletes, but the environment usually sends a different message. Athletes often live in athletic dorms, have social support systems that are primarily composed of other athletes, and are exposed to an organization that can foster an "us–them" ("them" being the rest of the university population) viewpoint. Sport psychologists can be helpful in an athlete's struggle to form an identity, but the obstacles that are in place for such development are substantial.

Establishing intimate relationships is part of young adulthood and is strongly tied to identity. Identities are developed with the assistance of intimate others. In some collegiate sporting environments, the veneration of masculinity is pervasive (e.g., American football, basketball). Internalizing this sport culture's veneration of aggressive masculinity and denigrating passivity (e.g., male entitlement, femininity is a sign of weakness, viewing women as objects of gratification) work against the establishment of intimacy (cf. Gage, 2008). The locker room, fraternity house mentality that can be propagated by sports administrators, coaches, and other athletes can pose a serious challenge to those struggling with intimacy and self-identity. The world of the intercollegiate athlete can sometimes be inimical to the establishment of strong multifaceted identities and healthy, satisfying intimate relationships.

Pressures to Perform On and Off the Court and Field

The life of a student-athlete when school is in session is often a series of attempts to get caught up. It is the rare student-athlete who is well ahead in his or her studies. The pressures and demands of academic and sport performance combined often leave little time for student-athletes to engage in common student activities such as play and socializing. In the following subsections, we discuss academic pressure, time management concerns, academic challenges, injury, and dealing with the media, some of the special pressures faced by student-athletes.

ACADEMIC PERFORMANCE

NCAA, NAIA, and NJCAA eligibility rules require student-athletes to meet certain academic standards. For example, NCAA Division I eligibility rules require student-athletes to complete 40% of their graduation requirements with a grade point average (GPA) of at least 1.8 by the end of their second year, 60% with a GPA of 2.0 by the end of their third year, and 80% with a GPA of 2.0 by the end of their fourth year to maintain eligibility (see NCAA, 2009, or http://www.ncaastudent.org/NCAA_Guide.pdf for the latest NCAA regulations; these rules change regularly). At-risk student-athletes are often monitored by coaches and staff to determine whether they are attending classes, completing and turning in assignments, and meeting GPA standards. At some universities, the student-athletes who do not have a certain GPA must attend study hall and/or see tutors. A student-athlete's day might run something like this: classes 9:00 to 1:00, lunch 1:30, athletic training table 2:00 to 2:15, practice 2:30 to 5:30, dinner 6:00, study hall 7:00 to 10:00, and then maybe some more studying at home later. Time for scheduling extra activities such as sport psychology consultation is limited.

Although the amount of time student-athletes participate in their respective sports (i.e., practice, competition, workouts) is officially limited by the NCAA to no more than 4 hours per day, 20 hours per week (Abell, 2000; Wrisberg & Johnson, 2002), additional activities, including study hall, lifting weights, and viewing game film, are often strongly encouraged. Thus, sport-related demands can be at odds with academic needs and goals (e.g., study time, gaining internships, participating in independent study experiences; Hood, Craig, & Ferguson, 1992; Petrie, Hankes, & Denson, 2010). Efforts have been made to provide support services for student-athletes (see NCAA Student-Athlete Affairs at http://www.ncaa.org/) to facilitate academic success. However, a sports-over-academics culture still exists at many institutions such that athletes are excessively entitled, exploited, and effectively denied the opportunity to receive a legitimate college education (e.g., Oliard, 2009; Splitt, 2010).

Time Management

Organizing student-athletes' time is often not a problem. Much of their time is already scheduled. Pinkney (1996) made the wise suggestion that some common time management techniques are just not appropriate for many student-athletes. For example, one should not ask student-athletes to find more time in the day or set aside more time to get things done. They do not have "extra" time. In a true sense, they already have great time management skills—they get to practice on time; they use their time effectively in the pool or in the weight room. Time management for student-athletes needs to focus not on finding more time but on using the time they have more effectively and efficiently.

Academic Challenges

Many student-athletes miss classes and tests because of travel and competitions. This scheduling issue remains a thorny problem. Some university professors are accommodating and arrange for student-athletes to complete assignments and take exams in a way that fits their sport schedules, especially if student-athletes notify them in advance. Other professors, however, resent the request for special treatment.

Student-athletes with challenging academic circumstances may benefit from using support service personnel to facilitate interactions with professors. Some student-athletes are hesitant to take advantage of these resources (J. C. Watson, 2005) even though such interventions can be helpful. However, it should also be noted that interventions on behalf of the student-athlete by support service providers can also make the situation worse by irritating already unhappy professors and leading student-athletes to believe that other people are responsible for negotiating challenges related to their academic success when in fact student-athletes are responsible for themselves.

SPORT INJURY

Experiencing a sport injury can be challenging for athletes on a variety of levels. An injury brings up questions of athletic scholarships (they may not be renewed), friendships (teammates may become more distant), and self-esteem (identity issues mentioned previously). One positive note about injuries is that athletes are often particularly willing to meet with a sport psychologist because they have extra time and issues to discuss. Injury can be a catalyst for seeking service. Sport psychologists who are unfamiliar with injury issues may wish to do some homework in this field to gain knowledge about helping athletes with rehabilitation (e.g., Hamson-Utley, Martin, & Walters, 2008; Kolt, 2000; Kolt & Andersen, 2004; Tunick, Etzel, Leard, & Lerner, 1996; Wiese & Weiss, 1987) and working with sports medicine organizations (e.g., Andersen & Brewer, 1995).

DEALING WITH THE MEDIA

Many Division I schools require their athletes and coaches to attend seminars on how to appropriately communicate with the media. Ideally, this training includes expectations about student-athlete visibility and communication on social networking sites, blogs, and with communication tools such as Twitter. Such training is important as media mishaps can have lasting consequences for sport careers.

Switching focus from athletes to sport psychologists, we note that major athletic events at universities often provide opportunities for the press to bring up sport psychology and sport psychologists. On these occasions, the media and some athletes may attribute sport success to interactions with sport psychologists. This error can lead to resentment on the part of athletes and coaches who should be recognized for their performances. Excessive media attention also challenges sport psychologists attempting to maintain professional confidentiality boundaries. We recommend that sport psychologists remain in the background as much as possible when dealing with the media and inform athletes that this is where they wish to remain.

Common Clinical Issues With Intercollegiate Athletes

Intercollegiate athletes are, in general, a healthy group, but they are also subject to many of the same mental and social problems of their nonathlete peers. In some instances, student-athletes may actually be more at risk of developing mental and behavioral problems than other students (e.g., eating disorders, adjustment disorders). In the subsections that follow are some of the common clinical concerns that may occur in the student-athlete population.

MOOD AND ANXIETY DISORDERS

In addition to experiencing stress and low self-esteem (Hudd et al. 2000; Papanikolaou, Nikolaidis, Patsiaouras, & Alexopoulos, 2003), some athletes are at risk for other mood and anxiety disorders (e.g., panic disorder, depression; Baum, 2005; Hays, 2010; Humphrey, Yow, & Bowden, 2000; see also Chapter 14, this volume). College athletes who consider themselves students as well as athletes are likely to gain academic and psychological advantages over those who do not (see Killeya-Jones, 2005). This identification as a student and athlete may be susceptible to strain, however, when student-athletes feel incapable of achieving the expectations of significant others (e.g., peers, family members, coaches, boosters and fans, sport agents), which may result in stress and depression (Marx, Huffman, & Doyle, 2008). Depression is the "common cold" of mental disorders, and athletes may become depressed for a variety of reasons. The prevalence of depression and anxiety for female college athletes is slightly higher than that for nonathletes (Carr, Conway, Mundt, Brown, & Thein-Nissenbaum, 2007).

EATING DISORDERS

Athletes in some sports, especially those sports that emphasize appearance (e.g., diving, gymnastics) or have weight classes (e.g., wrestling), may be at greater risk of developing eating disorders than their nonathlete peers (Andersen & Peterson, 2005). In recent years, there has been a growing interest in eating disorders among both male and female student-athletes (Petrie & Greenleaf, 2010). That interest has grown from an increased concern for the health and welfare of ath-letes but also because of litigation brought against intercollegiate sports departments by athletes who developed eating disorders during their college years. The etiology and treatment of eating disorders is beyond the scope of this chapter, but there are many useful resources available to sport psychologists (e.g., Black & Burckes-Miller, 1988; Borgen & Corbin, 1987; Dosil, 2008; Parker, Lambert, & Burlington, 1994; Petrie, 1993; Petrie & Greenleaf, 2007; Rosen & Hough, 1988; Stice & Shaw, 2004; Thompson & Sherman, 1993). For descriptions of the diagnosis and cognitive–behavioral treatment of athletes with eating disorders, see Petrie and Greenleaf (2010).

The Practitioner and the NCAA, NAIA, and NJCAA

The NCAA, NAIA, and NJCAA have complex sets of ever-changing rules and regulations that apply to a wide range of behaviors and activities involving student-athletes. It behooves sport psychologists to become familiar with these rules, particularly rules that relate to student-athlete recruitment, academic progress, and allowable services to avoid putting the athlete or the team in jeopardy of rule violations (NCAA, 2009; NCAA Academic and Membership Affairs Staff, 2010). Depending on the rule infraction, the consequences can range from a warning to the loss of the student's eligibility to the whole team being placed on probation (or worse).

Current NCAA regulations have been interpreted as stating that sport psychology consultation should only occur in a group classroom-like setting or the sport psychologist's office (Bemiller & Wrisberg, 2011). Sport psychologists who go out on the playing field to work with ath-letes (e.g., helping athletes with on-site self-talk strategies) are con-sidered to be acting as extra coaches. The NCAA limits the number of coaches allowed for each sport, so teams with the maximum number of coaches that have a sport psychologist work on the field are in violation of NCAA rules. NCAA regulations do not prevent sport psychologists from attending and observing practice.

Sport psychologists who offer teams psychoeducational sessions on performance-enhancement topics in a classroom setting are in compli-ance with NCAA rules regarding the number of allowable coaches. How-ever, the time spent in these psychoeducational team sessions must be included in the weekly allotment of hours for practice and team meet-ings (i.e., 20 hours). General support services such as advisement, per-sonal counseling, career counseling, and tutoring are exempt from the

20-hour-per-week regulation. To reduce the risk of rule violations, sport psychologists can contact the institution's compliance coordinator, who can help answer questions about sport psychology service delivery and maintenance of compliance with relevant regulations. For the latest update on rules concerning eligibility, enforcement, and considerations for athletes with learning disabilities, refer to the NCAA (http://www.ncaa.org), the NAIA (http://naia.cstv.com), and the NJCAA (http://njcaa.org).

Who Works With College Student-Athletes

Academic athletic advisors, tutors, counseling center staff, academic department staff (e.g., exercise science professors), and university career center staff are generally available on campus to provide services of a psychological, academic, or counseling nature to student-athletes. For those sport psychologists who have little or no contact with intercollegiate sport (e.g., private practitioners, academics) and who wish to establish a relationship with athletes and coaches, there are several approaches to consider. The first approach involves academic athletic counselors who counsel athletes on academic matters, eligibility, registration, and so forth. Many academic athletic counselors are familiar with the factors that influence academic success for student-athletes (see Lapchick, 1989), are overworked, and might welcome a good referral source for athletes who want to work on performance enhancement or other personal issues. Forming a liaison with academic athletic counselors is probably one of the smarter moves a university counseling center psychologist or other sport psychology practitioner can make.

Another approach to developing a relationship with intercollegiate sports involves connections with the sports medicine unit. Studies (Francis, Andersen, & Maley, 2000; Hamson-Utley et al., 2008) have shown that athletic trainers and sport physical therapists would like to see more training in psychology and more psychological services in sports medicine settings. It appears that many athletic trainers would welcome contact with sport psychologists, especially those with experience and knowledge of psychological processes in injury rehabilitation (see Kolt & Andersen, 2004). However, sports medicine units in intercollegiate sports departments often have convoluted structures (Andersen & Brewer, 1995) and varying degrees of sport psychology knowledge (Hamson-Utley et al., 2008). Therefore, a thorough familiarity with the structure and reporting lines of such organizations may help avoid unintentional faux pas when offering services.

Working in Intercollegiate Sports

Sport psychologists often have boundaries that differ from the more traditional clinical or counseling psychology ones (Andersen, Van Raalte, & Brewer, 2001). Sport psychologists may attend practices and competitions and even travel to away games and meets. This rather "familiar" behavior may pose some problems. Sport psychologists might want to clarify their boundaries to themselves and their clients. There are some sport psychologists who travel, eat, and even work out with teams. The rationale behind this behavior involves getting the sport psychologist to be accepted as one of the team or coaching staff. Although the intentions seem good, the results of such familiar behavior may lead to NCAA violations and problematic dual relationships or other ethical concerns (Ellickson & Brown, 1990).

Awareness of these sorts of issues before beginning work with teams and athletes is valuable because intercollegiate athletics is a high-visibility field. Division I intercollegiate sport teams are in the entertainment business with an entertainment product to sell (often a football or basketball team). Understanding this truth can help sport psychology practitioners work more effectively with athletic department personnel. Athletics administrators, coaches, and athletes face different pressures and challenges than do faculty and administrators working "across the street" at the university, where teaching and research receive the most attention.

Large universities may have a chief athletic director and several associate and assistant athletic directors to cover areas such as marketing, sports information, contest management, and student support services. Whenever sport psychologists enter into the system, the assistant athletic director or other administrator responsible for the area of service (e.g., sports medicine) in which the sport psychologist is working needs to be advised that the sport psychologist is on board. Entering into the system without checking in with the "top brass" may set off the organizational immune system and get the sport psychologist hastily removed.

In addition to team contacts, administrators, coaches, or athletes may seek out sport psychology services directly. These various service seekers present challenges to sport psychologists, who must remain clear on who the client is. Unlike traditional counseling settings, services may be solicited by one person, paid for by another person, and delivered to a third person. Administrators and/or coaches who allocate money for services for an athlete may assume that they are entitled to information about what that money is buying and how the services are going. Sport psychologists who provide preemptive education about psychologists' ethical codes to coaches, administrators, and athletes tend to be more successful. Working with the athletic department to develop a holistic health and welfare team that involves coaches, medical staff members, strength trainers, student life counselors, dietitians and nutritionists, academic athletic counselors, and so forth may be a particularly effective way for sport psychologists to work in university sport settings.

Summary

College and university sports provide a potentially vast market for sport psychologists, but even today it is still a rather closed and guarded area. Sport psychologists may find all sorts of difficulties breaking into these unique subcultures. The good news is that more and more athletic departments and universities are paying closer attention to the health and welfare of athletes as they transition in and out of intercollegiate sports, and sport psychologists will likely continue to play a role in the humanizing of services for college student-athletes. The major take-home message from this chapter is that although the issues collegiate athletes deal with are often similar to those that other athletes face, sport psychologists need to know the distinct challenges that college and university sports present. Suitable education and training in the topics discussed in this chapter (and book) in addition to relevant experiences in intercollegiate sports are necessary not only for breaking into this marketplace but also for sustaining relationships with those involved in these higher education sport subcultures.

References

Abell, V. L. (Ed.). (2000). *2000–01 NCAA Division I manual.* Indianapolis, IN: National Collegiate Athletic Association.

Allen, E. J., & Madden, M. (2008, March). *Hazing in view: College students at risk. Initial findings from the National Study of Student Hazing.* Retrieved from http://www.hazingstudy.org/publications/hazing_in_view_web.pdf

Andersen, M. B., & Brewer, B. W. (1995). Organizational and psychological consultation in collegiate sports medicine groups. *Journal of American College Health, 44,* 63–69. doi:10.1080/07448481.1995.9937514

Andersen, M. B., & Peterson, K. (2005). "I have a friend who . . ." Group work on weight and body image. In M. B. Andersen (Ed.), *Sport psychology in practice* (pp. 61–74). Champaign, IL: Human Kinetics.

Andersen, M. B., Van Raalte, J. L., & Brewer, B. W. (2001). Sport psychology service delivery: Staying ethical while keeping loose. *Professional Psychology: Research and Practice, 32,* 12–18. doi:10.1037/0735-7028.32.1.12

Baum, A. L. (2005). Suicide in athletes: A review and commentary. *Clinics in Sports Medicine, 24,* 853–869. doi:10.1016/j.csm.2005.06.006

Bemiller, J., & Wrisberg, C. A. (2011). An overview and critique of NCAA policy regarding the use of sport psychology consultants at the Division I level. *Journal of Intercollegiate Sport, 4,* 227–242.

Berkowitz, S. (2008, May 16). Few athletics programs in black; most need aid. *USA Today,* 12C. Retrieved from http://www.usatoday.com/printedition/sports/20080516/c12schools16.art.htm

Black, D. R., & Burckes-Miller, M. E. (1988). Male and female college athletes: Use of anorexia nervosa and bulimia nervosa weight loss methods. *Research Quarterly for Exercise and Sport, 59,* 252–256.

Borgen, J. S., & Corbin, C. B. (1987). Eating disorders among female athletes. *The Physician and Sportsmedicine, 15*(2), 89–95.

Brown, S. J. (2006). The surge in online gambling on college campuses. *New Directions for Student Services,* No. 113, Wiley InterScience. Retrieved from http://www.ic.arizona.edu/ic/indv10258/readings/BrownSurge.pdf

Butki, B. D., Andersen, M. B., & Heyman, S. R. (1996). Knowledge of AIDS and risky sexual behaviors among athletes. *Academic Athletic Journal, 11*(1), 29–36.

Campo, S., Poulos, G., & Sipple, J. W. (2005). Prevalence and profiling: Hazing among college students and points of intervention. *American Journal of Health Behavior, 29,* 137–149. doi:10.5993/AJHB.29.2.5

Carr, K., Conway, K., Mundt, M., Brown, D., & Thein-Nissenbaum, J. (2007). *Division I female college athlete health.* Madison: University of Wisconsin, Department of Family Medical Research.

Coakley, J. (2009). *Sports in society: Issues and controversies* (10th ed.). New York, NY: McGraw Hill.

Dosil, J. (2008). *Eating disorders in athletes.* Chichester, England: Wiley InterScience. doi:10.1002/9780470725047

Ellickson, K. A., & Brown, D. R. (1990). Ethical considerations in dual relationships: The sport psychologist-coach. *Journal of Applied Sport Psychology, 2,* 186–190. doi:10.1080/10413209008406429

Engwall, D., Hunter, R., & Steinberg, M. (2004). Gambling and other risk behaviors on university campuses. *Journal of American College Health, 52,* 245–256. doi:10.3200/JACH.52.6.245-256

Erikson, E. H. (1968). *Identity: Youth and crisis.* New York, NY: Norton.

Francis, S. R., Andersen, M. B., & Maley, P. (2000). Physiotherapists' and male professional athletes' views on psychological skills for rehabilitation. *Journal of Science and Medicine in Sport, 3,* 17–29. doi:10.1016/S1440-2440(00)80044-4

Fulks, D. L. (2008). *Revenues and expenses of NCAA Division I intercollegiate athletics programs.* Retrieved from http://www.ncaapublications.com/ productdownloads/RE09.pdf

Gage, E. A. (2008). Gender attitudes and sexual behavior: Comparing center and marginal athletes and nonathletes in a collegiate setting. *Violence Against Women, 14,* 1014–1032. doi:10.1177/1077801208321987

Hamson-Utley, J. J., Martin, S. B., & Walters, J. (2008). Athletic trainers' and physical therapists' perceptions of the effectiveness of psychological skills within sport-injury rehabilitation programs. *Journal of Athletic Training, 43,* 258–264. doi:10.4085/1062-6050-43.3.258

Hays, K. F. (2010). Depression. In S. J. Hanrahan & M. B. Andersen (Eds.), *Routledge handbook of applied sport psychology: A comprehensive guide for students and practitioners* (pp. 250–259). London, England: Routledge.

Heyman, S. R., Varra, E. M., & Keahey, J. (1993, August). Comparison of high school varsity athletes and non-varsity students on measures of homophobia, sexual activity, and knowledge about AIDS. In S. R. Heyman (Chair), *Homophobia in sport: Confronting the fear.* Symposium conducted at the meeting of the American Psychological Association, Toronto, Ontario, Canada.

Hood, A. B., Craig, A. F., & Ferguson, B. W. (1992). The impact of athletics, part-time employment and other activities on academic achievement. *Journal of College Student Development, 33,* 447–453.

Hoover, N. C. (1999). *Initiation rites and athletics: A national survey of NCAA sports teams.* Retrieved from http://www.alfred.edu/sports_hazing/ docs/hazing.pdf

Hudd, S., Dumlao, J., Erdmann-Sager, D., Murray, D., Phan, E., Soukas, N., & Yokozuka, N. (2000). Stress at college: Effects on health habits, health status, and self-esteem. *College Student Journal, 34,* 217–227.

Humphrey, J. H., Yow, D. A., & Bowden, W. W. (2000). *Stress in college athletics: Causes, consequences, coping.* Binghamton, NY: Haworth Half-Court Press.

Jowett, S., Paull, G., Pensgaard, A. M., Hoegmo, P. M., & Riise, H. (2005). Coach-athlete relationship. In J. Taylor & G. S. Wilson (Eds.), *Applying sport psychology: Four perspectives* (pp. 153–170). Champaign, IL: Human Kinetics.

Killeya-Jones, L. A. (2005). Identity structure, role discrepancies, and psychological adjustment in male college athletes. *Journal of Sport Behavior, 28,* 167–185.

Koch, J. R., Roberts, A. E., Armstrong, M. L., & Owen, D. C. (2010). Body art, deviance, and American college students. *The Social Science Journal, 47,* 151–161. doi:10.1016/j.soscij.2009.10.001

Kokotailo, P. K., Henry, B. C., Koscik, R. E., Fleming, M. F., & Landry, G. L. (1996). Substance use and other risk behaviors in collegiate athletes. *Clinical Journal of Sport Medicine, 6,* 183–189. doi:10.1097/ 00042752-199607000-00008

Kolt, G. S. (2000). Doing sport psychology with injured athletes. In M. B. Andersen (Ed.), *Doing sport psychology* (pp. 223–236). Champaign, IL: Human Kinetics.

Kolt, G. S., & Andersen, M. B. (2004). *Psychology in the physical and manual therapies.* Edinburgh, Scotland: Churchill Livingstone. doi:10. 1016/B978-0-443-07352-6.50006-3

Lapchick, R. E. (1989). The high school student-athlete: Root of the ethical issues in college sport. In R. E. Lapchick & J. B. Slaughter (Eds.), *The rules of the game* (pp. 17–28). New York, NY: Macmillan.

Martens, M. P., Dams-O'Connor, K., & Beck, N. C. (2006). A systematic review of college student athlete drinking: Prevalence rates, sports-related factors, and interventions. *Journal of Substance Abuse Treatment, 31,* 305–316. doi:10.1016/j.jsat.2006.05.004

Marx, J., Huffman, S., & Doyle, A. (2008). The student-athlete model and the socialization of intercollegiate athletes. *Athletic Insight: The Online Journal of Sport Psychology, 10*(1). Retrieved from http://www. athleticinsight.com/Vol10Iss1/StudentAthleteModel.htm

Mayers, L. B., Judelson, D. A., Moriarty, B. W., & Rundell, K. W. (2002). Prevalence of body art (body piercing and tattooing) in university undergraduates and incidence of medical complications. *Mayo Clinic Proceedings, 77,* 29–34. doi:10.4065/77.1.29

McCabe, S. E., Brower, K. J., West, B. T., Nelson, T. F., & Wechsler, H. (2007). Trends in non-medical use of anabolic steroids by U.S. college students: Results from four national surveys. *Drug and Alcohol Dependence, 90,* 243–251. doi:10.1016/j.drugalcdep.2007.04.004

McGlone, C. A. (2005). Hazing in NCAA Division I women's athletics: An exploratory analysis. *Dissertation Abstracts International: Section A, The Humanities and Social Sciences, 66,* 1690.

National Collegiate Athletic Association. (2001). *NCAA study of substance use habits of college student-athletes.* Indianapolis, IN: Author.

National Collegiate Athletic Association. (2005). *NCAA study of substance use habits of college student-athletes.* Retrieved from http://www.ncaa publications.com/productdownloads/SAHS09.pdf

National Collegiate Athletic Association. (2009). *2009–10 NCAA guide for the college-bound student-athlete: Where academic and athletics success is your goal.* Retrieved from http://www.ncaastudent.org/NCAA_Guide.pdf

National Collegiate Athletic Association Academic and Membership Affairs Staff. (2010). *2010–2011 NCAA Division I Manual.* Indianapolis, IN: NCAA Academic and Membership Affairs Staff.

O'Brien, C. P., & Lyons, F. (2000). Alcohol and the athlete. *Sports Medicine, 29,* 295–300. doi:10.2165/00007256-200029050-00001

Oliard, M. (2009). *Bowled over: Big-time college football from the sixties to the BCS era.* Chapel Hill: University of North Carolina Press.

Oppenheimer, B. (1984). Short-term small group intervention for college freshmen. *Journal of Counseling Psychology, 31,* 45–53. doi:10.1037/0022-0167.31.1.45

Papanikolaou, Z., Nikolaidis, D., Patsiaouras, A., & Alexopoulos, P. (2003). The freshman experience: High stress-low grades. *Athletic Insight: The Online Journal of Sports Psychology.* Retrieved from http://www.athletic insight.com/Vol5Iss4/Commentary.htm

Parham, W. D. (1996). Diversity within intercollegiate athletics: Current profile and welcomed opportunities. In E. F. Etzel, A. P. Ferrante, & J. W. Pinkney (Eds.), *Counseling college student athletes: Issues and interventions* (2nd ed., pp. 27–54). Morgantown, WV: Fitness Information Technology.

Parker, R. M., Lambert, M. J., & Burlington, G. M. (1994). Pathological features of female runners presenting with pathological weight control behaviors. *Journal of Sport & Exercise Psychology, 16,* 119–134.

Petitpas, A. J., & France, T. (2010). Identity foreclosure in sport. In S. J. Hanrahan & M. B. Andersen (Eds.), *Routledge handbook of applied sport psychology: A comprehensive guide for students and practitioners* (pp. 282–291). London, England: Routledge.

Petrie, T. A. (1993). Disordered eating in female collegiate gymnasts: Prevalence and personality/attitudinal correlates. *Journal of Sport & Exercise Psychology, 15,* 424–436.

Petrie, T. A., & Greenleaf, C. (2007). Eating disorders in sport: From theory to research to intervention. In G. Tenenbaum & R. Eklund (Eds.), *Handbook of sport psychology* (3rd ed., pp. 352–378). New York, NY: Wiley. doi:10.1002/9781118270011.ch16

Petrie, T. A., & Greenleaf, C. (2010). Male and female athletes with eating disorders. In S. J. Hanrahan & M. B. Andersen (Eds.), *Routledge handbook of applied sport psychology: A comprehensive guide for students and practitioners* (pp. 224–232). London, England: Routledge.

Petrie, T. A., Hankes, D., & Denson, E. (2010). *A student athlete's guide to college success* (3rd ed.). Boston, MA: Wadsworth/Cengage Learning.

Pew Research Center for the People & the Press. (2007). How young people view their lives, futures and politics: A portrait of Generation Next. Retrieved from http://people-press.org/reports/pdf/300.pdf

Pinkney, J. W. (1996). Coaching student-athletes toward academic success. In E. F. Etzel, A. P. Ferrante, & J. W. Pinkney (Eds.), *Counseling college student athletes: Issues and interventions* (2nd ed., pp. 309–332). Morgantown, WV: Fitness Information Technology.

Rainie, L., & Horrigan, J. A. (2005). Decade of adoption: How the Internet has woven itself into American life. *Pew Internet and American Life*

Project. Retrieved from http://www.pewinternet.org/pdfs/Internet_Status_2005.pdf

Rosen, L., & Hough, D. (1988). Pathogenic weight control behaviors of female college gymnasts. *The Physician and Sportsmedicine, 16*(9), 141–144.

Schmidt, M., & Armstrong, M. (2007). Tattooing and body piercing. *UptoDate.* Retrieved from http://www.uptodate.com/patients/content/topic.do?topicKey=~F9D93_pPmRU_d9

Shanoff, D., & Lipsyte, R. (2005). Should college athletes be paid? *Espn. com.* Retrieved from http://sports.espn.go.com/espn/page2/story?page=shanoff/lipsyte/050316

Sperber, M. (1990). *College sports, Inc.: The athletic department vs. the university.* New York, NY: Holt.

Splitt, F. G. (2010). *Reclaiming academic primacy and integrity in higher education.* Retrieved from http://drakegroupblog.files.wordpress.com/2013/01/splitt_reclaiming_2010.pdf

Stice, E., & Shaw, H. (2004). Eating disorder prevention programs: A meta-analytic review. *Psychological Bulletin, 130,* 206–227. doi:10.1037/0033-2909.130.2.206

Thompson, R. A., & Sherman, R. (1993). *Helping athletes with eating disorders.* Champaign, IL: Human Kinetics.

Title IX, Education Amendments, 20 U.S. C. § 1681–1688 (1972).

Tunick, R., Etzel, E., Leard, J., & Lerner, B. (1996). Counseling injured and disabled student athletes: A guide for understanding and intervention. In E. F. Etzel, A. P. Ferrante, & J. W. Pinkney (Eds.), *Counseling college student athletes: Issues and interventions* (2nd ed., pp. 157–184). Morgantown, WV: Fitness Information Technology.

Van Raalte, J. L., Cornelius, A. E., Linder, D. E., & Brewer, B. W. (2007). The relationship between hazing and team cohesion. *Journal of Sport Behavior, 30,* 491–507.

Watson, A., & Martin, M. (1998). Sexual activity and condom use in female collegiate athletes versus non-athletes. *Journal of Athletic Training, 33*(Suppl. 2), S611.

Watson, J. C. (2002). Assessing the potential for alcohol-related issues among college student-athletes. *Athletic Insight: The Online Journal of Sport Psychology, 4*(3), 14–27. Retrieved from http://www.athletic insight.com/Vol4Iss3/AlcoholAssessment.htm

Watson, J. C. (2005). College student athletes' attitudes toward a help-seeking behavior and expectations of counseling services. *Journal of College Student Development, 46,* 442–449. doi:10.1353/csd.2005.0044

Watson, J. C., & Kissinger, D. B. (2007). Athletic participation and wellness: Implications for counseling college student-athletes. *Journal of College Counseling, 10,* 153–162. doi:10.1002/j.2161-1882.2007.tb00015.x

Wiese, D. M., & Weiss, M. R. (1987). Psychological rehabilitation and physical injury: Implications for the sportsmedicine team. *The Sport Psychologist, 1,* 318–330.

Wilson, R., & Wolverton, B. (2008, January 11). The new face of college sports. *The Chronicles of Higher Education.* Retrieved from http://thecollegeconnection.net/images/The_New_Face_of_College_Sports.pdf

Wrisberg, C. A., & Johnson, M. S. (2002). Quality of life. In M. Kellmann (Ed.), *Enhancing recovery: Preventing underperformance in athletes* (pp. 253–267). Champaign, IL: Human Kinetics.

Patrick H. F. Baillie, Henry Davis IV, and Bruce C. Ogilvie

Working With Elite Athletes 18

Working With Elite Athletes

If applied sport psychology has a particular area of glamour, it likely rests in the realm of providing services to elite athletes. We define *elite athletes* as those whose pursuit of excellence in sport has led to their participation and success in competition at the Olympic or professional level. Unfortunately, among some practitioners there is a tendency to promote themselves on the basis of the number of medals or championship teams

Dr. Ogilvie died in 2003. He was a coauthor on previous editions of this chapter and made innumerable important contributions to sport psychology, often through his work with elite athletes.

The authors thank Ken Ravizza, who provided commentary and suggestions on an earlier publication of this chapter.

Correspondence concerning this chapter should be addressed to Patrick Baillie, PhD, Alberta Health Services, 3500 26th Avenue N.E., Calgary, Alberta, Canada, T1Y 6J4.

http://dx.doi.org/10.1037/14251-018
Exploring Sport and Exercise Psychology, Third Edition, J. Van Raalte and B. Brewer (Editors)

with which they have been associated. More appropriately, in our view, working with elite athletes should be seen as an opportunity to work with talented and dedicated clients, athletes who have reached the pinnacle of their particular sports.

In this chapter, we address some of the unique issues facing both the sport psychology client and practitioner, including gaining entry and acceptance with Olympic and professional athletes, recognizing differences between work with teams and work with individuals, coping with the distractions and obligations that face athletes and sport psychology consultants at this level of competition, and evaluating the ongoing effectiveness of sport science consultation as related not only to the athlete psychologically but also to the full spectrum of sport performance. Although there is no doubt that there are special pleasures that may come from working with elite athletes, there are also specific perils about which a prepared consultant must be aware.

Work with elite athletes brings into play special challenges for the sport psychology consultant (McCann, 2008; Van Raalte, 1998, Wylleman & Johnson, 2012). It is more than an extension of services offered to amateur sports clubs and other competitors. Travel schedules can disrupt the regularity of involvement; the media may look to the sport psychology consultant for that extra insight or news tip; administrative structures may become increasingly burdensome; substance abuse issues may put the sport psychology consultant in an ethical or even a legal dilemma; and mental health issues may necessitate external psychiatric consultation. The sport psychology consultant at the contemporary elite level usually works within a multidisciplinary sport science team requiring essential, regular, time-consuming, and ethically challenging collaborations between professionals. At times, the consultation process fails, leading to changes in service delivery—changes that may even include abrupt termination of the consultation contract.

The Starting Point: Gaining Entry With Elite Athletes

The image that sport psychology consultants present at their first meeting with elite athletes will often characterize the nature and duration of the professional relationship. Honesty, genuineness, and the ability to earn athletes' trust are frequently mentioned as essential elements on which practitioners build their reputation (Ravizza, 1988). Gardner (2001) noted:

> In certain respects, those in professional sports are suspicious and cynical about the value of psychology. Many in the field have

previously oversold the value of their services or have been less than open and honest in describing the limits of their training and education. This has resulted in a situation in which those psychologists seeking to work in professional sports have had to overcome the negative experiences and misconceptions of others before even having the opportunity to demonstrate their skills. (p. 37)

STRATEGIES FOR ACCESS TO AND ACCEPTANCE BY PROFESSIONAL AND OLYMPIC ATHLETES

It is essential for sport psychology consultants to use a variety of methods to gain access to and acceptance by professional and Olympic athletes (see Exhibit 18.1). Many athletes and coaches realize the importance of sport psychology, but their enthusiasm for working with a mental training consultant may not be informed by a full appreciation of the skill-set differences between mental trainers and licensed and registered psychologists who work in sport. Moreover, coaches may feel that sport psychology techniques such as goal setting, focus control, and avoidance of burnout are basic skills that fall under the coach's purview. Athletes, on the other hand, may believe that consultation with a sport psychology consultant is an admission of weakness, although research has indicated that athletes (in this case, football players) do not derogate other athletes who consult sport psychologists (Van Raalte, Brewer, Brewer, & Linder, 1992). Other significant barriers to the involvement of a sport psychology consultant are negative connotations associated with the image of a

EXHIBIT 18.1

Strategies for Gaining Access to and Acceptance by Professional and Olympic Athletes

1. Gain experience working with athletes in a variety of settings, including schools and universities, local sports clubs, development teams, and other amateur organizations.
2. Develop name recognition by volunteering with sports teams, presenting at coaching clinics, working with individual athletes, making cold calls to sports organizations and following up with written materials, and giving public presentations or lectures to other interested audiences.
3. Accurately assess the needs of athletes, rather than imposing any sort of predetermined program developed elsewhere. Assessment includes identification of the athletes' strengths, requirements, experiences with applied sport psychology, and interests in performance enhancement and mental training.
4. Be sensitive to the needs of the athletes, be flexible in scheduling, provide support for the athletes, and provide clear strategies with a positive focus.
5. Use language that is appropriate to the sport setting, emphasizing plain language, direct communication, and simple ideas instead of psychological jargon. Knowledge and use of terms related to player positions, game rules, and sport strategies assists in the development of early rapport.

"shrink" (Linder, Brewer, Van Raalte, & De Lange, 1991), lack of sport-specific knowledge by the practitioner (Porter, 2008; Van Raalte, 1998), a practitioner's lack of experience in working with mental illness within the sport environment, and general lack of experience with the elite sport environment (Ravizza, 1988). Ravizza (1988) recommended using terms such as *mental training* or *mental toughness* instead of *sport psychology* because athletes are likely to be more comfortable with these alternatives. For athletes referred to a sport psychology consultant, feelings of paranoia are not uncommon (Ogilvie, 1979). These will be managed in most cases if the practitioner demonstrates an on-the-field comfort with working in the elite competitive and training settings. Supervised experience with amateur sports clubs or with college teams provides the practitioner with exposure to the sport and to introductory administrative issues. As the past several years have shown, with huge athlete contracts, constraints on Olympic program funding, and strikes or lock-outs in major professional team sports, elite athletics is business driven, and sport psychology consultants often need to immediately prove to be worth their fees. On-the-job training is almost nonexistent.

Sport psychology positions working with elite athletes are scarce and are rarely advertised. In North America, there are about half a dozen full-time positions working with Olympic athletes, perhaps 25 to 50 practitioners working with professional sports teams, and a slightly higher number consulting part time with Olympic athletes. For a handful of skilled practitioners, years of experience and a track record of proficiency may lead to unsolicited offers of employment. For slightly more, presentations at coaching conferences, publications in popular magazines or books, and involvement with development teams serve to provide name recognition when approaching teams or national governing bodies (NGBs), the organizations that allocate funding and determine policy for Olympic sports. Experience, in short, helps, but cold calls and other sales techniques are required before a novice practitioner is able to get a foot in the door. Among other strategies, experience with a single team member, collegiality with an administrator, or the willingness to start with volunteer services have proven to be useful approaches (Carr, 2007).

Care must be exercised, however, never to violate the principles of responsible caring embodied in the sport psychology consultant's or mental trainer's codes of professional conduct. These principles strike at the heart of responsible professionalism, and they are often contradicted when a practitioner uses an athlete to build his or her professional reputation or to gain a contract with a sport organization. The athlete must first fully understand and approve of the requisite limited disclosures and, in addition, must appreciate the consequences, foreseen and unforeseen, for the athlete if the practitioner gains this "foot in the door."

Understanding athletes' motivation and commitment is an important step in earning their respect and trust. As a result, Ravizza (1988), Orlick (1989), and some of the contributors to special editions of *The Sport Psychologist* (i.e., Botterill, 1990; Ravizza, 1990), *Psychology of Sport and Exercise* (Wylleman & Johnson, 2012), and the *Journal of Sport Psychology in Action* (Fletcher, 2012) have recommended that the consultation process include a focus on mental preparation (Stambulova, Stambulov, & Johnson, 2012) and detailed assessment of athlete and team needs rather than on the imposition of a packaged program and an evaluation of sport psychology consultant effectiveness (Haberl & McCann, 2012). Orlick (1989) stated, "I never begin an individual consultation session with a preconceived notion of what a particular high performance athlete might want or need. Each one has different needs, and these needs differ at various times in his or her career" (pp. 358–359). Orlick described beginning the assessment by discussing athletes' goals, their experiences with mental preparation, and identification of mental tasks that require focused work. This type of assessment can then form the basis of a working relationship between sport psychology consultant and athlete prior to the Olympic Games (Birrer, Wetzel, Schmid, & Morgan, 2012; Pensgaard & Abrahamsen, 2012). Ravizza (1988) added that the practitioner must also determine how to integrate mental skills training into the coach's schedule so as to minimize disruption. Coaches are likely to be more comfortable with a consultant who provides assurances that sport psychology interventions are intended to complement the coach's role and not to impinge on typical coaching domains such as skill acquisition, game strategy, and roster decisions.

In possibly the most comprehensive component analysis of service delivery to date, Poczwardowski and Sherman (2011) used interviews with expert consultants to expand on their earlier work and to outline a revised sport psychology service delivery (SPSD) heuristic. The (perhaps too) simplified understanding of the current expert opinion on the necessary elements of effective delivery may be summarized by two factors: the necessity for consultants to appreciate and evaluate clients' goals, needs, and personality and the importance of consultants' self-awareness and regulation of individual characteristics, capabilities, philosophy, and ethics (Henriksen & Diment, 2011; Poczwardowski & Sherman, 2011; Poczwardowski, Sherman, & Ravizza, 2004).

Athletes also may need sport psychology consultants to be sensitive to scheduling issues. Given the pressures and commitments of elite-level athletic competition, several authors (e.g., Botterill, 1990; Halliwell, 1990) have suggested that time with family is important for the athlete and that sport psychology interventions offered on road trips, when downtime is more common, may be better received. Other dimensions of access will likely reflect the practitioner's own values, such as being in the locker room before games, on the field during practices, or in a conveniently located arena office. Preferences vary.

> I have found that I can be most effective by keeping a low profile and being available on planes, buses, or in my hotel room. An open-door policy based upon a genuine interest in each player has proven to be the most effective approach for me. (Ogilvie, 1979, p. 51)

Working to develop a long-term relationship between a sport psychology consultant and a team (or individual athlete) enhances learning for the consultant and may create the opportunity for broader types of psychological interventions to be provided with the team (Shambrook, 2009).

Personality may also play a central role in determining the goodness of fit between an athlete or team and a practitioner. Orlick and Partington (1987) surveyed 75 Canadian Olympic athletes and found that sport psychology consultants were given positive evaluations when they were accessible, flexible, seen to have something concrete to offer, willing to provide athlete-specific input, and able to assist athletes in overcoming problems. Gould, Murphy, Tammen, and May (1991) found that effectiveness of consultants was highly correlated with their fitting in with the team, drawing on the athletes' strengths, being trustworthy, having a positive focus, and providing clear strategies—with some of these aspects being emphasized within the revised SPSD heuristic described previously (Poczwardowski & Sherman, 2011). Similarly, Anderson, Miles, Robinson, and Mahoney (2004) found that sport psychology consultants who were good communicators, were knowledgeable about sport, provided feedback, and used appropriate service delivery formats were viewed favorably by athletes. Negative evaluations were centered on sport psychology consultants who lacked sensitivity, failed to provide sufficient feedback, had poor application of psychology to sport, and whose interpersonal styles were described among other things as wimpy or domineering. Orlick and Partington concluded, "As a result of this study, . . . we have become acutely aware of the importance of having people with the right kind of personal qualities enter the field" (pp. 16–17).

For many elite athletes, appropriate service delivery includes performance as well as mental health issues. Although the prevalence of depression among intercollegiate athletes may be the same as or lower than that of nonathletes (Proctor & Boan-Lenzo, 2010; Storch, Storch, Killiany, & Roberti, 2005), data collected within a larger study (Davis, Liotti, Ngan, Smith, & Mayberg, 2008) indicated that the prevalence of depression among elite swimmers—defined as those with a reasonable expectation that their expert preparation provides them good odds of doing well at the Olympic Trials—may be higher than reported in studies that have not set a high enough standard for the classification of "elite" (e.g., Yang et al., 2007). Indeed, a study of 50 elite swimmers confirmed these earlier results, indicating a 34% prevalence of depression diagnosed according to the *Diagnostic and Statistical Manual of Mental Disorders* (4th ed., text revision; American Psychiatric Association, 2000) among those who had failed performances in major competition. This is roughly twice what is the widely reported prevalence for university students who are not classed as elite athletes (Hammen, Gialloreto, Kubas, & Davis, in press; Storch et al., 2005).

Sport psychology consultants who are trained to work with elite athletes' concerns with regard to performance, training, and mental health (up to and including postperformance suicidal ideation) may be particularly competent to work with elite performers (Davis & Baillie, 2009). However, those practicing from a clinical perspective should be cautious in the use of diagnostic labels and psychological terms that can be perceived unfavorably by coaches and athletes. Adjusting language to develop rapport and meet the needs of clients is a valuable approach.

NEGOTIATING AND DETAILING THE TERMS OF CONSULTATION

There are three broad categories of services widely offered by team sport psychology consultants: (a) performance enhancement, (b) clinical or counseling services, and (c) psychological testing (Gardner, 2001). Multiple models of service delivery exist within applied sport psychology, which are related to practitioners' self-perceived competencies, coaching philosophies, and team and athlete needs. For example, both Ravizza (1990) and Rotella (1990) presented educational models that consist of information, practice, and support for athletes that is performance-enhancement centered and avoids counseling and player selection. Dorfman (1990) offered a combined clinical and educational approach with personal and family counseling and encouraged referrals for drug rehabilitation, financial advice, and academic assistance. Neff (1990) described a wide-ranging employee assistance program with a professional sports organization, including personal counseling and testing. Gardner (2001) stated that informal discussion among sport psychology consultants "suggests that more teams use psychologists in . . . predraft testing . . . than [in] any other professional function" (p. 37). Ziemainz, Neumann, Rasche, and Stemmler (2006) reported that most sport psychology consultants (87.5% of a German sample) use standardized sport-specific tests in their work with athletes and coaches. Murphy (1988) compared medical, consultation, and educational models in applied sport psychology and recommended a consultation-type model drawn from a base in industrial and organizational psychology.

Service delivery models may be shaped by the needs of the team or NGB. Sport psychology consultants are generally brought in to meet a particular organizational need, although over time, their roles and responsibilities may grow. Gardner (2001) provided a personal example of being brought into a professional sports organization for the purpose of providing predraft assessments. His work with the team later developed into the provision of performance enhancement services and coach–athlete relationship development.

The issue of philosophy of service delivery should be clarified before a contract between practitioner and client is formalized. Recommendations regarding the content of the contract are presented in Exhibit 18.2. Essential elements include financial terms, clarification of access, clarification of role, and details of the referral process. Specific services to be provided will vary, as will the amount of time to be provided by the practitioner, the term of the contract, and the level of compensation.

When using an employee assistance program as the model of service, the sport psychology consultant should take extra care to clarify referral procedures and payment of costs associated with outside services, (e.g., substance abuse programs, family counseling, financial management professionals). Because confidentiality issues can limit the ability of practitioners to make referrals (e.g., the sport psychology consultant may be put in a position of having to disclose personal information about an athlete before the team or NGB may authorize funds for other treatment), consultants may have to make independent decisions to spend a significant amount of a team's or an NGB's money or to affect training and travel schedules should the needs of the athlete include comprehensive treatment alternatives.

EXHIBIT 18.2

Recommendations for the Content of a Contract for Sport Psychology Services With Elite Athletes

---

1. Financial terms
   a. Determine an appropriate level of compensation for services rendered.
   b. Attempt to avoid contracts based on barter, particularly with individual athletes.
   c. Specify the time period during which the contract is in effect.
   d. Identify escape clauses through which either side may prematurely terminate services, with associated periods of notification.
2. Contract for sufficient orientation
   a. Present orientation workshops for the entire coaching staff.
   b. Schedule individual meetings with each athlete.
3. Professional issues
   a. Detail professional boundaries (e.g., confidentiality, access to the sport psychology consultant including online methods such as Skype or instant messaging, potential research or testing activities).
   b. Describe specific competencies.
   c. Explain the referral process.

In addition to service delivery issues, contracts generally list fees for services provided per session or per season. Rates may be similar to those charged for psychological services or, in the case of season-long contracts, business consultation. Some sport psychology consultants use a barter system for payment, for example, accepting season tickets in trade for sport psychology consulting. Sport psychology consultants are advised to review the relevant literature on the impact of remuneration on therapeutic outcome (e.g., Cerney, 1991; Yoken & Berman, 1987) before accepting this type of payment. Barter should be avoided when clinically contraindicated and/or when exploitative.

Even less financially rewarding than barter are *reverse contracts*. Here, in exchange for being allowed to promote association with an especially prominent athlete or team, sport psychology consultants actually compensate the team for the privilege of that association. A cash payment to the team or providing services for no fee may be part of these contracts. We believe that a fee-for-services model is ideal because the value that the team or athlete writes into the practitioner's contract is an early reflection of the importance or relevance that the client is giving to sport psychology consulting.

The contract is also an appropriate place to clarify issues around competencies of the sport psychology consultant. For example, sport psychology consultants might offer services that are in high demand by athletes, such as concentration and attention training, stress management, relaxation, self-talk, competition planning, monitoring and evaluation, imagery, precompetition planning, goal setting, and interpersonal communication (Gould et al, 1991; Partington & Orlick, 1991). Practitioners might also address career transition planning, eating disorders, substance abuse concerns, personal development issues, and crisis management, depending on their training and the needs and interests of the athletes or teams.

Crises are inevitable, and sport psychology consultants can be expected, with little warning, to be called on to aid in the resolution of complex critical problems. For example, McCabe (2010) described the role played by mental training consultant Wayne Halliwell with Joannie Rochette when Ms. Rochette's mother died suddenly, just days before Ms. Rochette was scheduled to compete in the 2010 Winter Olympic Games in Vancouver.

This situation and others like it are most easily handled by sport psychology consultants who have defined their roles and developed relationships with athletes, teams, medical personnel, sport science staff (e.g., exercise physiologists, nutritionists, strength trainers, biomechanists), sport organizations, and NGBs. When meeting with athletes, sport psychology consultants generally describe sport psychology strategies and interventions and detail the nature of privileged communication. The central theme of conversations with teams and athletes may be that sport psychology services are tailored to match their interests and concerns. Meetings with relevant team personnel such as coaches, athletic trainers, sport scientists, and team physicians can be used to introduce sport psychology services, answer questions, discuss how services can best be provided, explain how referrals are effectively made, and convey the idea that sport psychology practitioners can help team personnel meet their personal goals while respecting their individual expertise and needs. Protocols are often developed to ensure proper support for elite athletes and teams and for the full and appropriate use of sport psychology consultants, medical staff, and sport science practitioners. Specification of professional boundaries relating to test materials, the voluntary nature of athlete involvement, confidentiality, and the referral process should be included in such protocols to ensure that services will be delivered within the ethical framework of the field. Many problems will be prevented through the development of an appropriate contract such as that presented in Exhibit 18.3.

Working Ethically With Elite Athletes

The single most important ethical issue to face a sport psychology consultant working with elite athletes is clarification of exactly who is the client. Is the practitioner's primary allegiance to the athlete, coach, general manager, or NGB? The nature of the relationship to the primary client, subsumed within this issue, is the protection of the privacy of the client. It is an important but manageable challenge to design a collaborative model that balances a respect for privacy with competition goals. The basic framework must be clarified during initial negotiations but is likely to require careful modification throughout the term of the contract.

Haberl and Peterson (2006) summarized the most predictable domains of sport psychology practice in which ethics questions are likely to arise. These include travel and accommodation with teams, together with dual and multiple relationships. For example, at an Olympic Games, a sport psychology consultant might sit at a meal with an athlete who makes negative comments about a teammate who has choked under pressure. "Is it possible for a sport psychology consultant to help teammates who are chokers?" the athlete asks. All eyes turn to the sport psychology consultant, who may be working with the teammate in question and possibly also with the athlete speaking and members of the coaching staff.

Andersen, Van Raalte, and Brewer (2001) noted that the looser boundaries often involved in working with elite athletes can contribute to complicated ethical dilemmas. Vernacchia and Henschen (2008) also

EXHIBIT 18.3

Sample Contract for the Provision of Sport Psychology Services

1. This agreement is between [the sport psychologist(s)] and [the client(s)] for the provision of sport psychology services by [the sport psychologist(s)] with [the client(s)].
2. The agreement covers the period between [the present date or the first day of the season] and [1 year less a day from the present date or the last possible day of competition]. Either party may terminate services at any time on written notice [1 month] prior to the termination.
3. Areas in which [the sport psychologist] is competent to provide service include (add or delete as applicable) goal setting, stress management, substance abuse counseling, focus control, psychometric assessment, marital or couples counseling, imagery, precompetition and competition planning, crisis management, interpersonal communication, self-talk strategies, and regulation of arousal. Data collection for research by the sport psychologist, assessments of draft prospects, and other services will be negotiated separately.
4. Required services outside of these areas of competence will be accessed through referrals at the discretion of [the sport psychologist], wherever possible in consultation with [the client] and with the chief physician. Costs associated with additional treatment resources will be paid by [the client]. Such services may include substance abuse treatment, family or marital counseling, or career transition programs.
5. Fees for the provision of sport psychology services by [the sport psychologist] will be in the amount of $[   ], to be paid in [   ] equal installments, on [date(s)] by [the client].
6. The nature and content of all services provided by [the sport psychologist] to an individual athlete are privileged and will not be disclosed by [the sport psychologist] to anyone without the written consent of the athlete. The nature and content of services provided to the team as a whole are also privileged and will not be disclosed outside of the team by [the sport psychologist] without the written consent of [the head coach].
7. (When working with a team or national governing body) [The sport psychologist] will consult [every 2 weeks] with [the head coach] to discuss issues of team cohesion, communication, mental focus, and other topics determined by mutual concern.
8. At a time agreed on by the parties, [the sport psychologist] will hold an introductory meeting with [the athlete(s)] to outline expectations for the provision of sport psychology services. This meeting will outline the training and background of [the sport psychologist], services to be offered, relevant readings, ethical standards, and scheduling and will include time to answer questions from [the athlete(s)]. Meetings with each individual athlete will be arranged at times of mutual convenience.
9. At a time agreed on by the parties, [the sport psychologist] will meet separately with the coaching staff, the medical staff, and any other team personnel as may be appropriate, to outline the training and background of [the sport psychologist], services to be offered, procedures for interdisciplinary consultation, relevant readings, ethical standards, and scheduling, and to answer questions from each of these groups.
10. Any modifications to this agreement must be made by mutual consent of the parties.
    Dated [date] at [city]
    Signed [the sport psychologist] [name of the sport psychologist printed]
    [the athlete or head coach] [name of the signatory/client printed]

Note. Fees may cover all or part of the services to be provided. When the fees cover preseason training and regular contact during the season but not crisis management issues or other circumstances such as attendance at nonlocal competitions, additional fees should be specified in the contract. An informal survey by Patrick H. F. Baillie and Henry Davis IV suggests that fees for a season of service to a professional team range from barter for a pair of season tickets to over $50,000. Fees for a year of service with college and university teams range from $0 for pro bono work covered by primary employment in the counseling center to over $200,000 for private sport psychology consultants.

identified myriad consulting challenges that can contribute to ethical challenges at an Olympic Games, such as staff stress, "physical bankruptcy," drug testing, and injury. More specifically, Vernacchia and Henschen recounted the experience of working with an athlete who was in need of an immediate X-ray before being cleared to compete in the Olympic Games. As a result of bureaucratic issues, the test would not be paid for by the team, and therefore the athlete would not be cleared and would have to withdraw from the Games. Although the sport psychologist could have afforded to pay for the test, he instead was able to help facilitate treatment with the physician, thus avoiding a dual relationship (i.e., sport psychology consultant and financial supporter).

RESPECTING BOUNDARIES BETWEEN ADMINISTRATORS, COACHES, AND ATHLETES

In working with teams, the sport psychology consultant may find varying levels of acceptance among the athletes. Issues such as history with other consultants, overall trust, cultural background, and personal motivation influence the comfort of athletes in seeking mental skills training. Ravizza (1988) suggested that three groups may arise: "In general, I find that about one third of the athletes on a team are very receptive to the program in the beginning, one third will seek it out when they are struggling, and one third are not receptive" (p. 249). Put simply, not all members of a team will feel comfortable in accessing sport psychology services. Practitioners must identify whether they need to address this reluctance or allow for a more gradual building of acceptance by the team. Goodness of fit applies to the whole team and the sport psychology consultant, not necessarily each team member.

Working with individual athletes may result in a reduction of the number of extraneous factors that can disrupt the sport psychology consultant–athlete relationship. For example, when golf or tennis professionals seek service, responsibility is usually restricted to the clients and their agents. Clarification of the role of the sport psychology consultant is relatively straightforward. There are notable occasions, however, when sponsors or parents have, by the nature of their relationship to the athlete, influenced the implementation of mental skills training programs. When service is extended to an entire team or NGB, functioning within established ethical guidelines can be an ongoing challenge. Confidentiality issues often arise as coaches and administrators, understandably seeking accountability from the sport psychology consultant, may ask for information pertaining to services provided to a given athlete, including the content or frequency of sessions. Coaches who use the sport psychology consultant as a sounding board may disclose pending personnel decisions that affect individual athletes but that the sport psychology consultant may not disclose to athletes. As noted, when the trade or cut then comes, athletes may raise hard questions about the allegiances of the sport psychology consultant.

Work with teams generally proceeds only with the approval of the coach. As a result, some practitioners view allegiance to the coach as being a prerequisite to work with sports teams (Ogilvie, 1979; Ravizza, 1990). However, sport psychology consultants who are seen as agents of the coaching staff and who focus primarily on issues raised by coaches are unlikely to be effective. On the other hand, sport psychology consultants who emphasize athlete needs at the expense of the team are not particularly successful. When working with teams and athletes, maintaining a balance between various constituencies and professional ethics can be challenging. Ongoing supervision and a network of professional mentors and colleagues are essential for sport psychology practitioners attempting to manage these myriad challenges and to provide optimal services.

MAINTAINING CONFIDENTIALITY

As stated, potentially one of the most difficult issues facing the sport psychology consultant relates to information gained through work with an individual athlete and about which the coach, other sport science or medical consultants, or team administrators may seek disclosure. Porter (2008) surveyed experienced sport psychology consultants and concluded that maintaining confidentiality was a core ethical challenge in sport psychology service delivery. Similarly, Stapleton, Hankes, Hays, and Parham (2010) noted that maintaining competence, confidentiality, and boundary issues are among the more commonly faced ethical issues in applied sport psychology.

Explicating and reiterating the limits of disclosure in person and in writing as part of a contractual agreement is a good way to start work as a sport psychology consultant. For some athletes, complete confidentiality within legal limits is preferred. For other athletes, such as an athlete with an eating disorder who meets with a physiologist, physician, strength trainer, nutritionist, and sport psychology consultant, limited disclosure among experts to enhance treatment may be preferred. Many athletes choose informed disclosure when the potential benefits are explained, but care must be taken to assure that no athlete feels pressured into giving consent.

Overall, athletes' right to complete privacy is sabotaged by membership on elite teams that receive public attention and, at an Olympic level, public financial support. Even behind the training room door, at this level, athletes are discussed and treated by multidisciplinary teams—not simply by coaches and doctors—and many consider the athletes to be accepting of the open sharing of their personal information. This is not the context described by family practice doctors who practice traditional medical ethics and usually see patients on a 1:1 basis (Bewley, 1997), and it is not the context defined by medical ethicists who delineate patient confidentiality protections that are required by the common practice of sharing patient information electronically (Goldstein, 2010). Rules governing what is known as *autonomous authorization*—wherein a patient deliberates without bias or pressure over whether to accept a medical intervention—are usually not practicable. Elite athletes are expected to consent to as extensive a level of sport science collaboration deemed necessary to maximize the chances to win. This expectation undermines the fundamental principles inherent in informed consent, and this expectation itself must be addressed when the sport psychology consultant and athletes meet to discuss confidentiality. Patrick H. F. Baillie worked in a professional sport with a substance abuse policy that provided for fines "of any team official knowing of a player's drug use and not reporting such use." To respect confidentiality, the contract stated that the team would pay any fines levied against the consultant. This policy was agreed to after extensive discussion and collaboration with administrators. It is advisable that sport psychology consultants repeatedly engage athletes in dialogue over confidentiality so that athletes are afforded an issue-by-issue opportunity to consent to the scope and the way in which their confidential information will be shared.

Distractions and Obligations: Factors That May Impair Peak Performance for Elite Athletes

Competition at the Olympic or professional level may offer athletes the ultimate showcase for their talents. It is also likely to bring into play new time demands; new sources of competitive stress; and other challenges, such as dealing with the media, life on the road, and heightened pressure, either self-imposed or external, for consistent excellence. For the sport psychology consultant, these issues must be addressed to assist athletes in maintaining focus during training and competitions. However, the disturbances also interfere with athletes' time and may, therefore, impinge on access to and the availability of suitable consultation sessions.

COPING WITH TRAVEL, OUTSIDE EMPLOYMENT, AND OTHER DISTRACTIONS

At multisport competitions such as the Olympic Games, the Pan American Games, or the World University Games, athletes are often faced with personal, situational, and an interaction of personal and situational factors

(Gould & Maynard, 2009), such as significant disruptions to training schedules; crowded accommodations; time spent travelling to and from practice venues; and hours spent waiting, eating, making travel arrangements, and trying to e-mail or connect by Skype to home. Greenleaf (1999) found that Olympic athletes responded best to these negative distractions when a plan had been prepared, addressing, for example, how to access friends and family and how and when to interact with media. In short, when the athlete had a sense of control amid changes that sometimes included working with different coaches, such preparation seemed to help. As Canadian diver Eryn Bulmer stated, "Whoever can ignore the distractions the best is going to perform the best. I've learned how to compete under pressure and how to block those things out" (Jones, 2000, p. 8). Giges and Petitpas (2000) offered a framework for brief-contact sport psychology interventions in the field, describing them as time limited, action oriented, and present focused. The advent of convenient and inexpensive communication via texting, e-mail, cell phones, and Skype may assist sport psychology consultants in maintaining contact with clients when they are away for competitions, but the cautious user must consider issues of confidentiality and of interstate (or international) service delivery that are inherent in these technologies.

Most professional sports teams spend half of their season on the road. For golfers, bowlers, and tennis players, among others, the entire season may be spent traveling. Unless well sponsored, Olympic and semiprofessional athletes may need to balance training and competition with the demands of earning a living outside of sport. These and other factors not only conspire against the best performances of the athletes but also affect the delivery of sport psychology services.

Michelle Mullen, a professional bowler interviewed by Gould and Finch (1990), described life on tour as being extremely stressful as a result of struggling to make a living and to maintain a healthy perspective on the role of sport:

> You must be able to keep your bowling in the right regard and not let it become your total life. Sometimes the tour can become so all consuming, and in many ways it has to be. However, you must remember that it's just part of your life and not necessarily the total essence of it (p. 422).

Discussing possible research areas for sport psychology, Mullen noted:

> Interesting things to study have to do with lifestyle and getting an understanding for the stressful lifestyle. It's different in every sport for different reasons. Finances have a lot to do with it, depending on what you're competing for. Understanding what kind of roller coaster it is as a professional athlete, especially the uncertainty . . . dealing with different issues like that, the stress levels are underestimated by far. (Gould & Finch, 1990, p. 426)

Gould and Finch also noted that the stresses related to competing on television in front of audiences of millions, more prevalent in the professional rather than the amateur ranks, can also affect elite athletes' performance.

Botterill (1990) described the importance of spouses, families, and friends in the life of the professional athlete, and therefore, when serving as a sport psychology consultant, he offers his services to these people. Botterill also noted the difficulty of scheduling interventions:

> Road trips often contain unique challenges to work through and players can be more receptive to spending additional time on things on the road. Professional players spend so much time away from home they are often well advised to maximize time with their families when at home. (p. 366)

A broader analysis of the scheduling of interventions suggests that team meetings or coach referrals after a home practice are likely to be met with annoyance and disinterest from team members. Athletes, as noted earlier, like a consultant to be available but flexible. When a program is truly supported by the coaching staff, mental training exercises may replace some or all of the allotted practice time or may be integrated into on-the-field or on-the-court training. Other times for less intrusive interventions include travel times (e.g., at airports or bus stations, en route, at hotels) and during meals. Sport psychology consultants should discuss the issue of scheduling as part of the introductory stage of the consultation. Sensitivity to scheduling so as to avoid adding to the demands on the athlete is likely to be favorably received.

DEALING WITH THE MEDIA

Just as professional sport is a business, so is the media's function in covering it. For this reason, athletes and sport psychology consultants should learn to interact effectively with writers and reporter. Exposure on television, in print, or online (e.g., Facebook, *TMZ Sports,* Twitter, YouTube) may improve the marketability of athletes and consultants, but an ongoing relationship with the media also increases the risk of making a potentially damaging off-the-cuff comment (never off the record—reporters are always researching, even if not actually quoting). The simple fact that an athlete is seeing the shrink or commented about a fellow athlete's or coach's situation may become a story.

In most elite sport organizations, there are public relations staff members who provide excellent counsel regarding media contacts. Reporters gain access to athletes only at limited times, although they may freely editorialize about issues that, when read or seen by athletes, can interfere with their training and competitive focus. Among the worst mistakes that an athlete might make are comments that suggest dissension among team members or that insult opponents, thereby offering a grudge motivation to others. Athletes are, therefore, well-advised to make only comments that describe personal disappointment (e.g., "I felt that I didn't play up to my potential this evening") or that offer positive reflections on team members (e.g., "Mike played hard today and we capitalized on the opportunities he created") or the competition (e.g., "Our opponents played well, so we had to beat a good team"). Generally, athletes should remember that members of the media are dependent on the quotes they receive from their subjects. Athletes who have nothing to say will not be quoted. However, reporters ultimately must find and file a story and will do the best they can with the information offered. Complete avoidance of the media has worked only for rare athletes and is likely to hamper athletes in developing community involvement and potential revenues from endorsements. Careful management of media interactions, then, becomes an asset.

The same concerns that affect athletes with regard to the media may be raised for sport psychology consultants. Directing media to the press officer is often the safest way to avoid an errant comment. When the practitioner becomes the focus of a story, extreme caution must be exercised by the team and by the consultant. Although the original story may be a favorable account of the sport psychology consultant's activities, competing media sources are likely to reframe the idea to boost their own sales. Sport psychology consultants who answer media questions by serving in a broad educational role, for example, describing the purpose and techniques of applied sport psychology in performance enhancement, may serve both their athletes and the field well. Discussing team dynamics, coaching styles, and athlete preparedness may lead to a quick end to the consultant relationship with the sports organization.

Win or Lose, the Season Ends: Reflecting on the Consultation and Planning for the Future

After each involvement with elite athletes, it is important that practitioners undertake an evaluation of the consultation process, including self-assessment and the eliciting of feedback from athletes and/or coaches and administrators. Such a procedure is likely to provide valuable insights that can prepare consultants for future opportunities or for marketing themselves in another setting. The Consultant Evaluation Form developed by Partington and Orlick (1987) and the Characteristics of Effective Sport Psychology Consultants Inventory developed by Lubker, Visek, Geer, and Watson (2008) may be useful tools for this evaluation process.

ASSESSING THE EFFECTIVENESS
OF THE CONSULTATION

In a study of consultants, administrators, coaches, and athletes, Gould et al. (1991) used the Consultant Evaluation Form to assess the characteristics of effective services provided to 25 NGBs. A similar process was used by Orlick and Partington (1987), with both studies providing a practical basis for comparing the results of self-evaluation. The Characteristics of Effective Sport Psychology Consultants Inventory (Lubker et al., 2008) consists of five factors of effective consultants: (a) positive interpersonal skills (e.g., friendly, approachable, trustworthy), (b) physical characteristics (e.g., looks physically fit, dresses similar to coaching staff, of same gender as the sport team), (c) athletic background (e.g., background as competitive athlete, has competed in that sport), (d) professional status (e.g., possesses advanced degree in performance enhancement, is certified), and (e) sport culture (e.g., intelligent, has knowledge of mental skills, able to fit into sport environment).

Ultimately, the goodness of fit with the organization and the use of the sport psychology consultant by the athlete are the measures of overall effect. Shortcomings, however, may be the result of various elements that are beyond the control of the practitioner. Athletes, for example, may fear their coach and, hence, fear the sport psychology consultant whose allegiance has been demanded by the coach. Beginning a consultation in a crisis management mode is also likely to influence its positive utility. The length of the relationship with an athlete or team may affect effectiveness. "Establishing initial rapport with coaches takes time. Yet the pressure on coaches of elite teams is for quick results," wrote Ravizza (1988, p. 247). In contrast, Orlick (1989) stated,

> In my best or most effective consulting situations I have enough time to make a difference, which means multiple contacts at the individual level. . . . Usually it takes about 3 years of ongoing work before things really come together mentally for highly committed athletes. (p. 363)

The evaluation process should include comprehensive assessment of the sport psychology services. This might include assessment of the sport psychology consultant, athletes, coaches, families, and administrators. The information gleaned can help identify program strengths and determine what changes might enhance the implementation of consulting services in the future, even if these are with other athletes, teams, and coaches. For example, the following questions could be posed: Were adequate facilities made available to the consultant? What support did the coach provide for learning and practice of mental skills strategies? Could the issue of confidentiality and privilege have been better introduced or explained? Was enough time made available for consultations? Were team meetings (if any) appropriately scheduled and attended? Were the athletes receptive to sport psychology services? Did athletes and coaches benefit from having a sport psychology consultant on board? If so, how? What were the sport psychology consultant's strengths? What could be done to strengthen the program and delivery of sport psychology services? It should be noted that evaluation of service delivery can occur during as well as after the season.

CONTENDING WITH THE END OF A RELATIONSHIP AND MARKETING ONESELF AGAIN

Athletes retire or are traded; coaches resign or are fired; teams shift priorities or look for scapegoats in seasons of underachievement. For these and other reasons, the job of sport psychology consultant may come to an abrupt end. On occasion, consultants may make decisions to fire themselves.

Whether the practitioner's relationship continues with a team or NGB after significant personnel changes depends on the consultant's ability to market services to the new power brokers. When possible and appropriate, an introduction to the new coach, for example, is best made by the general manager or other team official and done privately, with discussion about the effectiveness of the previous consultation. Sometimes, of course, the departure of a coach or general manager spells the beginning of a major housecleaning that is likely to include the sport psychology consultant. "The sign that you should take your Rorschach cards and run will be when you go to the box office for your free tickets to the game and find that the attendant has forgotten your name" (Ogilvie, 1979, p. 55).

The end of a consulting relationship also offers an appropriate opportunity for self-evaluation. Before heading in search of a new contract, the consultant may find it helpful to reflect on his or her success (or failure) in achieving the objectives of the previous consultation. Even if won–lost ratios and excellence in competition have not changed, more internal variables may be analyzed. These variables include the athletes' knowledge of sport psychology strategies, effective use of the techniques, rapport between the athlete(s) and the sport psychology consultant, utilization of sport psychology services, team cohesion, and athletic skill development, among others. Between contracts is also a good time to consult and connect with colleagues; to attend professional meetings; to catch up with the most recent literature; and to consider necessary changes in service delivery, such as accessibility and availability of the consultant, communication with coaches, team versus individual sessions, and the model of consultation.

Letters of introduction or reference may be a suitable way to mark the end of a positive consultation process while laying the foundation for the next contract. Testimonials, although sometimes acceptable under the American Psychological Association's *Ethical Principles of Psychologists and Code of Conduct* (American Psychological Association, 2010), draw a range of responses from practitioners. Loehr (1990), for example, described negotiating endorsements by athlete-clients in lieu of financial remuneration. Because of the issues of confidentiality and barter raised by this approach, it is widely discouraged. Written evaluations by coaches and NGBs, instead of from athletes themselves, may be a more acceptable method for presenting documentation of previous experiences and accomplishments to potential clients. Cold calls, submission of proposals, networking, updating of websites and blogs, and other procedures used previously may be needed to search for another position.

No doubt, the end of a consultation may begin a trying time for the sport psychology consultant. There may be financial implications and feelings of loss. Trying to find the next job can be just as difficult as trying to find the first. Even a positive reputation as a sport psychology consultant will not necessarily create a new elite- or professional-level position. As a result, the process of marketing, gaining access, and establishing the trust and respect of athletes and coaches begins again.

Summary

In this chapter, we have provided a perspective on the role of the sport psychology consultant working with Olympic and professional athletes. Although this level of competition offers athletes the pinnacle of sport excellence, it introduces challenges for the provision of mental training and interventions. Intervening for performance-enhancement reasons is a routine aspect of working with elite athletes and teams. Less frequent, but often more challenging, is the management of mental health issues, including eating disorders, depression, and on occasion, suicidal gestures. Practitioners intending to work at this level usually must first gain experience in other sport settings to clarify for themselves issues such as the model of service delivery, negotiation of contracts, guarantees regarding confidentiality, and the scope of skills and programs they are competent to offer.

The difficulties of gaining access, earning the trust of athletes and coaches, providing effective service, and evaluating the usefulness of the consultation may make the provision of sport psychology with elite athletes a demanding and, at times, perilous process. As Ravizza (1990) wrote, "In every situation there is an ideal way to do your job, and then there is reality" (p. 331). In their profiles of 10 leading sport psychology consultants, Straub and Hinman (1992) cited the opinion of Tara Scanlan that sport psychology is not for the faint hearted. She advises prospective sport psychologists to seriously assess the strength of their "pioneering spirit." Sport psychologists, Scanlan continues, often have to travel uncharted routes, and they should make sure they can handle the challenges. (p. 307)

References

American Psychiatric Association. (2000). *Diagnostic and statistical manual of mental disorders* (4th ed., text revision). Washington, DC: Author.

American Psychological Association. (2010*). Ethical principles of psychologists and code of conduct (2002, Amended June 1, 2010).* Retrieved from http://www.apa.org/ethics/code/index.aspx

Andersen, M. B., Van Raalte, J. L., & Brewer, B. W. (2001). Sport psychology service delivery: Staying ethical while keeping loose. *Professional Psychology: Research and Practice, 32,* 12–18. doi:10.1037/0735-7028.32.1.12

Anderson, A., Miles, A., Robinson, P., & Mahoney, C. (2004). Evaluating the athlete's perception of the sport psychologist's effectiveness: What should we be assessing? *Psychology of Sport and Exercise, 5,* 255–277. doi:10.1016/S1469-0292(03)00005-0

Bewley, S. (1997). Family secrets: Patients have right to privacy and confidentiality [Letter to the editor]. *BMJ, 315,* 1380. doi:10.1136/bmj.315.7119.1380b

Birrer, D., Wetzel, J., Schmid, J., & Morgan, G. (2012). Analysis of sport psychology consultancy at three Olympic Games: Facts and figures. *Psychology of Sport and Exercise, 13,* 702–710. doi:10.1016/j.psychsport.2012.04.008

Botterill, C. (1990). Sport psychology and professional hockey. *The Sport Psychologist, 4,* 358–368.

Carr, C. M. (2007). A psychologist in the world of intercollegiate sports: Professional development issues. *Journal of Clinical Sport Psychology, 1,* 293–303.

Cerney, M. S. (1991). Reduced fee or free psychotherapy: Uncovering the hidden issues. *Psychotherapy Patient, 7,* 53–65. doi:10.1300/J358v07n01_07

Davis, H., & Baillie, P. H. F. (2009, September). *Mental training and sport psychology at the summer Olympic Games: Ethics and collaboration.* Paper presented at the meeting of the Association of Applied Sport Psychology, Salt Lake City, Utah.

Davis, H., Liotti, M., Ngan, E., Smith, A., & Mayberg, H. S. (2008). fMRI BOLD signal changes in elite swimmers while viewing videos of personal failure: Effects of cognitive reappraisal (CBT). *Brain Imaging and Behavior, 2*, 84–93. doi:10.1007/s11682-007-9016-x

Dorfman, H. A. (1990). Reflections on providing personal and performance enhancement consulting services in professional baseball. *The Sport Psychologist, 4*, 341–346.

Fletcher, D. (2012). An introduction to the special edition: Sport psychology in action at the Olympic and Paralympic Games. *Journal of Sport Psychology in Action, 3*, 61.

Gardner, F. L. (2001). Applied sport psychology in professional sports: The team psychologist. *Professional Psychology: Research and Practice, 32*, 34–39. doi:10.1037/0735-7028.32.1.34

Giges, B., & Petitpas, A. (2000). Brief contact interventions in sport psychology. *The Sport Psychologist, 14*, 176–187.

Goldstein, M. M. (2010). Health information technology and the idea of informed consent. *The Journal of Law, Medicine & Ethics, 38*, 27–35. doi:10.1111/j.1748-720X.2010.00463.x

Gould, D., & Finch, L. (1990). Sport psychology and the professional bowler: The case of Michelle Mullen. *The Sport Psychologist, 4*, 418–430.

Gould, D., & Maynard, I. (2009). Psychological preparation for the Olympic Games. *Journal of Sports Sciences, 27*, 1393–1408. doi:10.1080/02640410903081845

Gould, D., Murphy, S., Tammen, V., & May, J. (1991). An evaluation of U.S. Olympic sport psychology consultant effectiveness. *The Sport Psychologist, 5*, 111–127.

Greenleaf, C. A. (1999, August). Individual interviews with 1998 Nagano Olympic athletes. In D. Gould (Chair), *Factors influencing 1998 U.S. Olympic athlete and coach performance.* Symposium conducted at the meeting of the American Psychological Association, Boston, MA.

Haberl, P., & McCann, S. (2012). Evaluating USOC sport psychology consultant effectiveness: A philosophical and practical imperative at the Olympic Games. *Journal of Sport Psychology in Action, 3*, 65. doi:10.1080/21520704.2012.683095

Haberl, P., & Peterson, K. (2006). Olympic-size ethical dilemmas: Issues and challenges for sport psychology consultants on the road and at the Olympic Games. *Ethics & Behavior, 16*, 25–40. doi:10.1207/s15327019eb1601_4

Halliwell, W. (1990). Providing sport psychology consulting services in professional hockey. *The Sport Psychologist, 4*, 369–377.

Hammen, T., Gialloreto, C., Kubas, H., & Davis, H. (in press). The prevalence of failure based depression among elite athletes. *Clinical Journal of Sport Medicine.*

Henriksen, K., & Diment, G. (2011). Professional philosophy: Inside the delivery of sport psychology service at Team Denmark. *Sport Science Review, 20*, 5–21. doi:10.2478/v10237-011-0043-6

Jones, T. (2000, September 14). Calmer waters: Bulmer a veteran in the Olympic battle of nerves. *Calgary Sun*, Olympics, p. 8.

Linder, D. E., Brewer, B. W., Van Raalte, J. L., & De Lange, N. (1991). A negative halo for athletes who consult sport psychologists: Replication and extension. *Journal of Sport & Exercise Psychology, 13,* 133–148.

Loehr, J. (1990). Providing sport psychology consulting services to professional tennis players. *The Sport Psychologist, 4,* 400–408.

Lubker, J. R., Visek, A. J., Geer, J. R., & Watson, J. C., II. (2008). Characteristics of an effective sport psychology consultant: Perspectives from athletes and consultants. *Journal of Sport Behavior, 31,* 147–165.

McCabe, D. (2010). The mental work behind medals. *McGill News*. Retrieved from http://publications.mcgill.ca/mcgillnews/2010/03/15/the-mental-work-behind-medals/

McCann, S. (2008). At the Olympics everything is a performance issue. *International Journal of Sport and Exercise Psychology, 6,* 267–276. doi:10.1080/1612197X.2008.9671871

Murphy, S. M. (1988). The on-site provision of sport psychology services at the 1987 U.S. Olympic Festival. *The Sport Psychologist, 2,* 337–350.

Neff, F. (1990). Delivering sport psychology services to a professional sport organization. *The Sport Psychologist, 4,* 378–385.

Ogilvie, B. (1979). The sport psychologist and his professional credibility. In P. Klavora & J. V. Daniel (Eds.), *Coach, athlete and the sport psychologist* (pp. 44–55). Champaign, IL: Human Kinetics.

Orlick, T. (1989). Reflections on sportpsych consulting with individual and team sport athletes at Summer and Winter Olympic Games. *The Sport Psychologist, 3,* 358–365.

Orlick, T., & Partington, J. (1987). The sport psychology consultant: Analysis of critical components as viewed by Canadian Olympic athletes. *The Sport Psychologist, 1,* 4–17.

Partington, J., & Orlick, T. (1987). The sport psychology Consultant Evaluation Form. *The Sport Psychologist, 1,* 309–317.

Partington, J., & Orlick, T. (1991). An analysis of Olympic sport psychology consultants' best-ever consulting experiences. *The Sport Psychologist, 5,* 183–193.

Pensgaard, A. M., & Abrahamsen, F. E. (2012). Potentials and pitfalls: Short-term involvement versus long-term involvement in sport psychology with Olympic and Paralympic athletes. *Journal of Sport Psychology in Action, 3,* 119. doi:10.1080/21520704.2012.683088

Poczwardowski, A., & Sherman, C. P. (2011). Revisions to the sport psychology service delivery (SPSD) heuristic: Explorations with experienced consultants. *The Sport Psychologist, 25,* 511–531.

Poczwardowski, A., Sherman, C. P., & Ravizza, K. (2004). Professional philosophy in the sport psychology service delivery: Building on theory and practice. *The Sport Psychologist, 18,* 445–463.

Porter, T. D. (2008). Attitudes and opinions of sport psychologists on training and ethics in sport psychology. *Dissertation Abstracts International: Section B, Sciences and Engineering, 69,* 1340.

Proctor, S. L., & Boan-Lenzo, C. (2010). Prevalence of depressive symptoms in male intercollegiate student-athletes and nonathletes. *Journal of Clinical Sport Psychology, 4,* 204–220.

Ravizza, K. (1988). Gaining entry with athletic personnel for season-long consulting. *The Sport Psychologist, 2,* 243–254.

Ravizza, K. (1990). Sportpsych consultation issues in professional baseball. *The Sport Psychologist, 4,* 330–340.

Rotella, R. J. (1990). Providing sport psychology consulting services to professional athletes. *The Sport Psychologist, 4,* 409–417.

Shambrook, C. (2009). Delivering sport psychology to Olympic rowers: Beyond psychological skills training. In B. Hemmings & T. Holder (Eds.), *Applied sport psychology: A case-based approach* (pp. 111–138). Hoboken, NJ: Wiley-Blackwell.

Stambulova, N., Stambulov, A., & Johnson, U. (2012). Believe in yourself, channel energy, and play your trumps': Olympic preparation in complex coordination sports. *Psychology of Sport and Exercise 13,* 679–686.

Stapleton, A. B., Hankes, D. M., Hays, K. F., & Parham, W. D. (2010). Ethical dilemmas in sport psychology: A dialogue on the unique aspects impacting practice. *Professional Psychology: Research and Practice, 41,* 143–152.

Straub, W. F., & Hinman, D. A. (1992). Profiles and professional perspectives of 10 leading sport psychologists. *The Sport Psychologist, 6,* 297–312.

Storch, E. A., Storch, J. B., Killiany, E. M., & Roberti, J. W. (2005). Self-reported psychopathology in athletes: A comparison of intercollegiate student-athletes and non-athletes. *Journal of Sport Behavior, 28,* 86–98.

Van Raalte, J. L. (1998). Working in competitive sport: What coaches and athletes want psychologists to know. In K. F. Hays (Ed.), *Integrating exercise, sports, movement and mind: Therapeutic unity* (pp. 101–110). Binghamton, NY: Haworth Press. doi:10.1300/J358v10n03_09

Van Raalte, J. L., Brewer, B. W., Brewer, D. D., & Linder, D. E. (1992). NCAA Division II college football players' perceptions of an athlete who consults a sport psychologist. *Journal of Sport & Exercise Psychology, 14,* 273–282.

Vernacchia, R. A., & Henschen, K. P. (2008). The challenge of consulting with track and field athletes at the Olympic Games. *International Journal of Sport and Exercise Psychology, 6,* 254–266. doi:10.1080/1612 197X.2008.9671870

Wylleman, P., & Johnson, U. (2012). Sport psychology and the Olympic Games: An introduction in the special issue. *Psychology of Sport and Exercise, 13,* 658. doi:10.1016/j.psychsport.2012.04.004

Yang, J., Peek-Asa, C., Corlette, J. D., Cheng, G., Foster, D. T., & Albright, J. (2007). Prevalence of and risk factors associated with symptoms of depression in competitive collegiate student athletes. *Clinical Journal of Sport Medicine, 17,* 481–487. doi:10.1097/JSM.0b013e31815aed6b

Yoken, C., & Berman, J. S. (1987). Third-party payment and the outcome of psychotherapy. *Journal of Consulting and Clinical Psychology, 55,* 571–576. doi:10.1037/0022-006X.55.4.571

Ziemainz, H., Neumann, G., Rasche, F., & Stemmler, M. (2006). The application of psychological assessment methods in sport psychology: A survey of sport psychologists in the BISP [German Federal Institute of Sport Science] Sport Psychology Expert Database. *Zeitschrift für Sportpsychologie, 13,* 53–59. doi:10.1026/1612-5010.13.2.53

Stephen P. Gonzalez, Ariane L. Smith Machin, and Karen D. Cogan

Diversity in Sport 19

> If the mental health profession is to receive acceptance from racial/ethnic minority groups, it must demonstrate, in no uncertain terms, its good faith and ability to contribute to the betterment of a group's quality of life.
> —*Sue & Sue (1999, p. 24)*

Despite a long-held belief within the field of counseling psychology concerning the importance of understanding and appreciating individual differences, constructive change in how many mental health professionals work with issues of diversity at the individual and community level has been slow in coming. In 1992, Sue, Arredondo, and McDavis noted that minority clients may be in therapy with professionals who, because of inadequate training, lack the basic competencies for working ethically and effectively with diverse populations. Although there is room for improvement, current accreditation standards of the American Psychological Association (APA) now require that all counseling and clinical psychology graduate programs include relevant course work and ensure that students demonstrate competency in their understanding of and ability to work with issues of diversity. Similarly, the Council for Accreditation of Counseling and Related Educational Programs also requires master's level psychology students to demonstrate competencies in relation to diversity

http://dx.doi.org/10.1037/14251-019
Exploring Sport and Exercise Psychology, Third Edition, J. Van Raalte and
B. Brewer (Editors)

and equity and is required to advocate and be responsive to multicultural students. Furthermore, social and cultural diversity is one of eight core curricular areas required by the Council for Accreditation of Counseling and Related Educational Programs. Finally, the National Association for School Psychologists also requires programs to have students maintain a commitment to understanding and responding to human diversity as reflected in a program's philosophy and mission, goals, and objectives practiced throughout all aspects of the program, including admissions, faculty, course work, practica, and internship experiences. Human diversity is recognized as a strength that is valued and respected.

Unfortunately, the field of sport and exercise psychology has lagged behind with respect to diversity issues. The Association for Applied Sport Psychology's (AASP) *Code of Ethical Principles and Standards* (AASP, 1994) includes awareness of individual differences in Principle D of the APA Ethics Code (APA, 2010), Respect for People's Rights and Dignity, but the requirements to become a Certified Consultant, AASP, include no specific training related to diversity. Furthermore, little attention has been paid to diversity issues in sport and exercise psychology research, theory, and practice (Kamphoff, Gill, Araki, & Hammond, 2010). For example, an analysis of AASP conference program abstracts from 1986 to 2007 found that only 10.5% of all abstracts included a discussion of cultural diversity, and 31.9% included a diverse sample. Of those abstracts that addressed cultural diversity issues, the majority addressed gender, with almost no attention to race and ethnicity, nationality, sexual orientation, disability, or age (Kamphoff et al., 2010). The purpose of this chapter is to provide (a) a brief description of diverse groups' involvement in sport, (b) an overview covering the current status of these groups, and (c) practical suggestions for how sport psychology professionals might enhance their awareness of diversity and work more effectively with diverse groups.

Gender

Historically, girls' and women's roles were focused on family and motherhood, with little attention paid to sport and exercise performance (Bernstein & Blain, 2003). It was not until the early 1970s in the United States that women's and girls' participation in sport increased dramatically in large part as a result of legislative changes demanding equal treatment (Title IX, Education Amendments, 1972) for female athletes (Coakley, 2009). For example, at the Moscow Olympics in 1980, women athletes constituted 21.5% of the total athletes in the games (1,115 women, 4,064 men). Accordingly, there were only 50 women's events compared with 146 for men. However, by the 2010 Vancouver Olympic Games, women constituted 40% of the total participants in the games (1,060 women, 1,572 men); there were 39 women's events offered and 47 men's events.

CURRENT STATUS

Increasing opportunities and rewards for women athletes have contributed to new controversies. In particular, who may compete in sport as a woman? The International Olympic Committee's current position is that male athletes who have undergone a sex change operation after puberty, have completed appropriate hormone replacement therapy for 2 years, and have undergone a medical evaluation are eligible to compete as women. However, identifying female athletes for the purposes of competition has been problematic. In 2000, systematic gender testing to identify athlete gender was banned in part because it was humiliating for athletes, socially and culturally insensitive, expensive, difficult, and unclear or potentially inaccurate for people with unusual genetic configurations such as a male genetic makeup and female anatomy or body chemistry (Simpson et al., 2000).

Some women athletes have expressed concern that their opponents are in fact men. In 2009, Caster Semenya, a young 800-meter runner, won the World Championships and was "accused" of being a man. The International Association of Athletics Federations, the governing body of international track and field, ordered Semenya to undergo gender tests that involved a physical medical evaluation and reports from a gynecologist, endocrinologist, psychologist, internal medical specialist, and gender expert. Comments about Semenya brought up questions about the standards used to determine sex and gender and the ethical issues that arise in the process of gender testing (Wiesemann, 2011). Ultimately, Semenya returned to competition as a woman athlete who has naturally occurring male and female characteristics. The experiences of Semenya with regard to gender issues led sporting bodies such as the International Olympic Committee to further discuss and clarify gender-related guidelines. Currently, a panel of medical experts is called on to examine individual athletes about whom concerns have been raised and make recommendations on whether these athletes are eligible to compete as women. This secret process contains the potential for bias and inconsistency but may serve to protect athletes' right to privacy while helping to ensure a fair playing field for all.

With regard to sport psychology research related to gender, much of the literature has focused on male athletes' experiences, limiting the generalizability of findings to female athletes (Gill & Kamphoff, 2010). Fortunately, current research and scholarship are addressing gender issues (e.g., Hanrahan & Cerin, 2009; Norman, 2010; Steinfeldt, Wong, Hagan, Hoag, & Steinfeldt, 2011; Wiesemann, 2011), beginning the process of clarifying relevant sport psychology topics as they apply to male, female, and intersex people. Keeping sport psychology within a multicultural perspective challenges one's worldview, enriches one's scholarship and practice, and advances sport psychology in the public interest (Gill, 2007). Overall, the barriers for women from the past may not always be as visible and obstructive as they have been in the past, but they may still be in place (J. Harris, 2007).

INTERVENTION STRATEGIES

Working With Female Athletes

Guidelines for working competently with women have been suggested for psychologists (APA, 2007) and can be applied to sport psychology consultants working with female athletes. First, sport psychology consultants should have some knowledge of how men's and women's socialization and sport experiences differ because of gender. People are socialized into multiple groups including those based on gender, and within their groups, people have both shared and unique identities and developmental pathways (Brody & Hall, 2010). Second, sport psychology consultants should be sensitive to circumstances in which an athlete might work best with a same-sex or opposite-sex counselor and make referrals as needed. With issues such as sexual abuse or eating disorders, a female athlete might feel more comfortable working with a female consultant. On the other hand, some female athletes may relate better to or be more comfortable consulting with a man. In the end, the sport psychology consultant should respect athletes' wishes and assist them in determining who might best meet their individual needs. Third, sport psychology consultants should seek supervision or consultation with colleagues who are knowledgeable about gender issues.

Female Sport Psychology Consultants Working With Male Athletes

Female sport psychology consultants working with male athletes may face a variety of stereotypes because of their gender. On the plus side, female psychology consultants are perceived as being more attractive and trustworthy and are rated more highly on general "good counselor" dimensions than are their male counterparts (Petrie, Cogan, Van Raalte, & Brewer, 1996). On the negative side, athletes or coaches may question female consultants' knowledge of sport, competence, and acceptability to athletes; have concerns about the possibility of attraction and transference; cite the impression that women like to gossip and will not honor confidentiality; and worry that women will be manipulative to get athletes to comply (Yambor & Connelly, 1991). Because sport remains primarily a male domain (Coakley, 2009; Hardin & Greer, 2009), it is important for female consultants to recognize that these misperceptions exist and can interfere with their work with athletes and sport teams. It is useful to address the issues proactively at the beginning of consultation, exploring any concerns the male athlete or coach has about a female consultant's potential effectiveness.

Race and Ethnicity— Cultural Diversity

It is hard to imagine watching a televised sporting event—football, baseball, basketball, track and field, and boxing—without seeing a wide array of athletes from many different cultural and ethnic backgrounds. These images suggest that sport participation is diverse in all sports at high levels. Or do they? Outside of certain sports, such as professional football, baseball, and basketball, rates of participation among racially and ethnically diverse athletes are quite low (Coakley, 2009). In fact, in many sports at elite levels, athletes of color are underrepresented or even nonexistent (Coakley, 2009).

There are many reasons for this underrepresentation in sport, including a long history of discrimination, denial of opportunities, stereotypes, immigration patterns of certain racial and ethnic groups, and inconsistencies among expectations in sport and cultural value systems (Coakley, 2009). In some sporting contexts, teams may appear segregated by race and ethnicity (e.g., O. Harris, 1994) and racially and ethnically diverse individuals are denied opportunities to advance in management positions (Coakley, 2009). Clearly, changes should occur within the structure of sport organizations, among coaches, and with athletes if racially and ethnically diverse individuals are to gain full access to opportunity in sport.

CURRENT STATUS

Duda and Allison's (1990) review of the sport and exercise psychology literature sparked a concern that racially and ethnically diverse athletes were rarely included in research either at a conceptual or descriptive level. This analysis was presented as a wake-up call to the field, providing direction for how to examine the influences of racial, ethnic, and cultural factors in sport and exercise. Attention to diversity issues related to race and ethnicity increased with journal articles (Gano-Overway, 1995; Hall, 1996;

O. Harris, 1994; Hayashi, 1996; Kontos & Arguello, 2005; Kontos & Breland-Noble, 2002; Morgan, Griffin, & Heyward, 1996; Ram, Starek, & Johnson, 2004; Solomon et al., 1996), book chapters (Gill, 2000, 2007; Hanrahan, 2010; Parham, 2005), and books dedicated to the practice of cultural sport psychology and sports in different societies (Managan, Fan, & Gersting, 2003; Schinke & Hanrahan, 2009). The increase in scholarship is important, but the sport psychology field still needs to work toward more cultural awareness in consulting with racially and ethnically diverse athletes (Gill, 2007).

INTERVENTION STRATEGIES

To be effective in multicultural contexts, sport psychology consultants should realize that their work (and athletes' reactions to this work) is influenced by larger social-political factors in society (Sue & Sue, 1999). Gill (2007) added that to best serve athletes in multicultural contexts, consultants should avoid narrow definitions of culture because they emphasize ethnicity and should instead use a holistic approach that encompasses an intersection of experiences, race, gender, and the like. Consistent with these statements, we offer the following suggestions for working more competently with racially and ethnically diverse athletes. In doing so, we freely acknowledge that consultants also should seek other sources of information, supervision, and continuing education if they want to work effectively in multicultural contexts.

Acknowledge Biases and Racism

All individuals have biases and racial attitudes that are products of growing up in a racist society. Practitioners who become aware of their attitudes and biases can work to limit their negative influence and be better able to develop new and broader assumptions about human behavior (Sue & Sue, 1999) extending beyond traditional views.

Recognize Within-Group Differences

Practitioners should not assume that all the members of any racial or ethnic group are the same or that every athlete of color experiences race or ethnicity in the same manner. For example, the broad category of Asian Americans is made up of individuals of the following nationalities: Chinese, Japanese, Korean, Vietnamese, Thai, Hmong, Cambodian, Philippine, and East Indian, to name just a few. Likewise, Kontos and Arguello (2005) noted that Latin athletes are Venezuelan, Colombian, Mexican, Dominican, and Chilean, to name a few. Clearly, tremendous variation exists within racial and ethnic minority groups, some of which may be due to acculturation (Atkinson, Morten, & Sue, 1993), racial identity development (e.g., Helms, 1995), or ethnic group affiliation. To understand an athlete solely (or even primarily) through the prism of his or her racial or ethnic group is to do that individual a disservice. Racial or ethnic group is but one factor to consider when trying to understand an individual's worldview (Speight, Myers, Cox, & Highlen, 1991).

Develop Multicultural Skills and Knowledge

In addition to understanding within-group differences, consultants need to develop knowledge, counseling skills, and interventions that are multiculturally sensitive and take into account the social, environmental, and cultural factors that broadly influence racially and ethnically diverse athletes (Sue & Sue, 2007). Certain cultural groups tend to share viewpoints that focus on family, community, respect for elders, religion, mutual trust, and the endurance of stress (Kontos & Arguello, 2005). Learning about different worldviews, models of acculturation and racial identity, cultural mistrust, communication styles, family systems, indigenous healing methods, and the histories and values of each specific racial or ethnic group will be an important first step in developing a multicultural knowledge base.

This knowledge may be particularly useful when working with athletes who are participating in elite sport in a location that is different from their birthplace or home of origin. Popp, Hums, and Greenwell (2009) studied how international athletes and native-born U.S. athletes viewed the purpose of sport. International athletes described the purpose of sport as less about competition than domestic U.S.-born athletes. Popp and colleagues suggested that more research is necessary to understand the values and experiences of international athletes. Although this area of research is developing, it seems clear that sport psychology consultants working with international athletes have additional issues to consider, not the least of which may be international athletes' perceptions of and attitudes toward sport psychology consultation.

Address Societal Racism and Promote Institutional Change

This strategy involves the consultant moving beyond the role of individual change agent to confront problems at a societal and institutional level. Being an advocate for an oppressed group may be the most effective role for the sport psychology consultant, depending on the circumstances (Atkinson, Thompson, & Grant, 1993). If consultants who have credibility and influence do not work to make changes in racist and discriminatory institutional policy and social practices, then racially and ethnically diverse athletes will continue to be oppressed by these powerful forces. Such advocacy can be as simple as providing diversity training to coaches and athletic department officials or as complex as helping sport organizations change policies regarding the recruitment and hiring of racial and ethnic minorities. If sport psychologists truly believe in the importance of developing positive, supportive sport environments for all athletes, then they should be willing to step forward to confront the racist and discriminatory practices, whether overt or subtle, that unfold around them.

Sexual Orientation: Gay, Lesbian, Transgender, and Bisexual Athletes

The Williams Institute, an organization dedicated to the field of sexual orientation and gender-identity-related law and public policy, estimates the size of the lesbian, gay, bisexual, and transgender (LGBT) community in the United States as 3.5% of the adult population. In sport, it is difficult to estimate exact numbers for the population that identifies as LGBT. For example, out of the nearly 10,000 athletes who participated in the Beijing Olympics in 2008, only 10 publicly indicated that they were part of the LGBT population (Buzinski, 2008). As V. Krane (personal communication, August 30, 2000) noted, it may be impossible to determine accurate prevalence rates because most athletes are not open about their sexual orientation. In fact, many men wait until retirement to come out about their sexuality to reduce the negative repercussions of homophobia in many men's sports (Coakley, 2009).

In the Current Status section that follows, we focus primarily on the experiences of lesbian athletes because most research has been conducted in this area. The Current Status section also touches on the experiences of gay male athletes, but research is limited in this area (Lucyk, 2011). In the Intervention Strategies section, however, we offer general comments about working with LGBT athletes as a group, although we recognize that differences may exist among these groups of athletes.

CURRENT STATUS

At the 2008 National Collegiate Athletic Association (NCAA) convention, the NCAA hosted a session titled "Time Out! A Conversation About Including Lesbian, Gay, Bisexual, and Transgender (LGBT) Student Athletes." The session was a wake-up call to the intercollegiate athletic community: Participants shared information related to the current culture and climate within collegiate athletics for LGBT student athletes. Within this presentation, participants discussed the fear that exists, the energy that it takes to hide and live a double life, disparaging comments heard in everyday conversations, and the personal and emotional toll on athletes. As reported by the NCAA, the session "helped provide awareness of how homophobia adversely affects student-athlete well-being" (Ensign, Yiamouyiannis, White, & Ridputh, 2011).

The NCAA has taken legislative action and developed programming initiatives with the intent of providing an inclusive collegiate environment for all students, including the LGBT students. The NCAA adopted Constitution 2.6 (the Principle of Nondiscrimination) in 1993 and amended it in 2000 to include reference to sexual orientation. Because of general societal homophobia and heterosexual biases, an LGBT athlete is likely to deal with the same issues that any other LGBT individual would encounter (Cogan & Petrie, 1996). Such issues include but are not limited to (a) the need to conceal sexual orientation; (b) difficulty trusting others; (c) overt and subtle pressure from society, self, family, and/or friends to change sexual orientation; (d) reconciliation of religious beliefs that may not condone an LGBT lifestyle; and (e) a general assumption of a heterosexual life. Although a positive support system and strong self-identity can provide some protection (Krane, 1996), as a result of these pressures, LGBT individuals may experience depression, anger, isolation, shame, anxiety, confusion, and for athletes, poor sport performance.

LGBT athletes and coaches also likely experience stressors that are unique to the sport environment (Krane, 1996, 1997; Krane & Barber, 2005; Lenskyj, 1991; Rotella & Murray, 1991), such as avoiding success for fear of being "outed" by the media, losing endorsement contracts because of their sexual orientation, balancing what is right for themselves or their careers, and being encouraged (subtly and overtly) to leave the team or their sport. In addition, female athletes have been passed over in selection processes because they have the appearance of being a lesbian, and coaches have not been hired because of a lesbian label (Krane & Barber, 2005; Wellman & Blinde, 1997). Another recent source of stress examined in the literature involves the support staff of athletes, specifically athletic trainers (Ensign et al., 2011). Ensign and colleagues (2011) found that despite an overall acceptance of homosexual athletes, 15% of all athletic trainers in the NCAA had unfavorable views of LGBT athletes. Although 15% is a minority of athletic trainers, the fact that support staff team members are biased adds another layer of instability and fear for LGBT athletes. Coaches also can make it difficult for athletes to come out, especially those who endorse specific Christian values opposed to homosexuality (Jacobson, 2002).

For lesbian athletes, homonegativity and heterosexual bias are experienced not only from the broader society but also from the sport environment as well. Negative stereotypes in the forms of labeling, vulgarities, and derogatory media depictions likely affect all lesbian athletes to some degree (Krane, 1996). In fact, Krane in 1997 and later with Barber in 2003 argued that the sport environment in its current masculine form is hostile toward lesbian athletes. She found that lesbian college athletes experience three major forms of homonegativism: (a) pressure to adhere to a feminine gender role and image (e.g., athletes may be dismissed from the team if they "look" too masculine), (b) labeling female athletes as lesbian as a way of stigmatizing them (e.g., athletes being assumed that they are lesbian because they are part of a specific team or teammates gossiping about other teammates or coaches), and (c) pressure to distance oneself from the lesbian label (e.g., making fun of other lesbians or not speaking out against homonegative or derogatory comments; Krane, 1997). These experiences help shape the social identity perspective of lesbian athletes, or simply how people behave individually and socially because of perceptions of group membership (Krane & Barber, 2003). With pressures and expectations from the self and others, the experience of lesbian athletes is one that is guarded because of the masculinity of sport.

Although Krane's (1996, 1997) theoretical model and research focused on the experiences of lesbian athletes, one can see how the previously stated components of homonegativism could apply to gay and bisexual athletes as well. An article titled "The Loneliest Athletes" in *The Chronicle of Higher Education* highlighted the fact that athletes rarely come out during their competitive careers, especially males (Jacobson, 2002). Jacobson (2002) noted that individuals who are gay and do choose to come out tend to be those who participate in individual sports such as swimming, tennis, golf, skiing, and cross-country running. Athletes who participate in team sports such as football, baseball, and hockey often find that the sport environment is too homophobic and dangerous to come out. Another reason it is difficult for LGBT athletes to come out is because the institution of sport reinforces and promotes homophobia through heteronormatives and muscular Christianity (Lucyk, 2011). Despite the difficult environment sport poses for athletes to come out in, if a gay athlete is successful, he can challenge the rigid hegemonic masculinity and expose that masculinity in sport is not as streamlined as it appears (Anderson, 2002). It is sad that a gay athlete must be successful to make strides in the sporting environment for equality, but until there is a culture of acceptance and more athletes come out, the sport environment remains one of uncertainty for gay athletes. Clearly, more research and scholarly discussion is needed to "transform the silence" (Ensign et al., 2011; Stevenson, Rowe, & Markwell, 2005) surrounding LGBT athletes. Through such a dialogue, sexual orientation may become a nonissue or simply a part of one's identity and not the accusation, label, vulgarity, or stigma it currently is for many athletes.

A movement that is working to "transform the silence" is the Gay Games, an Olympic-style competition held every 4 years that is open to all sexualities (Krane, Barber, & McClung, 2002). According to the Federation of Gay Games, participation in the 2010 games in Cologne,

Germany, was approximately 10,000 athletes from over 70 countries. Krane et al. (2002) studied gay female participants in the Gay Games to understand the social psychological benefits from participating in the games and found that women felt empowered to come out and work toward social change and felt comfortable being themselves rather than what society expects them to be. Clearly, the Gay Games provided an empowering experience for these women, and the event in and of itself serves to affect perceptions of LGBT athletes in sport. Although the Gay Games had a positive impact on its participants, Lucyk (2011) cautioned that "gay sports reinforce gender and sexual binaries" and that "because the Gay Games practice inclusivity, they may be undervalued by hegemonic society when compared to athletes who had to 'earn' their position on a team" (p. 76). Whereas Lucyk spoke from a dominant view in society standpoint, Krane et al. (2002) examined participation on an individual level and found participation to encourage change, thus benefiting the movement to make sport more inclusive globally.

INTERVENTION STRATEGIES

Although not an exhaustive list, strategies for assisting LGBT athletes at the individual and societal level are provided in the following subsections.

Self-Awareness

Sport psychology consultants who work with LGBT athletes should be comfortable with their own as well as others' same-gender attractions. If the consultant is struggling with the acceptability of these feelings, supervision or a referral is in order.

Be Aware That Sexual Orientation Is Not Always an Issue

Sport psychology consultants should not assume that an athlete's sexual orientation is the primary reason for seeking assistance. Like any other athlete, LGBT athletes will seek assistance from a sport psychology consultant for issues that are not directly linked to their sexual orientation. It is important to be open to discussing sexual orientation but to realize that LGBT athletes may only want to focus on developing specific mental skills to enhance their performance.

Be Open and Supportive When Sexual Orientation Is an Issue for the Athlete

For athletes, sexual orientation may be a concern for several reasons. First, athletes may be in the early stages of their sexual identity development and may be confused about their feelings or behaviors. In such situations, normalizing their confusion and feelings and educating them on the process of developing a healthy sexual identity is in order. In addition, consultants can help LGBT athletes develop a positive support system (D. Clark, 1997) to counter the sense of aloneness and isolation from teammates that they may be feeling. To accomplish this goal, consultants need to be aware of available community resources as well as knowledgeable about LGBT athlete role models (e.g., Gareth Thomas, Billy Bean, Sheryl Swoopes, Martina Navratilova, Greg Louganis) and sport competitions, such as the Gay Games (Krane & Waldron, 2000).

Second, athletes may be in the process of making decisions regarding coming out to friends, family, teammates, and/or coaches. Such disclosure should always be the individual's decision, and the athlete should never be pressured to do so too hastily. If the athlete chooses to come out, it will be important to offer support, encouragement, patience, and understanding. Furthermore, the athlete might role play coming out with the consultant to become more comfortable with the process and to better anticipate reactions from others.

Third, because of homonegative team or athletic department environments, LGBT athletes may feel pressure to "go along" with the negativity or face ridicule and isolation if they speak out against it. Thus, LGBT athletes may seek counseling concerning how to cope with the situation in which they find themselves. If that is the case, the consultant can support athletes in decision making that may range from doing nothing to directly confronting the offending individuals to leaving the environment altogether. If athletes choose to confront homonegativity, consultants may help by role playing different approaches and discussing possible reactions.

Becoming an Advocate

As advocates, sport psychology consultants can speak out against discrimination and prejudice (Kauer & Krane, 2010; Krane, 1996) and educate those in positions of authority, such as coaches and athletic administrators, about the toxic effects of homophobia and heterosexual bias. Although such an approach may have negative repercussions, such as being labeled "gay" and denigrated as a result, sport psychology professionals have an ethical and moral responsibility to make sport a positive environment for all participants. To limit such potential negative consequences and help their message be received, sport psychology professionals should be open, positive, and nonevaluative in their educational efforts. Kauer and Krane (2010) emphasized that practitioners should encourage coaches and athletes to create a sense of "inclusive excellence," in which the label "team member" is paramount to inclusion. Practitioners should provide resources to coaches and their teams as well as encourage dialogue so as to create a safe zone. A final note is that sport psychology consultants should never assume that they are allies of the LGBT community simply because they support social justice. Earning the trust of LGBT individuals (as well as any group of people) is paramount in creating a safe and welcoming environment for providing the best possible care.

Athletes With Disabilities

Athletes with disabilities, including but not limited to athletes who are blind or deaf or have cerebral palsy, spinal cord injuries, intellectual disabilities, and amputations, compete in local, regional, and national competitions in many sports (Asken, 1989). In many countries, organized sport programs exist for persons with disabilities in such sports as alpine skiing, archery, athletics, biathlon, boccia, cross-country skiing, cycling, equestrian competitions, football, goalball, ice sledge hockey, judo, para-canoeing, powerlifting, rowing, sailing, shooting, swimming, table tennis, para-triathlon, volleyball (sitting), wheelchair basketball, wheelchair curling, wheelchair dance sport, wheelchair fencing, wheelchair rugby, and wheelchair tennis. At the international level, athletes can compete in the Paralympics, a major elite-level multisport event similar in format to the Olympics. In 2008, approximately 3,951 athletes with disabilities competed in the Beijing Paralympics, and in 2010, approximately 502 athletes participated in the Vancouver Paralympic Games (International Paralympic Committee, 2011). With so many athletes interested in reaching the highest levels of performance at national and international competitions, this is a population that may be particularly receptive to sport psychology services.

Although people with disabilities can participate in physical activity on a variety of levels, the information in this section is focused on competitive athletes with disabilities. Since 1986, the U.S. Olympic Festival has offered opportunities for athletes with disabilities to compete (Paciorek, Jones, & Tetreault, 1991), as have the Olympics for the Physically Disabled, the Special Olympics, and the Paralympics.

CURRENT STATUS

Most research related to athletes with disabilities has compared athletes with and without disabilities on a variety of indicators. In general, this research has shown that the two groups of athletes across sports such as marathoning, track and field, swimming, weightlifting, and table tennis are similar in terms of mood states and psychological health (Henschen,

Horvat, & Roswal, 1992; Horvat, Roswal, & Henschen, 1991) and their commitment to sport (Fung, 1992). R. A. Clark and Sachs (1991) found that the psychological skills of athletes who are deaf are more similar to than different from those of hearing athletes. Gregg (2010) reported that athletes with intellectual disabilities experience anxiety prior to competing and that imagery is one of the most used skills for athletes with intellectual disabilities. Martin (1999) found that athletes with disabilities were as goal oriented as able-bodied athletes. When looking at disengagement from sport, Martin (1999) found that life transition models were applicable to both athletes with disabilities and able-bodied athletes, with both groups noting that transitions out of sport were related to self-identity, postcareer planning, sport goal achievement, voluntary withdrawal, and social support. Overall, there are few differences in psychological variables between able-bodied athletes and those with disabilities (Hanrahan, 2007). Although there are few differences in psychological variables, practitioners must be sensitive to the individual and his or her specific needs rather than taking a blanket approach to the disability.

With regard to physical issues, research on sport injury indicates that athletes with disabilities tend to lose more training time as a result of injury than do athletes without disabilities (Davis & Ferrara, 1995; Martin, 2010). This may be because many injuries (e.g., pressure sores) and illnesses (e.g., bladder infections) are directly related to physical disability. Spinal cord injuries provide a serious challenge to athletes with disabilities because of daily chronic pain and the inability to regulate body temperature (Martin, 2010). Thus, research and applied intervention guidelines indicate that it is valuable to be cognizant of athletes' disability and physical limitations; however, athletes with disabilities are likely to have many of the same psychological needs and abilities as their counterparts without disabilities.

INTERVENTION STRATEGIES

Historically, athletes with disabilities have been underserved by sport psychology consultants (Martin, 1999). Recently, however, consultants have acknowledged the importance of psychological skills training for this population (Gregg, 2010; Hanrahan, 1998, 2004, 2007, 2010; Martin, 1999, 2010; Vose, Clark, & Sachs, 2010). Furthermore, because athletes with disabilities are generally receptive to sport psychology interventions (Martin, 1999), sport psychology consultants may find working with these athletes a winning situation for all involved.

To be effective when working with athletes with intellectual disabilities, Gregg (2010) suggested that practitioners provide safe environments for athletes to push themselves and experience adversity within the athlete's abilities, provide opportunities to facilitate communication and socializing, and focus on and reinforce a limited number of psychological skills. Practitioners working with athletes who are visually impaired or blind should not be afraid to ask how much an athlete can see so as to better assess the athlete's visual abilities (Vose et al., 2010). After assessing visual abilities or past history, a practitioner might be able to incorporate imagery exercises into the mental training program. Practitioners should also be mindful of their language and use as colorful and descriptive communications as possibly, especially with athletes who are visually impaired.

Athletes who are deaf or hard of hearing require a practitioner to be mindful of the athlete's preferred communication style (e.g. sign language, writing). Vose et al. (2010) also recommended using as many practical visual aids as possible when communicating and teaching mental skills to athletes who are deaf and hard of hearing. It is important to make eye contact with the athletes and remember that they will not be able to hear instructions during a task, so one must use preperformances and time outs wisely and effectively so as to provide the best services possible (Vose et al., 2010).

When working with athletes with physical disabilities, sport psychology consultants should recognize the unique needs of this population and have special knowledge in the following areas (Asken, 1991):

- the psychology of physical disability and the physical and psychological trauma athletes may have experienced;
- the physiological and medical considerations unique to the disability that can influence future injury and performance;
- the complexities in motivation to compete, which range from the usual desires for challenge and/or fitness to denial of the physical disability;
- performance problems, such as anxiety, that result from limitations associated with the disability;
- the organizational structure of wheelchair and competitive sport for people with disabilities (e.g., restricted funding and financial rewards so athletes may have mixed priorities with job demands, limited training time and facilities, dealing with several sports at a time); and the social environment such as physical and social barriers (e.g., a disability may get a negative reaction from the community, the individual may be stigmatized).

In addition, Hanrahan (2007) recommended the following actions:

- If a person acquires the disability from an accident or illness, do not rush sport participation on the athlete. Allow individuals to develop an interest on their own.
- Focus on ability rather than disability. These individuals are *athletes*. There is no need to discuss the disability or to bring attention to it unless the athlete feels comfortable or it affects training.
- Do not avoid failure. Provide a safe environment for the athletes to fail, and provide support to encourage psychological growth.

Although standard interventions may need to be adapted to fit the unique needs of the disability, athletes with disabilities can benefit from a wide range of performance enhancement skills, such as arousal control, attention and concentration, goal setting, self-talk, negative thought stopping, interpersonal and assertiveness skills training, confidence enhancement, imagery, and precompetition preparation (Asken, 1989; Hanrahan, 1998; Martin, 1999). Furthermore, Martin (1999) suggested that sport psychology consultants work to create an environment that emphasizes the whole person in which mental skills are taught such they can be easily transferred to other life areas.

Masters Athletes

Masters athletes are "competitors who exceed a minimum age specific to each sport and who participate in competitive events designed for masters athletes" (Spiriduso, 1995, p. 390). Hawkins (2005) gave some examples of different sports and ages that constitute a masters athlete. For example, swimmers who are 25 years old and older are considered masters swimmers. Additionally, masters rowers must be at least 27 years of age, weight lifters 40, and golfers 50 and older. Some sports, such as track and field, have specific age requirements for different genders, with women considered masters athletes at 35 years of age and men at 40 (Hawkins, 2005). Given that there are multiple age requirements for a variety of different sports and not just one universal age requirement, individuals working with athletes need to educate themselves as to what constitutes a masters athlete for the athlete's sport and gender.

CURRENT STATUS

The World Masters Games is the largest international competition exclusively for masters athletes held every 4 years (Hodge, Allen, & Smellie, 2008). With over 32,000 athletes competing at the 2009 World Masters Games in Edmonton, Alberta, Canada (World Masters Games, 2011), it is one of the biggest multievent sporting events in the world. Touting the mission of promoting "sport for life," masters athletes are some of the most highly motivated athletes (Hodge et al., 2008). Masters athletes compete for many reasons, such as for social bonding and sharing interests with others, to feel competent and belong, to give purpose and meaning to life, and to promote giving back to the community through coaching others (Hodge et al., 2008; Lyons & Dionigi, 2007). In addition to examining the motives and reasons for masters athletes to compete in sports, Baker, Fraser-Thomas, Dionigi, and Horton (2010) found that masters sport participants had positive development through better negotiating the aging process and enhancing motivation to stay physically active, and participation helped to challenge stereotypes of older sport participants.

Overall, the limited research on masters athletes reveals that masters athletics are generally positive experiences for participants. Hodge et al. (2008) found that most masters athletes competed with a task orientation, competing to better themselves and master skills or tasks rather than competing with an ego orientation that emphasizes outperforming others. Gaining attention from others motivated some masters athletes, but the sense of community and the value of sharing experiences with others were evident across several research studies (Baker et al., 2010; Hodge et al., 2008; Lyons & Dionigi, 2007). Research suggests that masters athletes tend to be intrinsically motivated (Hodge et al., 2008; Newton & Fry, 1998), train for personal reasons, and embrace the "fit for life" slogan of masters athletics rather than cutthroat competition.

INTERVENTION STRATEGIES

With limited research available on masters athletes, it is important for sport psychology consultants to approach each athlete as a unique individual. Assuming that all masters athletes seek community and are task oriented might undermine these athletes. Although many masters athletes compete for intrinsic reasons, others compete to battle stereotypes and gain recognition for their accomplishments (Hodge et al., 2008). To effectively consult with masters athletes, consultants should consider the points presented in the subsections that follow.

Examine Personal Biases

Sport psychology consultants should self-reflect and consider their attitudes toward older adults competing in sport. *Ageism* is the stereotyping of or showing prejudice toward individuals simply because they are old (APA, 2004). Masters athletes are competitive individuals who often compete on a global stage, and sport psychology consultants should view masters athletes as legitimate athletes or refer interested athletes to a consultant who can offer supportive services.

Become Aware of the Challenges Facing Older Athletes

It is important for consultants to familiarize themselves with the challenges that are unique to athletes as they age and progress in their masters careers. Some athletes find that it takes more time and effort to maintain endurance, strength, and skill, which can cause stress and frustration. Consultants may work with masters athletes to set realistic goals, to incorporate appropriate amounts of rest and recovery into training, and to consider a task-oriented mind-set to offset potential frustrations related to the aging process.

Provide the Services That Masters Athletes Need and Want

Masters athletes may be particularly motivated to take advantage of sport psychology techniques that can enhance performance. Self-talk, imagery, and relaxation can be effective for many athletes, and research to date does not dispute using mental skills training to consult with masters athletes. However, sport psychology consultants should be aware of the needs and motivations of the masters athlete they are working with and tailor any mental skills programs to best serve those motives and needs.

Conclusion

Knowledge of characteristics related to gender, race and ethnicity, sexual orientation, disability, and age are important for sport psychology consultants working with athletes to consider. However, we caution sport psychology consultants against using general information on any given population as the primary criterion for guiding assessment and interventions. Instead we encourage sport psychology professionals to approach athletes as individuals, recognizing that culture or group membership is but one important factor that defines each person. As Sue and Sue (1999) and Gill (2007) have noted, generalizations are a necessary part of human interaction, but they need to be applied tentatively and be open to change. Each individual comes from an intersection of backgrounds and experiences, and taking each background and experience into consideration will best serve athletes from all walks of life.

References

American Psychological Association. (2004). Guidelines for psychological practice with older adults. *American Psychologist, 59,* 236–260.

American Psychological Association. (2007). Guidelines for psychological practice with girls and women. *American Psychologist, 62,* 949–979. doi:10.1037/0003-066X.62.9.949

American Psychological Association. (2010*). Ethical principles of psychologists and code of conduct (2002, Amended June 1, 2010).* Retrieved from http://www.apa.org/ethics/code/index.aspx

Anderson, E. (2002). Gays in sport: Contesting hegemonic masculinity in a homophobic environment. *Gender & Society, 16,* 860–877. doi:10.1177/089124302237892

Asken, M. J. (1989). Sport psychology and the physically disabled athletes: Interview with Michael D. Goodling, OTR/L. *The Sport Psychologist, 3,* 166–176.

Asken, M. J. (1991). The challenge of the physically challenged: Delivering sport psychology services to physically disabled athletes. *The Sport Psychologist, 5,* 370–381.

Association for Applied Sport Psychology. (1994). *AASP Code of Ethical principles and standards.* Retrieved from https://www.appliedsportpsych.org/about/ethics/code

Atkinson, D. R., Morten, G., & Sue, D. W. (1993). *Counseling American minorities: A cross-cultural perspective.* Dubuque, IA: Brown & Benchmark.

Atkinson, D. R., Thompson, C., & Grant, S. (1993). A three-dimensional model for counseling racial/ethnic minorities. *The Counseling Psychologist, 21,* 257–277. doi:10.1177/0011000093212010

Baker, J., Fraser-Thomas, J., Dionigi, R. A., & Horton, S. (2010). Sport participation and positive development in older persons. *European Review of Aging and Physical Activity, 7,* 3–12. doi:10.1007/s11556-009-0054-9

Bernstein, A., & Blain, N. (Eds.). (2003). *Sport, media, culture: Global and local dimensions.* London, England: Frank Cass.

Brody, L., & Hall, J. (2010). Gender emotion, and socialization. In J. C. Chrisler & D. R. McCreary (Eds.), *Handbooks of gender research in psychology: Vol. 1. Gender research in general and experimental psychology* (pp. 429–454). New York, NY: Springer.

Buzinski, J. (2008). Number of gay and lesbian athletes at the 2008 Games is on par with 2004 but includes only one man. In addition, there is one bisexual softball player. *OutSports*.com. Retrieved from http://www.outsports.com/os/index2.php?option=com_content&task=view&id=111&pop=1&page

Clark, D. (1997). *Loving someone gay.* Berkeley, CA: Celestial Arts.

Clark, R. A., & Sachs, M. (1991). Challenges and opportunities in psychological skills training in deaf athletes. *The Sport Psychologist, 5,* 392–398.

Coakley, J. (2009). *Sport in society: Issues & controversies* (10th ed.). Boston, MA: McGraw-Hill.

Cogan, K. D., & Petrie, T. A. (1996). Counseling women college student-athletes. In E. Etzel, A. Ferrante, & J. Pinkney (Eds.), *Counseling college student athletes* (pp. 77–106). Morgantown, WV: Fitness Information Technology.

Davis, R. W., & Ferrara, M. S. (1995). Sports medicine and athletes with disabilities. In K. P. DePauw & S. J. Gavron (Eds.), *Disability and sport* (pp. 133–149). Champaign, IL: Human Kinetics.

Duda, J. L., & Allison, M. (1990). Cross-cultural analysis in exercise and sport psychology: A void in the field. *Journal of Sport & Exercise Psychology, 12,* 114–131.

Ensign, K. A., Yiamouyiannis, A., White, K. M., & Ridpath, B. D. (2011). Athletic trainers' attitudes toward lesbian, gay, and bisexual National Collegiate Athletic Association student-athletes. *Journal of Athletic Training, 46,* 69–75. doi:10.4085/1062-6050-46.1.69

Fung, L. (1992). Commitment to training among wheelchair marathon athletes. *International Journal of Sport Psychology, 23,* 138–146.

Gano-Overway, L. (1995). *Goal perspectives and their relationships to beliefs, affective responses and coping strategies among African and Anglo American athletes* (Unpublished master's thesis). Purdue University, West Lafayette, IN.

Gill, D. L. (2000). *Psychological dynamics of sport and exercise* (2nd ed.). Champaign, IL: Human Kinetics.

Gill, D. L. (2007). Gender and cultural diversity. In G. Tenenbaum & R. C. Eklund (Eds.), *Handbook of sport psychology* (3rd ed., pp. 823–844). Hoboken, NJ: Wiley.

Gill, D. L., & Kamphoff, C. S. (2010). Gender and cultural considerations. In J. M. Williams (Ed.), *Applied sport psychology* (pp. 417–433). Boston, MA: McGraw-Hill.

Gregg, M. (2010). Athletes with intellectual disabilities. In S. J. Hanrahan & M. B. Andersen (Eds.), *Routledge handbook of applied sport psychology: A comprehensive guide for students and practitioners* (pp. 432–449). New York, NY: Routledge.

Hall, R. (1996). *Ethnic identity and cross racial experiences of college athletes* (Unpublished master's thesis). Temple University, Philadelphia, PA.

Hanrahan, S. J. (1998). Practical considerations for working with athletes with disabilities. *The Sport Psychologist, 12,* 346–357.

Hanrahan, S. J. (2004). Sport psychology and athletes with disabilities. In T. Morris & J. Summers (Eds.), *Sport Psychology: Theory, applications, and issues* (pp. 572–583). Hoboken, NJ: Wiley.

Hanrahan, S. J. (2007). Athletes with disabilities. In G. Tenenbaum & R. C. Eklund (Eds.), *Handbook of sport psychology* (3rd ed., pp. 845–858). Hoboken, NJ: Wiley.

Hanrahan, S. J. (2010). Culturally competent practitioners. In S. J. Hanrahan & M. B. Andersen (Eds.), *Routledge handbook of applied sport psychology: A comprehensive guide for students and practitioners* (pp. 460–468). New York, NY: Routledge.

Hanrahan, S. J., & Cerin, S. (2009). Gender, level of participation, and type of sport: Differences in achievement goal orientation and attributional style. *Journal of Science and Medicine in Sport, 12,* 508–512. doi:10.1016/j.jsams.2008.01.005

Hardin, M., & Greer, J. (2009). The influence of gender-role socialization, media use, and sports participation on perceptions of gender-appropriate sports. *Journal of Sport Behavior, 32,* 207–226.

Harris, J. (2007). Gender issues in sport. *International Review for the Sociology of Sport, 42,* 217–221. doi:10.1177/1012690207084754

Harris, O. (1994). Race, sport, and social support. *Sociology of Sport Journal, 11,* 40–50.

Hawkins, S. A. (2005). Training masters athletes. In G. J. Jones & D. J. Rose (Eds.), *Physical activity instruction of older adults* (pp. 263–279). Champaign, IL: Human Kinetics.

Hayashi, C. (1996). Achievement motivation among Anglo-American and Hawaiian male physical activity participants: Individual differences and social contextual factors. *Journal of Sport & Exercise Psychology, 18,* 194–215.

Helms, J. (1995). An update of Helms's White and people of color racial identity models. In J. G. Ponterotto, J. M. Casas, L. A. Suzuki, & C. M. Alexander (Eds.), *Handbook of multicultural counseling* (pp. 181–198). Thousand Oaks, CA: Sage.

Henschen, K., Horvat, M., & Roswal, G. (1992). Psychological profiles of the United States wheelchair basketball team. *International Journal of Sport Psychology, 23,* 128–137.

Hodge, K., Allen, J. B., & Smellie, L. (2008). Motivation in masters sport: Achievement and social goals. *Psychology of Sport and Exercise, 9,* 157–176. doi:10.1016/j.psychsport.2007.03.002

Horvat, M., Roswal, G., & Henschen, K. (1991). In the field: Psychological profiles of disabled male athletes before and after competition. *Clinical Kinesiology, 45,* 14–18.

International Paralympic Committee. (2011). *Paralympic Games.* Retrieved from http://www.paralympic.org/Paralympic_Games/

Jacobson, J. (2002, November 1). The loneliest athletes. *The Chronicle of Higher Education, 49*(10), A36.

Kamphoff, C., Gill, D., Araki, K., & Hammond, C. (2010). A content analysis of cultural diversity in the association for applied sport psychology's conference programs. *Journal of Applied Sport Psychology, 22,* 231–245. doi:10.1080/10413201003673153

Kauer, K., & Krane, K. (2010). Diverse sexual and gender identities in sport. In S. J. Hanrahan & M. B. Andersen (Eds.), *Routledge handbook of applied sport psychology: A comprehensive guide for students and practitioners* (pp. 414–422). New York, NY: Routledge.

Kontos, A. P., & Arguello, E. (2005). Sport psychology consulting with Latin American athletes. *Athletic Insight: The Online Journal of Sport Psychology, 7*(3), 36–49.

Kontos, A. P., & Breland-Noble, A. M. (2002). Racial/ethnic diversity in applied sport psychology: A multicultural introduction to working with athletes of color. *The Sport Psychologist, 16,* 296–315.

Krane, V. (1996). Lesbians in sport: Toward acknowledgment, understanding, and theory. *Journal of Sport & Exercise Psychology, 18,* 237–246.

Krane, V. (1997). Homonegativism experienced by lesbian collegiate athletes. *Women in Sport & Physical Activity Journal, 6,* 141–163.

Krane, V., & Barber, H. (2003). Lesbian experiences in sport: A social identity perspective. *Quest, 55,* 328–346. doi:10.1080/00336297.2003.10491808

Krane, V., & Barber, H. (2005). Identity tensions in lesbian intercollegiate athletics. *Research Quarterly for Exercise and Sport, 76,* 67–81. doi:10.5641/027013605X13076330976803

Krane, V., Barber, H., & McClung, L. R. (2002). Social psychological benefits of Gay Games participation: A social identity theory explanation. *Journal of Applied Sport Psychology, 14,* 27–42. doi:1041-3200/02

Krane, V., & Waldron, J. (2000). The Gay Games: Creating our own sport culture. In K. Schafer & S. Smith (Eds.), *The Olympics at the millennium: Power, politics, and the Olympic Games* (pp. 147–164). Piscataway, NJ: Rutgers University Press.

Lenskyj, H. (1991). Combating homophobia in sport and physical education. *Sociology of Sport Journal, 8,* 61–69.

Lucyk, K. (2011). Don't be gay, dude: How the institution of sport reinforces homophobia. *Constellations: An International Journal of Critical and Democratic Theory, 2,* 66–80.

Lyons, K., & Dionigi, R. (2007). Transcending emotional community: A qualitative examination of older adults and masters' sports participation. *Leisure Sciences, 29,* 375–389. doi:10.1080/01490400701394881

Managan, J. A., Fan, H., & Gersting, J. L. (Eds.). (2003). *Sports in Asian society: Past and present.* London, England: Frank Cass.

Martin, J. J. (1999). A personal development model of sport psychology for athletes with disabilities. *Journal of Applied Sport Psychology, 11,* 181–193. doi:10.1080/10413209908404199

Martin, J. J. (2010). Athletes with physical disabilities. In S. J. Hanrahan & M. B. Andersen (Eds.), *Routledge handbook of applied sport psychology: A comprehensive guide for students and practitioners* (pp. 432–440). New York, NY: Routledge.

Morgan, L., Griffin, J., & Heyward, V. (1996). Ethnicity, gender, and experience effects on attributional dimensions. *The Sport Psychologist, 10,* 4–16.

Newton, M., & Fry, M. (1998). Senior Olympians' achievement goals and motivational responses. *Journal of Aging and Physical Activity, 6,* 256–270.

Norman, L. (2010). Feeling second best: Elite women coaches' experiences. *Sociology of Sport Journal, 27,* 89–104.

Paciorek, M. J., Jones, J., & Tetreault, P. (1991). Disabled athlete participation at the 1990 U.S. Olympic Festival. *Palaestra, 7,* 18–25.

Parham, W. D. (2005). Raising the bar: Developing an understanding of athletes from racially, culturally, and ethnically diverse backgrounds. In M. Andersen (Ed.), *Sport psychology in practice* (pp. 201–222). Champaign, IL: Human Kinetics.

Petrie, T. A., Cogan, K. D., Van Raalte, J. L., & Brewer, B. W. (1996). Gender and the evaluation of sport psychology consultants. *The Sport Psychologist, 10,* 132–139.

Popp, N., Hums, M. A., & Greenwell, T. C. (2009). Do international student-athletes view the purpose of sport differently than United States student-athletes at NCAA Division I universities? *Journal of Issues in Intercollegiate Athletics, 2,* 93–110.

Ram, N., Starek, J., & Johnson, J. (2004). Race, ethnicity, and sexual orientation: Still a void in sport and exercise psychology? *Journal of Sport & Exercise Psychology, 26,* 250–268.

Rotella, R., & Murray, M. (1991). Homophobia, the world of sport, and sport psychology consulting. *The Sport Psychologist, 5,* 355–364.

Schinke, R. J., & Hanrahan, S. J. (Eds.). (2009). *Cultural sport psychology.* Champaign, IL: Human Kinetics.

Simpson, J. L., Ljungqvist, A., Ferguson-Smith, M. A., de la Chapelle, A., Elsas, L. J., Ehrhardt, A. A., . . . Carlson, A. (2000). Gender verification in the Olympics. *JAMA, 284,* 1568–1569. doi:10.1001/jama.284.12.1568

Solomon, G., Wiegardt, P., Yusuf, F., Kosmitzki, C., Williams, J., Stevens, C., & Wayda, V. (1996). Expectancies and ethnicity: The self-fulfilling prophecy in college basketball. *Journal of Sport & Exercise Psychology, 18,* 83–88.

Speight, S. L., Myers, L. J., Cox, C. I., & Highlen, P. (1991). A redefinition of multicultural counseling. *Journal of Counseling & Development, 70,* 29–36. doi:10.1002/j.1556-6676.1991.tb01558.x

Spiriduso, W. W. (1995). *Physical dimensions of aging.* Champaign, IL: Human Kinetics.

Steinfeldt, J., Wong, Y., Hagan, A., Hoag, J., & Steinfeldt, M. (2011). A contextual examination of gender role conflict among college football players. *Psychology of Men & Masculinity, 12,* 311–323. doi:10.1037/a0023722

Stevenson, D., Rowe, D., & Markwell, K. (2005). Explorations in 'event ecology': The case of the International Gay Games. *Social Identities: Journal for the Study of Race, Nation, and Culture, 11,* 447–465.

Sue, D. W., Arredondo, P., & McDavis, R. J. (1992). Multicultural competencies/standards: A call to the profession. *Journal of Counseling and Development, 70,* 477–486. doi:10.1002/j.1556-6676.1992.tb01642.x

Sue, D. W., & Sue, D. (1999). *Counseling the culturally different: Theory and practice* (3rd ed.). New York, NY: Wiley.

Sue, D. W., & Sue, D. (2007). *Counseling the culturally diverse: Theory and practice* (5th ed.). Hoboken, NJ: Wiley.

Title IX, Education Amendments, 20 U.S. C. § 1681–1688 (1972).

Vose, J. E., Clark, R. A., & Sachs, M. L. (2010). Athletes who are blind/visually impaired or deaf/hard of hearing. In S. J. Hanrahan & M. B. Andersen (Eds.), *Routledge handbook of applied sport psychology:*

A comprehensive guide for students and practitioners (pp. 450–459). New York, NY: Routledge.

Wellman, S., & Blinde, E. (1997). Homophobia in women's intercollegiate basketball: Views of women coaches regarding coaching careers and recruitment of athletes. *Women in Sports and Physical Activity Journal, 6,* 165–188.

Wiesemann, C. (2011). Is there a right not to know one's sex? The ethics of 'gender verification' in women's sports competition. *Journal of Medical Ethics, 37,* 216–220. doi:10.1136/jme.2010.039081

World Masters Games. (2011). *Events: Past masters events.* Retrieved from http://www.imga.ch/

Yambor, J., & Connelly, D. (1991). Issues confronting female sport psychology consultants working with male students athletes. *The Sport Psychologist, 5,* 304–312.

PROFESSIONAL ISSUES | V

Penny McCullagh, John M. Noble, and Steve Portenga

Education for Sport and Exercise Psychology

20

A lthough many think that the field of sport and exercise psychology is an outgrowth of the 21st century, an examination of the literature indicates a far longer history than that. In fact, some argue that sport and exercise psychology has been present since the beginning of recorded time (Kremer & Moran, 2008). For example, Gardiner (1930) suggested that as early as A.D. 200 a system had been developed to help athletes optimize performance. In 1900, de Coubertin published an article titled "La Psychologie du Sport"—perhaps the first time the term *psychology of sport* was used in modern scientific literature (Kornspan, 2007). Through the first half of the 20th century, sport and exercise psychology continued to develop around the world. The International Society of Sport Psychology was established in 1965 under the direction of Dr. Ferruccio Antonelli of Italy. The Second International Society of Sport Psychology World Congress was held in Washington, DC, in 1968, and in his opening address, Antonelli (1970) indicated that more than 1,400 individuals

http://dx.doi.org/10.1037/14251-020
Exploring Sport and Exercise Psychology, Third Edition, J. Van Raalte and
B. Brewer (Editors)

from 47 nations were members of the organization. Numerous historical accounts of the field have been written, and readers can refer to some of these sources for further recounts of the field (e.g., McCullagh, 1995; Ryba, Stambulova, & Wrisberg, 2005; Wiggins, 1984).

The growth in the field has continued, and some countries have more than one primary professional association dedicated to sport and exercise psychology. This expansion has led to the need for formal training of students. Educational paths for sport and exercise psychology students stemmed primarily from two disciplines: kinesiology and psychology. The purpose of this chapter is to highlight some of the educational routes available for individuals interested in careers and/or formal training in sport and exercise psychology.

Training in Kinesiology

Historically, most of the academic work in sport and exercise psychology was conducted in kinesiology departments (formerly known as departments of physical education). Since the 1970s, departments studying human movement have had a variety of names and emphases and have been housed in a various colleges on university campuses. Departments are now most likely to be titled kinesiology but may also be departments of human movement studies, health and human performance, or exercise science (see Wallace, 2011, for a more exhaustive list of names). These departments are generally housed in colleges of arts and sciences but may be in colleges of health science, education, or others.

UNDERGRADUATE TRAINING IN KINESIOLOGY

At the undergraduate level, kinesiology students in broad-based programs take courses in the humanities (e.g., philosophy, history, sociology of sport), in the behavioral and social areas (e.g., motor development, sport and exercise psychology, motor learning), and in the life science area (e.g., structural kinesiology, exercise physiology, biomechanics). Students are generally expected to also take prerequisites in the parent disciplines of psychology, biology, chemistry, physics, and sociology. Finally, courses within the sport and exercise psychology area may include such titles as Psychology of Physical Activity, Sport and Exercise Psychology, Psychological Kinesiology, or Mental Skills Training for Performance. Initially, the emphasis in this field was on sport psychology. However, over time, the field has expanded to include exercise and physical activity. In most undergraduate kinesiology programs, students might only get one class in this area, although some programs may offer further upper division electives in sport and exercise psychology. This is not necessarily the case, however, in other countries. In some Asian universities, for example, there may be as many as 11 undergraduate classes in applied sport psychology that specifically lead to a degree in sport psychology in contrast to a generalist kinesiology degree (the Hong Kong Society of Sport and Exercise Psychology and the Japanese Society of Sport Psychology are examples of two professional associations in Asia that can be a resource for more information on education and training in those countries).

Around the world there is a fair amount of variability in undergraduate training that may lead to professional opportunities as a sport psychologist. For example, some universities in Australia provide the opportunity for specialization in sport and exercise psychology at the undergraduate level through their honors programs. These programs may provide 2 years of course work in general education and exercise science education, a 3rd year of interdisciplinary course work in both psychology and sport science, and a 4th-year joint honors focus on the scientist-practitioner model. Other Australian and European universities provide an opportunity for a 4th-year specialist program in sport and exercise psychology that is not necessarily connected to their honors programs.

Depending on the focus of a particular department, students in North America may be offered the opportunity to specialize their kinesiology program toward a professional career, including athletic training, fitness management, strength and conditioning, cardiac rehabilitation, or teaching physical education. Other departments may not take a professional-based approach to training undergraduates and instead take a liberal arts approach that may lead to graduate training in physical or occupational therapy, becoming a physician assistant, nursing, medicine, or graduate study in kinesiology that may have a research or applied emphasis. Very few departments in North America offer an emphasis in sport and exercise psychology at the undergraduate level.

Although it is not our aim to debate the relative merits of obtaining undergraduate training in a kinesiology department versus a psychology department (addressed later in the chapter), there are some valid reasons that students may want to obtain training in kinesiology prior to embarking on a career track in this area. For example, a sport and exercise psychology practitioner should understand the *physiological* (exercise physiology) principles that affect bodies during human movement to fully understand the complexities of issues facing a runner hoping to improve psychological skills for maximizing marathon performance. Likewise, the sport and exercise psychology consultant benefits from knowledge of the *mechanical* (biomechanics) influences on the high jump when helping a high jumper maintain focus during an entire competition. An exercise psychology consultant who understands the impact that *feedback* (motor learning) from the exercise leader can have on both the skills of the developing exerciser, the drives of the individuals within the exercise class, and the motivational orientations of the entire exercise group (sport sociology) is likely to be effective. Finally, the practitioner who is familiar with the training requirements and expectations within specific sports and physical activities such as diving is more likely to notice if an athlete is engaged in usual training or demonstrating the symptoms of an eating disorder.

Although the core courses in kinesiology may cover the basics, numerous other classes could complement the future sport and exercise psychology consultant's movement-based education. Courses in sports medicine and sport nutrition as well as classes that focus on the teaching of sport skills may be useful. Taking courses in these specialty areas by no means makes one an expert. However, increased knowledge may provide a foundation on which consultants and researchers can build effective relationships with athletes, clients, coaches, and participants.

GRADUATE PROGRAMS IN KINESIOLOGY

At the graduate level, training in sport and exercise psychology becomes more specialized. Rather than study "just" sport and exercise psychology, the program of study typically takes on a more focused appearance. For example, students need to determine if they are more interested in pursuing a research or applied emphasis. Not that one precludes the other, but an emphasis on primarily research or applied work generally becomes apparent. Furthermore, within this broad research versus applied emphasis, students also begin focusing on a more specific topic such as team cohesion, perceptions of competence, motivation, imagery, or aggression. Each of these distinctions is present at both the master's and doctoral level but is more pronounced at the doctoral level.

Typically, students complete a master's degree before being selected for a doctoral program. To gain admission to a master's program, students generally must provide evidence that they have completed prerequisites in kinesiology-based courses. If students come from another discipline, such as psychology, they may need to complete these courses as part of their graduate training. The *Directory of Graduate Programs in Applied Sport Psychology* (Sachs, Burke, & Schweighardt, 2010) lists more than 100 programs with an emphasis in sport and exercise psychology. The information provided in the *Directory of Graduate Programs in Applied Sport Psychology* and in *The World Sport Psychology Sourcebook* (Salmela, 1991) is particularly useful because doctoral degrees are not granted in sport and exercise psychology; rather they are awarded in kinesiology (or some similar label). However, just because a university has a doctoral program in kinesiology, that does not mean that it provides a specialization in sport and exercise psychology. Adding to the problem of the Internet search is the fact that kinesiology departments may have a variety of names and exist in a variety of colleges. One of the best ways to select a graduate program is to select an individual to study with. This can be accomplished by reviewing the research literature in an area of interest, contacting authors who publish in areas of interest, and discussing graduate training opportunities with the authors at their or other academic institutions.

A typical sport and exercise psychology graduate program (master's or doctoral) in a kinesiology department includes courses in research methods and statistics, motor behavior (including motor development, motor control, and motor learning), and other advanced courses in the humanities (e.g., sociology) and life science (e.g., exercise physiology) areas. In addition to these classes taken through the kinesiology department, other supportive courses might also be required in departments of psychology, sociology, or others. At the graduate level, students typically enroll in two or more sport and exercise psychology courses that focus on such topics as applied issues in sport and exercise psychology, youth sport, social psychological aspects of physical activity, psychophysiological approaches, or exercise motivation. Depending on the emphasis of the program, students may also engage in internships doing applied sport and exercise psychology work under the supervision of an adviser.

The basic purpose of most graduate programs in kinesiology departments is to conduct research and train researchers. At the doctoral level, students may become involved with various aspects of their adviser's research program before moving on to more independent experiences. Training students to conduct research that can be presented at professional meetings or published in scientific journals is an important concern within graduate programs. Some of this research may be applied research, and many programs offer opportunities to practice sport and exercise psychology consulting.

In many countries, the training and accreditation to become an applied sport psychology consultant is directly linked to that country's professional organization that oversees the licensure process for clinical and counseling psychologists. However, in other countries, training and credentialing is open to those trained in both psychology and kinesiology. See more about the requirements for accreditation in the chapter by Zizzi, Zaichkowsky, and Perna (Chapter 21, this volume).

In Europe, the European Federation of Sport Psychology provides oversight to the European Master's in Sport and Exercise Psychology program. This program consists of a consortium of four European universities that aim to educate highly qualified researchers and professionals for the field. The curriculum is interdisciplinary and research based and integrates the learning concepts into the programs of the consortium schools. In China, sport psychology students train in departments of sport psychology that include faculty in kinesiology and psychology. In the United States, the Association for Applied Sport Psychology (AASP) offers certification for consultants who complete requisite course work, earn master's and doctoral degrees, and garner applied experience under the guidance of an appropriately trained mentor. Graduate programs in North America have increasingly offered course work that enables graduates to complete the academic and applied requirements necessary for AASP certification primarily in departments of kinesiology but also in some departments of psychology (see Chapter 21, this volume).

Most, but not all, of the sport psychology faculty positions in higher education are housed in kinesiology programs. This does not preclude a person trained in psychology from obtaining these positions, and there are certainly some sport psychology faculty positions for those trained in psychology in psychology departments (held almost always by those with psychology doctoral degrees). It behooves most candidates to have training in kinesiology if they aspire to a university professor position.

Training in Psychology

Most psychology departments in the United States are housed in a college of arts and sciences and provide students with a liberal arts undergraduate degree. *Psychology* has been described as "the scientific study of behavior and mental processes" (Atkinson, Atkinson, Smith, & Hilgard, 1987, p. 13). Psychologists can serve a variety of functions, and an array of course work is necessary to adequately encompass the field. For example, subdisciplines within psychology include cognitive, social, clinical, counseling, neuropsychological, developmental, forensic, and organizational specialization areas, to name just a few.

UNDERGRADUATE PROGRAMS IN PSYCHOLOGY

Typically, undergraduate students take course work across this entire spectrum of psychology. Of course, the emphasis and course offerings vary depending on the expertise of faculty members at any particular college or university. According to the American Psychological Association's (APA's) *APA Guidelines for the Undergraduate Psychology Major*, "A baccalaureate degree in psychology should document that students have the ability to think scientifically about behavior, the skills related to the conduct of research, and the values that reflect psychology as both a science and an applied discipline" (2007a, p. 1). Thus, the purpose of an undergraduate psychology degree is an exposure to the breadth of the field of psychology and the development of the general knowledge, skills, and values necessary for successful completion of graduate education or other career options. This broad exposure is very helpful as a foundation for understanding the principles of human performance and behavior change that are taught in graduate programs in sport and exercise psychology.

The emphasis in undergraduate psychology departments typically does not address the psychology of sport and exercise. Some psychology programs offer a course or two in sport and exercise psychology; however, students may need to explore their school's kinesiology department to find additional sport and exercise psychology and related courses. Those students seeking to continue to a graduate program in psychology will find an undergraduate major in psychology to be an advantage in the application process. Some students with undergraduate degrees in psychology may choose graduate study in kinesiology. A minor in kinesiology or dual major in psychology and kinesiology can provide a strong background for graduate study in these areas.

GRADUATE PROGRAMS IN PSYCHOLOGY

Graduate students in psychology departments focus on any one of the previously mentioned specialization areas. Unfortunately, only a few psychology departments (e.g., Springfield College, University of Denver) offer specialties in sport psychology. This requires students to be proactive in planning for their career development, identifying faculty who might be supportive of their sport and exercise psychology interests.

Most graduate students in psychology departments who are interested in sport and exercise psychology choose to earn a PhD or PsyD in clinical or counseling psychology. *Clinical psychology* is the "application of psychological principles to the diagnoses and treatment of emotional and behavioral problems" (Atkinson et al., 1987, p. 15). Clinical psychologists typically work with people with mental illness, personality disorders, criminal behavior, drug addiction, eating disorders, or other behavioral problems. Clinical psychologists work in hospitals, juvenile courts, mental health clinics, prisons, medical schools, or private practice. *Counseling psychologists* work to facilitate "personal and interpersonal functioning across the life span with a focus on emotional, social, vocational, educational, health-related, developmental, and organizational concerns" (APA, Division 47 [Exercise and Sport Psychology], n.d., para. 1). Counseling psychologists often work with people who are having normal struggles with abnormal situations in their lives. They typically work in university counseling centers, academia, or in private practice. Information about graduate training in psychology is available in *Getting In: A Step-by-Step Plan for Gaining Admission to Graduate School in Psychology* (2nd ed.; APA, 2007b).

Both clinical and counseling psychology doctoral students complete a series of supervised practica and internships prior to graduation. These experiences are generally in mainstream areas of psychology, although some internships offer opportunities for work in sport and exercise psychology (see http://www.apa47.org). The balance of applied work versus research that clinical and counseling psychology doctoral students experience during their training is determined, in part, by the degree that they choose to pursue. The PhD is based on a scholar-practitioner model that generally includes a strong focus on research. The PsyD is based on a practitioner-scholar model with a primary emphasis on practice. Completion of a PhD, PsyD, or certain master's degrees in clinical or counseling psychology or social work can make a graduate eligible to become licensed as a psychologist, clinical mental health counselor, or social worker, credentials required by most states for providing reimbursable psychological services. Students who plan their course work and a plan of study carefully can also become Certified Consultants, AASP. It should be noted that admission to clinical and counseling programs is highly competitive and requires excellent undergraduate grades, high scores on standardized tests, letters of recommendation, and personal statements. Many programs have several hundred applicants for only a handful of positions.

Although there are many similarities in sport and exercise psychology education and training around the world, there are also important differences. For example, a doctorate is required to be licensed as a psychologist in the United States, but a master's degree is required to practice psychology in most of mainland Europe and in South Africa. In Australia, the Australian Psychological Association has designated the master's degree in psychology as the terminal degree for practitioners and the doctorate for researchers. State legislation regulates the practice of psychology, and it is illegal to use the title psychologist in Australia without being registered. Registration requires a bachelor's degree from an accredited university and either a master's degree or 2 years of supervised work experience. A similar arrangement linking training for sport and exercise psychology consultants to that of general psychology practitioners exists in the United Kingdom. In Asia, there are programs that provide credentialing and recognition for psychology practitioners. However, sport psychology credentialing in China, Japan, and Taiwan currently requires degrees and training primarily earned through sport psychology or kinesiology departments.

How Do Psychologists Supplement Their Training

What options do individuals have if they already have been trained in clinical or counseling psychology and want to make a transition and include sport and exercise psychology as part of their practice? It is recommended that they start by learning about the field, reading books like this one, viewing relevant videos (e.g., http://www.vbvideo.com), and attending conferences and conventions of sport and exercise psychology organizations. A formal mechanism for supplementing training is to review and meet the requirements for certification by the AASP. This typically requires the completion of additional courses in kinesiology and sport and exercise psychology and experience providing supervised applied sport and exercise psychology services under the mentorship of a professional who is a Certified Consultant, AASP. AASP publishes a list of kinesiology courses offered online (http://www.appliedsport psych.org) that can be used to meet certification requirements as well as a list of certified consultants available to mentor applied experiences.

Employment Opportunities

Most of the positions conducting research and teaching sport and exercise psychology are in kinesiology departments, although there are some positions in psychology departments. Faculty positions are advertised online at various websites (see Exhibit 20.1). For those interested in practice, the greatest opportunities appear to be for those with a psychology license. The U.S. Olympic Committee requires that all full-time sport psychology consultants on staff be licensed psychologists. The number of athletic departments in the United States with full-time sport psychology consultants on staff continues to grow. Almost all of these positions require a licensed psychologist with sport psychology training. The preference for licensed psychologists is due to the wider range of services a person who is licensed can legally provide, the ability to help with difficult issues and in crisis situations, and for legal liability concerns (Zillmer & Gigli, 2007).

Other career options include working in group or private practice as a clinical or counseling psychologist and meeting with athlete or exercise clients. Graduates with master's degrees may find positions as academic athletic advisors or CHAMPS (Challenging Athletes' Minds for Personal Success) life skills coordinators for intercollegiate athletic departments. Those with a specialty in exercise psychology may work as fitness coaches or corporate wellness coaches. American citizens with training in sport

---

EXHIBIT 20.1

Online Sources for Employment Opportunities

American Kinesiology Association (http://www.americankinesiology.org)
American Psychological Association, Division 47, Sport and Exercise Psychology
 (http://www.apa47.org)
Association for Applied Sport Psychology (http://www.appliedsportpsych.org)
Canadian Society for Psychomotor Learning and Sport Psychology (http://www.scapps.org)
Chronicle of Higher Education (http://www.chronicle.com)
National Academy of Kinesiology (http://www.nationalacademyofkinesiology.org)
National Association of Kinesiology and Physical Education in Higher Education
 (http://www.nakpehe.org)
National Collegiate Athletic Association (http://www.mcaamarket.mcaa.org/jobs)
North American Society for the Psychology of Sport and Physical Activity
 (http://www.naspspa.org)

Note. Many professional organizations publish job announcements. However, some are only available to dues-paying members of the society.

---

psychology that includes a performance focus may work with the Army's Comprehensive Soldier Fitness-Performance and Resilience Enhancement Program providing mental skills and related training to soldiers, department of the Army civilians, and their families.

In 2010, APA Division 47 (Lutkenhouse, 2010) created an ad hoc committee to describe a host of career opportunities in sport and exercise psychology. The report detailed descriptions of jobs and included interviews with individuals currently performing jobs as certified consultants, university athletic department consultants, clinical psychologists working with athletes, individuals employed by the Army Center for Enhanced Performance, sport and exercise psychology faculty, academic advisors, and fitness and lifestyle coaches. This report provides an inside look at many of these career options and should be helpful in gaining an understanding of the wide array of career options available.

Training in Kinesiology Versus Psychology— Integration is the Key

To become a competent professional in the field of sport and exercise psychology, it is necessary to have training in both kinesiology and psychology. To determine the right primary field of study, it is useful to determine one's ideal career. For those who choose to teach and conduct research in sport and exercise psychology, pursuing a doctorate in kinesiology is a good option because most academic jobs are available in kinesiology departments. However, those who want to spend the majority of their working career providing clinical or counseling services to individuals (including athletes, exercisers, or performers) with the possibility of doing some teaching should consider psychology training.

Table 20.1 provides a taxonomy for the education and roles of individuals trained in psychology and kinesiology with a focus on research and practice. Carefully examining the roles will help determine where one wants to get one's primary training. It should be noted that the quadrants are not independent. Rather, there is overlap and having information from all perspectives is fruitful.

TABLE 20.1

Taxonomy for Education and Roles

Academic training area			
Kinesiology		Psychology	
Employment opportunities	Typical issues	Employment opportunities	Typical issues
Research			
1. Academic 2. Medical setting	1. Theory testing 2. Scale development 3. Data collection with scientific method 4. Data analysis 5. Publication 6. Undergraduate/ graduate teaching 7. Training doctoral students	1. Academic 2. Clinical institution 3. Medical setting	1. Theory testing 2. Scale development 3. Data collection with scientific method 4. Data analysis 5. Publication 6. Undergraduate/ graduate teaching 7. Intervention testing 8. Training doctoral students
Practice			
1. Part-time academic 2. Comprehensive Soldier Fitness-Performance and Resilience Enhancement Program 3. Allied health field 4. Sport coaching 5. Life skills training for athletes	1. Mental skills training with athletes ▪ Arousal management ▪ Concentration ▪ Imagery ▪ Self-talk ▪ Routines ▪ Goal setting 2. Consultation with coaches 3. Consultation with teams	1. NCAA athletic department 2. Academic (full time or part time) 3. Private practice 4. University counseling center 5. Hospital 6. Clinic 7. Law enforcement 8. Social services 9. Life skills training for student athletes	1. Individual differences accounting for performance 2. Behavior change 3. Individualized counseling in sport or nonsport settings ▪ Anxiety disorders ▪ Depression ▪ Eating disorders ▪ Substance abuse ▪ Relationship issues ▪ Crisis intervention

Conclusion

There are numerous educational avenues that can be followed in sport and exercise psychology. Before deciding which path is best, it can be valuable to meet with individuals in the field and to discuss opportunities and options. Reading books, professional journals, and attending professional meetings are also valuable ways to identify the area of study. The availability of online courses has increased the opportunity for students and professionals to supplement their current training. Determining the best path for training is highly dependent on the desired outcome.

References

American Psychological Association. (2007a). *APA guidelines for the undergraduate psychology major.* Washington, DC: Author. Retrieved from http://www.apa.org/ed/resources.html

American Psychological Association. (2007b). *Getting in: A step-by-step plan for gaining admission to graduate school in psychology* (2nd ed.). Washington, DC: Author.

American Psychological Association, Division 47. (n.d.). *What is counseling.* Retrieved from http://www.div17.org/about/what-is-counseling-psychology/

Antonelli, F. (1970). Opening address. In G. S. Kenyon & T. M. Grogg. (Eds.), *Contemporary psychology of sport: Proceedings of the Second International Congress of Sport Psychology* (pp. 3–6). Washington, DC: The Athletic Institute.

Atkinson, R. L., Atkinson, R. C., Smith, E. E., & Hilgard, E. R. (1987). *Introduction to psychology* (9th ed.). New York, NY: Harcourt Brace Jovanovich.

Gardiner, E. N. (1930). *Athletics of the ancient world.* Oxford, England: Oxford University Press.

Kornspan, A. S. (2007). The early years of sport psychology: The work and influence of Pierre de Coubertin. *Journal of Sport Behavior, 30,* 77–93.

Kremer, J., & Moran, A. (2008, August). Swifter, higher, stronger. The history of sport psychology. *The Psychologist, 21,* 740–743

Lutkenhouse, J. (2010). *Career opportunities in the field of exercise and sport psychology.* Retrieved from http://www.apadivisions.org/division-47/about/resources/students/careers.pdf

McCullagh, P. (1995). Sport psychology: A historical perspective. *The Sport Psychologist, 9,* 363–365.

Ryba, R. V., Stambulova, N. B., & Wrisberg, C. A. (2005). The Russian origins of sport psychology: A translation of an early work of A. C. Puni. *Journal of Applied Sport Psychology, 17,* 157–169. doi:10.1080/10413200590932461

Sachs, M. L., Burke, K. L., & Schweighardt, M. A. (2010). *Directory of graduate programs in applied sport psychology* (10th ed.). Madison, WI: Association for Applied Sport Psychology.

Salmela, J. H. (1991). *The world sport psychology sourcebook.* Champaign, IL: Human Kinetics.

Wallace, S. (2011). *Introduction to kinesiology: The science of physical activity.* San Diego, CA: Cognella.

Wiggins, D. K. (1984). The history of sport psychology in North America. In J. M. Silva & R. S. Weinberg (Eds.), *Psychological foundations of sport* (pp. 9–22). Champaign, IL: Human Kinetics.

Zillmer, E. A., & Gigli, R. W. (2007). Clinical sport psychology in intercollegiate athletics. *Journal of Clinical Sport Psychology, 1,* 210–222.

Samuel Zizzi, Leonard Zaichkowsky, and Frank Perna

Certification in Sport and Exercise Psychology

21

S port and exercise psychology is a multidisciplinary profession. Scientists, educators, and practitioners of sport and exercise psychology share a common interest, but most have received their primary training in an array of general disciplines spanning psychology, kinesiology, and medicine and including a variety of subspecialties such as clinical and counseling psychology, exercise physiology, and biomechanics to name but a few of the possibilities other than a distinct sport and exercise psychology track.

Similar to other applied disciplines in their early stage of development, sport and exercise psychology faced the task of generating a mutually accepted model of professional training, code of practice, and core knowledge base. Because the practice of a profession serves as the primary interface of the field with the general public and encompasses both legal and professional issues, no other area in an applied profession generates as much attention and controversy as codifying standards for professional preparation and practice (see

http://dx.doi.org/10.1037/14251-021
Exploring Sport and Exercise Psychology, Third Edition, J. Van Raalte and B. Brewer (Editors)

Brooks & Gerstein, 1990, on the credentialing of counselors; see Cummings, 1990, and Fretz & Mills, 1980, on credentialing of professional psychologists). The general public views the educational background and professional behavior of those who practice as the model for the field. The field of sport and exercise psychology is no exception. There has been considerable debate as to the range of services that should be provided within sport and exercise psychology (Kirschenbaum, 1994; Morgan, 1988), who should provide those services, and how these individuals should be trained (Andersen, Van Raalte, & Brewer, 2001; Danish & Hale, 1981; Heyman, 1993; May, 1993; Monahan, 1987; Morris, Alfermann, Lintunen, & Hall, 2003; Silva, 1989).

Certification is a function of a professional organization that attempts to codify a common standard of preparation and practice. At a beginning stage, these standards must serve the dual purpose of recognizing the experience of members currently in the field and setting guidelines for those newer members who wish to pursue sport and exercise psychology. The purpose of this chapter is to (a) define terminology associated with certification, which in our opinion has been at the root of much controversy; (b) provide a history of certification from an international perspective; (c) provide a rationale for the existence of the certification process; (d) outline and respond to criticisms that have been levied against certification; and (e) explore future improvements in certification that could further develop the field.

Defining Certification and Related Terms

The terminology associated with the credentialing process in general and in sport and exercise psychology in particular is complicated. For instance, confusion exists regarding statutory versus nonstatutory designations and regarding certification versus licensure. The following sections define many terms that are related to the credentialing process.

CREDENTIALING

Credentialing is a broad generic term that is commonly defined as a process of giving a title or claim of competence. Credentialing includes *statutory* designations that are protected by codified law and enacted by a legislative body or as a function of administrative law or executive order as well as *nonstatutory* designations, such as recognition by organizations and registries, that are not protected by law. In the mental health field, credentialing appears to take five basic forms: association membership, accreditation of educational and training programs, certification by a nongovernmental agency, government licensure and chartered membership, and registration on an official roster (Anchor, 1988).

CERTIFICATION

Certification is generally a nonstatutory designation granted by an organization rather than by a legislative body. However, some states use the label *certification* in reference to statutory designations (e.g., certified teacher, certified psychologist). Certification is usually a transitional designation that may serve as a preliminary step toward statutory standards for that profession (Smith, 1986). The National Coaching Certification Program in Canada and Association for Applied Sport Psychology (AASP) certification are examples of nonstatutory certification, whereas public school certification and certified mental health counselors are examples of statutory certification.

REGISTRY

Registry is generally a nonstatutory designation indicating "that an individual has been publicly identified as meeting qualifications as specified by the organization and is eligible for formal listing" (Smith, 1986, p. 13). The U.S. Olympic Committee Sport Psychology Registry and the former Canadian Mental Training Registry are examples of registries.

LICENSURE AND CHARTERED MEMBERSHIP

Licensure and *chartered membership* are statutory processes and are the most restrictive of all these terms. The statutory designations of licensure and chartered membership indicate state or provincial processes that are designed to regulate professional conduct within a particular field. At times, a state may adopt a professional organization's admission standards or code of ethics, and it may even relegate the monitoring of the field to a professional board of the organization. However, the state legislature retains legal authority and determines the professional organization's involvement. Licensure and chartered membership as a psychologist are examples of statutory processes that protect the use of titles (i.e., licensed psychologist, chartered psychologist) and scope of practice (e.g., psychological test interpretation).

PSYCHOLOGIST

The title *psychologist* is restricted in Australia, Canada, the United Kingdom, and the United States. This title is generally reserved for those who are licensed, chartered, registered, or certified to offer services to the public. Psychologists generally have a doctoral degree in counseling or clinical psychology. Exceptions to this restricted use of the title include individuals who teach and conduct research in psychology and individuals from selected states and provinces that recognize master's level psychologists. Internationally, the requirements to become a psychologist vary dramatically and often do not require completion of a doctoral degree.

COUNSELOR

Any person who is helping another is in fact offering counseling services. For instance, there are academic counselors, drug and alcohol counselors, career counselors, marriage counselors, and so forth. In many cases, little or no training is provided for these "lay" counselors; however, in other cases, counselors undergo rigorous training, making them eligible for statutory designations such as *licensed mental health counselor* or *licensed professional counselor*.

ACCREDITED OR APPROVED PROGRAM

The terms *accredited* and *approved* generally refer to an educational, training, or service program that has met certain standards that may or may not be related to certification or licensure. Accreditation is usually the result of a review of relevant documentation (e.g., course syllabi, learning objectives, job placement data, curriculum and practicum offerings) and a site visit by a team of reviewers from the accreditation agency. The American Psychological Association (APA) has an accreditation program that approves training programs in counseling, school, and clinical psychology. It should be emphasized, however, that by participating in an APA-approved program one does not automatically become licensed to practice psychology. This point is particularly confusing to aspiring young professionals because they may be unaware of the fact that licensing is a state function. Typically, state licensing boards require applicants to complete a standardized exam and a set number of postdoctoral clinical hours (e.g., 2,000 hours) along with graduation from a doctoral level program and completion of a predoctoral clinical hour requirement. In 2003, after the efforts of many members of APA Division 47 (Exercise and Sport Psychology), APA established a proficiency in sport psychology. This proficiency outlines a set of competencies that professionals should acquire, in addition to their licensure as a psychologist, if they desire to practice in sport and exercise settings. A full description of the proficiency can be found online at http://www.apa.org/ed/graduate/specialize/sports.aspx.

A Brief History of Sport Psychology Certification

The question of who is qualified to be a *sport psychologist* has been an issue ever since the field of sport psychology expanded from being primarily a topic for research and teaching in universities to providing professional services to athletes and coaches. A number of position papers were written on the topic beginning in the late 1970s (Harrison & Feltz, 1979) and writing on this topic has continued to the present (Andersen et al., 2001; Meyers, Coleman, Whelan, & Mehlenbeck, 2001; Silva, Conroy, & Zizzi, 1999; Tod, Andersen, & Marchant, 2011; Watson, Zizzi, Etzel, & Lubker, 2004).

UNITED STATES

The U.S. Olympic Committee (USOC) initiated the first systematic attempt in North America to credential sport and exercise psychologists. In August 1982, the USOC brought together a committee that proposed that a sport psychology registry be established that would include the names of qualified workers in three separate categories of sport psychology. These categories included (a) clinical and counseling sport psychologists, (b) educational sport psychologists, and (c) research sport psychologists. The committee provided criteria for the three categories ("U.S. Olympic Committee establishes," 1983) and invited sport psychologists to apply for membership in the registry. In 1995, the USOC and AASP formed a certification partnership (Association for the Advancement of Applied Sport Psychology, 1995) allowing AASP-certified consultants who are also members of APA to apply for acceptance on the registry. As of January 2011, 133 sport psychologists are listed on the registry (K. Cogan, personal communication, January 24, 2011).

In 1989, the AASP approved a certification program. The AASP Executive Board, Certification Committee, and fellows focused particular attention on matters pertaining to *role definition* (i.e., What can sport and exercise psychologists do?) and *title* (i.e., What is the most appropriate legally acceptable title for members working in sport and exercise psychology?). After extensive deliberation, it was concluded that if AASP certified individuals as sport psychologists, the AASP might be in violation of state and provincial laws. Because of this legal issue, AASP fellows voted to use the title Certified Consultant, AASP, rather than a title supported by many members—certified sport psychologist. The criteria for AASP certification are presented in Exhibit 21.1, and updated application

EXHIBIT 21.1

Criteria for Association of Applied Sport Psychology Certification

1. Completion of a master's or doctoral degree from an accredited institution of higher education. In Canada, an institution of higher education must be recognized as a member in good standing of the Association of Universities and Colleges of Canada. Programs leading to a doctoral degree must include the equivalent of 3 full-time academic years of graduate study, 2 years of which are at the institution from which the doctoral degree is granted and 1 year of which is in full-time residence at the institution from which the doctoral degree is granted.

2. Completion of 400 hours of mentored experience with a qualified person (i.e., one who has an appropriate background in applied sport psychology), during which the individual receives training in the use of sport psychology principles and techniques (e.g., mentored practica in applied sport psychology in which the recipients of the assessments and interventions are participants in physical activity, exercise, or sport). Master's level applicants who complete the course work requirements and 400 hours of mentored experience will be granted provisional certification. On completing an additional 300 hours of mentored experience, they will be granted full status as a certified consultant.

3. Knowledge of professional ethics and standards. This requirement can be met by taking one course on these topics or by taking several courses in which these topics constitute parts of the courses or by completing other comparable experiences.

4. Knowledge of the sport psychology subdisciplines of intervention and performance enhancement, health and exercise psychology, and social psychology as evidenced by three courses or two courses and one independent study in sport psychology (two of these courses must be taken at the graduate level).

5. Knowledge of the biomechanical and/or physiological bases of sport (e.g., kinesiology, biomechanics, exercise physiology).

6. Knowledge of the historical, philosophical, social or motor behavior bases of sport (e.g., motor learning and control, motor development, issues in sport and physical education, sociology of sport history, and philosophy of sport and physical education).

7. Knowledge of psychopathology and its assessment (e.g., abnormal psychology, psychopathology).

8. Training designed to foster basic skills in counseling (e.g., graduate-level course work on basic intervention techniques in counseling; mentored practica in counseling, clinical, or industrial and organizational psychology).

9. Knowledge of skills and techniques within sport or exercise (e.g., skills and techniques courses, clinics, formal coaching experiences, or organized participation in sport or exercise).

10. Knowledge and skills in research design, statistics, and psychological assessment attained in graduate-level course work.

    At least two of the following four criteria must be met through educational experiences that focus on general psychological principles (rather than sport specific ones).

11. Knowledge of the biological bases of behavior (e.g., biomechanics and kinesiology, comparative psychology, exercise physiology, neuropsychology, physiological psychology, psychopharmacology, sensation).

12. Knowledge of the cognitive–affective bases of behavior (e.g., cognition, emotion, learning, memory, motivation, motor development, motor learning and control, perception, thinking).

13. Knowledge of the social bases of behavior (e.g., cultural or ethnic and group processes, gender roles in sport, organization and system theory, social psychology, sociology of sport).

14. Knowledge of individual behavior (e.g., developmental psychology, exercise behavior, health psychology, individual differences, personality theory).

Note. Data from the Association for Applied Sport Psychology (2012).

requirements can be found online at http://www.appliedsportpsych.org. As of January 2011, the number of certified consultants was 355, a pattern of slow but steady growth of approximately 20 new consultants per year (S. Castillo, personal communication, January 19, 2011).

CANADA

Under the leadership of Dr. Murray Smith, Canada instituted the Canadian Registry for Sport Behavioral Professionals in 1987. This national registry was a part of the Canadian Association of Sport Sciences and was designed to provide a list of names of providers who were qualified to offer professional services to the sport community, including athletes, coaches, parents, teams, administrators, agencies, and sport governing bodies (Canadian Association of Sport Sciences, 1994). The registry was similar to the USOC registry in that it listed qualified professionals in three categories: (a) licensed psychologists, (b) sport educators/counselors, and (c) sport researchers. The Canadian registry was replaced by the Canadian Mental Training Registry in 1994 and by the Canadian Sport Psychology Association directory in 2000. The Canadian Sport Psychology Association serves two primary roles: (a) recognizing professionals from a variety of backgrounds who are competent to deliver sport psychology services in Canada and (b) providing mentoring and supervision opportunities for aspiring professionals. The 2011 directory lists 76 professional members as either a registered psychologist or a mental performance consultant (Canadian Sport Psychology Association, 2011), following a model of certification similar to the Certified Consultant, AASP requirements, which include course work, applied experiences, and attainment of at least a master's degree.

AUSTRALIA

Like their colleagues in North America, Australians have struggled with the question of who can be a sport psychologist. Jeffrey Bond was appointed the first *applied* sport psychologist at the Australian Institute of Sport in 1982. For the next 20 years, educational programs as well as opportunities in the field of sport and exercise psychology grew at a rapid rate. Although there is wide acceptance of sport psychology services at many levels of sport in Australia, currently only two accredited master's programs exist because of such programs' failure to make money for universities (S. Hanrahan, personal communication, January 20, 2011).

To practice as a sport psychologist in Australia, one must be a full member of the Australian Psychological Society and accepted as a member of the College of Sport and Exercise Psychologists. The college has been sanctioned by and is held directly accountable to the Australian

Psychological Society (see http://www.groups.psychology.org.au/csep/). As such, sport and exercise psychology is closely linked to the profession of psychology ("Chairperson's Report," 1993), although it also has strong links with Sports Medicine Australia. The standard route to become a registered psychologist is to first complete an Australian Psychological Society–accredited 4-year degree in psychology and then a 2-year accredited master's program. Accredited master's programs include course work, research, and 1,000 hours of supervised practice.

UNITED KINGDOM

The British Association of Sport and Exercise Sciences (1994) developed accreditation criteria that were designed to "set, maintain and enhance the professional and ethical standards of its members who are actively involved in the sport and exercise sciences." Accreditation was initially available in two categories: (a) research accreditation (i.e., carrying out research in sport and exercise science); and (b) support accreditation (i.e., providing appropriate guidance and service to client groups). Since 2009, the Health Professions Council serves as the clearinghouse to "maintain and publish a register of health professionals who meet our standards" (Health & Care Professions Council, 2011). This register serves as a governing body, thereby legally protecting all forms of health services and psychological practice, including the designation *sport and exercise psychologist.* Thus, people who are trained in fields other than psychology are ineligible for accreditation as sport and exercise psychologists. Individuals can obtain membership on this registry via three routes: voluntary register transfer (members from British Psychological Society or Association of Educational Psychologist prior to 2009), completion of a United Kingdom-approved degree program, or an international application.

FRANCE

The French Society for the Psychology of Sport initiated an accreditation process for professionals in 2000. To earn certification in sport psychology, professionals must complete credentialing as a psychologist in France, agree to the ethics charter of the organization, and document 720 hours of supervised experience in a sport setting over a 3-year period (French Society for the Psychology of Sport, 2010). As of December 2010, the registry listed 28 certified professionals.

NETHERLANDS

The Dutch Society for Sport Psychology started its accreditation program in 2004. From 2005 to 2008 there was an extended transition period in which all the current members had the opportunity to meet the criteria that were set. After November 2008, new applicants were required to complete a bachelor's degree in psychology or movement sciences and a master's degree in sport psychology. After that, one could choose to become a *teacher sport psychologist* or continue as a *research sport psychologist*. To earn status as an applied sport psychologist, students need to follow a part-time 2-year program with applied work and supervision. Certified sport psychologists are registered as a trademark: SPORTPSYCHOLOOG VSPN. The current number of certified sport psychologists is 61 (R. Schuijers, personal communication, January, 2011).

SWEDEN

In Sweden, the National Sport Federation established a certification procedure in 2010, which is administered by the Swedish Sport Federation in collaboration with universities and major sports. Only individuals who meet this standard are given contracts from the National Sport Federation to work with elite-level athletes. The National Sport Federation cohosts a 2-year educational program that focuses on elite-level sport together with the Swedish School of Sport and Health Science. In 2011, Umeå University served as the first University in Sweden to educate licensed psychologists with an emphasis on sport and exercise psychology (G. Kentta, personal communication, January 2011).

JAPAN

Beginning in the year 2000, the Japanese Society of Sport Psychology has certified 120 mental training consultants (Suzuki, 2010). To qualify for the basic level of Certified Assistant Mental Training Consultant in Sport, an applicant must have a master's degree, be a member of the Japanese Society of Sport Psychology for 2 years, and complete course requirements in sport psychology, general psychology, and sport science. The sport science training includes required workshops offered at the Japanese Society of Sport Psychology annual conference, previous athletic experience, and ongoing supervised hours of consulting and/or teaching experience with athletes or coaches in the past 5 years. Practitioners with additional experience may qualify to become Certified Mental Training Consultants in Sport and Certified Master Training Consultants in Sport. Additional training is required for recertification every 5 years.

CHINA

The 2008 Beijing Olympic Games provided the momentum needed for the Sport Psychology Committee of the Chinese Sport Science Society to establish a preliminary certification system in October 2006. This hierarchical system established a three-tiered certification framework including doctoral level (psychological counseling expert of sport, 400 hours of practical experience spanning 5 years), master's level (sport psychological consultant, 200 hours of experience across 2 years), and bachelor's level (underlying sport psychological consultant) requirements. Aspiring consultants are also required to publish research, pass a qualifying examination, and complete an oral defense. The initial grandparenting process restricted admission to only 20 to 25 *experts,* but the pool of certified consultants in China continues to grow at each level.

TAIWAN

The Society of Sport and Exercise Psychology of Taiwan certification program in sport psychology requires a bachelor's degree in physical education or psychology as well as a master's degree in sport psychology. Applicants must complete 12 required courses with 95% attendance and an average score of 80/100 in their course work. Once applicants complete a 150-hour supervised internship, they are eligible to receive the *elementary* credential and may earn *medium* and *advanced* credentials after 3 and 5 years of practice, respectively. This credential allows consultants to practice in sport and exercise settings with all age groups but does not allow consultants to work with mental disorders or to prescribe medication. There are currently 20 certified consultants with approximately 40 additional professionals working toward this credential in Taiwan (C. Huang, personal communication, December 1, 2010).

The Benefits of Certification

The AASP notes several benefits of certification on its website (AASP, 2011), which are integrated into the following discussion.

ACCOUNTABILITY AND PROFESSIONALISM

The primary objective of a certification program is to provide a standard that sport administrators, coaches, psychologists, other health care professionals, the media, and the public accept as reliable evidence that an individual has attained specified professional competency. In this way, certifying associations assume accountability for high standards of performance in sport and exercise psychology. Certification also attests to the professionalism of the practicing individual, thereby protecting the public interest by promoting quality control.

RECOGNITION AND PUBLIC AWARENESS

Certification means that each individual certified as a consultant is listed in a registry of accredited specialists. Each is recognized as having fulfilled prescribed standards of performance and conduct. This registry is made publicly available to all amateur and professional sport organizations as well as other professional groups. In this way, certification serves to provide a vehicle for identifying qualified practitioners.

CREDIBILITY

The certification process affords credibility because certification procedures for identifying qualified professionals are rigorous and based on peer review. In many cases, the public can be assured that sport and exercise psychology is maintaining high standards of performance because of recertification procedures that require the continuing education of consultants.

PROACTIVE SELF-DETERMINATION

Another benefit to certification is that of *proactive self-determination* (Smith, 1987). There is clearly an advantage to having the sport and exercise psychology profession proactively define education and training, roles, ethical standards, and so forth, rather than having external professional organizations define conditions in possibly unacceptable ways. It is expected that as more people become certified in sport and exercise psychology, the marketing efforts of this credential will become more effective, which will result in greater recognition of this credential.

Criticisms of Certification

Considering that sport and exercise psychology is a relative newcomer as an applied science, it is not surprising that attempts to codify guidelines for professional practice have been met with both favorable and unfavorable reactions. For a full discussion of the pros and cons of AASP certification, we refer readers to Anshel (1992, 1994) and Zaichkowsky and Perna (1992).

The two most common criticisms of certification programs in any discipline are that they are overexclusionary and that the specific guidelines may harm the profession. For example, Anshel (1994) argued correctly that certification "fails to recognize the expertise of individuals who meet many, but not all, of the criteria for certification" (p. 345). However, because certification is a nonstatutory designation, the credential is voluntary and not a prerequisite for practice. This argument holds little or no weight as a legitimate criticism of any certification program because these designations are developed by professional organizations that are responsible for managing the best interests of the field, and they are meant to represent a minimum standard of competence.

A second criticism is based largely on the premise that certification may create the illusion of sanctioning fraudulent practice (Anshel, 1992; Zaichkowsky & Perna, 1992). Although it is true that certified consultants who make fraudulent claims, misapply techniques, and generally practice outside of their area of expertise would likely damage the field of sport and exercise psychology, there is no evidence to suggest that certification promotes this occurrence. More arguments can be made supporting the opposite view that certification likely reduces unethical practice.

The course work and supervised practica required for certification are intended to document that not only are applicants for certification exposed to the interventions used in the provision of sport and exercise psychology services but also that they demonstrate proficient skill and judgment in their application (e.g. Blakeslee & Goff, 2007; Fournier, Calmels, Durand-Bush, & Salmela, 2005; Greenspan & Feltz, 1989; Gucciardi, Gordon, & Dimmock, 2009; Sheard & Golby, 2006; Thelwell & Greenlees, 2003; Thelwell, Greenlees, & Weston, 2006). Present certified sport and exercise psychology practitioners, similar to other applied professionals, are encouraged to regularly apprise themselves of new developments through journals, conferences, workshops, and consultation. To maintain certified status, consultants generally are required to complete continuing education credits to keep abreast of new information and applications within the field.

It is true that certification, similar to all credentialing processes, can only minimally define competent practice. Whether consultants seek to adjust their practice as new evidence accumulates or to engage in consultation and referral when appropriate is not an issue plaguing certification but rather an issue of professional integrity. We contend that certification standards serve to promote competent practice by providing training guidelines for students and professionals seeking to expand their practice.

A related criticism that often arises concerns the belief that licensed mental health practitioners without requisite experience in the practice of sport and exercise psychology, specifically psychologists, would be eligible for certification as sport and exercise psychology practitioners. This is simply not the case. Nor is it appropriate to assume that a psychologist without demonstrated expertise may opt to advertise and practice as a sport and exercise psychologist without the potential for censure. Although statutes typically protect the title *psychologist* and permutations thereof, state regulatory boards prohibit psychologists and other mental health professionals from practicing and advertising in areas outside of their expertise. Professionals may be reported to their respective certifying or licensing boards for practicing outside of their area of expertise. Therefore, although sport and exercise psychology credentialing organizations have no legal jurisdiction over professionals who practice unethically, by having publicly stated certification criteria, individuals and sport and exercise psychology organizations are in a better position to curtail practice that is detrimental to the field of sport psychology.

It is our view that certification provides the public with standard criteria that consultants have met and a means by which certified and noncertified professionals can be compared. With time, professional sport and exercise psychology organizations and the public will decide if certification is important. In the interim, the public is protected to the greatest extent possible from fraud. However, as is the case with credentialing in other professional fields, certification does not and never was intended to guarantee expertise or personal integrity. All professional organizations contain isolated individuals who have engaged in unethical and at times criminal conduct. Any allegation that certification promotes inappropriate behavior detrimental to the field is unsubstantiated. On the contrary, to dispense with certification and let "the market" determine quality, as has been suggested (Anshel, 1992), would likely be a professional disaster.

Future Developments in Certification

For certification credentialing to significantly improve the quality of training and services provided within applied sport psychology, it must be supported by a large number of professionals within the field. In the past 10 years, the percentage of the professional membership holding Certified Consultant, AASP status, has increased from 25% to 41% of the membership, showing a strong emphasis within the organization to grow this credential. In the Netherlands, 28% of the members of the Dutch Society for Sport Psychology are certified. However, it should be noted that more than half of all professional members in these organizations are not certified.

The following subsections highlight issues that are challenges for those hoping to become certified in sport and exercise psychology. Addressing these issues would not simply increase the number of certified consultants but also would facilitate the application process to allow for qualified consultants to become certified more efficiently.

MEETING THE PRACTICUM HOURS REQUIREMENTS

Many applicants struggle to get enough supervised hours working in sport and exercise settings, and this struggle includes candidates from both sport science and psychology backgrounds. One key issue involves finding qualified supervisors for applied work with sport and exercise clients. The AASP recently changed the terminology associated with this requirement from *supervision* to *mentorship*. This seemingly simple change has the potential to create many more willing mentors who are currently licensed psychologists and interpret supervision as a protected legal term that holds them responsible for their trainees' work. Licensed psychologists may be more able to serve as mentors but for important legal reasons must be cautious about whom they choose to supervise. To provide additional support for those seeking certification, it may be useful to establish a clearinghouse wherein certified consultants could offer mentorship or supervision over the telephone and/or other electronic media to those consultants who are unable to acquire such support in their geographic area. This indirect mentoring model may be effective in encouraging applicants to complete their applied hours and could establish a more direct mentoring relationship beyond the boundaries of graduate programs. As more countries begin to develop a pool of certified professionals, adopting this flexible model of mentoring may allow their certification programs to grow more rapidly compared with a more rigid approach to supervision.

Aside from supervision issues, students also often struggle to get a diverse set of experiences across sport and exercise settings. To ensure comprehensive training, opportunities need to be developed within graduate programs to ensure that students have access to youth sport participants, elite athletes, adult and older adult exercisers, and possibly chronic disease populations (e.g., those with obesity, cancer, diabetes, heart disease). For instance, some sport psychology or counseling programs have already developed relationships with other academic units (community medicine, exercise physiology) to provide practicum opportunities for their students. Developing new applied opportunities would increase the likelihood that students could not only meet the minimum hour requirements for certification but also get experience providing interventions to several different populations.

MEETING THE COURSE WORK REQUIREMENTS

In addition to their struggles with practicum hours, students in some countries preparing to apply for certification have difficulty completing courses in all required curricular areas. Two general approaches may help students get the courses they need for certification. The first approach involves encouraging programs to develop course work that mirrors the requirements for certification. Some authors have argued that certification will not be able to sustain itself in the future without the support of quality graduate training programs (Silva et al., 1999). Thus, in addition to support from professional members, certification programs also need the support of sport psychology graduate programs to help produce a greater number of consultants who have the requisite training to become certified. Finally, on an institutional level, and regardless of programmatic change (which can be slow and costly), the minimal involvement for faculty advisors and department chairs interacting with sport psychology students should include teaching students about the requirements of certification early in their careers and considering the course work components of certification when developing plans of study with their students. Then, if the program or department does not offer a particular class, students could proactively seek out their remaining requirements in other departments, online, or through continuing education workshops. Internet-based and workshop-centered training methods could create an efficient model through which professionals who are lacking only a few classes or competencies could be eligible for certification.

Summary

In this chapter, we attempted to provide an overview of key issues related to certification in sport and exercise psychology. We defined nomenclature associated with certification, emphasized legal issues concerned with the title psychologist, and presented arguments for and against the process. We also provided a brief history of certification of sport and exercise psychologists and reviewed recent international developments in certification. Future directions and improvements in certification were explored, which we hope will help the field of applied sport psychology continue to provide quality service in the public domain.

References

Anchor, K. N. (1988). Professional regulation in the U.S.: Task force on issues and problems in current credentialing practices. *Medical Psychotherapy: An International Journal, 1,* 173–180.

Andersen, M. B., Van Raalte, J. L., & Brewer, B. W. (2001). Sport psychology service delivery: Staying ethical while keeping loose. *Professional Psychology: Research and Practice, 32,* 12–18. doi:10.1037/0735-7028.32.1.12

Anshel, M. H. (1992). The case against the certification of sport psychologists: In search of the phantom expert. *The Sport Psychologist, 6,* 265–286.

Anshel, M. H. (1994). *Sport psychology: From theory to practice.* Scottsdale, AZ: Gorsuch Scarisbrick.

Association for Applied Sport Psychology. (2011). *Benefits of certification.* Retrieved from http://appliedsportpsych.org/consultants/benefits-of-certification

Association for Applied Sport Psychology, (2012). *Become a certified consultant.* Retrieved from http://www.appliedsportpsych.org/Consultants/become-certified

Association for the Advancement of Applied Sport Psychology. (1995). A new USOC–AASP partnership. *AASP Newsletter, 10*(3), 9.

Blakeslee, M. L., & Goff, D. M. (2007). The effects of a mental skills training package on equestrians. *The Sport Psychologist, 21,* 288–301.

British Association of Sport and Exercise Sciences. (1994). *Accreditation criteria for sport and exercise scientists—Psychology section.* Unpublished manuscript.

Brooks, D. K., & Gerstein, L. H. (1990). Counselor credentialing and interprofessional collaboration. *Journal of Counseling & Development, 68,* 477–484. doi:10.1002/j.1556-6676.1990.tb01394.x

Canadian Association of Sport Sciences. (1994). *Canadian mental training registry.* Gloucester, Ontario, Canada: Author.

Canadian Sport Psychology Association. (2011). *Professional membership.* Retrieved from http://www.en.cspa-acps.ca/membershipdirectory/professionalmembership.html

Chairperson's report. (1993). *Australian Sport Psychology Association Bulletin, 2,* 4–6.

Cummings, N. A. (1990). The credentialing of professional psychologists and its implication for the other mental health disciplines. *Journal of Counseling & Development, 68,* 485–490. doi:10.1002/j.1556-6676.1990.tb01395.x

Danish, S. J., & Hale, B. D. (1981). Toward an understanding of the practice of sport psychology. *Journal of Sport Psychology, 3,* 90–99.

Fournier, J. F., Calmels, C., Durand-Bush, N., & Salmela, J. H. (2005). Effects of a season-long PST program on gymnastic performance and psychological skills development. *International Journal of Sport and Exercise Psychology, 3,* 59–78. doi:10.1080/1612197X.2005.9671758

French Society for the Psychology of Sport. (2010). *Accreditation procedure* [Translated online]. Retrieved from http://www.psychodusport.com/ProcedureAccredit.php

Fretz, B. R., & Mills, D. H. (1980). *Licensing and certification of psychologists and counselors: A guide to current policies, procedures and legislation.* San Francisco, CA: Jossey-Bass.

Greenspan, M. J., & Feltz, D. L. (1989). Psychological interventions with athletes in competitive situations: A review. *The Sport Psychologist, 3,* 219–236.

Gucciardi, D. F., Gordon, S., & Dimmock, J. A. (2009). Evaluation of a mental toughness training program for youth-aged Australian footballers: I. A quantitative analysis. *Journal of Applied Sport Psychology, 21,* 307–323. doi:10.1080/10413200903026066

Harrison, R. P., & Feltz, D. L. (1979). The professionalization of sport psychology: Legal considerations. *Journal of Sport Psychology, 1,* 182–190.

Health & Care Professions Council. (2011). *About registration.* Retrieved from http://www.hpc-uk.org/aboutregistration

Heyman, S. (1993, August). *The need to go slowly: Educational and ethical issues in proposed sport psychology certification.* Paper presented at the meeting of the American Psychological Association, Toronto, Ontario, Canada.

Kirschenbaum, D. S. (1994, August). *Helping athletes improve sport performance—Best guesses.* Division 47 Presidential Address at the meeting of the American Psychological Association, Los Angeles, CA.

May, J. (1993, August). *Issues concerning certification of sport psychologists.* Paper presented at the meeting of the American Psychological Association, Toronto, Ontario, Canada.

Meyers, A. W., Coleman, J. K., Whelan, J. P., & Mehlenbeck, R. S. (2001). Examining careers in sport psychology: Who is working and who is making money? *Professional Psychology: Research and Practice, 32,* 5–11. doi:10.1037/0735-7028.32.1.5

Monahan, T. (1987). Sport psychology: A crisis identity? *The Physician and Sportsmedicine, 15,* 203–212.

Morgan, W. P. (1988). Sport psychology in its own context: A recommendation for the future. In J. S. Skinner, C. B. Corbin, D. M. Landers, P. E. Martin, & C. L. Wells (Eds.), *Future directions in exercise and sport science* (pp. 97–110). Champaign, IL: Human Kinetics.

Morris, T., Alfermann, D., Lintunen, T., & Hall, H. (2003). Training and selection of sport psychologists: An international review. *International Journal of Sport and Exercise Psychology, 1,* 139–154. doi:10.1080/1612 197X.2003.9671708

Sheard, M., & Golby, J. (2006). Effect of a psychological skills training program on swimming performance and positive psychological development. *International Journal of Sport and Exercise Psychology, 4,* 149–169. doi:10.1080/1612197X.2006.9671790

Silva, J. M. (1989). Toward the professionalization of sport psychology. *The Sport Psychologist, 3,* 265–273.

Silva, J. M., Conroy, D. C., & Zizzi, S. J. (1999). Critical issues confronting the advancement of applied sport psychology. *Journal of Applied Sport Psychology, 11,* 298–320. doi:10.1080/10413209908404206

Smith, M. F. R. (1986, October). *Background to the proposal for a Canadian registry for sport psychology.* Paper presented at the meeting of the Canadian Association of Sport Science. Ottawa, Ontario, Canada.

Smith, M. F. R. (1987). *Canadian Association of Sport Sciences: Registry for sport behavioral professionals.* Unpublished manuscript.

Suzuki, M. (2010). Certification and contents of mental training consultant in sport. In Certification Committee in Japanese Society of Sport Psychology and Japanese Society of Certified Mental Training Consultant in Sport (Eds.), *Sports mental training guidebook* (pp. 27–30). Tokyo, Japan: Baseball Magazine.

Thelwell, R. C., & Greenlees, I. A. (2003). Developing competitive endurance performance using mental skills training. *The Sport Psychologist, 17,* 318–337.

Thelwell, R. C., Greenlees, I. A., & Weston, N. J. (2006). Using psychological skills training to develop soccer performance. *Journal of Applied Sport Psychology, 18,* 254–270. doi:10.1080/10413200600830323

Tod, D., Andersen, M. B., & Marchant, D. B. (2011). Six years up: Applied sport psychologists surviving (and thriving) after graduation. *Journal of Applied Sport Psychology, 23,* 93–109. doi:10.1080/1041320 0.2010.534543

U.S. Olympic Committee establishes guidelines for sport psychology services (1983). *Journal of Sport Psychology, 5,* 4–7.

Watson, J. C., II, Zizzi, S. J., Etzel, E. F., & Lubker, J. R. (2004). Applied sport psychology supervision: A survey of students and professionals. *The Sport Psychologist, 18,* 415–429.

Zaichkowsky, L. D., & Perna, F. M. (1992). Certification of consultants in sport psychology: A rebuttal to Anshel. *The Sport Psychologist, 6,* 287–296.

Kate F. Hays and Jack J. Lesyk

Incorporating Sport and Exercise Psychology Into Clinical Practice

22

T he expanding field of sport and exercise psychology offers considerable promise for individuals contemplating a career in psychology (Helms & Rogers, 2010; Wegenek & Buskist, 2010). Graduate and postgraduate training opportunities in sport psychology are increasing on a regular basis (Sachs, Burke, & Schweighardt, 2011). For established practitioners, however, the route to sport and exercise psychology may be somewhat more circuitous. This chapter is intended to address questions such as the following: What opportunities are available for the practice of sport and exercise psychology? How can sport and exercise psychology be incorporated into a clinical practice? What present clinical skills are applicable, and what new skills should be acquired? What are the most salient business issues? What practitioner concerns need to be addressed?

We would like to acknowledge the contributions made by Robert J. Smith to this chapter in the prior two editions of this volume.

http://dx.doi.org/10.1037/14251-022

Exploring Sport and Exercise Psychology, Third Edition, J. Van Raalte and B. Brewer (Editors)

The Public and Professional Climate

Sports interest and participation has been expanding in recent years: More individuals are participating in sport; previously underserved members of the population, such as youth and seniors, women, and persons with disabilities, are actively engaged; and more money is being spent on sporting equipment and participation fees. At the professional level, teams and leagues are being created; there is increased attendance; and more media time and space are devoted to sports coverage (Fort, 2011; National Sporting Goods Association, http://www.nsga.org/i4a/pages/index.cfm?pageid=3346).

With regard to health and exercise behaviors among the general public, there has been considerable interest in and promotion of active lifestyles through engagement in sport and exercise ("ACSM and AMA Launch 'Exercise is Medicine' Program," http://certification.acsm.org/exercise-is-medicine-credential). The benefits of exercise and sport participation are now frequent topics in electronic and print media. Popular books and articles extoll the physical, emotional, and cognitive benefits of exercise (e.g., Krucoff & Krucoff, 2009; Ratey & Hagerman, 2008).

Along with the increased interest in sport and exercise, there has been a concomitant increase in public awareness of the importance of the mental aspects of performance at all levels. Olympic and professional athletes and coaches speak openly and positively about their use of sport psychology consultants. Many recreational and young athletes wish to emulate those they admire; they want to use some of the same methods as their heroes and therefore seek the services of sport and exercise psychologists. Professionals in domains such as law enforcement, performing arts, medicine, the military, and business also have expressed interest in applying the principles and practices of sport psychology (Hays & Brown, 2004). It seems likely that this trend will continue well into the future, providing additional new markets for the development and expansion of sport and exercise psychology services.

Because the field of sport and exercise psychology holds considerable appeal both for the public and practitioners, this is a good time for mental health practitioners who wish to transition into this practice (Hays, 2012). Opportunities are available for those who accept the challenge and are willing to add new skills, knowledge, and credentials to their existing ones.

Practice Opportunities in Sport

Practitioners may engage in sport and exercise psychology in three somewhat distinctive ways: addressing the mind-to-body aspect (i.e., the use of mental techniques within sports), focusing on the body-to-mind component (i.e., the positive impact of exercise on mental health), and practicing psychotherapy with athletes. The majority of this chapter focuses on the first because it is the area that people tend to think of when they think of applied sport psychology. The other two areas are also worth noting and are addressed, briefly, here as well as in other chapters of this volume.

MIND TO BODY: PEAK PERFORMANCE TRAINING

Peak performance training, often described as psychological skills training (PST), is based on the assumption that aspects of thoughts and feelings (the mind) can improve or inhibit performance effectiveness (the body). Mental skills techniques are designed to enhance optimal performance. Considerable research, especially with competitive athletes, suggests that educational psychological skills intervention improves competitive performance (Harmison, 2006; Krane & Williams, 2006).

PST programs typically include training in relaxation, imagery, goal setting, concentration, and cognitive self-management. Largely adapted from cognitive–behavioral theory and therapy, these techniques have become such a standard element of sport psychologists' repertoire as to be considered a "canon" of PST (Andersen, 2000b). They are consonant with a specific, goal-focused, time-limited frame, one that can result in marked behavior change. These methods are most effective when individually prescribed rather than packaged or presented en masse (Fifer, Henschen, Gould, & Ravizza, 2008). Most practitioners augment their PST work with other forms of service, whether academic or clinical (Greene, 2010; Meyers, Coleman, Whelan, & Mehlenbeck, 2001). Although some develop a solo practice, others find it most effective to offer services within a multidisciplinary establishment, such as a sports medicine facility (Petitpas, 1998), medical organization (Heil, 1993), or university health setting (Pargman, 1999). A special section of the American Psychological Association's (APA's) *Monitor on Psychology* ("Keeping Athletes on Track," 2008) offered descriptions of psychologists' work with athletes ranging from Olympians to those with intellectual disabilities.

BODY TO MIND: EXERCISE AND MENTAL HEALTH

Moderate exercise performed regularly (e.g., aerobic exercise three times a week for one-half hour at a time) has profound effects not only on the cardiovascular system but also on mood and sense of well-being (Berger & Motl, 2000). Exercise is associated with a reduction in depression, the amelioration of anxiety, and improvements in self-esteem, mastery, body image, and socialization, all contributory to improvements in mental and emotional functioning (Landers & Arent, 2001; Tkachuk & Martin, 1999). Detailed descriptions of the use of exercise with various clinical populations form the basis of several books on the mental benefits of physical activity (Hays, 1999; Johnsgard, 2004; Leith, 1998; Marcus & Forsyth, 2008; Ratey & Hagerman, 2008).

Exercise can be used for a number of purposes in the psychotherapy setting, whether as a form of therapy, an adjunct to psychotherapy, or the medium in which the therapy is conducted (see Chapter 10, this volume). Therapists' roles in relation to the client in regard to exercise may involve consultation, modeling, or participation. The client's own level of involvement in sport or exercise may range from the sedentary nonathlete to the competitive or professional athlete (Gulli, 2011).

PSYCHOTHERAPY WITH ATHLETES

In an early prospective study, Pierce (1969) found that college athletes were less likely than other students to seek psychotherapy. Athletes were considered to be mentally healthier than the general population; by the time they sought services, however, levels of psychopathology could be fairly severe (Morgan, 1985). The stigma often associated with seeking assistance for mental health problems seemed to be reflected and perhaps exacerbated among collegiate athletes (e.g., Linder, Brewer, Van Raalte, & De Lange, 1991). This earlier aversion to help seeking may be shifting as a result of the active public health destigmatization of mental health problems, increased public information concerning sport psychology, and increased numbers of well-known athletes' public comments regarding their work with sport psychologists.

Typical presenting problems include anxiety, depression, eating disorders, substance abuse, fears of success or failure, and relationship and motivational concerns, suggesting that there is substantial overlap between athletic and nonathletic clinical populations (see Chapter 10, this volume). The athlete seeking psychotherapy may be more comfortable working with a therapist who is knowledgeable about sport and appreciative of its role in the athlete's life. Psychotherapists should be sensitive to the client in context, respecting his or her identification as an athlete, taking seriously the client's engagement in competitive sport, and recognizing the legitimacy of time constraints created by competition schedules (Andersen, 2000a; "Keeping Athletes on Track," 2008).

It has been suggested (e.g., Aoyagi & Portenga, 2010) that a distinction should be made between the practice of sport or performance psychology (i.e., performance enhancement) and psychotherapy with athletes. In real life, however, the distinction between PST and counseling or psychotherapy is arbitrary (Haberl, 2012; S. McCann, 2008). In the only large-scale survey of its kind, Meyers, Whelan, and Murphy (1995) found that even though the initial focus of services at the U.S. Olympic Training Center concerned performance, 85% of all cases seen by the sport psychology staff involved personal counseling with athletes. Detailed case descriptions of this combination of PST and psychotherapy or counseling provide interesting examples of intentional, flexible adaptation (see, e.g., Andersen, 2000a, 2005; Herzog & Hays, 2012).

Transitioning Oneself and One's Practice Toward Exercise and Sport Psychology

Few psychologists enter the field with an entrepreneurial focus, and fewer still obtain graduate training in the business of practice. An initial phase of the shift toward a sport and exercise psychology practice may involve coming to terms with the issue of selling, or marketing, oneself and one's product (Grodzki, 2000).

Incorporating sport and exercise psychology into clinical practice raises a number of issues that can be subsumed under three central self-assessment questions: (a) Where am I now, that is, what is my level of interest, skill, and knowledge? (b) Where do I want to be, that is, what are my goals? and (c) How do I get there, or in business terms, how do I market this practice? Careful consideration of these questions will facilitate the transition necessary to integrate sport and exercise consultation into a practice.

INTEREST, SKILL, AND KNOWLEDGE DEVELOPMENT

Although sport psychology consulting has a well-developed history, contentions over "turf" and content mean that the path to such practice often does not follow a straight trajectory. Practitioners become involved in sport and exercise psychology for a number of reasons and at different points in their professional lives. Some are or have been athletes and wish to combine that experience with the knowledge and skills of graduate training in clinical or counseling psychology. Others become involved because of tangential but related areas of knowledge, for example, motivation, talent development, a wellness perspective, or health psychology. Still others are drawn to sport psychology, recognizing the value of a niche practice especially in light of the current limitations on health care reimbursement.

Because sport psychology involves knowledge both in psychology and the sport sciences, people developing a practice in sport psychology will need to have some systematic knowledge of both. The relative balance of knowledge and skill in counseling or therapy compared with motor learning or kinesiology will depend on the practitioner's professional and practice goals, including types of work settings, clientele, and practice focus (Andersen, Van Raalte, & Brewer, 2001; C. H. Brown, 2001). As with other areas of knowledge and skill, practitioners can develop expertise by knowing what they need to know, learning it systematically, and practicing it deliberately (Davis & Critchfield, 2010).

Guidance with regard to the development of necessary skills can be found in the criteria for certification as a sport psychology practitioner, such as those of the Association for Applied Sport Psychology (http://appliedsportpsych.org/consultants/become-certified) and the APA's Proficiency in Sport Psychology (http://www.apa.org/ed/graduate/specialize/sports.aspx). The Association for Applied Sport Psychology certification is bestowed at an individual level in recognition of the completion of relevant course work in both sport sciences and psychology and supervised training in applied sport psychology. The British Association of Sport and Exercise Sciences, similarly, accredits individual sport and exercise scientists (http://www.bases.org.uk). The APA proficiency designates a subset of the practice of psychology. To make this latter information more pertinent to the individual, Lesyk "translated" the proficiency into a self-directed study checklist of relevant knowledge and skills (http://www.apa47.org/pdfs/KnowSkills_Check_10_10.pdf). Included are particular knowledge and skills in, for example, the history of sport psychology; methods of assessment, treatment, and consultation; organizational behavior; specific sports populations; and specific mental skills. Further information regarding definitions and criteria regarding designation of title can be found in Chapter 21, this volume.

A model of *contextual intelligence* (C. H. Brown, Gould, & Foster, 2005) suggests that in working with athletes, practitioners need three levels of knowledge in a pyramidal structure that moves from the general to the specific. *Foundational knowledge* forms the base of the pyramid. Graduate education often provides foundational skills, including training in relationship skills; models of change, such as the transtheoretical model (Prochaska, Norcross, & DiClemente, 1995); knowledge and skills regarding performance excellence, including PST such as arousal regulation, cognitive control, mental imagery, goal setting, and attentional control (Weinberg & Gould, 2011; Williams, 2009); understanding of organizations and systems; and knowledge of the physiological aspects of performance. Sport sciences—exercise physiology, biomechanics, and motor learning—provide consultants with important knowledge about physiological contributions to athletic performance.

At a second level of specificity, *issues knowledge* involves understanding the typical issues or concerns encountered by athletes. Sport and exercise psychologists must have specialized knowledge regarding such matters as the management of competitive anxiety and stress, dealing with injuries, career longevity and retirement, and team cohesion and leadership (Andersen, 2000a; C. H. Brown et al., 2005).

Contextual intelligence, or "knowing what works with which persons in which situations" (C. H. Brown et al., 2005, p. 51), forms the apex of the pyramid. It includes "not only knowing the culture of the sport domain in general, but also knowing the culture and context of the specific setting in which the individual operates" (C. H. Brown et al., 2005, p. 54).

Sport and exercise psychologists with firsthand experience in specific sports or forms of exercise are often at an advantage when consulting. They are familiar with the explicit and implicit rules of the game and with sport culture and language (C. H. Brown et al., 2005; Fifer et al., 2008), which is likely to enhance their credibility with athlete consultees (Hays & Brown, 2004). Because practitioners are likely to encounter some sports or situations with which they are not familiar, they can gain experience and learn more about a particular sport through reading, observation, and discussion with athletes, coaches, and others who are knowledgeable about that sport. Athletes generally are less concerned with whether a consultant has specific knowledge of their sport than with the consultant's openness to learning the common terms used and willingness to help the athletes achieve their goals (Fifer et al., 2008; Gould, 2009).

In sum, aspiring sport and exercise psychology consultants can gain knowledge and experience by (a) obtaining graduate training in sport psychology (Sachs et al., 2011), (b) reading texts on sport psychology (e.g., Horn, 2008; Weinberg & Gould, 2011; Williams, 2009) and practitioner applications (e.g., Andersen, 2000a, 2005), (c) pursuing continuing education offerings (e.g., conference presentations, postgraduate online education, workshops, teleconsultation; Belar et al., 2001; Hays, 2010; Lesyk, 2010), and (d) participating in formal or informal supervision or consultation.

GOAL DEVELOPMENT

In *The Seven Habits of Highly Effective People,* Covey (1989) advised people pursuing a goal to "begin with the end in mind." If one begins with the goal of incorporating sport and exercise psychology into clinical practice, what does an ideal sport and exercise psychology practice look like? From a personal perspective, one may ask questions such as the following: Why do I want to change my practice? How would I like my practice to be different in the future? What am I willing to invest to bring this about? From a business perspective, important areas to address include the product, that is, the services to be offered; the target market, or type of clientele; and the financial and practical integration of sport psychology into one's general clinical practice.

Product

As indicated earlier, the services provided by sport and exercise psychologists vary greatly. There is no standard pathway, template, or job description for applied sport psychology. The "product" should be determined by a mix that includes the clinician's current skills, personal preferences, and commitment to expanding skills as well as the needs of the market. Once these are determined, it will be important to enumerate these specific professional activities in promotional materials.

Determining one's focus is key to the development of any consulting practice (Eldridge & Eldridge, 2004), and sport psychology is no exception (Lesyk, 1998). Developing a particular niche, a "unique combination of interests, skills, talents, experience, background and contacts" (Edwards & Edwards, 1998, p. 8), makes business, economic, and personal sense (Dean, 2000; Foster, 1999; Grodzki, 2000). A niche needs to be narrow enough to distinguish the practitioner from the competition but wide enough to sustain sufficient business. It is, of course, critical that the practitioner is competent and finds the niche enjoyable (Port, 2010; Stout & Grand, 2005).

Target Market

The search for a target market can begin with a written description of an ideal client (Grodzki, 2000; Port, 2010). Demographic and other relevant variables may include age group, gender, race and ethnicity, ability level, type of sport or exercise, and type of client (e.g., team, individual athlete, coach, parent, official, administrator). Work setting preferences (e.g., developmental, collegiate, or professional sports; fitness; country clubs; business) also help shape the target market and sources of referrals. One may also select particular kinds of issues, for example, injured athletes, athletes with eating disorders, the challenges of retirement, or parents of young athletes (Lesyk, 1998).

The successful sport and exercise psychology practice involves ensuring a good match between the practitioner's interests and competencies and the characteristics of the local sport and exercise scene: Who participates in what sports or exercise activities at what ability levels, and how are these sport and exercise activities organized? For example, Jack J. Lesyk has developed a significant clientele in figure skating, equestrian sports, and golf, partially because these sports have widespread levels of participation in his locale.

The concept of *unarticulated need* (Lambin, Chumpitaz, & Schuiling, 2007) suggests that the potential consumer is unaware of the need until new information creates awareness. Once awareness is attained, there is an increased demand for services. In many instances, this two-step educational approach is vital to sport psychology practice. Because potential consumers may have a limited understanding of the role and value of sport psychologists, the sport psychologist (a) explains the ways that mental skills are essential to good performance and (b) informs the potential consumer of the ways that he or she can assess, plan, and execute mental skills interventions, whether among individuals or teams.

Financial Goals and Practice Balance

Clinicians beginning to incorporate sport psychology into their practices will probably do so gradually. Continued attention to one's "bread-and-butter" practice allows a progressive phasing in of sport and exercise psychology practice. It is not unusual to experience some temporary reduction in income while devoting time to the non-income-generating tasks of acquiring new skills and marketing sport psychology services. Typically, sport and exercise psychology work develops slowly enough that the desirable balance between consultations with athletes and other work can emerge over time (Lesyk, 1998).

Different segments of the sport and exercise psychology market offer varying levels of financial remuneration. Professional athletes and coaches provide one such market, although entrée may be more of a challenge. Among amateur enthusiasts, certain sports draw athletes with more financial viability. Many golfers, tennis players, figure skaters, rowers, marksmen, polo players, and equestrians are more affluent; college athletes and recreational exercisers, on the other hand, may have fewer resources of their own to spend on mental training.

MARKETING

Acquiring the requisite competencies and identifying target populations are necessary but not sufficient means to start and sustain a solid sport psychology practice. Marketing is designed to bring appropriate clients to the practice while at the same time maintaining the confidence and trust of present and former clients (Blann, Shelley, & Gates, 2011; Grodzki, 2000; Stout & Grand, 2005). As with clinical services, successful practitioners market their practices on an ongoing basis.

Although professionals often present themselves in terms of their credentials and services, a basic principle of marketing suggests that it is essential to focus instead on the benefits that the client will derive from such services (Grodzki, 2000). Key elements in positioning oneself involve standing out in one way or another and offering a service to one's "audience" (a) that they need (b) in a way that no one else is offering.

Although marketing a sport or sport and exercise psychology practice takes into account general principles of marketing, at the same time, there are unique features to this field. In particular, these include the following:

- Community and referral sources need to know what sport and exercise psychology is, what services are available, and what kinds of clients are appropriate.
- Community and referral sources need to understand that not every psychologist (or mental health professional) is qualified to deliver all sport and exercise psychology services.
- The practitioner needs to become known as a competent, qualified, ethical provider of sport and exercise psychology services in the community.

Overall, thanks to favorable media coverage and popular interest, today's public and members of the sport community seems to have a more complete and accurate understanding of sport and exercise psychology than in times past. Some persistent misunderstandings, nonetheless, should be addressed (e.g., that sport and exercise psychology is only for troubled athletes or "head cases," that sport and exercise psychology is only for elite athletes, that sport and exercise psychology is just another form of talk therapy). Fortunately, ample educational materials that address these issues are available on the websites of various sport psychology organizations, for example, the Association for Applied Sport Psychology (http://www.appliedsportpsych.org), APA's Division 47 (Exercise and Sport Psychology; http://www.apa47.org), the British Association of Sport and Exercise Sciences (http://www.bases.org.uk), the European Federation of Sport Psychology (http://www.fepsac.com), and the International Society of Sport Psychology (http://www.issponline.org).

Before engaging in marketing activities, it is advisable to "tool up," preparing marketing materials in a variety of formats (Blann et al., 2011). For many small (as well as large) businesses these days, a website and ancillary electronic presence (e.g., LinkedIn, Facebook, Twitter, blog) is often the centerpiece of all marketing efforts—and for good reason: A modest and yet effective website can be created and maintained at a relatively low cost and with a small investment of time. It will describe the services offered and the practitioner's qualifications and will often include useful information that can turn browsers into buyers. Unlike print brochures, electronic marketing can use a variety of media and can be updated regularly to reflect the practitioner's activities and accomplishments. Needless to say, the most important aspect of one's web presence is to make it easy for the prospective customer to be able to know how to contact the practitioner.

Because sport and exercise psychology is a highly specialized service that is useful and affordable to only a small segment of the general population, advertising should, likewise, target specific audiences and address them as directly as possible. Such audiences might include coaches, parents of young athletes, and specific athlete or exercise groups. In addition to providing direct contacts with potential clients, often organizations will promote guest speakers in their newsletters and in local media releases. Perhaps the most important aspect of presenting to live audiences is the personal presentation and contact with audience members. Seeing, hearing, and interacting with a sport psychologist can be much more effective in bringing clients to a practice than many dollars spent on formal advertising.

Another valuable yet inexpensive avenue of marketing a practice involves writing for club newsletters, sports websites, or local news media. Although these sources may not offer direct financial remuneration, an article or regular column on sport psychology may turn readers into clients and/or referral sources.

Systematic networking with coaches, athletic directors, athletic trainers, fitness instructors, sports medicine personnel, sport and exercise scientists, nutritionists, and sports agents is reciprocally important: Not only are these professionals potential referral sources, they also can form the basis of one's own referral network, thus benefitting clients and increasing one's credibility. When networking, one should ask oneself: How can I present myself as a useful resource to this referral source (Grodzki, 2003)? To maintain and retain potential referral sources and collegial connections, as with marketing in general, networking should be an ongoing activity built into one's schedule.

Ultimately, the most effective marketing strategy is to conduct a practice that is based on doing excellent, competent, ethical work and genuinely caring about clients. The majority of referrals over many years, for both of us, have come from current and former clients who are pleased with their services and have referred others. Unlike clinical clients, who may be embarrassed to share their positive therapy experiences, athletes and exercisers appear to feel less stigma and be more willing to tell their coaches, teammates, and friends about their positive experiences with a sport psychologist.

DEVELOPING PROFESSIONAL SUPPORTS

Solo practitioners know all too well how isolated consultants can feel. Nurturing connections with professionals from sport and exercise psychology and other related fields is therefore critical. A professional support network can be developed by (a) identifying colleagues who can provide supervision or consultation services, whether face-to-face or at a distance (Hays, 2010); (b) creating prospective informal networks or legal partnerships with other sport and exercise psychologists, sports medicine professionals, fitness professionals, or sports agents; (c) identifying professionals in other fields who can provide guidance in setting up a practice, such as attorneys, certified public accountants, marketing consultants, public relations consultants; and (d) joining local, national, and international sport and exercise psychology associations for continuing education, referrals, credentialing, electronic resources, and visibility. Organizations such as the Association for Applied Sport Psychology, APA's Division 47, the British Association of Sport and Exercise Science, the European Federation of Sport Psychology, and the International Society of Sport Psychology offer the practitioner support, education, and the opportunity to assist in shaping the field.

Practitioner Issues

The inclusion of sport and exercise psychology in one's practice offers considerable promise, yet a number of issues need to be addressed. Salient concerns include coping with becoming a novice again, suffering setbacks, scheduling, and managing diagnostic concerns and ethical issues.

HUMILITY, AMBIGUITY, AND HUBRIS

Expanding one's practice into an unfamiliar area involves the acquisition of new information and skills as well as their integration into existing knowledge and practice. The seasoned practitioner may experience discomfort in being placed in the position of learner once again. Acknowledging ignorance, however, can assist in lowering the barriers so that learning can occur, whether through reading, coursework, or supervised practice. An attitude of humility, openness, and curiosity makes this process not only more interesting but also more effective. It is important to remember that the professional "half-life" of graduate-level knowledge retention is fairly short (Wise, 2010).

PRACTICAL CONCERNS

Working with amateur and professional athletes may require some flexibility and variation in scheduling, as a function of the particular sport and the nature and length of the contact with the athlete. Because some sports are seasonal, an athlete may not see the relevance of contact during the off-season. It may be useful, though, to encourage such athletes to work on their mental game precisely because it is the off-season and they can devote time to such work. Some athletes may require intensive work before important events. Athletic teams may expect the sport and exercise psychologist to travel with them (S. C. McCann, 2000; Stapleton, 2010). The psychologist who has other clients or contracts needs to develop backup services to ensure sufficient and appropriate coverage when necessary. If sport psychology obligations occur at predictable times, it may be helpful to print up a schedule beforehand so that other clients know these plans well in advance. As when clinicians take vacations, it is important to pay attention to clients' subjective experience of such absences.

Involvement in seasonal sport and exercise activities can create a "boom-or-bust" cycle. To smooth out the cycle, the practitioner can become involved with athletes and exercisers whose sports and activities have different seasons or adapt other aspects of the overall practice to these demands.

PSYCHOPATHOLOGY AND DIAGNOSIS

The clinical practitioner working in sport and exercise psychology often operates on the cusp of the wellness–illness continuum (Herzog & Hays, 2012). Clients may not be seeking psychotherapy; they may not have definable psychopathology. Although therapeutic, the services provided may not be psychotherapy. The practitioner accustomed to diagnosis and third-party billing thus confronts both ethical and legal dilemmas in considering the source of payment for services, particularly with individuals. Can the practitioner bill insurance for sport psychology services? In the United States, if the clinician provides a diagnosis for the client using psychological or behavioral disorders listed in the *Diagnostic and Statistical Manual of Mental Disorders* (American Psychiatric Association, 2000) and if the client is interested and willing to be given a diagnostic label, it is appropriate to bill the client's insurance company for these services, regardless of whether the client is an athlete. If, however, the psychologist is providing mental skills training or performance enhancement services, rather than treatment for a disorder deemed *medically necessary,* it would both be inappropriate and illegal to bill the client's insurance company.

The financial stability of a practice that has been predominately insurance-based could be threatened by a radical shift to performance enhancement work. For the clinician who wishes to transition away from insurance and managed care, however, sport psychology may provide the opportunity to do so (Greene, 2010). Furthermore, sport psychology services are often of shorter duration than traditional clinical treatment. These clients are often willing to self-pay for highly specialized services that offer practical and fairly rapid results.

In the United States, all health services must comply with federal Health Insurance Portability and Accountability Act of 1996 regulations (http://www.hhs.gov/ocr/privacy), which are designed to protect the patient's right to privacy and regulate the storage and transmission of the patient's medical information. Although these regulations apply to all clinical services, they may not be required for psychological skills or performance enhancement services. It is prudent, however, for sport and exercise psychologists to voluntarily treat all client records in a manner that conforms to the Health Insurance Portability and Accountability Act of 1996 regulations. This avoids possible legal ambiguities and is consistent with ethical principles and respect for the client's privacy.

ETHICAL CONCERNS FOR PRACTITIONERS

Boundary Issues

Concerns about boundaries, present for all sport and exercise psychologists (see Chapter 23, this volume), take on particular significance for the practitioner entering this field (Andersen et al., 2001; J. L. Brown & Cogan, 2006; Stapleton, 2010). As one's practice moves toward consultation, it is important to note changes in the relationship between psychologist and client and how those shifts are understood and monitored. The possibility for loss of traditional structures and for a more casual relationship increases with changes in level and type of engagement between client and practitioner. Exercising with clients, observing them on the playing field (whether during practice or competition), traveling with a team, and working with high-profile clients all involve changes from the standard therapist–client, in-office, 50-minute hour. Sport and exercise psychologists need to recognize possible shifts in role relationships, levels of self-disclosure, and power and gender imbalances. It is vital to have an ongoing way to review these questions, whether through reflection, supervision, or consultation (Andersen et al., 2001; Stapleton, Hankes, Hays, & Parham, 2010).

Sport and Exercise Psychologist as a Title

The professionalization of applied sport and exercise psychology has brought increased attention to the complex issues that surround use of the title *sport and exercise psychologist*. In North America, the title *psychologist* is restricted for use by psychologists who have met the qualifications and are licensed within their jurisdiction. Beyond this restriction, psychologists are additionally bound by ethics to practice within their level of competence (APA, 2010). By virtue of specialized education, training, and experience in exercise and sport, it becomes appropriate for psychologists to claim the sport psychologist title ("How Can a Psychologist Become a Sport Psychologist?" http://www.apa47.org/ pracPro.php). Those with training primarily in the sport sciences are not legally eligible to identify themselves as sport and exercise psychology practitioners or to maintain an independent counseling or psychotherapy practice (for additional discussion, see Chapter 21, this volume).

Confidentiality

Confidentiality issues are reflected in many aspects of sport and exercise psychology. Psychologists are obligated not to disclose information concerning clients, except as that privilege is waived by clients (APA, 2010). In contrast, coaches are routinely quoted in the press discussing their players. Does psychologists' commitment to confidentiality change when they work in the arena of sport and exercise psychology? The temptation of disclosure to the media becomes increasingly seductive the more important or famous the client is (Lesyk, 1998; S. C. McCann, 2000). As in other contractual or consultative contexts, a common ethical challenge is that of disclosure if one is hired by a team administrator to work with team members. It is important to specify how confidentiality will be handled, preferably in writing and before the work begins.

Confidentiality issues can also arise as a function of the entrepreneurial nature of sport psychology and the high public visibility of some athletes. For example, client endorsements and the public identification of those clients present a marketing and ethical dilemma. At present, no standard exists; practitioners handle these issues in decidedly different ways. We suggest that it is valuable to err on the side of caution and respect for privacy: Even if clients waive their rights to confidentiality, such decisions may reflect the power differential between the sport psychologist and the client rather than a freely accepted agreement. Additionally, placing the client in a position of endorsing one's services in essence creates a dual relationship in which the client serves as the sport and exercise psychologist's marketing agent. Therefore, the sport and exercise psychologist should weigh carefully the implications and effects of any decision that does not fully protect the client's identity.

Conclusion

The opportunities to include sport and exercise psychology in clinical practice are rich and varied. The professional who is retooling combines the inquiry of the scientist with the practitioner's attention to individual differences. Practice opportunities range from prevention and performance enhancement to psychotherapy and remedial treatment.

The business of learning and developing a new practice in sport and exercise psychology involves an assessment of both current practice and future goals. Various potential problem areas also require careful consideration and proactive planning.

It cannot be overemphasized that for one's own protection as well as growth in regard to all of these issues, it is critical to have networks of colleagues, whether informally or formally designated, with whom to consult. To the extent that one's education in this field has been "on-the-job training," it is even more important to develop viable ways to anticipate and address troublesome issues before they arise.

References

American Psychiatric Association. (2000). *Diagnostic and statistical manual of mental disorders* (4th ed., text revision). Washington, DC: Author.

American Psychological Association. (2010). *Ethical principles of psychologists and code of conduct (2002, Amended June 1, 2010).* Retrieved from http://www.apa.org/ethics/code/index.aspx

Andersen, M. B. (Ed.). (2000a). *Doing sport psychology: Process and practice.* Champaign, IL: Human Kinetics.

Andersen, M. B. (2000b). Introduction. In M. B. Andersen (Ed.), *Doing sport psychology: Process and practice* (pp. xiii–xvii). Champaign, IL: Human Kinetics.

Andersen, M. B. (Ed.). (2005). *Sport psychology in practice.* Champaign, IL: Human Kinetics.

Andersen, M. B., Van Raalte, J. L., & Brewer, B. W. (2001). Sport psychology service delivery: Staying ethical while keeping loose. *Professional Psychology: Research and Practice, 32,* 12–18. doi:10.1037/0735-7028.32.1.12

Aoyagi, M. W., & Portenga, S. T. (2010). The role of positive ethics and virtues in the context of sport and performance psychology service delivery. *Professional Psychology: Research and Practice, 41,* 253–259. doi:10.1037/a0019483

Belar, C. D., Brown, R. A., Hersch, L. E., Hornyak, L. M., Rozensky, R. H., Sheridan, E. P., . . . Reed, G. W. (2001). Self-assessment in clinical health psychology: A model for ethical expansion of practice. *Professional Psychology: Research and Practice, 32,* 135–141. doi:10.1037/0735-7028.32.2.135

Berger, B. G., & Motl, R. W. (2000). Exercise and mood: A selective review and synthesis of research employing the profile of mood states. *Journal of Applied Sport Psychology, 12,* 69–92. doi:10.1080/10413200008404214

Blann, W. F., Shelley, G., & Gates, S. C. (2011). Marketing sport psychology consulting services. *Journal of Sport Psychology in Action, 2*, 33–52. doi:10.1080/21520704.2011.564719

Brown, C. H. (2001). Clinical cross-training: Compatibility of sport and family systems psychology. *Professional Psychology: Research and Practice, 32*, 19–26. doi:10.1037/0735-7028.32.1.19

Brown, C. H., Gould, D., & Foster, S. (2005). A framework for developing contextual intelligence (CI). *The Sport Psychologist, 19*, 51–62.

Brown, J. L., & Cogan, K. D. (2006). Ethical clinical practice and sport psychology: When two worlds collide. *Ethics & Behavior, 16*, 15–23. doi:10.1207/s15327019eb1601_3

Covey, S. R. (1989). *The seven habits of highly effective people.* New York, NY: Fireside/Simon & Schuster.

Davis, M. J., & Critchfield, K. L. (2010). Practicing deliberately: Could we all be expert therapists? *Psychotherapy Bulletin, 3*, 7–10.

Dean, B. (2000). Niche criteria for a successful coaching practice. *In Practice, 20*, 112–114.

Edwards, P., & Edwards, S. (1998). *Getting business to come to you.* New York, NY: Tarcher.

Eldridge, E., & Eldridge, M. (2004). *How to position yourself as the obvious expert: Turbocharge your consulting or coaching business now.* West Palm Beach, FL: MasterMind.

Fifer, A., Henschen, K., Gould, D., & Ravizza, K. (2008). What works when working with athletes. *The Sport Psychologist, 22*, 356–377.

Fort, R. (2011). *Sports economics* (3rd ed.). Boston, MA: Prentice Hall.

Foster, S. (1999). Creating a theme-based practice specialization outside of managed care. *In Practice, 19*, 118–121.

Gould, D. (2009). Confidence. In K. F. Hays (Ed.), *Performance psychology in action: A casebook for working with athletes, performing artists, business leaders, and professionals in high-risk occupations* (pp. 57–76). Washington, DC: American Psychological Association.

Greene, M. (2010). Developing a sport psychology practice. In S. Walfish (Ed.), *Earning a living outside of managed mental health care: 50 ways to expand your practice* (pp. 215–218). Washington, DC: American Psychological Association. doi:10.1037/12138-048

Grodzki, L. (2000). *Building your ideal private practice: How to love what you do and be highly profitable too!* New York, NY: Norton.

Grodzki, L. (2003). *Twelve months to your ideal private practice: A workbook.* New York, NY: Norton.

Gulli, C. (2011, May 19). Concussions: The untold story. *Maclean's.* Retrieved from http://www2.macleans.ca/2011/05/19/concussions-the-untold-story

Haberl, P. (2012). Peter Haberl. In A. Poczwardowski & M. Aoyagi (Eds.), *The chronicle of expert approaches to sport & performance psychology* (pp. 51–70). Morgantown, WV: Fitness Information Technology.

Harmison, R. J. (2006). Peak performance in sport: Identifying ideal performance states and developing athletes' psychological skills. *Professional Psychology: Research and Practice, 37,* 233–243. doi:10.1037/0735-7028.37.3.233

Hays, K. F. (1999). *Working it out: Using exercise in psychotherapy.* Washington, DC: American Psychological Association. doi:10.1037/10333-000

Hays, K. F. (2010, October). That's why we're called practitioners: Tele-consultation groups for lifelong learning in sport psychology. In J. J. Lesyk (Chair), *Continuing professional education: Three alternative approaches.* Symposium conducted at the conference of the Association for Applied Sport Psychology, Providence, RI.

Hays, K. F. (2012). Sport psychology. In C. E. Stout (Ed.), *Getting better at private practice* (pp. 412–425). New York, NY: Wiley. doi:10.1002/9781118089972.ch27

Hays, K. F., & Brown, C. H. (2004). *You're on! Consulting for peak performance.* Washington, DC: American Psychological Association. doi:10.1037/10675-000

Health Insurance Portability and Accountability Act of 1996, Pub. L. No. 104-191 Stat. 1936 (1996).

Heil, J. (1993). *Psychology of sport injury.* Champaign, IL: Human Kinetics.

Helms, J. L., & Rogers, D. T. (2010). *Majoring in psychology.* New York, NY: Wiley-Blackwell. doi:10.1002/9781444320718

Herzog, T., & Hays, K. F. (2012). Therapist or mental skills coach? How to decide. *The Sport Psychologist, 26,* 486–499.

Horn, T. S. (Ed.). (2008). *Advances in sport psychology* (3rd ed.). Champaign, IL: Human Kinetics.

Johnsgard, K. (2004). *Conquering depression & anxiety through exercise.* Amherst, NY: Prometheus.

Keeping athletes on track. (July/August, 2008). *Monitor on Psychology, 39*(7), 54–69.

Krane, V., & Williams, J. M. (2006). Psychological characteristics of peak performance. In J. M. Williams (Ed.), *Applied sport psychology: Personal growth to peak performance* (5th ed., pp. 207–227). New York, NY: McGraw-Hill.

Krucoff, C., & Krucoff, M. (2009). *Healing moves* (2nd ed.). Monterey, CA: Healthy Learning.

Lambin, J., Chumpitaz, R., & Schuiling, I. (2007). *Market-driven management: Strategic and operational marketing* (2nd ed.). New York, NY: Palgrave Macmillan.

Landers, D. M., & Arent, S. M. (2001). Physical activity and mental health. In R. N. Singer, H. A. Hausenblas, & C. Janelle (Eds.), *Handbook of research on sport psychology* (2nd ed., pp. 740–765). New York, NY: Wiley.

Leith, L. M. (1998). *Exercising your way to better mental health.* Morgantown, WV: Fitness Information Technology.

Lesyk, J. J. (1998). *Developing sport psychology within your clinical practice: A practical guide for mental health professionals.* San Francisco, CA: Jossey-Bass.

Lesyk, J. J. (2010, October). An intensive two-day workshop in applied sport psychology: Transitioning into sport psychology. In J. J. Lesyk (Chair), *Continuing professional education: Three alternative approaches.* Symposium conducted at the conference of the Association for Applied Sport Psychology, Providence, RI.

Linder, D. E., Brewer, B. W., Van Raalte, J. L., & De Lange, N. (1991). A negative halo for athletes who consult sport psychologists: Replication and extension. *Journal of Sport & Exercise Psychology, 13,* 133–148.

Marcus, B., & Forsyth, L. (2008). *Motivating people to be physically active* (2nd ed.). Champaign, IL: Human Kinetics.

McCann, S. (2008). At the Olympics, everything is a performance issue. *International Journal of Sport and Exercise Psychology, 6,* 267–276. doi:10 .1080/1612197X.2008.9671871

McCann, S. C. (2000). Doing sport psychology at the really big show. In M. B. Andersen (Ed.), *Doing sport psychology: Process and practice* (pp. 209–222). Champaign, IL: Human Kinetics.

Meyers, A. W., Coleman, J., Whelan, J., & Mehlenbeck, R. (2001). Examining careers in sport psychology: Who is working and who is making money? *Professional Psychology: Research and Practice, 32,* 5–11. doi:10.1037/0735-7028.32.1.5

Meyers, A. W., Whelan, J. P., & Murphy, S. (1995). Cognitive behavioral strategies in athletic performance enhancement. In M. Hersen, R. M. Eisler, & P. M. Miller (Eds.), *Progress in behavior modification* (pp. 137–164). Pacific Grove, CA: Brooks/Cole.

Morgan, W. P. (1985). Selected psychological factors limiting performance: A mental health model. In D. H. Clarke & H. M. Eckert (Eds.), *Limits of human performance* (pp. 70–80). Champaign, IL: Human Kinetics.

Pargman, D. (Ed.). (1999). *Psychological bases of sport injuries* (2nd ed.). Morgantown, WV: Fitness Information Technologies.

Petitpas, A. (1998). Practical considerations in providing psychological services to sports medicine clinics. *Journal of Applied Sport Psychology, 10,* 157–167. doi:10.1080/10413209808406383

Pierce, R. A. (1969). Athletes in psychotherapy: How many, how come? *Journal of the American College Health Association, 17,* 244–249.

Port, M. (2010). *Book yourself solid: The fastest, easiest, and most reliable system for getting more clients than you can handle even if you hate marketing and selling* (2nd ed.). New York, NY: Wiley.

Prochaska, J. O., Norcross, J., & DiClemente, C. (1995). *Changing for good.* New York, NY: Harper.

Ratey, J., & Hagerman, E. (2008). *Spark: The revolutionary new science of exercise and the brain.* New York, NY: Little, Brown.

Sachs, M. L., Burke, K. L., & Schweighardt, S. L. (2011). *Directory of graduate programs in applied sport psychology* (10th ed.). Madison, WI: Association for Applied Sport Psychology.

Stapleton, A. B. (2010). Ethical considerations in applied sport psychology. *Professional Psychology: Research and Practice, 41,* 143–152. doi:10.1037/a0017976

Stapleton, A. B., Hankes, D. M., Hays, K. F., & Parham, W. D. (2010). Ethical dilemmas in sport psychology: A dialogue on the unique aspects impacting practice. *Professional Psychology: Research and Practice, 41,* 143–152. doi:10.1037/a0017976

Stout, C., & Grand, L. (2005). *Getting started in private practice: The complete guide to building your mental health practice.* Hoboken, NJ: Wiley.

Tkachuk, G. A., & Martin, G. L. (1999). Exercise therapy for patients with psychiatric disorders: Research and clinical implications. *Professional Psychology: Research and Practice, 30,* 275–282. doi:10.1037/0735-7028.30.3.275

Wegenek, A. R., & Buskist, W. (2010). *The insider's guide to the psychology major: Everything you need to know about the degree and profession.* Washington, DC: American Psychological Association.

Weinberg, R. S., & Gould, D. (2011). *Foundations of sport and exercise psychology* (5th ed.). Champaign, IL: Human Kinetics.

Williams, J. M. (Ed.). (2009). *Applied sport psychology* (6th ed.). New York, NY: McGraw-Hill.

Wise, E. H. (2010). Maintaining and enhancing competence in professional psychology: Obsolescence, life-long learning, and continuing education. *Professional Psychology: Research and Practice, 41,* 288–297. doi:10.1037/a0020424

James P. Whelan, Maggie Hill, Meredith Ginley, and Andrew W. Meyers

Ethics in Sport and Exercise Psychology

23

S tanding on the pool deck at her son's first competitive swim meet, a mother's booming voice wills her 6-year-old through his 50-yard backstroke. At his finishing touch, the mother's head drops, her shoulders slump, and she sighs over his slow time and last-place finish. The son's reaction, however, is strikingly different. He leaps from the pool, smiling, and runs to his mother asking, "Did I win? Did I win?" The mother hesitates but then enthusiastically affirms his success. As he skips away, she turns to no one in particular and says, "Sometimes it's okay to lie."

For a brief moment, our swim mom found herself facing a dilemma. She had to make a decision between two competing values that were both important to her: loving support and honesty. Both are values that most parents cherish and teach. It is true that she could have attempted to fulfill both values. Somehow she could have created a loving way to tell him he had not succeeded. Or perhaps she could have made some vague statement about how he did his best. No matter

http://dx.doi.org/10.1037/14251-023

Exploring Sport and Exercise Psychology, Third Edition, J. Van Raalte and B. Brewer (Editors)

which way she answered, she still had to prioritize these two parental values. Of course, in other situations she might not always make the decision she made on the pool deck that day. For example, the next time her son misinformed her about the completion of his homework, she might decide to emphasize honesty over support. Philosophically, this mother can be considered a moral particularist rather than generalist (Dancy, 2006; Hooker & Little 2000). Rather than holding on to an ordered list of values or a firm set of guidelines that apply in every situation, she considers context as important when choosing the right thing to do. Then she hopes that the outcome will fulfill her expectations.

Sport and exercise psychology professionals also face ethical dilemmas in specific contexts or roles. Some wish for the simplicity and ease of a hierarchical list of values or obvious rules for how to act. However, ethical dilemmas are often complex. Effective decision making in these situations may be informed by the traditions of clinical and counseling psychology (e.g., Stainback, Moncier, & Taylor, 2007; Whelan, Meyers, & Donovan, 1995) and/or an educational perspective that emphasizes skill development consultation (Vealey, 2007). Previous versions of the American Psychological Association's (APA's) *Ethical Principles of Psychologists and Code of Conduct* (Ethics Code) were clearly applicable to sport-psychology-related work, but there were also philosophical and practical gaps in those codes that sometimes left sport and exercise psychology professionals unsure of their ethical foundations.

Because the APA Ethics Code (APA, 2010) is the foundation of many ethics codes used by sport and exercise psychology professionals worldwide, we have chosen to use it as a focus for this discussion. In this chapter, we argue that the APA Ethics Code is useful for professionals who have incorporated it into their professional work. Our discussion begins with a declaration on the purpose of professional ethics and a brief history of the APA Ethics Code. Next, we explore the primary traditions in philosophical theories of right and wrong. In the final section of the chapter, we address a few of the ethical issues that are unique challenges for sport psychology work. Although the APA Ethics Code provides a strong ethical foundation for applied work, interested readers may want to consider the ethics codes of other professional organizations such as the Canadian Psychological Association. The Canadian *Code of Ethics for Psychologists* (Canadian Psychological Association, 2000) is based on the APA Ethics Code but has been extensively revised to address specific values and concerns. For example, the Canadian code emphasizes the process of ethical decision making by delineating a 10-step ethical-decision-making process that incorporates culture and other contexts. Furthermore, the code highlights challenges that can arise when specific ethical principles conflict and identifies the principles that deserve greater weight when making ethical decisions (for more ethics codes and related information, see http://kspope.com/ethcodes/index.php).

Purpose of Professional Ethics Codes

Questions about ethical conduct permeate modern culture. People expect that professionals can judge between right and wrong and should behave in accordance with those judgments. However, one need only go online, pick up a news magazine or newspaper, or spend a few evenings watching television to find aggressive inquiries into the ethics of politicians, lawyers, physicians, psychologists, and a variety of other professionals. Society, with good reason, has become mistrusting and cynical about the judgments of its professionals and experts. In turn, this mistrust and cynicism has led to decreased tolerance for professional misbehavior and increased demands for ethical reform (Krause, 1996; Windt, 1989). Partly as a consequence of this cultural mistrust, the study of ethics and the development of written codes of ethics in the social sciences and helping professions has absorbed much energy and generated a great deal of debate (Ellickson & Brown, 1990; Windt, Appleby, Battin, Francis, & Landesman, 1989). This activity in the realm of professional ethical behavior reflects the concerns felt by many that a professional code of ethics needs to address the cultural concerns and fears articulated by society.

To address these concerns, a profession and its members must accept that it and they have a fiduciary duty to society and particularly those members of society who call on the profession for services. Professions must therefore attend to both the privileges and the responsibilities of professional status (Fisher, 2010; Koocher & Keith-Spiegel, 2008). Privileges derive from society's agreement to designate a group of trained individuals as possessing specialized knowledge and the power implicit in this knowledge. The profession's responsibilities result from society's expectation that the profession will regulate itself to "do no harm" and will govern itself to ensure the dignity and welfare of individuals and the public. The profession and its members also agree to ensure the quality of their interactions with society.

Professional organizations are therefore obligated to develop and enforce guidelines that regulate their members' professional conduct. Professional groups, especially those engaged in the helping professions, must demonstrate to society that they hold themselves accountable for their professional behavior (Pryzwansky & Wendt, 1999). Ethical principles, which go above and beyond personal ethics, are one such set of self-regulatory guidelines. These principles, written and adopted by the profession, guide members to act responsibly as they use the privileges granted by society. The adoption of a code of ethics also establishes a community standard and thereby impacts all who practice in the profession regardless of membership status. A profession's inability to regulate itself violates the public's trust and creates cultural and societal cynicism toward the profession.

To realize professional responsibility, members need to embrace their commitment to behaving ethically. As Fisher (2010) emphasized, this commitment is "a strong desire to do what is right because it is right" (p. 34). All members of the profession should be committed to knowing and understanding ethical obligations, correcting ethical mistakes, and resolving ethical dilemmas as they arise. Ethical mistakes occur when someone accidentally behaves in a manner inconsistent with an ethics code. Such mistakes occur with some frequency even when professionals understand their ethical obligations. For example, one study on ethical behaviors revealed that over 60% of psychologists admitted that they had unintentionally disclosed confidential information even though 75% of the respondents understood that to do so was unquestionably unethical (Pope, Tabachnick, & Keith-Spiegel, 1987). When such mistakes occur, committed professionals accept responsibility for the mistake, adopt corrective actions if possible, and take active steps to prevent such mistakes in the future. Ethical dilemmas, by contrast, take place when ethical values and principles are in conflict or are less than fully clear. To be aware of situations in which such conflicts occur and to carefully consider the best way to reach resolution means understanding the code and how to problem solve around the commitment to do what is best.

Before we turn to codes of ethics, it is important to differentiate professional ethics from other standards of behavior. It is reasonable that professional ethical decision making is influenced by other guidelines, including personal moral standards and legal regulation. These guidelines affect decision making about what is right and wrong in a particular situation. Personal morals, like professional ethics, are based on important core values and specific rules for reaching decisions about personal behavior. Morals typically develop from cultural contexts, religious education, and personal experiences (Midgley, 1993). These morals define personal integrity. In contrast, professional ethics are a collective agreement among the members of a profession about the how the professional behaves. Ideally, personal morals and professional ethics are in agreement, although the two might sometimes conflict. A thorough understanding of professional ethics and a separate awareness of personal value systems help prepare the professional for conflicts between the professional and the personal.

Equally common is the blending of ethical considerations and legal responsibilities (Pryzwansky & Wendt, 1999). In fact, ethical and legal issues are frequently united to help professionals manage the risks of independent professional practice (Knapp, Gottlieb, Berman, & Handelsman, 2007; Koocher & Keith-Spiegel, 2008; Pettifor, 1996). It is not uncommon for ethics to be part of state licensing laws for psychologists. The standards of the APA Ethics Code have been adopted to regulate psychologist's professional conduct by 49 of the 50 state licensing boards in the United States (Bass et al., 1996). However, an ethical foundation as a reason for a behavioral decision can be different from the legal reason for such a decision. For example, legal informed consent is a signed document. Ethical informed consent requires that the consenting individuals understand what they are agreeing to and why. It is valuable for any professional engaged in ethical-decision-making processes to have an independent understanding of the operative moral, ethical, and legal issues before choosing how to act in a particular situation.

The American Psychological Association's Ethics Code

Psychology as a field has a long and successful history of acting responsibly and proactively on issues of ethical conduct. Since 1953, there have been 11 published versions of the APA Ethics Code. Each version included language noting that the primary purpose of the code was to protect the public trust in psychology. These documents also were developed to establish professional integrity, educate and socialize members of the profession, and regulate the profession.

The first version was adopted in 1952, 60 years after the formation of the APA (APA, 1953). The Committee on the Ethical Standards for Psychology began the process by defining a set of objectives (see Hobbs, 1948) that included taking an empirical approach to developing the original code by using critical incidents to define the boundaries of behavior. Specifically, this committee asked the membership to submit personal situations in which, as psychologists, they had to make decisions that had ethical implications. The collection of approximately 1,000 critical incidents was used to develop six categories of rules and prohibitions to ensure that psychologists' behavior was moral, professional, and courteous. The document, including case examples, was, as one might expect, 170 pages long. An important lesson learned by the APA was that even at this length there could not be a proscriptive code of ethics that would address every situation in which psychologists might find themselves dealing with ethical challenges. As a consequence, the value of this first code was really the initiation of a dialog about the values and ethical principles that psychologists share.

The 10 revisions that followed the 1953 APA Ethics Code did not use this empirical approach but maintained many of the original committee's objectives. All revisions retained an emphasis on an explicit set of values embodied as principles and a set of decisional and behavioral rules, or standards. The code was to be applied to all activities, settings, and roles related to the work of the psychologist. Each revision offered members avenues to participate in the process of revising the document. Finally, revisions attempted to ensure that the code continued to reflect moral values as the foundation of psychology's professional obligations.

The 1992 Ethics Code (APA, 1992) was a significant departure from the previous versions. Before the 1992 version, the code had blended statements of aspirational principles and enforceable standards. Although this format provided clarity on the differences between the principles and the rules, psychologists involved in charges of ethical violations offered legal challenges to the use of the code by state regulatory boards (Bersoff, 1994). These challenges centered on the fairness of using subjective interpretations of the code's aspirational wording. To make the code more enforceable, the 1992 revision separated the aspirational principles and enforceable standards. Despite adding clarity to what are enforceable rules, the relationship between the rules and values was less clear. This format also affected how psychologists may have come to understand and use the code. Specifically, professionals could learn a set of rules or enforceable standards but fail to understand the reasons or values behind these rules or standards (Jordan & Meara, 1991).

The major changes in 2002 (APA, 2002) served to address criticism that the 1992 Ethics Code was too focused on protecting the profession rather than the public (Bersoff, 1994), indifferent about concerns of diverse groups (Payton, 1994), equivocal about multiple relationships (Sonne, 1994), and generally vague (Bersoff, 1994). In addition, revisions were influenced by the increased presence of HMOs, increased reliance on the Internet and other electronic devices in practice and research, and the need to better address cultural and language diversity in presenting populations (Fisher, 2010). The underlying principle of "do no harm" was retained, but of significant note was the revision of the general principles to increase their clarity, concision, and connection to the standards (Fisher, 2010; Knapp & VandeCreek, 2004).

As with previous editions, the 2002 Ethics Code (and its amended version; see APA, 2010) begins with an introduction. This section addresses important questions about the code's applicability. This text clarifies that the document applies to the broad types of activities that are part of a psychologist's work. Relevant to sport and exercise psychology, such activities include individual and group or team interventions, health promotion, skill building and educational efforts, organizational consulting, research, and teaching. The introduction highlights a distinction between professional activities and the professional's private life. Care should be taken to be aware of how these two spheres merge. For example, the sport and exercise psychology professional traveling with a team might think that drinking alcohol with dinner is a personal decision; however, for athletes with team rules that forbid alcohol use during the competitive season, such a choice may appear problematic. The introduction notes that the code applies to association members. Although this is true, there is also a statement that other organizations may adopt the code. Such organizations might include a regulatory agency. In addition, the code establishes a community standard for professional behavior that may be applied to the professional. The introduction also addresses the topic of language used in the code. Modifiers such as *reasonably* and *appropriate* are used to note the importance of context-specific judgment and remove inequality that might occur without the modifier. Finally, the introduction provides that practice and research guidelines adopted by the APA or other professional organizations should be considered when using the ethical standards.

The code's preamble and five general principles follow the introduction and provide a foundation for the personal commitment of the professional to the scientific and professional roles of psychologists. The five aspirational principles are then defined. They are presented alphabetically with no principle valued more highly than the others.

- Principle A: Beneficence and Nonmalfeasance concerns the balancing of obligations to do good and not harm. This principle challenges the professional to be aware of and to minimize possible harm while striving to do good.
- Principle B: Fidelity and Responsibility centers on the importance of trust and professionals' obligation to understand and fulfill their commitments.
- Principle C: Integrity stresses the need to be honest, accurate, and truthful.
- Principle D: Justice is about fairness, awareness of biases, and the importance of competence.
- Principle E: Respect for People's Rights and Dignity calls for the professional to respect the dignity, worth, and privacy of all people regardless of individual, cultural, and role differences and the need for safeguards to protect individuals' with special vulnerabilities.

Following the definition of these principles are 10 sections of 151 enforceable standards. These standards provide descriptions of specific behaviors that identify the difference between ethical and unethical conduct (Fisher, 2010). Essentially, these rules help psychologists identify behaviors that are ethically unacceptable. It is essential to understand that these are not the only possible unacceptable behaviors but rather a delineation of ethical boundaries. To accomplish this goal, each standard is focused on a unitary concept and is written to provide for the enforcement of that concept (Fisher, 2010).

Ethical Theory and Ethical Codes

Professional codes of ethics, although not direct products of the academic tradition, are grounded in the ideas and debates found in the theories of ethics and morality. The philosophical study of ethics involves the inquiry into principles and presuppositions that operate in moral judgments. Traditionally, this field has been concerned with the study of the virtuous person and what is good and bad, right, and wrong. It concerns defining the values that contribute to the "good life." Professional codes of ethics are an attempt to put into practice this good life. Codes of ethics may exist for many different populations and diverse situations; different cultures, religions, and professions may have quite different codes of ethics. One common factor underlying all ethics codes, however, is the definitional acceptance of the code as a moral guide to self-regulation (O'Donohue & Mangold, 1996; Windt, 1989). Thus, the function of ethics in general and professional ethics codes in particular is to define and illustrate right and wrong behavior for a given population, especially as that population interacts with other populations.

Philosophy of ethics is theory driven. In other words, one cannot make a determination of what is right or wrong behavior on the basis of personal whim. If that were the case, then ethics and, by implication, professional codes of ethics would merely be the fickle voice of the majority. Codes of ethics cannot exist without some sort of theory behind them, informing them, grounding them, and providing for their application. This does not mean, however, that codes of ethics are therefore vastly different from ordinary morality. Indeed, professional codes of ethics do not have a "hierarchy of values" that is different from ordinary morality (O'Donohue & Mangold, 1996, p. 394).

In the history of philosophy one can find many distinct sources for ethics and ethics codes. From the Judeo–Christian ethic to Aristotle to Nietzsche, philosophies of ethics have abounded. However, the perspectives of consequentialism, deontology, and virtue ethics have been described as particularly influential in the field of psychology and especially on the APA Ethics Code (Eyde & Quaintance, 1988; Knapp & VandeCreek, 2004; O'Donohue & Mangold, 1996). In the following sections, we present a brief description of these competing ethical philosophies.

CONSEQUENTIALISM

Proponents of consequentialism argue that the ethical nature of behavior cannot be determined in an a priori manner. Actions are judged ethical or not on the basis of their consequences. It is the end that is important, not the means by which one arrives at the end. To be ethical, an individual must follow specific rules that increase the likelihood that the consequences of actions will be ethical. Although this principle has been stated in many ways, it can be summarized in the well-known statement, "the greatest good for the greatest number." John Stuart Mill (1861/1979), a principal representative of this school, assumed that human beings do not solely desire lofty objectives such as virtue and duty or only desire base things like wealth. What human beings desire is happiness, and when goals such as virtue and wealth increase happiness, people seek them. The goal of morality, then, becomes one of maximizing happiness, and happiness is maximized when the greatest number of people experience it.

In creating moral and ethical codes, consequentialism stresses the necessity of maximizing positive outcome for the majority of human beings. The way to maximize this happiness is by ensuring that the rules that are developed for this purpose are followed. If it can be shown that a particular action produces the greatest good for the greatest number, then people should engage in that action. Hence, this approach leads to rules or ethical codes that, when followed, are believed to lead to the most positive results for all.

DEONTOLOGY

In contrast to consequentialism, the deontological viewpoint holds that it is the intent of the actor and not the outcome of the action that matters. The deontologists argue that ethics needs to be founded on firm and lasting principles that can be applied to all situations. These principles lead to a sense of duty that motivates ethical behavior. Ethics, for the deontologists, is concerned with what should be, not with what is; therefore, what needs to be established is the ideal, or what ought to be. The ideal is encapsulated in principles that are not specific to any one situation but can be applied to many different areas. For example, philosophers of this school would prefer to have general principles, such as "Respect other people," than a litany of narrow rules that apply to specific situations. The problem becomes one of determining the guiding principles that lead to the good and the right.

Perhaps the best known philosopher from the deontological school was Immanuel Kant. He argued that morality entails duty to one's conscience. Kant stated that rationality exists in every human and that reason is capable of generating the possibilities of future experiences. People have the ability to plan ahead and judge whether an action will be ethical or not on the basis of past experiences. Morality, therefore, is a duty to the future possibilities of experience and is based on the general principle of respect for other human beings.

In *Grounding for the Metaphysics of Morals*, Kant (1785/1977) described the categorical imperative, which has several qualifications and conditions.

It states that a moral action is one that is universal and consistent. Stated differently, a moral action must be able to be applied to all human beings and must involve no contradictions. The categorical imperative is then used to test whether actions are moral or not. One can test a maxim (e.g., I will borrow money and never repay it) by reasoning; if everyone were to do this, could they continue to do it forever? In this example, everyone could of course borrow money without repaying, but everyone could not continue to engage in the behavior forever without damage to self and others. Out of this example comes a basic and underlying moral principle: respect for human beings. Actions that are destructive to human beings are not moral because they cannot be universalized. The work of Kant provides philosophical justification for the grounding of morals and a framework from which specific moral maxims can be generated for diverse situations.

VIRTUE ETHICS

Virtue ethics has emerged as a rival to the impersonal and universal dictates of consequentialism and deontology. Rather than acting to bring the greatest good or prioritizing rules for moral action, *virtue ethics* is a broad term for theories that emphasize the role of character and virtue. In this theory, *character* refers to the development of virtues or values that lead to moral behavioral choices.

The centerpiece of this approach to moral behavior is the advice to act as the virtuous person would act (Beauchamp & Childress, 2001). The historical foundation of virtue ethics is found in Aristotle, who proposed that the virtuous person possesses ideal character traits. According to Artistotle (MacIntyre, 1984), character traits are dispositional but can also be nurtured and matured. Unlike deontological and consequentialist theories, virtue ethics does not aim primarily to identify universal principles that can be applied in any moral situation or specific sets of rules for specific situations. This approach has been challenged by questions such as, What is a virtue? What are the primary virtues? Can one teach someone to become virtuous?

Integrating Philosophy and Ethics

Philosophers from each of these schools of ethics have unique relations to the APA Ethics Code. Deontologists, particularly Kant, might argue for the code's general principles; with his emphasis on duty to conscience and the use of reason to test all possible actions, Kant's view of ethics supports the understanding and documentation of general principles, or general plans of action, that would guide future tests of ethical behavior. Kant's philosophy offers no need for particular rules. It is a dynamic system that is constantly capable of evaluating every possible action that can be thought of at any moment.

Consequentialists come at the problem from quite a different direction. This philosophy points to the necessity of specific codes and standards that deal with specific situations. Only by dealing with the specific contingencies of the environment and behavior can the happiness and the good of the greatest number be ensured. By looking to past experiences, rules can be generated that will cover future experiences. Mill, for example, would make no provisions for general principles that inform ethics in a global sense. Rather, his framework requires specific directives that contribute to the greatest good for the greatest number. Thus, the work of the consequentialists can be seen as supporting the creation of specific rules or enforceable standards that govern behavior.

The applicability of virtue ethics for an ethics code requires a shift of focus away from the individual as moral agent and to the profession as a whole. The profession can serve as the moral agent, adopting and promoting a set of identifiable virtues that should be upheld by its members. This approach provides a cultural moral grounding for both general principles and more specific statements of moral action. For example, Principle A: Beneficence and Nonmaleficence in the APA Ethics Code has been described as based in the virtues of compassion, prudence, and respect for humanity. Specific ethical standards drawn from this principle would also represent these virtues. For example, the standards on confidentiality establish the obligation to respect and defend the privacy of the individual therapy or assessment client as well as the research participant. Examples of other standards that enforce the virtues of this general principle are those related to avoidance of conflicts of interest, the prohibition of exploitative relationships, and the use of deception in research.

It can be argued that the APA Ethics Code operates according to all of these assumptions. Functionally, the APA Ethics Code is an amalgam of these different philosophical frameworks. From deontology, the APA Ethics Code derives its five general principles, all of which operate as ethical maxims capable of being universalized and consistent without resorting to individual rules for specific cases. These principles are intended to be portable; they transcend specific situations and therefore are capable of influencing a wide range of behaviors. Likewise, the APA Ethics Code follows the consequentialism philosophy with its enforceable standards. These are specific rules that are thought to flow out of the general principles and that apply to specific situations within the broad field of psychology. The problem with attempting to create an exhaustive list is that one cannot anticipate every problematic circumstance. Undoubtedly, the standards as they are currently written do not represent all of the possible rules that a professional would need to follow to behave ethically. However, the APA Ethics Code claims to be enforceable, and ethics codes can be enforceable only if specific rules are spelled out. The question of other rules that are also enforceable but have not yet been codified naturally arises. The APA Ethics Code recognizes this dilemma and provides for the creation of additional rules: "The Ethical Standards are not exhaustive. The fact that a given conduct is not specifically addressed by an Ethical Standard does not mean that it is necessarily either ethical or unethical" (APA, 2010, Introduction and Applicability). Finally, virtue ethics promotes an understanding of the values at the foundation of the APA Ethics Code. An understanding of these values or virtues allows the professional to more effectively problem solve when dilemmas arise or novel situations occur.

This dynamic model of ethics in which principles give guidance across context areas but standards fail to fit perfectly each situation may make some people inside and outside of the profession uncomfortable. People seem naturally to desire specificity and the ease of applicability that a list of rules provides. However, codes of ethics continue to move away from the unreachable goal of a finite list of rules and toward a dynamic model that treats ethics in a thematic sense by emphasizing general guiding principles.

Ethical Concerns in Sport and Exercise Psychology

Sport and exercise psychology professionals working with athletes and athletic organizations certainly encounter ethically challenging situations that differ from those encountered in other settings and with other client populations. Consider the experience of Carla, a collegiate athlete who eventually realized her goal of completing a doctoral degree in counseling psychology. Her academic and professional program provided training in sport and exercise psychology. She also attended sport and exercise psychology conference continuing education workshops. Her first job was at a university counseling center where the director considered it a coup to add a professional who could be a liaison with the athletic department. Not a month into the job, Carla was asked to contact the coach of the women's volleyball team. The coach was excited to have Carla's services because she felt her team really needed the help of a sport psychologist. She requested mental skills training for her team, assistance with a couple of "head cases," information about the psychology of coaching, and feedback about her coaching. Her coaching concerns centered on more effective communication with her team. The coach said that several players seemed to be upset and discouraged by her feedback. Carla very carefully talked with the coach about the boundaries of her roles with the team and her commitment to confidentiality for both team members and the coach. The coach assured Carla that she was familiar with sport psychology and was confident that Carla would be able to help.

Carla's initial experiences were positive and apparently effective, but a month later the situation became much more challenging. Early on, the coach was receptive to Carla's psychoeducational efforts around team communication and suggestions about how to use specific feedback with the unhappy student-athletes. Regular mental skills training sessions with the team also went well. Carla began meeting individually with two of the new players who were experiencing difficulty adjusting to school. Unfortunately, the pressure of conference play precipitated the coach returning to an authoritarian style. Carla's meetings with team members included more and more complaints about the coach. Then, several players spoke confidentially with Carla about leaving the team. They felt psychologically abused, and with their parent's support, they wanted to be released from the team. One morning, Carla arrived at her office to find the coach waiting for her. The coach had heard about the team, small group, and individual meetings and now wanted to know "exactly what was going on." Carla thought she had prepared well and informed everyone of her role with the team and her commitment to confidentiality. But at this moment none of that mattered. The angry coach was standing in Carla's office demanding answers.

People sometimes question why working with athletes would be different from working with any other population. The answer is that athletes and athletic preparation and competition generate challenging experiences, often under high stress in visible settings (e.g., Moore, 2003; Petitpas, Brewer, Rivera, & Van Raalte, 1994; Stapleton, Hankes, Hays, & Parham, 2010). Complicated situations and behavioral and emotional responses also affect professionals working with medical patients (Hanson, Kerkhoff, & Bush, 2005); military veterans (Johnson et al., 2011); people who are gay, lesbian, or bisexual (Lyons, Bieschke, Dendy, Worthington, & Georgemiller, 2010); religious individuals (Rosenfeld, 2011); and many other client populations. For those working in diverse settings, such challenges test professionals' knowledge of the meaning and the application of ethics codes. These situations call for sport and exercise psychology professionals to identify and clarify their personal values as well as their professional and institutional guidelines. For competent individuals like Carla, a careful consideration of the ethical implications of the population being served and the situations in which these services are provided matter greatly.

Unfortunately, in this instance Carla failed to fully anticipate ethical challenges that can arise when working within sport organizations. Sport settings are often public (e.g., practice fields, swimming pools, stadiums) and involve complicated interrelationships among individuals, groups, and systems. Athletes are typically embedded in organizations with sports administrators, coaches, trainers, teammates, family, fans, and journalists who may be unfamiliar with the role and have different agendas than those of sport and exercise psychology professionals. Moore (2003) and others (e.g., Aoyagi & Portenga, 2010; Etzel, Watson, & Zizzi, 2004; Petitpas et al., 1994; Stapleton et al., 2010) have reviewed the ethical challenges sport and exercise psychology professionals face when working with athletes and provide a comprehensive source of common ethical topics encountered in these situations. These reviews identify three prevalent ethical issues: competence, confidentiality, and relationship boundaries. It is valuable for sport and exercise psychology practitioners to be knowledgeable about and prepared for these ethical challenges in sport settings (Van Raalte & Anderson, 2000).

COMPETENCE

Competence is clearly a cornerstone of ethical practice in any profession. It is essential to the APA Ethics Code's Principle A: Beneficence and Nonmaleficence as well as to Principle B: Fidelity and Responsibility. There are least six ethical standards detailing how boundaries and maintenance of competence are essential to sport and exercise psychology work. For example, take Rick, who is hired to help a group of high school golfers deal with competitive stress. Rick has a master's degree in sport psychology and is a Certified Consultant, Association for Applied Sport Psychology. He is using a series of relaxation exercises to help a golfer develop her preshot routine. One golfer comments on how she hates to imagine herself in the exercises because she thinks she looks so fat. She also mentions that she has been skipping meals and has passed out recently while out on the course. Rick begins to believe that more than relaxation exercises are needed. Knowledgeable about promoting positive health behavior, he offers psychoeducational information on healthy dieting that the athlete seems to appreciate. Because of her response to this effort, he decides not to pursue a referral to evaluate the possibility of an eating disorder (see Standard 6.07, Referrals and Fees; APA, 2010).

In this case, Rick does not have the necessary training to assess or treat an athlete for an eating disorder, so to work within the boundaries of his competency he should seek a consultation for this athlete (see Standard 2.01, Boundaries of Competency; APA, 2010). Additionally, Rick should carefully consider his role with the team. He has been hired to teach relaxation exercises to athletes. As such, if he spends a good deal of his time on nutrition counseling with this one athlete, he could be neglecting his responsibilities to other athletes in the organization. Remaining within the boundaries of one's competence and role can be greatly assisted by maintaining relationships with consulting colleagues or supervisors. Ethically, referrals should be made regardless of whether the psychological symptoms are affecting athletic performance.

The use of telehealth or new technologies can challenge sport and exercise psychology professionals' competence. Nickelson (1998) defined *telehealth* "as the use of telecommunications and information technology to provide access to health assessment, diagnosis, intervention, consultation, supervision, education, and information across distance" (p. 527). Activities that traditionally would take place face-to-face between a professional and a client can now be conducted using telephone or Internet technologies. Application to sport and exercise psychology work is particularly intriguing as a traveling athlete or coach can establish and maintain communication with the sport and exercise psychology professional. Critical questions about provider competence, confidentiality, and consumer protection need to be carefully considered before professionals use these technologies. The APA Ethics Committee (1997) issued a statement that stressed the relevance of the APA Ethics Code to psychologists engaged in telehealth. Specifically, this committee warned that psychologists are required to work within the bounds of their competence. Although some believe that greater guidance is needed (e.g., Humphreys, Winzelberg, & Klaw, 2000; Jerome & Zaylor, 2000), the APA Ethics Code states that principles and standards apply to all settings and all communication contexts. Specific standards that are important to consider include 3.10a, Informed Consent; 4.02c, Discussing the Limits of Confidentiality; 5.01a, Avoidance of False or Deceptive Statements; and 5.04, Media Presentations.

CONFIDENTIALITY

Professionals working in sport and exercise psychology frequently encounter challenges to confidentiality. Some could be accidental, such as a sportswriter observing a sport and exercise psychology professional interacting with a struggling sport star. Others can occur from lack of knowledge or poor judgment as when the professional believes that a disclosure might be beneficial. Sports communities often emphasize the internal sharing of information. Sports scientists may gain the favor of organizational leaders when they reveal even incidental information about the health of an athlete. The awareness of when these challenges arise and how to manage them is essential to ethical practice. Release of a client's private information can certainly do that individual harm as well as violate the charge to be responsible for one's actions and work. These violations can erode the integrity of the practice of psychology. Confidentiality is a significant component of all seven standards of Section 4, Privacy and Confidentiality, of the APA Ethics Code. It is also important to remember that divulging private health information may be illegal under Health Insurance Portability and Accountability Act guidelines.

It is helpful to consider the following case. A doctoral level psychologist is contracted by a major university to work with a team and particularly with an athlete who reports anxiety. After a month of consultation, the head coach asks for a meeting to evaluate the effectiveness of the sport psychology program. The coach asks specific questions about the team and about the individual athlete's progress. How should the sport psychologist respond? Refusing to answer the coach's questions to maintain confidentiality might result in termination from the team, but divulging confidential information is unethical. One possibility is to redirect the conversations with the coach. What are the coach's concerns? What has the coach been seeing at practice and competitions? Perhaps supporting a meeting between the coach and athlete would be helpful. It is possible that the sport psychologist could get permission from the athlete to share information, but misunderstandings are more likely when indirect communication methods are used. This scenario highlights an area in which confidentiality issues are complex; even though the professional is under contract to the university, the professional's primary fiduciary responsibility lies with the athlete.

MULTIPLE RELATIONSHIPS

Boundary violations are another area in which potential ethical dilemmas arise, especially in the unique settings in which sport and exercise psychologists often practice. Before delving into this topic further, it is necessary to first differentiate between a boundary crossing and a boundary violation. According to Aoyagi and Portenga (2010), a *boundary crossing* occurs when interactions deviate from the traditional therapist–client interaction such as holding sessions with athletes in locker rooms or maintaining multiple relationships within the team context that do not cause harm and may actually be helpful. *Boundary violations,* however, such as violating confidentiality guidelines, deviate from the traditional therapist–client interaction and also cause harm. Before interacting with the client in a nontraditional manner, the sport and exercise psychologist must fully inventory the possible consequences on objectivity, effectiveness, and the potential effect on the client (Moore, 2003). In the sports arena, it can be particularly beneficial to address proactively how the sport and exercise psychologist will respond to individuals in settings outside of the office (e.g., during travel to competitions, in the practice setting, around campus). For example, if a sport and exercise psychologist travels with the team to a competition and the coaches invite her to join the team for dinner, how will she respond, and what will the consequences be if she accepts or declines? In this instance, if she declines, she may alienate herself from the coaching staff and make interaction with them more difficult. By accepting the invitation, she may be seen by team members as an extension of the coaching staff and that may create barriers for team members to interact with her.

Fidelity in relationships with clients is another cornerstone of the APA Ethics Code. In different ways, all of the general principles address the need to prioritize relationships with clients, students, and research participants. Multiple relationships open the possibility of distorting the professional relationship, creating conflicts of interest and undermining the fiduciary nature of the consultation process (Sonne, 1994). Section 3, Human Relations, of the standards of the APA Ethics Code highlights the obligations to avoid conflict, not misuse position, prevent erosion of objectivity, and guard against exploitation. Further, it is the professional who has the burden of responsibility to ensure that harm is avoided.

For the professional, the solution lies in thinking through relationships before and as they develop. Certainly, it would be helpful if there were specific rules that clearly delineate all possible multiple-role relationships; unfortunately, there are not. Professional navigation of complex relationships requires conservative acceptance of responsibilities, explicit conversation about roles and requirements, an understanding of limits, and the opportunity to consult more experienced professionals when needed. In our opening vignette about Carla working with the volleyball team, Carla's assumption that everyone involved understood the boundaries of her work was probably a mistake. Her early conversations with the coach were valuable, but ongoing discussion about her role within the team might have prevented the situation from imploding. Carla would probably have benefitted from considering the ongoing demands of both general ethical principles and specific standards to clearly define roles and responsibilities to all involved.

Conclusion

An ethics code is an essential professional document that can help sport and exercise psychology professionals to regulate behavior and fulfill their societal contract and obligations. As developing fields emerge, psychologists may encounter ethical situations that existing ethics codes may not fully address. A clear grasp of the philosophical principles underlying professional ethics codes and an understanding of how to integrate a code's general principles and ethical standards can help members of the profession anticipate and navigate novel professional situations. It is clear from the examination of such situations that behaving ethically does not involve simply following the rules of an ethics code, especially one designed for a broader psychology. But understanding the philosophy of ethics helps to guide the professional toward increasingly ethical behavior.

References

American Psychological Association. (1953). *Ethical standards of psychologists.* Washington, DC: Author.

American Psychological Association. (1992). Ethical principles of psychologists and code of conduct. *American Psychologist, 47,* 1597–1611. doi:10.1037/0003-066X.47.12.1597

American Psychological Association. (2002). Ethical principles of psychologists and code of conduct. *American Psychologist, 57,* 1060–1073. doi:10.1037/0003-066X.57.12.1060

American Psychological Association. (2010). *Ethical principles of psychologists and code of conduct (2002, Amended June 1, 2010).* Retrieved from http://www.apa.org/ethics/code/index.aspx

American Psychological Association, Ethics Committee. (1997). *Services by telephone, teleconferencing, and Internet.* Retrieved from http://www.apa.org/ethics/education/telephone-statement.aspx

Aoyagi, M. W., & Portenga, S. T. (2010). The role of positive ethics and virtues in the context of sport and performance psychology service delivery. *Professional Psychology: Research and Practice, 41,* 253–259. doi:10.1037/a0019483

Bass, L. J., DeMers, S. T., Ogloff, J. R. P., Peterson, C., Pettifor, J. L., & Reaves, R. P., . . . Tipton, R. M. (1996). *Professional conduct and discipline in psychology.* Washington, DC: American Psychological Association; and Montgomery, AL: Association of State and Provincial Boards of Psychology.

Beauchamp, T. L., & Childress, J. F. (2001). *Principles of biomedical ethics* (5th ed.). Oxford, England: Oxford University Press.

Bersoff, D. N. (1994). Explicit ambiguity: The 1992 ethics code as an oxymoron. *Professional Psychology: Research and Practice, 25,* 382–387. doi:10.1037/0735-7028.25.4.382

Canadian Psychological Association. (2000). *Code of ethics for psychologists* (3rd ed.). Ottawa, Ontario, Canada: Author.

Dancy, J. (2006). *Ethics without principles.* Oxford, England: Oxford University Press.

Ellickson, K. A., & Brown, D. R. (1990). Ethical considerations in dual relationships: The sport psychologist-coach. *Journal of Applied Sport Psychology, 2,* 186–190. doi:10.1080/10413209008406429

Etzel, E., Watson, J., & Zizzi, S. (2004). A web-based survey of ethical beliefs and behaviors of AAASP members in the new millennium. *Journal of Applied Sport Psychology, 16,* 236–250. doi:10.1080/10413200490485595

Eyde, L. D., & Quaintance, M. K. (1988). Ethical issues and cases in the practice of personnel psychology. *Professional Psychology: Research and Practice, 19,* 148–154. doi:10.1037/0735-7028.19.2.148

Fisher, C. B. (2010). *Decoding the ethics code: A practical guide for psychologist* (2nd ed.). Thousand Oaks, CA: Sage.

Hanson, S. L., Kerkhoff, T. R., & Bush, S. S. (2005). *Health care ethics for psychologists: A casebook.* Washington, DC: American Psychological Association. doi:10.1037/10845-000

Hobbs, N. (1948). The development of a code of ethical standards for psychology. *American Psychologist, 3,* 80–84. doi:10.1037/h0060281

Hooker, B. W., & Little, M. (Eds.). (2000). *Moral particularism.* Oxford, England: Oxford University Press.

Humphreys, K., Winzelberg, A., & Klaw, E. (2000). Psychologists' ethical responsibilities in Internet-based groups: Issues, strategies, and a call for dialogue. *Professional Psychology: Research and Practice, 31,* 493–496. doi:10.1037/0735-7028.31.5.493

Jerome, L. W., & Zaylor, C. (2000). Cyberspace: Creating a therapeutic environment for telehealth applications. *Professional Psychology: Research and Practice, 31,* 478–483. doi:10.1037/0735-7028.31.5.478

Johnson, W. B., Johnson, S. J., Sullivan, G. R., Bongar, B., Miller, L., & Sammons, M. T. (2011). Psychology in extremis: Preventing problems of professional competence in dangerous practice settings. *Professional Psychology: Research and Practice, 42,* 94–104. doi:10.1037/a0022365

Jordan, A. E., & Meara, N. M. (1991). The role of virtues and principles in moral collapse: A response to Miller. *Professional Psychology: Research and Practice, 22,* 107–109. doi:10.1037/0735-7028.22.2.107.b

Kant, I. (1977). Grounding for the metaphysics of morals. In S. M. Cahn (Ed.), *Classics of Western philosophy* (pp. 925–976). Indianapolis, IN: Hackett. (Original work published 1785)

Knapp, S., Gottlieb, J., Berman, J., & Handelsman, M. M. (2007). When law and ethics collide: What should psychologists do? *Professional Psychology: Research and Practice, 38,* 54–59. doi:10.1037/0735-7028.38.1.54

Knapp, S., & VandeCreek, L. (2004). A principled-based analysis of the 2002 American Psychological Association Ethics Code. *Psychotherapy: Theory, Research, Practice, Training, 41,* 247–254. doi:10.1037/0033-3204.41.3.247

Koocher, G. P., & Keith-Spiegel, P. (2008). *Ethics in psychology: Professional standards and cases* (3rd ed.). New York, NY: Oxford University Press.

Krause, E. A. (1996). *Death of the guilds: Professionals, states and the advance of capitalism, 1930 to the present.* New Haven, CT: Yale University.

Lyons, H. Z., Bieschke, K. J., Dendy, A. K., Worthington, R. L., & Georgemiller, R. (2010). Psychologists' competence to treat lesbian, gay and bisexual clients: State of the field and strategies for improvement. *Professional Psychology: Research and Practice, 41,* 424–434. doi:10.1037/a0021121

MacIntyre, A. (1984). *After virtue: A study of moral theory.* Notre Dame, IN: University of Notre Dame Press.

Midgley, M. (1993). The origins of ethics. In P. Singer (Ed.), *A companion to ethics* (pp. 3–13). Cambridge, MA: Blackwell.

Mill, J. S. (1979). Utilitarianism. In G. Sher (Ed.), *John Stuart Mill: Utilitarianism* (pp. 1–63). Indianapolis, IN: Hackett. (Original work published 1861)

Moore, Z. (2003). Ethical dilemmas in sport psychology: Discussion and recommendations for practice. *Professional Psychology: Research and Practice, 34,* 601–610. doi:10.1037/0735-7028.34.6.601

Nickelson, D. W. (1998). Telehealth and the evolving health care system: Strategic opportunities for professional psychology. *Professional Psychology: Research and Practice, 29,* 527–535. doi:10.1037/0735-7028.29.6.527

O'Donohue, W., & Mangold, R. (1996). A critical examination of the ethical principles of psychologists and code of conduct. In W. T. O'Donohue & R. F. Kitchener (Eds.), *Psychology and philosophy: Interdisciplinary problems and responses* (pp. 371–380). New York, NY: Allyn & Bacon.

Payton, C. R. (1994). Implications of the 1992 ethics code for diverse groups. *Professional Psychology: Research and Practice, 25,* 317–320. doi:10.1037/0735-7028.25.4.317

Petitpas, A., Brewer, B., Rivera, P., & Van Raalte, J. (1994). Ethical beliefs and behaviors in applied sport psychology: The AAASP ethics survey. *Journal of Applied Sport Psychology, 6,* 135–151. doi:10.1080/10413209408406290

Pettifor, J. L. (1996). Maintaining professional conduct in daily practice. In L. J. Bass, S. T. DeMers, J. R. P. Ogloff, C. Pettifor, J. L. Reaves, R. P. Rétfalvi, . . . R. M. Tipton (Eds.), *Professional conduct and discipline in psychology* (pp. 91–100). Washington, DC: American Psychological Association; and Montgomery, AL: Association of State and Provincial Boards of Psychology.

Pope, K. S., Tabachnick, B. G., & Keith-Spiegel, P. (1987). Ethics of practice: The beliefs and behaviors of psychologists as therapists. *American Psychologist, 42,* 993–1006. doi:10.1037/0003-066X.42.11.993

Pryzwansky, W. B., & Wendt, R. N. (1999). *Professional and ethical issues in psychology.* New York, NY: Norton.

Rosenfeld, G. W. (2011). Contributions from ethics and research that guide integrating religion and psychotherapy. *Professional Psychology: Research and Practice, 42,* 192–199. doi:10.1037/a0022742

Sonne, J. L. (1994). Multiple relationships: Does the new ethics code answer the right questions. *Professional Psychology: Research and Practice, 25,* 336–343. doi:10.1037/0735-7028.25.4.336

Stainback, R. D., Moncier, J. C., & Talyor, R. E. (2007). Sport psychology: A clinician's perspective. In G. Tenenbaum & R. C. Eklund (Eds.), *Handbook of sport psychology* (3rd ed., pp. 310–331). Hoboken, NJ: Wiley.

Stapleton, A. B., Hankes, D. M., Hays, K. F., & Parham, W. D. (2010). Ethical dilemmas in sport psychology: A dialogue on the unique aspects impacting practice. *Professional Psychology: Research and Practice, 41,* 143–152. doi:10.1037/a0017976

Van Raalte, J. L., & Anderson, M. (2000). Supervision I: From models to doing. In M. B. Anderson (Ed.), *Doing sport psychology* (pp. 153–165). Champaign, IL: Human Kinetics.

Vealey, R. S. (2007). Mental skills training in sport. In G. Tenenbaum & R. C. Eklund (Eds.), *Handbook of sport psychology* (3rd ed., pp. 287–309). Hoboken, NJ: Wiley.

Whelan, J. P., Meyers, A. W., & Donovan, C. (1995). Interventions with competitive recreational athletes. In S. Murphy (Ed.), *Sport psychology interventions* (pp. 71–116). Champaign, IL: Human Kinetics.

Windt, P. Y. (1989). Professions and professional ethics: The theoretical background. In P. Y. Windt, P. C. Appleby, M. P. Battin, L. P. Francis, & B. M. Landesman (Eds.), *Ethical issues in the professions* (pp. 1–24). Englewood Cliffs, NJ: Prentice-Hall.

Windt, P. Y., Appleby, P. C., Battin, M. P., Francis, L. P., & Landesman, B. M. (Eds.). (1989). *Ethical issues in the professions.* Englewood Cliffs, NJ: Prentice-Hall.

Index

About the Editors

Judy L. Van Raalte, PhD, is a professor of psychology at Springfield College; a certified consultant, Association for Applied Sport Psychology; and listed in the United States Olympic Committee Sport Psychology Registry. She has worked with athletes, coaches, and sport organizations around the world. Dr. Van Raalte has presented at conferences in 16 countries, produced sport psychology videos, and published more than 80 articles in peer-reviewed journals on topics such as self-talk, body image, and professional issues in sport and exercise psychology. She is a fellow of the American Psychological Association and the Association for Applied Sport Psychology.

Britton W. Brewer, PhD, received his doctorate in clinical psychology from Arizona State University. He is a professor of psychology at Springfield College; a certified consultant, Association for Applied Sport Psychology; listed in the United States Olympic Committee Sport Psychology Registry; and a fellow of the American Psychological Association and the Association for Applied Sport Psychology. His research focuses on psychological aspects of pain and injury in sports. As CEO of Virtual Brands, LLC, he has been an executive producer of more than 20 sport psychology videos.